T0184921

Lecture Notes in Business Information Processing 241

Series Editors

More information about this series at http://www.springer.com/series/7911

Slimane Hammoudi · Leszek Maciaszek
Ernest Teniente · Olivier Camp
José Cordeiro (Eds.)

Enterprise Information Systems

17th International Conference, ICEIS 2015
Barcelona, Spain, April 27–30, 2015
Revised Selected Papers

Editors
Slimane Hammoudi
MODESTE/ESEO
Angers
France

Olivier Camp
MODESTE/ESEO
Angers
France

Leszek Maciaszek
Macquarie University, Sydney
Wroclaw University of Economics, Poland
Wroclaw
Poland

José Cordeiro
INSTICC
Instituto Politécnico de Setúbal
Setúbal
Portugal

Ernest Teniente
Despatx Omega-132
Polytechnic University of Catalonia
Barcelona
Spain

ISSN 1865-1348 ISSN 1865-1356 (electronic)
Lecture Notes in Business Information Processing
ISBN 978-3-319-29132-1 ISBN 978-3-319-29133-8 (eBook)
DOI 10.1007/978-3-319-29133-8

Library of Congress Control Number: 2015944743

Printed on acid-free paper

This Springer imprint is published by SpringerNature
The registered company is Springer International Publishing AG Switzerland

Empowering the Knowledge Worker: End-User Software Engineering in Knowledge Management

Witold Staniszkis(✉)

Rodan Development, Wyczółki 89, 02-820 Warsaw, Poland
Witold.Staniszkis@rodan.pl

Abstract. We present a novel architecture of a knowledge management system meeting the end-user software engineering requirements, thus empowering the knowledge worker to eliminate such intermediaries as system analysts and application programmers. Advantages of direct representation of user requirements in executable knowledge management application specifications, as well as the resulting system agility and ease of maintenance are highlighted. The state-of-the-art in the end-user software engineering area pertaining to the knowledge management systems realm comprises information about the on-going research and development efforts. The principal features of a knowledge management system toolbox are described, comprising among others, such functional areas as semantic modelling of knowledge object repositories, and adaptive management of knowledge management processes. Finally we succinctly discuss the end-user oriented methodology guiding specification of the knowledge management application solutions.

Keywords: Knowledge management · End-user software engineering · Dynamic workflow · Semantic content modelling · Knowledge maps · Adaptive case management

1 Introduction

Rapid growth of the international trade and cooperation on the one hand and the global Information and Communication Technology (ICT)-driven communication powered by the Internet have fuelled unprecedented expansion of global collaboration in practically all walks of human activity. Virtual organisations spanning not only diverse countries but also entire regions become an ubiquitous and dynamic phenomenon. A good example are the European research programmes based on international project consortia, i.e. virtual organisations, characterised by well-defined goals to be attained within a specific time frame.

Also the nature of human activities has undergone a dramatic change resulting in more than 50 % of workers being classified as "knowledge workers", a termed coined by Peter Drucker over half of century ago, whose productivity underlies the competitive advantage of all developed economies. Indeed, again according to Peter Drucker [13], productivity of the knowledge workers represents the major management challenge of the 21st century.

Notwithstanding the ubiquity of such ICT environments as networking, email, social media and content management enhancing the capability of goal-oriented collaborating

S. Hammoudi et al. (Eds.): ICEIS 2015, LNBIP 241, pp. 3–19, 2015.
DOI: 10.1007/978-3-319-29133-8_1

teams, jointly known as organization 2.0 platforms, much needs to be done to leverage investment in the intellectual capital represented and produced by the knowledge workers.

A survey of knowledge worker activities reported by Nathaniel Palmer [41] reveals that over 60 % of the working day is spent in unstructured and often unpredictable work patterns. This telling result explains, at least partially, the common fallacies of the business process management (BPM) projects aiming at supporting human collaboration within the knowledge-intensive work activities. Clearly a novel approach is needed to support the non-production (in the Fredric Taylor sense) work processes of the knowledge worker.

The major advantage of the end-user-driven design and development of the knowledge management application solutions is the elimination of intermediaries, such as system analysts and application programmers, thus enabling the direct representation of the user requirements in executable application specifications. Direct involvement of the end-users in the development process leads to increased system agility and ease of maintenance. The ubiquitous cloud environments provide flexibility, and relative low cost, of computing and storage resources, that can be readily obtained and easily adjusted to the current application workload. All of the above characteristics are a perfect match for the requirements of the transient and goal-oriented knowledge management application solutions.

The non-IT users of the knowledge management development tools should be able to design and implement fully functional knowledge management solutions comprising a repository of information objects organized according to a semantic model, providing the principal view of the repository information to the system users, as well as the process management functionality supporting execution of the knowledge workers' procedures and tasks.

The substantial impact of the end-user development is exemplified by data published by the US Bureau of Labour and Statistics in 2012, quoted in [24], showing that there have been in the United States fewer than 3 million professional programmers but more than 55 million people have been using spreadsheets and databases at work, many of whom write formulae and queries to support their job.

A significant challenge in involving non-IT professional developers creating complex application solutions, notwithstanding the scope of automated development tools support (e.g. application generating wizards), is the notorious lack of sound software engineering practices, such as quality assurance of implemented solutions, which often precludes sufficient reliability and robustness of the resulting applications.

Our research and development work in the area of the knowledge management software tools initiated within the ICONS FP5 research project [20] and further expanded within the eGovBus FP6 research project [14], as well as the ensuing engineering of the research results resulting in development of the OfficeObjects® knowledge management platform [37], provided us with the solid basis for design, construction, and implementation of agile end-user-oriented knowledge management application solutions.

OfficeObjects® is a proprietary JEE (Java Enterprise Edition) framework integrated with several specialized open source components supporting such functionality as the full text search, business intelligence and reporting, as well as the portal environment.

In the following sections we discuss the principle user requirements, defining the functional scope of the knowledge management software tools, and the underlying application development methodology, which had provided the guidelines for design and development of the OfficeObjects® knowledge management software tools, as well as the pertinent state-of-the-art research and development results.

Further we succinctly present the end-user-oriented development features of the OfficeObjects® architecture highlighting the strengths and challenges of the knowledge management software tools, and finally we present the end-user oriented development methodology.

2 The Knowledge Management Application Requirements

The challenges facing knowledge workers, particularly those having direct negative effect on their productivity, have been identified in the already mentioned study performed by Nathaniel Palmer [41] repeatedly in 2011 and 2013. Table 1 summarizes the results obtained in the 2013 survey, where column "%" provides the proportion of respondents giving the positive answer, and the remaining columns refer to the KMS feature areas, shown in Fig. 1, relevant to the corresponding challenge.

Table 1. Knowledge worker challenges vs. the KMS features.

Knowledge workers' challenge[a]	%	1	2	3	4	5	6
Lack of visibility into the current state or status of others' work supporting your own	71			X	X	X	X
Difficulty tracking "to do" items or task lists	45			X	X		
Difficulty organizing and assembling the right team	51	X	X	X			
Difficulty managing documentation and information needed for a given project	57		X	X			
Difficulty finding co-workers/collaborators with the right experience	53		X	X		X	X
Difficulty determining the next step or course of action	36			X	X		X

1. Enterprise 2.0 Ontology
2. Knowledge Representation
3. Content Repository
4. Workflow Process Management
5. Enterprise 2.0
6. Knowledge Integration

[a] [41]

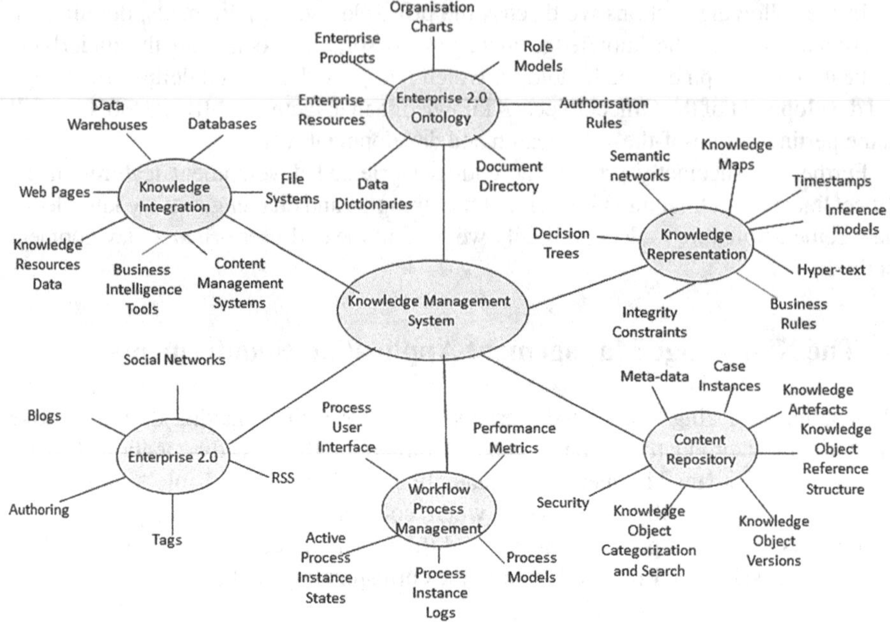

Fig. 1. Feature requirements of the knowledge management system.

The analysis results clearly indicate the importance of the "Content Repository" features providing means to alleviate obstructions impeding the knowledge worker productivity, immediately followed by such feature areas as "Workflow Process Management" and "Knowledge Representation".

The KMS feature model has been introduced in [20], serving subsequently as the road map of the OfficeObjects® development project, undergoing revisions motivated by experience derived from a number of large scale knowledge management applications. Another important lesson learnt in the course of these application projects was the utmost importance of empowering the KMS end-users to ensure their active participation, not only in the user requirements analysis, but first of all in the KM solution development and maintenance processes.

The rapidly growing end-user software engineering (EUSE) field has also influenced the focus of the OfficeObjects® software architecture design to embrace the EUSE techniques and methodologies. The user-oriented assessment of the eGovernment service bus system [14] developed with the use of the OfficeObjects® platform, in particular of its service design and development tools, has shown that non-programming IT technicians were able to develop complex services published in the Web.

The ensuing development of the subsequent versions of the OfficeObjects® platform has been concentrated on the ergonomic aspects of end-user interfaces, both in the area of application solution development tools, and the functional system areas, such as the content repository, workflow process graphic interfaces, and the HCI features.

The existent and emerging software standards pertaining to the OfficeObjects® platform have been incorporated in the software design in order to facilitate high acceptance level of the end-users and IT professionals, as well as to support interoperability with information systems and data sources that may be integrated within the knowledge management application solutions.

3 The KMS Research Activities

The **architecture of knowledge management systems** is a field of intensive research and development effort. Notwithstanding the research and innovation currently under way, the comprehensive integrated end-user development tools supporting agile development of advanced KM application solutions are rarely meeting the advanced knowledge management system requirements. Apart from the OfficeObjects® platform [37], the closest example is a prototype of the knowledge management platform presented in [27]. Analogously to our approach, the above authors propose a distributed platform replicating functional components to achieve system scalability through the use of load balancing under the varying workload conditions. Also the virtual organizations, possibly involving several independent partners, are envisaged as the prime users of the proposed system. The system is supporting advanced content management solutions, but it does not provide application development tools oriented towards the end-user software engineering community. System security is a significant concern in knowledge management as well as in the generic collaborative systems, these issues are discussed at length in [47, 58] respectively.

The **End-User Software Engineering (EUSE)** field has been growing significantly over the last several years, evolving from the spreadsheet financial models, through the graphic user interface implementations, to the end-user developed mashup applications. The Service-Oriented Architecture (SOA), providing an integration platform for accessing domain-specific application environments, has enabled development of complex and robust applications by non-programmers.

It is the common believe that the knowledge management application design and specification tools are to provide an abstraction level concealing the underlying technological complexity of a KMS platform, thus enabling the end-user developer to concentrate on the application requirements of the KM solution. A comprehensive overview of current end-user development tools has been presented in [24]. The field has been growing considerably over the last several years and a number of important research initiatives have been published. A composition model facilitating the programming-illiterate knowledge workers to develop rich internet applications, integrating pre-existing software components to be published in a graphic web interface (a mashup), has been presented in [30]. Other mashup frameworks bridging the perspective of the service based software development and the end-user development have also been presented in [35, 36].

Development of Web 2.0 tools and techniques has enabled end-users to move from content and personalization to functionality supported by the user-developed web services. A number of such projects, spanning from ambient intelligence, through to wizard-based process development, have been presented at the AVI Workshop held in Rome on May 25–29 2010 [9]. The use of design patterns in the end-user development projects has also been growing as presented in [61]. A good example of a design pattern repository is the MIT process library described in [31].

Semantic Knowledge Content Modelling, similar to the OfficeObjects® knowledge map approach, has been proposed in [12]. The platform, serving the cultural heritage applications, is a closed software system providing no development tools for the system users. The corporate knowledge management domain is represented by an advanced prototype of a knowledge management system SKMS (Smart Knowledge Management System) presented in [32]. The platform provides a powerful document structuring mechanism in the form of dynamic categorization trees, but similarly to the above solutions, it neither provides tools for specification of the knowledge management or scientific workflow processes, nor it allows for semantic modelling of the knowledge repository content.

Several KM systems currently under development are equipped with formal ontology models in the form of semantic nets, as represented by the Topic Maps ISO standard (ISO 13250), mostly supporting semantic browsing features referencing the repository and external information objects. An example of Topic Maps-based semantic net implementation is the DREAM platform presented in [4] utilized for semantic indexing and search of visual objects. Topic Maps are also used for categorization of documents on the basis of their meta-data attribute values. Examples of such architectures may be found in [6] as well as in [10, 42, 60].

The role of an ontology model in the knowledge management system has been extensively discussed in [11, 59]. It is generally agreed that an ontology specification language can be seen as a knowledge representation language, which should guarantee that every concrete ontology enjoys the following properties: (i) it is a surrogate for the things in the real world; (ii) it is a set of ontological commitments; and (iii) it is a medium for human expression. In other words, an ontology may be specified without any particular reasoning paradigm in mind, and it does not necessarily have to be a theory of representational constructs plus inferences it recommends, or a medium for efficient computation.

Many tailor-made ontology specification languages have been defined so far. In the context of the DARPA Knowledge Sharing Effort, for example, Gruber defined *Ontolingua* [17]. The language was developed as an ontology layer on top of KIF [16], which allowed frame style definition of knowledge representation models (such as classes, slots, and subclasses). Other languages, such as *Conceptual Graphs* [52, 59], have also been popular for specifying ontologies.

Recently, the XML-based W3C Web Ontology Language (OWL) [38, 59] has gained wide popularity. The language is characterized by very high expressiveness, but to get some guarantees with respect to computability, a user has to limit herself to a well-understood fragment of OWL, called OWL DL, based on Description Logics (DL) [2, 3, 7, 59].

The **Human Computer Interaction** field, enriched by ubiquity and growing computing power of mobile devices, such as smartphones and tablets, as well as the new mobile context-aware software standards exemplified by HTML5, offers significant opportunities for new intelligent applications based on knowledge management systems, such as the OfficeObjects® platform. Development of the graphic user interface, as well as configuring of the mobile device apps serving as clients, represents important challenges for the end-user KM application development. The field is rich with research projects concentrating on issues of automatic generation of mobile device graphic interfaces on the server side, as described in [8, 26], as well as the component-based end-user development of complex graphic interfaces integrating heterogeneous data sources and application functions, such as mashups described in [30, 35].

The Ambient Intelligence field is a growing application area to be supported by the end-user software development tools, like those available in the OfficeObjects® platform, either as a new solution development by parameterization of the existing design patterns, or as an application of the off-the-shelf components. Examples of such application solutions have been presented in [1, 28].

Workflow Management Platforms available as the cloud computing services are subject of many research efforts, and consequently quite widely published, in particular in the eScience area. Many projects concentrate on workflow tools and run-time platforms supporting scientific workflows moving vast amounts of data resulting from scientific experiments. Automation of data interchange is a subject of many publications in particular related to the field of HPC (High Performance Computing), among others interesting results are presented in [21, 49, 62, 63].

All of the presented system prototypes use the workflow management platforms as a middleware layer responsible for coordination of scientific computation tasks, providing facilities for parallel scheduling of complex computations, and passing intermediate result data among such computations. Ubiquity of these solutions in the scientific computation community bodes well for other application areas, such as among others the knowledge management field.

New workflow paradigms are being proposed in response to the growing need to support and measure efficiency of the knowledge work. Working methodologies, such as SCRUM for example, are becoming ubiquitous not only in the software development work. One of the significant proposals of the new workflow paradigm is the Role Model developed by Keith Harrison-Broninski [18, 19].

A set of lightweight methods called "agile" are being developed in recent years [37] to better fit the dynamic nature of projects and organizations. Agile methods adopt a dynamic process control model, which is meant for processes that are not always well defined and are sometimes unpredictable and unrepeatable.

A comprehensive discussion of the scientific workflow models is provided in [57] highlighting a number of issues that are still open. Among others according to D. Talia, the outstanding problems include (a) adaptive/dynamic workflow models. (b) service-oriented workflows in cloud computing infrastructures, and (c) workflow provenance and annotation mechanisms and systems.

Adaptive Case Management (ACM) is a fast growing area of management innovation, rather than the computer science research, fuelled by the widely believed constatation that the classic graph-oriented workflow models are incompatible with the nature of the knowledge work. A convincing proof is provided by the already presented results of the survey conducted by Nathaniel Palmer [41], as well as by explicit calls for the BPM paradigm shift in [5, 50, 56]. Additional argumentation, calling for a major overhaul of the presently available workflow process and content management architectures, may be found in [33, 34, 39, 40, 45, 46, 53–55]. Another important line of thought, discussed in [22, 23, 25], is the data orientation of the ACM platforms considering the rich knowledge object repository structures and the semantic modelling to be the principal support vehicles of the knowledge work. Indeed for a growing engineering field anchored in purely practical issues, the intensity of general interest, exemplified by the number of publications, is astonishing. In fact, this vouches for the real practical impact of the knowledge worker efficiency issues, as stated by Peter Drucker at the turn of the 20th century [13].

The ACM field, notwithstanding its practical flavor, attracted the attention of the computer science research community approaching the existing issues from a theoretical vantage point. One of such projects, initiated at the Sorbonne University in Paris has been presented in [48].

4 The OfficeObjects® KM Architecture

The OfficeObjects® software architecture, presented in Fig. 2, has been evolving over the last 4 years to provide the comprehensive set of features required for the knowledge management application development. As we stressed in the preceding discussion, the end-user orientation has been the major focus of our design and development effort. The presented software architecture meets the application requirements included in the knowledge management feature model shown in Fig. 1.

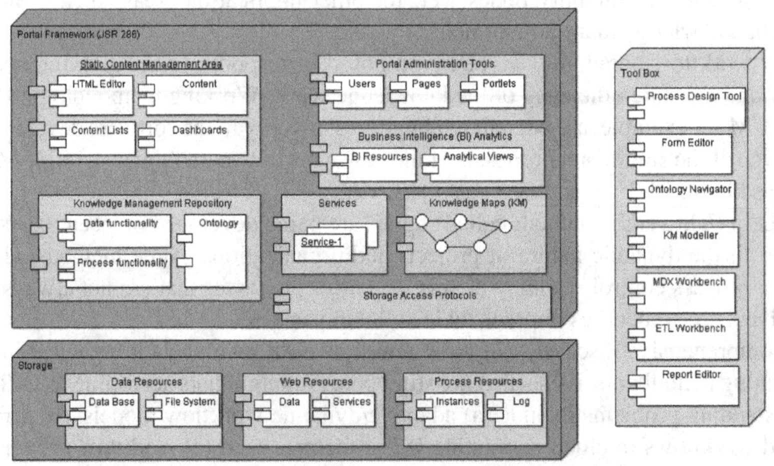

Fig. 2. OfficeObjects® platform architecture.

The OfficeObjects® functional modules are deployed within three principal packages installed in the virtualized processing environment. The user-visible functionality, representing the application solutions, is deployed within the **JSR 286 Portal Framework** [29] providing a rich and mature environment for the end-user-oriented mush up application development.

A rich and extensible library of portlets supports the state-of-the-art Enterprise 2.0 solutions packaged within the **Static Content Management Area**. The portal administration tools are available within the **Portal Administration Tools** pages. Both functional areas render themselves readily for the end-user software development, which is usually based on the use of assorted web applications.

The knowledge management functionalities, comprising the OfficeObjects® components, as well as the integrated open source software components, such as, among others, the community TIBCO Jaspersoft report server incorporating the Mondrane ROLAP engine [43] executing the Multidimensional Expressions (MDX) analytical language [51]. The above functionalities may be deployed as portlets, depending on the knowledge management solution requirements, respectively within the **Knowledge Management Repository** and the **Business Intelligence (BI) Analytics** areas.

The Knowledge Management Repository publishes all OfficeObjects® services dedicated to content, process and ontology management. An important knowledge management tool the **Knowledge Maps,** based on the Topic Maps ISO 12350 standard, supports creation and delivery of semantic models, superimposed on the knowledge repository content, providing semantically enriched knowledge artefact navigation and selection functionality. A knowledge map may comprise references to the repository information objects as well as to the external information objects, such as web pages, Wikipedia entries, database queries etc. The knowledge maps and the dynamic object categorization trees used in advanced knowledge management systems prove to be intuitive and user-friendly.

The KMS features concerned with the integration of the external knowledge resources, data, and services are supported by the OfficeObjects® Service Broker module facilitating deployment of complex services within the Portal Framework developed with the use of OfficeObjects® tools and deployed in the OfficeObjects® WorkFlow platform.

The **Ontology** model, supported by the Topic Maps Ontology Navigator, comprises all information concerning the KMS user environment, such as the organization structure, user accounts and access rights, role models, etc., as well as the semantic model features comprising controlled vocabularies, data dictionaries, information object class specifications, and the knowledge map definitions.

All of the above components of the run-time OfficeObjects® architecture are supported by the **OfficeObjects® Tool Box** providing design and development functions for the users specifying a knowledge management application solution. The **Process Design Tool** coupled with the **Form Editor** provide tools to specify the workflow process BPMN model and the corresponding process GUI. The **Knowledge Maps (KM) Modeller** may be based on any available UML Class Diagram tool exporting the XMI notation to be subsequently processed by the OfficeObjects® Ontology Manager module and mapped onto the ontology structure to form a Knowledge Maps definition.

The scope of design specifications supported by the Tool Box components becomes apparent in the context of the design decision trees, discussed in Sect. 5.

The **MDX Workbench,** the **Extract-Transform-Load (ETL) Workbench**, and the **Report Editor**, are used to develop data marts, and the associated ROLAP models, within the integrated **Business Intelligence** solution. Although, all of these tools require data analysis skills, they may be used by no-IT personnel, hence they fall into the broad class of the EUSE tools.

The underlying data **Storage** package represents systems and facilities, such as data base management systems, file systems, web services, and web pages, that may be referenced to select and retrieve information objects accessible via the Knowledge Management Repository reference structures.

The **workflow process instances** managed by the OfficeObjects® WorkFlow platform are stored in a WfMC run-time meta-model format. Event data resulting from execution of workflow process instances are recorded in the form of process logs, which subsequently may be used to generate process execution reports and ROLAP models. The workflow process definitions are available via the OfficeObjects® Process Design Tool and may be exported/imported with the use of the WfMC XPDL notation.

The OfficeObjects® Repository data model is presented in Fig. 3 as the UML class diagram of information resources coupled with a set of interfaces representing the repository referential structure. The repository contains instances of information object classes, where an object may belong to only one object class determined by the meta-data model. The physical structure of an information object instance, i.e. the number, size and type of binary artefacts (files), stored in an object, is completely arbitrary, thus independent of the corresponding information object class.

Semantics of the KM repository are dependent on its referential structure, i.e. on information object classification and assignment to respective object collections. The classification and assignment actions are subdivided into three principal modes, namely the **Automatic** mode, the **Manual** mode, and the **Knowledge Map** mode. The last variant may be considered a variation of the Automatic mode.

The automatic collection represents the following object collection semantics; (a) Full Text Retrieval pertain to the entire population of all information classes automatically indexed and made eligible for retrieval on the basis of their textual content, (b) the remaining three automatic collections, i.e. the **Categorization Tree**, the **Meta-data Search**, and the **Register**, pertain to the population of a single object class only. The categorization trees support a hierarchical access path to information objects selected on the basis of the meta-data attribute values, and the registers are a chronological ordering of objects within the corresponding class or a subordinated sub-class defined by a selection predicate referencing the meta-data attributes.

The manual collections, such as the case files or repository folders, represent a manual, information-bearing classification process, since most often the allocation activities may not be reproduced on the basis of the meta-data values. In fact, the allocation decisions are implemented by the direct user actions. However, in some applications it may be possible to perform such allocations automatically, if appropriate information, such as for example the case file identifier, are present in the meta-data of the information object to be categorized.

The knowledge map is constructed and maintained automatically, controlled by the construction rules, defined on the meta-data attributes, and by the appropriate mapping rules. The mapping rules decide, which meta-data attributes are to be represented in the corresponding knowledge map topics (nodes), and the construction rules determine the

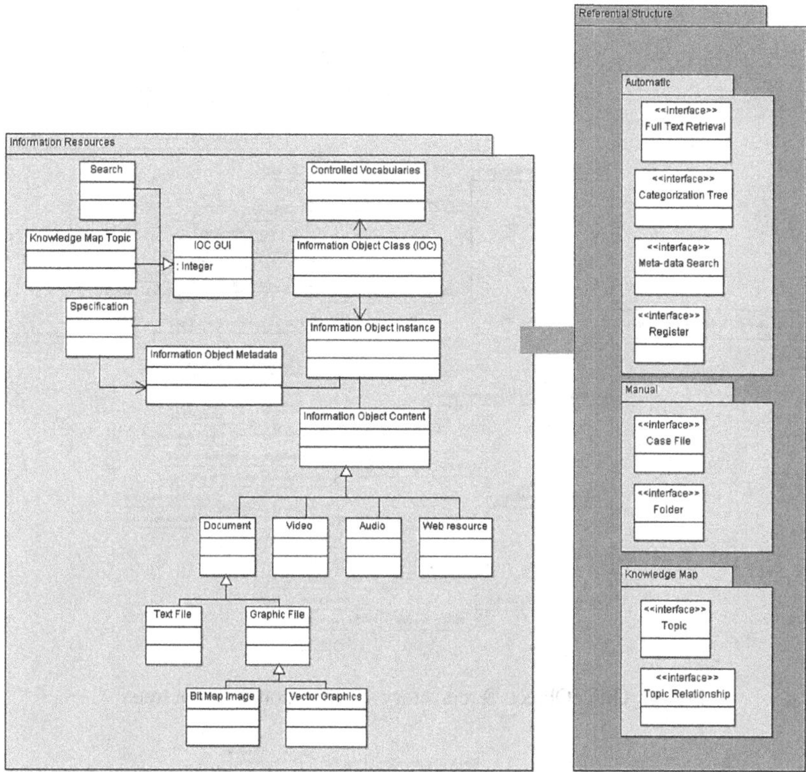

Fig. 3. OfficeObjects® repository data model.

relationships maintained among the knowledge map topics, thus establishing the required traversal path within the map.

5 The KMS Solution End-User Specification Methodology

We have selected two knowledge management application design and specification areas to illustrate the merits and limitations of the OfficeObjects® application development tools, in particular their eligibility for the end-user. We need to make a reservation, that we expect the computer literacy of the end-user system developer, often such a role being called the power-user, at least on the level of an expert spreadsheet user or a personal database user. As we mentioned before, such qualifications are ubiquitous among the professionals using computers for their work.

We concentrate on two principal design areas of the knowledge management system functional spectrum, namely on the knowledge repository and on the workflow management platform, shown in Figs. 4 and 5 respectively. A convention used in both mind maps is the **X** symbol meaning that the decision branch and all descending children are ineligible for the end-user, due to their complexity calling for the professional IT skills.

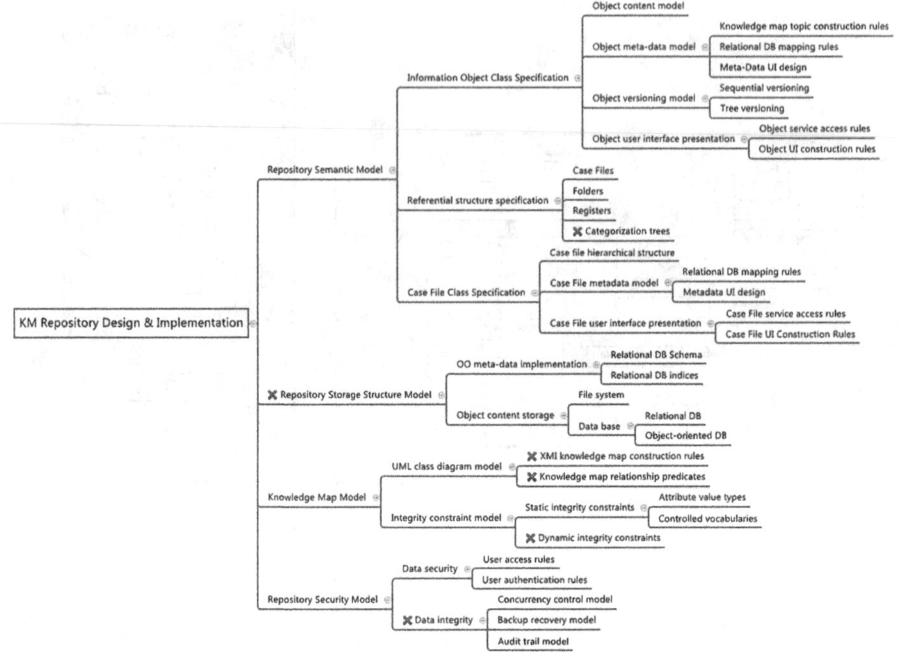

Fig. 4. OfficeObjects® repository specification decision tree.

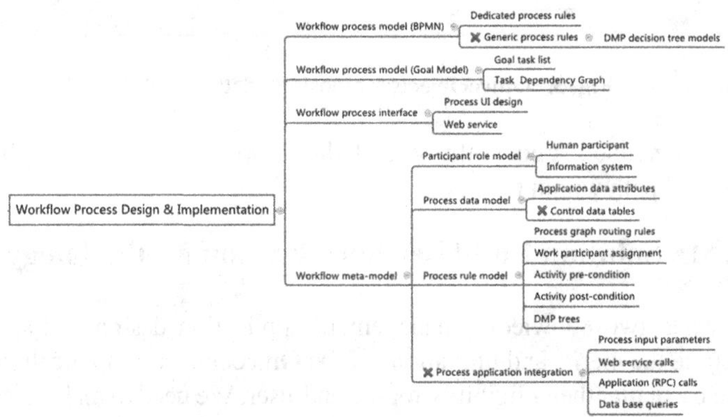

Fig. 5. OfficeObjects® Workflow specification decision tree.

The **Repository Semantic Level** includes all design decisions, either pertaining to the conceptual model of the repository knowledge resources, or to the underlying data structure specifications providing the building blocks for the higher level constructs, such as the meta-data specifications of an information object class. Design specification, which we believe might be too complex for the non-programming user, are the categorization tree materialization queries, since they require advanced SQL operations such as the JOIN and GROUP BY queries.

All of the other design specifications pertaining to the semantic modelling of the knowledge resources, such as the automatic assignment predicates aligning information objects within the target referential objects, such as **Registers** and **Case Files**, are well within the grasp of the power-user. All in all, it is quite possible, that the power-users define a complex repository data model, albeit some OfficeObjects® methodology and tools training is advisable.

On the other hand, definition of the **Repository Storage Structure Model** requires decisions calling for the specialized data management skills, hence it usually rests beyond capabilities of even advanced power-users. The solution here is to apply default physical data structure configurations, pre-configured in the software distribution version, offering good performance support for typical repository usage patterns.

The **Knowledge Maps Model** is a critical feature of the most of the knowledge management applications supporting semantic views over the information objects stored in the knowledge repository. Superimposing an UML class diagram model over the Topic Maps ontology, and maintaining references between topics and information objects, allows the repository user to select and manipulate the knowledge resources, i.e. the information objects, according to a domain-oriented semantic data model. Navigation in the network of binary topic relationships, linking internal and external knowledge artefacts, constitutes a powerful search platform guiding navigation along the associative selection paths.

The knowledge map design may proceed in a "top down" manner, starting from the UML class diagram referencing the information object classes and linking them within appropriate relationships, or using a "bottom up" method, defining the topic relationships and the associated relationship predicates directly using the Topic Maps formalism. The latter method may not be advisable for the power-users.

The recommended design methodology is to define the UML class diagram of a knowledge map, tag the relationships with the selected association predicates defined over meta-data attributes of the associated classes, and to automatically generate the Topic Maps specifications via the XMI interface.

We also assume that both **Dynamic integrity constraints** as well as **Data integrity** rules and procedures may be too complex for a non-IT professional and they will usually require help from the system administration staff. Notwithstanding the above limitations, we may safely claim that a working knowledge management repository may be designed, specified and maintained by non-IT professionals possibly supported by the system familiarization rudimentary training.

The second important design realm of the knowledge management application solution implementation is the **Workflow Process Design & Implementation** area. The scope of design decisions facing the system designer is depicted in Fig. 5. Most of the application specification tools, such as the process graph specification, the graphic user interface form editor, the functional rule specification language, and the process participant role model, have proven to be sufficiently user friendly to be productively employed by the power-users.

We find that specifying generic workflow models, employing the dynamic process modification features [14], may exceed the capabilities of the power-user. On the other hand, parameterizing such processes, available in the process pattern library, is quite straightforward and may readily be performed by the users.

In order to address the requirements identified in Sect. 2, rather than utilizing the BPMN graphical process model, one may specify the **Goal Model** workflow process [37] much more suitable for planning and executing the project-oriented activities. The Goal Model processes are specified as the check list of all process tasks, the participant assignment rules for each task, and the dependency graph representing the precedence relationships among tasks. Task execution is scheduled only for tasks that are not bound by any precedence relationship.

The process goal is met when all tasks have been executed. Such process specification and maintenance tasks as interpreting the process **control data tables** comprising the workflow process run-time meta-models, for diagnostic and performance-oriented process design purposes, may require assistance from the process administration staff. Also the **process application integration** specifications, may either require the power-users to undergo substantial training, or collaboration with the process administration staff.

6 Conclusions

The end-user oriented methodology underlying development of the knowledge management application solutions has been verified in the course of a number of application projects. Among others, a large-scale knowledge management application system had been implemented in the period of 2010–2012 serving a community of 2000 scientists working for 20 research organizations.

The knowledge management system is currently used as a networking tool to support co-operation of industrial organizations and research institutes according the recommendations of the Open Innovation model.

The platform, which serves as a tool supporting communication and cooperation, as well as providing information pertaining to the resources and skills possessed by the participating organizations, facilitates their co-operation and the dissemination of best practices in the area of the research work and management.

The lessons learnt during design and development of the above system confirm, that all major application functions were indeed developed without the recourse to classic application programming languages, such as Java or C ++. The only hurdle to overcome by the non-programming developers were the Java Script validation codes. Although the power-users were successfully involved in the system development effort, provision of sufficiently thorough training materials, as well as of the technical help available on-line could significantly improve the implementation process.

References

1. Aggarwal, J.K., Ryoo, M.S.: Human activity analysis: a review. ACM Comput. Surv. **43**(3) (2011)
2. Baader, F., Sattler, U.: An overview of tableau algorithms for description logics. Stud. Logica **69**(1), 5–40 (2001)
3. Baader, F., Calvanese, D., McGuinness, D.L., Nardi, D., Patel-Schneider, P.F. (eds.): The Description Logic Handbook: Theory, Implementation, and Applications. Cambridge University Press, Cambridge (2003)

4. Badii, A., Chattun, L., Meng, Z., Crouch, M.: The DREAM framework: using a network of scalable ontologies for intelligent indexing and retrieval of visual content. In: Proceedings of the International Conference on Web Intelligence and Intelligent Agent Technology. IEEE (2009)
5. Bider, I., Johannesson, P., Perjons, E.: Justifying ACM: why we need a paradigm shift in BPM. In: Fischer, L. (ed.) Empowering Knowledge Workers – New Ways to Leverage Case Management. Future Strategies Inc., New York (2014)
6. Cahier, J-P., Ma, X., Zaher, L.: Document and item-based modeling; a hybrid method for a socio-semantic web. In: Proceedings of the ACM DocEng Conference, Manchester, UK, 21–24 September 2010
7. Calvanese, D., De Giacomo, G., Lenzerini, M., Nardi, D.: Reasoning in expressive description logics. In: Robinson, A., Voronkov, A. (eds.) Handbook of Automated Reasoning. Elsevier Science Publishers, Amsterdam, Chap. 23 (2001)
8. Wiza, W., Walczak, K., Chmielewski, J.: Mobile interfaces for building control surveyors. In: Cellary, W., Estevez, E. (eds.) Software Services for e-World. IFIP AICT, vol. 341, pp. 29–39. Springer, Heidelberg (2010)
9. Costabile, M.F., De Ruyter, B., Mehandjiev, N., Mussio, P.: End-user development of software services and applications. In: AVI 2010, Rome, 25–29 May 2010
10. Damen, D., Pinchuk, R., Fontaine, B.: Creating topic maps ontologies for space experiments. In: Proceedings of the International Conference on Topic Maps Research and Applications (TMRA) (2009)
11. Davis, R., Shrobe, H., Szolovits, P.: What is a knowledge representation? AI Mag. **14**(1), 17–33 (1993)
12. Doerr, M., Iorizzo, D.: The Dream of a global knowledge network – a new approach. ACM J. Comput. Cult. Herit. **1**(1), 1–23 (2008)
13. Drucker, P.F.: Management Challenges for the 21st Century. Elsevier Ltd., Oxford (1999)
14. The Administrative Process Generator Design report, FP6-IST-2004-26727, Advanced eGovernment Information Service Bus (eGovBus), March 2006
15. User-oriented assessment of the eGovBus prototype, FP6-IST-2004-26727, Advanced eGovernment Information Service Bus (eGovBus), December 2008
16. Ginsberg, M.L.: Knowledge interchange format: the KIF of death. AI Mag. **12**(33), 57–63 (1991)
17. Gruber, T.R.: A translation approach to portable ontology specifications. Knowl. Acquis. **5**, 99–220 (1993)
18. Harrison-Broninski, K.D.: Human Interactions – The Heart and Soul of Business Process Management. Meghan-Kiffer Press, Tampa (2005)
19. Harrison-Broninski, K.: Types of business process. In: Fischer, L. (ed.) How Knowledge Workers get Things Done-Real World Adaptive Case Management. Future Strategies Inc., New York (2012)
20. Intelligent Content Management System (ICONS) Project Presentation, FP5 IST-2001-32429 (2002)
21. Juve, G., Deelman, E.: Scientific workflows and clouds. Crossroads Plugging Cloud **16**(3), 14–18 (2010). http://www.acm.org/crossroads
22. Khoyi, D.: Data orientation. In: Swenson, K.D. (ed.) Mastering the Unpredictable. Future Strategies Inc., New York (2010)
23. Khoyi, D., Swenson, K.D.: Templates, not programs. In: Swenson, K.D. (ed.) Mastering the Unpredictable. Future Strategies Inc., New York (2010)
24. Ko, A.J., et al.: The state of the art in end-user software engineering. ACM Comput. Surv. **43**(3), 44 (2011)

25. Kraft, F.M.: Improving knowledge work. In: Swenson, K.D. (ed.) Mastering the Unpredictable. Future Strategies Inc., New York (2010)
26. Lakshman, T.K., Thuijs, X.: Enhancing enterprise field productivity via cross platform mobile cloud apps. In: Proceedings of the MCS 2011, Bethesda, Maryland, USA, 28 June 2011
27. Langenberg, D., Kind, C., Darnes, M.: The KnowledgeCloud Project, BMWi, Germany (2011)
28. Lee, Y., et al.: MobiCon: a mobile context-monitoring platform. Comm. ACM **55**(3), 54–65 (2012)
29. Sezov, R.: Liferay, Portal Administrator's Guide. Liferay Inc., Los Angeles (2009)
30. Lizcano, D., Alonso, F., Soriano, J., Lopez, G.: A new end-user composition model to empower knowledge workers to develop rich internet applications. J. Web Eng. **10**(3), 197–233 (2011)
31. Malone, T.W., Crowston, K., et al.: Organizing Business Knowledge: The MIT Process Handbook. MIT Press, Cambridge (2003)
32. Mancilla-Amaya, L., Sanin, C., Szczerbicki, E.: The e-decisional community: an integrated knowledge sharing platform. In: Proceedings of the 7th Asia-Pacific Conference on Conceptual Modelling (APCCM 2010), Brisbane, Australia (2010)
33. Matthias, J.T.: User requirements for a new generation of case management systems. In: Fischer, L. (ed.) Taming the Unpredictable – Real World Adaptive Case Management: Case Studies and Practical Guidance. Future Strategies Inc., New York (2011)
34. McCauley, D.: Achieving agility. In: Swenson, K.D. (ed.) Mastering the Unpredictable. Future Strategies Inc., New York (2010)
35. Mehandjiev, N., De Angeli, A.: End-user mashups – analytical framework. In: WAS4FI 2012, Bertinoro, Italy, 19 September 2012
36. Nestler, T., Namoun, A., Schill, A.: End-user development of service-based interactive web applications at the presentation layer. In: EICS 2011, Pisa, 13–16 June 2011
37. OfficeObjects® Software Product, Rodan Systems S.A., Warsaw, Poland (2010). www.rodan.pl
38. W3C, The XML-based Web Ontology Language. http://www.w3.org/TR/owl-features/
39. Palmer, N.: BPM and ACM. In: Fischer, L. (ed.) Taming the Unpredictable – Real World Adaptive Case Management: Case Studies and Practical Guidance. Future Strategies Inc., New York (2011)
40. Palmer, N.: Case management megatrends. In: Fischer, L. (ed.) How Knowledge Workers Get Things Done – Real World Adaptive Case Management. Future Strategies Inc., New York (2012)
41. Palmer, N.: Where is ACM today? realities and opportunities. In: Fischer, L. (ed.) Empowering Knowledge Workers – New Ways to Leverage Case Management. Future Strategies Inc., New York (2014)
42. Park, J.: Topic maps, dashboards and sensemaking. In: Proceedings of the International Conference on Topic Maps Research and Applications (TMRA) (2008)
43. Mondrian 3.0.4 Technical Guide, Pentaho Org., USA (2009)
44. Pepper, S.: The TAO of topic maps: finding the way in the age of infoglut (2009). http://www.ontopia.net/topicmaps/materials/tao.html
45. Pucher, M.J.: The elements of adaptive case management. In: Swenson, K.D. (ed.) Mastering the Unpredictable. Future Strategies Inc., New York (2010)
46. Pucher, M.J.: The strategic business benefits of adaptive case management. In: Fischer, L. (ed.) How Knowledge Workers Get Things Done – Real World Adaptive Case Management. Future Strategies Inc., New York (2012)

47. Ruiz, C., Alvaro, G., Gomez-Perez, J.: A framework and implementation for secure knowledge management in large communities. The ACTIVE project website (2011). http://www.active-project.eu/
48. Rychkova, I., Kirsch-Pinheiro, M., Le Grand, B.: Automated guidance for case management: science or fiction? In: Fischer, L. (ed.) Empowering Knowledge Workers – New Ways to Leverage Case Management. Future Strategies Inc., New York (2014)
49. Shams, K.S., Powell, M.W., Crockett, T.M., Norris, J.S., Rossi, R., Soderstrom, T.: Polyphony: a workflow orchestration framework for cloud computing. In: Proceedings of the 2010 10th IEEE/ACM International Conference on Cluster, Cloud and Grid Computing. IEEE, New York (2010)
50. Silver, B.: Case management: addressing unique BPM requirements. In: Fischer, L. (ed.) Taming the Unpredictable – Real World Adaptive Case Management: Case Studies and Practical Guidance. Future Strategies Inc., New York (2011)
51. Spofford, G.: MDX Solutions. Wiley, New York (2001)
52. Sowa, J.F.: Conceptual graphs for a database interface. IBM J. Res. Dev. **20**(4), 336–357 (1976)
53. Swenson, K.D.: The nature of knowledge work. In: Swenson, K.D. (ed.) Mastering the Unpredictable. Future Strategies Inc., New York (2010)
54. Swenson, K.D.: Advantages of agile BPM. In: Fischer, L. (ed.) Taming the Unpredictable – Real World Adaptive Case Management: Case Studies and Practical Guidance. Future Strategies Inc., New York (2011)
55. Swenson, K.D.: Case management: contrasting production vs. adaptive. In: Fischer, L. (ed.) How Knowledge Workers Get Things Done – Real World Adaptive Case Management. Future Strategies Inc., New York (2012)
56. Swenson, K.D.: Innovative organizations act like systems, not machines. In: Fischer, L. (ed.) Empowering Knowledge Workers – New Ways to Leverage Case Management. Future Strategies Inc., New York (2014)
57. Talia, D.: Workflow systems for science: concepts and tools. ISRN Softw. Eng. (2013). doi: 10.1155/2013/404525
58. Tolone, W., Ahn, G.J., Tanusree, P.: Access control in colaborative systems. ACM Comput. Surv. **37**(1), 29–41 (2005)
59. van Harmelen, F., van Harmelen, F., Lifschitz, V., Porter, B.: Handbook of Knowledge Representation. Elsevier Science, San Diego (2007)
60. Vatant, B.: Managing complex environments with topic maps. In: Proceedings of the Knowledge Technologies Conference 2001, Austin, USA (2001)
61. Verginadis, Y., Papageorgiou, N., Apostolou, D., Mentzas, G.: A review of patterns in collaborative work. In: Proceedings of the ACM GROUP 2010 Conference, Sanibel Island, Florida, USA, 7–10 November 2010
62. Vockler, J-S., Juve, G., Deelman, E., Rynge, M., Berriman, G.B.: Experiences using cloud for a scientific workflow application. In: Proceedings of the ACM ScienceCloud 2011 Conference, San Jose, California, USA, 8 June 2011
63. Zinn, D., McPhillips, T., Ludascher, B., Simmhan, Y., Giakkoupis, M., Prasanna, V.K.: Towards reliable, performant workflows for streaming-applications on cloud platforms. In: Proceedings of IEEE/ACM International Symposium on Cluster, Cloud and Grid Computing. IEEE, New York (2011)

[illegible] Knowledge Web [illegible]

47. Ru[illegible] C[illegible] [illegible] A framework and model [illegible] [illegible] project [illegible]

48. [illegible] M. [illegible] In: [illegible] New York (2011)

49. [illegible] Powell, M.W. [illegible] In: [illegible] IEEE/ACM International Conference on Cluster, Cloud and Grid Computing. IEEE, New York (2011)

50. [illegible] Management: Case Studies and Practical Guidance [illegible] New York (2010)

51. [illegible] New York (2011)

[illegible]

[illegible] New York (2011)

[illegible]

[illegible] New York (2010)

[illegible]

[illegible]

60. [illegible]

61. Vergnaud [illegible] In: Proceedings of the ACM [illegible] Florida, USA [illegible]

62. [illegible]

64. [illegible] In: Proceedings of IEEE/ACM International Symposium on Cluster, [illegible] Computing. IEEE, New York (2011)

Databases and Information Systems Integration

Fire Detection from Social Media Images by Means of Instance-Based Learning

Marcos Vinicius Naves Bedo(✉), William Dener de Oliveira, Mirela Teixeira Cazzolato, Alceu Ferraz Costa, Gustavo Blanco, Jose F. Rodrigues Jr., Agma J.M. Traina, and Caetano Traina Jr.

Institute of Mathematics and Computer Science, University of São Paulo, P.O. Box 668, São Carlos/SP, Brazil
{bedo,willian,alceufc,junio,agma,caetano}@icmc.usp.br,
{mirelac,gublanco}@usp.br
http://www.gbdi.icmc.usp.br

Abstract. Social media can provide valuable information to support decision making in crisis management, such as in accidents, explosions, and fires. However, much of the data from social media are images, which are uploaded at a rate that makes it impossible for human beings to analyze them. To cope with that problem, we design and implement a database-driven architecture for fast and accurate fire detection named FFireDt. The design of FFireDt uses the instance-based learning through indexed similarity queries expressed as an extension of the relational Structured Query Language. Our contributions are: (*i*) the design of the Fast-Fire Detection (*FFireDt*), which achieves efficiency and efficacy rates that rival to the state-of-the-art techniques; (*ii*) the sound evaluation of 36 image descriptors, for the task of image classification in social media; (*iii*) the evaluation of content-based indexing with respect to the construction of instance-based classification systems; and (*iv*) the curation of a ground-truth annotated dataset of fire images from social media. Using real data from Flickr, the experiments showed that system *FFireDt* was able to achieve a precision for fire detection comparable to that of human annotators. Our results are promising for the engineering of systems to monitor images uploaded to social media services.

Keywords: Fire detection · Image descriptors · Social media · Extended-SQL

1 Introduction

Fire incidents represent a serious threat to industries, crowded events and densely populated areas. This kind of incident may cause impacts in property, environment, and danger to human life. Therefore, a fast response of the authorities is essential to prevent and reduce injuries and financial losses, when crises situations strike. The management of such situations is a challenge that requires fast and effective decisions using all available data, because decisions based on

S. Hammoudi et al. (Eds.): ICEIS 2015, LNBIP 241, pp. 23–44, 2015.
DOI: 10.1007/978-3-319-29133-8_2

incomplete information may lead to more damages [1]. Software systems can be used to support expert and rescue forces in the decision making during crises, by improving information correctness and availability [2].

Systems aimed at supporting salvage and rescue teams often rely on images to understand the crisis scenario and to determine the actions that will reduce losses [3]. Crowdsourcing and social media, as massive sources of images, possess a great potential to assist such systems. Users from social media such as Flickr, Twitter, and Facebook upload pictures from mobile devices in many situations, generating a flow of images with valuable information. Such information may reduce the time spent to make decisions, especially when used along with other information sources. In order to benefit from massive volume of social media images, automatic image analysis is an important technique to grasp the dimensions, type, objects and people involved in an incident.

Despite the potential benefits, we observed that there is still a lack of studies concerning automatic content-based processing of crisis images [3]. In the specific case of fire – which is observed during explosions, car accidents, forest and building fire, to name a few, there is an absence of studies to identify the most adequate content-based retrieval techniques (image descriptors) able to identify and retrieve relevant images captured during crises. Therefore, our objective in this work is to fill this gap with the aid of a prototype system for fire monitoring. Our system sets up an extension of the relational model [4] to store images collected from social media at the same time that it employs similarity queries to classify them.

This work reports on one of the steps of the project *Reliable and Smart Crowdsourcing Solution for Emergency and Crisis Management – Rescuer*[1]. The project goal is to use crowdsourcing data (image, video, and text captured with mobile devices) to assist in rescue missions. Here, we evaluate a set of techniques for fire detection by image content, one of the project targets. We use real images from Flickr[2], a well-known social media website from where we collected a large set of images that were manually annotated as having fire, or not. We used this dataset as a ground-truth to evaluate image descriptors in the task of detecting fire. Our contributions are the following:

1. **Design of FFireDt:** we introduce the Fast-Fire Detection architecture, a scalable system for automatic fire detection that rivals the state-of-the-art methods and whose accuracy compares to that of human annotation;
2. **Evaluation:** we soundly compare the precision and performance of 36 image descriptors for image classification. Additionally, we show that indexing similarity querying is necessary to make instance-based learning scalable;
3. **Flickr-Fire Dataset:** a vast human-annotated dataset of real images, suitable as ground-truth for the development of content-based techniques for fire detection – distributed online at http://icmc.usp.br/pessoas/junio/DatasetFlicker/DatasetFlickr.htm.

[1] http://www.rescuer-project.org/.
[2] https://www.flickr.com/.

The groundwork of the *FFireDt* architecture is described in [5]. This paper's contribution extends the latter publication with a number of new results. Specifically, we introduce: *(i)* an extended description of the *FFireDt* logical design; *(ii)* the *FFireDt* schema fully integrated into the relational model; *(iii)* an extended analysis of the *FFireDt* image classification, which includes the use of indexing techniques; and *(iv)* a comprehensive presentation of the experimental results.

The rest of this paper is organized as follows. Section 2 introduces the related work; Sect. 3 presents the main concepts regarding fire-detection in images; Sect. 4 presents the proposed architecture and the *FFireDt* relational schema. Section 5 describes the experiments and discusses their results; finally, Sect. 6 presents the conclusions.

2 Related Work

In this paper we are interested in the following problem:

Problem 1. Given a collection of photos, possibly obtained from a social media service, how can we efficiently and effectively detect fire?

There are interesting approaches related to this problem concerning motion analysis on video, but they are not applicable for still images [6], and most of these approaches do not present satisfactory performance [7–9]. Other works have a different focus, as in the case of [10], whose work aims at mining information from sets of images originated from social events at the same time that its corresponding related topics are detected (e.g. touristic attractions).

In the literature, there are studies proposing particular color models focused on fire detection, based on Gaussian differences [7] or in spectral characteristics to identify fire, smoke, heat or radiation. The spectral color model has been used along with spatial correlation and stochastic modeling in order to capture fire motion [9]. However, such technique requires a sequence of images and is not suitable for individual images, which are common in social media.

Other studies employ a variation of the combination given by a color model transform and a classifier. This combination is employed in the work of Dimitropoulos *et al.* [11], which represents each frame of a video according to the most prominent texture and shape features. It also combines such representation with spatio-temporal motion features to employ SVM classification to detect fire in videos. However, this approach is neither scalable nor suitable for fire detection on still images.

On the other hand, the feature extraction methods available in the MPEG-7 Standard have been used for image representation in fast-response systems that deal with large amounts of data [12–14]. Nevertheless, to the best of our knowledge, there is no study employing those extractors for fire detection. Despite the multiple approaches seen in this section, there is no conclusive work about which image descriptors are suitable to identify fire in images. Thus, it is a demand to have means to accurately evaluate the most appropriate method, as we pursue in the present research.

3 Background

3.1 Content-Based Model for Retrieval and Classification

The use of queries based on similarity is a well-known approach to retrieve images by content, relying on the representation of such data through feature extraction techniques [15,16]. After the extraction of a vector of representative numerical features, the images can be retrieved by comparing their vectors using a distance function, which is usually a metric or a divergence function; the Euclidean distance is the most common one. Such a comparison is a necessary step in image retrieval systems. However, it is possible to employ this same method, the similarity-based retrieval, in the task of image classification. This is called Instance-Based Learning (IBL). IBL classifiers label a given image according to the labels of its most similar images as informed by a similarity query [17]. Formally, these concepts can be expressed as follows:

Definition 1. Feature Extraction Method (FEM): *A feature extraction method is a non-bijective function that, given an image domain $\mathbb{I}$, is able to represent any image $i_q \in \mathbb{I}$ in a domain $\mathbb{F}$ as f_q. Each value f_q is called a feature vector (FV) and represents characteristics of the image i_q.*

We use FEMs to represent images in multidimensional domains. Therefore, the image feature vectors can be compared according to the next definition:

Definition 2. Evaluation Function (EF): *Given the feature vectors f_i, f_j and $f_k \in \mathbb{F}$, an evaluation function $\delta : \mathbb{F} \times \mathbb{F} \rightarrow \mathbb{R}$ is able to compare any two elements from $\mathbb{F}$. The EF is said to be a metric distance function if it complies with the following properties:*

- *Symmetry:* $\delta(f_i, f_j) = \delta(f_j, f_i)$.
- *Non-negativity:* $0 < \delta(f_i, f_j) < \infty$.
- *Triangular inequality:* $\delta(f_i, f_j) \leq \delta(f_i, f_k) + \delta(f_k, f_j)$.

The FEM defines the element distribution in the multidimensional space. On the other hand, the evaluation function defines the behavior of the searching functionalities. Therefore, the combination of FEM and EF is the main parameter to improve or decrease the accuracy and quality for both classification and retrieval. Formally, this association can be defined as:

Definition 3. Image Descriptor (ID): *An image descriptor is a pair $\langle \epsilon, \delta \rangle$, where ϵ is a composition of FEM and δ is a weighted EF.*

By employing a suitable *image descriptor*, it is possible to inspect the neighborhood of a given element considering previously labeled cases. This course of action is the principle of the Instance-Based Learning algorithms, which rely on previously labeled data to classify new elements according to their nearest neighbors. The sense of what "nearest" means is provided by the EF. Formally, the nearest elements correspond to the following definition:

Definition 4. k-Nearest-Neighbors - kNN: *Given an image i_q summarized as $f_q \in \mathbb{F}$, an image descriptor $ID = \langle \epsilon,\ \delta \rangle$, a number of neighbors $k \in \mathbb{N}$ and a set F of represented images, the k-Nearest Neighbors set is, generically, the subset of $F \subset \mathbb{F}$ such that $kNN = \{f_n \in \mathbb{F} \mid \forall\ f_i \in F;\ \delta(f_n,\ f_q) < \delta(f_i,\ f_q)\}$.*

The fast execution of kNN queries is crucial to a system that handles images arriving from a social media service. Similarity kNN queries using extended-SQL [18] satisfies this need as they lead to huge performance gains [19,20] if planned as an extension of a Relational Database Management System. Once part of a database system, the similarity retrieval mechanism is also able to store the automatic classification and the results of the kNN queries. Similarity queries rely on the properties of the *image descriptor* to define the image representations and the search space. Therefore, the choice of suitable descriptors becomes the critical point to be defined in a fire detection system. The next section reviews the possibilities of image descriptors for this task as well as how similarity queries can be used to support IBL over the relational model.

3.2 MPEG-7 Feature Extraction Methods

The MPEG-7 standard was proposed by the ISO/IEC JTC1 [21]. It defines expected representations for images regarding color, texture and shape. The set of proposed feature extraction methods was designed to process the original image as fast as possible, without taking into account specific image domains. The original proposal of MPEG-7 is composed of two parts: high and low-level values, both intended to represent the image. The low-level value is the representation of the original data by a FEM. On the other hand, the high-level feature requires examination by an expert.

The goal of MPEG-7 is to standardize the representation of *streamed* or stored images. The low-level FEMs are widely employed to compare and to filter data, based purely on content. These FEMs are meaningful in the context of various applications according to several studies [12,14]. They are also supposed to define objects by including color patches, shapes or textures. The MPEG-7 standard defines the following set of low-level extractors [22]:

- **Color:** Color Layout, Color Structure, Scalable Color and Color Temperature, Dominant Color, Color Correlogram, Group-of-Frames;
- **Texture:** Edge Histogram, Texture Browsing, Homogeneous Texture;
- **Shape:** Contour Shape, Shape Spectrum, Region Shape;

We highlight that shape FEMs' usually depends on previous object definitions. As the goal of this study relies on defining the best setting for automatic classification and retrieval for fire detection, user interaction in the extraction process is not suitable for our proposal. Thus, we focus only on the color and texture extractors. In this study we employ the following MPEG-7 extractors: Color Layout, Color Structure, Scalable Color, Color Temperature, Edge Histogram, and Texture Browsing. They are explained in the next Sections.

Color Layout. The MPEG-7 Color Layout (CL) [23] describes the image color distribution considering spatial location. It splits the image in square sub-regions (the number of sub regions is a parameter) and label each square with the average color of the region. Next, the average colors are transformed to the YCbCr space and a Discrete Cosine Transformation is applied over each band of the YCbCr region values. The low-frequency coefficients are extracted through a zig-zag image reading. In order to reduce dimensionality, only the most prominent frequencies are employed in the feature vector.

Scalable Color. The MPEG-7 Scalable Color (SC) [24] aims at capturing the prominent color distribution. It is based on four stages. The first stage converts all pixels from the RGB color-space to the HSV space and a normalized color histogram is constructed. The color histogram is quantized using 256 levels of the HSV space. Finally, a Haar wavelet transformation is applied over the resulting histogram [13].

Color Structure. The MPEG-7 Color Structure (CS) expresses both spatial and color distribution [25]. This paper splits the original image in a set of color structures with fixed-size windows. Each fixed-size window selects equally spaced pixels to represent the local color structure. The window size and the number of local structures are parameters of CS [24]. For each color structure, a quantization based on the HMMD - a color-space derived from HSV that represents color differences - is executed. Then a local "histogram" based on HMMD is built. It stores the presence or absence of the quantized color instead of its distribution along with the window. The resulting feature vector is the accumulated distribution of the local histograms according to the previous quantization.

Edge Histogram. The MPEG-7 Edge Histogram (EH) aims at capturing local and global edges. It defines five types of edges regarding $N \times N$ blocks, where N is an extractor parameter. Each block is constructed by partitioning the original image into square regions. After applying the square masks to an image, it is possible to compute the local edge histograms. At this stage, the entire histogram is composed of $5 \times N$ bins, but it is biased by local edges. To circumvent this problem, a variation [26] was proposed to capture also semi-local edges. The resulting feature vector is composed of N plus thirteen edge-histograms, which represents the local and the semi-local distribution, respectively.

Color Temperature. The main hypothesis supporting the MPEG-7 Color Temperature (CT) is that there is a correlation between the "feeling of image temperature" and illumination properties. Formally, the proposal considers a theoretical object called *black body*, whereupon its color depends on the temperature [27]. According to Planck's formula, the locus of the theoretical black body changes from 2,000 Kelvin (red) to 25,000 Kelvin (blue). The feature vector represents the linearized pixels in the XYZ space. This is performed by interactively discarding every pixel with luminance Y above the given threshold – a FEM's parameter. Thereafter, the average color coordinates in XYZ are converted to UCS. Finally, the two closest isotemperature lines is calculated from the given color diagrams [27]. The formula for the resulting color temperature depends on the average point, the closest isolines and the distances among them.

Texture Browsing. The MPEG-7 Texture Browsing extractor (TB) is obtained from Gabor filters applied to the image [28]. This FEM parameters' are the same used in Gabor filtering. The Texture Browsing feature vector is composed of 12 positions: 2 to represent regularity, 6 for directionality and 4 for coarseness. The regularity features represent the degree of regularity of the texture structure as a more/less regular pattern, in such a way that the more regular a texture, the more robust the representation of the other features is. The directionality defines the most dominant texture orientation. This feature is obtained providing an orientation variation for the Gabor filters. Finally, the coarseness represents the two dominant scales of the texture.

3.3 Evaluation Functions

An Evaluation Function expresses the proximity between two feature vectors. We are interested in feature extractor that generates the same amount of features for each image, thus we account only for evaluation functions for multidimensional spaces. Particularly, we employed distance functions (metrics) and divergences as evaluation functions. Suppose two feature vectors $X = \{x_1, x_2, \ldots, x_n\}$ and $Y = \{y_1, y_2, \ldots, y_n\}$ of dimensionality n. Table 1 shows the EFs implemented, according to their evaluation formulas. The most widely employed metric distance functions are those related to the Minkowski family: the Manhattan, Euclidean and Chebyshev [29]. A variation of the Manhattan distance is the Canberra distance that results in distances in the range $[0, 1]$. These four EFs satisfy the properties of Definition 2. Therefore, they are metric distance functions. However, there are non-metric distance functions that are useful for image classification and retrieval. The Kullback-Leibler Divergence, for instance, does not follow the triangular inequality neither the symmetry properties. A symmetric variation of the Kullback-Leibler is the Jeffrey Divergence, yet it still is not a metric due to the lack of the triangular inequality compliance.

3.4 Similarity Queries Support on RDBMS

Relational Database Management Systems (RDBMS) do not offer support to content-retrieval and similarity queries. Accordingly, several works have proposed an extension of the relational model to provide this support [19,20]. In this research, we use the *framework* SimbA [30], of our authorship, for the content-based retrieval functionalities. In accordance to the aforementioned benefits of this approach, this design choice improves the fire detection in our architecture, which focus on social media images. This extended-RDBMS tool enables the

Table 1. Evaluation functions: their classification as metric distance functions and respective formulas.

Name	Metric	Formula
City-Block	Yes	$\sum_{i=1}^{n} \|x_i - y_i\|$
Euclidean	Yes	$\sqrt{\sum_{i=1}^{n}(x_i - y_i)^2}$
Chebyshev	Yes	$\lim_{p\to\infty}(\sum_{i=1}^{n} \|x_i - y_i\|^p)^{\frac{1}{p}}$
Canberra	Yes	$\sum_{i=1}^{n} \frac{\|x_i - y_i\|}{\|x_i\|+\|y_i\|}$
Kullback Leibler divergence	No	$\sum_{i=1}^{n} x_i \ln(\frac{x_i}{y_i})$
Jeffrey divergence	No	$\sum_{i=1}^{n}(x_i - y_i)\ln(\frac{x_i}{y_i})$

improvement of the logical design and capabilities of the original proposal of the *FFireDt* architecture. It defines a relational schema to store the images arriving from a social network as well as their classifications and nearest neighbors. In this arrangement, the SimbA *framework* permits to create image descriptors and to store the images and their descriptive data into tables. It also enables to query images by content using extended SQL according to a given *image descriptor* and to employ the `GROUP BY` clause to perform the classification task. The advantages of using SimbA are: *(i)* the definition of a new *image descriptor* through extended-SQL as well new feature extractor methods and evaluation functions; *(ii)* query images by content through Selection and Join operations; and *(iii)* automatic indexing according to the *image descriptor*. Unlike its competitors FMI-SiR and Sim-DB, SimbA does not depend on a specific RDBMS and is able to handle regular and extended-SQL queries alike. Moreover, SimbA is flexible enough to provide support for several image file formats.

3.5 Instance-Based Learning - IBL

The main hypothesis for IBL classification is that the unlabeled feature vectors (FV) pertain to the same class of its k Nearest-Neighbors, according to a predefined rule. Such classifier relies on three components:

1. An evaluation function, which evaluates the proximity between two FVs;
2. A classification function, which receives the nearest FVs to classify the unlabeled one – commonly considering the majority of retrieved FVs;
3. A concept description updater, which maintains the record of previous classifications.

Variations of this strategy define different IBL versions. For instance, the IB1 adopts the majority of the retrieved elements as the classification rule and keeps no record of previous classifications. kNN similarity queries are sufficient to achieve IB1 classification. Moreover, it can be seamlessly expressed as an extended-SQL statement to be submitted to *framework* SimbA. This database-driven approach reduces the total time to execute the IB1 processing by using indexing techniques.

3.6 Dataset Flickr-Fire

For experimentation, we built the Flickr-Fire dataset, which consists of 5,962 images (no duplicates), obtained under license Creative Commons, using the Flickr API[3]. To retrieve the images we used textual queries such as: "fire car accident", "criminal fire", and "house burning". Figure 1(a) and (b) illustrate samples of the obtained images. After the retrieval, we excluded images with low quality.

Fig. 1. Sample images labeled as (a) `fire` and (b) `not_fire` from dataset `Flickr-Fire`.

Even with queries related to fire, some of the images did not present visual traces of fire, so each image was manually annotated in order to construct a coherent ground-truth dataset. To perform the annotation, we selected 7 subjects, all of them aging between 20 and 30 years, and non-color-blinded. The annotation was planned in a manner that each image was classified for at least two subjects as containing, or not, traces of fire. For the images with divergence in the annotation process, we asked a third subject to act as a tiebreaker. The average disagreement between the subjects was of 7.2 %. Aiming at balancing the class distribution of the dataset, we randomly removed images so to end up with 1,000 images containing fire and 1,000 images without fire. This dataset was named `Flickr-Fire` and employed in the experiments of Sect. 5.

4 FFireDt Physical Design

Here we introduce the Fast-Fire Detection (*FFireDt*) architecture, which depends on the *framework* SimbA, proposed in a previous work of ours, to perform image retrieval and classification. Figure 2 illustrates the relationship

[3] The Flickr API is available at: www.flickr.com/services/api/.

among the modules, their communication, and how they relate to SimbA. The feature extraction methods module (the FEM module) accepts any kind of feature extractor. For this work, we implemented six extractors following the MPEG-7 standard: Color Layout, Scalable Color, Color Structure, Edge Histogram, Color Temperature, and Texture Browsing – explained in Sect. 3.2. The evaluation functions module (the EF module) is also designed for general implementations; for this work, we implemented six functions: City-Block, Euclidean, Chebyshev, Jeffrey Divergence, Kullback-Leibler Divergence, and Canberra. The feature extractors methods and evaluation functions acronyms are listed in Table 2(a) and (b).

Table 2. Acronyms used in the experiments for (a) Feature Extracted Methods, and (b) Evaluation Functions.

(a)

Feature Extractor Method	Acronym
Color Layout	CL
Scalable Color	SC
Color Structure	CS
Color Temperature	CT
Edge Histogram	EH
Texture Browsing	TB

(b)

Evaluation Function Name	Acronym
City-Block	CB
Euclidean	EU
Chebyshev	CH
Canberra	CA
Kullback Leibler	KU
Jeffrey Divergence	JF

The *FFireDt* system heavily relies on image descriptors, which must be first defined and integrated into the system. By using the extended-SQL syntax provided by SimbA, the *FFireDt* image descriptors can be expressed as high-level commands as follows:

```
CREATE METRIC ID_<fem>_<ef> USING <ef>
FOR STILLIMAGE (<fem> (<fem_setting>));
```

The above command creates an *image descriptor*, a `''METRIC''` named `''ID_<fem>_<ef>''`, by associating one feature extractor method (`<fem>`) and one evaluation function (`<ef>`). Additionally, it is possible to define the parameters of the FEM through the `<fem_setting>` command option. The tuple corresponding to the metric just created is stored inside the user-transparent SimbA data-dictionary (which is not a table of the *FFireDt* system) and is used as basis for the creation of further tables: the "KnowledgeBase" (`Know_Base`) table that contains the ground-truth set of images of `Flickr-Fire`, and the `Data` table to store the incoming flow of images arriving from the social network service. The tables can be defined through the extended-SQL commands as follows:

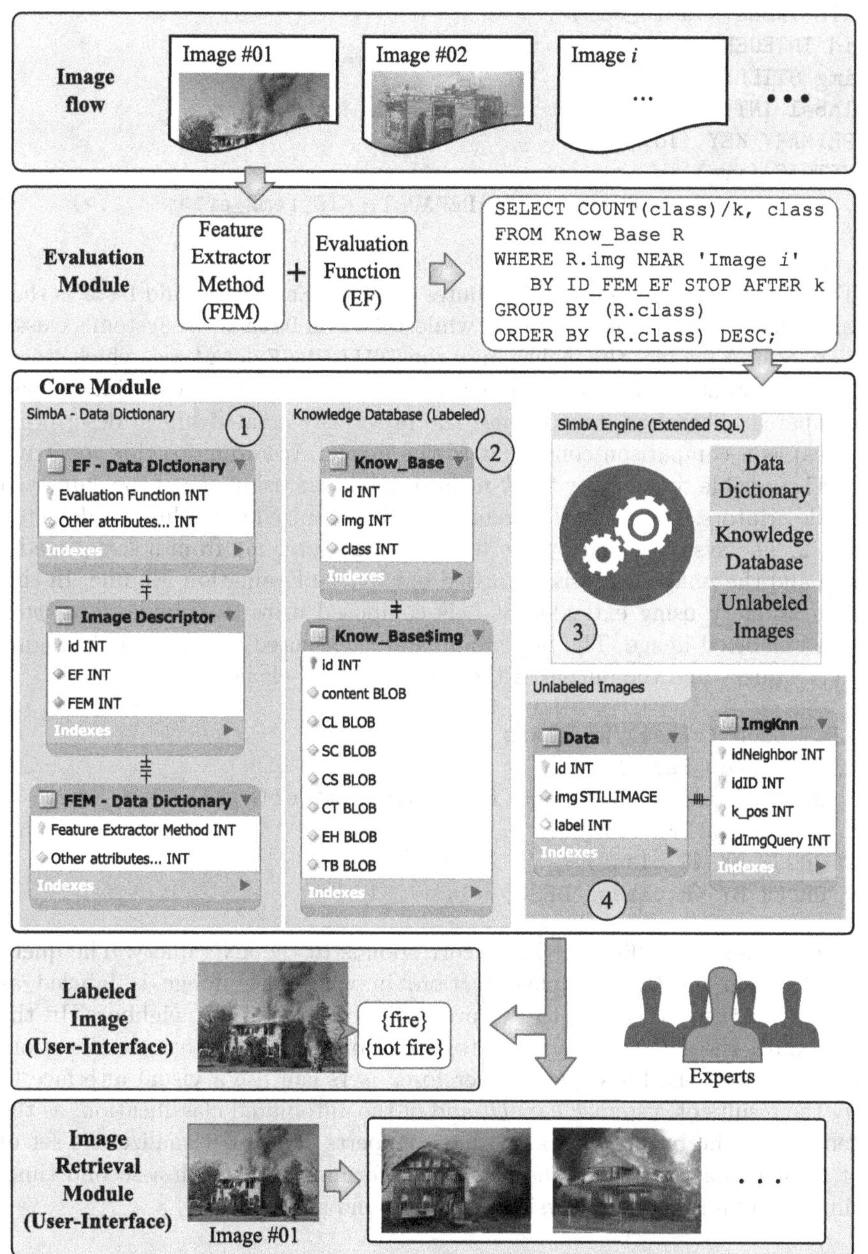

Fig. 2. *FFireDt* physical Design. A flow of images feeds the system, which generates an extended-SQL statement to perform a kNN query. The Core Module uses the SimbA Engine (3) to solve the query. It relies on the image descriptors stored in the Data-Dictionary (1) and in a ground-truth dataset to perform the classification (2). The SimbA Engine output for each unlabeled image is stored in two separated tables (4).

```
CREATE TABLE <Table_Name>(
   id INTEGER,
   img STILLIMAGE,
   label INT,
   PRIMARY KEY (id),
   METRIC (img)
          USING (<ID_fem1_ef1> DEFAULT, <ID_fem2_ef1>, <...>)
);
```

The differences between the attributes of tables Know_Base and Data is that class on Know_Base cannot be null, while label on Data is the system's classification. SimbA enables the inclusion of the STILLIMAGE data type, which stores the image content. Notice that, it is also necessary to specify how the images will be compared. Therefore, here we use the previously created image descriptors (metrics) as a comparison constraint to the image. According to this construction, it is possible to query by the k-nearest neighbors using one of the employed image descriptors. The *FFireDt* architecture is organized in modules as depicted by Fig. 2. The system is fed by the flow of images arriving from a social media service and the image analysis is carried out by the Evaluation Module. In this module, a query using extended-SQL is composed using an *image descriptor* and an unlabeled image. The SQL command is executed by the SimbA Engine as a kNN query and the output is the set of grouped elements:

```
SELECT COUNT(class)/k, class
    FROM Know_Base R
    WHERE R.img NEAR <Image i> BY <ID_fem1_ef1>
       STOP AFTER <k>
    GROUP BY (R.class)
    ORDER BY (R.class) DESC;
```

In this query, the NEAR predicate corresponds to the kNN query. The query output is used for the IB1 classification, in which the image is labeled as {fire, not_fire} according to the predominant class of its neighbors. In the core module, the *FFireDt* system stores the image, the system classification, and the result of the kNN query. Therefore, users can use a visual interface to verify the results of system *FFireDt* and of the automated classification; as the system stores the results of a kNN query, experts can also visualize the set of most similar images without the need of performing the search a second time. All images submitted for analysis are labeled and stored.

5 Experiments

In this section, we analyze the combination of classifiers and image descriptors to identify the most suitable ones for the social media domain. We evaluate the impact of the image descriptors creating a candidate set of 36 descriptors, given by the combination of the 6 feature extractors with the 6 evaluation functions – as introduced in Sect. 4, and executing the IB1 classifier over the `Flickr-Fire` dataset.

We also measured the average time to perform the $FFireDt$ image classification over SimbA to evaluate the performance improvement achieved with a relational database. The experiments were performed using the following procedure:

1. Calculate the F-measure metric to evaluate the efficacy of each image descriptor (FEM-EF combination);
2. Select the top-six image descriptors, according to the F-measure; proceed by generating Precision-Recall plots, bringing more details about the behavior of the techniques;
3. Validate our partial findings using Principal Component Analysis to plot the feature vectors of the extractors;
4. Employ the top-three image descriptors, according to the previous results, to perform a ROC curve evaluation and to determine the most accurate $FFireDt$ setting;
5. Evaluate the efficiency of the $FFireDt$ architecture, measuring the wall-clock time, considering the multiple configurations of the descriptors;
6. Measure the average time to perform the fire detection strategy to evaluate the performance improvement regarding the use of *framework* SimbA.

5.1 Obtaining the F-Measure

We calculated the F-measure for the 36 image descriptors using 10-fold cross validation, in order to detect fire over the $Flickr - Fire$ dataset. That is, for each round of evaluation, we used one tenth of the dataset to test the IB1 classifier and the remaining data to train. It was performed 10 times and then the average F-measure was calculated. Table 3 presents the F-measure values for all the 36 combinations of feature extractor/evaluation function. The highest values obtained for each row are highlighted in bold. The experiment revealed that distinct descriptor combinations impact on fire detection. More specifically, we observed that the accuracy of extractors based on color is better than that of the extractors based on texture (Edge Histogram, and Texture Browsing).

Moreover, the extractors Color Layout and Color Structure have shown the best efficacy for fire detection, in combination respectively with the evaluation functions Euclidean and Jeffrey Divergence. The highlighted values are pointed out as the best settings for tuning the $FFireDt$ system. We considered the results adequate, since the best descriptor achieved an F-Measure up to 0.866, while the human labeling process accuracy was of 92.8 %.

We also compared the best combination achieved by the IB1 classifier, as reported in Table 4, with other classifiers. Those experimental evidences suggest that the instance-based learning (the $FFireDt$ approach) is the most adequate classification strategy for fire detection. To compare the $FFireDt$ classification with other classification paradigms, we experimented system $FFireDt$ with the best EF of each FEM, as reported in Table 3. The comparison results were

Table 3. F-measure for each pair of feature extractor method (rows) versus evaluation function (columns). For each feature extractor, the evaluation function with the highest F-Measure is highlighted.

FEM	Evaluation functions					
	CB	EU	CH	CA	KU	JF
CL	0.834	**0.847**	0.807	0.828	0.803	0.844
SC	**0.843**	0.827	0.811	0.835	0.671	0.798
CS	0.853	0.849	0.821	0.848	0.746	**0.866**
CT	0.799	0.798	0.798	**0.800**	0.734	0.799
EH	0.808	0.806	0.795	0.806	0.462	**0.815**
TB	**0.766**	0.762	0.745	0.751	0.571	0.755

Table 4. System *FFireDt* obtained the highest F-Measure for all but one FEM when compared to other classifiers. For each feature extractor, we highlighted strategy with the highest F-Measure.

FEM	Classifiers			
	FFireDt	Naïve-Bayes	J48	Random forest
CL	**0.847**	0.787	0.751	0.829
SC	0.843	0.808	0.845	**0.864**
CS	**0.866**	0.406	0.842	0.866
CT	**0.800**	0.341	0.800	0.774
EH	**0.815**	0.522	0.711	0.787
TB	**0.766**	0.476	0.706	0.723

grouped according to the employed FEM. Table 4 shows the *FFireDt* results compared to Naïve-Bayes, J48, and RandomForest classifiers. The results show that *FFireDt* achieved the best F-Measure among the competitors in every setting, but for FEM Scalable Color. In this case, the Random Forest strategy beats the *FFireDt* classification, although by a narrow F-Measure margin.

5.2 Precision-Recall

In order to detail the analysis of Sect. 5.1, we also measured the Precision and Recall of the *image descriptors* employed as the settings of system *FFireDt*. This type of graphical analysis enables to better understand the behavior of the image descriptors and, more specifically, the behavior of the feature extractors.

A Precision vs. Recall (P×R) curve is suitable to measure the number of relevant images regarding the number of retrieved elements. We used Precision vs. Recall as a complementary measure to determine the potential of each image descriptor in the *FFireDt* setting. A rule of thumb on reading P×R curves is: the closer to the top the better the result is. Accordingly, we consider only the

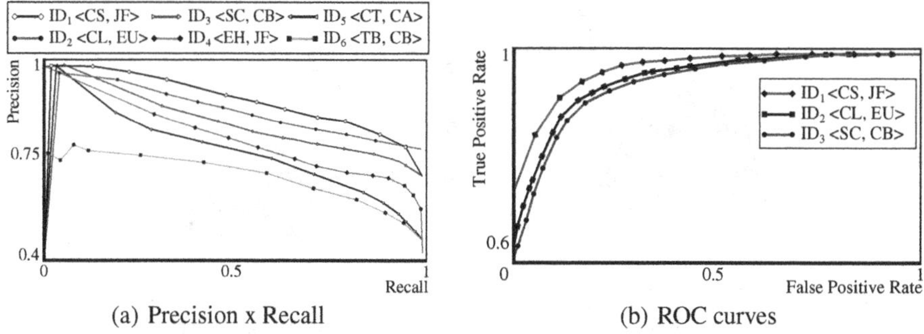

(a) Precision x Recall

(b) ROC curves

Fig. 3. Evaluation of the descriptors: (a) *Precision vs. Recall* graphs for each of the most precise image descriptor combinations according to F-measure; and (b) ROC curves for the top three image descriptors in the task of fire detection.

most efficient combination of each feature extractor, as highlighted in Table 3: $ID_1\langle$CS, JF$\rangle$, $ID_2\langle$CL, EU$\rangle$, $ID_3\langle$SC, CB$\rangle$, $ID_4\langle$EH, JF$\rangle$, $ID_5\langle$CT, CA$\rangle$ and $ID_6\langle$TB, CB$\rangle$. Figure 3(a) confirms that the image descriptors ID_1, ID_2, and ID_3 are in fact the most effective combinations for fire detection. It also shows that, for those three descriptors, the precision is at least 0.8 for a recall of up to 0.5, dropping almost linearly with a small slope, which can be considered acceptable. This observation reinforces the findings of the F-measure metric, indicating that the behavior of the descriptors is homogeneous and well-suited for the task of retrieval and, consequently, for classification purposes.

5.3 Visualization of Feature Extractors

Based on the results observed so far, we hypothesize that the most adequate extractors to be used in system *FFireDt* are Color Structure, Color Layout, and Scalable Color. In this section, we look for further evidence, using visualization techniques to better understand the feature space of the extractors using Principal Component Analysis (PCA). The PCA analysis takes as input the extracted features, which may have several dimensions according to the FEM domain, and reduces them to two features. Such reduction allows us to visualize the data as a scatter-plot. Our hypothesis shall gain more credibility if the corresponding visualizations allow seeing a better separation of the classes *fire* and *not-fire*, in comparison to the other three extractors. Figure 4 presents the two-dimensional projection of the data, plotting the two principal components of the space generated by each extractor. Figure 4(a) depicts the representation of the data space generated by CL, the extractor that presented the better separability in the classification process. The two clusters can be seen as two well-formed clouds with a reasonably small overlapping, splitting the images as containing fire or not. Figure 4(b) shows the data visualization of the space generated by CS, which was the FEM that obtained the highest F-measure on previous experiments. The data projection shows that each cluster forms a cloud

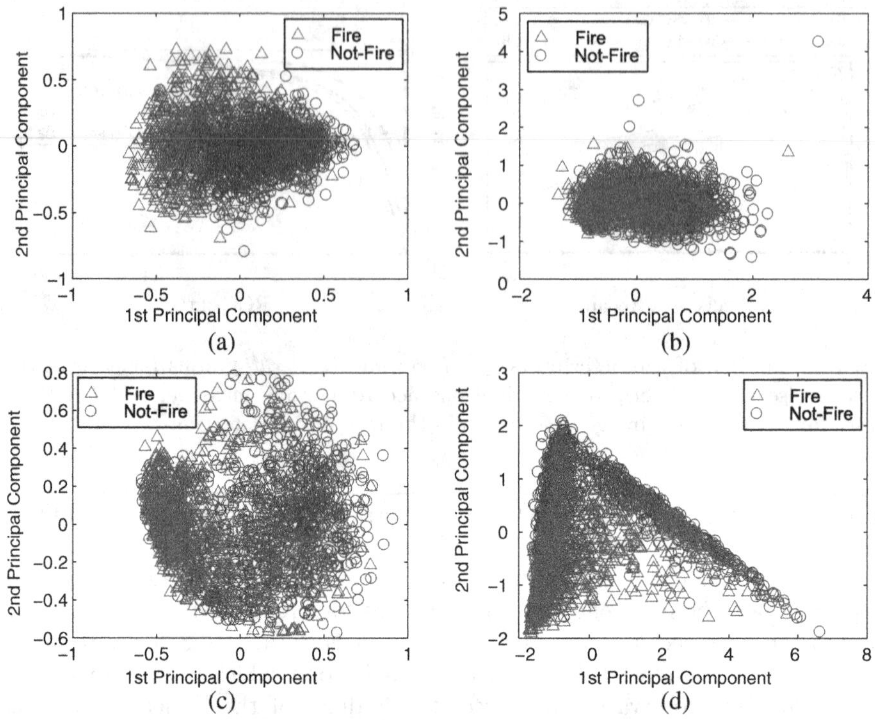

Fig. 4. PCA projection of fire and not-fire images: (a) Color Layout, (b) Color Structure, (c) Scalable Color and (d) Edge Histogram. The Color Layout visually separates the dataset into two clusters.

clearly identifiable, having the centers of the clouds distinctly separated. However, this figure reveals that there is a large overlap between the two classes. Figure 4(c) presents the projection of the space generated by the SC extractor. Again, it can be seen that there are two clusters, but with an even larger overlap between them. Visually, the CL outperformed the other color FEMS: the CS and SC, when drawing the border between the two classes. Figure 4(d) depicts the visualization generated by the EH extractor. It can be seen that indeed it has two clouds: one almost vertical to the left and another along the "diagonal" of the figure. However, the two clouds are not related to the existence of fire, as the elements of both clusters are distributed over both clouds. Figure 4(a), (b) and (c) show the visualization of the extractors based on color. The four visualizations show that the corresponding CL, SC and SC indeed generate clusters. However, there are increasing larger overlaps between fire and not-fire instances. Regarding the TB and CT features, the PCA projection was not able to separate the fire and not-fire classes. Concluding, the visualization of the feature spaces shows that extractors based on color are able to separate the data into visual clouds related to the expected clusters. Particularly, Color Layout has shown the best visualization, followed by Color Structure, and Scalable Color, which also have shown to significantly separate the classes. However, the extractors based on texture identify characteristics that are not related to fire, thus presenting the worst separability, as expected.

5.4 ROC Curves

In order to determine the best setting for the *FFireDt* system, we employed one last accuracy measure: the ROC curve. It allows us to determine the experiments overall effectiveness, using measures of sensitivity (recall) and specificity. Figure 3(b) presents the detailed ROC curves for image descriptors $ID_1 = \langle$CS, JF$\rangle$, $ID_2 = \langle$CL, EU$\rangle$, and $ID_3 = \langle$SC, CB$\rangle$, the top three best combinations according to the F-Measure, Precision-Recall and Visualization experiments. For fire-detection, the area under the ROC curve was up to 0.93 for ID_1; up to 0.87 for ID_2; and up to 0.85 for ID_3. These results indicate that the top three image descriptors have similar and satisfactory accuracy. Therefore, the choice of which descriptor to use becomes a matter of performance.

5.5 Processing Time and Scalability

When monitoring images originated from social media, the time constraint is important because of the high rate at which new images arrive. Thus, we also evaluate the efficiency, given in wall-clock time, of the candidate image descriptors. We ran the experiments in a personal computer equipped with a processor Intel Core i7 R 2.67 GHz with 4GB memory using the Ubuntu 14.04 LTS operating system.

Feature Extractors. Figure 5(a) shows the average time required to perform the feature extraction on system *FFireDt* regarding `Flickr-Fire` dataset. Color Structure, the most precise extractor, was the second fastest. The second and third most precise extractors were Color Layout and Scalable Color: the former was three times slower than Color Structure, and the latter was the fastest extractor. Thus, we are now able to state the that extractors Color Structure and Scalable Color are the best choices for fire detection in image streams. Meanwhile, the texture-based extractors Edge Histogram, and Texture Browsing presented low performances, so they are definitely dismissed as possible choices.

Evaluation Functions. Figure 5(b) shows the time required to perform 2 trillion evaluation calculations for each evaluation function on feature vectors of 256 dimensions. The plot *average precision vs. wall-clock time* shows that, although the Jeffrey Divergence demonstrated the highest precision, it was the least efficient. In their turn, City-Block and Euclidean distances presented excellent performance and a precision only slightly below the Jeffrey Divergence. Therefore, we can say that they are the most adequate evaluation functions when performance is on concern, such as is the case in our problem domain. Finally, we conclude that the image descriptors given by the combinations $\langle$CS, SC$\rangle \times \langle$CB, EU$\rangle$ are the best options in terms of both efficacy (precision) and efficiency (wall-clock time). In Table 5 we reproduce the F-measure results highlighting the most adequate combinations according to our findings.

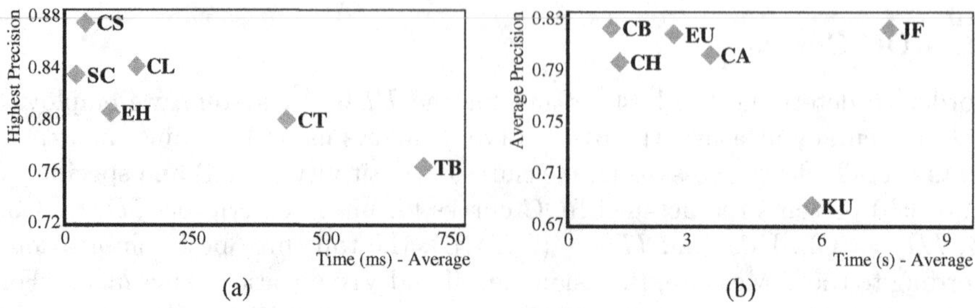

Fig. 5. Evaluation of the descriptors: (a) Plot *Highest precision when classifying dataset* `Flickr-Fire` *vs. Average time to extract the features of one image* for the six feature extractors; and (b) Plot *Average precision when classifying dataset* `Flickr-Fire` *vs. Time to perform 2 trillion calculations* for the six evaluation functions.

Therefore, according to all the experiments, we point out that the best image descriptor for fire detection, considering our social media dataset `Flickr-Fire`, is given by the combinations of extractors MPEG-7 Color Structure and Scalable Color with distance function City-Block. This combination provides not only more efficacy, but also more efficiency. In general, we noticed that feature extractors based on color were more effective than extractors based on texture. We also identified that the Jeffrey divergence was the most accurate, however, it was also the most expensive evaluation function. The next section presents the performance improvements achieved by the incorporation of similarity queries on system *FFireDt*.

Table 5. F-measure for each pair of feature extractor method (rows) and evaluation function (columns), now highlighting the best combinations according to our experiments.

FEM	Evaluation functions					
	CB	**EU**	CH	JF	KU	CA
CL	0.834	0.847	0.807	0.844	0.803	0.828
CS	**0.853**	**0.849**	0.821	0.866	0.746	0.848
SC	**0.843**	**0.827**	0.811	0.798	0.671	0.835
EH	0.808	0.806	0.795	0.815	0.462	0.806
CT	0.799	0.798	0.798	0.799	0.734	0.800
TB	0.766	0.762	0.745	0.755	0.571	0.751

5.6 Performance Improvement

We used the most suitable *image descriptor* defined by the previous experiments to run the performance evaluation experiments. According to this, we measured the average time of the *FFireDt* system with the setting $ID = \langle SC, CB \rangle$ with and without the use of similarity queries to solve the Instance-Based Learning classification. We used the *Flickr – Fire* dataset of Sect. 3.6 as the knowledge database of system *FFireDt*. Next, we performed a set of k-Nearest Neighbor queries for an increasing number of neighbors (k) over this knowledge database to label new 350 images obtained with the Flickr API. Figure 6 presents the average time demanded to perform fire detection using the *FFireDt* system with and without the similarity queries, for k varying from 15 to 53.

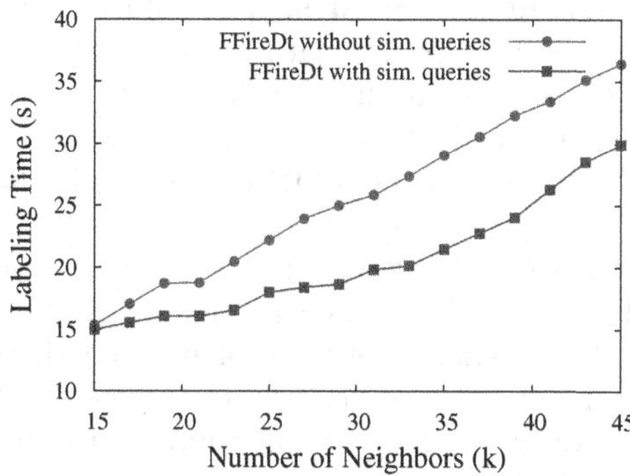

Fig. 6. The *FFireDt* performance improvement due to the use of indexed similarity queries to solve the IB1 classification. The similarity queries are implemented by *framework* SimbA.

As it can be observed, the adoption of a similarity query engine (SimbA) that employs indexing techniques leads to a performance gain of 30 %, on average, if compared to using a bare brute-force scan strategy. Besides, the integration of this methodology to an extended-SQL syntax allows for a rapid experimentation environment, which allowed the wide-scope evaluation (36 image descriptor combinations) reported in this paper. The indexing techniques internal to SimbA lead to performance improvements because they employ metric space properties to prune the search space when solving a kNN query, reducing the number of distance computations.

6 Conclusions

In this work we studied the problem of quickly identifying fire in social-media images, in order to assist rescue services during emergencies. The approach was based on an architecture for content-based image storage, retrieval, and classification, relying on database relational technology. Using this architecture, we compared the accuracy and performance (processing time) of 36 image descriptors (feature extractor and evaluation function) in the task of identifying fire in the images. Since we used supervised machine learning (instance-based learning), we built a ground-truth dataset with 2,000 human-annotated images obtained from website Flickr. The results allowed us not only to achieve a high-efficacy classification system, but also to elucidate the adequacy of a vast set of image descriptor possibilities in relation to the social media domain. Our contributions are summarized as follows:

1. **Fast-Fire Detection (FFireDt) Architecture:** we designed and implemented a database-driven, scalable, and accurate architecture for content-based image retrieval and classification that was able to achieve a precision for fire detection that is comparable to that of human annotators;
2. **Evaluation of Existing Techniques:** we soundly compared 36 combinations of MEPG-7 image descriptors (feature extractor + evaluation function) considering their potential for accurate retrieval as indicated by metrics F-measure and Precision-Recall. As a result we achieved an accuracy of 85 %, precise classification (as shown by ROC curves) and efficient performance (wall-clock time);
3. **Improved Instance-based Learning:** we described and evaluated the design of a classification architecture (*FFireDt*) for fire detection, whose performance suggests the mandatory use of indexed similarity querying in the construction of instance-based classification systems;
4. **Dataset Flickr-Fire:** we built a human-annotated dataset of real images suitable as ground-truth to foster the development of more precise techniques for automatic identification of fire – available online at http://icmc.usp.br/pessoas/junio/DatasetFlicker/DatasetFlickr.htm.

We conclude by stressing that detecting fire in social media images could help decision making during emergency situations. To this end, it is required to have automated tools that can flag relevant images from the social media as soon as possible. This work is a significant step towards this goal.

Acknowledgements. This research is supported, in part, by FAPESP, CNPq, CAPES, STIC-AmSud, the RESCUER project, funded by the European Commission (Grant: 614154) and by the CNPq/MCTI (Grant: 490084/2013-3).

References

1. Russo, M.R.: Emergency management professional development: Linking information communication technology and social communication skills to enhance a sense of community and social justice in the 21st century. In: Crisis Management: Concepts, Methodologies, Tools and Applications, pp. 651–663. IGI Global (2013)
2. Kudyba, S.: Big Data, Mining, and Analytics: Components of Strategic Decision Making. Taylor & Francis Group, London (2014)

3. Villela, K., Breiner, K., Nass, C., Mendonća, M., Vieira, V.: A smart and reliable crowdsourcing solution for emergency and crisis management. In: Interdisciplinary Information Management Talks, Podebrady, Czech Republic, pp. 213–220 (2014)
4. Sumathi, S., Esakkirajan, S.: Fundamentals of Relational Database Management Systems, vol. 47. Springer, Heidelberg (2007)
5. Bedo, M.V.N., Blanco, G., Oliveira, W.D., Cazzolato, M., Costa, A.F., Rodrigues, J., Traina, A.J.M., Traina Jr., C.: Techniques for effective and efficient fire detection from social media images. In: International Conference on Enterprise Information Systems, Barcelona, Spain, pp. 34–46 (2015)
6. Chunyu, Y., Jun, F., Jinjun, W., Yongming, Z.: Video fire smoke detection using motion and color features. Fire Technol. **46**, 651–663 (2010)
7. Celik, T., Demirel, H., Ozkaramanli, H., Uyguroglu, M.: Fire detection using statistical color model in video sequences. J. Vis. Commun. Image Represent. **18**, 176–185 (2007)
8. Ko, B.C., Cheong, K.H., Nam, J.Y.: Fire detection based on vision sensor and support vector machines. Fire Saf. J. **44**, 322–329 (2009)
9. Liu, C.B., Ahuja, N.: Vision based fire detection. In: International Conference on Pattern Recognition, vol. 4, pp. 134–137 (2004)
10. Tamura, S., Tamura, K., Kitakami, H., Hirahara, K.: Clustering-based burst-detection algorithm for web-image document stream on social media. In: IEEE International Conference on Systems, Man, and Cybernetics, pp. 703–708. IEEE (2012)
11. Dimitropoulos, K., Barmpoutis, P., Grammalidis, N.: Spatio-temporal flame modeling and dynamic texture analysis for automatic video-based fire detection. IEEE Trans. Circ. Syst. Video Technol. **25**(2), 7–14 (2014)
12. Doeller, M., Kosch, H.: The mpeg-7 multimedia database system (mpeg-7 mmdb). J. Syst. Softw. **81**, 1559–1580 (2008)
13. Ojala, T., Aittola, M., Matinmikko, E.: Empirical evaluation of mpeg-7 xm color descriptors in content-based retrieval of semantic image categories. In: International Conference on Pattern Recognition, vol. 2, pp. 1021–1024 (2002)
14. Tjondronegoro, D., Chen, Y.P.: Content-based indexing and retrieval using mpeg-7 and x-query in video data management systems. World Wide Web **5**, 207–227 (2002)
15. Silva, Y.N., Aly, A.M., Aref, W.G., Larson, P.Å.: SimDB: a similarity-aware database system. In: ACM International Conference on Management of Data, Indianapolis, Indiana, USA, pp. 1243–1246 (2010)
16. Guyon, I., Gunn, S., Nikravesh, M., Zadeh, L.A.: Feature Extraction: Foundations and Applications (Studies in Fuzziness and Soft Computing). Springer-Verlag New York, Inc., Secaucus (2006)
17. Aha, D.W., Kibler, D., Albert, M.K.: Instance-based learning algorithms. Mach. Learn. **6**, 37–66 (1991)
18. Barioni, M.C.N., Razente, H.L., Traina, A.J.M., Traina Jr., C.: Seamlessly integrating similarity queries in sql. Softw. Pract. Exp. **39**, 355–384 (2009)
19. Silva, Y.N., Aref, W.G., Larson, P.Å., Pearson, S., Ali, M.H.: Similarity Queries: their conceptual evaluation, transformations, and processing. VLDB J. **22**, 395–420 (2013)
20. Kaster, D.S., Bugatti, P.H., Traina, A.J.M., Traina Jr., C.: FMI-SiR: a flexible and efficient module for similarity searching on Oracle database. J. Inf. Data Manage. **1**, 229–244 (2010)
21. IEEE MultiMedia: Mpeg-7: the generic multimedia content description standard, part 1. IEEE MultiMedia **9**, 78–87 (2002)

22. Sato, M., Gutu, D., Horita, Y.: A new image quality assessment model based on the MPEG-7 descriptor. In: Qiu, G., Lam, K.M., Kiya, H., Xue, X.-Y., Kuo, C.-C.J., Lew, M.S. (eds.) PCM 2010, Part I. LNCS, vol. 6297, pp. 159–170. Springer, Heidelberg (2010)
23. Kasutani, E., Yamada, A.: The mpeg-7 color layout descriptor: a compact image feature description for high-speed image/video segment retrieval. In: International Conference on Image Processing, vol. 1, pp. 674–677 (2001)
24. Manjunath, B.S., Ohm, J.R., Vasudevan, V.V., Yamada, A.: Color and texture descriptors. IEEE Circ. Syst. Video Technol. **11**, 703–715 (2001)
25. Sikora, T.: The mpeg-7 visual standard for content description-an overview. IEEE Circ. Syst. Video Technol. **11**, 696–702 (2001)
26. Park, D.K., Jeon, Y.S., Won, C.S.: Efficient use of local edge histogram descriptor. In: ACM Workshops on Multimedia, pp. 51–54. ACM (2000)
27. Wnukowicz, K., Skarbek, W.: Colour temperature estimation algorithm for digital images - properties and convergence. Opto Eletron. Rev. **11**, 193–196 (2003)
28. Lee, K.L., Chen, L.H.: An efficient computation method for the texture browsing descriptor of mpeg-7. Image Vis. Comput. **23**, 479–489 (2005)
29. Zezula, P., Amato, G., Dohnal, V., Batko, M.: Similarity Search - The Metric Space Approach. Advances in Database Systems, vol. 32. Springer, Berlin, Heidelberg (2006)
30. Bedo, M.V.N., Traina, A.J.M., Traina Jr., C.: Seamless integration of distance functions and feature vectors for similarity-queries processing. J. Inf. Data Manage. **5**, 308–320 (2014)

Querying Time Interval Data

Philipp Meisen[1(✉)], Diane Keng[2], Tobias Meisen[1], Marco Recchioni[3], and Sabina Jeschke[1]

[1] Institute of Information Management in Mechanical Engineering, RWTH Aachen University, Aachen, Germany
philipp@meisen.net

[2] School of Engineering, Santa Clara University, Santa Clara, USA

[3] Airport Devision, Inform GmbH Aachen, Aachen, Germany

Abstract. Analyzing huge amounts of time interval data is a task arising more and more frequently in different domains like resource utilization and scheduling, real time disposition, as well as health care. Analyzing this type of data using established, reliable, and proven technologies is desirable and required. However, utilizing commonly used tools and multidimensional models is not sufficient, because of modeling, querying, and processing limitations. In this paper, we address the problem of querying large data sets of time interval data, by introducing a query language capable to retrieve aggregated and analytical results from such a database. The introduced query language enables analysis of time interval data in an on-line analytical manner. It is based on requirements stated by business analysts from different domains. In addition, we introduce our query processing, established using a bitmap-based implementation. Finally, we present and critically discuss a performance analysis.

Keywords: Time interval data · Query language · On-line analytical processing · Bitmap · TidaQL

1 Introduction

Managers and business analysts, among others, use business intelligence and analytical tools for data-driven decision support on tactical and strategical level. An important technology used within this field is OLAP, i.e., on-line analytical processing. It enables the user to interact with the stored data by querying for answers. This is achieved by selecting dimensions, applying different operations to selections (e.g., roll-up, drill-down, or drill-across), or comparing results. The heart of every OLAP system is a multidimensional data model (MDM), which defines the different dimensions, hierarchies, levels, and members [1].

In this paper, we focus on time interval data. Enterprises of the public and private sector record, collect, and generate such data every day, in various situations, different areas and huge amounts. Some examples are the resource utilization in production environments, deployment of personnel in service sectors, or courses of diseases in healthcare. Thereby, time interval data is used to represent observations, utilizations or measures over a period. Put in simple terms, time interval data is defined by two time values (i.e., start and end), as well as descriptive values associated to the interval: like

S. Hammoudi et al. (Eds.): ICEIS 2015, LNBIP 241, pp. 45–68, 2015.
DOI: 10.1007/978-3-319-29133-8_3

labels, numbers, or more complex data structures. Figure 1 illustrates a sample database containing five such data records.

key	resources	type	location	start	end
2285954	3	cleaning	POS F6	2015/01/01 16:21	2015/01/01 17:13
2285965	5	maintenance	POS F5	2015/01/01 16:25	2015/01/01 17:10
2285971	1	maintenance	POS F5	2015/01/01 17:02	2015/01/01 17:17
2285972	3	room service	POS F5	2015/01/01 16:42	2015/01/01 16:55
2285990	4	miscellaneous	POS F6	2015/01/01 16:20	2015/01/01 17:05

Fig. 1. A sample time interval database with intervals defined by [start, end), an id, and three descriptive values.

The need of handling and analyzing time interval data using established, reliable, and proven technologies like OLAP is desirable in this respect and an essential acceptance factor. Nevertheless, the MDM needed to model time interval data, normally makes use of many-to-many relationships that have been shown led to problems of summarizing. Several solutions solving these problems on different modeling levels have been introduced over the last years. They lead to increased integration effort, enormous storage needs, usually inacceptable query per performances, memory issues, and complex multidimensional expressions [2, 3]. Considering real-world scenarios, these solutions are only applicable to many-to-many relationships having a small cardinality. However, this is mostly not the case when dealing with time interval data. As a result, the usage of MDM and available OLAP systems is not sufficient, even though business analysts desire the operations (e.g., roll-up, drill-down, slice, or dice) made available through such systems.

Enabling such OLAP like operations in the context of time interval data, requires the provision of extended filtering and grouping capabilities. The former is achieved by matching descriptive values against known filter criteria logically connected using operators like *and*, *or*, or *not*, as well as a support of temporal relations like *starts with*, *during*, *overlapping*, or *within* [4]. Known aggregation operators like *max*, *min*, *sum*, or *count* apply the latter, as well as temporal aggregation operators like *count started* or *count finished* [5]. Figure 2 exemplifies the application of the *count* aggregation operator for time interval data. The color code identifies the different types of a time interval (e.g., cleaning, maintenance, room service, miscellaneous). Furthermore, the swim-lanes show the location. The figure illustrates the count of intervals for each type over one day across all locations (e.g., POS F5 and POS F6) using a granularity of minutes (i.e., 1,440 aggregations are calculated).

In this paper, we first present a query language allowing the analysis of time interval data in an OLAP manner. Our query language includes DDL, a data definition language, DCL, a data control language, and DML, a data manipulation language. The former uses the TIDAMODEL (our time interval data model) introduced in [6], whereby the latter supports the two-step aggregation technique mentioned in [5]. Second, we outline our query processing which utilizes a bitmap-based implementation.

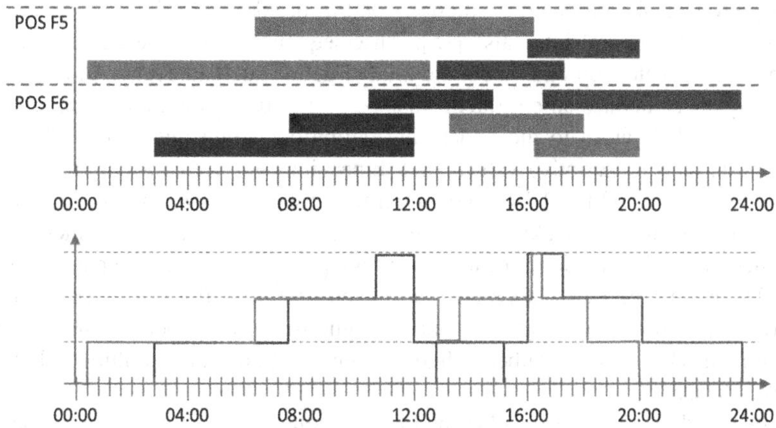

Fig. 2. On top the time interval data (10 records) shown in a Gantt-Chart, on the bottom the aggregated time-series.

This paper is an extended version of [7]. In Sect. 2, we discuss related work done in the field of time interval data. In particular, this section provides a concise overview of research dealing with the analyses of time interval data. We provide an overview of time interval models. Furthermore, we discuss related work done in the field of OLAP, and present query languages. In Sect. 3, we introduce our query language and processing. The section presents among other things how to define a model and load it, how to apply temporal operators, how to support the two-step aggregation, how to define groups, and how to use filters. In the ensuing chapter, we introduce implementation issues, empirically evaluate the performance regarding the query processing, and outline possible performance gains using a distributed query processing. We conclude with a summary and directions for prospective work in Sect. 5.

2 Related Work

When defining a query language, it is important to have an underlying model, which defines the foundation for the language (e.g., the relational model for SQL, different interval-based models for, e.g. IXSQL or TSQL2, the multidimensional model for MDX, or the graph model for Cypher). Over the last years several models have been introduced in the field of time intervals, e.g., for temporal databases [8], sequential pattern mining [9, 10], association rule mining [11], or matching [12].

Chen et al. introduced the problem of mining time interval sequential patterns [13]. The defined model uses events to derive time intervals, whereby a time interval is determined by the time between two successive time-points of events. The definition is based on the sequential pattern mining problem introduced by Agrawal and Srikant [14]. The model neither includes any dimensional definitions, nor addresses the labeling of time intervals with descriptive values.

Papapetrou et al. presented a solution for the problem of "discovering frequent arrangements of temporal intervals" [15]. An e-sequence is an ordered set of events. Whereby, a start value, an end value and a label define such an event. Additionally, a set of e-sequences defines an e-sequence database. The definition of an event given by Papapetrou et al. is close to the underlying definition within this paper (cf. Fig. 1). Nevertheless, facts, descriptive values, and dimensions are not considered.

Mörchen introduced the TSKR model defining tones, chords, and phrases for time intervals [16]. Roughly speaking, the tones represent the duration of intervals, the chords the temporal coincidence of tones, and the phrases represent the partial order of chords. The main purpose of this model is to overcome limitations of Allen's temporal model (cf. [4]) considering robustness and ambiguousness when performing sequential pattern mining. The model neither defines dimensions, considers multiple labels, nor recognizes facts.

Summarized, models presented in the field of sequential pattern mining, association rule mining or matching do generally not define dimensions. Moreover, they focuses on generalized interval data, or support only non-labelled data. Thus, these models are not suitable considering OLAP of time interval data, but are a guidance to the right direction.

The research community of temporal databases has also defined different interval-based models [8]. Thereby, a categorization in weak and strong models is applicable. A weak model is one, in which the intervals are used to group time-points, whereas the intervals of the latter carry semantic meaning. Thus, from an analytical point of view, a weak interval-based model is not of further interest, because it is transformable into an equivalent point-based model. Nevertheless, a strong model and the involved meaning of the different operators – especially aggregation operators – are of high interest. Strong interval-based models presented in the field of temporal databases lack to define dimensions, but present important preliminary work.

In the field of OLAP, several systems capable of analyzing sequences of data have been introduced over the last years. Chui et al. introduced S-OLAP for analyzing sequence data [17]. Liu and Rundensteiner analyzed event sequences using hierarchical patterns, enabling OLAP on data streams of time point events [18]. Bebel et al. presented an OLAP like system enabling time point-based sequential data to be analyzed [19]. Nevertheless, the system supports neither time intervals, nor temporal operators.

Recently, Koncilia et al. presented I-OLAP, an OLAP system to analyze interval data [20]. They claim to be the first who proposed a model for processing interval data. The definition is based on the interval definition presented in [13], which defines the intervals as the gap between sequential events. However, Koncilia et al. assume that the intervals of a specific event-type (e.g., temperature) for a set of specific descriptive values (e.g., POS G2) are non-overlapping and consecutive. Considering the sample data shown in Fig. 1, the assumption of non-overlapping intervals is not valid in general (cf. record 2,285,965 and 2,285,971). Figure 3 illustrates the model of Koncilia et al. showing five temperature events for POS G2 and the intervals determined for the events. Koncillia et al. also mention the support of dimensions, hierarchies, levels, and members, but lack to specify what types of hierarchies are supported and how, e.g., non-strict relations are handled.

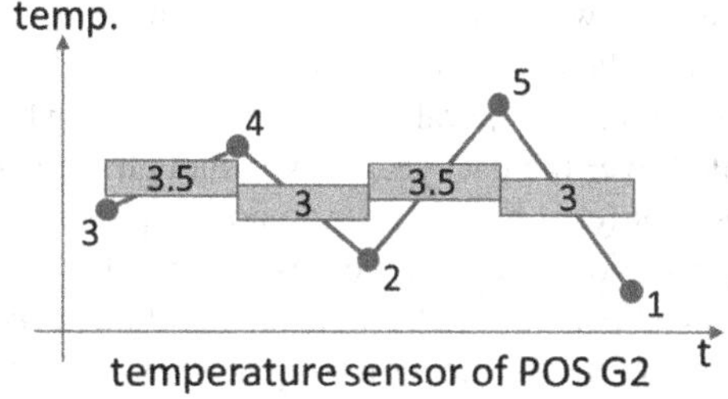

Fig. 3. Illustration of the model introduced by Koncilia et al. [20]. The intervals (rectangles) are created for each two consecutive events (dots). The facts are calculated using the average function as the *compute value function.*

Also recently, Meisen et al. introduced the TIDAMODEL "enabling the usage of time interval data for data-driven decision support" [7]. The presented model is defined by a 5-tuple (P, Σ, τ, M, Δ) in which P denotes the time interval database, Σ the set of descriptors, τ the time axis, M the set of measures, and Δ the set of dimensions. P contains the raw time interval data records and a schema definition of the contained data. The schema associates each field of the record (which may contain complex data structures) to one of the following categories: temporal, descriptive, or bulk. Each descriptor of the set Σ is defined by its values (more specific its value type), a mapping- and a fact-function. The mapping-function is used to map the descriptive values of the raw record to one or multiple descriptor values. The mapping to multiple descriptor values allows the definition of non-strict fact-dimension relationships. Additionally, the model defines the time axis to be finite and discrete, i.e., it has a start, an end, and a specified granularity (e.g., minutes). The set of dimensions Δ can contain a time dimension (using a rooted plane tree for the definition of each hierarchy) and a dimension for each descriptor (using a directed acyclic graph for a hierarchy's definition). Figure 4 illustrates the modeled sample database of Fig. 1 using the TIDAMODEL. The figure shows the five intervals, as well as the values of the descriptors location (cf. swim-lane) and type (cf. legend). It does not show dimensions. All descriptors use the identity function as mapping function. The used granularity for the time dimension is minutes.

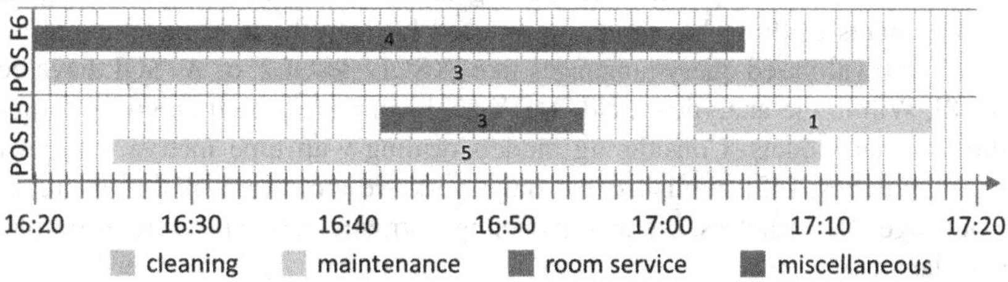

Fig. 4. Data of the sample database shown in Fig. 1 modeled using the TIDAMODEL [7].

Another important aspect when dealing with time interval data in the context of OLAP is the aggregation of data and the provision of temporal aggregation operators. Kline and Snodgrass introduced temporal aggregates [21], for which several enhanced algorithms were presented over the past years. Even though the solutions focus on one specific aggregation operator (e.g., SUM), they do not support multiple filter criteria, or do not consider data gaps. Koncilia et al. address shortly how aggregations are performed using the introduced *compute value functions* and *fact creating functions* [20]. Nevertheless, they neither define nor mention temporal operators. Koncilia et al. further point out that some queries need special attention when aggregating the values along time, but a more precise problem statement is not presented. Meisen et al. introduce a two-step aggregation technique for time interval data [6]. The first step aggregates the facts along the intervals of a time granule and the second one aggregates the values of the first step depending on the selected hierarchy level of the time dimension. In Fig. 5, the two-step aggregation technique is illustrated. It depicts how the technique is used to determine the needed resources within the interval [16:30, 16:34]. Within the first step, the sum of the resources for each granule is determined and within the second step the maximum of the determined values is calculated, i.e., 14. Additionally, they introduce temporal aggregation operators like *started* or *finished count*.

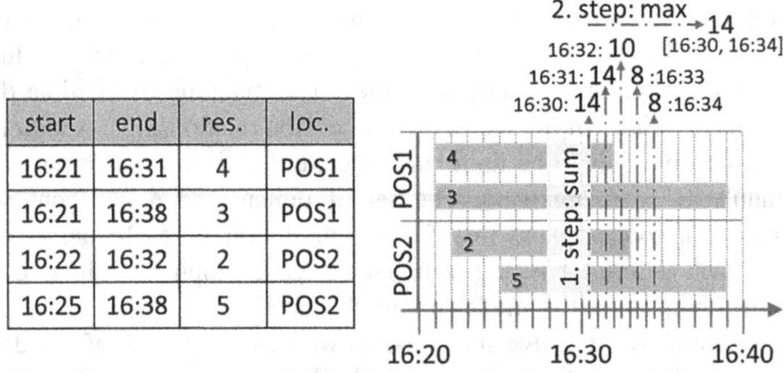

start	end	res.	loc.
16:21	16:31	4	POS1
16:21	16:38	3	POS1
16:22	16:32	2	POS2
16:25	16:38	5	POS2

Fig. 5. Two-step aggregation technique presented by [6].

The definition of a query language based on a model and operators (i.e., like aggregations), is common practice. Regarding time-series, multiple query languages and enhancements of those have been introduced [22]. In the field of temporal databases, time interval-based query languages like IXSQL, TSQL2, or ATSQL have been defined [8]. Within the analytical field, MDX [23] is a widely used language to query multidimensional models. Considering models dealing with time interval data in the context of analytics, [20] published the only work we are aware of that mentions a query language. Nevertheless, the authors neither formally define nor further introduce the query language.

Overall, it can be stated that recent research and requests from industry indicate that the handling of time interval data in an analytical context is an important task. Thus, a query language is required capable of covering the arising requirements. Koncilia et al.

and Meisen et al. (cf. [6, 7, 20]) introduced two different models useful for OLAP of time interval data. Meisen et al. also present different temporal aggregation operators, as well as standard aggregation operators [6]. Nevertheless, a definition of a query language useful for OLAP and an implementation of the processing are not formally introduced.

3 The TIDA Query Language (TidaQL)

In this section, we introduce our time interval data analysis query language (TidaQL). We designed the language to query time interval data from an analytical point of view. The language is based on aspects of the previously discussed TidaModel. Nevertheless, the language should be applicable to any time interval database system, which is capable of analyzing time interval data, whereby some adaptions may be necessary or some features may not be supported by any system.

3.1 Requirements

During several workshops with over 70 international business analysts from different domains (i.e., aviation industry, logistics providers, service providers, as well as language and gesture research), the requirements concerning the query language and its processing were specified. We aligned the results of the workshop with an extended literature research. Table 1 summarizes the selected results.

3.2 Data Definition Language

The DDL is used to define, add, or remove the models known by the system. [DDL1] requires a command within the DDL that enables the user to load or unload a model. The LOAD and UNLOAD command is exemplified in the following listing.

```
LOAD [modelId|"modelId"|FROM 'location']
   [SET autoload = [true|false] [, force = [true|false]]]

UNLOAD [modelId|"modelId"]

DROP MODEL [modelId|"modelId"]
```

A model can be loaded by using a model identifier already known to the system (e.g., if the model was unloaded), or by specifying a location from which the system can retrieve a model definition to be loaded. Additionally, properties can be defined (e.g., the *autoload* property can be set, to automatically load a model when the system is started). In addition, the *force* property is used to load a model, even if it is already loaded (e.g., to force a model to be reloaded). In the following subsection, we present an XML used to define a TidaModel.

Table 1. Summary of the requirements concerning TIDAQL (selected results).

Requirement	Description
Data Control Language (DCL)	
[DCL1]: authorization aspects	It is expected that the language encompass authorization features, e.g., user deletion, role creation, granting, and revoking permissions
[DCL2]: permissions grantable on global and model level	Permissions must be grantable on a model and a global level. It is expected that the user can have the permission to add data to one model but not to another. For simplicity, it should be possible to grant or revoke several permissions at once
Data Definition Language (DDL)	
[DDL1]: loading and unloading	The language has to offer a construct to load new and unload models. The newly loaded model has to be available without any restart of the system. An unloaded model has to be unavailable after the query is processed. However, queries currently in process must still be executed
[DDL2]: non-onto, non-covering, non-strict hierarchies	Each descriptor dimension must support hierarchies that may be non-onto, non-covering, and/or non-strict [24]
[DDL3]: raster levels	A raster level is a level of the time dimension. For example: the *5-minute raster*-level defines members like [00:00, 00:05) … [23:55, 00:00). Several raster levels can form a hierarchy (e.g., 5-min → 30-min → 60-min → half-day → day)
Data Manipulation Language (DML)	
[DML1]: raw data records	The language must provide a construct to select the raw time interval data records
[DML2]: time-series by time-windows	The language must support the specification of a time-window for which time-series of different measures can be retrieved
[DML3]: temporal operators	It must be possible to use temporal operators for filtering as, e.g., defined by Allen (1983). Depending on the type of selection (i.e., raw records or time-series), the available temporal operators may differ
[DML4]: The two-step aggregation technique	Meisen et al. (2015) present a two-step aggregation technique that has to be supported by the language. Both aggregation operators (see Fig. 5) must be specified by a query selecting time-series, no pre-defined measure should be necessary
[DML5]: complete time-series	A time-series is selected by specifying a time-window (e.g., 01.01.2015, 02.01.2015) and a level (e.g., minutes). The resulting time-series must contain a value for each member of the selected level, even if no time interval covers the specified member. The value may be *N/A* or *null* to indicate missing information

(*Continued*)

Table 1. (*Continued*)

Requirement	Description
[DML6]: insert, update and delete	The language must offer constructs to insert, update and delete time interval data records
[DML7]: open, half-open, or closed intervals	The system should be capable of interpreting intervals defined as open, e.g. (0, 5), closed, e.g. [0, 5], or half-opened, e.g. (0, 5]
[DML8]: meta-information	It is desired that the language supports a construct to receive meta-information from the system, e.g. actual version, available users, or loaded models
[DML9]: bulk load	It is desired, that the language provides a construct to enable a type of bulk load, i.e., increased insert performance

3.2.1 The XML TidaModel Definition

As mentioned in Sect. 2, the TidaModel is defined by a 5-tuple (P, Σ, τ, M, Δ). The time interval database P contains the raw record inserted using the API or the `INSERT` command introduced later in Sect. 3.4.1. From a modelling perspective, it is important for the system to retrieve the descriptive and temporal values from the raw record. According to that, it is essential to define the descriptors Σ and the time axis τ within the XML definition. Below, an excerpt of an XML file defining the descriptors of our sample database shown in Fig. 1 is presented:

```
<model id="myModel">
 <descriptors>
  <string id="LOC" name="location" />
  <string id="TYPE" name="type" />
  <int id="RES" null="true" />
 </descriptors>
</model>
```

The excerpt shows that a tag specifying the type (i.e., the descriptor implementation to be used), an id-attribute, and an optional name-attribute defines a descriptor. Additionally, it is possible to define if the descriptor allows *null* values (default) or not. To support more complex data structures (and one's own mapping functions), it is possible to specify one's own descriptor-implementations:

```
<descriptors>
 <ownImpl:list id="D4" />
</descriptors>
```

Our implementation looks for descriptor implementations by scanning the class-path automatically. An added implementation must provide an XSLT file, placed into the same package and named as the concrete implementation of the descriptor-class. This type of file is used to create the instance of the own implementation using a Spring Bean configuration (http://spring.io/).

```
<!-- File: my/own/desc/List.xslt -->
<xsl:template match="ownImpl:list">
 <xsl:call-template name="beanDesc">
  <xsl:with-param name="class">
    my.own.desc.List
  </xsl:with-param>
 </xsl:call-template>
</xsl:template>
```

The time axis of the TIDAMODEL is defined by:

```
<model id="myModel">
 <time>
  <timeline start="20.01.1981"  end="20.01.2061"
            granularity="MINUTE" />
 </time>
</model>
```

The time axis may also be defined using integers, i.e., [0, 1000]. Our implementation includes two default mappers applicable to map different types of temporal raw record value to a defined time axis. Nevertheless, sometimes it is necessary to use different time-mappers (e.g., if the raw data contains proprietary temporal values). These can be achieved by using the same mechanism as described previously for descriptors.

Due to the explicit time semantics, the measures M defined within the TIDAMODEL are different from the ones typically known from an OLAP definition. The model defines three categories for measures, i.e., *implicit time measures*, *descriptor bound measures*, and *complex measures*. The categories determine when which set of data is provided during the calculation process of the measures. Our implementation offers several aggregation operators useful to specify a measure, i.e., *count*, *average*, *min*, *max*, *sum*, *mean*, *median*, or *mode*. Besides, we implemented two temporal aggregation operators *started count* and *finished count*, as suggested by Meisen et al. (2015). We introduce the definition and usage of measures in Sect. 3.4.2.

The TIDAMODEL also defines the set of dimensions Δ. The definition differs between descriptor dimensions and a time dimension, whereby every dimension consists of hierarchies, levels, and members. It should be mentioned that, from a modelling point of view, each descriptor dimension fulfills the requirements formalized in [DDL2] and that the time dimension supports raster-levels as requested in [DDL3]. The definition of a dimension for a specific descriptor or the time dimension can be placed within the XML definition of a model using:

```
<model id="myModel">
 <dimensions>
  <dimension id="DIMLOC" descId="LOC">
   <hierarchy id="LOC">
    <level id="HOTEL">
         <member id="DREAM" rollUp="*" />
         <member id="STAR" rollUp="*" />
     <member id="ADV" reg="TENT" rollUp="*" />
        </level>
        <level id="ROOMS">
         <member id="POSF" reg="POS F\d" rollUp="DREAM" />
         <member id="POSG" reg="POS G\d" rollUp="DREAM" />
        </level>
        <level id="STARROOMS">
         <member id="POSA" reg="POS A\d" rollUp="STAR" />
    </level>
   </hierarchy>
  </dimension>
 </dimensions>
</model>
```

In Fig. 6, the descriptor dimension defined by the previously shown XML excerpt is illustrated. The circled nodes are leaves that are associated with descriptor values known by the model (using regular expressions). Additionally, it is possible to add dimensions for analytical processes to an already defined model, i.e., to use it only for a specific session or query. The used mechanism to achieve that is similar to the loading of a model and is not be introduced further.

The definition of a time dimension is straightforward to the one of a descriptor dimension. Nevertheless, we added some features in order to ease the definition. Thus, it is possible to define a hierarchy by using pre-defined levels (e.g., templates like 5-min-raster, day, or year) and by defining the level to roll up to, regarding the hierarchy. The following XML excerpt exemplifies the definition:

```
<model id="myModel">
 <dimensions>
  <timedimension id="DIMTIME">
   <hierarchy id="TIME5TOYEAR">
    <level id="YEAR" template="YEAR"
       rollUp="*" />
    <level id="DAY" template="DAY"
       rollUp="YEAR" />
    <level id="60R" template="60RASTER"
        rollUp="DAY" />
    <level id="5R" template="5RASTER"
        rollUp="60R" />
    <level id="LG" template="LOWGRAN"
        rollUp="5R" />
   </hierarchy>
  </timedimension>
 </dimensions>
</model>
```

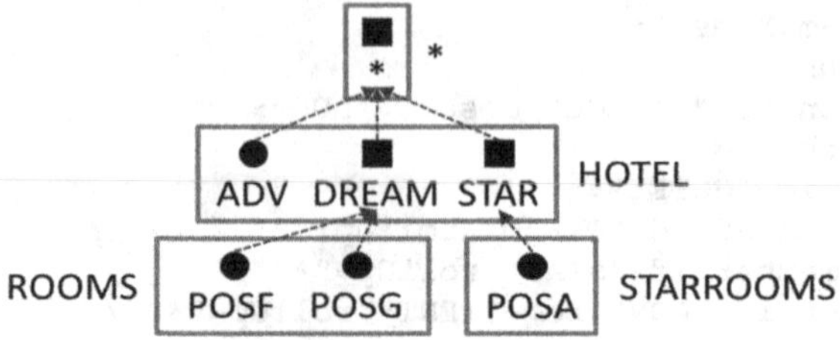

Fig. 6. Illustration of the dimension created with our web-based dimension-modeler as defined by the XML excerpt.

A defined model is published to the server using the `LOAD` command. The following subsection introduces the command, focusing on the loading of a model from a specified location.

3.2.2 Processing the LOAD Command

The loading of a model can be triggered from different applications, drivers, or platforms. Thus, it is necessary to support different loaders to resolve a specified location. In the following, we illustrate the issue by some examples. When firing a `LOAD` query from a web-application, it is necessary that the model definition be uploaded to the server, prior to executing the query. While running on an application server, it may be required to load the model from a database instead of loading it from the file-system.

Thus, we added a resource-loader, which can be specified for each context of a query. Within a servlet, the loader resolves the specified location against the upload-directory. Thereby our JDBC driver implementation is capable of sending a client's file to the server using the data stream of the active connection. After retrieving and validating the resource, the implementation uses a model-handler to bind and instantiate the defined model. As already mentioned, the bitmap-based implementation presented by [5] is used. The implementation instantiates several indexes and bitmaps for the defined model. After the instantiation, the model is marked to be up and running by the model-handler and accepts DML queries. Figure 7 exemplifies the initialized bitmap-based indexes filled with the data from the database of Fig. 1.

3.3 Data Control Language

The definition of the DCL is also straightforward to the DCL known from other query languages (e.g., SQL). As defined by requirement [DCL1], the language must encompass authorization features. Hence, the language contains commands like `ADD`, `DROP`, `MODIFY`, `GRANT`, `REVOKE`, `ASSIGN` and `REMOVE`. In our implementation, the execution of a DCL command always issues a direct commit, i.e., we currently do not support any roll back. The following listing shows the syntax of the commands.

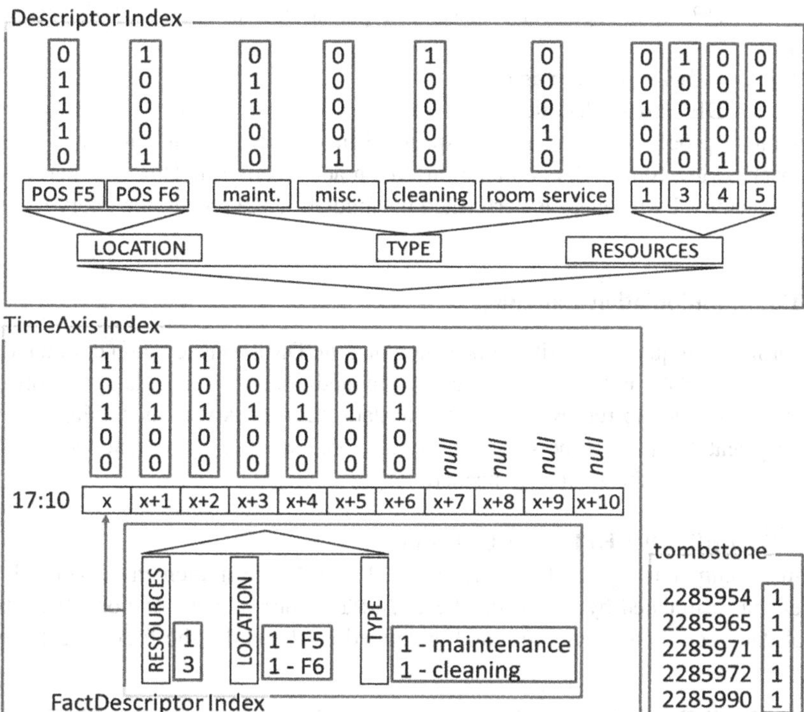

Fig. 7. Example of a loaded model filled with the data shown in Fig. 1 (cf. [6]).

```
ADD USER 'name' WITH PASSWORD 'password'
    [WITH PERMISSIONS 'permission1' [, 'permission2', ...]]
    [WITH ROLES 'role1' [, 'role2', ...]]

ADD ROLE 'name'
  [WITH PERMISSIONS 'permission1' [, 'permission2', ...]]

DROP [ROLE|USER] 'name'

MODIFY USER 'name' SET PASSWORD = 'name'

GRANT 'permission1' [, 'permission2', ...]] TO [ROLE|USER]

REVOKE 'permission1' [, 'permission2', ...]]
 FROM [ROLE|USER]

ASSIGN [ROLE|ROLES] 'role1' [, 'role2', ...]]
 TO USER 'name'

REMOVE [ROLE|ROLES] 'role1' [, 'role2', ...]]
 FROM USER 'name'
```

To fulfill the [DCL2] requirement, we define a permission that consists of a scope-prefix and the permission itself. We determine two permission-scopes GLOBAL and MODEL. Thus, a permission of the GLOBAL scope is defined by

```
GLOBAL.<permission>
```

(e.g., GLOBAL.manageUser). Instead, a permission of the MODEL scope is defined by

```
MODEL.<model>.<permission>
```

(e.g., MODEL.myModel.query).

For query processing, we use the Apache Shiro authentication framework (http://shiro.apache.org/). Shiro offers annotation driven access control. Thus, the permission to, e.g., execute a DML query is performed by annotating the processing query method.

3.4 Data Manipulation Language

Considering the requirements, it can be stated that the DML must contain commands to `INSERT`, `UPDATE`, and `DELETE` records. In addition, it is necessary to provide `SELECT` commands to retrieve time interval data records, as well as results retrieved from aggregation (i.e., time-series). Furthermore, a `GET` command to retrieve meta-information of the system is needed.

3.4.1 INSERT, DELETE, and UPDATE

The three commands `INSERT`, `DELETE`, and `UPDATE` are implemented to fulfill the requirement formulated by [DML6]. The `INSERT` command adds one or several time interval data records to the system and is defined as shown by the following listing.

```
INSERT INTO [modelId|"modelId"] (id1 [, id2, ...]) VALUES
   (value1 [, value2, ...]) [,(value1 [, value2, ...]), ...]
```

The processing of an insert statement is done in several steps. First, the system parses the structure of the data that has to be inserted. The query-parser validates the correctness of the structure, i.e., the structure must contain exactly one field marked as *start* and exactly one field marked as *end*. Additionally, the parser verifies if a descriptor (referred by its id) really exists within the model. Finally, it reads the values and invokes the processor by passing the structure, as well as the values. The processor iterates over the defined values, validates those against the defined structure, uses the mapping functions of the descriptors to receive the descriptor values, and calls the mapping function of the time-axis. The result is a so-called *processed record* that is used to update the indexes. The persistence layer of the implementation ensures that the raw record and the indexes are persisted. Finally, the tombstone bitmap is updated which ensures that the data is available within the system.

A deletion is performed by setting the tombstone bitmap for the specified id to zero. This indicates that the data of the record is not valid. In this manner, any query processors will not consider the data anymore. The internally scheduled clean-up process removes the deleted records and releases the space. In the following listing, we exemplify a delete statement.

```
DELETE recordId FROM [modelId|"modelId"]
```

By deleting the record with the specified identifier and inserting the record as described above an update is performed. The following listing exemplifies an update statement.

```
UPDATE recordId FROM [modelId|"modelId"]
   SET (id1 [, id2, ...]) VALUES (value1 [, value2, ...])
```

To support bulk load, as desired by [DML9], an additional statement is introduced. The `MODIFY MODEL` command is used to modify properties of the model, e.g., to enable the bulk load. The following listing shows the statement.

```
MODIFY MODEL [modelId|"modelId"]
   SET bulkload = [true|false]
```

When enabling the bulk load, the system waits until all currently running `INSERT`, `UPDATE`, or `DELETE` queries of other sessions are performed. New queries of that type are rejected across all sessions during the waiting and processing phase. By the time the system has handled all queries, it responds to the bulk-enabling query and expects an insert-like statement, whereby the system directly starts to parse the incoming data stream. As soon as the structure is known to the system, all incoming values are inserted. The indexes are generally only updated in memory. If the memory capacity reaches a specified threshold, the persistence-layer is triggered and memory is released. In this circumstance, the system flushes the current data in memory and persists it using the configured persistence-layer (e.g., using the file-system, a relational database, or any other NoSQL database). Whenever the system finishes a bulk load, it flushes the memory and persists the data as well.

3.4.2 SELECT Raw Records and Time-Series

The `SELECT` command is addressed by the requirements [DML1], [DML2], [DML3], [DML4], [DML5], and [DML7].

```
SELECT [TRANSPOSE(TIMESERIES)|TIMESERIES]
  OF msrExp1 [AS "alias1"] [, msrExp2 [AS "alias2"], ...]
  [ON timeDimExp] FROM [modelId|"modelId"] IN interval
  [WHERE logicalExp] [GROUP BY groupExp]

SELECT [RECORDS|COUNT(RECORDS)|IDS(RECORDS)]
  FROM [modelId|"modelId"]
  [EQUALTO|STARTINGWITH|FINISHINGWITH|MEETING|DURING|
   CONTAINING|BEFORE|AFTER|OVERLAPPING|WITHIN] interval
  [WHERE [logicalExp |idExp]] [LIMIT int[, int]]
```

We support the definition of the intervals as open, half-open or closed (cf. [DML7]). The processing of the intervals is possible, thanks to the discrete time-axis used by the model. Using a discrete time-axis with a specific granularity makes it easy to determine the previous or following granule. Thereby, every half-open or open interval can be transformed into a closed interval using the previous or following granule. Hence, the result of the parsing always results in a closed interval that is used during further query processing.

As illustrated in the listing, the SELECT RECORDS statement allows to retrieve records satisfying a logical expression (logicalExp) based on descriptor values (e.g., LOC="POS F5" OR (TYPE="cleaning" AND DIMLOC.LOC.HOTEL="DREAM")) and/or fulfilling a temporal relation (cf. [DML3]). Following Allen [5], the query language supports ten different temporal relations, e.g., EQUALTO, BEFORE, or AFTER. The interested reader may notice that Allen introduced thirteen temporal relationships. We removed some inverse relationships (i.e., inverse of meet, overlaps, starts, and finishes). When using a temporal relationship within a query, the user is capable of defining one of the intervals used for comparison. Thus, the removed inverse relationships are not needed. Instead, the user just modifies the self-defined interval. Besides, we added the WITHIN relationship which is a combination of several relationships and allows an easy selection of all records within the user-defined interval (i.e., at least one time-granule is contained within the user-defined interval).

When processing a SELECT RECORD query, the processor initially evaluates the filter expression and retrieves a single bitmap specifying all records fulfilling the filter's logic (cf. [6]). In a second phase, the implementation determines a bitmap of records satisfying the specified temporal relationship. The two bitmaps are combined using the *and*-operator to retrieve the resulting records. Depending on the requested information (i.e., count, identifiers, or raw records (cf. [DML1])), the implementation creates the response using bitmap-based operations (i.e., count and identifiers) or retrieving the raw records from the persistence layer. Figure 8 depicts the evaluation of selected temporal relationships using bitmaps and the database shown in Fig. 1.

The SELECT TIMESERIES statement specifies a logical expression equal to the one exemplified in the SELECT RECORDS statement. In addition, the statement specifies a GROUP EXPRESSION that defines the groups to create the time-series for (e.g., GROUP BY DIMLOC.LOC.ROOMS). Furthermore, it specifies the measures that have to be calculated for the time-series and the time-window (cf. [DML2]). It is also possible to specify several comma-separated measures. Some measure expressions are exemplified in the following listing, using the descriptors DESC1, DESC2, and DESC3.

```
SUM(DESC1 * DESC2) + MIN(DESC3)
MAX(SUM(DESC1 * DESC2) + MIN(DESC3)) + MIN(COUNT(DESC1))
```

A simple (considering the measures) example of a SELECT TIMESERIES query is as follows:

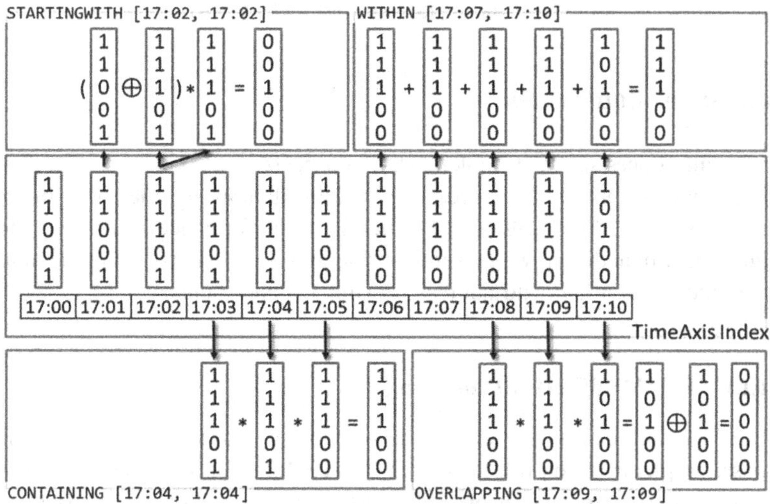

Fig. 8. Examples of the processing of temporal relationships using bitmaps (and the sample database of Fig. 1).

```
SELECT TRANSPOSE(TIMESERIES)
    OF MAX(SUM(RESOURCES)) AS "needed Res"
    ON DIMTIME.TIME5TOYEAR.5RASTER
 FROM myModel IN [01.01.2015, 02.01.2015)
 WHERE DIMLOC.LOC.HOTEL="DREAM" GROUP BY TYPE
```

As required by [DML4], a measure can be defined using the two-step aggregation technique. The first aggregation (in the example SUM) is specified for a specific descriptor and the second optional aggregation function (in the example MAX) aggregates the values across the stated level of the time-dimension.

When processing the query, the system retrieves the bitmaps for the filtering and the grouping conditions. The system iterates over the bitmaps of the specified groups and the bitmaps of the granules of the selected time-window. For each iteration, the implementation combines the filter-bitmap, group-bitmap, and the time-granule-bitmap and applies the first aggregation function. The second aggregation function is applied whenever all values of a member of the specified time-level are determined by the first step. This processing technique ensures that for each time-granule a value is calculated, even if no interval covers the granule (cf. [DML5]).

3.4.3 GET Meta-Information

Like the version of the system, [DML8] demands the existence of a command which enables the user to retrieve meta-information. This requirement is fulfilled by adding a GET command to the query language. A GET statement can be utilized to retrieve the version, models, users, roles, or permissions known by the system;

```
GET [VERSION|MODELS|USERS|ROLES|PERMISSIONS]
```

4 Implementation Issues

This section introduces selected implementation aspects of the language and its query processing. First, we introduce processing implementations for the most frequently used query-type SELECT TIMESERIES and show performance results for the different algorithms. In addition, we present considerations of analysts using the language to analyze time interval data and address possible enhancements.

4.1 SELECT TIMESERIES Processing

In Sect. 3, we outlined the query processing based on the TIDAMODEL and its bitmap-based implementation (cf. Sects. 3.2.2 and 3.4.2). For a detailed description of the bitmap-based implementation, we refer to [5]. In this section, we introduce three additional algorithms which are capable to process the most frequently used SELECT TIMESERIES queries, introduced in Sect. 3.4.2.

Prior to explaining the algorithms, it should be stated, that we did not implement any algorithm based on AGGREGATIONTREES [21], MERGESORT, or other related aggregation algorithms defined within the research field of temporal databases. Such algorithms are optimized to handle single aggregation operators (e.g., count, sum, min, or max). Thus, the implementation would not be a generic solution usable for any query. Nevertheless, such algorithms may be useful to increase query performance for specific, often used measures. It may be reasonable to add a language feature, which allows to define a special handling (e.g., using an AGGREGATIONTREE) for a specific measure. Furthermore, none of the presented algorithms support queries using group by, multiple measures, or multi-threading scenarios. To support these features, techniques like iterations and locks could be used.

First, we introduce our naive implementation. The algorithm filters the records of the database, which fulfill the defined criteria of the IN (row 04) and WHERE clause (row 06). Next, it calculates the measure for each defined range (row 10). The calculation of each measure depends mainly on its type (i.e., measure of lowest granularity (e.g., query #1 in Table 2), measure of a level (e.g., query #2), or two-step measure (e.g., query #3)). Because of space limitations, we state the complexity of the

Table 2. The shortened queries used for testing.

#	Query
1	**OF** COUNT(TASKTYPE) **IN** [01.JAN, 01.FEB) **WHERE** WA.LOC.TYPE = 'Gate'
2	**OF** SUM(TASKTYPE) **ON** TIME.DEF.DAY **IN** [01.JAN, 01.FEB) **WHERE** WORKAREA = 'SEN13'
3	**OF** MAX(COUNT(WORKAREA)) **ON** TIME.DEF.DAY **IN** [01.JAN, 01.FEB) **WHERE** TASKTYPE = 'short'
4	**OF** MAX(SUM(PERSON)/COUNT(PERSON)) **ON** TIME.DEF.MIN5DAY IN [01.JAN, 01.FEB) **WHERE** TASKTYPE = 'long'

calc-method instead of presenting it. The complexity is O(k.n), with k being the number of granules covered by the TimeRange and n being the number of records.

```
01 TimeSeries naive(Query q, Set r) {
02   TimeSeries ts = new TimeSeries(q);
03   // filter time def. by IN [a, b]
04   r = filter(r, q.time());
05   // filter records def. by WHERE
06   r = filter(r, q.where());
07   // it. ranges def. by IN and ON
08   for (TimeRange i : q.time()) {
09     // filter records for the range
10     r' = filter(r, i);
11     // det. measures def. by OF
12     ts.set(i, calc(i, r', q.meas()));
13   }
14   return ts;
15 }
```

The other algorithms we implemented are based on INTERVALTREES (INTTREE) as introduced by [25]. The first version (A) uses the tree to retrieve the relevant records considering the IN-clause (row 05 of the naive algorithm). Further, the algorithm proceeds as the naive algorithm. The second implementation (B) differs by creating a new INTTREE for every query.

```
01 TimeSeries iTreeB(Query q, Set r) {
02   TimeSeries ts = new TimeSeries(q);
03   // filter records def. by WHERE
04   IntervalTree iTree = createAndFilter(r, q.in(),
                                           q.where());
05   // it. ranges def. by IN and ON
06   for (TimeRange i : q.time()) {
07     // use iTree to filter by i
08     r' = filter(iTree, i);
09     // det. measures def. by OF
10     ts.set(i, calc(i, r', q.meas());
11   }
12   return ts;
13 }
```

As shown, the algorithm filters the records according to the IN- and WHERE-clause and creates an INTTREE for the filtered records (row 04). The created iTree is used to retrieve the relevant records for each range (row 08), when iterating over the defined ranges.

4.2 Performance

We ran several tests on an Intel Core i7-4810MQ with a CPU clock rate of 2.80 GHz, 32 GB of main memory, an SSD, and running 64-bit Windows 8.1 Pro. As Java implementation, we used a 64-bit JRE 1.6.45, with XMX 4,096 MB and XMS 512 MB. We tested the parser (implemented using ANTLR v4) and processing considering correctness. In addition, we measured the runtime performance of the processor for the three introduced algorithms (cf. Sect. 4.2), whereby the data and structures of all algorithms were held in memory to obtain CPU time comparability.

We used a real-world data set containing 1,122,097 records collected over one year. The records have an average interval length of 48 min and three descriptive values: person (cardinality: 713), task-type (cardinality: 4), and work area (cardinality: 31). The used time-granule was minutes (i.e., time cardinality: 525,600). We tested the performance using the `SELECT TIMESERIES` queries shown in Table 2. Each query specifies a different type of query (i.e., different measure, usage of groups, or filters) and was fired 100 times against differently sized sub-sets of the real-world data set (i.e., 10, 100, 1,000, 10,000, 100,000, and 1,000,000 records).

The results of the runtime performance tests are shown in Fig. 9. As illustrated, the bitmap-based implementation performs better than the naive and INTTREE algorithms when processing query #1 and #3. Regarding query #2 the INTTREE-based implementations perform best. As stated in Table 3, the most important criterion to determine the performance is the selectivity. Regarding a low selectivity, the INTTREE-based algorithm (B) performs best.

Nevertheless, considering persistency and reading of records from disc the algorithm may perform worse. We would also like to state briefly, that other factors (e.g., kind of aggregation operators used) influence the performance of the bitmap algorithm, so that it outperforms the INTTREE-based implementation, even if a low selectivity is given.

4.3 Considerations

The query language and processing introduced in this paper, is currently used within different projects by analysts and non-experts of different domains to analyze time-interval data. In the majority of cases, the introduced language and the processing is capable of satisfying the user's needs. Nevertheless, there are limitations, issues, and preferable enhancements. In the following, we introduce selected requests/improvements:

1. The presented query language and its processing do not support any type of transactions. A record inserted, updated, or deleted is processed by the system as an atomic operation. Therefore, after several operations rollbacks have to be performed manually. This typically increases implementation effort on the client-side.
2. The presented XML definition of dimensions (cf. 3.2.1) uses regular expressions to associate a member of a level to a descriptor value. Regular expressions are sometimes difficult to be formalized (especially for number ranges). An alternative, more user-friendly expression language is desired.

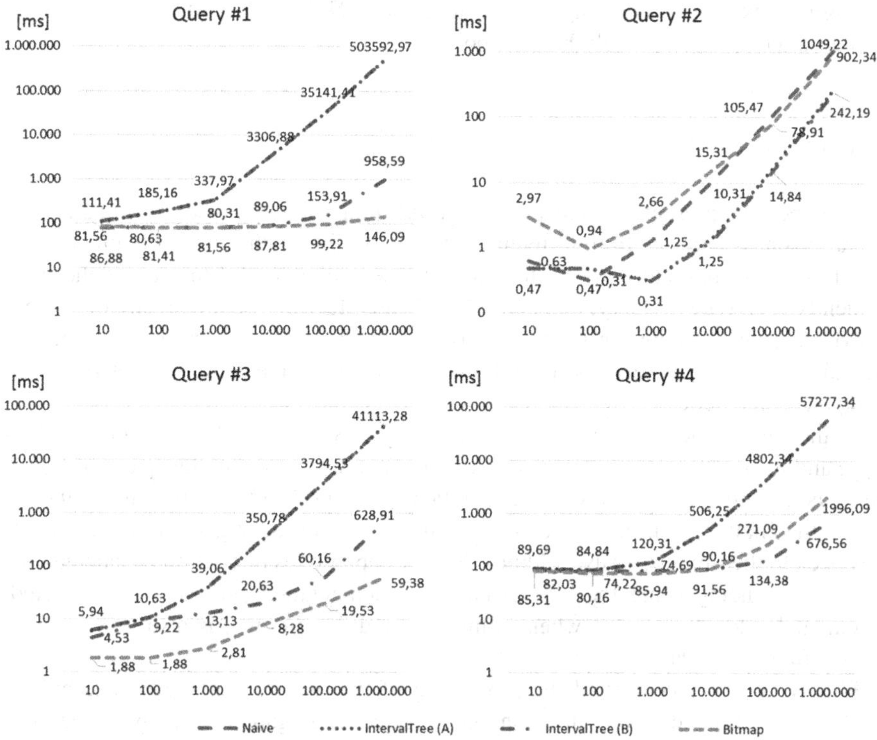

Fig. 9. The measured average CPU-time performance (out of 100 runs per query).

Table 3. Statistics of the test results.

Number of records					*Selectivity*			
in DB	Selected by query				Selected/in DB			
	#1	#2	#3	#4	#1	#2	#3	#4
10^1	1	0	0	0	0.1000	0.0000	0.0000	0.0000
10^2	5	0	7	1	0.0500	0.0000	0.0700	0.0100
10^3	12	2	46	9	0.0120	0.0020	0.0460	0.0002
10^4	147	9	480	95	0.0147	0.0009	0.0480	0.0021
10^5	1.489	121	5.148	996	0.0149	0.0012	0.0515	0.0223
10^6	15.378	1.261	51.584	9710	0.0154	0.0013	0.0516	0.2175

3. The `UPDATE` and `DELETE` commands (cf. 3.4.1) need the user to specify a record identifier. The identifier can be retrieved from the result-set of an `INSERT`-statement or using the `SELECT RECORDS` command. Nevertheless, users requested to update or delete records by specifying criteria based on the records' descriptive values.
4. When a model is modified, it has to be loaded to the system as new, the data of the old model has to be inserted and the old model has to be deleted. Users desire a

language extension, allowing to up-date models. Nevertheless, the implications of such a model update could be enormous.

5 Conclusions

In this paper, we presented a query language fulfilling the requirements formalized by several business analysts from different domains, dealing with time interval data on a daily basis. We introduced four different implementations useful to process the most frequently used type of query, i.e., `SELECT TIMESERIES`. The processing of a query is performed by fetching the relevant records utilizing a naïve approach, one of two interval tree based approaches, or a bitmap based implementation to determine an aggregated time series.

In the future, the mentioned considerations (cf. Sect. 4.3) of the introduced language and its implementation should be investigated. Furthermore, this query language should be extended to support on-line analytical mining (OLAM) on time interval data. One of the challenges in that field is the remapping from aggregated time-series patterns back to the time-intervals. Additionally, the capabilities of distributed calculations and load balancing using the bitmap based implementation should be investigated. Incremental calculations, i.e., when rolling-up or drilling-down, is also an important task for future studies.

Finally, an enhancement of the processing of the two-step aggregation technique should be considered. Depending on the selected aggregations, an optimized processing strategy may be reasonable. Such an enhancement could also be achieved by utilizing known aggregation techniques like an AggregationTree (cf. Sect. 4.1).

Acknowledgements. The approaches presented are supported by the German Research Foundation (DFG) within the Cluster of Excellence "Integrative Production Technologies for High-Wage Countries" and the project "ELLI – Excellent Teaching and Learning in Engineering Sciences" as part of the Excellence Initiative at the RWTH Aachen University.

References

1. Codd, E.F., Codd, S.B., Salley, C.T.: Providing OLAP (on-line analytical processing) to user-analysts: an IT mandate. E.F. Codd and Associates (sponsored by Arbor Software Corporation) (1993)
2. Mazón, J.-N., Lichtenbörger, J., Trujillo, J.: Solving summarizability problems in fact-dimension relationships for multidimensional models. In: 11th International Workshop on Data Warehousing and OLAP (DOLAP 2008), pp. 57–64, Napa Valley, California, USA, 26–30 October 2008
3. Kimball, R., Ross, M.: The Data Warehouse Toolkit: the Definitive Guide to Dimensional Modeling, 3rd edn. Wiley Computer Publishing, New York (2013)
4. Allen, J.F.: Maintaining knowledge about temporal intervals. Commun. ACM **26**(11), 832–843 (1983)

5. Meisen, P., Keng, D., Meisen, T., Recchioni, M., Jeschke, S.: Bitmap-based on-line analytical processing of time interval data. In: 12th International Conference on Information Technology, Las Vegas, Nevada, USA, 13–15 April 2015
6. Meisen, P., Meisen, T., Recchioni, M., Schilberg, D., Jeschke, S.: Modeling and processing of time interval data for data-driven decision support. In: IEEE International Conference on Systems, Man, and Cybernetics. San Diego, California, USA, 04–08 October 2014
7. Meisen, P., Keng, D., Meisen, T., Recchioni, M., Jeschke, S.: TIDAQL: a query language enabling on-line analytical processing of time interval data. In: 17th International Conference on Enterprise Information Systems (ICEIS 2015). Barcelona, Spain (2015)
8. Böhlen, M.H., Busatto, R., Jensen, C.S.: Point-versus interval-based temporal data models. In: 14th International Conference on Data Engineering, pp. 192–200. Orlando, Florida, USA, 23–27 February 1998
9. Papapetrou, P., Kollios, G., Sclaroff, S., Gunopulos, D.: Mining frequent arrangements of temporal intervals. Knowl. Inf. Syst. **21**(2), 133–171 (2009)
10. Mörchen, F.: Temporal pattern mining in symbolic time point and time interval data. In: IEEE Symposium on Computational Intelligence and Data Mining (CIDM 2009), Nashville, Tennessee, USA, 30 March–2 April 2009
11. Höppner, F., Klawonn, F.: Finding informative rules in interval sequences. In: Hoffmann, F., Adams, N., Fisher, D., Guimarães, G., Hand, D.J. (eds.) IDA 2001. LNCS, vol. 2189, pp. 125–134. Springer, Heidelberg (2001)
12. Kotsifakos, A., Papapetrou, P., Athitsos, V.: IBSM: interval-based sequence matching. In: 13th SIAM International Conference on Data Mining (SDM13), Austin, Texas, USA, 02–04 May 2013
13. Chen, Y.-L., Chiang, M.-C., Ko, M.-T.: Discovering time-interval sequential patterns in sequence databases. Expert Syst. Appl. **25**(3), 343–354 (2003)
14. Agrawal, R., Srikant, R.: Mining sequential patterns. In: International Conference Data Engineering, pp. 3–14. Taipei, Taiwan (1995)
15. Papapetrou, P., Kollios, G., Sclaroff, S., Gunopulos, D.: Discovering frequent arrangements of temporal intervals. In: 5th IEEE International Conference on Data Mining (ICDM 2005), pp. 354–361. IEEE Press (2005)
16. Mörchen, F.: A better tool than Allen's relations for expressing temporal knowledge in interval data. In: 12th ACM SIGKDD International Conference on Knowledge Discovery and Data Mining, Philadelphia, Pennsylvania, USA (2006)
17. Chui, C.K., Kao, B., Lo, E., Cheung, D.: S-OLAP: An OLAP system for analyzing sequence data. In: ACM SIGMOD International Conference on Management of Data, Indianapolis, Indiana, USA (2010)
18. Liu, M., Rundensteiner, E., Greenfield, K., Gupta, C., Wang, S., Ari, I., Mehta, A.: E-cube: multi-dimensional event sequence analysis using hierarchical pattern query sharing. In: ACM SIGMOD International Conference on Management of Data, Athens, Greece (2011)
19. Wrembel, R., Królikowski, Z., Będbel, B., Morzy, T., Morzy, M.: OLAP-like analysis of time point-based sequential data. In: Castano, S., Vassiliadis, P., Lakshmanan, L.V., Lee, M.L. (eds.) ER 2012 Workshops. LNCS, vol. 7518, pp. 153–161. Springer, Heidelberg (2012)
20. Morzy, T., Koncilia, C., Eder, J., Wrembel, R.: Interval OLAP: analyzing interval data. In: Bellatreche, L., Mohania, M.K. (eds.) DaWaK 2014. LNCS, vol. 8646, pp. 233–244. Springer, Heidelberg (2014)
21. Kline, N., Snodgrass, R.T.: Computing temporal aggregates. In: 11th International Conference on Data Engineering (ICDE 1995), pp. 222–231, Taipei, China, 06–10 March 1995
22. Rafiei, D., Mendelzon, A.O.: Querying time series data based on similarity. IEEE Trans. Knowl. Data Eng. **12**(5), 675–693 (2000)

23. Spofford, G., Harinath, S., Webb, C., Huang, D.H., Civardi, F.: MDX-Solutions: With Microsoft SQL Server Analysis Services 2005 and Hyperion Essbase. Wiley, New York (2006). ISBN 0471748080
24. Pedersen, T.B.: Aspects of data modeling and query processing for complex multidimensional data. Ph.D. thesis, Department of Computer Science, Aalborg Universitetsforlag, Aalborg. Publication, No. 4 (2000)
25. Kriegel, H.-P., Pötke, M., Seidl, T.: Object-relational indexing for general interval relationships. In: Jensen, C.S., Schneider, M., Seeger, B., Tsotras, V.J. (eds.) SSTD 2001. LNCS, vol. 2121, pp. 522–542. Springer, Heidelberg (2001)

Collaborative Knowledge Management Using Wiki Front-End Modules

Catarina Marques-Lucena[1,2(✉)], Carlos Agostinho[1,2], Sotiris Koussouris[3], João Sarraipa[1,2], and Ricardo Jardim-Gonçalves[1,2]

[1] Centre of Technology and Systems, CTS, UNINOVA, 2829-516 Caparica, Portugal
{cml,ca,jfss,rg}@uninova.pt

[2] Departamento de Engenharia Eletrotêcnica, Faculdade de Ciências e Tecnologia, Universidade Nova de Lisboa, 2829-516 Lisbon, Portugal

[3] School of Electrical and Computer Engineering, NTUA, 9 Iroon Polytechniou Street, 15780 Athens, Greece
skous@me.com

Abstract. Nowadays organizations have been pushed to speed up the rate of industrial transformation to high value products and services. The capability to agilely respond to new market demands became a strategic pillar for innovation, and knowledge management could support organizations to achieve that goal. However, such knowledge management approaches tend to be over complex or too academic, with interfaces difficult to manage, even more if cooperative handling is required. Nevertheless, in an ideal framework, both tacit and explicit knowledge management should be addressed to achieve knowledge handling with precise and semantically meaningful definitions. Contributing towards this direction, this paper proposes a framework capable of gathering the knowledge held by domain experts through a widespread wiki look interface, and transforming it into explicit ontologies. This enables to build tools with advanced reasoning capabilities, able to provide contextualized recommendation of resources, facilitating communities' coordination and supporting decision-making activities. A scenario where the framework was successfully applied is provided to show the pertinence of the proposed framework.

Keywords: Semantic wiki · Tacit knowledge · Explicit knowledge · Knowledge management · Recommendation systems

1 Introduction

In the past, employees used to stay in a company for their entire professional life, and consequently, their knowledge as well. However, nowadays employees are switching jobs several times and when they leave, they take their knowledge with them [1]. As a consequence, organizations must be able to capture their employees knowledge and experience to be able to change their personal knowledge into organizational knowledge, so it can be used when they are no longer with them [2].

S. Hammoudi et al. (Eds.): ICEIS 2015, LNBIP 241, pp. 69–86, 2015.
DOI: 10.1007/978-3-319-29133-8_4

Knowledge can be considered as information that has been understood and embedded in the brain. Thus, it is difficult to transfer between individuals due its individual oriented nature [3]. In this context, researchers consider tacit knowledge as the background knowledge a person uses when trying to understand anything that is presented to him [4]. Explicit knowledge is another type of knowledge, which can be expressed in words and numbers, and can be easily communicated and shared in the form of hard data, scientific formulae, codified procedures or universal principles [5]. By transforming tacit knowledge into explicit knowledge, it can be consulted and used by a full community, instead of being locked in a single community's element. However the transformation of tacit knowledge into explicit knowledge can be considered one of the most challenging steps under knowledge management.

The more communication, involvement, and interaction of people, more is the chance for organizations to expose tacit knowledge residing in individuals' heads. Thus, the importance of developing services or mechanisms to gather knowledge from domain experts has increased. As main actors, they are who better know how to characterize their domain. The result of involving them directly in the knowledge acquisition process and transformation into explicit knowledge is the possibility to software applications to adjust in accordance to specific objectives and have the notion of context. This will contribute, as an instance, to help domain experts to find others to interact about a specific topic of interest and/or expertise based on the shared knowledge.

Collective awareness refers to a common and shared vision of the whole teams or community context which allows members to coordinate implicitly their activities and behaviors through communication [6]. Making decisions with awareness will reduce the effort to coordinate tasks and resources by providing a context in which to interpret utterances and to anticipate actions [7]. This is also an objective that the authors intend to achieve, where collective awareness is supported by the explicit knowledge gather from domain experts and trough specific reasoning it. This facet will facilitate resources coordination by helping domain experts in the decision-making.

In this paper, an initial assessment related to the necessity of gathering individual's tacit knowledge and transforming it into explicit is conducted. Based on this necessity, a knowledge based establishment process is proposed where both knowledge engineers and domain experts contribute to increase communities' knowledge (explicit knowledge). This approach will support a framework for knowledge management using simple wiki-based front-end modules where tacit knowledge can be expressed in a form of explicit knowledge directly by the different employees. Afterwards, an application scenario of the proposed framework followed by some conclusions and future work statements are presented.

1.1 Related Work

Knowledge management tools are pieces of software that enable the user to create, edit or perform other operations over explicit knowledge forms (e.g. ontologies). In [8], is stated that ontology tools can be applied in all the stages of the ontology life cycle (creation, population, validation, deployment, maintenance and evolution). Some ontology management tools to consider are Ontopia[1], TM4L [9], and Protégé[2]. They are all very complete, since they all provide support to several types of ontology languages (OWL, RDF, XML) and graphic visualization methods. However, in what concerns domain experts usage, they may be difficult to use without knowledge engineers support. For that reason, the suggested knowledge management approach relies in the collaborative aspects of Semantic wikis to allow collaborative knowledge management in a iterative way by domain experts, which might not have the technical skill required for complex solutions. By using widespread and well-accepted wiki technology, domain experts are able to model and update their knowledge in a familiar environment by reusing externalized knowledge already stored in wikis.

Semantic wikis enrich wiki systems for collaborative content management with semantic technologies [10]. An overview of relevant research can be found in [11], where is possible to verify that prominent wikis like Semantic MediaWiki [12], ikeWiki [13], and SemperWiki [14], manage to disseminate semantic technologies and are used to support several semantic applications. Thus, domain experts and ontologies are able to cooperate in one system while wiki pages are presented in a human-readable format in parallel to the formal ontologies. Some works to consider are [15], and also [16]. In the first work, the authors gather wiki knowledge by defining a set of relations between Semantic MediaWiki annotations and OWL DL concepts [15]. In the latter, the authors also focus on Semantic MediaWiki annotations, but with some interactive assistance to support users in the knowledge representation process [16]. They provide functionality for collaboratively authoring, querying and browsing Semantic Web information. In both their works, explicit knowledge is achieved through a set of mappings that relate with ontological concepts. This is very powerful when one is aiming to build machine reasoning and intelligence capabilities. Nevertheless, in their proposal, all the textual and descriptive information is lost, which can be a major drawback when a feedback loop based on natural language needs to be maintained with Human users. The proposed work addresses this challenge complementing the state of the art by building a knowledge base where not only annotations are used to create ontological relations, but also content from wiki articles, gathering natural language descriptions in data properties, and consequently obtaining a richer representation of a domain.

2 Knowledge Base Establishment Process

The proposed knowledge base establishment process intends to enable knowledge management features, able to facilitate the gathering of tacit knowledge and transforming it into explicit knowledge, ready to be used by a specific community. It is a fact that when an information system intends to represent a domain's knowledge it needs to be aligned to the community that it represents.

[1] http://www.ontopia.net/page.jsp?id=about.
[2] http://protege.stanford.edu/.

Consequently it is required to have a solution where community members could present their knowledge about the domain and discuss it with their peers. Additionally, such knowledge must be available and dynamically maintained by all the involved actors. The proposed knowledge base establishment process is based on [17] and it is presented in Fig. 1. As can be observed, one of the knowledge management approach components is an explicit information front-end, where the knowledge is kept in a format that allows domain experts to utilize it. In turn, domain experts need to be able to use the explicit information to turn it into their own personal knowledge in order to create and share additional (explicit) knowledge from it. This corresponds to the bottom cycle of Fig. 1, which is aggregated through automatic synchronization with the upper cycle of the figure, in such way that if there is new knowledge added by a domain user, it would smoothly be available in the knowledge base for any further community application (e.g. enhanced searching or reasoning services).

The result is an ontology, whose model is constantly refined accordingly with the explicit information front-end module in order to better handle the knowledge provided by the domain experts. Depending on the ontology structure, synchronization services between the front-end and the ontology are implemented.

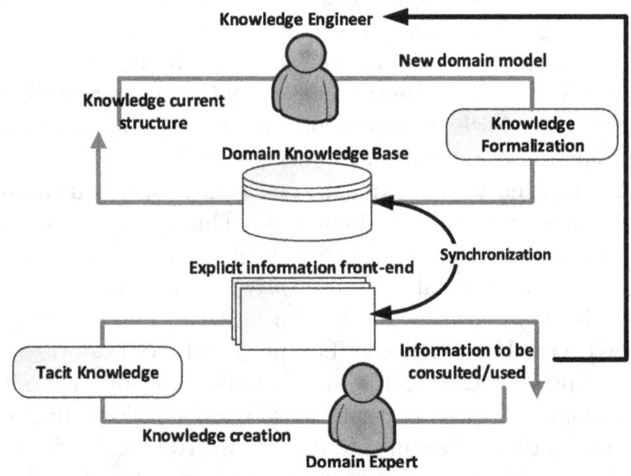

Fig. 1. Knowledge management approach.

2.1 Framework for Knowledge Management

The framework instantiates the knowledge management approach and uses ontologies and wiki front-end modules, able to facilitate the achievement of explicit knowledge from domain experts' tacit knowledge. Since the knowledge is constantly refined and updated by the domain experts' community, it would allow to make decisions based on individual's tacit knowledge. As can be observed in Fig. 2, the proposed framework is composed by four modules: (1) wiki-based front-end; (2) Synchronization module; (3) Knowledge Base; and (4) Reasoning and Decision Making module. Framework's input is the front-end user's knowledge, which is processed and consumed by the community that uses it to re-feed this cycle with more knowledge.

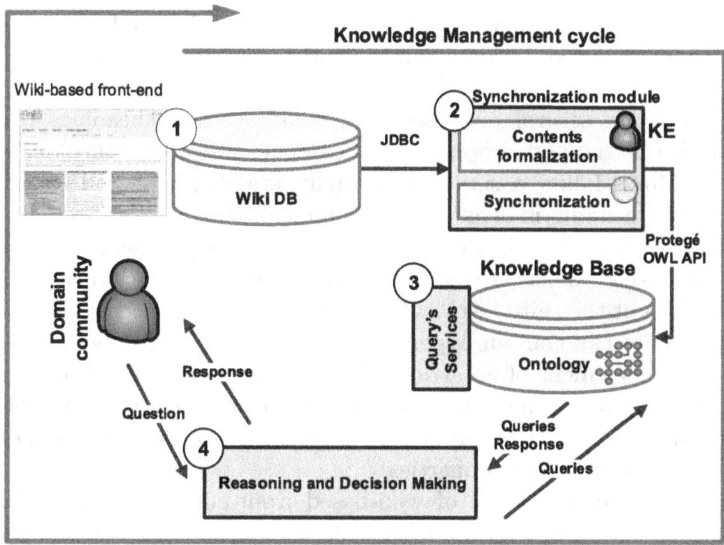

Fig. 2. Framework for knowledge management using wiki-based front-end modules.

The first module is a wiki-based front-end which corresponds to the explicit information front-end of the knowledge base establishment process presented in Fig. 1. It is characterized by being collaboratively edited by domain experts based on the knowledge consulted. However, the content of wiki-based front-ends is characterized by being human readable only. This means that its content is not formalized to facilitate computerized use (e.g. reasoning). For that reason, the synchronization module is composed by 2 sub-modules: (1) Contents formalization; and (2) Synchronization. In the contents formalization sub-module a knowledge formalization methodology is required and will be presented in the next sub-section. The synchronization sub-module is responsible for the synchronization itself between the knowledge provided by the domain experts in the front-end and the domain knowledge base.

The purpose of the ontology, modeled by knowledge engineers, is to hold the explicit knowledge about a domain in a formalized way so that it can be used by the community for reasoning purposes. Such functionality is performed by the module Reasoning and Decision making, which is able to provide structured and useful contextual information.

Wiki-Based Front-End Contents Formalization Methodology. Wiki-based front-ends are encyclopaedias that are collaboratively edited by its users, which contribute with their (tacit) knowledge. A key factor to extract knowledge from wiki-based front-ends is that such pages often follow a global template that facilitates the retrieval of information. Such front-ends provide categories that are used to classify articles and other pages. These categories are implemented by MediaWiki[3]. They help readers to find, and navigate around, a subject area, to see pages sorted by title, and thus find articles relationships. One particularity is that the resulting category system can consist in a hierarchical representation of categories related, as an example, by the relation 'is a', as the classes in an ontology.

Organized using several body sections, wikis use their headings to clarify articles and break the text, organizing its content, and populating the table of contents. Headings follow a six-level hierarchy, starting at 1 and ending at 6. The level of the heading is defined by the number of equal signs on either side of the title. Heading 1 (= Heading 1 =) is automatically generated as the title of the wiki front-end article. Sections start at second level (== Heading 2 ==), with subsections at the third level (=== Heading 3 ===), and so on [18]. Some sections of articles can contain hyper-links, and they point to a whole category, article or specific element of an article. A hyperlink between several pages, can somehow, be compared to a relation between instances of an ontology. Therefore, the organization of an article can be seen as a characterization by properties of its content (object and data properties).

Based on that organization of wiki-based front-ends the methodology for contents formalization of Fig. 3 is proposed. As can be observed, the step 0 of the methodology consists in the creation of a wiki root class in the ontology. It will handle the knowledge represented by the domain experts in the wiki-based front-end. The process of assigning categories to other categories, in the proposed methodologies (step 1), will be used by the knowledge engineers to build ontology's classification taxonomy, being the tagging between them handled as the ontological relation 'is a'. The classification of categories' contents can be facilitated if a classification taxonomy of those contents is defined (step 2). This will allow to better structure the gathered knowledge and visualize relations between knowledge base's instances.

In this methodology it is assumed that the content of all pages under a specific category follows the same structure. With that assumption, it is possible to follow with the steps 3 and 4 of the methodology. In step 3 and 4, for each article section is created a data property or object property to represent that knowledge in the ontology. The object properties created will connect the classes under the wiki root class and those under the classifiers taxonomy previously defined. Data properties will represent knowledge that is not under that taxonomy.

The process of assigning articles to categories, in the proposed methodology (steps 5 and 6) will be used to instantiate the ontology. This is done by creating an instance under the class with the article's category name (step 5). Then, based

[3] http://en.wikipedia.org/wiki/MediaWiki.

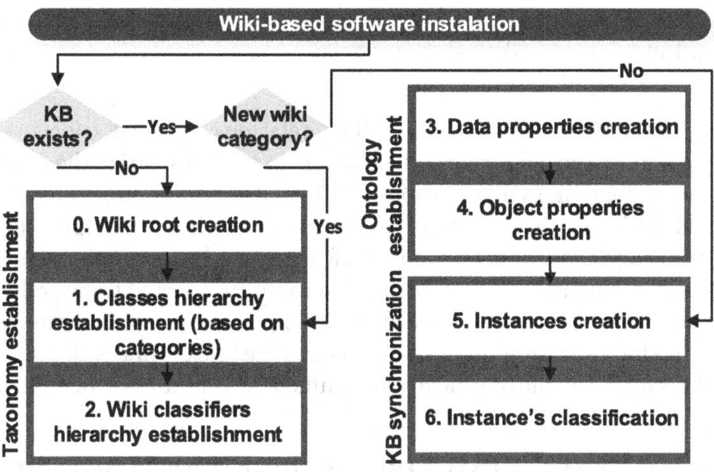

Fig. 3. Methodology for wiki-based front-end contents formalization.

on HTML analysis of articles' content, the knowledge of its sections can be represented in the data and object properties of the previously created instance (step 6).

The methodology also covers the creation of a new category on the front-end after the knowledge base is defined. It is aligned with the necessity of domain experts to share new kind of knowledge, which is not formalized yet. An example of how the methodology here presented is used can be found on Sect. 3.2.

Synchronization Between Wiki-Based Front-End Modules and Ontologies. The synchronization module runs periodically and starts by connecting to the wiki front-end database in order to verify if any changes occurred since its last run. JDBC (Java Database Connectivity) is used to querying the front-end database[4]. By querying the wikimedia table 'recentchanges', the authors have access to the set of changed pages, and its type: edition, creation, or removal. If the change is an edition or a creation, through the link to the table text (links to new & old page text) it is possible to have access to the current content of the front-end page.

After the collection of the recent changes the HTML of each article or category's page is processed in order to create/ populate the necessary instances, data properties and object properties in the knowledge base (steps 5 and 6 of the proposed methodology). In these steps of the execution flow it is also verified if the information remains consistent (e.g. the pages (articles) of the same category have the same structure). After the processing of all detected changes, the update of the ontology is made. This update is made using Jena OWL API.

[4] http://upload.wikimedia.org/wikipedia/commons/4/41/Mediawiki-database-schema.png.

It provides the necessary classes and methods to load and save OWL files and to query and manipulate OWL data models.

Reasoning and Decision-Making. The relations between concepts established, as a result of knowledge formalization, help to characterize the community resources (e.g. domain experts, topics). Thus, the Reasoning and Decision-Making module is able to use that knowledge, together with specific patters of knowledge usage to recommend specific features and support decisions. As an example, if a domain expert constantly participates in specific topics refinement, he can be interested in interact with domain experts with similar interests and participate in the discussion of similar topics. Thus, next time a domain expert enters in the system, it automatically recommends to him a set of resources.

3 Supporting the EISB During the ENSEMBLE Project

ENSEMBLE (Envisioning, Supporting and Promoting Future Internet Enterprise Systems Research through Scientific Collaboration)[5], was a Support Action funded by the European Commission (EC) that coordinated and promoted research activities in the domain of Future Internet Enterprise Systems (FInES), providing a sustainable infrastructure for the FInES community to contribute and support the EISB (Enterprise Interoperability Science Base) initiative [19], as well the 2015 Roadmap [20]. The FInES cluster, now DBI community[6], has been supported by the EC in support of the Digital Agenda for Europe, a flagship initiative of the Europe 2020 strategy.

The following scenario is related to the gathering of tacit knowledge from the FInES community and transforming it into explicit knowledge, so that it could be available to the full community, and support knowledge intensive initiatives such as the EISB. To achieve that, a wiki-based front-end (explicit information front-end) has been used, the FInESPedia[7]. It provides explicit knowledge to the community users and allows them based on that, to create new tacit knowledge and post it in the front-end. Moreover, the knowledge provided by the users is formalized in the EISB reference ontology.

3.1 FinESPedia

FInESPedia aims at providing an overview of the state of the art in Future Internet Enterprises Systems. This source of knowledge, more focused on the collaborative gathering and sharing of information from domain experts, is accessible through the FInES cluster portal[8]. As can be observed in Fig. 4, its homepage

[5] http://www.fines-cluster.eu/jm/ENSEMBLE-Public-Category/ensemble-objectives.html.
[6] http://www.dbi-community.eu.
[7] http://finespedia.epu.ntua.gr/.
[8] http://www.fines-cluster.eu/jm/.

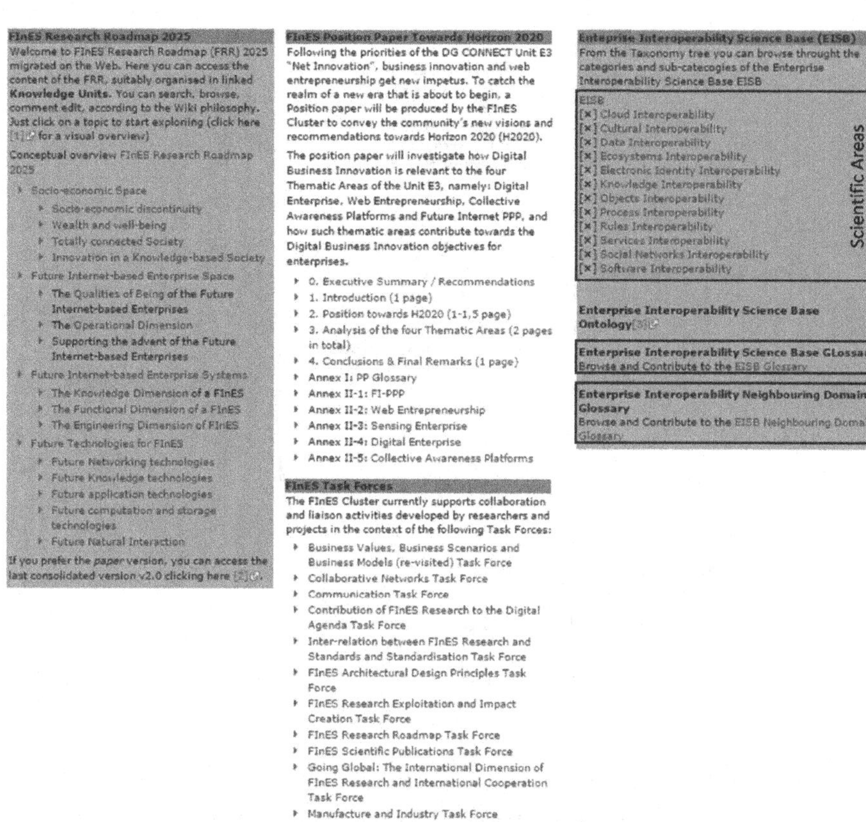

Fig. 4. FinESPedia Main Page.

is dived into four main sections, namely: (1) FInES Research Roadmap 2025; (2) FInES Position Paper Towards Horizon 2020; (3) Enterprise Interoperability Science Base (EISB) where this use case is focused; and (4) FInES Task Forces.

Going into further detail (on the EISB), the FInESPedia is essentially composed by Scientific Areas, EISB Glossary and also the Neighbouring Domains Glossary, that are being synchronized with the EISB ontology, as explained next. To the formalization of FInESPedia front-end knowledge, the methodology of Sect. 2.1 was followed.

3.2 Application of the Methodology

The EISB knowledge base is a component that intends to capture ENSEMBLE community knowledge with precise and semantically meaningful definitions. As explained along the paper, it also serves as a facilitator for knowledge reasoning, allowing different views of the information gathered from the wiki. Having this

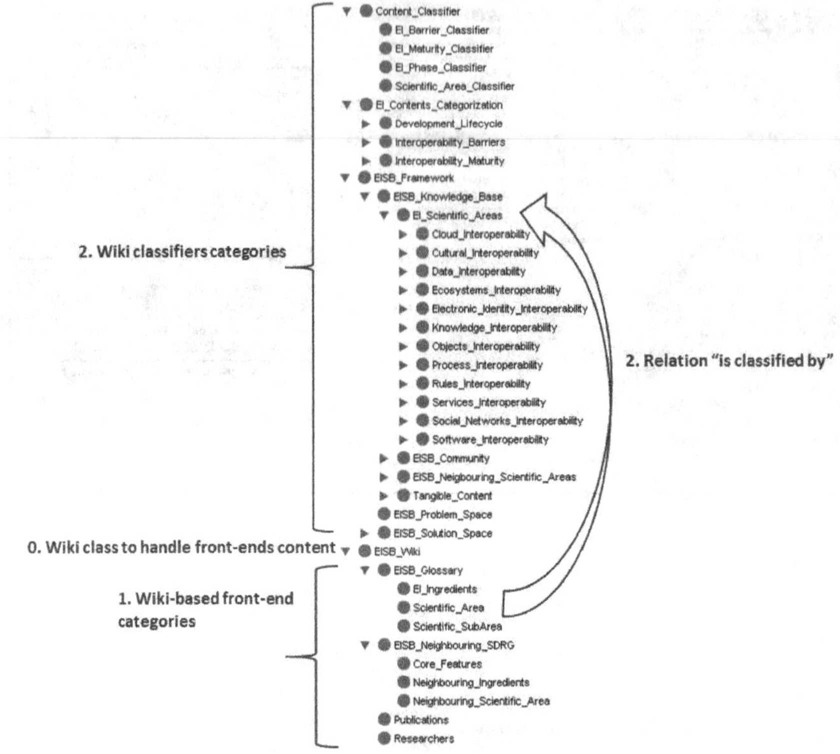

Fig. 5. Knowledge Base's taxonomy establishment.

kind of knowledge would facilitate the search of specific information, for instance papers or methods of a specific EISB area, or a specific set of tutorials related to a specific EISB topic, or even a set of expert researchers. Furthermore, this ontology can be a valuable asset for the scientific base itself, gathering meta-information relevant to both Enterprise Interoperability and the neighbouring domains [21].

Taxonomy Establishment Based on the Methodology. Fig. 5 represents the application of the methodology to establish the knowledge base taxonomy. As can be observed, step 0 of the methodology consists in the creation of the class 'EISB_Wiki', which will handle the categories' taxonomy represented in the wiki-based front-end.

The step 1 of the methodology was accomplished by navigating in the front-end articles' category classification, as was explained in Sect. 2.1 It results in the identification of four main classes to be handled under the class 'EISB_Wiki':

- EISB Glossary - Representation of the contents of the glossary page of FInES-Pedia, including: EI Ingredients, including the detailed information about the

various EISB ingredients (e.g. methods, tools, experiments); Scientific Area, regarding the EISB scientific areas represented in the wiki page; and Scientific SubAreas, regarding scientific sub areas represented in the FInESPedia [22];
- EISB Neighbouring SDRG - Serves the same purpose of the EISB Glossary, but refers to the Neighbouring domains instead; (see [23] for technical details on the neighbouring domains);
- Publication - Information regarding the publications presented in FInESPedia;
- Researchers - Information about the researchers acting in the EISB community.

Step 2 of the methodology consists in the categories contents' classifiers. This is a knowledge engineers' works in which they analyze the knowledge that the domain experts want to represent in order to create a classifiers taxonomy from it. The four main classes of the classifiers taxonomy are:

- EI Contents Categorization - that aims to represent the information about the different categories that the content of the wiki can take, namely: Interoperability Maturity, which holds the information about the various maturity models available; Development Lifecycle, which houses the information about the different development phases of certain publication (Assessment, Design, Implementation); and Interoperability Barriers, Indicating which type of EI barrier is targeted accordingly with the image of the ISO standard 11354 [24];
- Content Classifier - which stores information relative to classifications of the EISB contents: EI Barrier Classifiers, which assigns (High-Low) relevance of a certain content regarding its interoperability barrier (e.g. Technical- High); EI Maturity Classifier, which has the information relative to the maturity of the wiki content (e.g. mature, infant); Phase Classifier, which classifies publications relatively to its development lifecycle (e.g. Design-High); and Scientific Area Classifier, which classifies a wiki content with the relevance pertaining to a certain scientific area (e.g. Data Interoperability - Medium);
- EISB Framework - the purpose of this class is to hold information about the elements that compose the EISB universe. It handles the knowledge about the framework components: EISB Knowledge Base (the scope of the previous descriptions); EISB Problem Space; and EISB Solution Space (Hypothesis, Laws, etc.) [21].

On example of a relation 'is classified by' is represented in Fig. 5. It illustrated that the Scientific Areas represented in the wiki-based front-end can be classified by the subclasses under the class 'EI_Scientific_Areas' of the wiki classifiers taxonomy.

Ontology Properties Establishment Based on the Methodology. In this subsection, the steps 3 and 4 of the methodology are demonstrated. The type of pages that were selected to exemplify the methodology were those under the category 'Publications'. It was assumed that the articles under this category follow the same structure of the page illustrated in the top of Fig. 6. Concerning

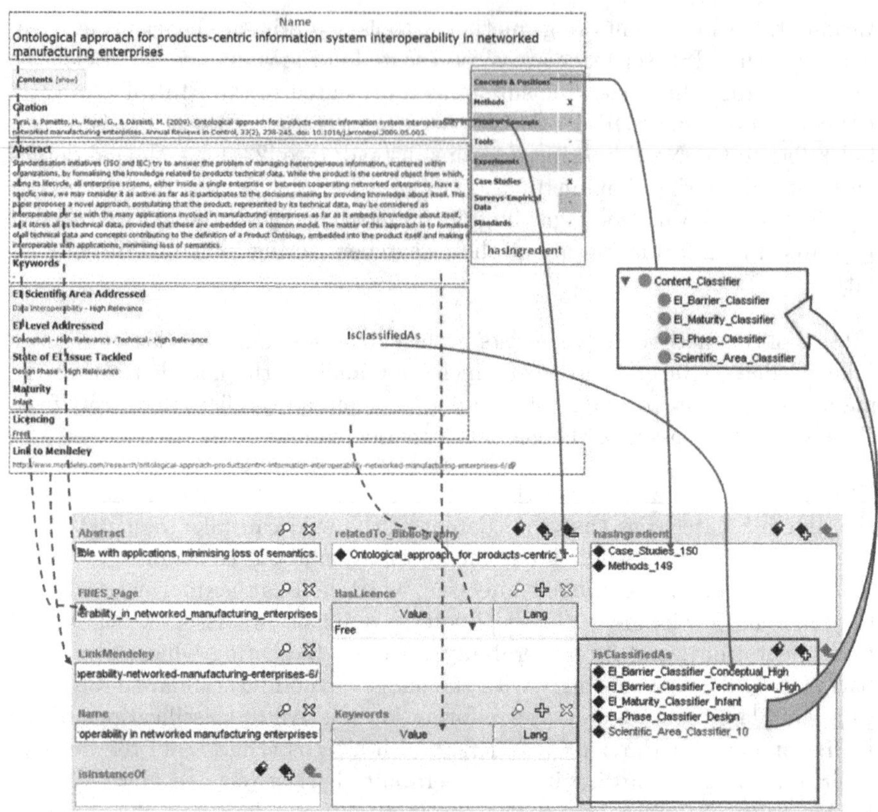

Fig. 6. New publication demonstration scenario.

its content and the classifiers taxonomy established on step 2, the data properties (green dotted areas of Fig. 6) defined are: 'Abstract'; 'FINES_Page'; 'Keywords'; 'HasLicence'; 'Link_Mendeley'; and 'Name' (step 3 of the methodology). The object properties (blue line continued areas) defined were: 'hasIngredient'; 'IsClassifiedAs'; and 'related_to_Bibliography'.

3.3 Ensemble's Knowledge Base Synchronization

After structuring the information retrieved from the wiki front-end, and concerning the scenario of a new publication creation, it is possible to do the synchronization between the front-end and the ontology in order to populate the knowledge base with domain experts' knowledge. The synchronization tool is triggered by a 'cron job' that runs daily. Then, the recent changes are analysed in order to verify if there is any new publication in the FInESPedia. That verification is made by analysis of the HTML content of the pages to verify in which category the page belongs.

The wiki front-end to ontology synchronization of a new publication is illustrated in Fig. 6. It is possible to verify that the various sections of the wiki page have a direct correspondence in the ontology (result of knowledge engineers work), and all the contents are therefore successfully migrated. It is also possible to verify that the object property 'IsClassifiedAs' relates the wiki pages content with a taxonomy under the classifiers defined in step 2.

After contents formalization, the knowledge management framework is capable of handle articles' creation, edition and elimination without the intervention of knowledge engineers. However, if other non-modelled category occurs (other type of tacit knowledge), knowledge engineers need to re-follow the proposed knowledge structuring methodology. In such way, the new sub-domain knowledge inserted by the domain experts can be transformed into explicit knowledge to be presented to the community.

3.4 Recommendation Services

The recommendation services, part of the Reasoning and Decision-making module, have the goal to search for the most appropriate features to provide to domain experts. The recommendation is based on the analysis of several patterns (e.g. history of edition and consulting of resources) of the formalized knowledge. As an instance, the FInESPedia publications could be related through several different characteristics (e.g. *Keywords*, *Ingredients*, *Licensing*, and *Researchers*) to researchers and topics of interest. This knowledge together with the historical information of resource consulting, allows the reasoning and decision-making module to recommend resources to interact with taking into account domain experts profile (see Fig. 7).

One of the searching features provided is related to the retrieval of publications with the biggest level of similarity with the publications consulted by a domain expert. It is done following the cycle represented in Fig. 8. This cycle starts with the definition of the set of characteristics considered as relevant for

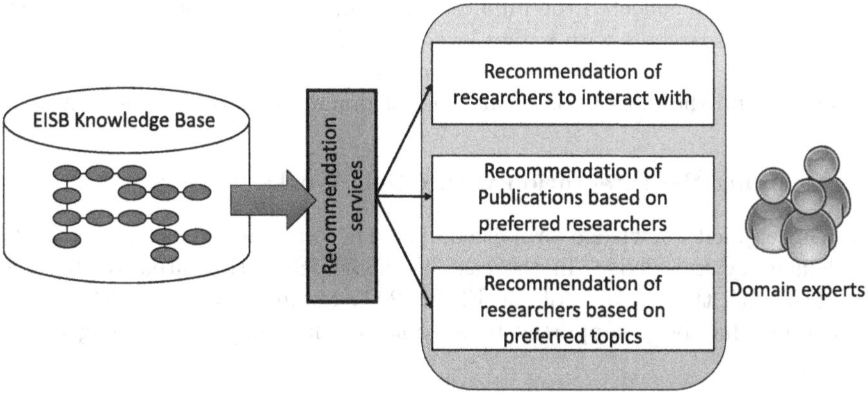

Fig. 7. EISB recommendation systems.

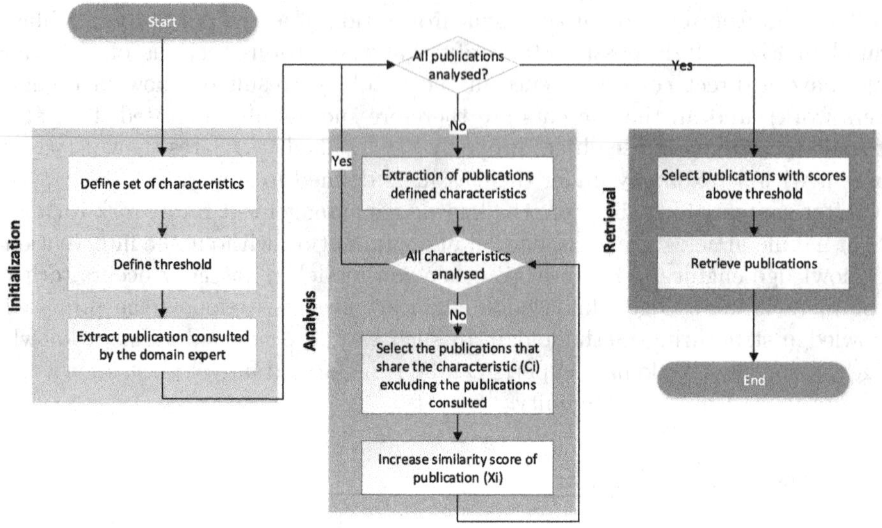

Fig. 8. Methodology for publications recommendation.

common publications identification and a thresholf defining the minimum score for witch publications are considered as similar. Then, all the publications consulted or edited in the past by the domain expert are collected.

In the analysis phase, for each publication of the previous set, the values of the characteristics defined in the previous phase are collected and the similarity scores for the publications with identical values increased. When all the publications and corresponding characteristics are analyzed, the publications with scores above the defined threshold are recommended to the author to interact with.

The recommendation system is also capable to recommend researchers (domain experts) to interact with (e.g. collaborate, consult work). It is done following the same path explained previously and then the inverse one. That means, at first are collected the publications of interest to a user, and then, are collected the researchers with higher level of participation in these publications. In this way, the system is able to have context awareness of the resources usage and recommend the most appropriate one for domain experts interact with.

3.5 Enabling the Integration with Other Works

By having explicit knowledge formalized, it also becomes much easier to integrate complementary knowledge. In the case of ENSEMBLE this situation became very clear with the example of the FInES 2025 roadmap. Like the EISB, also the roadmap has been supported by an ontology for knowledge management[9]

[9] (https://webbrain.com/brainpage/brain/CBEB302D-2971-659C-4D49-2EB9CF575C49;jsessionid=4CBA3002E17F081303C3A45BA84821A0).

with a wiki front-end (in this case only to visualize information[10]). Due to both ontologies links were easily defined between knowledge domains, enabling readers to navigate through the wiki between the roadmap and the EISB knowledge, increasing their awareness of the FInES and enterprise interoperability domains.

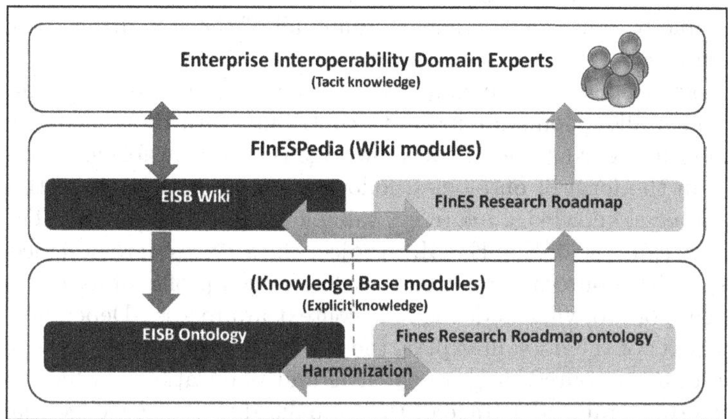

Fig. 9. Integration between EISB knowledge base and FInES research roadmap.

The described scenario is illustrated in Fig. 9. The collaborative knowledge management described here is related to the left part of the figure, where the domain experts are able to directly contribute to community knowledge by deploying it in the EISB wiki. This knowledge is then formalized in the EISB Ontology (obtained using the methodology of Fig. 3). Thank to this formalization, and following a harmonization process [25], direct links can be established between EISB and FInES Research Roadmap concepts. These established links are then represented in the FInESPedia allowing the navigation between the two domains [21].

4 Conclusions

To increase the competitiveness level, organizations must be able to keep its employees knowledge inside the organization, even when they leave. The same happens with researchers and scientists so that the community can capitalize their knowledge. Hence, responding to those needs, a knowledge management framework based on wiki front-end modules was implemented. With the proposed framework, domain experts can actively contribute to the knowledge of their community through a simple and, considerably well-known interface, as wiki-based front-ends. This kind of front-ends are known by being easy to setup and use, tracking of changes, and on-the-fly publishing. Thus are being largely

[10] http://finespedia.epu.ntua.gr/FInES_Research_Roadmap_2025.html.

selected to share knowledge in several areas like teaching [26], collaborative modeling [27], process development [28], and others. However, beside the mentioned advantadges, wikis are also characterized for being human readable only. This means that its content is not formalized to facilitate computerized use, an issue addressed by Semantic wikis. Most of the state of the art solutions are based on mappings between semantic annotations and ontological relations. The presented solution is able to complement that, handling all of the wiki articles content in natural language.

This paper proposes to use simple web-based interfaces, in the form of wiki modules, which allow domain experts to contribute with their tacit knowledge through an intuitive front-end. That knowledge is then transformed into explicit knowledge, in the form of ontologies, following a semi-automatic methodology. With this process, knowledge becomes available for querying and intelligent reasoning. In the example of ENSEMBLE project the services were designed to recommend specific resources in relation to a determined profile of user. Thus they give some support to what is defined as 'context awareness'. Depending on the profile (context) of the domain expert, the system is able (aware) to suggest the most appropriate resources (e.g. researchers and publications), which will help domain experts to take advantage of the formalized tacit knowledge shared.

Other knowledge bases can be integrated, providing users extended awareness of the domain and enriched feedback information that can motivate the refinement of the front-end and more suitable decisions. In the exemple provided, trough harmonization, relations between concepts from EISB and FInES Research Roadmap were established. These allow user to navigate between both domains and increasing their awareness of the FInES and enterprise interoperability domains.

The Authors applied successfully these ideas in the ENSEMBLE case and are currently working on forms to decrease the level of participation of knowledge engineers in tacit knowledge gathering. Currently, in order for a new concept to be detected and formalized in the ontology, knowledge engineers need to be constantly verifying the wiki contents and manually instruct the synchronization tool to recognize and handle such knowledge. In future work, the authors plan to automatize such procedure. Moreover, when the knowledge is gathered by a full community, an article can be edited several times and, it may be useful to keep track of those changes in the ontology (e.g. versioning mechanism). As an instance, the amount of changes that a page suffers in a specific period of time can be an indicator of a community interest in a specific topic. Also, the authors intend to apply this approach to other domains of knowledge management (e.g. requirements engineering, collaborative education curriculum creation, etc.).

Acknowledgements. The research leading to these results have received funding from the European Union 7th Framework Programme (FP7/2007-2013) under grant agreement: ENSEMBLE (http://www.fines-cluster.eu/jm/ENSEMBLE-Public-Category/ensemble-objectives.html) n 257548, ALTERNATIVA (DCI-ALA/19.09.01/10/21526/245-575/ALFA III (2010) 88), and also through OSMOSE (http://www.osmose-project.eu) nr 610905 which is enabling to continue this line of research.

References

1. Kim, S.: Factors affecting state government information technology employee turnover intentions. Am. Rev. Pub. Adm. **35**, 137–156 (2005)
2. Jones, K., Leonard, L.N.K.: From tacit knowledge to organizational knowledge for successful KM. In: King, W.R. (ed.) Knowledge Management and Organizational Learning, pp. 27–39. Springer, Heidelberg (2009)
3. Osterloh, M., Frey, B.S.: Motivation, knowledge transfer, and organizational form. Technical report, Institute for Empirical Research in Economics - University of Zurich, IEW - Working Papers (2000)
4. Polanyi, M.: The Tacit Dimension. Anchor Books, New York (1967). Terry lectures
5. Nonaka, I., Takeuchi, H.: The Knowledge-Creating Company: How Japanese Companies Create the Dynamics of Innovation. Oxford University Press, New York (1995)
6. Daassi, M., Favier, M.: Groupware and team aware: bridging the gap between technologies and human behaviour. In: The Encyclopedia of Virtual Communities and Technologies (2005)
7. Gutwin, C., Greenberg, S., Roseman, M.: Workspace awareness in real-time distributed groupware: framework, widgets, and evaluation. In: Sasse, M.A., Cunningham, R.J., Winder, R.L. (eds.) HCI 1996, pp. 281–298. Springer, London (1996)
8. Youn, S., Arora, A., Chandrasekhar, P., Mestry, P., Sethi, A.: Survey about ontology development tools for ontology-based knowledge management. University of South California (2009)
9. Dicheva, D., Dichev, C.: Tm4l: creating and browsing educational topic maps. Br. J. Educ. **37**, 391–404 (2006)
10. Schaffert, S., Krötzsch, M., Vrandečić, D.: Reasoning in semantic wikis. In: Antoniou, G., Aßmann, U., Baroglio, C., Decker, S., Henze, N., Patranjan, P.-L., Tolksdorf, R. (eds.) Reasoning Web. LNCS, vol. 4636, pp. 310–329. Springer, Heidelberg (2007)
11. Völkel, M., (ed.): Proceedings of the First Workshop on Semantic Wikis - From Wiki To Semantics. Workshop on Semantic Wikis, ESWC 2006 (2006)
12. Völkel, M., Vrandečić, D., Krötzsch, M.: Semantic mediawiki. In: Cruz, I., Decker, S., Allemang, D., Preist, C., Schwabe, D., Mika, P., Uschold, M., Aroyo, L.M. (eds.) ISWC 2006. LNCS, vol. 4273, pp. 935–942. Springer, Heidelberg (2006)
13. Schaffert, S.: IkeWiki: a semantic wiki for collaborative knowledge management. In: 15th IEEE International Workshops on Enabling Technologies: Infrastructure for Collaborative Enterprises, WETICE 2006, pp. 388–396 (2006)
14. Oren, E.: SemperWiki: a semantic personal Wiki. In: Proceedings of the 1st Workshop on The Semantic Desktop at the ISWC 2005 Conference, Galway, pp. 107–122 (2005)
15. Vrandecic, D., Krötzsch, M.: Reusing ontological background knowledge in semantic Wikis. In: SemWiki (2006)
16. Dello, K., Simperl, E.P.B., Tolksdorf, R.: Creating and using semantic web information with makna. In: Proceedings of the First Workshop on Semantic Wikis - From Wiki To Semantics, Workshop on Semantic Wikis, ESWC 2006 (2006)
17. Sarraipa, J.A., Marques-Lucena, C., Baldiris, S., Fabregat, R., Aciar, S.: The ALTER-NATIVA knowledge management approach. J. Intell. Manufact. 1–17 (2014). doi:10.1007/s10845-014-0929-0
18. Wikipedia: Wikipedia: Manual of Style/Layout (2014)

19. Jardim-Goncalves, R., Grilo, A., Agostinho, C., Lampathaki, F., Charalabidis, Y.: Systematisation of interoperability body of knowledge: the foundation for enterprise interoperability as a science. Enterp. IS **7**, 7–32 (2013)
20. FInES Research Roadmap Force: FInES Research Roadmap 2015 (2012)
21. Agostinho, C., Jardim-Goncalves, R., Sarraipa, J.A., Lampathaki, F.: EnSEMBLE Envisioning, Supporting and Promoting Future Internet Enterprise Systems Research through Scientific Collaboration EISB Models & Tools Report (2009)
22. Lampathaki, F., Koussouris, S., Agostinho, C., Jardim-Goncalves, R., Charalabidis, Y., Psarras, J.E.: Infusing scientific foundations into enterprise interoperability. Comput. Ind. **63**, 858–866 (2012)
23. Agostinho, C., Jardim-Goncalves, R., Steiger-Garcao, A.: Underpinning EISB with enterprise interoperability neighboring scientific domains. In: Revolutionizing Enterprise Interoperability through Scientific Foundations. IGI Global, pp. 41–76 (2014)
24. ISO, TC 184, SC 5: Advanced automation technologies and their applications Part 1 : Framework for enterprise interoperability. (ISO/DIS 11354–1: 2011) (2011)
25. Sarraipa, J., Jardim-Goncalves, R., Steiger-Garcao, A.: MENTOR: an enabler for interoperable intelligent systems. Int. J. Gen. Syst. **39**, 557–573 (2010)
26. Parker, K.R., Chao, J.T.: Wiki as a teaching tool. Interdisc. J. Knowl. Learn. Objects **3**, 57–72 (2007)
27. Dengler, F., Happel, H.J.: Collaborative modeling with semantic mediawiki. In: Proceedings of the 6th International Symposium on Wikis and Open Collaboration, WikiSym 2010, Article no. 23. ACM, New York (2010)
28. Dengler, F., Lamparter, S., Hefke, M., Abecker, A.: Collaborative process development using semantic mediawiki. In: Proceedings of the 5th Conference of Professional Knowledge Management, Solothurn, Switzerland, GI (2009)

Anything Relationship Management and Early Stage Prototype

Jonathan P. Knoblauch, Rebecca Bulander(✉), and Bernhard Kölmel

Hochschule Pforzheim, Tiefenbronner Straße 65, 75175 Pforzheim, Germany
{jonathan.knoblauch, rebecca.bulander, bernhard.koelmel}@hs-pforzheim.de

Abstract. The internet of people, virtual and physical things as well as data and processes in between– also called the Internet of Everything with its different entities– is continuously growing every day. This offers on the one side the possibility for new business models; on the other side organizations are faced with the challenge to manage this variety of entities. Not only for the own organization relevant individual entities must be detected but out of the relationships between these entities a lot of valuable information can be collected. This article describes how Anything Relationship Management provides a solution to manage the different relationships and to gain information to optimize the business. Therefore an Anything Relationship Management framework is provided and an early stage prototype of a possible scenario in the smart factory environment is shown.

Keywords: Anything Relationship Management · Stakeholder relationship management · Customer Relationship Management · Relationship management · Internet of everything

1 Introduction

An increasing interconnectedness of people, physical objects and virtual objects through ICT (information and communication technology) has been observable for years. This is reflected in various fields such as business contacts (e.g. LinkedIn and Xing), social media (e.g. Facebook, WhatsApp and Twitter) or the emerging Internet of Everything. Cisco estimates that in 2020 50 billion devices and objects will be connected to the internet [1]. Particularly companies and organizations have a variety of relationships with their stakeholders, as well as other physical things (cars, machines etc.) and virtual objects (cloud services, documents etc.) today. All those things have to be managed with appropriate approaches. xRM can be used for this purpose as a further evolution of Customer Relationship Management, allowing the management of any kind of objects with appropriate mechanisms on a IT platform. Compared to existing relationship management systems, which usually only represent a partial area of a company, the xRM approach is implemented on a flexible and generic xRM platform that enables a uniform mapping of all relationship management areas of a company. While there are a lot of offers of xRM platforms (Microsoft Dynamics CRM, SugarCRM etc.), there is still a lack of appropriate management strategies and concepts

S. Hammoudi et al. (Eds.): ICEIS 2015, LNBIP 241, pp. 87–107, 2015.
DOI: 10.1007/978-3-319-29133-8_5

for xRM. Britsch et al. (2012) see this as "one of the central research questions of Anything Relationship Management" [2]. The lack of management strategies has often emerged in the ICT sector.

The objective of this document is the presentation of a conceptual framework for xRM as an associated management concept. This document summarizes the results of a research project. Some basic background about xRM, the difference between xRM and CRM and some theoretical foundations of management concepts are described for this purpose. Additionally, the main objectives and principles of xRM will be explained. The conceptual framework for xRM is explained. The conceptual framework gets validated by an implemented example at an early stage prototype in the environment of a smart fact. Finally a conclusion and an outlook for further use are given.

2 Fundamentals of xRM

2.1 Definition of xRM

In literature we find different definitions of the term xRM like [2–4]. In most definitions xRM is seen as the further stage of CRM as well as the implementation of the theoretical foundations of relationship management. In addition, xRM includes a technological component (IT system or platform) and a conceptual component (management concept and management strategy). In newer definitions xRM is seen as an opportunity to manage objects in the internet of everything [5]. The following definition covers the main aspects of past and previous definitions of xRM: "Anything Relationship Management (xRM), as an advancement of CRM, is a consistent and holistic concept of Relationship Management between and in-between enterprises, people, physical things and virtual assets. It is based on one or more flexible, modular and scalable IT platforms, which can be focussed on different branches. xRM helps enterprises to capture, coordinate and analyse entities and their relationships as well as processes in the Internet of Everything" [5].

2.2 Differences Between CRM and xRM

The graph below illustrates in what layers CRM will advance towards. Therefore a three-layered architecture with a management layer, a middleware layer and a backend layer is depicted (see Fig. 1).

The management layer contains the basic factors and aspects of the Relationship Management concept of an organization. At the middleware layer of xRM the different relationships between the entities are managed. Therefore this layer contains mostly a highly efficiently and dynamical platform with the capability of interoperability. The main task of the back-end layer is to integrate various systems in a homogeneous system landscape. Besides ERP and SCM systems this layer also has to integrate intelligent physical things like Cyber Physical Systems (CPS) or virtual things such as cloud computing services.

Since xRM is a further stage of CRM a comparison is useful. Next these two terms are compared according to different criteria.

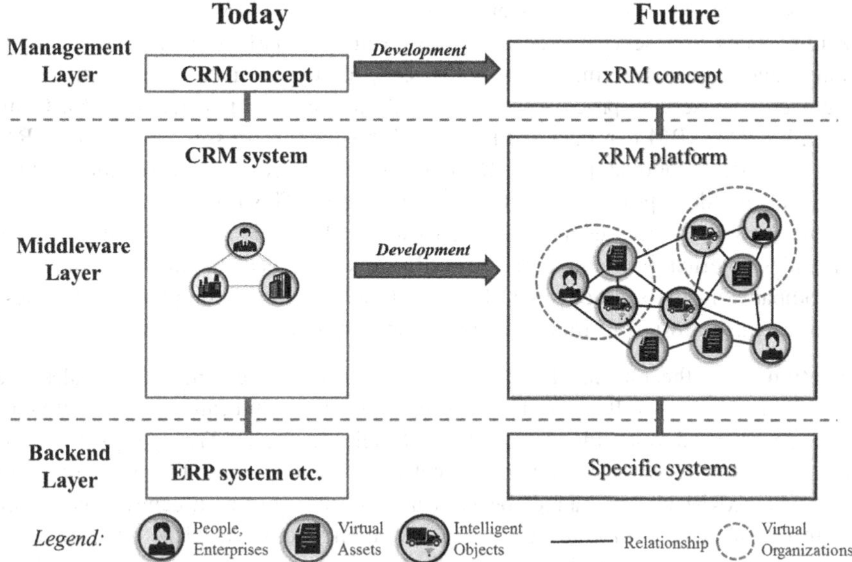

Fig. 1. Evolution of xRM [5].

Entities and Relationships. The main entities in CRM are the customers and their relationships to the company, the products and the services or the brand. In xRM the customers are only one of many entities, but still the most important one. Besides virtual assets and physical objects xRM also includes all relevant primary and secondary stakeholders of the company. Furthermore xRM connects stakeholders and physical objects in the real world with virtual assets in the virtual world (information world). Each relevant object of the real world always exists as a digital replication in the virtual world.

Management Tasks. A company serves a particular selection of customers. These customers can be differentiated by e.g. their buying behavior, revenue or customer value. Therefore it is important to manage them each in an individual way. An established approach, especially for marketing and sales, is to manage customers depending on their customer value [6]. With xRM, however, all relevant relationships of the company have to be managed systematically. This leads to a significantly higher complexity of relationships management. That complexity isn't contained in the individual relationships, but rather in the variation of the relationships.

Objectives. According to [7], the objectives of CRM are to establish profitable customer relationships and a holistic customer-oriented business strategy with CRM systems. The relevant departments of a company must be interconnected and aligned towards the customers for this purpose [7]. By contrast, the objectives of xRM are to identify and manage all profitable relationships of the company and to map them in a consistent and holistic approach with ICT. Additionally, xRM seeks to increase the relationship quality in all relevant stakeholder relationships, e.g. using quality Key Performance Indicators (KPIs).

Processes. The most important operational processes in CRM can be divided into marketing, sales and service processes. For example, marketing processes include campaign and lead management, sales processes, the opportunity, contract and order management and service processes the feedback and support management [8]. Compared with CRM, xRM can map and manage all business processes that involve xRM entities and their relationships [9]. xRM comprises interactive processes that include different stakeholders, physical objects and virtual assets. This leads to an improvement of internal business processes through a consistent and holistic mapping and managing [2]. Besides internal business processes xRM also enables the implementation of cross-company business processes [10]. Such functionality is important for business cooperation in the form of virtual enterprises and organizations.

Integration. On the one hand CRM systems merge isolated marketing, sales and service applications as well as specific internet applications and call center departments into one coordinated system landscape with a Single Source Of Truth (SSOT). On the other hand CRM systems are integrated between other systems like ERP or SCM systems [11]. xRM in turn cannot be seen as a system, but as a central integration platform that integrates all kind of systems and applications. An xRM platform has a high flexibility and can therefore adopt historically grown systems with their related structures [3]. Future xRM platforms must also integrate smart objects like cyber-physical systems (CPS) or virtual objects like cloud computing services [9].

2.3 xRM, Internet of Everything and Smart Factory

The Internet of Everything is a dynamic network, which is based on interoperable communication protocols and standards. Within this network each physical or virtual object can be identified and therefore integrated in a network [12]. Therefore it is possible to detect the relationship structure and to link real and virtual entities dynamically with the right context [2].

With the xRM approach organizations are able to connect stakeholders with other entities like physical things or virtual assets on a platform which allows the systematic management of all for the business case relevant business objects.

xRM can be applied on several business scenarios. One important of them is the smart factory. In the smart factory three integration scenarios can be differentiated: A horizontal integration through value networks, a holistic integration of engineering across the entire value chain and a vertical integration along networked manufacturing systems [13].

Implementing xRM in a vertical integration means e.g. to build powerful solutions across the vertical integration by reconfiguring whole manufacturing systems over an xRM user interface. Implementing xRM in the horizontal integration of interoperable xRM platforms can help to show connections between multiple companies as well as stakeholders, to share business context and to extend value networks.

2.4 Management Concepts for xRM

The authors [2] see xRM as "a strategic management approach that integrates and aligns all levels of relationships. In this sense xRM contributes to the systematic management of relationships to all partners, be they horizontal (e.g., joint ventures), vertical (e.g., franchising), or lateral co-operations (e.g., authorities)" [2]. One of the central research questions of Anything Relationship Management and BISE (Business & Information Systems Engineering) is how a strategic management concept may look and which design principles have to be used [2]. While there are plenty of xRM platforms offered through the ICT market, there is still a gap between appropriate management concepts for corresponding xRM platforms. Therefore, we want to introduce a conceptual framework for xRM consisting of a management concept and a general platform architecture that provides a comprehensive approach to manage xRM in connected society.

The main focus is on a strategic management concept for xRM. Generally, management concepts show interpretations of people, their behavior and the organization that is bound to market conditions, to create an order in the variety of goals, ideas, plans and methods. A management concept can be seen as an abstract design model of the reality, which refers to a desired future order that is achieved through the proper usage of the management concept. Therefore the essential components as well as the relationship and effect structures are mapped, without giving specific guidelines on the possible configurations. The particularly important elements are displayed and highlighted in a management concept. Especially in complex systems and environments, management concepts must have a sufficiently high level of abstraction [14]. Before the developed conceptual framework is introduced the most important principles and objectives of xRM are described in the next section. These principles and objectives as well as the general fundamentals of management concepts will be used to design the conceptual framework for xRM.

3 xRM Principles and Objectives

Despite the fact that there are different publications of xRM (e.g. [2] or [15]), there is still no clear analysis of core principles and objectives of xRM. In this section we want to point out which xRM principles and xRM objectives have to be considered when dealing with xRM. The results of these were investigated through literature research in books, scientific magazines and on the web as well as expert interviews and the visit of events with topics about xRM (e.g. the fairs: CeBIT 2014, CRM-expo 2014 and 2. Trendkonferenz forum!xRM). In addition, different xRM platforms and xRM systems were investigated and compared.

3.1 Principles of xRM

In this section the authors will give an overview about the most important principles of xRM.

Flexible, Scalable and Interoperable Platform. An xRM platform can be seen as a platform-as-a-Service (PaaS) with a software development environment for xRM applications [2]. Such a platform has a flexible and scalable infrastructure. Furthermore xRM platforms and their entities should have the ability of interoperability among themselves. Thus, the use of well-defined communication models and communication protocols is necessary [16].

Configurable Framework. A configurable framework is one of the basic elements of xRM. Such a framework provides an implementation of important application services like access management or administration function, a first area of application (typically CRM) and a development environment for function extension. The software development environment includes components like a repository or debug functions and has the ability to install plug-ins.

Point and Click Apps/Customization. One benefit of xRM is the possibility to build "Point & Click Apps" and to customize them easily out of the box. This is one of the core principles that xRM contributes and therefore allows the building of apps quickly and easily without having to have deeper implementation skills.

Flexible Schema and Extensibility. The underlying data model of xRM platforms does not have a fixed schema but a flexible and extensible one. This means that xRM platforms can hold any data model and can generate or extend the data model without much programming knowledge. The xRM platform undertakes the database adjustments and queries for the user.

Integration/Mapping of Various Entities. xRM enables the mapping of any kind of entity (stakeholder, virtual asset or physical object) in an application. This allows the fulfillment of comprehensive business requirements on one platform. The next level of xRM is integrating smart objects or shared virtual objects through the internet of everything. As mentioned in point one a standard for communication is required.

Implementation of Service Orientation Capabilities and Architecture. Many xRM platforms follow the service orientation paradigm and are built on a service-oriented architecture (SOA). This allows serving the platform consumer with service orientated capabilities like immediate availability and well-defined behavior of servicers or service composition.

Company-Wide and Cross-System Workflows. Company-wide and cross-system workflows can be established more easily with xRM since one or more interoperable platforms or well-defined communication standards are in place. This leads to less workflow disruptions and a faster flow time as well as a more consistent management of workflows and business processes.

Custom GUIs for Each User. Any graphical user interface (GUI) of an xRM application can be customized by the user. Depending on user preferences and access restrictions one and the same xRM application can have a completely different GUI.

New Software Releases Do Not Affect the Customized Data Model and Application. A customized and extended data model has to be safe for new software releases of the xRM platform. This means that if the platform provider publishes new updates, these updates do not lead to problems regarding the customized data model and application.

3.2 Objectives of XRM

While several of the xRM objectives depend on the respective organization or the business sectors, there are also a number of general objectives that can be identified. Those objectives are primarily conceptual ones since the intention of this paper is to create a management concept for xRM.

1. **Identification and Segmentation of Entities and Relationships**

   To handle the different entities in xRM it is necessary to identify and segment them. In addition to a basic classification according to their characteristic (stakeholder type etc.) a second step has to be taken to evaluate them depending on criteria such as profitability or potential. Furthermore all relevant relationships must also be identified and segmented. Unique identification of entities can be implemented by URI (Uniform Resource Identifier), IPv6 or similar concepts and technologies. The identification of people will be the big challenge in terms of uniqueness and the privacy policy. Projects such as "Integrated digita.me User goods" are enormously important for this purpose (see http://www.dime-project.eu/).

2. **Control and Management of Entities and Relationships**

   The right level for control and management for all entities should be found through xRM. Since companies and their organizational structures can be quite complex, appropriate mechanisms are needed that allow the control and management of entities, relationships and corporate structures on different levels.

3. **Reduction of Complexity and Consolidation of Data**

   Using the concepts of xRM should help to deal with enormous amounts of data (big data) the company is faced with. Structured data as well as unstructured data has to be assigned to the corresponding entities and relationships for this. The correct assignment of unstructured data is thereby the big challenge. New knowledge is gained (like the supplier who is also customer) and less storage space is needed through merging data in one entity of the same actor that acts in different roles or is used in different ways. Furthermore the reduction of complexity and the dealing with big data needs appropriate methods like predictive analytics, prescriptive analytics and data mining.

4. **Differentiated Stakeholder Approaches**

   Just as in CRM, where there are differentiated customer approaches, these principles have to be extended to all stakeholders in the organization. With xRM (concept and platform) a foundation can be given to build and establish differentiated approaches in a systematical and holistic way.

5. **Enhancing of Relationship Quality and Contact Maintenance**

With xRM, relationship quality and contact maintenance should be enhanced for all relevant stakeholders (customers, suppliers, employees etc.). This will lead to a higher loyalty, better relationships and finally it will increase the profitability of the organization. Furthermore it will help to ensure long-term competitiveness and will lead to a continuous improvement of business through the creation of new relationships with stakeholders and the stabilization or the termination of existing ones [17].

6. **Identify and Know Stakeholder Objectives**

An important objective is to know the individual goals and expectations of your stakeholders, to document them and to coordinate them among themselves in order to strive for win-win situations.

7. **Using xRM on the Internet of Everything**

The future goal of xRM platforms will be to build a well-defined link to the infrastructure of the IoE, to objects of the IoE as an xRM entity as well as to manage them systematically and to provide stakeholders access and availability to them. This also means that xRM platforms have to be flexibly expandable in terms of their entities and interfaces [18]. The concepts of the Semantic Web and the Web of Things are therefore becoming increasingly important.

8. **Horizontal Integration with Smart Factory**

Horizontal integration is a term to link various IT systems used for the different process steps in manufacturing and business planning processes within a company or across multiple companies towards an integrated solution [13]. xRM concepts and platforms can be used to build such a solution, if they have capabilities like interoperable. But, more importantly, xRM is not just an IT platform, it is a business strategy and a management concept combined with an IT platform. Thus, xRM can help to implement the horizontal integration of an organization across multiple companies (value added networks) to an integrated solution.

9. **Privacy Policy**

Since xRM is all about data from entities (stakeholders etc.) and relationship management, it is necessary to ensure privacy policy. This requirement is more important than ever. Data and information have become the oil of the twenty-first century. Therefore, a more comprehensible and transparent handling of personal data must be present for protection and trust building.

10. **Real-Time Communications and Data Safety**

To exploit optimization potential in the interconnection of distributed entities and the value creation processes the exchange of data in real time is required. However, real-time integration and communication leads to numerous security threats. These threats can mostly be eliminated by caching incoming data on an isolated server and verifying the data through security software. But in turn this influences real-time communication. Real-time communications and data safety are affected by each other [19].

4 Structure and Components

4.1 Overview of the Conceptual Framework

Based on the principles and objects of xRM an xRM conceptual framework has been created with the primary purpose to structure and systematically order the various areas of application, use cases, entities and relationships of an organization.

The xRM conceptual framework includes several components with various elements, methods and models that build an abstract structure of a higher management layer to manage different areas of application. The following figure shows the components and their structure in the xRM conceptual framework (see Fig. 2).

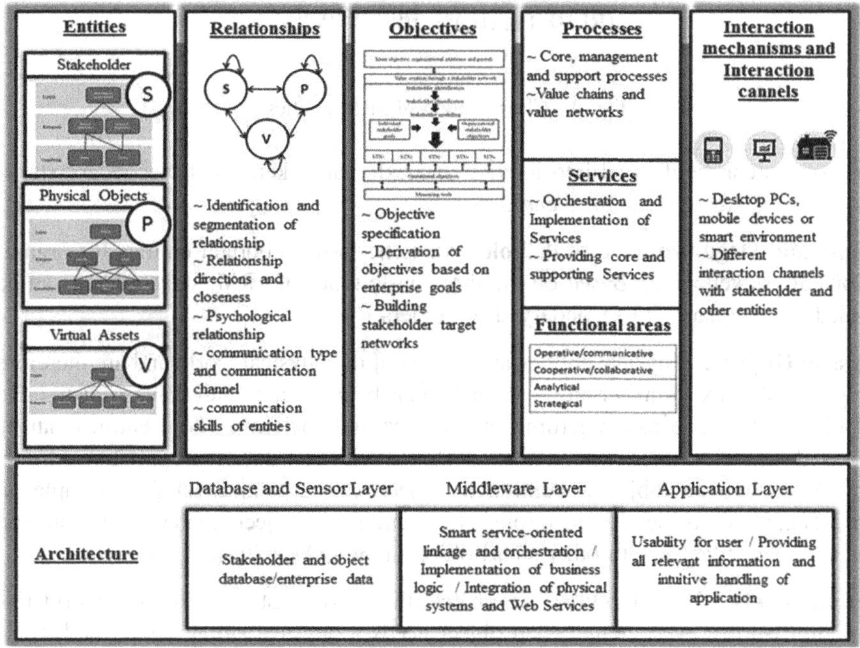

Fig. 2. The conceptual framework of xRM.

4.2 Components

4.2.1 Entities

The entities in xRM include three basic forms: people and organizations (stakeholders), physical objects and virtual assets (see Fig. 3).

According to [20] primary stakeholders are people, groups and organization "without whose continuing participation the corporation cannot survive as a going concern. [Secondary Stakeholders however are] those who influence or affect, or are influenced or affected by, the corporation, but they are not engaged in transactions with the corporation and are not essential for its survival" [20]. Moreover primary

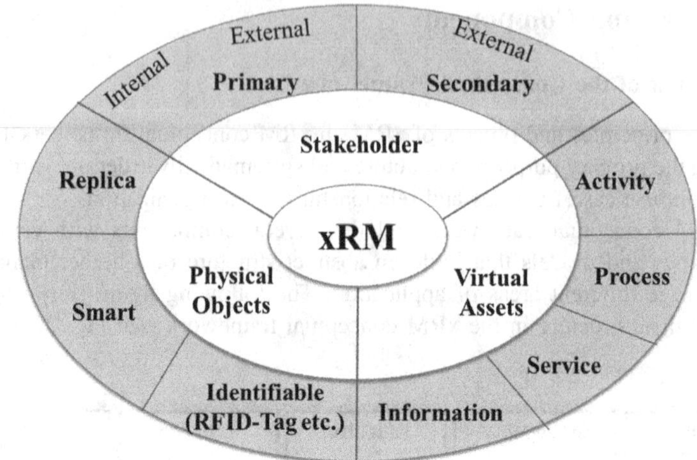

Fig. 3. Classification of xRM entities.

stakeholders can be divided into internal and external stakeholders. Secondary stakeholders are always external stakeholders.

People and Organizations (Stakeholders). The most important entities for organizations are stakeholders. Based on the three basic types of xRM, stakeholders can be divided into primary and secondary stakeholders.

Physical Objects. Physical entities are objects of the physical world and are therefore everything that exists materially, except human beings, since they have a distinctive and clearly definable role regarding intelligence and sociality. These entities can be classified regarding their communication ability with ICT into representation (digital copy of an existing object), identifiable object (has a unique ID for example an RFID-Tag, which is identifiable through ICT) and smart object (can communicate and interact independently with other smart objects (e.g. cyber-physical systems).

Virtual Assets. Virtual entities are objects that only exist in the digital world (information world), even though each object needs a physical storage (e.g. hard disk). A virtual entity is made up of digital data and can be divided into information (e.g. data base, document), service (e.g. cloud service), process (e.g. business process) or activity (e.g. machine activity, machine state).

4.2.2 Relationships

In the component "Relationships" the connections between the entities are identified, described, restricted, and managed. While relationships of virtual assets and physical things can be identified through documentation, logs files or ICT tools, it is more difficult to identify stakeholder relationships. Basic approaches like employee or expert surveys, checklist procedures, analysis of contractual relations, environmental monitoring, analysis of resource relationships and network analysis must be implemented for this purpose [21].

A basic classification of relationships can take place according to [22] who divides relationships into P2P (people-to-people), M2M (machine-to-machine) and P2M divides (people-to-machine) [22]. Virtual assets and physical things are grouped together as "Machine".

Communication Skills are the primary size for a classification for M2M relations. Hence the relationships of entities can have non communication ability, passive communication ability (e.g. RFID), and active communication ability.

Furthermore there will be a future communication classification according to standard communication characteristics of entities. For example the I40-compliant communication ability which requires certain skills such as communication-capable software components, a unique identification in a network or standardized service functions [23].

Several dimensions have to be considered for stakeholders. The first dimension is the **relationship direction**. This dimension has on the one hand a vertical, horizontal and lateral relationship view and on the other hand an external as well as an internal view (see Fig. 4) [24].

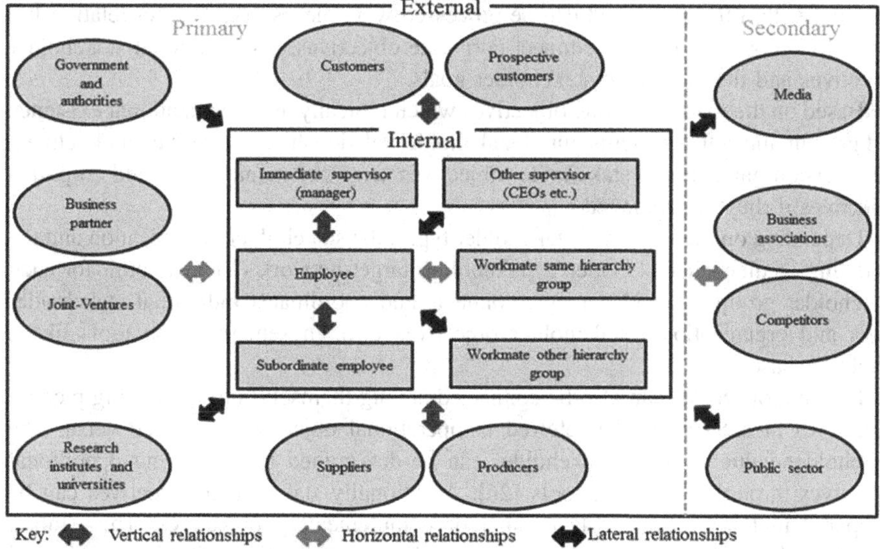

Fig. 4. Overview of stakeholder relationships.

Another important dimension is the **relationship closeness** which describes how strongly a stakeholder can be influenced by another person or organization. Thereby influence can be made through a direct relationship (stakeholders can be addressed directly) or an indirect relationship (stakeholders can only be addressed through one or more intermediate entities).

Next the **psychological relationship** dimension has to be considered for relationship quality [25]. A basic classification is done by dividing relationships into weak ones (some interaction existing) and strong ones (fulfilling defined criteria which measures the quality) [17].

Finally, the **communication type** (personal, digital etc.) and **communication channel** have to be considered. This describes how the communication with stakeholders is achieved (personal, digital etc.) and through which tools. This dimension also brings people and machines together (P2M). According to the communication ability of machines people can interact with them through different channels of communication (e.g. user interfaces, speech recognition etc.).

4.2.3 Objectives

Different objectives have to be defined to highlight the purpose they are needed for based on the entities and their relationships. In the component "Objectives" this definition is done. Therefore it is necessary to clearly specify the objectives, to derive different objectives based on the corporate objectives and to build objective relationship networks.

Particularly important are the objectives of stakeholders. Here two views can be differentiated: the individual goals that stakeholders have and the objectives the organization has with stakeholders. Information about individual stakeholder goals can be saved within the entity and can be processed when necessary. "Target relationship networks" should be built to connect corporate objectives, organizational stakeholder objectives and the individual stakeholder goals.

Based on the main corporate objectives which typically are organizational existence and growth, the actual benefits out of stakeholder relationships are derived and defined. Vice versa organizational stakeholder objectives serve the management and corporate objectives if they are achieved.

Depending on the identified stakeholder types, the stakeholder classification and the modeling of their characteristics a stakeholder target network (STN) is built for each stakeholder group. The STN maps, connects and coordinates individual stakeholder goals and organizational stakeholder objectives through semantic web tools like a graph database.

Furthermore STNs can also be connected among themselves to see the big picture. Objectives in a STN can be referred to operational objectives and vice versa. The stakeholder value for each stakeholder can be determined by measuring operational objectives through measuring tools [26]. Additionally stakeholder objectives can be compared in terms of possible conflict or complementary objectives. Thus, future issues can be detected early and counteracted. The connection of objectives in and between STNs will allow seeing the big picture and will allow implementing the right services and processes.

4.2.4 Processes and Services

Processes and services are designed to achieve the defined business goals. A process has an input at the beginning, which was triggered by another process or an event and an output at the end, which returns a result. In addition, various entities, relationships and information are involved in processes. Methods and rules are necessary to effectively and efficiently accomplish processes [27]. The result of a process may be a service (like a customer service). But a service can also be a partial step of a process. Services serve a consumer (Stakeholder or other process step) with a specific need.

There are different areas of applications in xRM (e.g. CRM, ERM or smart machine management). Each area of applications has a number of use cases (e.g. sales order, recruitment or real-time analysis of machine data). These use cases again consist of different scenarios depending on criteria like input, rules, methods and time. The correlation between xRM applications, xRM use cases and xRM scenarios as well as processes and services is shown in the following Fig. 5.

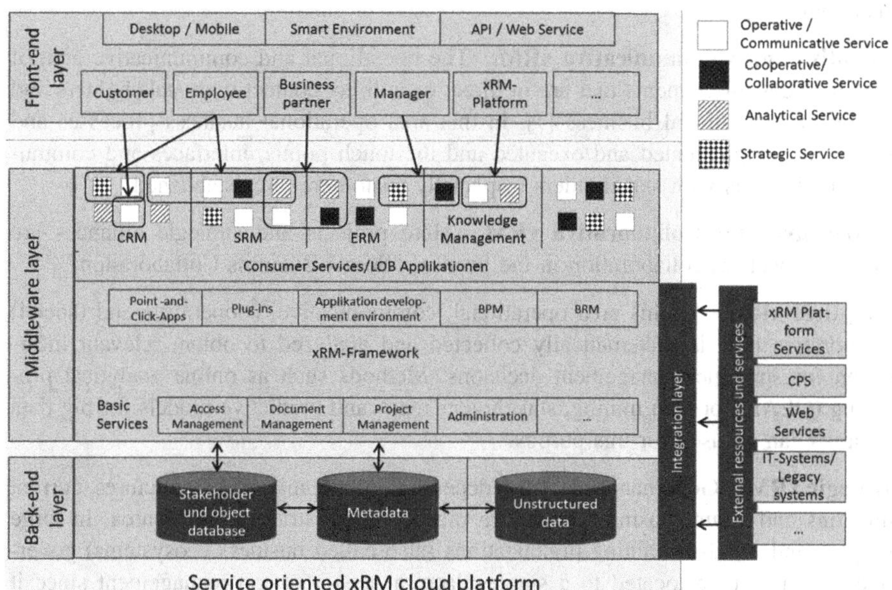

Fig. 5. Basic architecture of xRM platforms.

Basically, business processes can be distinguished between core processes, management processes and supporting processes. But, processes can also be distinguished by their structure.

One variety is the process that consists of a sequence of activities (chain) and which leads to clear predictable results. Such business processes are important when certain quality standards have to be accomplished. A disadvantage of this type of business processes is that the individual process steps are interdependent. If a process step performs incorrectly, this has an impact on all other process steps. In addition, modification, innovation and new outcomes can only carefully be tried, because the effects are often not predictable. The second form of business processes is a network business process. Thereby business activities and business tasks are spread across multiple business services which in turn are not sequenced in a business process, but services that serve other services referring to their respective business goals.

The entities (especially people) that are part of such a service solve problems and deliver solutions through creativity and innovation, instead of executing pre-defined activities. The objective is to give the customer what he wants. The structure can be seen as a network with various connections. Just like in the internet architecture, business processes can take several possible ways towards their outcome. This structure is useful when business process activities cloud fail or are too slow when taking a certain path. The disadvantage however, is that redundancy in the tasks, activities and services have to exist [28].

4.2.5 Functional Areas

The objectives, processes and services of xRM can be assigned to one of the following functional areas.

Operative and Communicative xRM. The operational and communicative area of xRM includes all elements that are in direct or indirect contact with stakeholders and include the operational business [7]. In this area operational business processes and services are implemented and executed and the touch points, interfaces and communication channels with stakeholders (especially customers) are established.

Cooperative and Collaborative xRM. Here projects and strategic alliances are mapped as well as collaboration in the form of "Social Business Collaboration".

Analytical xRM. In this area operational, communicative, cooperative and (social) collaborative data is systematically collected and analyzed to obtain relevant information for strategic management decisions. Methods such as online analytical processing (OLAP), or data mining, stakeholder maps and predictive models for big data scenarios can be used for this purpose.

Strategic xRM. Governance activities depending on organizational structures, current situations and future business goals are placed in the strategic xRM area. In large complex and rapidly chaining organizations (also called business ecosystems) governance can never be located to a single place, a person or top management since it always depends on many different aspects (habits, informal rules, attitudes, external circumstances etc.) and therefore happens simultaneously in many places at the same time [29]. To manage such an environment effectively governance impulses have to be performed relaying on information about the entities, relationships and individual goals. Governance impulses are not just commands they are mechanics that take all elements and organizational structures into account.

4.2.6 Interaction Channels and Mechanisms

The interaction with the components and their elements mapped on an xRM platform can be done through different mechanisms and interaction channels. Three basic approaches can be distinguished.

Desktop and Mobile. The desktop and mobile access is the most common interaction interface for xRM. Here content is presented to the user through a graphical user interface. The user performs actions (read, save, update and delete) on the GUI using devices (e.g. mouse and keyboard) or touch screens. In xRM a user can also customize his own individual GUI depending on his used services and preferences.

Smart Environment. A smart environment is typically provided with CPS and corresponding sensors that can interact with the environment and are able to exchange data over networks. People can interact with a smart environment through language, motions or gestures (e.g. smart home scenarios).

API (Application Programming Interface). Here access to the xRM platform can be performed via a programming interface used for M2M communication. Such an interface provides accessible services and functions for other systems and machines.

4.2.7 Architecture

The architecture of the xRM platforms can have different forms and layers depending on xRM provider. The future architecture of xRM will follow the principles of service-oriented architecture and cloud computing. In consideration of these trends a general three-tier architecture is shown in Fig. 5, since it is a common way to illustrate the platform elements.

Back-End Layer. All relevant data of entities and business is stored in the back-end layer. Besides a stakeholder and object database, in which all entities with their attributes are stored, unstructured data such as documents, social media data and machine data are also stored in this layer and addressed through appropriate metadata if able.

Theoretically, any databases could be used in this layer. But, probably databases like SAP HANA, which also is a platform with many basic services and a strong linkage of data and business logic or NoSQL databases like MongoDB, which is a document-oriented database, will be used in the future.

Middleware Layer. The business logic for xRM applications is implemented in this layer. Therefore this layer offers a framework with basic services (administration, access management etc.) as well as a development environment to implement application via point-and-click or programming. Furthermore the development environment and existing software modules can be extended through plug-ins. Tools for business process management (BPM) and business rules management (BRM) are also provided. Services can be orchestrated, processes can be implemented and finally consumer applications for several stakeholders can be built based on all of these elements.

Integration Layer. A connection to external resources and services is set through the integration layer. This enables the integration of web services, xRM platform services or cyber-physical systems besides legacy-systems.

Front-End Layer. Access mechanisms to the xRM platform applications are provided by the use of the front-end layer through desktops, mobile apps, smart environments, web services and APIs. Each consumer can create his own service bundle, and customize its interface individually. Thus, the different requirements of consumers can be satisfied flexibly and fully.

5 Validation and xRM Use Case Example

To validate the developed conceptual framework for xRM an experimental validation was chosen by implementing an xRM prototype with the open source xRM software SugerCRM. SugarCRM is a Customer Relationship Management application that was founded in 2004 as an open source project for Silicon Valley companies. [30] SugarCRM has evolved into an xRM platform over the last years, fulfilling xRM principles like the existence of a configurable framework, a plugin installation module and a Point-and-Click functionality. There are other xRM platforms e.g. Microsoft Dynamics CRM, CAS platform or Salesforce that likewise could have been used for implementing an xRM prototype.

5.1 Use Case

The chosen use case is part of the smart factory vision (industrial internet) and connects the production of mixing liquids with important business processes. The use case describes a top-down approach that recreates the structure of an existing machine for mixing liquids as a service on an xRM platform and connecting that service to other business entities. Furthermore typically data exchange activities (sensor data, sales order, and production tasks) are simulated. The main objective is to demonstrate how the xRM conceptual framework could be used as a management concept in the smart factory of the future.

5.2 Utilization of the Configurable Framework

The following table gives the overview of the utilization of the conceptual framework to the described use case (Table 1).

5.3 Implementation Steps

The primary goals of the use case were to easily give customers and employees access to a mixing liquid service on the xRM platform as well as to view random created sensor and actuator values through an xRM user interface. At the beginning an entity relationship model was defended and automatically transferred through a created package of the SugarCRM Module Builder to a database schema of the MySQL database. The sales order process and the production process of mixing liquids were implemented through the SugarCRM Module Builder and by added more functionality to the extensions. Besides mapping the described processes on the xRM platform an additional function was implemented that enabled all relevant information of each order item to be saved via XML to transmit it to an existing mixing machine. The main service was the CPPS-Service, mixing two chosen ingredients in a designated mixing ratio, volume per filling and amount. Another service we implemented allowed sending sensor data directly to the REST/SOAP API to continuously update the sensor values of a CPPS-Component. This function is part of the analytical xRM. The other functions

Table 1. Utilization of the conceptual framework.

Entities

The use case includes the following entities.

Name	Type	Description
Customer	Primary stakeholder	The customer who wants to order a mixed liquid.
Sales Order	Activity	The sales order that is created by the customers.
Order item	Information	Order items are part of the sales order and have the relevant information for a production task.
Ingredient	Product	The products that will gets mixed.
Supplier	Primary stakeholder	The supplier that delivers products.
CPPS-Service	Service	A service that delivery a specific outcome for the customer
CPPS-Module	Smart object	Is a plug-and-produce part of a CPPS-Service.
CPPS-Component	Smart object	Is an addressable object (sensor, actuator) of a CPPS Module.
Owner	Primary stakeholder	An owner is responsible or a CPPS-Service and/o CPPS-Module.

Relationships

These entities are related among themselves.

Main Relationships	Description
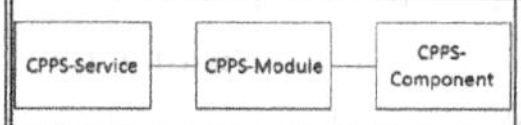 CPPS-Service — CPPS-Module — CPPS-Component	A CPPS-Service is built up out of one-to-many CPPS- Modules which in turn are built up out of one-to-many CPPS-Components (sensors and actuators).
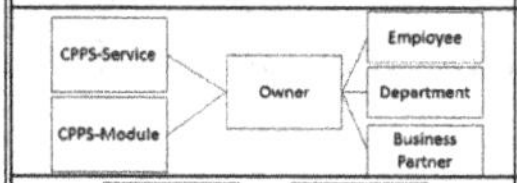 CPPS-Service, CPPS-Module — Owner — Employee, Department, Business Partner	Additionally, a CPPS-Service and a CPPS-Module both have a many-to-one relationship to an owner who is responsible for an entity. The owner can be an employee, department or business partner.
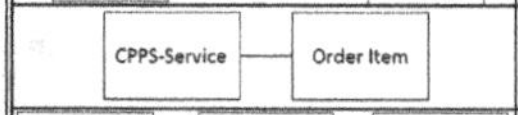 CPPS-Service — Order Item	The production task is saved in an order item and can be taken over by one CPPS-Service. A CPPS - Service can take over many production tasks.
 Order Item — Sales Order — Customer	Each order Item belongs to a sales order. The sales order is initiated by a customer.
 Order Item — Products — Supplier	Every order item is made up out of products that will get mixed during the production task. These products get delivered by a supplier.

Objectives

The two main entities to look at when identifying the objects are the customers and the company.

Customer	Company
A fast and flexible delivery.	Mass customization.
The ability to change the sales order after the production has begun.	A flexible and intelligent production and manufacturing plant.
Individual products with high quality.	Cost efficiency maintenance.

Processes

The main processes in the use case are:

1. Smart production processes.
2. Sales processes.
3. Purchase processes.

Services

The main services in this use case are:

1. Production services (e. g. mixture of own beverages).
2. A Service for automated notification of maintenance.
3. Web-enabled monitoring service for the production process.

Functional Areas

The main functional areas of this use case are:

1. The operative and communicative function areas involving the customer and the production process.
2. The analytic function areas for maintenance and monitoring.

Interaction Channels and Mechanisms

The interaction channels and mechanisms are:

1. Displays in factories and on the manufacturing plant.
2. Displays in factories and on the manufacturing plant.
3. Internal (employee) and external (customer, business partner) PCs.
4. Mobile devices (e. g. maintenance of worker, reports for manager).

Architecture

Use the three-tier architecture and the Module Builder function of SugarCRM to build:

1. Entities and relationships in the back-end layer (SugarCRM Module Builder: Fields, Labels, Relationships)
2. Processes and services in the middleware layer (implementation of extension in ...\sugarcrm custom\Extension\modules)
3. Integrating end points of sensor and actuator values through the integration layer (REST and SOAP)
4. Customized user interface in the front-end layer (SugarCRM Module Builder: Layouts, Dashlets)

can be related to the operative and communicative xRM. Access to interaction channels and mechanisms were enabled through the inbuilt SugarCRM user interfaces via web browser. These interfaces can get extended. For example a new SugarCRM Dashlet was defined in the home screen, allowing viewing sensor and actuator values in real time or as specified in the "Auto-Refresh" section. Due to SugarCRM basic functionality the programming effort was easily manageable.

5.4 Overview of the Business Scenario

The following figure gives an overview of the implemented business scenario regarding the sales order process and production process. Thereby, only the important aspects are depicted.

The business scenario starts with an event of a customer who wants to mix liquids. This customer has access to the xRM-platform through a customer interface like a web shop and places a sales order with order items. The customer interface is the access point to the customer service and triggers the sales order process. Typically during the

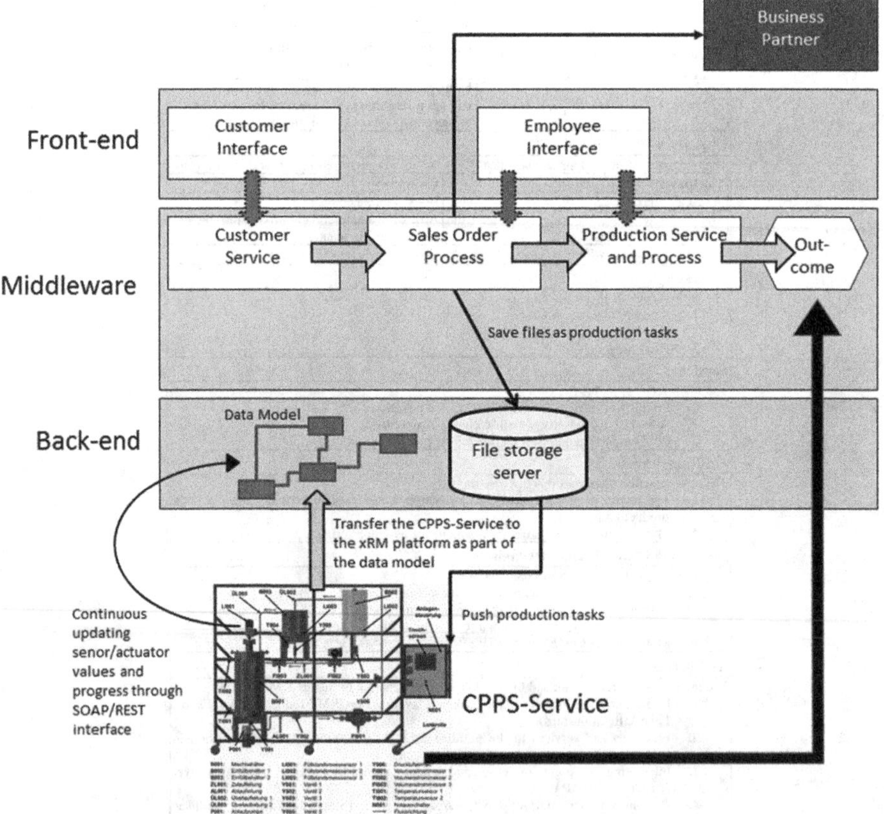

Fig. 6. Overview xRM business scenario [according to [31]].

sales order process it is also verified if necessary ingredients are in stock. If not, they are ordered from a supplier through a purchase system (not shown in Fig. 6). With respect to customer permissions, customer skills and environment settings either the customer or an employee can choose a CPPS-Service for mixing liquids as a Service. Depending on the chosen CPPS-Service the business process can be forwarded to a business partner (e.g. if the own organization cannot accept the sales order concerning above capacity) or keep the business process and save the resulting production tasks in a file storage server. If the sales order was transferred to a business partner this is registered and will lead to a brokerage for the organization. The further process steps in the own organization are the final saving of sales order with an acknowledgment via email, the scheduling for the manufacturing and the start of the manufacturing process by pushing the production tasks to the production machine with an implemented logic like FIFO (First In – First Out) or HIFO (Highest In – First Out). During the production the production machine (CPPS-Service) updates sensor values and progress on the xRM-platform. This information can be use for maintenance or to send notification to the customer (e.g. notification when manufacturing is finished). After the manufacturing process is finish the mixed liquid (outcome) is prepared for getting shipped to the customer.

6 Conclusion

At the beginning of this paper we described the purpose of xRM and defined the term. After that a comparison of CRM and xRM was given. We also highlighted the need for management concepts and explained what they are. By using the principles and objectives of xRM, we presented a conceptual framework for xRM. This conceptual framework has the primary purpose to structure and systematically order the various areas of application, use cases, scenarios of xRM in organizations. This conceptual framework provides a systematic approach to build xRM application and to reduce the complexity of business areas and relationship varieties in relationship management. After that we provided an early stage prototype in the area of the smart factory and also presented additional a suitable business scenario.

The connections through ICT between people and machines and among each other will expand in the future. This will lead to a significant increase in data volume and data traffic. Furthermore, the Internet of Everything, the cloud computing technology and the mobile internet as well as the digitization and automation of knowledge work will lead to an enormous economic potential. We will have future challenges in data transmission infrastructure and privacy policy. But the future progress will also lead to new innovative business models. xRM will become more and more important in business and in private use (e.g. smart home). The quick and secure connection of entities to xRM platforms, as well as the interoperability of these platforms is one of the future technological challenges in the ICT sector.

We see need for further research in the following areas:

- How can such an xRM platform in such an flexible and connected environment be made secure against any kind of attacks.

- How can we make sure that the communication takes place in real time?
- How can the interoperability between all entities be endured?
- How can the benefits of xRM and the relationship structure enriched with context better proven and promoted?
- How can any kind of objects, people and virtual assets be easily and automatically integrated in an xRM-platform without much effort?

Acknowledgements. The authors would like to thank the research program of Karl Steinbuch of the MFG Innovation Agency for ICT and Media for the financial support of the research project "Ma-x-RM – Management concept of Anything Relationship Management".

References

1. Evans, D.: The internet of everything. How More Relevant and Valuable Connections will Change the World. Cisco (2012). https://www.cisco.com/web/about/ac79/docs/innov/IoE.pdf
2. Britsch, J., Schacht, S., Mädche, A.: Anything Relationship Management. Bus. Inf. Syst. Eng. BISE **4**(2), 85–87 (2012)
3. Radjou, N., Orlov, L. M., Child, M.: Apps for dynamic collaboration, the forrester report. In: Forrester Research, Cambridge, MA (2001)
4. Microsoft. The xRM Advantage for Solution Builders, p. 8 (2010). http://microsoftaucrm.wordpress.com/2010/05/20/new-dynamics-crm-white-paper-the-xrm-advantage-for-solution-builders/
5. Knoblauch, J.P., Bulander, R.: Literature review and an analysis of the state of the market of Anything Relationship Management (xRM) – xRM as an extension of customer relationship management. In: Proceedings of 11th International Conference on E-Business and Telecommunications (ICE-B), 28–30 August, 2014, pp. 236–244. INSTICC, Wien, Austria (2014)
6. Günter, B., Helm, S.: Kundenwert: Grundlagen – Innovative Konzepte – Praktische Umsetzungen. Gabler Verlag, Wiesbaden (2006)
7. Hippner, H., Wilde, K.D.: Grundlagen des CRM. Konzepte und Gestaltung, pp. 8–58. Gabler Verlag, Wiesbaden (2006)
8. Hippner, H., Leußer, W., Wilde, K.D.: CRM – grundlagen, konzepte und prozesse. In: Hippner, H., Hubrich, B., Wilde, K.D. (eds.) Grundlagen des CRM, Strategie. Geschäftsprozesse und IT-Unterstützung, pp. 15–55. Gabler Verlag, Wiesbaden (2011)
9. Britsch, J., Kölmel, B.: From CRM to xRM: managerial trends and future challenges on the way to anything relationship management. In: IIMC, International Information Management Corporation Dublin (2011)
10. CAS Software AG, 2012. xRM – Use the strength of your network, white paper. http://www.itselector.nl/wpcontent/files_mf/1370607159CASCRMxRM_Whitepaper_EN.pdf
11. Hippner, H., Wilde, K.D., Rentzmann, R., Hesse, F.: IT-Unterstützung durch CRM-systeme. In: Hippner, H., Hubrich, B., Wilde, K.D. (eds.) Grundlagen des CRM. Strategie, Geschäftsprozesse und IT-Unterstützung, pp. 129–155. Gabler Verlag, Wiesbaden (2011)
12. Martinez, C.: Objective ICT-2013.1.4 - A reliable, smart and secure Internet of Things for Smart Cities (2012). http://www.oko-ist.cz/calls/ncp-infoday_12-06-19/Obj_1_4.pdf

13. acatech. Recommendations for implementing the strategic initiative INDUSTRIE 4.0 (2013). http://www.forschungsunion.de/pdf/industrie_4_0_final_report.pdf
14. Zielowski, C.: Managementkonzepte aus Sicht der Organisationskultur. Auswahl, Ausgestaltung und Einführung. Deutscher Universitätsverlag, Wiesbaden (2006)
15. Alexakis, S., Bauer, M., Britsch, J., Kölmel, B.: Interoperability in service-oriented production networks: managing n:n relationships with xRM. In: Charalabidis, Y., Lampathaki, F., Jardim-Goncalves, R. (eds.) Revolutionizing Enterprise Interoperability through Scientific Foundations, pp. 119–136. Business Science Reference, Hershey (2014)
16. Günthner, W., Hompel, M.: Internet der Dinge in der Intralogistik. (VDI-Buch). Springer, Heidelberg (2010)
17. Riemer, K.: Sozialkapital und Kooperation. Mohr Siebeck, Tü-bingen (2005)
18. Uckelmann, D., Harrison, M., Michahelles, F.: Architecting the Internet of Things, pp. 12–13. Springer, Heidelberg (2011)
19. Federal Ministry of Education and Research, Zukunftsbild Industrie 4.0, pp. 26–27 (2013). http://www.bmbf.de/pubRD/Zukunftsbild_Industrie_40.pdf
20. Clarkson, M.B.E.: A stakeholder framework for analyzing and evaluating corporate social performance. Acad. Manage. Rev. **20**(1), 92–117 (1995)
21. Tewes, G.: Signaling Strategien im Stakeholder Management. Kommunikation und Wertschöpfung, pp. 139–145. Gabler, Wiesbaden (2008)
22. Evans, D.: The Internet of Things. How the Next Evolution of the Internet is Changing Everything, Cisco (2011). https://www.cisco.com/web/about/ac79/docs/innov/IoT_IBSG_0411FINAL.pdf
23. VDI e. V.: Industrie 4.0 Statusreport. Gegenstände, Entitäten, Komponenten. In: The Association of German Engineers (VDI) (2014). http://www.vdi.de/fileadmin/vdi_de/redakteurdateien/sk_dateien/VDI_Industrie_4.0_Komponenten_2014.pdf
24. Diller, H.: Beziehungs-marketing. WiSt **24**(9), 442–447 (1995)
25. Lorenz, B.: Beziehungen zwischen Konsumenten und Marken. Eine empirische Untersuchung von Markenbeziehungen. Gabler Verlag, Wiesbaden (2009)
26. Görlitz, J.: Die Bedeutung des Anspruchsgruppenkonzepts im strategischen Management. Zeitschrift für Planung Unternehmenssteuerung **17**(4), 411–431 (2007)
27. Bach, N.: Wertschöpfungsorientierte Organisation Architekturen, Prozesse Strukturen. Springer Gabler, Wiesbaden (2012)
28. Gray, D., Vander Wal, T.: The connected company, pp. 148–149. O'Reilly Media Inc, Sebastopol (2012)
29. Exner, A., Exner, H., Hochreiter, G.: Selbststeuerung von Unternehmen. Ein Handbuch für Manager und Führungskräfte. Frankfurt, New York: Campus-Verl, pp. 44–50 (2009)
30. Mertic, J.: The Definitive Guide to SugarCRM Better Business Applications, p. 3. Apress, New York (2009)
31. Damjanac, A.: INDUSTRIE 4.0 – Geschäftsmodelle und Prozesse in der vierten industriellen Revolution. Thesis, Pforzheim University, p. 50 (2015)

How Can We Implement a Multidimensional Data Warehouse Using NoSQL?

Max Chevalier[1], Mohammed El Malki[1,2(✉)], Arlind Kopliku[1], Olivier Teste[1], and Ronan Tournier[1]

[1] Université de Toulouse, IRIT, UMR 5505, Toulouse, France
{Max.Chevalier,Mohammed.ElMalki,Arlind.Kopliku, Olivier.Teste,Ronan.Tournier}@irit.fr
[2] Capgemini, Toulouse, France

Abstract. The traditional OLAP (On-Line Analytical Processing) systems store data in relational databases. Unfortunately, it is difficult to manage big data volumes with such systems. As an alternative, NoSQL systems (Not-only SQL) provide scalability and flexibility for an OLAP system. We define a set of rules to map star schemas and its optimization structure, a precomputed aggregate lattice, into two logical NoSQL models: column-oriented and document-oriented. Using these rules we analyse and implement two decision support systems, one for each model (using MongoDB and HBase).We compare both systems during the phases of data (generated using the TPC-DS benchmark) loading, lattice generation and querying.

Keywords: NoSQL · OLAP · Aggregate lattice · Column-oriented · Document-oriented

1 Introduction

Nowadays, analysis data volumes are reaching critical sizes [17] challenging traditional data warehousing approaches. Current implemented solutions are mainly based on relational databases (using R-OLAP approaches) that are no longer adapted to these data volumes [8, 12, 27, 28]. With the rise of large Web platforms (e.g. Google, Facebook, Twitter, Amazon, etc.) solutions for "Big Data" management have been developed. These are based on decentralized approaches managing large data amounts and have contributed to developing "Not only SQL" (NoSQL) data management systems [27]. NoSQL solutions allow us to consider new approaches for data warehousing, especially from the multidimensional data management point of view. This is the scope of this paper.

In this paper, we investigate the use of NoSQL models for decision support systems. Until now (and to our knowledge), there are no direct mapping rules that transform a multi-dimensional conceptual model (i.e. a description of data in a generic way regardless of information technologies) into a NoSQL logical model (i.e. using a specific technique for implementing the conceptual level). Existing research implement OLAP systems in NoSQL using an intermediate relational logical model (called R-OLAP). In this paper, we define a set of rules to translate automatically and directly a

S. Hammoudi et al. (Eds.): ICEIS 2015, LNBIP 241, pp. 108–130, 2015.
DOI: 10.1007/978-3-319-29133-8_6

conceptual multidimensional model into two alternative NoSQL logical models: one column-oriented and one document-oriented. For each model, we define mapping rules translating from the conceptual level to the logical one.

Our motivation is multiple. Implementing OLAP systems using NoSQL systems is a relatively new alternative and is justified by the promising advantages of these systems such as flexibility and scalability. However, the increasing research in this direction demands for formalization, common models and empirical evaluation of different NoSQL systems. In this scope, this work investigates two logical models, their respective mapping rules and also data loading issues including pre-computing data aggregates.

Traditionally, decision support systems use data warehouses [31] to centralize data in a uniform fashion [18]. Within data warehouses, interactive data analysis and exploration is performed using On-Line Analytical Processing (OLAP) [2, 7]. Data is often described using a conceptual multidimensional model, such as a star schema [2]. We illustrate this multidimensional model with a case study on RSS (*Realy Simple Syndication*) feeds of news bulletins from an information website. We study the *Content* of news bulletins (the subject of the analysis or fact) using three dimensions of those bulletins (analysis axes of the fact, or dimensions): *Keyword* (contained in the bulletin), *Time* (publication date) and *Location* (geographical region concerned by the news). The fact has two measures (or analysis indicators):

- The number of news bulletins (*NewsCount*).
- The number of keyword occurrences (*OccurrenceCount*).

The conceptual multidimensional schema of our case study is described in Fig. 1, using a graphical formalism based on [14, 25].

One of the most successful implementation of OLAP systems uses relational databases. In these implementations, the conceptual schema is transformed into a logical schema (here a relational schema, called in this case a denormalized Relational-OLAP schema) using two transformation rules:

- Each dimension is a table that uses the same name. Table attributes are derived from attributes of the dimension (called parameters and weak attributes). The root parameter is the primary key.
- Each fact is a table that uses the same name, with attributes derived from (1) fact attributes (called measures) and (2) the root parameter of each associated dimension. Attributes derived from root parameters are foreign keys linking each dimension table to the fact table and form a compound primary key.

Due to the huge amount of data that can be stored in OLAP systems, it is common to pre-compute some aggregated data to speed up common analysis queries. In this case, fact measures are aggregated using different combinations of either dimension attributes or root parameters only. This generates a *lattice of pre-computed aggregates* [15] or *aggregate lattice* for short. The lattice is a set of nodes, one per dimension combinations. Each node (e.g. the node called "*Time, Location*") is stored as a relation called an aggregate relation (e.g. the relation *time-location*). This relation is composed of attributes corresponding to the measures and the parameters or weak attributes from

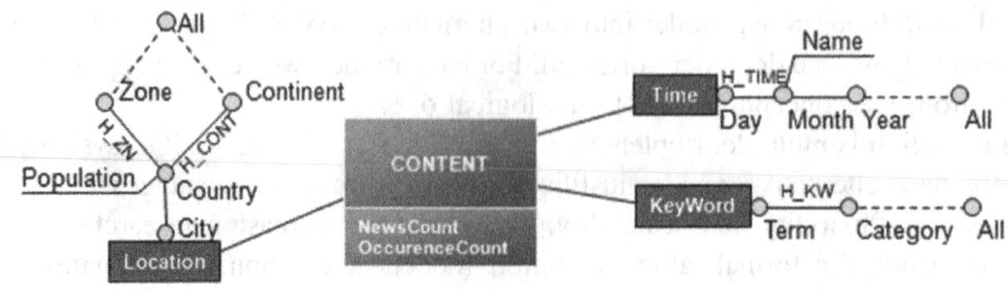

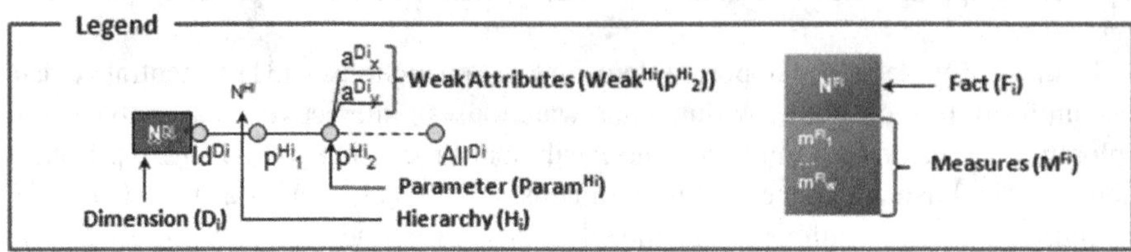

Fig. 1. Multidimensional conceptual schema of our example, news bulletin contents according to keywords, publication time and location concerned by the news.

selected dimensions. Attributes corresponding to measures are used to store aggregated values computed with functions such as SUM, COUNT, MAX, etc.

When using NoSQL systems for implementing OLAP systems, we must consider the above issues. In this paper and, in order to deal with these issues, we use two logical NoSQL models for the logical implementation; we define mapping rules (that allows us to translate a conceptual design into a logical one) and we study the lattice computation.

The rest of this paper is organized as follows: in Sect. 2, we present existing approaches that allow getting a NoSQL implementation from a data warehouse conceptual model using a pivot logical model; in Sect. 3 we define our conceptual multidimensional model, followed by a section for each of the two NoSQL models we consider along with their associated transformation rules, i.e. the column-oriented model in Sect. 4 and the document-oriented model in Sect. 5. Finally, in Sects. 6 and 7, we detail our experiments and discuss them.

2 Related Work

To our knowledge, there is no work for automatically and directly transforming data warehouses defined by a multidimensional conceptual model into a NoSQL model.

Several research works translate data warehousing concepts to a relational R-OLAP logical level [23]. Today, multidimensional databases are mostly implemented using relational technologies. Mapping rules are used to convert structures of the conceptual level (facts, dimensions and hierarchies) into a logical model based on relations. Moreover, many works have focused on implementing logical optimization methods based on pre-computed aggregates (also called materialized views) as in [15, 23]. However, R-OLAP implementations suffer from scaling-up to large data volumes (i.e. "Big Data"). Research is currently under way for new solutions such as using NoSQL systems [19]. Our approach aims at revisiting these processes for automatically implementing multidimensional conceptual models directly into NoSQL models.

The NoSQL term was first used in 1998 to define a lightweight open source relational database that did not expose the standard SQL interface [29, 32]. Today, NoSQL is interpreted as "Not only SQL" meaning that SQL can be supported but not only. Google's BigTable database is one of the first commercially successful NoSQL systems [1]. It corresponds to a distributed sparse database and maps a row key, a column key and a timestamp to an arbitrary byte array. Since then, many comparisons with Relational DataBases Management Systems (RDBMS) have been done. In [13], the authors compare a distributed RDBMS with NoSQL systems on On-Line Transaction and Analytical Processing (OLTP and OLAP) queries. In [24], the authors compare query execution using map-reduce on NoSQL systems with query execution on distributed RDBMS and identify the advantages on both architectures. In [27], the authors announced the end of relational era architecture; hence, an increasing attention towards implementing data warehouses [8].

As stated in introduction, other studies investigate the process of transforming relational databases into a NoSQL logical model. In [21], the author has proposed an approach for transforming a relational database into a column-oriented NoSQL database using HBase [16], a column-oriented NoSQL database. In [30], an algorithm is introduced for mapping a relational schema to a NoSQL schema in MongoDB [9], a document-oriented NoSQL database. However, these approaches never consider the conceptual model of data warehouses. They are limited to the logical level, i.e. transforming a relational model into a column-oriented model. More specifically, the duality fact/dimension requires guaranteeing a number of constraints usually handled by the relational integrity constraints and these constraints cannot be considered in these logical approaches.

This study highlights that there is currently no approaches for automatically and directly transforming a data warehouse multidimensional conceptual model into a NoSQL logical model. It is possible to transform multidimensional conceptual models into a logical relational model, and then to transform this relational model into a logical NoSQL model. However, this transformation using the relational model as a pivot model has not been formalized as both transformations were studied independently of each other. Also, this indirect approach can be tedious.

We can also cite several recent works that are aimed at developing data warehouses in NoSQL systems whether columns-oriented [11, 12], or key-values oriented [35]. However, the main goal of these papers is to propose benchmarks. These studies have not put the focus on the model transformation process. Likewise, they only focus one NoSQL model, and limit themselves to an abstraction at the HBase logical level. Both models [12, 35], require the relational model to be generated first before the abstraction step. By contrast, we consider the conceptual model as well as two orthogonal logical models that allow distributing multidimensional data either vertically using a column-oriented model or horizontally using a document-oriented model.

Finally we take into account hierarchies in our transformation rules by providing transformation rules to manage the aggregate lattice.

3 Conceptual Multi-Dimensional Model

To ensure robust translation rules we first define the multidimensional model used at the conceptual level.

A **multidimensional schema**, namely E, is defined by (F^E, D^E, $Star^E$) where:

- $F^E = \{F_1, \ldots, F_n\}$ is a finite set of facts,
- $D^E = \{D_1, \ldots, D_m\}$ is a finite set of dimensions,
- $Star^E$: $F^E \rightarrow 2^{D^E}$ is a function that associates each fact F_i of F^E to a set of D_i dimensions, $D_i \in Star^E(F_i)$, along which it can be analyzed; note that 2^{D^E} is the *power set* of D^E.

A **dimension**, denoted $D_i \in D^E$ (abusively noted as D), is defined by (N^D, A^D, H^D) where:

- N^D is the name of the dimension,
- $A^D = \{a_1^D, \ldots, a_u^D\} \cup \{id^D, All^D\}$ is a set of dimension attributes,
- $H^D = \{H_1^D, \ldots, H_v^D\}$ is a set hierarchies.

A **hierarchy** of the dimension D, denoted $H_i \in H^D$, is defined by (N^{Hi}, $Param^{Hi}$, $Weak^{Hi}$) where:

- N^{Hi} is the name of the hierarchy,
- $Param^{H_i} = <id^D, p_1^{H_i}, \ldots, p_{v_i}^{H_i}, All^D>$ is an ordered set of $v_i + 2$ attributes which are called **parameters** of the relevant graduation scale of the hierarchy, $\forall k \in [1..v_i]$, $p_k^{Hi} \in A^D$.
- $Weak^{Hi}$: $Param^{Hi} \rightarrow 2^{A^D - Param^{Hi}}$ is a function associating with each parameter zero or more **weak attributes**.

A **fact**, $F \in F^E$, is defined by (N^F, M^F) where:

- N^F is the name of the fact,
- $M^F = \{f_1(m_1^F), \ldots, f_v(m_v^F)\}$ is a set of measures, each associated with an aggregation function f_i.

Example. Consider our case study where news bulletins are loaded into a multidimensional data warehouse described by the conceptual schema in Fig. 1.

The multidimensional schema E^{News} is defined by:

- $F^{News} = \{F_{Content}\}$, $D^{News} = \{D_{Time}, D_{Location}, D_{Keyword}\}$ and $Star^{News}(F_{Content}) = \{D_{Time}, D_{Location}, D_{Keyword}\}$.

The fact represents the data analysis of the news feeds and uses two measures: the number of news (*NewsCount*) and the number of occurrences (*OccurrenceCount*); both for the set of news corresponding to a given term (or keyword), a specific date and a given location. This fact, $F_{Content}$ is defined by (*Content*, {*SUM*(*NewsCount*), *SUM* (*OccurrenceCount*)}) and is analyzed according to three dimensions, each consisting of several hierarchical levels (detail levels):

- The geographical location (*Location*) concerned by the news (with levels *City*, *Country*, *Continent* and *Zone*). A complementary information of the country being its *Population* (modeled as additional information; it is a weak attribute).
- The publication date (*Time*) of the bulletin (with levels *Day*, *Month* and *Year*); note that the month number is associated to its *Name* (also a weak attribute),
- The *Keyword* used in the News (with the levels *Term* and *Category* of the term).

For instance, the dimension $D_{Location}$ is defined by (*Location*, {*City*, *Country*, *Continent*, *Zone*, $ALL^{Location}$}, {H_{Cont}, H_{Zn}}) with $City = id^{Location}$ and:

- H_{Cont} = (HCont, {City, Country, Continent, $ALL^{Location}$}, (Country, {Population})); note that $Weak^{HCont}$ (Country) = {Population},
- H_{Zn} = (HZn, {City, Country, Zone, $ALL^{Location}$}, (Country, {Population})).

4 Conversion into a NoSQL Column-Oriented Model

The *column-oriented model* considers each record as a key associated with a value decomposed in several columns. Data is a set of lines in a table composed of columns (grouped in families) that may be different from one row to the other.

4.1 NoSQL Column-Oriented Model

In relational databases, the data structure is determined in advance with a limited number of typed columns (a few thousand) each similar for all records (also called "tuples"). Column-oriented NoSQL models provide a flexible schema (untyped columns) where the number of columns may vary between each record (or "row").

A column-oriented database (represented in Fig. 2, left) is a set of tables that are defined row by row (but whose physical storage is organized by groups of columns: column families; hence a "vertical partitioning" of the data). In short, in these systems, each table is a logical mapping of rows and their column families. A column family can contain a very large number of columns. For each row, a column exists if it contains a value.

A **table** $T = \{R_1,\ldots, R_n\}$ is a set of rows R_i. A row $R_i = (Key_i, (CF_i^1,\ldots, CF_i^m))$ is composed of a row key Key_i and a set of column families CF_i^j.

A **column family** $CF_i^j = \{(C_i^{j1}, \{v_i^{j1}\}),\ldots, (C_i^{jp}, \{v_i^{jp}\})\}$ consists of a set of columns, each associated with an atomic value. Every value can be "historised" thanks to a timestamp. This principle useful for version management [34] will not be used in this paper due to limited space, although it may be important.

The flexibility of a column-oriented NoSQL database allows managing the absence of some columns between the different table rows. However, in the context of multi-dimensional data storage, data is usually highly structured [22]. Thus, this implies that the structure of a column family (i.e. the set of columns defined by the column family) will be the same for all the table rows. The initial structure is provided by the data integration process called ETL, Extract, Transform, and Load [26].

Example: Let us have a table T^{News} representing aggregated data related to news bulletins with: $T^{News} = \{R_1, \ldots, R_x, \ldots, R_n\}$; due to lack of space, see [6] for a graphical

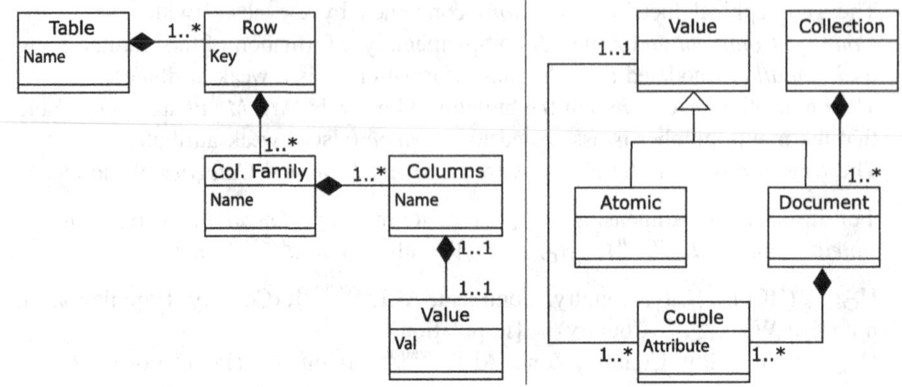

Fig. 2. UML class diagrams representing the concepts of NoSQL databases (left: column-oriented; right: document-oriented).

representation of the table. We detail the R_x row that corresponds to the number of news bulletins, and the number of occurrences where the keyword "Iraq" appears in those news bulletins, published at the date of 09/22/2014 and concerning the location "Toulouse" (south of France).

$R_x = (x, (CF_x^{Time} = \{(C_x^{Day}, \{V_x^{Day}\}), (C_x^{Month}, V_x^{Month}), (C_x^{Name}, V_x^{Name}), (C_x^{Year}, V_x^{Year})\}, CF_x^{Location} = \{(C_x^{City}, V_x^{City}), (C_x^{Country}, V_x^{Country}), (C_x^{Population}, V_x^{Population}), (C_x^{Continent}, V_x^{Continent}), (C_x^{Zone}, V_x^{Zone})\}, CF_x^{Keyword} = \{(C_x^{Term}, V_x^{Term}), (C_x^{Category}, V_x^{Category})\}, CF_x^{Content} = \{(C_x^{NewsCount}, V_x^{NewsCount}), (C_x^{OccurrenceCount}, V_x^{OccurrenceCount})\}))$

The values of the five columns of $CF_x^{Location}$, (C_x^{City}, $C_x^{Country}$, $C_x^{Population}$, $C_x^{Continent}$ and C_x^{Zone}), are (V_x^{City}, $V_x^{Country}$, $V_x^{Population}$, $V_x^{Continent}$ and V_x^{Zone}); e.g. V_x^{City} = Toulouse, $V_x^{Country}$ = France, $V_x^{Population}$ = 65991000, $V_x^{Continent}$ = Europe, V_x^{Zone} = Europe-Western.

More simply we note: $CF_x^{Location}$ = {(City, {Toulouse}), (Country, {France}), (Population, {65991000}), (Continent, {Europe}), (Zone, {Europe-Western})}.

4.2 Column-Oriented Model Mapping Rules

The elements (facts, dimensions, etc.) of the conceptual multidimensional model have to be transformed into different elements of the column-oriented NoSQL model (see Fig. 3).

- Each conceptual star schema (one F_i and its associated dimensions $Star^E(F_i)$) is transformed into a table T.
- The fact F_i is transformed into a column family CF^M of T in which each measure m_i is a column $C_i \in CF^M$.
- Each dimension $D_i \in Star^E(F^i)$ is transformed into a column family CF^{Di} where each dimension attribute $A_i \in A^D$ (parameters and weak attributes) is transformed into a column C_i of the column family CF^{Di} ($C_i \in CF^{Di}$), except the parameter All^{Di}.

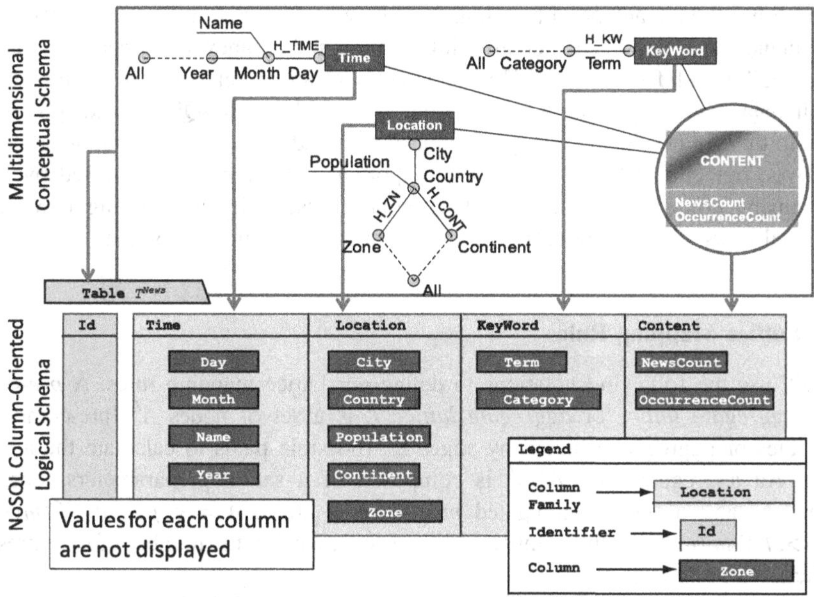

Fig. 3. Implementing a multidimensional conceptual model into the column-oriented NoSQL logical model.

Remarks. Each fact instance and its associated instances of dimensions are transformed into a row R_x of T. The fact instance is thus composed of the column family CF^M (the measures and their values) and the column families of the dimensions $CF^{Di} \in CF^{DE}$ (the attributes, i.e. parameters and weak attributes, of each dimension and their values).

As in a denormalized R-OLAP star schema [18], the hierarchical organization of the attributes of each dimension is not represented in the NoSQL system. Nevertheless, hierarchies are used to build the aggregate lattice. Note that the hierarchies may also be used by the ETL processes which build the instances respecting the constraints induced by these conceptual structures [22]; however, we do not consider ETL processes in this paper.

Example. Let E^{News} be the multidimensional conceptual schema implemented using a table named T^{News} (see Fig. 3). The fact ($F^{Contents}$) and its dimensions (D^{Time}, $D^{Localisation}$, $D^{Keyword}$) are implemented into four column families CF^{Time}, $CF^{Location}$, $CF^{Keyword}$, $CF^{Contents}$. Each column family contains a set of columns, corresponding either to dimension attributes or to measures of the fact. For instance the column family $CF^{Location}$ is composed of the columns $\{C^{City}, C^{Country}, C^{Population}, C^{Continent}, C^{Zone}\}$.

Unlike R-OLAP implementations, where each fact is translated into a central table associated with dimension tables, our rules translate the schema into a single table that includes the fact and its associated dimensions together. When performing queries, this approach has the advantage of avoiding joins between fact and dimension tables. As a consequence, our approach increases information redundancy as dimension data is duplicated for each fact instance. This redundancy generates an increased volume of the overall data while providing a reduced query time. In a NoSQL context, problems linked to this volume increase may be reduced by an adapted data distribution strategy. Moreover, our choice for accepting this important redundancy is motivated by data warehousing context where data updates consist essentially in inserting new data; additional costs incurred by data changes are thus limited in our context.

4.3 Lattice Mapping Rules

We will use the following notations to define our lattice mapping rules. A *pre-computed aggregate lattice* or *aggregate lattice* L is a set of nodes A^L (pre-computed aggregates or aggregates) linked by edges E^L (possible paths to calculate the aggregates). An aggregate node $A \in A^L$ is composed of a set of p_i parameters (one by dimension) and a set of aggregated m_i measures $f_i(m_i)$. $A = < p_1 \ldots . p_k, f_1(m_1), \ldots, f_v(m_v) >$, $k \leq m$ (m being the number of dimensions, v being the number of measures of the fact).

The lattice can be implemented in a column-oriented NoSQL database using the following rules:

- Each aggregate node $A \in A^L$ is stored in a dedicated table.
- For each dimension D_i associated to this node, a column family CF^{Di} is created, each dimension attribute a_i of this dimension is stored in a column C of CF^{Di},
- The set of aggregated measures is also stored in a column family CF^F where each aggregated measure is stored as a column C (see Fig. 4).

Example. We consider the lattice *News* (see Fig. 4). The lattice News is stored in tables. The node (*Keyword_Time*) is stored in a Table $T^{Keyword\_Time}$ composed of the column families $CF^{Keyword}$, CF^{Time} and CF^{Fact}. The attribute *Year* is stored in a column C^{Year}, itself in CF^{Time}. The attribute *Term* is stored in a column C^{Term}, itself in $CF^{Keyword}$. The two measures are stored as two columns in the column family CF^{fact}.

Many studies have been conducted about how to select the pre-computed aggregates that should be computed. In our proposition we favor computing all aggregates [18]. This choice may be sensitive due to the increase in the data volume. However, in a NoSQL architecture we consider that storage space should not be a major issue.

5 Conversion into a NoSQL Document-Oriented Model

The document-oriented model considers each record as a document, which means a set of records containing "attribute/value" pairs; these values are either atomic or complex (embedded in sub-records). Each sub-record can be assimilated as a document, i.e. a subdocument.

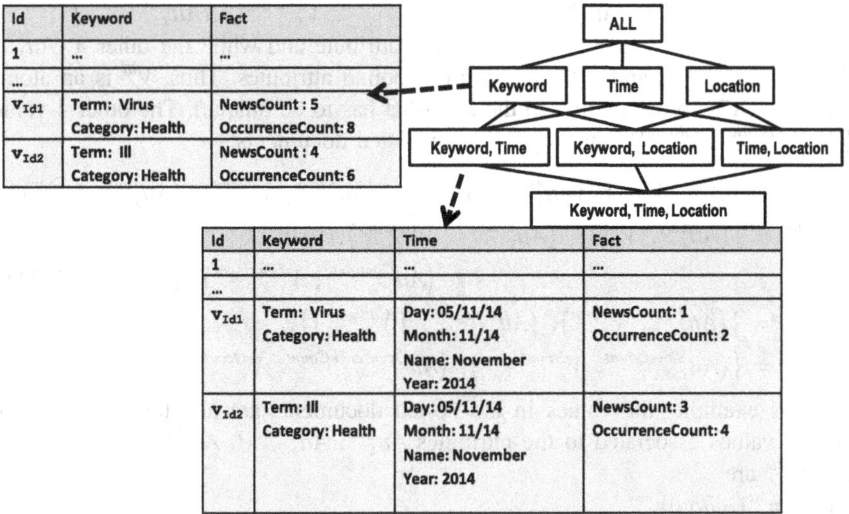

Id | Keyword | Fact
1 | ... | ...
...
v_{Id1} | Term: Virus Category: Health | NewsCount : 5 OccurrenceCount: 8
v_{Id2} | Term: Ill Category: Health | NewsCount : 4 OccurrenceCount: 6
ALL
Keyword
Time
Location
Keyword, Time
Keyword, Location
Time, Location
Keyword, Time, Location
Id | Keyword | Time | Fact
1 | ... | ... | ...
...
v_{Id1} | Term: Virus Category: Health | Day: 05/11/14 Month: 11/14 Name: November Year: 2014 | NewsCount: 1 OccurrenceCount: 2
v_{Id2} | Term: Ill Category: Health | Day: 05/11/14 Month: 11/14 Name: November Year: 2014 | NewsCount: 3 OccurrenceCount: 4

Fig. 4. Implementing the pre-computed aggregation lattice into a column-oriented NoSQL logical model.

5.1 NoSQL Document-Oriented Model

In the document-oriented model, each key is associated with a value structured as a document. These documents are grouped into collections. A document is a hierarchy of elements which may be either atomic values or documents. In the NoSQL approach, the schema of documents is not established in advance (hence the "schema less" concept).

Formally, a NoSQL document-oriented database can be defined as a collection C composed of a set of documents D_i, $C = \{D_1,\ldots, D_n\}$.

Each D_i **document** is defined by a set of pairs $D_i = \{(Att_i^1, V_i^1),\ldots, (Att_i^m, V_i^m)\}$, $j \in [1, m]$ where Att_i^j is an attribute (which is similar to a key) and V_i^j is a value that can be of two forms:

- The value is atomic.
- The value is itself composed by a nested document that is defined as a new set of pairs (attribute, value).

We distinguish **simple attributes** whose values are atomic from **compound attributes** whose values are documents called **nested documents** (see Fig. 2, right).

Example. Let C be a collection, $C = \{D_1,\ldots,D_x,\ldots,D_n\}$ in which we detail the document D_x; due to lack of space, see [6] for a detailed graphical representation of the document. Suppose that D_x provides the number of news and the number of occurrences for the keyword "Iraq" in the news having a publication date equals to 09/22/2014 and that are related to Toulouse. Within the collection $C^{News} = \{D_1,\ldots,D_x,\ldots,D_n\}$, the document D_x could be defined as follows:

D_x = {(Att_x^{Id}, V_x^{Id}), (Att_x^{Time}, V_x^{Time}), ($Att_x^{Location}$, $V_x^{Location}$), ($Att_x^{Keyword}$, $V_x^{Keyword}$), ($Att_x^{Content}$, $V_x^{Content}$)} where Att_x^{Id} is a simple attribute and while the other 4 (Att_x^{Time}, $Att_x^{Location}$, $Att_x^{Keyword}$, and $Att_x^{Content}$) are compound attributes. Thus, V_x^{Id} is an atomic value (e.g. "X") corresponding to the key (that has to be unique). The other 4 values (V_x^{Time}, $V_x^{Location}$, $V_x^{Keyword}$, and $V_x^{Content}$) are nested documents:

$$V_x^{Time} = \{(Att_x^{Day}, V_x^{Day}), (Att_x^{Month}, V_x^{Month}), (Att_x^{Name}, V_x^{Name}), (Att_x^{Year}, V_x^{Year})\},$$

$$V_x^{Location} = \{(Att_x^{City}, V_x^{City}), (Att_x^{Country}, V_x^{Country}), (Att_x^{Population}, V_x^{Population}), (Att_x^{Continent}, V_x^{Continent}), (Att_x^{Zone}, V_x^{Zone})\}$$

$$V_x^{Keyword} = \{(Att_x^{Term}, V_x^{Term}), (Att_x^{Category}, V_x^{Category})\},$$

$$V_x^{Contents} = \{(Att_x^{NewsCount}, V_x^{NewsCount}), (Att_x^{OccurenceCount}, V_x^{OccurenceCount})\}.$$

In this example, the values in the nested documents are all atomic values. For example, values associated to the attributes Att_x^{City}, $Att_x^{Country}$, $Att_x^{Population}$, $Att_x^{Continent}$ and Att_x^{Zone} are:

V_x^{City} = *"Toulouse"*,
$V_x^{Country}$ = *"France"*,
$V_x^{Population}$ = *"65991000"*,
$V_x^{Continent}$ = *"Europe"*,
V_x^{Zone} = *"Europe Western"*.

The other values are: V_x^{Day} = *"09/22/14"*, V_x^{Month} = *"09/14"*, V_x^{Name} = *"September"*, V_x^{Year} = *"2014"*; V_x^{Term} = *"Iraq"*, $V_x^{Category}$ = *"Middle-East"*; $V_x^{NewsCount}$ = *"2"*, $V_x^{OccurenceCount}$ = *"10"*.

5.2 Document-Oriented Model Mapping Rules

Under the NoSQL document-oriented model, the data is not organized in rows and columns as in the previous model, but it is organized in nested documents (see Fig. 5).

- Each conceptual star schema (one F_i and its dimensions $Star^E(F_i)$) is translated in a collection C.
- The fact F_i is translated in a compound attribute Att^{CF}. Each measure m_i is translated into a simple attribute Att^{SM}.
- Each dimension $D_i \in Star^E(F_i)$ is converted into a compound attribute Att^{CD} (i.e. a nested document). Each attribute $A_i \in A^D$ (parameters and weak attributes) of the dimension D_i is converted into a simple attribute Att^A contained in Att^{CD}.

Remarks. A fact instance is converted into a document d. Measures values are combined within a nested document of d. Each dimension is also translated as a nested document of d (each combining parameter and weak attribute values).

The hierarchical organization of the dimension is not preserved. But as in the previous approach, we use hierarchies to build the aggregate lattice.

Example. The document noted D_x is composed of 4 nested documents, $Att^{Content}$, that groups measures and $Att^{Location}$, $Att^{Keyword}$, Att^{Time}, that correspond to the instances of each associated dimension.

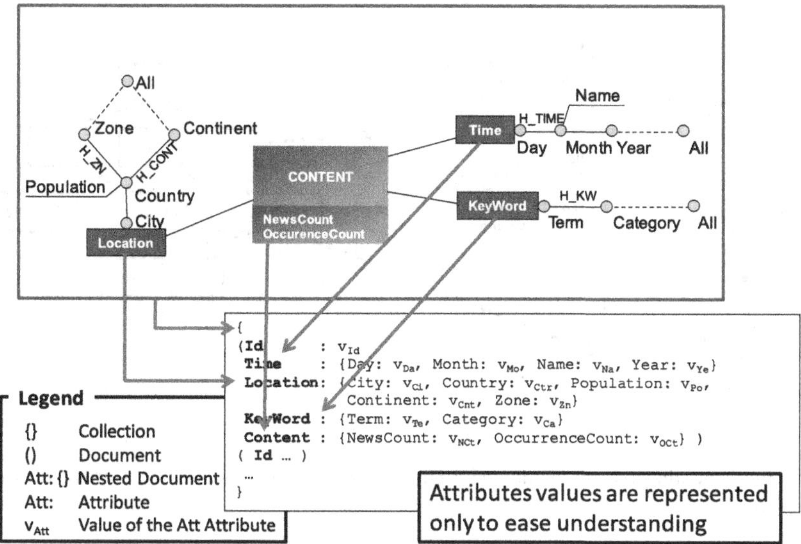

Fig. 5. Implementing the conceptual model into a document-oriented NoSQL logical model.

As the previous model, the transformation process produces a large collection of redundant data. This choice has the advantage of promoting data querying where each fact instance is directly combined with the corresponding dimension instances. The generated volume can be compensated by an architecture that would massively distribute this data.

5.3 Lattice Mapping Rules

As in the previous approach, we store all the pre-computed aggregates in a separate unique collection.

Formally, we use the same definition for the aggregate lattice as above (see Sect. 4.3). However, when using a document oriented NoSQL model, the implementation rules are:

- Each node A is stored in a collection.
- For each dimension D_i concerned by this node, a compound attribute (nested document) ${Att^{CD}}_{Di}$ is created; each attribute a_i of this dimension is stored in a simple attribute Att^{ai} of ${Att^{CD}}_{Di}$.
- The set of aggregated measures is stored in a compound attribute ${Att^{CD}}_F$ where each aggregated measure is stored as a simple attribute Att_{mi}.

Example. Let us Consider the lattice L^{News} (see Fig. 6). This lattice is stored in a collection $\mathrm{C}^{\mathrm{News}}$. The Node < *month_country* > is stored as a document d. The dimension *Time* and *Location* are stored in a nested document d^{date} and $d^{location}$ of d. The *month* attribute is stored as a simple attribute in the nested document d^{Time}.

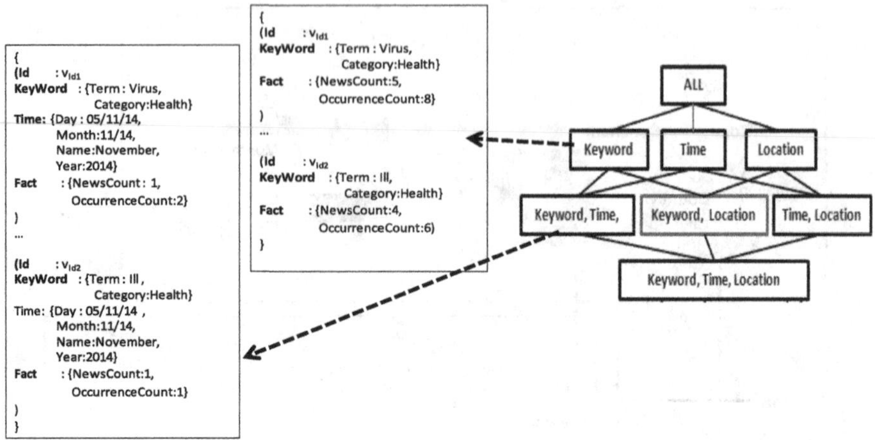

Fig. 6. Implementing the pre-computed aggregation lattice into a document-oriented NoSQL logical model.

The country attribute is stored in a nested document $d^{location}$ as simple attribute. The two measures are also stored in a nested document denote d^{fact}.

As in the column-oriented model, we choose to store all possible aggregates of the lattice; hence, a large potential decrease in terms of query response time.

6 Experiments

Our experimental goal is to illustrate the instantiation of our models as well as the lattice. Thus, our experiments concern data loading, lattice generation and querying.

We use HBase (respectively MongoDB) for testing the column-oriented (resp. document-oriented) model. Data is generated with a reference benchmark [33]. We generate datasets of sizes: 1 GB, 10 GB and 100 GB. After loading data, we compute the aggregate lattice using map-reduce/aggregations offered by both HBase and MongoDB. The details of the experimental setup are as follows:

Dataset. The *TPC-DS benchmark* is used for generating our test data. This is a reference benchmark for testing decision support (including OLAP) systems. It involves a total of 7 fact tables and 17 shared dimension tables. Data is meant to support a retailer decision system. We use the *store_sales* fact and its 10 associated dimensions tables (the most used ones). Some of its dimensions tables are higher hierarchically organized parts of other dimensions. We consider aggregations on the following dimensions: date (day, month, year), customer address (city, country), store address (city, country) and item (class, category).

Data Generation. Data is generated by the DSGen generator (1.3.0) that produces separate CSV-like files (Coma Separated Values), one per table (whether dimension or fact). This data is processed to keep only the *store_sales* measures and associated dimension values (by joining across tables and projecting the data). Data is then formatted as CSV files and JSon files, used for loading data in respectively HBase and MongoDB. We obtain successively *1 GB, 10 GB* and *100 GB* of random data. The JSon format being verbose, these files turn out to be approximately 3 times larger for the same data. The entire process is shown in the Fig. 7.

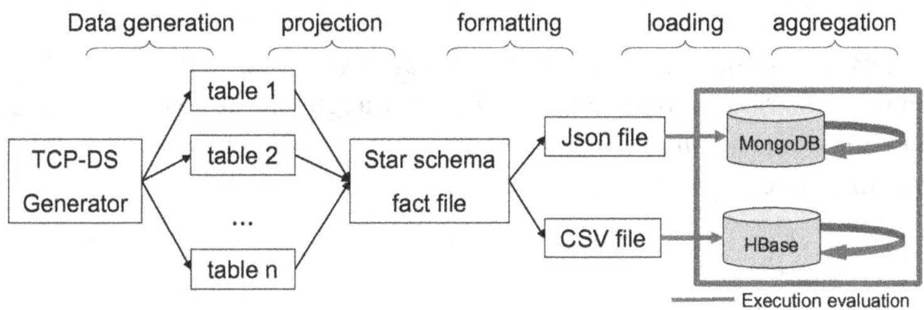

Fig. 7. Broad schema of the data preparation and measurements of our experimental setup.

Data Loading. Data is loaded into HBase and MongoDB using native instructions. These are supposed to load data faster when loading from files. The current version of MongoDB would not load data with our logical model from CSV file, thus we had to use JSON files.

Querying. We generated 12 queries organized by dimension and selectivity. The dimension is the number of dimensions in the grouping clauses (Equivalent to the SQL "Group By"): 1D = 1 dimension, 2D = two dimensions, 3D = three dimensions (Table 1).

Table 1. Query filters/restrictions.

Filter/Restriction	Number of rows	Selectivity level
store.c_city='Midway', date.d_year='2002'	883641	L
store.c_city='Midway', item.i_class='bedding'	31165	A
customer.ca_city='Sullivan', date.d_year='2003'	31165	H
customer.ca_city='Sullivan', item.i_class='bedding'	27	VH

The selectivity is a degree of filtering data when we apply the clauses (equivalent to the SQL "Where"). The level of selectivity is divided into 4 groups according to the following formula (in the following, *k* is defined according to the size of the collection $|C|$; we use $k = \frac{\ln|C|}{4}$):

Very High (VH) : selecting from 0 to e^k rows,

High (H) : selecting from e^k to e^{2k} rows,

Average (A) : selecting from e^{2k} to e^{3k} rows,

Low (L) : selecting from e^{3k} to e^{4k} rows,

The 12 queries are such that there are 4 queries per dimension and 3 per selectivity level. The experiments used a dataset of 1 GB. Query computing is done according to two strategies: *wL* (with lattice) using the optimal available aggregate node, *nL* (no lattice) without the use of the lattice i.e. aggregation is computed live on detailed data.

Lattice Computation. To compute the aggregate lattice, we use map-reduce functions from both HBase and MongoDB. Four levels of aggregates are computed on top of the detailed facts. These aggregates are: all combinations of 3 dimensions, all combinations of 2 dimensions, all combinations of 1 dimension, all data.

MongoDB and HBase allow aggregating data using map-reduce functions which are efficient for distributed data systems. At each aggregation level, we apply aggregation functions: *max, min, sum* and *count* on all dimensions. For MongoDB, instructions look like:

```
db.ss1.mapReduce(
  function(){
    emit({item:{i_class: this.item.i_class,
                i_category: this.item.i_category},
          store:{s_city: this.store.s_city,
                s_country: this.store.s_country},
          customer:{ca_city: this.customer.ca_city,
                ca_country: this.customer.ca_country}},
          this.ss_wholesale_cost);
  },
  function(key, values){
    return { sum: Array.sum(values),
             max: Math.max.apply(Math, values),
             min: Math.min.apply(Math, values),
             count: values.length};
  },
  {out: 'ss1_isc'}
);
```

Here data is aggregated using the item, store and customer dimensions.

For HBase, we use Hive on top to ease the query writing for aggregations. Queries with Hive are SQL-like. The below illustrates the aggregation on item, store and customer dimensions.

```
INSERT OVERWRITE TABLE out
select sum(ss_wholesale_cost), max(ss_wholesale_cost),
      min(ss_wholesale_cost), count(ss_wholesale_cost),
      i_class,i_category,s_city,s_country,ca_city,ca_country
from  store_sales
group by
      i_class,i_category,s_city,s_country,ca_city,ca_country;
```

Hardware. The experiments are done on a cluster composed of 3 PCs, (4 core-i5, 8 GB RAM, 2 TB disks, 1 Gb/s network), each being a worker node and one node acts also as dispatcher.

Data Management Systems. We use two NoSQL data management systems: HBase (v.0.98) and MongoDB (v.2.6). They are both successful key-value database management systems respectively for column-oriented and document-oriented data storage. Hadoop (v.2.4) is used as the underlying distributed storage system.

6.1 Experimental Results

Loading Data. The data generation process produced files respectively of 1 GB, 10 GB, and 100 GB. The equivalent files in JSon where about 3.4 times larger due to the extra format. In the table below, we show loading times for each dataset and for both HBase and MongoDB. Data loading was successful in both cases. It confirms that HBase is faster when it comes to loading. However, we did not pay enough attention to tune each system for loading performance. We should also consider that the raw data (JSon files) takes more space in memory in the case of MongoDB for the same number of records. Thus we can expect a higher network transfer penalty (Table 2).

Table 2. Dataset loading times (minutes) for each NosQL database.

Dataset size	1 GB	10 GB	100 GB
MongoDB	9.045 m	109 m	132 m
HBase	2.26 m	2.078 m	10,3 m

Lattice Computation. We report here the experimental observations on the lattice computation. The results are shown in the schema of Fig. 8. Dimensions are abbreviated (D: date, C: customer, I: item, S: store). The top level corresponds to IDCS (detailed data). On the second level, we keep combinations of only three dimensions and so on. For every aggregate node, we show the number of records/documents it contains and the computation time in seconds respectively for HBase (H) and MongoDB (M).

In HBase, the total time to compute all aggregates was 1700 s with respectively 1207 s, 488 s, 4 s and 0.004 s per level (from more detailed to less). In MongoDB, the total time to compute all aggregates was 3210 s with respectively 2611 s, 594 s, 5 s and 0.002 s per level (from more detailed to less). We can easily observe that computing the lower levels is much faster as the amount of data to be processed is smaller. The size of the aggregates (in terms of records) decreases too when we move down the hierarchy: 8.7 millions (level 2), 3.4 millions (level 3), 55 thousand (level 4) and 1 record in the bottom level.

Querying. The Table 3 summarizes the results for each query (1 to 12). Queries are described according to their dimension grouping, selectivity level and execution time on both MongoDB and HBase platforms. In the table, we indicate which pre-computed aggregate of the lattice is used to optimze the query execution. Results are compared in two cases: using the nodes of the pre-computed aggregate lattice or the base elements either C^{store_sales} or T^{store_sales}.

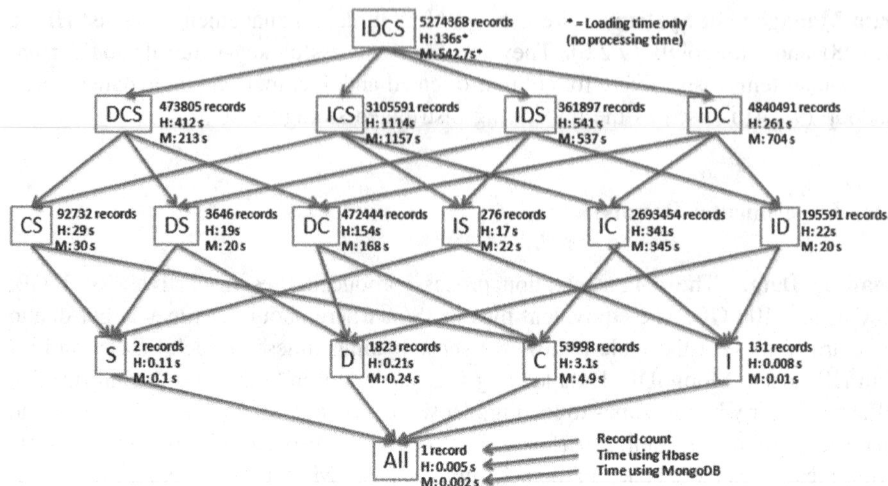

Fig. 8. The pre-computed aggregate lattice with processing time (seconds) and size (records/documents), using HBase (H) and MongoDB (M). The dimensions are abbreviated (D: Date, I: item, S: store, C: customer).

Table 3. Execution time of user queries (the last column is in seconds), Q = Query number, Dim = dimensions (I = Item, C = Customer, D = Date, S = Store), Agg = optimal aggregate, Slct = selectivity level, M = MongoDB, H = Hbase, +L = with lattice, -L = without lattice.

Q	Dim	Agg	Slct	M +L	M -L	H +L	H -L
1	I	DIS	L	*254 ms*	*3640 ms*	*976 ms*	*120 s*
2	S	IS	A	*5 ms*	*1881 ms*	*28 ms*	*79 s*
3	D	CD	H	*138 ms*	*1810 ms*	*414 ms*	*74 s*
4	C	CI	VH	*1008 ms*	*1797 ms*	*3528 ms*	*75 s*
5	IS	DIS	H	*115 ms*	*2060 ms*	*356 ms*	*76 s*
6	CI	CIS	A	*905 ms*	*2237 ms*	*2986 ms*	*90 s*
7	DS	DS	L	*16 ms*	*3921 ms*	*59 ms*	*75 s*
8	CD	CDI	VH	*1406 ms*	*2049 ms*	*4246 ms*	*73 s*
9	DIS	DIS	L	*249 ms*	*4311 ms*	*781 ms*	*91 s*
10	CIS	Base	A	*2198 ms*	*2198 ms*	*8754 ms*	*89 s*
11	CDI	CDI	L	*1420 ms*	*2052 ms*	*4261 ms*	*74 s*
12	CDS	Base	VH	*2051 ms*	*2051 ms*	*6094 ms*	*74 s*
Total				*9368 ms*	*30007 ms*	*26395 ms*	*990 s*

We can see that whenever the use of the lattice is ignored, the more selective queries (i.e. those where more rows are selected) require more execution time. This observation does not apply when the lattice is used to speed the results up. Thus, we can assume that using an aggregate lattice allows a query execution time improvement for all queries. The more data has to be read from the disk, the more significant is the improvement.

6.2 Complementary Experiments on the Column-Oriented Architecture

In order to go further in our research for an optimized logical NoSQL model, we have adapted the Start Schema Benchmark (SSB) which is based on the classical TPC-H benchmark, to be used in NoSQL systems [5]. This benchmark models a simple product retail sales case structured as a star schema. It contains one fact (LineOrder) and 4 dimensions (Customer, Supplier, Part and Date) each organized according to one or more hierarchies.

We have extended SSB to generate raw data specific to our models in JSon file format. This is convenient for our experimental purposes as JSon is the best file format for loading data in the column-oriented NoSQL system we use, i.e. MongoDB. Data loading was done according to three different scales: 15 GB, 150 GB and 375 GB of data; and took 1 306 s, 16 680 s and 46 704 s respectively. These complementary experiments were executed on a single machine (one of the nodes of our cluster described above). Hardware was upgraded and there were 2 × 2 TB disks and allowed us to lower a little bit the disk read/write bottleneck.

Query execution was also analyzed, where we generated three query sets with our SSB extension. The three sets correspond to variants of the three following queries:

```
Q1: select sum(l_extendedprice*l_discount) as revenue
    from lineorder, date
    where l_orderdate = d_datekey  and d_year = '1993'
          and l_discount between 1 and 3 and l_quantity < 25;
Q2: select sum(lo_revenue), d_year, p_brand1
    from lineorder, date, part, supplier
    where lo_orderdate = d_datekey and lo_partkey = p_partkey
        and lo_suppkey = s_suppkey and p_category = 'MFGR#12'
                               and s_region_name = 'AMERICA'
    group by d_year, p_brand1 order by d_year, p_brand1;
Q3: select c_nation_name, s_nation_name, d_year,
                                  sum(lo_revenue) as revenue
    from customer, lineorder, supplier, date
    where lo_custkey = c_custkey and lo_suppkey = s_suppkey
       and lo_orderdate = d_datekey and c_region = 'ASIA' and
      s_region = 'ASIA' and d_year >= 1992 and d_year <= 1997
    group by c_nation_name, s_nation_name, d_year
    order by d_year asc, revenue desc;
```

The query complexity increases from Q1 to Q3, as each manipulates one, two and three dimensions respectively. Note that we observed that the query generator produces a high selectivity, i.e. queries return relatively few documents. To counterbalance, we created a query Q4, similar to Q1 but with a much lower selectivity. This is done for analysis purposes. When a query has lower selectivity (i.e. we returns more records/documents), a significant impact on query execution can exist. Higher selectivity impacts operations such as "joins", storage of intermediary results, group by-s and network transfer. For queries Q2 and Q3, it was impossible to produce low selectivity results because the "group by" and "where" clauses reduce significantly the amount of returned records.

Query writing complexity turned out to be the same as using normalized vs denormalized R-OLAP implementations (i.e. snowflake schema vs star schema, [18]. When data is denormalized not only are queries supposed to be accelerated, but writing SQL queries usually turn out to be simpler. Here, in NoSQL, the same applies: as our model (nicknamed "flat") is fully denormalized (i.e. similar to the star schema), query complexity writing is lower than in a normalized version of our logical implementation.

Query execution time was compared to our alternative document-oriented logical models [3]. And results proved that the current "flat" model described here allows faster query execution: on average Q1 required 144 s, Q2, 140 s, Q3, 139 s and Q4, 173 s; all the other models described in [3, 4] require more execution time. Note that this execution time would have been approximately halved if we had run the queries on our three-node cluster (which was unfortunately partly unavailable due to hardware and network maintenance).

7 Discussion

In this section, we discuss our results and we want to answer three questions:

- Are the proposed models convincing?
- How can we explain performance differences between MongoDB and HBase?
- Are column-oriented or document-oriented approaches recommended for OLAP systems? If not systematically, when?

The choice of our logical NoSQL models can be criticized for being simple. However, we argue that it is better to start from the simpler and most natural models before studying more complex ones. The two models we studied are simple and intuitive, easing implementation. Processing and adapting the TPC-DS benchmark data was not difficult and successfully mapped and inserted into MongoDB and HBase proving the simplicity and effectiveness of the approach.

Our experiments concluded that, in our environment, HBase outperforms MongoDB with respect to data loading. This is not surprising as other studies highlight the good performance when loading data in HBase. We should also consider that data fed to MongoDB is larger due to additional markup (JSon) as MongoDB does not support CSV-like files when the data contains nested fields. Current benchmarks produce data in a columnar format (CSV like), giving an advantage to relational DBMS. The column-oriented model we propose is closer to the relational model with respect to the document-oriented model. This remains an advantage for HBase compared to MongoDB. We can observe that it becomes useful to have benchmarks that produce data that are adequate for the different NoSQL models.

As there was no comparable previous work, we initially started using simple logical models to implement our NoSQL experimental solutions. As this paper is an extension of [6], our research has advanced and we were able to introduce more advanced logical implementation solutions in both document-oriented [3] and column-oriented [4] systems. Both experiments compared their advanced models to the one described here. This model still proved to have interesting results during those complementary experiments and our initial intuition for implementing an OLAP system using a very simple logical solution was not completely wrong. Note also that in the meantime, a similar paper presented experiments on logical structures for column-oriented systems and although experiments are different, their conclusions seem similar to ours [10].

Still at this stage, it is difficult to draw detailed recommendations with respect to using column-oriented or document-oriented approaches for implementing OLAP systems. However, for the moment, we can recommend HBase if data loading is a major consideration. HBase uses also less disk space and it is known for effective data compression (due to column redundancy). Computing aggregates takes a reasonable time for both systems and the many aggregates take a "reasonable" disk space with respect to the "bigdata" scale. A major difference between the different NoSQL systems concerns querying. For queries that demand multiple attributes of a relation, the column-oriented approaches might take longer because data is not be available in the same place and joins are not recommended. For some queries, nested fields supported by document-oriented approaches can be an advantage while for others it would be a disadvantage (depending on the nesting order of the fields and the order required to access them by the query). A more in depth study of query performance is future work currently underway. Our complementary experiments [3, 4] also confirm these results where query performance is highly dependent on the storage path (different in Hbase and MongoDB) required to access the different query attributes. This is one of the major if not the major drawback of "schema free" storage such as NoSQL where the way data is to be stored depends on the way it will be accessed during query execution. Our complementary experiments on column-oriented systems and presented here in Sect. 6.2 shows us that the basic model designed here will require more time for data loading in the system and will use more disk space than more advanced models [3]. However, queries run faster on this type of simple model, and as a consequence, the lattice generation will be faster. Generating a complete lattice is materializing all queries using all possible combinations of dimension parameters. Moreover, is a fact, not to be neglected, that query writing is usually easier to write due to the simple logical structure.

8 Conclusion

This paper is about an investigation on the instantiation of OLAP systems through NoSQL approaches namely: column-oriented and document-oriented approaches. We have proposed respectively two NoSQL logical models for this purpose. Each model is associated to a set of rules that permits to transform a multi-dimensional conceptual model into a NoSQL logical model. We also show how to speed up queries using a lattice of pre-computed aggregations. This entire lattice is produced using map-reduce functions. This is done for illustrative purposes as it is not always necessary to compute the entire lattice. This kind of deeper optimizations is not the main goal of the paper.

Experiments were carried out initially with data from the TPC-DS benchmark. We generate respectively datasets of size 1 GB, 10 GB and 100 GB. The experimental setup shows how we can instantiate OLAP systems with column-oriented and document-oriented databases respectively with HBase and MongoDB. This process includes data transformation, data loading and aggregate computation. The entire process allows us to compare the different approaches with each other. Results show that both NoSQL systems we considered perform well. Experiments confirm that data loading and aggregate computation is faster with HBase. In complementary experiments, we used an extension of the SSB benchmark [5] for our column-oriented logical model, producing datasets of 15 GB, 150 GB and 375 GB. These experiments showed that the "flat" document-oriented logical model described in this paper is a relevant alternative solution in comparison to more advanced models we experimented [3, 4].

We are currently considering several future work. We wish to extend our approach for switching from one NoSQL model to another [20] and also consider more complex analytical queries to optimize our logical models in order to maximise query performance and combine these with the pre-computed aggregate lattice. In addition, we would like to see if current model transformation architectures such as MDA (Model Driven Architecture) could be used for generalizing our model to model transformations.

Acknowledgements. This work is supported by the ANRT funding under CIFRE-Capgemini partnership.

References

1. Chang, F., Dean, J., Ghemawat, S., Hsieh, W.C., Wallach, D.A., Burrows, M., Chandra, T., Fikes, A., Gruber, R.E.: Bigtable: a distributed storage system for structured data. ACM Trans. Comput. Syst. (TOCS) **26**(2), 4 (2008). ACM
2. Chaudhuri, S., Dayal, U.: An overview of data warehousing and OLAP technology. ACM SIGMOD Rec. **26**, 65–74 (1997)
3. El Malki, M., Teste, O., Kopliku, A., Chevalier, M., Tournier, R.: Implementation of multidimensional databases with document-oriented NoSQL. In: Madria, S., Hara, T. (eds.) DaWaK 2015. LNCS, vol. 9263, pp. 379–390. Springer, Heidelberg (2015)
4. Kopliku, A., Chevalier, M., Malki, M.E., Teste, O., Tournier, R.: Implementation of multidimensional databases in column-oriented NoSQL Systems. In: Morzy, T., Valduriez, P., Ladjel, B. (eds.) ADBIS 2015. LNCS, vol. 9282, pp. 79–91. Springer, Heidelberg (2015)
5. Chevalier, M., El Malki, M., Kopliku, A., Teste, O., Tournier, R.: Benchmark for OLAP on NoSQL technologies. In: IEEE International Conference on Research Challenges in Information Systems (RCIS), pp. 480–485. IEEE (2015)
6. Chevalier, M., El Malki, M., Kopliku, A., Teste, O., Tournier, R.: Implementing multidimensional data warehouses into NoSQL. In: 17th International Conference on Enterprise Information Systems (ICEIS), vol. 1, pp. 172–183. SciTePress (2015)
7. Colliat, G.: Olap, relational, and multidimensional database systems. ACM SIGMOD Rec. **25**(3), 64–69 (1996)
8. Cuzzocrea, A., Bellatreche, L., Song, I.-Y.: Data warehousing and OLAP over big data: Current challenges and future research directions. In: 16th International Workshop on Data Warehousing and OLAP (DOLAP), pp. 67–70. ACM (2013)
9. Dede, E., Govindaraju, M., Gunter, D., Canon, R.S., Ramakrishnan, L.: Performance evaluation of a MongoDB and hadoop platform for scientific data analysis. In: 4th Workshop on Scientific Cloud Computing, pp. 13–20. ACM (2013)
10. Dehdouh, K., Boussaid, O., Bentayed, F., Kabachi, N.: Using the column oriented NoSQL model for implementing big data warehouses. In: 21st International Conference on Parallel and Distributed Processing Techniques and Applications (PDPTA), pp. 469–475 (2015)

11. Bentayeb, F., Boussaid, O., Kabachi, N., Dehdouh, K.: Towards an OLAP environment for column-oriented data warehouses. In: Bellatreche, L., Mohania, M.K. (eds.) DaWaK 2014. LNCS, vol. 8646, pp. 221–232. Springer, Heidelberg (2014)
12. Bentayeb, F., Dehdouh, K., Boussaid, O.: Columnar NoSQL star schema benchmark. In: Ait Ameur, Y., Bellatreche, L., Papadopoulos, G.A. (eds.) MEDI 2014. LNCS, vol. 8748, pp. 281–288. Springer, Heidelberg (2014)
13. Floratou, A., Teletia, N., Dewitt, D., Patel, J., Zhang, D.: Can the elephants handle the NoSQL onslaught? In: International Conference on Very Large Data Bases (VLDB) 5(12), 1712–1723. VLDB Endowment (2012)
14. Golfarelli, M., Maio, D., Rizzi, S.: The dimensional fact model: A conceptual model for data warehouses. Int. J. Coop. Inf. Syst. (IJCIS) **7**(2–3), 215–247 (1998)
15. Gray, J., Bosworth, A., Layman, A., Pirahesh, H.: Data cube: a relational aggregation operator generalizing group-by, cross-tab, and sub-total. In: International Conference on Data Engineering (ICDE), pp. 152–159. IEEE Computer Society (1996)
16. Han, D., Stroulia, E.: A three-dimensional data model in Hbase for large time-series dataset analysis. In: 6th International Workshop on the Maintenance and Evolution of Service-Oriented and Cloud-Based Systems (MESOCA), pp. 47–56. IEEE (2012)
17. Jacobs, A.: The pathologies of big data. Commun. ACM **52**(8), 36–44 (2009)
18. Kimball, R., Ross, M.: The Data Warehouse Toolkit: The Definitive Guide to Dimensional Modeling, 3rd edn. Wiley, Indianapolis (2013)
19. Kim, J., Moon, Y.-S., Lee, S., Lee, W.: Efficient distributed parallel top-down computation of R-OLAP data cube using mapreduce. In: Cuzzocrea, A., Dayal, U. (eds.) DaWaK 2012. LNCS, vol. 7448, pp. 168–179. Springer, Heidelberg (2012)
20. LeFevre, J., Sankaranarayanan, J., Hacigumus, H., Tatemura, J., Polyzotis, N., Carey, M.J.: MISO: souping up big data query processing with a multistore system. In: International Conference on Management of data (SIGMOD), pp. 1591–1602. ACM (2014)
21. Li, C.: Transforming relational database into Hbase: A case study. In: International Conference on Software Engineering and Service Sciences (ICSESS), pp. 683–687. IEEE (2010)
22. Malinowski, E., Zimányi, E.: Hierarchies in a multidimensional model: From conceptual modeling to logical representation. Data Knowl. Eng. (DKE) **59**(2), 348–377 (2006). Elsevier
23. Morfonios, K., Konakas, S., Ioannidis, Y., Kotsis, N.: R-OLAP implementations of the data cube. ACM Comput. Surv. **39**(4), 12 (2007). ACM
24. Pavlo, A., Paulson, E., Rasin, A., Abadi, D.J., DeWitt, D.J., Madden, S., Stonebraker, M.: A comparison of approaches to large-scale data analysis. In: International Conference on Management of data (SIGMOD), pp. 165–178. ACM (2009)
25. Ravat, F., Teste, O., Tournier, R., Zurfluh, G.: Algebraic and Graphic Languages for OLAP Manipulations. Int. J. Data Warehouse. Min. (IJDWM) **4**(1), 17–46 (2008). IGI Publishing
26. Simitsis, A., Vassiliadis, P., Sellis, T.: Optimizing ETL processes in data warehouses. In: International Conference on Data Engineering (ICDE), pp. 564–575. IEEE (2005)
27. Stonebraker, M.: New opportunities for new SQL. Commun. ACM **55**(11), 10–11 (2012)
28. Stonebraker, M., Madden, S., Abadi, D.J., Harizopoulos, S., Hachem, N., Helland, P.: The end of an architectural era: (it's time for a complete rewrite). In: 33rd International Conference on Very large Data Bases (VLDB), pp. 1150–1160. ACM (2007)
29. Strozzi, C.: NoSQL – A relational database management system (2007–2010). http://www.strozzi.it/cgi-bin/CSA/tw7/I/en_US/nosql/Home%20Page
30. Vajk, T., Feher, P., Fekete, K., Charaf, H.: Denormalizing data into schema-free databases. In: 4th International Conference on Cognitive Infocommunications (CogInfoCom), pp. 747–752. IEEE (2013)

31. Vassiliadis, P., Vagena, Z., Skiadopoulos, S., Karayannidis, N.: ARKTOS: A Tool For Data Cleaning and Transformation in Data Warehouse Environments. IEEE Data Engineering Bulletin, 23(4), IEEE, pp. 42–47, 2000
32. Tahara, D., Diamond, T., Abadi, D.J.: Sinew: a SQL system for multi-structured data. In: International Conference on Management of data (SIGMOD), pp. 815–826. ACM (2014)
33. TPC-DS. Transaction Processing Performance Council, Decision Support benchmark, version 1.3.0 (2014). http://www.tpc.org/tpcds/
34. Wrembel, R.: A survey of managing the evolution of data warehouses. Int. J. Data Warehouse. Min. (IJDWM) **5**(2), 24–56 (2009). IGI Publishing
35. Zhao, H., Ye, X.: A practice of TPC-DS multidimensional implementation on NoSQL database systems. In: Nambiar, R., Poess, M. (eds.) TPCTC 2013. LNCS, vol. 8391, pp. 93–108. Springer, Heidelberg (2014)

International ERP Teaching Case: Design and Experiences

Jānis Grabis[1(✉)], Kurt Sandkuhl[2,3], and Dirk Stamer[2]

[1] Institute of Information Technology, Riga Technical University, Kalku 1, Riga, Latvia
grabis@rtu.lv

[2] Institute of Computer Science, University of Rostock, A.-Einstein-Str. 22, Rostock, Germany
{kurt.sandkuhl,dirk.stamer}@uni-rostock.de

[3] School of Engineering, Jönköping University, Jönköping, Sweden

Abstract. Enterprise Resource Planning (ERP) systems are among the most widely used large-scale information systems. Industry and students in IT-related subjects expect that ERP training is part of the studies during university education. However, traditional teaching materials use somewhat simplified multi-role and cross-organizational processes which do not fully reflect reality in enterprises, for example with respect to role-based permissions or coordination challenges in international organizations. This paper reports on an attempt to extend the SAP ERP GBI case study towards an international dimension. For this purpose an international ERP case study was developed which is presented in the paper with its didactical approach, the technical way how to implement the case study in SAP, and the teaching environment. The work is a joint effort by University of Rostock and Riga Technical University which has a focus on enhancing introductory ERP training for study programs in information technology and business informatics. One of the key features of the international ERP case study is that students of both universities work collaboratively on running business processes in the SAP ERP system. Evaluations suggest that the students appreciate the case study as suitable means to get an insight in real-life challenges connected to ERP use in an international context.

Keywords: ERP · Collaborative teaching · ERP internationalization · Case study

1 Introduction

Enterprise Resource Planning (ERP) systems are one of the most widely used large-scale information systems [1, 2]. They are often implemented at large international companies operating in many countries with different regulatory requirements and regional and cultural differences [3]. Given importance of the ERP systems, higher education establishments have incorporated them in study programs [4]. A range of training materials has been elaborated very often with a help of vendors of the ERP systems. However, the traditional teaching materials lack the international dimension and often follow a one-user-does-it-all approach. As a result, students are able to complete long-running, multi-role and cross-organizational processes in a relatively short time and ignoring permissions associated with

S. Hammoudi et al. (Eds.): ICEIS 2015, LNBIP 241, pp. 131–150, 2015.
DOI: 10.1007/978-3-319-29133-8_7

various roles. Therefore, they do not gain a good understanding of the ways processes are executed in practice. Additionally, the traditional teaching materials often focus on step-by-step instructions reducing a need for in-depth exploration of the features of the ERP systems and dealing with potential pitfalls.

This paper reports a collaborative effort by University of Rostock (UR) and Riga Technical University (RTU) to provide ERP teaching in an international environment. The objective of the paper is to elaborate an international ERP teaching case and to reflect on initial experiences in studying collaboratively ERP systems.

The international ERP case is used for practical exercises in a study course devoted to enterprise applications or business information systems. The course is given to both computing and business students and focuses on functional aspects of the ERP systems. A sales and distribution process performed by organizational units in different countries is at the core of the case. The case study is designed and carried out following case-based teaching principles [5]. The SAP ERP system is used for executing the international sales and distribution process. The case is developed as an extension of the standard SAP training material using the GBI case study [6] and students have knowledge of the standard case prior starting the international case. This way the international ERP is a natural continuation of previous exercises and the students work in the familiar environment. The other key principles used in the design of the international ERP case are usage of structured case execution instructions instead of the step-by-step type of instruction to facilitate inductive learning (see Sect. 5.2). Student groups located in different countries are jointly responsible for the case execution and a joint troubleshooting is promoted to facilitate peer learning. The sales process is executed in an asynchronous manner to resemble real life business operations where partners do not respond immediately.

The main contribution of the paper is development of the didactical approach to studying ERP systems in the international environment and elaboration of a new type of template for presenting case studies and training instructions. The didactical approach is based on a mix of deductive and inductive teaching approaches including collaborative work by teams of the students in different countries. The template for presenting training instructions is based on using structured task specifications rather than step-by-step guides.

The rest of the paper is organized as follows. Section 2 reviews related work on ERP studying. Section 3 describes context of development of the international ERP case study. Sections 4 and 5 described didactical and technical approaches to the international ERP case, respectively. Section 6 reports initial case study execution experiences and Sect. 7 concludes.

2 Literature Review

Boyle and Strong [7] have identified skill requirements of ERP graduates. The skills are categorized as ERP technical knowledge, technology management knowledge, business functional knowledge, interpersonal skills and team skills. The international ERP case focuses developing skills systems design/integration, knowledge of business functions, ability to understand the business environment to interpret business problems, ability to accomplish assignments, ability to be proactive, ability to work cooperatively in a team environment. More importantly ERP skills have direct impact on ERP implementation success [8].

Hepner and Dickson [4] provide a summary of business processes taught using ERP-integrated curricula and an ERP curriculum assessment. They focus on value of ERP-integration. Hayes and McGilsky [9] report on introducing ERP systems in the business core courses. They specifically emphasize importance of developing training curriculum and faculty competences showing that the standard materials are a good starting point and these can be later on elaborated for specific needs. An ERP simulation game is one of the ways of illustrating characteristics of ERP systems, especially, to business students [10]. The game focuses on comprehension of conceptual foundations of the ERP systems. Léger [11] implemented a turn-based simulation game approach for both undergraduate and graduate business administration students focusing on information technologies. The students were running five national companies during this simulation, which sell their products independently on three different marketplaces. The affected processes were: procurement, production and sales.

Cronan et al. [12] compared two different methods — an objective measure and a self-assed one — to measure cognitive learning effects in an ERP simulation game. To obtain knowledge about ERP systems and business processes a simulation game is more appropriate than other learning types like lab exercises or lectures [12]. Theling and Loos [13] proposed a multi-perspective approach to teach ERP systems to take into account that different roles were involved. They integrated four different perspectives on ERP systems in their curriculum like software engineer's, software consultant's, business analyst's and end-user's view. The hands-on experience was given by a case study using standard learning material provided by SAP. Monk and Lycett [14] described a work in progress multi-method approach to measure the effectiveness of ERP teaching. They combined a quantitative analysis of an experimental simulation game using a t-test and a qualitative analysis of interviews about the gained knowledge. They run their simulation game both in the UK and the US.

Dealing with complexity of ERP systems is a major challenge in studying ERP systems. Hussey et al. [15] propose a methodology for facilitating active learning so that students can attain in-depth understanding of the ERP systems. O'Sullivan [16] perceives usage of ERP systems as a way of bringing in real-world tools and experience in the classroom. ERP training can contribute to development of a wide range of professional skills for engineering students [17]. International collaboration is shown be particularly beneficial. Although modern information systems are used in the global context, information systems curriculum often does not follow the suite [18]. The internationalization framework proposed in that paper emphasizes importance of collaboration, communication and project management to achieve curriculum internationalization objectives.

Chang et al. [19] investigated the influence of post-implementation learning on ERP systems. They used a cross-sectional mail survey including 47 companies for their quantitative research. The number of returned questionnaires was 659. The main finding is that post-implementation learning has a significant influence on ERP usage including the dimensions like decision support, work integration and customer service. Furthermore, ERP usage is also shown to have significant effects on individual performance including areas like individual productivity, customer satisfaction and management control [19].

The literature survey provides evidence that ERP training plays an important role in information systems curriculum. The training has to provide a wide range of skills and internationalization is one of major challenges. Capturing complexity of using and developing large scale information systems is also important and challenging in the classroom environment. According to our literature research there is no cross-country collaborative case study using an ERP system including a setting with multiple roles and limited permissions in order to deepen the students' knowledge on cross-organizational business processes. This applies also to ERP systems taught by double loop learning and peer learning.

3 Teaching Environment

The international ERP studies are implemented as a collaborative effort between Riga Technical University and University of Rostock. Both universities are engaged in teaching advanced information systems and enterprise applications.

3.1 Background

The international ERP is a part of courses devoted to introduction to ERP systems. At RTU, the ERP Systems course is given to master students in the Information Technology study program. At UR, the course is given to both Master students in Business Informatics and students in the "Service Management" program which leads to a Master degree in business administration. The Information Technology as well as Business Informatics study programs deal with application of ICT in business environment and the ERP systems is one of the key aspects of using ICT at companies. The introductory ERP courses at both universities focus on general characteristics and functional aspects of the ERP systems. This founding knowledge is used as a prerequisite in related courses devoted to ERP development and implementation of enterprise applications.

Table 1 lists topics covered in the courses at RTU and UR, respectively. Every topic consists of lectures and practical exercises in the lab following the standard GBI curriculum. The international ERP process is executed as a part of the topic on ERP internationalization. This topic is given using the extended international case. It consists of an introductory overview of international ERP, independent work by students' teams of international ERP process execution and reflections on the process execution.

Table 1. Topics of the introductory ERP courses.

RTU	UR
Enterprise business processes	Process-oriented organizations
General characteristics of enterprise applications	General characteristics of information systems in enterprises
Data in ERP systems	ERP systems
Sales and distribution process	Sales and distribution processes
Financial accounting processes	Material management processes
Sales and financial accounting integration	Financial accounting processes
Production and inventory management processes	Integration of business processes
ERP internationalization	Electronic business in general
	e-procurement

Further details of the collaborative learning process are provided in Section 5. Completion of the international ERP process yields credits towards the final grade of the course.

3.2 Case Study

The functionality of the ERP system is explored with a help of the GBI case study. The GBI case is about a fictional bicycles manufacturing company operating in Germany and the United States. It manufactures and sells high end bicycles as well as cycling accessories. The case study covers all major operations of the company. It is comprehensive enough to give a good overview of these operations and at the same time hides some of the complexities characteristic to ERP systems making them less efficient for classroom usage. Its main teaching objective is to provide understanding of enterprise business process as implemented in the SAP ERP system. The case study comes with a set of teaching materials. These include lecture slides, case execution slides, SAP ERP systems configured to execute GBI's processes, GBI data set as well as some teaching support materials and utilities.

The GBI case covers sales and distribution, materials management, production planning, finance, warehouse management and human capital management processes. Despite being configured to represent global operation of the company, the teaching materials assume process execution within a single company code.

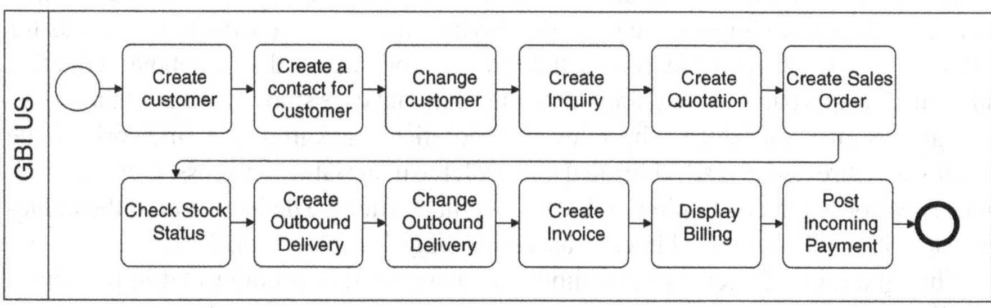

Fig. 1. Sales and distribution process in GBI.

The sales process is the most important process in the framework of this paper. Figure 1 shows an overview of the sales process as defined in the standard GBI case. Note that the process does not consider exceptional situations and decisions (e.g. stock is not available).

4 Didactical Approach

Development of the didactical approach including the selection of suitable methods and instruments started from the learning outcomes the international case study was supposed to establish. Learning outcomes are what the students can reliably demonstrate at the end of the module, i.e. what can be assessed in exams or is manifested by oral presentation or written documentation of the students' results.

The specific learning objectives for the international ERP relate to the required ERP skills as identified in [7]. The learning objectives for the case are:

- Strengthening general ERP usage skills,
- Strengthening knowledge of the sales and distribution process,
- Ability to track the process execution progress,
- Improving communication skills and foreign language skills,
- Business process execution in the collaborative setting and
- Understanding of roles and user permissions in ERP systems.

This section will motivate the use of inductive teaching approaches in teaching ERP and discuss features of the case study from a teaching perspective. In this context, the above learning objectives will be revisited and their implementation will be discussed.

4.1 Teaching Method

Traditional engineering instruction usually follows a deductive approach, which starts with theories introduced in lectures or homework and progresses to the applications of those theories. The deductive approach is based on the viewpoint that a solid understanding of theories is required for being able to apply them. From the learners' perspective, a drawback of this approach is that they have to learn a theory before knowing why it is important and for what purpose to apply it – which is not an optimal motivation [20].

Alternative teaching approaches are more inductive and include methods, such as problem-based learning, project-based learning or case-based teaching [5]. As inductive teaching methods are found to be more effective than traditional deductive methods for achieving a broad range of learning outcomes [21] we decided to combine deductive and inductive approaches. Teaching in the international case study started with a deductive part: lectures introduced the relevant theoretical background; homework of the students was directed to read additional material; the material was discussed in question-answer sessions at the beginning of the next lecture. After the deductive part, the inductive part followed manifested in case-based teaching (see also Sect. 4.2).

When planning the teaching method, we also took into account that in particular in ICT there is a tendency to a competence perspective on personal qualification, as manifested in the European e-Competence Framework [22]. The term competence is defined by the e-CF 3.0 as: "Competence is a demonstrated ability to apply knowledge, skills and attitudes for achieving observable results." [22, p. 5]. Typically a distinction is made between technical, method and social competences. The technical and method competences for our teaching module correspond to the learning outcomes defined at the beginning of this section. However, the teaching module also has the objective to develop social competences. Social competences are difficult to express in "assessable" learning outcomes but nevertheless need to be taken into account when planning the teaching methods. For our case, the social competences are the ability to actively contribute to distributed and international group work, which includes understanding that work with partners in other locations and countries usually cannot be solely performed by using ERP systems but also requires communication with people and coordination of group work and to train the ability to coordinate problem solving in distributed teams.

In order to support the inductive part of our teaching module, we decided to support different learning situations: collaborative learning, peer learning and tutoring. Collaborative learning can be very broadly defined as "a situation in which two or more people learn or attempt to learn something together" [23, p. 1]. In our case, we formed groups of students who got a joint assignment which included initial guidelines how to proceed. Some of the advantages attributed to collaborative learning are, e.g., that students come to a more complete understanding by comparing their views with other group members, having to explain to others requires elaboration and students with better skills serve as promoters in the groups [24].

Tutoring basically means to guide the students or group of students to the point in the learning process at which they become independent learners. Tutoring was provided by having a subject teacher from the field as "stand-by" for inquiries of the students during the course of the case study. At each university, a tutor was available who could be contacted by e-mail or visiting the tutor's office. Online-tutoring by using video-links was also possible.

Peer learning basically is the "acquisition of knowledge and skill through active helping and supporting among status equals or matched companions" [25]. We envisioned that peer learning situations would emerge between the collaborating groups at the two universities, i.e. that the groups from Riga would help the corresponding group from Rostock to understand issue and solve problems in the case study and vice versa. Support for peer learning was provided by offering document sharing, joint editing platforms and communication support for the groups.

For the above learning situations, computer support is provided, e.g. by providing groupware and learning management systems. The students were made aware of these instruments and used the computer support for peer learning and tutoring as part of their collaborative learning.

In order to develop the social competences, we designed the case material in a way that enforced communication between groups in Riga and Rostock, e.g. by including exceptions in the work flow which could not be remedied just by using the ERP system. Furthermore, the groups were forced to agree on an internal way of working, i.e. we did not define the "inner" roles and tasks of the teams. In Rostock, we also formed teams with mixed backgrounds, as the participants were from business information systems (engineering-oriented) and service management (purely business-oriented) programs. The tutor actively focused on technical and method support and promoted discussions within the teams for solving communication problems or conflicts.

4.2 Features of the Case Study

When developing the case study for the inductive part of teaching module, we looked for guidance regarding the didactical set-up in literature. Our focus was on important attributes of cases we had to implement and on principles of effective instruction to keep in mind. Much work on inductive teaching is based on a constructivist view which assumes that meaning is created from experiences where interaction with others plays an essential role [26]. In this context, some principles for effective instruction were identified and summarized in [21]. We applied these principles as follows:

- "*Instruction should begin with content and experiences likely to be familiar to the students, so they can make connections to their existing knowledge structures. New material should be presented in the context of its intended real-world applications [...]*" - The case study started from concepts, methods and theories introduced in previous courses or modules, which included, e.g., the terminology used in the ERP system of SAP, the flow of the SD process and the information required for this process. New material is motivated by established practice in real-world enterprises.
- "*Material should not be presented in a manner that requires students to alter their cognitive models abruptly and drastically. [...]*"- Both, case material and task to be performed, build upon knowledge from previous modules and the theories, terminology and methods continually established in these modules. Change in this knowledge happens gradually when students realize that distributed execution of the SD process requires different rights assigned to roles and that exceptions in processes are common and have to be treated by additional work steps or communication with the partners involved in the process. Thus, students frequently have to revisit essential concepts, improving their cognitive models with each visit.
- "*Instruction should require students to fill in gaps and extrapolate material presented by the instructor. [...]*"- The case description by intention is not fully exhaustive, leaves some gaps and requires additional tasks. These tasks can partly be completed by studying additional documentation and partly require interpretation and extrapolation of case material. For the students this means that the instructors and the provided material no longer are the primary sources of required information, which causes self-learning activities of the students.
- "*Instruction should involve students working together in small groups. [...]*"- The case includes elements of collaborative and cooperative learning in student groups with different complementary competence backgrounds.

For the actual case development, we implemented the core attributes of cases identified by [27]:

- Relevant: Goals and objectives of the case were stated explicitly to help students understand the relevance. The setting of the case was described in text and enriched with real world examples in an accompanying lecture. The case was developed with the previous knowledge of the students in mind to address learner level appropriate for the participation students.

- Realistic: the case was derived from an authentic real-world scenario avoiding over-simplification or too many uncommon features. The case description included small parts not necessarily relevant for the tasks (distractors). The full scope of the case becomes only clear when working on it, i.e. the content is gradually disclosed.
- Engaging: the SD process and role distribution on different locations opens multiple perspectives and different variations caused by the possible exceptions and required interactions with other parties. This makes the content rich and requires the student groups' engagement.
- Challenging: how to solve the built-in difficulty is not obvious but requires study of material and communication with other team members. The case structure also allows different ways to solve certain problems.
- Instructional: the case is anchored in previous teaching modules and prior knowledge of the students. Feedback from the instructors to the students is either possible on demand (tutor) or at defined steps in the process (assessment of results). Teaching aids including documentation and help systems are provided.

At the beginning of Sect. 4, learning objectives have been introduced. Our didactical approach and the case developed will support achievement of the learning objectives as follows: The ERP usage skills and knowledge of the sales and distribution process are strengthened by the need to go beyond standard tasks described in the step-by-step instructions. The process execution progress should be tracked to ensure communication among the distributed teams and to comply with the reporting requirements. The student teams work together thus improving their teamwork skills reinforced by working in the international environment. By using the structured case requirements and instructions, the students also learn about design of ERP implementation artefacts. The technical objective of understanding roles and permissions in the ERP systems is achieved by limiting a number of functions each student team can perform.

5 Technical Approach

In order to achieve learning outcomes, the standard GBI training instructions were extended and restructured, alternative variants of ERP setup were identified and appropriate user roles were created in the ERP system.

5.1 Extended Case Study

The international ERP case is based on the standard GBI case. The standard case is extended for application in the international environment (Fig. 2). It covers the sales and distribution process starting with a customer inquiry and finishing with customer payment. It is assumed that GBI has outsourced several business functions to another country. The operations in another country are performed by a business services provider on behalf of GBI. The outsourcing service provider company is called GBI BPO. GBI is responsible for the customer relationship management and billing activities, while

GBI is responsible for preparing initial sales documents and the warehousing activities. Activities performed in one country depend upon activities completed in other country. The process involves Sales and Distribution (SD), Materials Management (MM) and Financial Accounting (FI) activities.

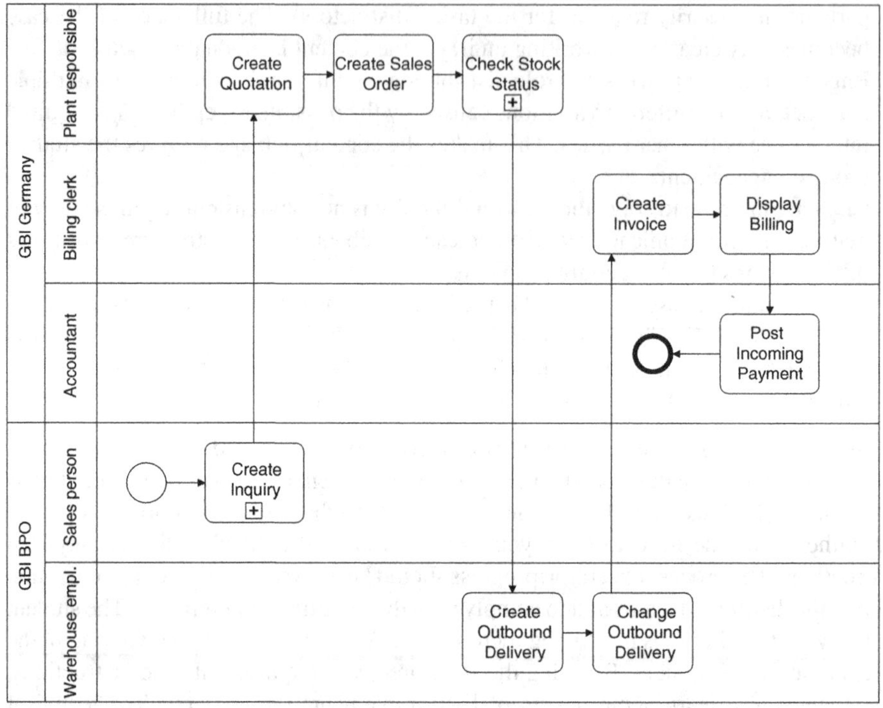

Fig. 2. The international sales and distribution process.

The international ERP process is initiated by one of the GBI customers inquiring about buying bicycles (Fig. 2). In the case of a new customer or changing customer contact information, the customer master data are updated (a part of the Create Inquiry sub-process). A new customer can only be created by the Plat responsible but customer data also can be changed by the Sales person. The customer also requests GBI to issue a legally binding sales quotation. During the process, employees use SAP ERP reporting and analytic functions to analyze the sales process. For instance, the employees evaluate the order probability of success and check the stock level. Once the customer has accepted the quotation, a sales order is created and the shipping and billing activities are initiated. The Warehouse employee creates an outbound delivery document and indicating the materials pick-up data in this document. The Billing clerk creates an invoice for the materials delivered, and the Accountant settles the invoice by posting incoming payments. If customers request products, which are currently not available in the stock, than the procurement processes should be invoked. The procurement operations are performed by GBI BPO.

5.2 Design of Instructions

Given that the students already have had an introduction into working with the ERP system following the standard GBI guidelines, the international GBI instructions are created to resemble ERP implementation specification documents rather than the step-by-step instructions. That is intended to promote self-learning and deeper understanding. At the same time, the students always can consult the standard GBI training materials.

In a fashion similar to ERP specification documents, each process activity is described by providing:

1. Short description,
2. Role performing the activity,
3. Input received from the previous activity,
4. Tasks,
5. Results of the activity execution and
6. Data definitions specifying data values to complete the tasks in the ERP system.

Additionally, scenarios to be explored are defined and assignments to be completed are given. The assignments' completion results are reported using a reporting template. This template defines main outcomes of the activity execution to be reported.

The activity execution tasks and the data definitions are the most important parts of the instructions. A sample definition of tasks in a form of the BPMN diagram is shown in Fig. 3. The sample elaborates the Create Inquiry activity. The corresponding data definition is given in Table 2. For instance, the customer information should be provided to create an inquiry. Meaning and purpose of these tasks are explained in the instructions. However, the students are left to their own devices to choose appropriate features of the ERP system to perform the task. Some of the data definitions have constant values while

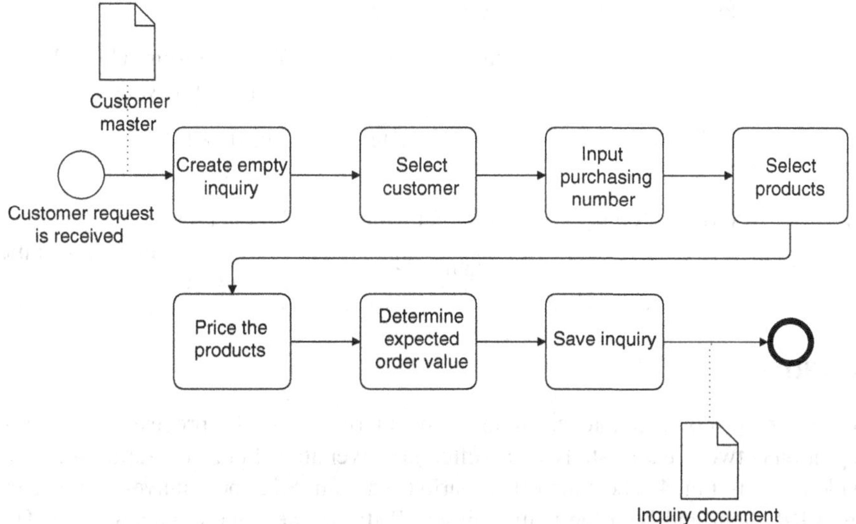

Fig. 3. Elaboration of tasks of the Create Inquiry activity.

others are taken from the individual assignment given to the students or chosen by the students themselves.

Table 2. Input data for performing tasks of the Create Inquiry activity.

Nr	Data item	Value	Description
Task 1			
1	Inquiry type	IN	A classification that distinguishes between different types of sales document.
2	Sales organization	US East	An organizational unit responsible for the sale of certain products or services.
3	Distribution channel	WH	
4	Division	Bicycles	
Tasks 2, 3, 4			
5	Customer	<customer>	Customer from the initial data of the assignment
6	PO number	<any string>	Number that the customer uses to uniquely identify a purchasing document
7	PO day	<today's date>	
8	Valid from	<today's date>	The date from which the inquiry is valid.
9	Valid to	<today's date + 30 days>	The date till which the inquiry is valid.
10	Inquiry items	<product name> <quantity>	Product name and quantity from the initial data of the assignment

5.3 ERP Setup

The ERP setup should enable execution of the international sales process by providing integration between teams studying at different universities. Four integration scenarios are identified in Fig. 4. The simplest scenario (a) assumes that both universities use the same ERP client and both the main unit and BSP use the same company code. This scenario implies that the identical configuration is used and there is no need establishing an information integration link. The single client two company codes scenario (b) implies that both companies might have different configuration allowing to represent specific localization requirements while application integration is not necessary. The remaining two scenarios (c) and (d) include application integration and most closely resemble real-life execution of cross-enterprise business processes.

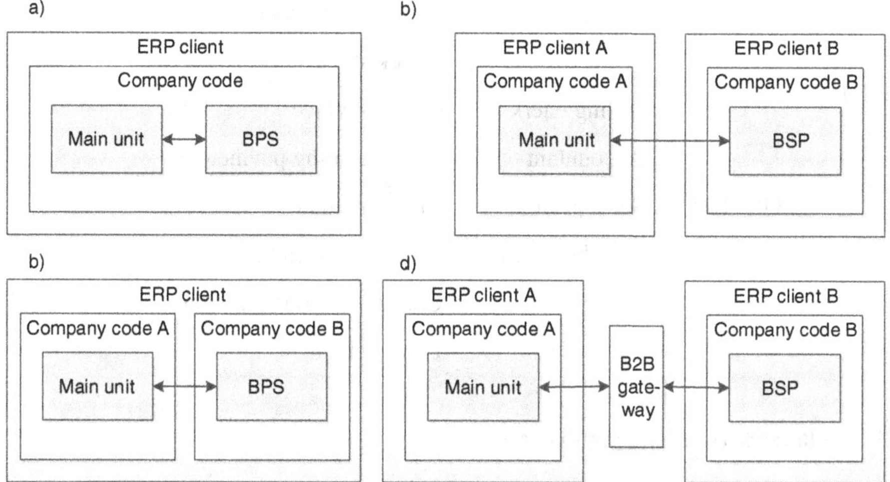

Fig. 4. Integration scenarios.

Currently, the simplest scenario of integration is used implying that both universities use the same ERP client and work within a single company code though with limited permissions to execute certain tasks as described in the next section.

5.4 Role Setup

Every university involved in the case represents one of the companies (i.e., GBI or GBI BPO). Every company is responsible for a certain list of activities, and these activities are performed by certain role in the company (Table 3).

To delimitate the roles, two composite SAP ERP roles are create. The composite SAP ERP role SAP_GBI_SD_MAIN is assigned to GBI and the composite SAP ERP role SAP_GBI_SD_BPO is assigned to GBI BPO. Thus, every company can perform only activities assigned to their composite role (e.g., Create inquiry is available only to GBI BPO). There is no separation of roles within the company (e.g., Plat representative and Billing clerk use the same composite role SAP_GBI_SD_MAIN).

Table 3. Assignment of the roles between GBI and GBI BPO.

Company	Role	Activity
GBI	Plant rep.	Create new customer
		Create quotation
		Create sales order
		Check stock status
	Billing Clerk	Create invoice
	Accountant	Post incoming payment
GBI BPO	Sales person	Create inquiry
	Warehouse Emp.	Create outbound delivery
		Change outbound delivery
		Procurement

5.5 Collaborative Learning Process

The international ERP collaborative learning takes place in three stages: (1) kick-off; (2) process execution; and (3) evaluation. During the kick-off phase, an introductory lecture on international ERP is given, teams of students are formed and individual assignment is given to the teams. The introductory lecture gives an overview of the case study and explains the collaborative learning process.

Students organize teams of 3–4 students at both universities. The teams are randomly paired together and they exchange the contact information. The individual assignment is given to each pair of the teams. The individual assignments represent three different customer inquiries and it includes cases of a new customer and out-of-stock situations.

Execution of fulfillment processes is initiated by GBI BPO and subsequently every team has 2 working days for completing its activities. During the evaluation phase, the teams finalize the process execution report and fill out a questionnaire providing their feedback on the assignment.

6 Evaluation

The international ERP case study is evaluated using a qualitative assessment and in practice. In the qualitative assessment, elements of the didactical and technical approaches are evaluated according to their expected contribution to the learning objectives. The practical evaluation is performed by actually using the case in the studies and gathering students' feedback.

6.1 Qualitative Assessment

The teaching objectives were formulated in Sect. 4. The didactical and technical techniques described in Sects. 4 and 5, respectively, contribute to achieving these objectives. The expected contributions are summarized in Table 4. The didactical and technical techniques presumably cover all learning objectives. The technically oriented objectives such as process tracking, data retrieval and access rights are achieved using the technical

Table 4. Techniques used to achieve the learning objectives.

Learning objectives	Contributing didactical and technical techniques
Strengthening knowledge of the sales and distribution process	Instructions begin with content and experiences familiar to the student
	Extension of the familiar case
Ability to track the process execution progress	Design of instructions including reporting requirements
Ability to use various data retrieval and lookup methods in SAP ERP	Finding information created by other team members
Ability to use various sales and distribution features provided in SAP ERP	Extrapolation of material presented by the instructor
	Dealing with exceptional occurring during the process execution
	Observing different features used by team members
Improving communication skills and foreign language skills	Students work together in teams
	International pairs of team perform the process and are jointly responsible for process execution
Business process execution in the collaborative setting	Alteration of cognitive model
	ERP setup to represent B2B links among the companies involved in process execution
	Data input/output dependencies among the process's activities performed by different team members
Understanding of roles and access rights in SAP ERP	The restricted access rights are used

means. The broader objectives of strengthening process knowledge, usage of different features, communication and collaboration are achieved by combing the didactical and technical methods. The learning process and progress towards achieving the learning objectives is guided by combining familiarity with the case and the need to change cognitive models and extrapolate information provided in the case. Teaming-up students from different countries strengthens communication skills, makes ERP usage more realistic and exposes students to different backgrounds and styles of work.

6.2 Practical Experiences

The international ERP assignment was used in the study process in Fall of 2014. 46 students organized in 7 teams and every university participated in the exercise. All 7 pairs of the team were able to complete the process using data from at least two initial customer inquiries though 3 teams were not able to complete the process using data from one initial customer inquiry because of incorrectly setup master data or lack of coordination in inventory replenishment.

The learning experience is evaluated by summarizing responses from the questionnaire (Table 5). The students mostly agree with statements from the questionnaire. Several questions indicate that the international ERP exercise was more engaging led to better understanding of the SAP ERP systems and the sales process. However, a significant number of students indicate that having specific roles did not improve their understanding of the sales process execution in the ERP system. The students stated that actions of the other team were not sufficiently transparent. This issue could be resolved by having the team to switch their roles. There is also a significant spread of options concerning the improvement of problem-solving skills. On several occasions troubleshooting was done remotely by the instructors. It is suggested that it should be done jointly by the instructors and the students' team working together. Not all team interacted smoothly and this issue could be resolved by organizing an initial virtual get-together for the team members from all universities so that they can discuss their background and studying approach.

A number of potential improvements in the instructions and organization of the collaborative learning process were also identified to reduce thè need for frequent outside assistance from the instructors.

The learning objectives stated in Sect. 3 were achieved. The knowledge of the sales process was improved by resolving different exceptional situations not considered in the standard GBI case. The teams were able to track the process execution and to exchange the necessary process execution data as well as to submit the final report. The students had very intense exchanges and jointly worked on problem solving. They experienced significant peer pressure to complete their activities on time and they approached that very dutifully. The cases of peer learning were observed both within the team and among team in both universities. The students also experience restrictions imposed by having different roles in the SAP ERP system.

Table 5. The surveying results as a percentage of all answers.

Question	Strongly Agree	Agree	Disagree	Strongly Disagree
International ERP was a more interesting way of studying than traditional exercises	36	42	19	3
Completing International ERP exercises was more complex than completing the standard GBI exercises	46	43	11	0
Completing International ERP exercises required more in-depth understanding of SAP ERP than completing the standard GBI exercises	43	46	9	3
Completing International ERP exercises improved my understanding of SAP ERP system	39	39	11	11
Having specific roles in the process execution improves understanding of the way enterprise applications work.	36	33	19	11
Communication with your other teams was positive	28	47	19	6
International ERP improved my collaboration and problem-solving skills.	17	47	25	11
International ERP consumed more time than I expected.	78	14	8	
We needed to communicate with the other team too often	31	42	19	8
We needed to seek outside assistance (e.g., from instructor) too often.	28	44	17	11

In general, the mix between deductive and inductive teaching methods proved suitable for our teaching module and the international ERP case study. A small part of the lectures was a repetition of content in information systems, ERP systems and process-oriented organizations that already was a part of earlier courses. Most of the lectures were dedicated to prepare case study work.

It is difficult to assess what individual progress and competence development the different students made. Here, we only can rely on the results of the assignments and exams. We also performed the international case study in autumn 2013. In 2013, the participation in the case study was not mandatory for in Rostock from MSc service management, i.e. they were allowed to participate in the e-Business module without the case study. When comparing the exam results between those students participating in the case study and those not participating, the results for the participating ones were much better in the ERP part. This is not surprising; nevertheless it indicates a certain value of the case study for learning success.

7 Conclusion

The international ERP case study was designed with a combination of deductive and inductive teaching methods in order to support achieving a broad range of learning outcomes. For this purpose, the case as such had to be challenging, engaging and realistic. Thus, we decided to provide a realistic representation of business process execution using ERP systems in the international environment and to encourage collaborative learning between student groups from both universities. The evaluation results suggest that the participating students recognized the value of having this kind of exercise. Although a number of improvement possibilities have been identified, our overall conclusion is that the case study served its instructional purposes, had a clear added value compared to the traditional teaching material and should be further elaborated and applied.

Future work will be directed to the areas of improvement which have been identified. One of our aims was to promote collaborative problem-solving in teams of students from both universities. This was only partially achieved and we intend to devote additional efforts on making students communicate and collaborate, i.e. to increase cohesion between team at different universities. In this context joint troubleshooting of students with the instructors is also important. Furthermore, we will put more emphasis going through the standard GBI curriculum before starting the case study. The students need to have this initial experience with SAP ERP system and for being able to fully appreciate the specifics of the case study and for being able to successfully complete the international ERP.

The use of a common e-learning platform also is part of the future work, since the e-learning systems currently established at both universities are not compatible and have different functionality. Although the information distributed to the students was identical, it was accessible in different ways which resulted in some information availability gaps.

From a technical perspective, we intend to also consider and integrate other ERP integration scenarios, e.g. based on other cross-company business processes. Such integration scenarios provide a more realistic insight of the way ERP systems are used in inter-company processes and transactions. Furthermore, we investigate the possibility to include examples exposing differences of ERP configurations in different countries.

Further evaluation of the international ERP case study will be performed in Fall 2015 and in collaboration with other universities interested in using the case study. The results of this evaluation will used to validate the qualitative assessment concerning relationships between the teaching approach and the learning outcomes.

Acknowledgements. The work presented in this paper was supported within the projects "KOSMOS (Konstruktion und Organisation eines Studiums in Offenen Systemen)" and "Studium Optimum" funded by the BMBF (Federal Ministry of Education and Research, Germany) and the European Social Funds of the European Union.

References

1. Shehab, E.M., Sharp, M.W., Supramaniam, L., Spedding, T.A.: Enterprise resource planning: an integrative review. Bus. Process Manag. J. **10**(4), 359–386 (2004)
2. Gronau, N.: Trends and future research in enterprise systems. International Workshops, Pre-ICIS 2010, St. Louis, MO, USA, December 12, 2010, Pre-ICIS 2011, Shanghai, China, December 4, 2011, and Pre-ICIS 2012, Orlando, FL, USA, December 16, 2012, Revised Selected Papers, LNBIP, 198, pp. 271–280 (2015)
3. Markus, M.L., Tanis, C., Van Fenema, P.C.: Multisite ERP implementations. Commun. ACM **43**(4), 42–46 (2000)
4. Hepner, M., Dickson, W.: The value of ERP curriculum integration: perspectives from the research. J. Inf. Syst. Educ. **24**(4), 309–326 (2013)
5. Prince, M., Felder, R.: The many faces of inductive teaching and learning. J. Coll. Sci. Teach. **36**(5), 14 (2007)
6. Magal, S.R., Word, J.: Integrated Business Processes with ERP Systems. Wiley, New York (2012)
7. Boyle, T.A., Strong, S.E.: Skill requirements of ERP graduates. J. Inf. Syst. Educ. **17**(4), 403–412 (2006)
8. Mohamed, S., McLaren, T.S.: Probing the Gaps between ERP Education and ERP implementation success factors. AIS Trans. Enterp. Syst. **1**(1), 8–14 (2009)
9. Hayes, G., McGilsky, D.E.: Integrating an ERP System into a BSBA curriculum at central michigan university. Int. J. Qual. Prod. Manag. **7**(1), 12–17 (2007)
10. Cronan, T.P., Douglas, D.E., Schmidt, P., Alnuaimi, O.: ERP Simulation Game: Learning and Attitudes toward SAP Samples of Company "First Time Hires". Technical Report, University of Arkansas (2009)
11. Leger, P.M.: Using a simulation game approach to teach ERP concepts. J. Inf. Syst. Educ. **17**(4), 441–447 (2006)
12. Cronan, T.P., Leger, P.M., Robert, J., Babin, G., Charland, P.: Comparing objective measures and perceptions of cognitive learning in an ERP simulation game: a research note. Simul. Gaming **43**(4), 461–480 (2012)
13. Theling, T., Loos, P.: Teaching ERP systems by a multiperspective approach. In: Association for Information Systems - 11th Americas Conference on Information Systems, AMCIS 2005: A Conference on a Human Scale 3, pp. 1043–1054 (2005)
14. Monk, E., Lycett, M.: Using a computer business simulation to measure effectiveness of enterprise resource planning education on business process comprehension. In: International Conference on Information Systems, ICIS 2011, 3, pp. 1876–1885 (2011)

15. Hussey, M., Wu, B., Xu, X.: Open and closed practicals for enterprise resource planning (ERP) learning. In: Software Industry-Oriented Education Practices and Curriculum Development: Experiences and Lessons, pp. 138–152 (2011)
16. O'Sullivan, J.: Does using real world tools in academia make students better prepared to enter the workforce as compared to a toy type simulation product? A look at ERP in academia, does using this real world tool make a difference to industry?. In: Proceedings IMSCI 2011 - 5th International Multi-Conference on Society, Cybernetics and Informatics, 102 (2011)
17. Moon, Y.B., Chaparro, T.S., Heras, A.D.: Teaching professional skills to engineering students with Enterprise Resource Planning (ERP): an international project. Int. J. Eng. Educ. **23**(4), 759–771 (2007)
18. Pawlowski, J.M., Holtkamp, P.: Towards an internationalization of the information systems curriculum. In: MKWI 2012 - Multiconference Business Information Systems, pp. 437–449 (2012)
19. Chang, H.H., Chou, H.W., Yin, C.P., Lin, C.I.: ERP post-implementation learning, ERP usage and individual performance impact. In: PACIS 2011 Proceedings 35 (2011)
20. Albanese, M.A., Mitchell, S.: Problem-based learning: a review of literature on its outcomes and implementation issues. Acad. Med. **68**, 52–81 (1993)
21. Prince, M.J., Felder, R.M.: Inductive teaching and learning methods: definitions, comparisons, and research bases. J. Eng. Educ. **95**, 123–138 (2006)
22. CEN: European e-Competence Framework 3.0: A common European Framework for ICT Professionals in all industry sectors. CWA 16234:2014 Part 1 (2014)
23. Dillenbourg, P.: What do you mean by collaborative learning? In: Dillenbourg, P. (ed.) Collaborative-learning: Cognitive and Computational Approaches, pp. 1–19. Elsevier, Oxford (1999)
24. Laal, M., Ghodsi, S.: Benefits of collaborative learning. Procedia Soc. Behav. Sci. **31**, 486–490 (2012)
25. Topping, K.J.: Trends in peer learning. Educ. Psychol. **25**(6), 631–645 (2005)
26. Vygotsky, L.S.: Mind in Society. Cambridge. Harvard University Press, Massachusetts (1978)
27. Kim, S., Phillips, W.R., Pinsky, L., Brock, D., Phillips, K., Keary, J.: A conceptual framework for developing teaching cases: a review and synthesis of the literature across disciplines. Med. Educ. **40**, 867–876 (2006)

Artificial Intelligence and Decision Support Systems

International Standard ISO 9001 – A Soft Computing View

José Neves[1(✉)], Ana Fernandes[2], Guida Gomes[1], Mariana Neves[3], António Abelha[1], and Henrique Vicente[4]

[1] Algoritmi, Universidade do Minho, Braga, Portugal
{jneves,abelha}@di.uminho.pt, mguida.mgomes@gmail.com
[2] Departamento de Química, Escola de Ciências e Tecnologia, Universidade de Évora, Évora, Portugal
anavilafernades@gmail.com
[3] Deloitte, London, UK
maneves@deloitte.co.uk
[4] Departamento de Química, Centro de Química de Évora, Escola de Ciências e Tecnologia, Universidade de Évora, Évora, Portugal
hvicente@uevora.pt

Abstract. In order to add value to ISO 9001, a Quality Management Systems that assess, measure, documents, improves, and certify processes to increase productivity, i.e., that transforms business at any level. On the one hand, this work focuses on the development of a decision support system, which will allow companies to be able to meet the needs of customers by fulfilling requirements that reflect either the effectiveness or the non-effectiveness of an organization. On the other hand, many approaches for knowledge representation and reasoning have been proposed using Logic Programming (LP), namely in the area of Model Theory or Proof Theory. In this work it is followed the proof theoretical approach in terms of an extension to the LP language to knowledge representation and reasoning. The computational framework is centered on Artificial Neural Networks to evaluate customer's satisfaction and the degree of confidence that one has on such a happening.

Keywords: International standard ISO 9001 · Knowledge representation and reasoning · Logic programming · Artificial neural networks · Normalization

1 Introduction

In 1987 the International Organization for Standardization (ISO) published the ISO 9000 series of standards. These standards aim to provide guiding principles and tools for the organizations that want, on the one hand, ensure that their products and services meet customers' needs, and one the other hand, guarantee that quality is consistently improved. The ISO 9000 series includes four different standards, namely ISO 9000:2005, ISO 9001:2008, ISO 9004:2009 and ISO 19011:2011. The ISO 9001:2008 addresses the requirements for a quality management system offering the possibility to the companies to demonstrate their capability to deliver products and services that fulfill customer and regulatory requirements and aims to increase customer satisfaction [1].

S. Hammoudi et al. (Eds.): ICEIS 2015, LNBIP 241, pp. 153–167, 2015.
DOI: 10.1007/978-3-319-29133-8_8

Quality Management (QM) is one of the practices that can bring competitive advantages to businesses, i.e., the implementation of QM effectively influences enterprises performance [2, 3]. Indeed, corporations that implement QM aim to add value to their customers, i.e., improvement of processes and products quality leads to reduce their costs and increase their profits [4, 5].

The ISO 9001 standard does not refer to the compliance with a given goal or result. This standard does not aim to measure the quality of the enterprises' products or services but rather point out the need to systematize a set of procedures and document such implementation [6]. The implementation of ISO 9001 standard is voluntary, although in some sectors it has become quasi-obligatory [6].

The International Standard ISO 9001 is applicable to all sectors and organizations, regardless of their type, size, product, or service. The standard is interpretative, not prescriptive, offering an independent system of managing and evaluation of companies' performance, allowing to improve either their management practices or their global recognition. ISO 9001 is based on eight quality management principles, which are incorporated within the requirements of the standard, and can be applied to develop organizational performance [1], in terms of:

- Customer focus, i.e., the customers are the main base of the organizations and therefore the companies should understand current and future customer needs, should meet customer requirements and make efforts to exceed customer expectations;
- Leadership, i.e., the leaders should define exactly the goals and the course of the organization. They must create the internal conditions in which workers can become involved in reaching the organization's goals;
- Involvement of people, i.e., the heart of an organization are the people and their participation permits their capacities to be used for the benefit of the organizations;
- Process approach, i.e., the management of the activities and resources as a process is the more efficient way to obtain a desired result;
- System approach to management, i.e., the identification, knowledge and management of interrelated processes as a system contributes to the effectiveness and efficiency of the organizations in attaining their objectives;
- Continual improvement, i.e., the continuous enhancement of the overall performance should be a permanent goal of the organization;
- Factual approach to decision making, i.e., the analysis of data/information is the fulcrum of effective decisions; and
- Mutually beneficial supplier relationships, i.e., the organizations and their suppliers are mutually dependent. Relationships reciprocally advantageous increase the ability of both to create value.

The derivative benefits are no less important, and include enhanced reputation, repeat business, ability to compete more effectively globally, both on quality and price, access to new markets, and improved customer and supplier relationships, enhanced employee morale, and better management control [7, 8]. According to Tarí [9] these benefits may be catalogued into internal and external. The former ones include improvements in corporate processes, having positive effects on operational and work forces issues (e.g. increase in productivity, improvement in efficiency, reduction in costs, training).

The external benefits, in turn, relate to effects on customers and society in general (e.g. customer satisfaction, better relationships with stakeholders, improved image).

The literature on ISO 9001 starts to appear at the end of 1980s and a large set of literature can be found nowadays. Some studies reveal positive effects on several performance metrics [10–12]. Contrariwise, a few studies highlight the negative effects of this standard on the performance of organizations [13, 14]. Other studies refer that ISO 9001 has no significant impact on performance [15–19] or has a contradictory impact, i.e., some organizations show benefits and others do not or, on the other hand, exhibit positive effects for some financial indicators and not for others [20–23].

The stated above shows that it is difficult to predict the organization's efficacy (or lack of efficacy), since it should be correlated with numerous variables and requires a multidisciplinary approach. Furthermore, it is necessary to consider different conditions with complex relations among them, where the available data may be incomplete, contradictory and even unknown. In order to overcome these drawbacks, the present work reports the founding of a computational framework that uses knowledge representation and reasoning techniques to set the structure of the information system and the associate inference mechanisms. We will centre on a *Logic Programming* (*LP*) method to knowledge representation and reasoning [24, 25], that is object of a formal proof, and look at a soft computing approach to knowledge processing based on Artificial Neural Networks (ANN) [26]. The requirements of ISO 9001 that can better predict the efficacy of an organization were selected. We take as example a company in the area of training where two management indicators, namely complaints and customer satisfaction were used and attained by questionnaires. Both indicators consider several items, namely Trainees' General Information; Trainees' Complaints; Quality of Support Materials; and Inquiries of Trainees' Satisfaction, which will be described later.

This paper is organized into five sections. In the former one an introduction to the problem presented is made. Then the proposed approach to knowledge representation and reasoning is introduced. In the third and fourth sections is introduced a case study and presented a solution to the problem. Finally, in the last section the most relevant conclusions are termed and the possible directions for future work are outlined.

2 Knowledge Representation and Reasoning

Knowledge and belief are generally incomplete, contradictory, or even error sensitive, being desirable to use formal tools to deal with the problems that arise from the use of partial, contradictory, ambiguous, imperfect, nebulous, or missing information [24, 25]. Some wide-ranging models have been presented where uncertainty is associated to the application of Probability Theory [27], Fuzzy Set Theory [28], Similarities [29, 30]. Other approaches for knowledge representation and reasoning have been proposed using the Logic Programming (*LP*) paradigm, namely in the area of Model Theory [31, 32] and Proof Theory [24, 25].

In present work it is followed the proof theoretical approach in terms of an extension to the *LP* language to knowledge representation and reasoning. An *Extended Logic Program* (*ELP*) is a finite set of clauses in the form:

$$
\begin{aligned}
&\{ \\
&\quad p \leftarrow p_1, \cdots, p_n, not\ q_1, \cdots, not\ q_m \\
&\quad ?\,(p_1, \cdots, p_n, not\ q_1, \cdots, not\ q_m)\ \ (n, m \geq 0) \\
&\quad exception_{p_1} \\
&\quad \ldots \\
&\quad exception_{p_j}\ \ (j \leq m, n) \\
&\}::\ scoring_{value}
\end{aligned}
$$

where "*?*" is a domain atom denoting falsity, the p_i, q_j, and p are classical ground literals, i.e., either positive atoms or atoms preceded by the classical negation sign ¬ [24]. According to this formalism, every program is associated with a set of abducibles [31, 32] given here in the form of exceptions to the extensions of the predicates that make the program. The term $scoring_{value}$ stands for the relative weight of the extension of a specific ***predicate*** with respect to the extensions of the peers ones that make the overall program.

In order to evaluate the knowledge that stems from a logic program an evaluation of the *Quality-of-Information* (*QoI*) was set in dynamic environments aiming at decision-making purposes [33, 34]. The objective is to build a quantification process of *QoI* and an assessment of the argument values of a given predicate with relation to their domains (here understood as *Degree-of-Confidence* (*DoC*), which stands for one's belief that its unknown values fits into the arguments ranges, taking into account their domains). The *QoI* with respect to the extension of a $predicate_i$ will be given by a truth-value in the interval [0,1] (for a detail discussion please see [35]).

The universe of discourse can be engendered according to the information given in the logic programs that endorse the information about the problem under consideration, according to productions of the type:

$$extensions - of - predicate_i = \bigcup_{1 \leq j \leq m} clause_j\,(x_1, \cdots, x_n)\ ::QoI_i::DoC_i \tag{1}$$

where ∪ and m stand, respectively, for set union and the cardinality of the extension of $predicate_i$. On the other hand, DoC_i denotes one's confidence on the attribute's values of a particular term of the extension of $predicate_i$, whose evaluation is given in [35].

3 A Case Study

As a case study, consider a database given in terms of the extensions of the relations (or tables) depicted in Fig. 1, which stands for a situation where one has to manage information about trainees' satisfaction assessment. Under this scenario some incomplete and/or unknown data is also available. For instance, in the *Trainees' Satisfaction* table, the opinion of trainee 1 about *Support Materials* is unknown, while the *Inquiries of Trainees' Satisfaction* ranges in the interval [16, 21]. In *Trainees' Complaints* table, 0 (zero) denotes absence and 1 (one) denotes existence of complaints, while in the *Gender* column of *Trainees' General Information* Table 0 (zero) and 1 (one) stand, respectively, for *female* and *male*. The issues of *Quality of Support Materials* and *Inquiries of Trainees' Satisfaction* tables range in the interval [0,5], i.e., range between Inadequate (0) and Excellent (5). In *Trainee Status* Column of the *Trainees' Satisfaction* Table 0, 1 and 2 stands respectively for *dropped out*, *ongoing* and *course finished*. The values presented in *Opinion About the Course* and *Willingness to Recommend the Company* columns ranges in the interval [0, 10]. In the former case 0 (zero) stands for *Strongly Negative Opinion* and 10 (ten) denotes a *Strongly Positive Opinion*. In the last case 0 (zero) stands for *None* and 10 (ten) denotes *Absolutely Sure*. The values presented in the remaining columns are the sum of the respective tables, ranging between [0, 6], [0, 10] and [0, 25] respectively for *Complaints*, *Support Materials* and *Inquiries of Trainees' Satisfaction* columns.

Now, applying the rewritten algorithm presented in [35], to all the tables that make the *Extension of the Relational Model for Trainees' Satisfaction Assessment* (Fig. 1), excluding of such a process the *Trainees' Satisfaction* one, and looking to the *DoCs* values obtained in this manner, it is possible to set the arguments of the predicate referred to below, that also denotes the objective function with respect to the problem under analyze.

$$satisfaction\!:\!Age,\, G_{ender},\, T_{rainee}S_{tatus},\, O_{pinion}A_{boutthe}C_{ourse},\\ W_{illingnessto}R_{ecommendthe}C_{ompany},\, Compl_{aints},\, S_{upport}M_{aterials}\\ I_{nquiriesof}T_{rainees'}S_{atisfaction} \rightarrow \{0,1\}$$

where 0 (zero) and 1 (one) denote, respectively, the truth values *false* and *true*.

The arguments of *satisfaction* predicate where set by a process of sensibility analysis, where the arguments chosen where those that present the higher DoC_s values, i.e., the ones that have a greater influence on the output of the objective function referred to above. Their terms also make the training and validation sets of the Artificial Neural Network (ANN) given in Fig. 2.

Trainees' General Information					
#	Age	Gender	Trainee Status	Opinion About the Course	Willingness to Recommend the Company
1	27	Female	finished	9	8
2	32	Male	dropped out	3	2
…	…	…	…	…	…
473	21	Female	ongoing	[8,9]	⊥

Trainees' Complaints						
#	Billing	Trainer	Infrastructures	Customer Service	Sale Arguments	Support Materials
1	0	0	0	0	0	0
2	1	1	1	0	1	1
…	…	…	…	…	…	…
473	1	0	1	0	0	0

Trainees' Satisfaction								
#	Age	Gender	Trainee Status	Opinion About the Course	Willingness to Recommend the Company	Complaints	Support Materials	Inquiries of Trainees' Satisfaction
1	27	0	2	9	8	0	⊥	[16, 21]
2	32	1	0	3	2	5	4	12
…	…	…	…	…	…	…	…	…
473	21	0	1	[8, 9]	⊥	2	8	22

Quality of Support Materials		
#	Syllabus	Materials
1	⊥	⊥
2	2	2
…	…	…
473	4	4

Inquiries of Trainees' Satisfaction					
#	Guidance	Trainer	Image of the Training Course	Customer Service	Methodologies
1	4	4	⊥	4	4
2	2	2	3	3	2
…	…	…	…	…	…
473	5	5	3	4	5

Fig. 1. Extension of the relational model for Trainees' satisfaction assessment.

Now, let us consider a record that presents the feature vector ($Age = 24$, $G_{ender} = 1$, $TS = 1$, $OAC = \perp$, $WRC = 7$, $Compl = 0$, $SM = 7$, $ITS = [14, 19]$), to which it is applied the rewritten algorithm presented in [35]. One may have:

Begin,

The predicate's extensions that make the Universe-of-Discourse for the record under observation are set ←

{

$$\neg\, satisfaction\,(Age, G, TS, OAC, WRC, Compl, SM, ITS) \leftarrow not\ satisfaction\,(Age, G, TS, OAC, WRC, Compl, SM, ITS)$$

$$satisfaction\Big(\underbrace{24,\ 1,\ 1,\ \perp,\ 7,\ 0,\ 7,\ [14, 19]}_{attribute's\ values}\Big) :: 1 :: DoC$$

$$\underbrace{[16, 34][0, 1][0, 2][0, 10][0, 10][0, 6][0, 10][0, 25]}_{attribute's\ domains}$$

}:: 1

The attribute's values ranges are rewritten ←

{

$$\neg\, satisfaction\,(Age, G, TS, OAC, WRC, Compl, SM, ITS) \leftarrow not\ satisfaction\,(Age, G, TS, OAC, WRC, Compl, SM, ITS)$$

$$satisfaction\Big(\underbrace{[24,24], [1,1], [1,1], [0,10], [7, 7], [0,0], [7,7], [14, 19]}_{attribute's\ values}\Big) :: 1 :: DoC$$

$$\underbrace{[16,34]\ [0, 1]\ [0, 2]\ [0, 10][0, 10][0, 6][0, 10]\ [0, 25]}_{attribute's\ domains}$$

}:: 1

The attribute's boundaries are set to the interval [0,1] ←

{

$$\neg\, satisfaction\,(Age, G, TS, OAC, WRC, Compl, SM, ITS) \leftarrow not\ satisfaction\,(Age, G, TS, OAC, WRC, Compl, SM, ITS)$$

$$satisfaction\Big(\underbrace{[0.4,0.4], [1,1], [0.5,0.5], [0,1], [0.7, 0.7], [0,0], [0.7,0.7], [0.6, 0.8]}_{attribute's\ values}\Big) :: 1 :: DoC$$

$$\underbrace{[0,1]\ \ [0, 1]\ \ [0, 1]\ \ [0, 1]\ \ [0, 1]\ \ [0, 1]\ \ [0, 1]\ \ [0, 1]}_{attribute's\ domains}$$

}:: 1

The DoC's values are evaluated ←

{

$$\neg\, satisfaction\,(Age, G, TS, OAC, WRC, Compl, SM, ITS) \leftarrow not\ satisfaction\,(Age, G, TS, OAC, WRC, Compl, SM, ITS)$$

$$satisfaction\Big(\underbrace{1,\ 1,\ 1,\ 0,\ 1,\ 1,\ 1,\ 0.98}_{attribute's\ confidence\ values}\Big) :: 1 :: 0.87$$

$$\underbrace{[0.4, 0.4][1, 1][0.5, 0.5][0, 1][0.7, 0.7][0, 0][0.7, 0.7][0.6, 0.8]}_{attribute's\ values\ ranges\ once\ normalized}$$

$$\underbrace{[0, 1]\ \ [0, 1]\ [0, 1]\ \ [0, 1]\ [0, 1]\ [0, 1]\ [0, 1]\ \ [0, 1]}_{attribute's\ domains\ once\ normalized}$$

}:: 1

End.

where its terms make the training and validation sets of the Artificial Neural Network (ANN) given in Fig. 2.

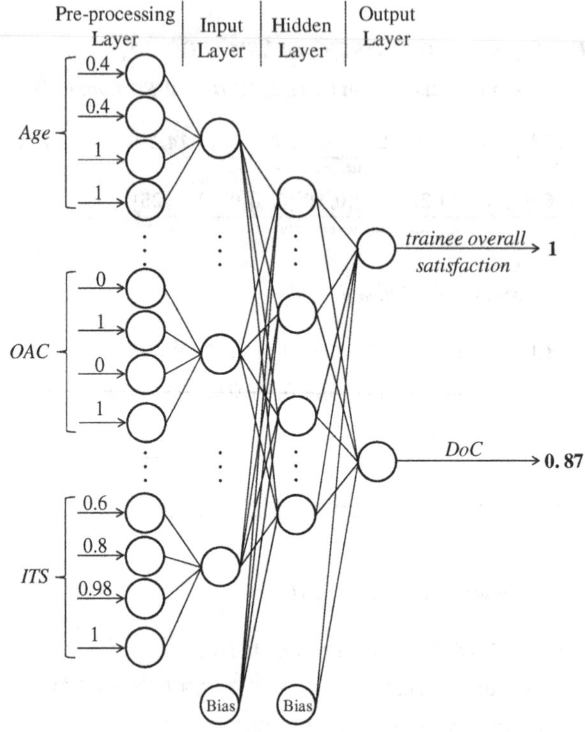

Fig. 2. The *ANN* topology.

Artificial Neural Networks. The previously presented model of trainees' satisfaction assessment shows how all the information is integrated into a normalized form. In this section, it is set a soft computing approach to model the universe of discourse based on ANNs, which are used to structure data and capture complex relationships between inputs and outputs [36, 37].

One of the main contributions of this work is related with the ability to deal with incomplete data/information. Besides to a classifier that enables to estimate the trainees' satisfaction, the approach intends also obtain the *DoC* associated to this inference. Thus, is necessary apply an algorithm that allows more than one output variable. The choice fell on ANNs due to their dynamics characteristics like adaptability, robustness and flexibility. ANNs simulate the structure of the human brain, being populated by multiple layers of neurons, with a valuable set of activation functions. As an example, let us consider the case listed above, where one may have a situation in which the trainees' satisfaction assessment is needed. In Fig. 2 it is shown how the normalized values of the interval boundaries and their *DoCs* and *QoIs* values (i.e., the tuple (*minimum*, *maximum*, *DoC*, *QoI*)) work as inputs to the ANN. Exemplifying with the arguments *Age*, *OAC* and *ITS* of the *satisfaction* predicate, one may have (0.4, 0.4, 1, 1); (0, 1, 0, 1); and (0.6,

0.8, 0.98, 1). The output depicts an evaluation of trainee's overall satisfaction, plus the confidence that one has on such a happening.

In this study 473 records were considered, coming from a vocational training company of the Lisbon region. The trainees' age average was 24.9 years, ranging from 16 to 34 years old. The gender distribution was 47.8 % and 52.2 % for male and female, respectively. Regarding the trainees' situation, 27.9 % completed their training, 11.8 % dropped out and 60.3 % are attending training. One hundred and seventeen trainees stated that the overall satisfaction about their training was negative, i.e., 24.7 % of the cases. The dataset holds information about the factors considered critical in the estimation of the trainees' satisfaction. Eighteen variables were selected allowing one to have a multi-variable dataset with 473 cases. These variables were grouped into four main categories, i.e., *Trainees' General Information*, *Trainees' Complaints*, *Quality of Support Materials* and *Inquiries of Trainees' Satisfaction* (Fig. 1). Thus, the number of variables used as input of the *ANN* model was reduced to eight (Table 1), i.e., the predicate's arguments were workout according to a process of sensibility analysis, based on their *DoC*s values. A technique used to determine how different values of an independent variable will impact a particular dependent variable under a given set of assumptions.

Table 1. Variables characterization.

Variable	Description	Data type
Age	Trainee's age	Numeric
Gender	Trainee's gender	Nominal
Trainee status	Reports the status of the trainees in the course (dropped out; course ongoing or course finished)	Nominal
Opinion about the course	Includes information related with the opinion of the trainees about the course, expressed in the interval [0, 10], where 0 stands for strongly negative opinion and 10 denotes a strongly positive opinion	Numeric
Willingness to recommend the company	Presents information related with the trainees' disposition to suggest the training company, expressed in the range [0, 10], where 0 denotes none while 10 stands for absolutely sure	Numeric
Complaints	Includes complaints presented by the trainees related with billing, trainer, infrastructures, customer service, sale arguments and/or support materials	Numeric
Support materials	Includes the issues related with the appreciation of the trainees about the syllabus and the support materials	Numeric
Inquiries of Trainees' Satisfaction	Presents the satisfaction of the trainees related with items like guidance, trainer, image of the training course, customer service and methodologies	Numeric

To ensure statistical significance of the attained results, 30 (thirty) experiments were applied in all tests. In each simulation, the available data was randomly divided into two mutually exclusive partitions, i.e., the training set with 400 of the available records, used during the modelling phase, and the validation set with the remaining 73 cases, used after training in order to evaluate the model performance and to validate it. The dataset used in the training phase it was divided in exclusive subsets through the 10-folds cross validation. In the implementation of the respective dividing procedures, ten executions were performed for each one of them. The back propagation algorithm was applied in the learning process of the *ANN*. The activation function used in the pre-processing layer was the *identity* one. In the other layers was used the *sigmoid* activation function.

A common tool to evaluate the results presented by the classification models is the coincidence matrix, a matrix of size $L \times L$, where L denotes the number of possible classes (two in the present case). Table 2 present the coincidence matrix (the values denote the average of the 30 experiments). A perusal of Table 2 shows that the model accuracy was 96.5 % (386 instances correctly classified in 400) and 90.4 % (66 instances correctly classified in 73) respectively for training and validation sets.

Table 2. The coincidence matrix for the ANN model.

Target	**Predictive**			
	Training set		Validation set	
	True (1)	False (0)	True (1)	False (0)
True (1)	TP = 293	FN = 8	TP = 50	FN = 5
False (0)	FP = 6	TN = 93	FP = 2	TN = 16

Based on coincidence matrix it is possible to compute sensitivity, specificity, Positive Predictive Value (PPV) and Negative Predictive Value (NPV) of the classifier:

$$sensitivity = TP/\,(TP + FN) \tag{2}$$

$$specificity = TN/\,(TN + FP) \tag{3}$$

$$PPV = TP/\,(TP + FP) \tag{4}$$

$$NPV = TN/\,(TN + FN) \tag{5}$$

where *TP*, *FN*, *TN* and *FP* stand, respectively, for *true positive*, *false negative*, *true negative* and *false positive*. In a few words, sensitivity and specificity are statistical measures of the performance of a binary classifier, while sensitivity measures the proportion of true positives that are correctly identified as such. Specificity measures the proportion of true negatives that are correctly identified. Moreover, it is necessary to know the probability of the classifier that give the correct answers. Thus, it is also calculated both *PPV* and *NPV*, while *PPV* stands for the proportion of cases with positive values that were correctly classified, NPV denotes the proportion of cases with negative values that were successfully labeled.

The corresponding *sensitivity*, *specificity*, *PPV* and *NPV* values are displayed in Table 3 for training and validation sets. A perusal of Table 3 shows that *sensitivity* ranges from 97.3 % to 90.9 %, while *specificity* ranges from 93.9 % to 88.9 %. *PPV* ranges from 98.0 % to 96.2 %, while *NPV* ranges from 99.2 % to 76.2 %. Moreover, the Receiver Operating Characteristic (ROC) curves for the training and validation sets are shown in Fig. 3(a). The areas under ROC curves are higher than 0.9 for both cases (0.96 and 0.90 respectively for training and validation sets), denoting that the model exhibits a good performance in the estimation of the trainees' overall satisfaction.

Table 3. Sensitivity, specificity, positive predictive value (PPV) and negative predictive value (NPV) for the ANN model and for the variables *Opinion About the Course* (*OAC*) and *Willingness to Recommend the Company* (*WRC*).

	Sensitivity (%)	Specificity (%)	PPV (%)	NPV (%)
ANN model				
Training set	97.3	93.9	98.0	99.2
Validation set	90.9	88.9	96.2	76.2
Variables OAC and WRC				
OAC	72.5	64.1	86.0	43.4
WRC	68.5	57.3	83.0	37.4

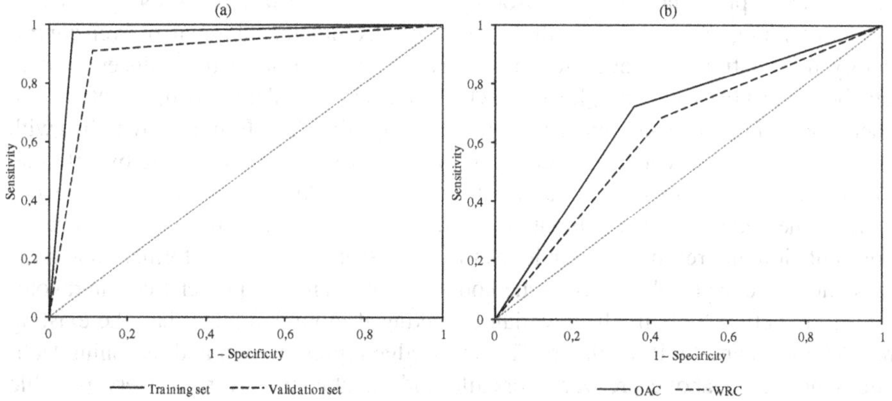

Fig. 3. The ROC curves for training and validation sets (a) and for the variables *Opinion About the Course* (*OAC*) and *Willingness to Recommend the Company* (*WRC*) (b).

In order to evaluate the capabilities of the model presented above, an attempt was made in order to estimate the trainees' overall satisfaction using the variables *opinion about the course* and *willingness to recommend the company*. The results are present in Table 3 and in Fig. 3(b). These results correspond to the best of the tests performed, in which a positive response was considered when the values of the mentioned variables were equal or higher than six.

The accuracy was 70.4 % (333 cases correctly classified in 473) and 65.8 % (311 cases correctly classified in 473) respectively for OAC and WRC, while the areas under ROC curves were 0.68 and 0.63. These results show that the performance of these two variables to discriminate the trainees' overall satisfaction is poor despite the acceptable values obtained for PPV (higher than 80 %). This value can be justified considering that it is the majority class, since the overall satisfaction of 75.4 % of the trainees was positive. Thus, the proposed model that put together the opinion of the trainees about the course and their willingness to recommend the company with other factors such as, age, gender and integrate them with the trainees status, their complaints, their appreciation of the support materials, and the satisfaction of the trainees related with items like guidance, trainer, image of the training course, customer service and methodologies, allowing to be assertive in the estimation of the trainees' overall satisfaction. This model showed a high sensibility, enabling the evaluation of overall satisfaction comparing with the trainees that really claimed a positive opinion as well classifying properly the negative ones (i.e., specificity). Therefore it can be a major contribution to estimate the trainees' overall satisfaction and contribute for the continuous improvement of the quality of the training courses and improve the services provided by the training companies.

4 Conclusions

This work starts with the development of a decision support system to assess trainees' overall satisfaction, centered on a formal framework based on Logic Programming for Knowledge Representation and Reasoning, complemented with an ANN approach to problem solving, which caters for the handling of incomplete, unknown, or even contradictory information. However, to set an early the estimation of the trainees' overall satisfaction is a hard and complex task, which needs to consider many different factors, where some of them are not represented by fully objective data. Being an area filled with incomplete and unknown data, information or knowledge it may be tackled by Artificial Intelligence based methodologies and techniques for problem solving. Indeed, this work presents the founding of a computational framework that uses powerful knowledge representation and reasoning techniques to set the structure of the information and the associate inference mechanisms. A method that brings a new approach that can revolutionize prediction tools in all its variants, making it more complete than the existing methodologies and tools available. The knowledge representation and reasoning techniques presented above are very versatile and capable of covering every possible instance by considering incomplete, contradictory, and even unknown data.

The model presented in this study showed a good performance in the estimation of the trainees' overall satisfaction, since their sensitivity and specificity exhibited values higher than 90 %. These findings were corroborated by the area under ROC curves (> 0.9). The main contribution of this work relies on the fact that at the end, the extensions of the predicates that make the universe of discourse are given in terms of *DoCs* values that stand for one's confidence that the predicates arguments values fit into their observable ranges, taking into account their domains. It also encapsulates in itself a new vision of Multi-value Logics, once a proof of a theorem in a conventional way, is evaluated to the interval [0, 1]. The ANNs were selected due to their dynamics characteristics like adaptability, robustness and flexibility. Future work may recommend that the same problem must be approached using others computational formalisms like Genetic Programming [25], Case Based Reasoning [38] or Particle Swarm [39], just to name a few.

References

1. Portuguese Institute of Quality: NP EN ISO 9001:2008 – quality management systems – requirements, 3rd edn. Portuguese Institute of Quality Edition, Caparica (2008)
2. Parast, M., Adams, S., Jones, E.: Improving Operation- al and business performance in the petroleum industry through quality management. Int. J. Q. Reliab. Manage. **28**, 426–450 (2011)
3. Shahin, A., Dabestani, R.: A feasibility study of the implementation of total quality management based on soft factor. J. Ind. Eng. Manag. **4**, 258–280 (2011)
4. Kaynak, H.: The relationship between total quality management practices and their effects on firm performance. J. Oper. Manage. **21**, 405–435 (2003)
5. Pignanelli, A., Csillag, J.: The impact of quality management on profitability: an empirical study. J. Oper. Supply Chain Manage. **1**, 66–77 (2008)
6. Braun, B.: Building global institutions: the diffusion of management standards in the world economy – an institutional perspective. In: Alvstam, C., Schamp, E. (eds.) Linking Industries Across the World, pp. 3–27. Ashgate, London (2005)
7. Heras, I., Casadesús, M., Dick, G.M.: ISO 9000 certification and the bottom line: a comparative study of the profitability of Basque region companies. Managerial Auditing J. **17**, 72–78 (2002)
8. Terlaak, A., King, A.: The effect of certification with the ISO 9000 quality management standard: a signaling approach. J. Econ. Behav. Organ. **60**, 579–602 (2006)
9. Tarí, J., Azorín, J., Heras, I.: Benefits of the ISO 9001 and ISO 14001 standards: a literature review. J. Ind. Eng. Manag. **5**, 297–322 (2012)
10. Corbett, C.J., Kirsch, D.A.: The financial impact of ISO 9000 certification in the United States: an empirical analysis. Manage. Sci. **51**, 1046–1059 (2005)
11. Naveh, E., Marcus, A.: Achieving competitive advantage through implementing a replicable management standard: Installing and using ISO 9000. J. Oper. Manage. **24**, 1–26 (2005)
12. Levine, D., Toffel, M.: Quality management and job quality: How the ISO 9001 standard for quality management systems affects employees and employers. Manage. Sci. **56**, 978–996 (2010)
13. Aarts, F.M., Vos, E.: The impact of ISO registration on New Zealand firms' performance: a financial perspective. TQM Mag. **13**, 180–191 (2001)
14. Yeung, A.C., Lo, C.K., Cheng, T.C.: Behind the Iron Cage: An Institutional Perspective on ISO 9000 Adoption and CEO Compensation. Organ. Sci. **22**, 1600–1612 (2011)
15. Lima, M., Resende, M., Hasenclever, L.: Quality certification and performance of Brazilian firms: An empirical study. Int. J. Prod. Econ. **66**, 143–147 (2000)
16. Sila, I.: Examining the effects of contextual factors on TQM and performance through the lens of organizational theories: an empirical study. J. Oper. Manage. **25**, 83–109 (2007)

17. Dick, G., Heras, I., Casadesús, M.: Shedding light on causation between ISO 9001 and improved business performance. Int. J. Oper. Prod. Manage. **28**, 687–708 (2008)
18. Martínez-Costa, M., Choi, T.Y., Martínez, J.A., Martínez-Lorente, Á.R.: ISO 9000/1994, ISO 9001/2000 and TQM: The performance debate revisited. J. Oper. Manage. **27**, 495–511 (2009)
19. Singh, P., Power, D., Chuong, S.: A resource dependence theory perspective of ISO 9000 in managing organizational environment. J. Oper. Manage. **29**, 49–64 (2011)
20. Singels, J., Ruel, G., van de Water, H.: ISO 9000 series – Certification and performance. Int. J. Q. Reliab. Manage. **18**, 62–75 (2001)
21. Yahya, S., Goh, W.: The implementation of an ISO 9000 quality system. Int. J. Q. Reliab. Manage. **18**, 941–966 (2001)
22. Terziovski, M., Power, D.: Increasing ISO 9000 certification benefits: a continuous improvement approach. Int. J. Q. Reliab. Manage. **24**, 141–163 (2007)
23. Benner, M.J., Veloso, F.M.: ISO 9000 practices and financial performance: a technology coherence perspective. J. Oper. Manage. **26**, 611–629 (2008)
24. Neves, J.: A logic interpreter to handle time and negation in logic databases. In: Muller, R., Pottmyer, J. (eds.) Proceedings of the 1984 Annual Conference of the ACM on the 5th Generation Challenge, pp. 50–54. Association for Computing Machinery, New York (1984)
25. Neves, J., Machado, J., Analide, C., Abelha, A., Brito, L.: The Halt Condition in Genetic Programming. In: Neves, J., Santos, M.F., Machado, J.M. (eds.) EPIA 2007. LNCS (LNAI), vol. 4874, pp. 160–169. Springer, Heidelberg (2007)
26. Cortez, P., Rocha, M., Neves, J.: Evolving time series forecasting ARMA models. J. Heuristics **10**, 415–429 (2004)
27. Li, R., Bhanu, B., Ravishankar, C., Kurth, M., Ni, J.: Uncertain spatial data handling: modeling, indexing and query. Comput. Geosci. **33**, 42–61 (2007)
28. Schneider, M.: Uncertainty management for spatial data in databases: fuzzy spatial data types. In: Güting, R.H., Papadias, D., Lochovsky, F.H. (eds.) SSD 1999. LNCS, vol. 1651, pp. 330–351. Springer, Heidelberg (1999)
29. Freire, L., Roche, A., Mangin, J.-F.: What is the best similarity measure for motion correction in fMRI time series? IEEE Trans. Med. Imaging **21**, 470–484 (2002)
30. Liao, T.: Clustering of time series data?– A survey. Pattern Recogn. **38**, 1857–1874 (2005)
31. Kakas, A., Kowalski, R., Toni, F.: The role of abduction in logic programming. In: Gabbay, D., Hogger, C., Robinson, I. (eds.) Handbook of Logic in Artificial Intelligence and Logic Programming, vol. 5, pp. 235–324. Oxford University Press, Oxford (1998)
32. Pereira, L.M., Anh, H.T.: Evolution prospection. In: Nakamatsu, K., Phillips-Wren, G., Jain, L.C., Howlett, R.J. (eds.) New Advances in Intelligent Decision Technologies. SCI, vol. 199, pp. 51–63. Springer, Heidelberg (2009)
33. Lucas, P.: Quality checking of medical guidelines through logical abduction. In: Coenen, F., Preece, A., Mackintosh, A. (eds.) Proceedings of AI-2003 (Research and Developments in Intelligent Systems XX), pp. 309–321. Springer, London (2003)
34. Machado, J., Abelha, A., Novais, P., Neves, J., Neves, J.: Quality of service in healthcare units. Int. J. Comput. Aided Eng. Technol. **2**, 436–449 (2010)
35. Neves, J., Fernandes, A., Gomes, G., Neves, J., Neves, M., Vicente, H.: International standard ISO 9001 – an artificial intelligence view. In: Hammoudi, S., Maciaszek, L., Teniente, E. (eds.) Proceedings of the 17th International Conference on Enterprise Information Systems (ICEIS 2015), vol. 1, pp. 421–428. Scitepress – Science and Technology Publications, Lisbon (2015)

36. Vicente, H., Dias, S., Fernandes, A., Abelha, A., Machado, J., Neves, J.: Prediction of the quality of public water supply using artificial neural networks. J. Water Supply: Res. Technol. – AQUA **61**, 446–459 (2012)
37. Vicente, H., Couto, C., Machado, J., Abelha, A., Neves, J.: Prediction of water quality parameters in a reservoir using artificial neural networks. Int. J. Design Nat. Ecodyn. **7**, 309–318 (2012)
38. Carneiro, D., Novais, P., Andrade, F., Zeleznikow, J., Neves, J.: Using case-based reasoning and principled negotiation to provide decision support for dispute resolution. Knowl. Inf. Syst. **36**, 789–826 (2013)
39. Mendes, R., Kennedy, J., Neves, J.: The fully informed particle swarm: simpler, maybe better. IEEE Trans. Evol. Comput. **8**, 204–210 (2004)

Possibilistic WorkFlow Net for Deadlock Avoidance in Interorganizational Business Processes

Leiliane Pereira de Rezende(✉) and Stéphane Julia

Computing Faculty, Federal University of Uberlândia, Uberlândia, MG, Brazil
leily_rezende@yahoo.com.br, stephane@ufu.br

Abstract. Soundness property is an important criterion which needs to be satisfied when treating workflow processes. However, a significant part of industrial business process models is not in fact sound, which can lead to deadlock situations due to message ordering mismatches, for example. In order to avoid deadlock situation in interorganizational business processes, an approach based on Siphon structures, possibilistic Petri nets and interorganizational WorkFlow nets is proposed. A deadlock situation is characterized by an insufficiently marked Siphon. Possibilistic Petri nets with uncertainty on the marking and on the transition firing are used to ensure the existence of at least one transition firing sequence enabling the completion of the process without encountering the deadlock situation. Routing patterns and communication protocols that exist in business processes are modeled by interorganizational Work-Flow nets. Combining these formalisms, a kind of possibilistic WorkFlow net is obtained.

Keywords: Interorganizational workflow net · Possibilistic petri net · Deadlocks · Siphon · Soundness · Process monitoring

1 Introduction

An organization produces value for its customers by executing various business processes. Business processes represent the sequences of activities that have to be executed within an organization to treat specific cases and to reach well defined goals [1]. Due to complexity and variety of business processes, contemporary organizations use information technology to support activities which may include automate their processes.

A workflow process corresponds to the automation of a business process, in whole or part, during which documents, information or tasks are passed from one participant to another for action, according to a set of procedural rules [2]. A Workflow Management Systems (WFMS) is a system that completely defines, manages and executes workflow processes through the execution of software whose sequence

L.P. de Rezende—Scholarship CAPES - Proc. n°. 99999.001925/2015-06.

S. Hammoudi et al. (Eds.): ICEIS 2015, LNBIP 241, pp. 168–191, 2015.
DOI: 10.1007/978-3-319-29133-8_9

of activities is driven by a computer representation of the workflow process logic [2]. They are a key technology for improving the effectiveness and efficiency of business processes within an organization [3].

Considering that modern organizations have to cope with complex administrative processes, WFMS have to deal with workflow processes shared among multiple organizations. These systems are critical to the functioning of many organizations. Most business information applications are large-scale software systems that provide essential support to companies in their business processes. Each business partner has to define private workflow processes that are connected to other workflow processes belonging to the other partners of the same organization [4]. An interorganizational workflow model corresponds then to a finite set of WorkFlow nets loosely coupled through asynchronous communication mechanisms [3].

Many papers have already considered Petri net theory as an efficient tool for the modeling and analysis of WFMS [1,5,6]. The WorkFlow nets, acyclic Petri net models used to represent business processes, are defined in [1].

Soundness property is an important criterion which needs to be satisfied when treating workflow processes. In fact, good properties of well-defined formal models such as WorkFlow nets can easily be proven, thus showing when business processes are following a rigid structure that does not allow deviations from the process description during real time execution. However, in [7], a case study revealed that, on average, only 46 % of 735 industrial business process models checked were in fact sound. In addition, as the synchronization of parallel processes can easily lead to a potential source of deadlock [8], it can be difficult to establish the soundness correctness of complex interorganizational workflow processes. As a matter of fact, even proving the soundness correctness of local workflow processes is not a guarantee of the soundness correctness of the whole system (the interorganizational workflow model) as was shown in [3]. Deadlock in this case comes generally from message ordering mismatches as shown in [9].

There exist many research papers devoted to the deadlock problem. Over the last two decades, a great deal of research has been focused on solving deadlock problems in resource allocation systems such as computer communication systems [10,11], WorkFlow systems [12,13], and flexible manufacturing systems [11,14], resulting in a wide variety of approaches. In addition, a variety of deadlock control policies based on Petri nets have been proposed for automated manufacturing system [15–23]. From a technical perspective, most of the control policies resolving deadlocks are developed via state space analysis or structural analysis of Petri nets. Deadlock control policies based on structural analysis can avoid the state explosion problem successfully, but always forbid some legal states [24].

Considering that a deadlock situation within the Petri net theory [25] is characterized as a zero marking for some structural objects called Siphons [26], several algorithms to detect the Siphons and efficient methods for the synthesis of supervisors enforcing that the marking of the Siphons never become completely empty and ensuring the Petri nets are free from deadlock, have been proposed in [4,27–32]. All these works are based on a kind of transformation of the process model and cannot be used at a monitoring level when a deadlock situation still exists in the control structure of the model.

In this paper, an approach based on Siphon structures, as well as possibilistic Petri nets and interorganizational WorkFlow nets is proposed to deal with deadlock situations in business processes. In particular, a kind of possibilistic WorkFlow net will be defined to treat in real time the deadlock situations that occur from message ordering mismatches between the local WorkFlow nets.

The remainder of this paper is as follow: in Sect. 2, the definition of interorganizational WorkFlow nets and soundness correctness criterion are provided. In Sect. 3, the definition of the objects Petri nets is presented. In Sect. 4, an overview of possibilistic Petri nets is given. In Sect. 5, the Siphon structure is defined. In Sect. 6, the possibilistic WorkFlow net is presented and an example based on a process that precedes the presentation of a paper at a conference illustrates the approach. Finally, Sect. 7 concludes this work with a short summary, an assessment based on the approach presented and an outlook on future work proposals.

2 Interorganizational WorkFlow Net

Before introducing the interorganizational WorkFlow nets (IOWF-net) and the soundness property for these nets, it is necessary to introduce the WorkFlow nets (WF-nets) and soundness in the single organizational context.

2.1 WorkFlow Net and Soundness

A Petri net that models a workflow process is called a WorkFlow net [1]. A WorkFlow net satisfies the following properties [5]:

- It has only one source place, named *Start* and only one sink place, named *End*. These are special places such that the place *Start* has only outgoing arcs and the place *End* has only incoming arcs.
- A token in *Start* represents a case that needs to be handled and a token in *End* represents a case that has been handled.
- Every task t (transition) and condition p (place) should be on a path from place *Start* to place *End*.

Following, the formal definition of WF-nets is presented.

Definition 1 ***(WorkFlow Net*** **[1]*).*** *A Petri net $PN = (P, T, F)$ is a WF-net if and only if:*

1. There is one source place $i \in P$ such that $\bullet i = \phi$;
2. There is one sink place $o \in P$ such that $o\bullet = \phi$;
3. Every node $x \in P \cup T$ is on a path from i to o.

A WF-net has one input place (i) and one output place (o) because any case handled by the procedure represented by the WF-net is created when it enters the WFMS and is deleted once it is completely handled by the WFMS, i.e., the WF-net specifies the life-cycle of a case. The third requirement in Definition 1 has been added to avoid "dangling tasks and/or conditions", i.e., tasks and conditions which do not contribute to the processing of cases [1].

Tasks can be optional, i.e. there are tasks that just need to be executed for some cases. The order in which tasks will be executed can vary from case to case [1]. Four basic constructions for routing are presented in [1,5]:

- *Sequential*: tasks are executed one after another sequentially, clearly demonstrating dependence among these tasks: one needs to finish for the other to start;
- *Parallel*: if more than one task can be executed simultaneously or in any order. In this case, both tasks can be executed without the result of one interfering in the result of the other;
- *Conditional* (or selective routing): when there is a choice between two or more tasks;
- *Iterative*: when it is necessary to execute the same task multiple times.

Soundness is a correctness criterion defined for WF-nets and is related to its dynamics. A WF-net is sound if, and only if, the following three requirements are satisfied [1]:

- For each token put in the place *Start*, one and only one token appears in the place *End*.
- When the token appears in the place *End*, all the other places are empty for this case.
- For each transition (task), it is possible to move from the initial state to a state in which that transition is enabled, i.e. there are no dead transitions.

Following, the formal definition of Soundness property in WF-nets context is presented.

Definition 2 ***(Soundness*** [1]***).*** *A procedure modeled by a WF-net* $PN = (P, T, F)$ *is Sound if and only if:*

1. For every state M reachable from state i, there exists a firing sequence leading from state M to state o. Formally:

$$\forall_M \left[(i \xrightarrow{*} M) \Rightarrow (M \xrightarrow{*} o) \right]$$

2. State o is the only state reachable from state i with at least one token in place o. Formally:

$$\forall_M \left[(i \xrightarrow{*} M \wedge M \geq o) \Rightarrow (M = o) \right]$$

3. There are no dead transitions in (PN, i). Formally:

$$\forall_{t \in T} \exists_{M,M'} \left[i \xrightarrow{*} M \xrightarrow{t} M' \right]$$

A method for the qualitative analysis of WF-nets (soundness verification) based on the proof trees of linear logic is presented in [6] and another based on a reachability graph is presented in [33].

The weak soundness property corresponds to the first requirement of the soundness property. Since the second requirement is implied by the first one, the only difference is the third requirement, i.e., for weak soundness property it is not required that there are no dead transitions, i.e. a WorkFlow net is weak sound if, and only if, for each token put in the place *Start* (i), one and only one token appears in the place *End* (o). This property states that starting from the initial state (just a token in place *Start*), it is always possible to reach the final state with one token in the place *End* [33].

2.2 Interorganizational WorkFlow Net and Soundness

An interorganizational WorkFlow net (IOWF-net) is essentially a set of loosely coupled workflow processes modeled by Petri nets. Typically, there exist n business partners which are involved in one "global" workflow process [34]. Each of these partners has its own "local" workflow process, that is private, and where full control exists over it. Therefore, an IOWF-net is composed of at least two local workflow processes.

The local workflows interact at certain points according to a communication structure. There exists two types of communication: asynchronous communication (corresponding to the exchange of messages between workflows) and synchronous communication (which forces the local workflows to execute specific tasks at the same time). Synchronous communication corresponds to the melting of some transitions [34].

In this paper, the synchronous case is not considered since we consider that each organization controls its own process. Only asynchronous communication protocols will be considered. Definition 3 formalizes the concept of an IOWF-net.

Definition 3 ***(IOWF-net*** [3]***).*** *An interorganizational WorkFlow net (IOWF-net) is a tuple* $IOWF = (PN_1, PN_2, ..., PN_n, P_{AC}, AC)$*, where:*

1. $n \in \mathbb{N}$ is the number of local WorkFlow nets (LWF-nets);
2. For each $k \in \{1, ..., n\} : PN_k$ is a WF-net with source place i_k and sink place o_k;
3. For all $k, l \in \{1, ..., n\} : if\, k \neq l$, then $(P_k \cup T_k) \cap (P_l \cup T_l) = \emptyset$;
4. $T^* = \bigcup_{k \in \{1,...,n\}} T_k$, $P^* = \bigcup_{k \in \{1,...,n\}} P_k$, $F^* = \bigcup_{k \in \{1,...,n\}} F_k$ (relations between the elements of the LWF-nets);
5. P_{AC} is the set of asynchronous communication elements (communication places);

6. $AC \subseteq P_{AC} \times \mathbb{P}(T^*) \times \mathbb{P}(T^*)$ corresponds to asynchronous communication relations[1].

Each asynchronous communication element corresponds to a place named in P_{AC}. The relation AC specifies a set of input transitions and a set of output transitions for each asynchronous communication element.

The workflow which precedes the presentation of a paper at a conference, presented in [3], will be used to understand the definition of IOWF-net shown below. "This workflow can be considered to be an interorganizational workflow with two loosely coupled workflow processes: (1) the process of an author preparing, submitting and revising a paper, and (2) the process of evaluating and monitoring submissions by the program committee. In this case, there exists two 'organizations' involved in the interorganizational workflow: the author (AU) and the program committee (PC). The author sends a draft version of the paper to the program committee. The program committee acknowledges the receipt and evaluates the submission. The paper is accepted or rejected by the program committee. In both cases the author is notified. If the paper is rejected, the workflow terminates, otherwise the author can start preparing the final version. After completing the final version, a copy is sent to the program committee and the program committee acknowledges the receipt of the final version. If the final version is not received by the program committee before a specific due date, the author is notified that the paper is too late. A paper which is too late will not be published in the proceedings".

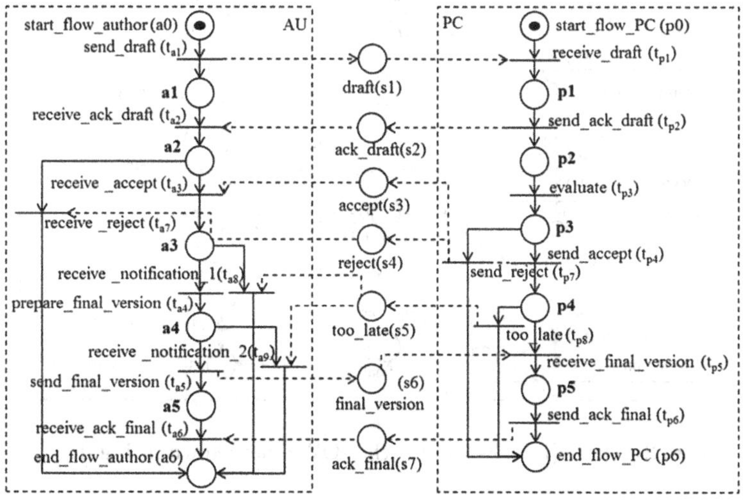

Fig. 1. An interorganizational workflow.

[1] $\mathbb{P}(T^*)$ is the set of all non-empty subsets of T^*.

Figure 1 shows the IOWF-net that models the process described above. This IOWF-net has two LWF-nets: *AU*, on the left, models the local workflow of the author and *PC*, on the right, models the workflow procedure followed by the program committee. Each of them has only one source and one sink place. In the LWF-net AU case, the source place is *start_flow_author* and the sink place is *end_flow_author*. In the LWF-net PC, the source and sink place are *start_flow_PC* and *end_flow_PC*, respectively. The places *draft*, *ack_draft*, *accept*, *reject*, *too_late*, *final_version* and *ack_final* are the communication places.

An IOWF-net which is composed of a number of sound local workflows may be subject to synchronization errors. In addition, it is also possible to have an interorganizational workflow which is globally sound but not locally sound [3]. To define a notion of soundness suitable for IOWF-nets, Aalst in [3] defined the *unfolding* of an IOWF-net into a WF-net.

In the *unfolded* net, i.e. the U(IOWF-net), all the local WF-nets are connected to each other by a start transition t_i and a termination transition t_o. Moreover, a global source place i and a global sink place o have been added in order to respect the basic structure of a simple WF-net. Asynchronous communication elements are mapped into ordinary places(P_{AC}) [3]. The result of the unfolding is the new WF-net shown in Fig. 2.

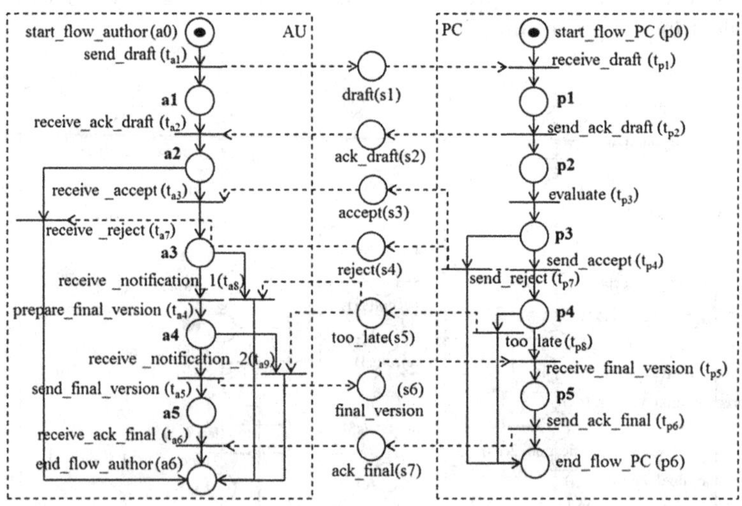

Fig. 2. The U(IOWF-net) for the IOWF-net shown in Fig. 1.

The soundness property definition for interorganizational workflows is given below:

Definition 4 ***Soundness.*** *An interorganizational WorkFlow net (IOWF-net) is sound iff it is locally sound and globally sound. IOWF-net is locally sound iff* *each of its local WorkFlow nets PN_k is sound. IOWF-net is globally sound iff U(IOWF-net) is sound.*

The IOWF-net shown in Fig. 1 is locally sound but is not globally sound given that the U(IOWF-net) of Fig. 2 is not Sound. One promptly notes that if the transition *too_late* of the LWF-net *PC* and the transition *send_final_version* of the LWF-net *AU* are fired, the messages *too_late* and *final_version* cross each other leading to a state of deadlock with a token in place $a5$ and the two messages are never received (a token in place *too_late* and a token in place *final_version*). Therefore, the IOWF-net does not satisfy the soundness property but satisfies the weak soundness property due to the fact that there exists at least one firing sequence, for example *send_draft*, *receive_draft*, *send_ack_draft*, *receive_ack_draft*, *evaluate*, *send_accept*, *receive_accept*, *prepare_final_version*, *send_final_version*, *receive_final_ version*, *send_ack_final*, *receive_ack_final*, that reaches the final state.

3 Objects Petri Nets

Ordinary Petri nets do not allow for the modeling of complex data structures. Many extensions have been proposed to model this specific aspect through high-level Petri net definitions.

The object Petri nets defined by Sibertin-Blanc [35] are based on the integration of predicate/transition Petri nets and the concept of the object oriented paradigm. The tokens are considered as *n-tuples* of instances for a class of objects and carries data structures defined as sets of attributes for specific classes. Preconditions and actions are associated with transitions, which respectively act on the attributes (eventually modifying their values) of the data structures transported by the tokens of the net. The object Petri nets can be formally defined by the 9 tuple:

$$N_0 =< P, T, C_{lass}, V, Pre, Post, A_{tc}, A_{ta}, M_0 > \tag{1}$$

where:

- C_{lass} is a finite set of classes of objects: for each class, a set of attributes is also defined;
- P is a finite set of places whose types are given by C_{lass};
- T is a finite set of transitions;
- V is a set of variables whose types are given by C_{lass};
- *Pre* is the function precedent place (an arc between a place and a transition which considers a formal sum of elements of V);
- *Post* is the next function place (an arc between a transition and a place which considers a formal sum of elements of V);
- A_{tc} is an application that associates to each transition a condition that involves the attributes of the formal variables associated with the input arcs of the transitions;

- A_{ta} is an application that associates to each transition an action that involves the formal attributes of the variables associated with the input arcs of the transition, and updates the attributes of the formal variables of the output arcs of the transition;
- M_0 is the initial marking which associates a formal sum of objects to each place (n-tuples of instances of classes that belong to C_{lass});

An example of object Petri net is presented in Fig. 3(a). The set of classes is defined as:

$$C_{lass} = \{Product, Request\}$$

The attributes of each class are described below:

$$\text{Product}\begin{cases} name = identifier; \\ code = integer; \\ cost = float; \end{cases} \quad \text{Request}\begin{cases} code : integer; \\ cost : float; \\ type : identifier; \end{cases}$$

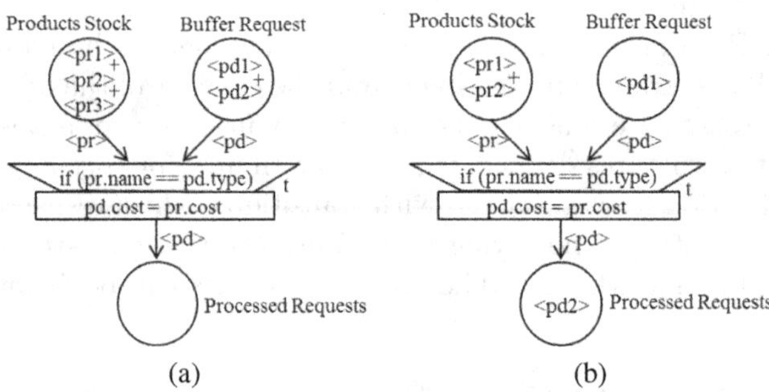

Fig. 3. Specification of a sale transaction: (a) before firing (b) after firing.

The variable *pr* belongs to the class *Product* and the variable *pd* belongs to the class *Request*. The place *Products Stock* belongs to the class *Product*, the place *Buffer Request* belongs to the class *Request* and the place *Processed Requests* belongs to the class *Request*. The initial marking M_0 is given by the objects that are in the places *Products Stock* and *Buffer Request* and is given by:

$$M_0 = \begin{bmatrix} <pr1> + <pr2> + <pr3>, \\ <pd1> + <pd2>, \\ 0 \end{bmatrix}$$

For example, the attributes of the objects (token) $pr1$ and *pd2* can be given by:

$$\begin{matrix} pr1 \\ (Product) \end{matrix} \begin{cases} name : hometheater; \\ code : 567544; \\ cost : 278,50; \end{cases} \qquad \begin{matrix} pd2 \\ (Request) \end{matrix} \begin{cases} code : 123440; \\ cost : 00,00; \\ type : hometheater; \end{cases}$$

The detailed definition of the dynamic behavior (firing rules) of the object Petri Net can be found in [35]. In Fig. 3(a), the transition t is enabled by the initial marking. The attributes of the variable *pr* associated with the arc connecting the place *Products Stock* to the transition t can be replaced by the attributes of the objects $pr1$ for example. Similarly, the attributes of the variable *pd* associated with the arc connecting the place $Buffer\ Request$ to transition t can be replaced by the attributes of the objects *pd2* for example. Considering that the attributes of the pair of objects *(pr1, pd2)* check the condition associated with the transition t, the transition can be fired. The action associated with the transition is then executed and a new object *pd2* can be produced in the place *Processed Requests*, as shown in Fig. 3(b), with the following attributes:

$$\begin{matrix} pd2 \\ (Request) \end{matrix} \begin{cases} code : 123440; \\ cost : 278,50; \\ type : hometheater; \end{cases}$$

In particular, when considering this new object *pd2*, the attribute *cost* has been modified after the firing of t.

4 Possibilistic Petri Net

Possibilistic Petri nets are derived from Object Petri nets [36]. In particular, in the approach presented in [37], a possibilistic Petri net is a model where a marked place corresponds to a possible partial state, a transition to a possible state change, and a firing sequence to a possible behavior. The main advantage in working with possibilistic Petri nets is that they allow for the updating of a system state at a supervisory level with ill-known information without necessarily reaching inconsistent states.

A possibilistic Petri net model associates a possibility distribution $\Pi_o(p)$ to the location of an object o, p being a place of the net. $\Pi_o(p) = 1$ represents the fact that p is a possible location of o, and $\Pi_o(p) = 0$ expresses the certainty that o is not present in place p. Formally, a marking in a possibilistic Petri net is then a mapping:

$$M : O \times P \longrightarrow \{0, 1\}$$

where O is a set of objects and P a set of places. If $M(o, p) = 1$, there exists a possibility of there being the object o in place p. On the contrary, if $M(o, p) = 0$, there exists no possibility of there being o in p. A marking M of the net allows one to represent:

- *A certain marking*: each token is located in only one place (well-known state). Then $M(o, p) = 1$ and $\forall p_i \neq p, M(o, p_i) = 0$.
- *An uncertain marking*: each token location has a possibility distribution over a set of places. It cannot be asserted that a token is in a given place, but only that it is in a place among a given set of places. For example, if there exists a possibility at a certain time to have the same object o in two different places, p_1 and p_2, then $M(o, p_1) = M(o, p_2) = 1$.

A possibilistic marking will correspond in practice to knowledge concerning a situation at a given time.

In a possibilistic Petri net, the firing (certain or uncertain) of a transition t is decomposed into two steps:

- *Beginning of a firing*: objects are put into output places of t but are not removed from its input places.
- *End of a firing*: that can be a firing cancellation (tokens are removed from the output places of t) or a firing achievement (tokens are removed from the input places of t).

A certain firing consists of a beginning of a firing and an immediate firing achievement. An uncertain firing (or a pseudo-firing) that will increase the uncertainty of the marking can be considered only as the beginning of a firing (there is no information to confirm whether the normal event associated with the transition has actually occurred or not). To a certain extent, pseudo-firing is a way of realizing abduction in a knowledge base system.

The interpretation of a possibilistic Petri net is defined by attaching to each transition an authorization function $\eta_{x_1,\ldots,x_n}$ defined as follows:

$$\eta_{x_1,\ldots,x_n} : T \longrightarrow \{False, Uncertain, True\}$$

where $x_1, ..., x_n$ are the variables associated with the incoming arcs of transition t (when considering the underlying Object Petri net).

If $o_1, ..., o_n$ is a possible substitution for $x_1, ..., x_n$ for firing t, then several situations can be considered:

- t is not enabled by the marking but the associated interpretation is true; an inconsistent situation occurs and special treatment process of the net is activated;
- t is enabled by a certain marking and the interpretation is true; then a classical firing (with certainty) of an object Petri net occurs;
- t is enabled by a certain marking and the interpretation is uncertain; then the transition is pseudo-fired and the imprecision is increased;
- t is enabled by an uncertain marking; if the interpretation is uncertain, t is pseudo-fired;
- t is enabled by an uncertain marking and the interpretation is true: a recovery algorithm, presented in [38], is called and a new computation of the possibility distribution of the objects involved in the uncertain marking is realized in order to go back to a certain marking.

Concepts about possibilistic Petri nets will be illustrated through a practical example in the Sect. 6.

5 Deadlock Situations Based on Empty Siphon

The presence of deadlock situations in Petri nets is due to the existence of particular structures called Siphons [27]. As special structures, Siphons are related to the liveness of a Petri net model and have been widely used in the characterization and prevention/avoidance of deadlock situations [39]. The definition of a Siphon is the following:

Definition 5 ***(Siphon*** **[40]*)***. *Let P' be a non empty subset of P (set of places). P' is a Siphon iff $\bullet P' \subseteq P'\bullet$. The set of the input transitions of P' is included in the set of the output transitions of P'. Siphon P' is said to be minimal iff it contains no other Siphons as its proper subset.*

As there exists more output transitions than input transitions in the subnet, the subset of places P' can be emptied of its tokens, which leads to a deadlock situation (no transitions enabled in the Petri net). In order that a Siphon is not completely emptied of its token, it needs to contain at least a trap. The definition of a trap is the following:

Definition 6 ***(Trap*** **[40]*)***. *Let P'' be a non empty subset of P(set of places). P'' is a trap iff $P''\bullet \subseteq \bullet P''$. The set of the output transitions of P'' is included in the set of the input transitions of P''.*

The necessary and sufficient condition for the liveness in a marked Petri net is that every Siphon in a net must contain at least a marked trap [41]. In addition, a necessary condition for the existence of a deadlock situation in a Petri net is for there to be at least an empty Siphon when considering the set of reachable markings [31].

Several algorithms have been presented by different authors for the automatic detection of Siphon structures in Petri nets, such as the procedures based on Incidence Matrix [25], inequalities [25], linear algebra [28], logic equations [42], and linear equations with slack variables [43].

An example of deadlock is presented in Fig. 4(a). The corresponding siphon is represented in Fig. 4(b). It is clear that if the firing sequence *send_draft* (t_{a1}), *receive_draft* (t_{p1}), *send_ack_draft* (t_{p2}), *receive_ack_draft* (t_{a2}), *evaluate* (t_{p3}), *send_accept* (t_{p4}), *receive_accept* (t_{a3}), *prepare_final_version* (t_{a4}), *send_final_version* (t_{a5}), *too_late* (t_{p8}) is fired, the Siphon in Fig. 4(b). becomes empty through the firing of transitions t_{a5} and t_{p8} and a deadlock situation (Fig. 4(a).) occurs for the marking *a5*, *too_late* (p_{s5}) and *final_version* (p_{s6}).

6 Possibilistic WorkFlow Net

As pointed out in the introduction, the synchronization of parallel processes can easily lead to a potential source of deadlock. In addition, most of the deadlocks in

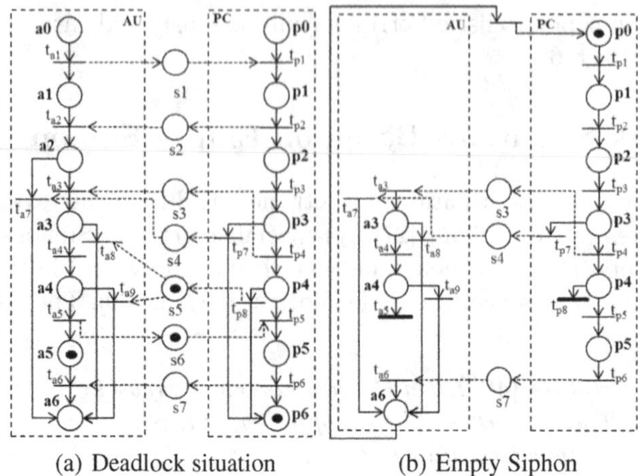

(a) Deadlock situation (b) Empty Siphon

Fig. 4. An example of deadlock.

a business process have structural causes that will not allow the process to reach its final state [13]. Another important point to be considered, is the fact that if a deadlock situation exists in a workflow process, the only solution to avoid the deadlock situation if the model of the process cannot be explicitly modified will be to avoid the sequence of transition firing leading to the deadlock situation and to follow with another firing sequence allowing the final marking corresponding to the goal to be reached.

A model of the process that considers the existing Siphons of the global business model and based on the firing rules of a kind of possibilistic Work-Flow net will eventually allow one to deviate from firing sequences that empty Siphon. Such a model will then be able to deal with deadlock situations when the workflow model respects the weak soundness property.

This approach is divided into three consecutive phases. The first phase is a kind of static analysis phase and determines which transitions are responsible by emptying of the Siphon structures. In particular, it specifies the transitions that will have an uncertain interpretation. Such transitions will have to be pseudo-fired to explore in a kind of forward reasoning of their effect on the Siphon marking. In the second phase, the workflow process will be transformed into a possibilistic WorkFlow net and uncertain interpretations will be attached to the transitions encountered in the previous phase. Finally, in the third phase, the possibilistic WorkFlow net will be executed following the behavior of the possibilistic token player algorithm given in Fig. 5. Such an inference mechanism will ensure that deadlock situations will be avoided during the execution of the process in the weak sound case, guaranteeing the existence of at least one firing sequence that will be able to reach the final marking of the process.

To illustrate the approach, the process that precedes the presentation of a paper at a conference, described in Subsect. 2.2 and represented in Fig. 1, will be

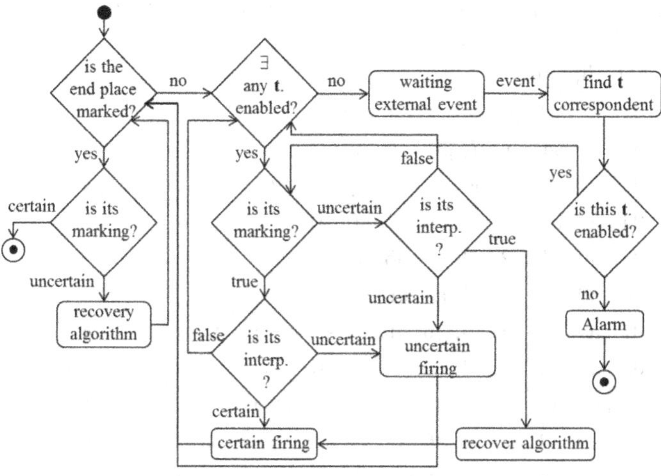

Fig. 5. Possibilistic token player algorithm associated with autonomous local processes.

considered. This IOWF-net, as pointed out in the Subsect. 2.2, is not globally sound; soon it may be subject to some synchronization errors that can generate some structural deadlocks during its execution. The first step to make the process free of deadlock during its execution is to determine the Siphon structures which can be emptied. As the focus of this paper is not to present a new algorithm for finding Siphon structures, the authors used the Petri net tool PIPE (Platform Independent Petri Net Editor) [44]. Through the use of the PIPE tool, 24 Siphon structures were found, from which 10 can be emptied (14 structures have trap and 10 do not). Table 1 shows the 24 Siphon structures. The symbol "•" in the Trap column indicates that the corresponding Siphon structure contain at least a trap. The Fig. 6 shows graphically the 10 Siphon structures without trap.

Not all the Siphons without traps will necessarily be emptied of theirs tokens. It will also depend on the global Petri net model behavior. Observing the reachability graph presented in the Fig. 7, it is possible to check that there exists only one deadlock state which is highlighted in gray. Such state occurs when the transitions *too_late* (t_{p8}) of the LWF-net *PC* and *send_final_version* (t_{a5}) of the LWF-net *AU* are fired in sequence. Considering this, $S_1 = 6$(a), (b), (c), (d), (e), (f) is the set of empty Siphons which lead to a deadlock situation in the Petri net model of Fig. 1.

In spite of the fact that all Siphons belonging to the set S_1 characterize deadlock situations, it is possible to verify that there exist some different characteristics between each one of them. Such characteristics are described below:

1. the Siphons 6(d), (e) and (d), (f) have as initial marking one token in the place *start_flow_author* ($a0$);
2. the Siphons 6(a) and (b) have as initial marking one token in the place *start_flow_PC* ($p0$);

Table 1. Siphon structures referring to Fig. 1.

ID	Siphon	Trap
01	p0, p1, p2, p3, p4, p5, p6	•
02	a6, s4, s5, s7, p0, p1, p2, p3, p4, p5	•
03	a3, a4, a5, a6, s3, s4, p0, p1, p2, p3	•
04	a2, a3, a4, a5, a6, s2, p0, p1	•
05	a0, a1, a2, a3, a4, a5, a6	•
06	a0, a2, a3, a4, a5, a6, s1, s2, p1	•
07	a0, a3, a4, a5, a6, s1, s3, s4, p1, p2, p3	•
08	a0, a1, a2, a3, a4, a6, s7, s6, p5	•
09	a2, a3, a4, a6, s2, s6, s7, p0, p1, p5	•
10	a0, a2, a3, a4, a6, s1, s2, s6, s7, p1, p5	•
11	a3, a4, a6, s3, s4, s6, s7, p0, p1, p2, p3, p5	•
12	a0, a3, a4, a6, s1, s3, s4, s6, s7, p1, p2, p3, p5	•
13	a0, a6, s1, s4, s5, s7, p1, p2, p3, p4, p5	•
14	a0, s1, p1, p2, p3, p4, p5, p6	•
15	a3, a4, a6, s3, s4, s7, p0, p1, p2, p3, p4, p5	
16	a2, a3, a4, a6, s2, s7, p0, p1, p2, p3, p4, p5	
17	a0, a1, a2, a3, a4, a6, s7, p0, p1, p2, p3, p4, p5	
18	a0, a1, a2, a3, a4, a6, s1, s7, p1, p2, p3, p4, p5	
19	a0, a2, a3, a4, a6, s1, s2, s7, p1, p2, p3, p4, p5	
20	a0, a3, a4, a6, s1, s3, s4, s7, p1, p2, p3, p4, p5	
21	a2, a6, s2, s5, s7, p0, p1, p2, p3, p4, p5	
22	a0, a1, a2, a6, s5, s7, p0, p1, p2, p3, p4, p5	
23	a0, a1, a2, a6, s1, s5, s7, p1, p2, p3, p4, p5	
24	a0, a2, a6, s1, s2, s5, s7, p1, p2, p3, p4, p5	

3. the Siphon 6(c) has as initial marking one token in the place *start_flow_author* ($a0$) and one token in the place *start_flow_PC* ($p0$);
4. the Siphons 6(a) and (f) become empty due to the firing of the transitions *send_final_version* (t_{a5}) and *late_late* (t_{p8});
5. the Siphons 6(b), (c), (d) and (e) become empty due to the firing of the transitions *send_final_version* (t_{a5}), *send_reject* (t_{p7}) and *late_late* (t_{p8});

Observing the characteristics cited above, it is possible to reduce the set S_1 to a single element corresponding to the Siphon 6(a). This occurs because the set of transitions responsible for emptying the Siphons associating with the fifth characteristic is the same in relation to Siphon 6(a) except by the presence of the transition t_{p7}; however the firing of the transition t_{p7} does not lead to a deadlock situation, only the firing of the transitions t_{a5} and t_{p8} are responsible

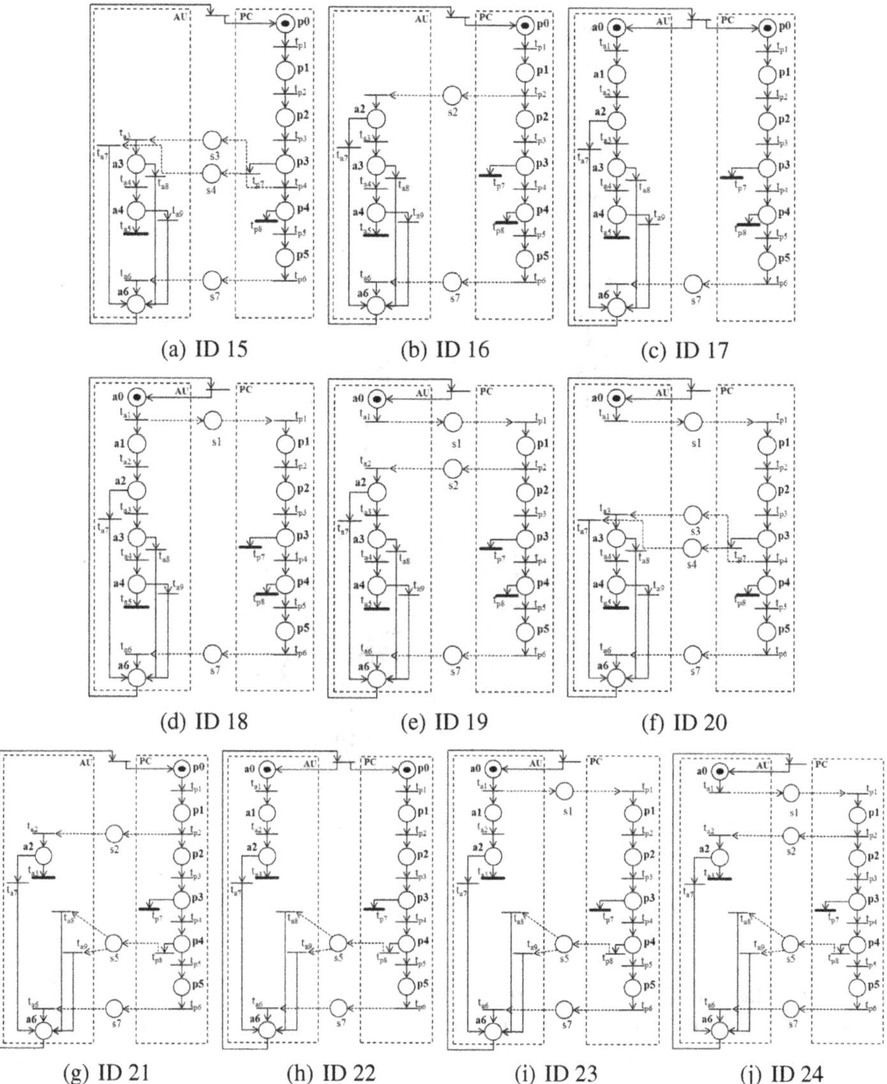

(a) ID 15 (b) ID 16 (c) ID 17

(d) ID 18 (e) ID 19 (f) ID 20

(g) ID 21 (h) ID 22 (i) ID 23 (j) ID 24

Fig. 6. The Siphon structures without trap.

for emptying the siphon. In addition, the difference between Siphons 6(a) and 6(f) is directly related to the initial marking.

Considering that the set of empty Siphons can be reduced to the single element containing the siphon 6(a), the interpretation of the transitions will then be classified as true or uncertain. As the transitions t_{a5} and t_{p8} are directly responsible for the emptying of the Siphon, they will have their interpretation classified as uncertain. The remaining transitions must be analyzed in order to verify if they are indirectly responsible for the emptying of the Siphon even-

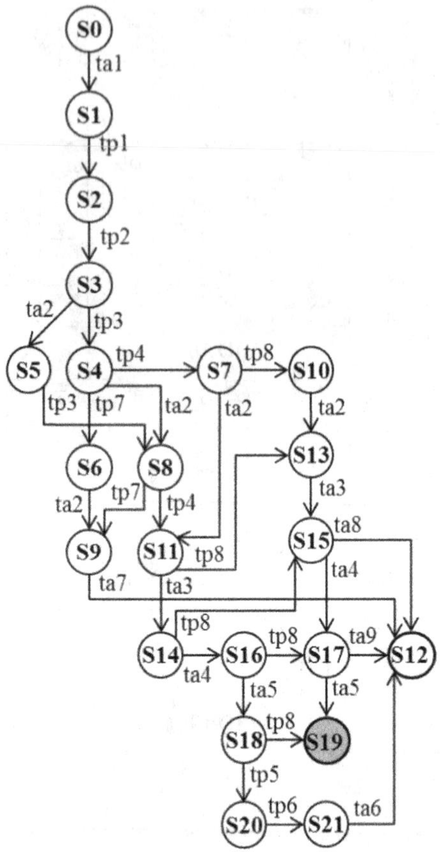

Fig. 7. Reachability graph.

tually. For classifying as uncertain the interpretation of a transition, the firing of the transition must be enabled by an uncertain marking and its firing must produce tokens in the places that do not belong to the Siphon. Considering this statement, each one of the remaining transitions are analyzed below:

- transition t_{a6}: enabled by uncertain marking when the transition t_{a5} is pseudo-fired, but its firing produces tokens only in the places that belongs to the Siphon 6(a). Its interpretation is then classified as true;
- transition t_{a9}: enabled by uncertain marking when the transition t_{a5} is pseudo-fired, but its firing produces tokens only in the places that belongs to the Siphon 6(a). Its interpretation is then classified as true;
- transition t_{p5}: enabled by uncertain marking when the transition t_{p8} is pseudo-fired, but its firing produces tokens only in the places that belongs to the Siphon 6(a). Its interpretation is then classified as true;

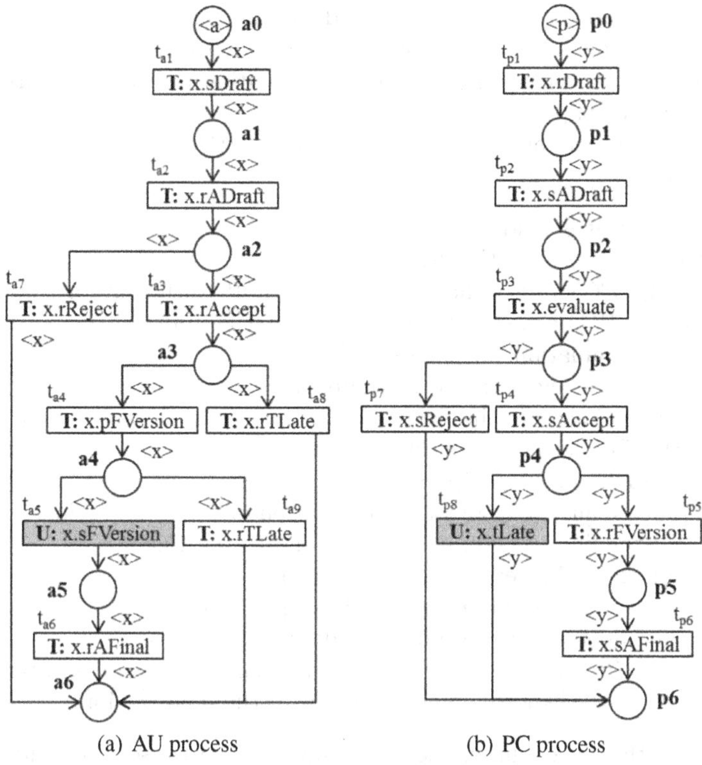

Fig. 8. *AU* and *PC* process using possibilistic WorkFlow net.

- transitions t_{a1}, t_{a2}, t_{a3}, t_{a4}, t_{a7}, t_{a8}, t_{p1}, t_{p2}, t_{p3}, t_{p4}, t_{p6} and t_{p7}: enabled by certain marking considering the actual classification. The interpretation of each one is then classified as true.

After defining the transitions that will be eventually pseudo-fired, in order to avoid a possible deadlock situation, the *PC* and *AU* processes can be transformed into possibilistic WorkFlow nets as illustrated in the Fig. 8(a) and (b), respectively. From the point of view of a local process, the communication places of the IOWF-net will be considered as simple external events associated with transitions. In particular, an interpretation will be attached with such transitions to indicate received messages. For example, the interpretation associated with the transition t_{p1} of the Fig. 8(b) is true if a message is received from the model of Fig. 1 through the communication place $draft$.

$< a >$ and $< p >$ are objects belonging to the class "Paper", as well as variables x and y and all the model's places. Each transition has an interpretation and an action attached to it defined by the designer. The interpretation is used to manage the occurrence of each event in the system by imposing conditions on the firing of transitions. An action corresponds to an application that involves the attributes of formal variables associated with incoming arcs, allowing for the modification of some specific attributes through the execution of some specific methods. In order to focus on the deadlock resolution problem, actions are not represented in this paper.

The interpretation of each condition used in the process *AU* or *PC* is described below:

- *sDraft*: the draft is ready to send to the *PC*;
- *rDraft*: the *PC* receives the draft;
- *sADraft*: the *PC* notifies the receipt of the draft to the author;
- *rADraft*: the *PC* acknowledges the receipt of the draft;
- *evaluate*: the evaluation was completed;
- *sAccept*: the *PC* decides to accept the paper;
- *rAccept*: the *PC* accepts the paper;
- *sReject*: the *PC* decides to reject the paper;
- *rReject*: the *PC* rejects the paper;
- *pFVersion*: the author begins the preparation of the final version;
- *sFVersion*: the final version is ready to send to the *PC*;
- *rFVersion*: the *PC* receives the final version;
- *tLate*: the deadline for submission of the paper is reached;
- *rTLate*: the paper is received after the deadline;
- *sAFinal*: the *PC* notifies the receipt of the final version to the author;
- *rAFinal*: the *PC* acknowledges the receipt of the final version.

Finally, in the third phase, the communicating processes *PC* and *AU* are executed considering the possibilistic token player algorithm given in Fig. 5. For this, let us assume that the transitions t_{a1}, t_{a2}, t_{a3} and t_{a4} of the LWF-net *AU* and the transitions t_{p1}, t_{p2}, t_{p3} and t_{p4} of the LWF-net *PC* have already been fired (Fig. 9(a) and (b)). If the transition t_{a5} of the LWF-net *AU* and the transition t_{p8} of the LWF-net *PC* are fired in sequence, the following scenario will occur:

- the transition t_{p8} of LWF-net *PC* is enabled by a certain marking and its interpretation is uncertain. Then, t_{p8} is pseudo-fired (Fig. 9(c));
- the transition t_{a5} of LWF-net *AU* is enabled by a certain marking and its interpretation is uncertain. Then, t_{a5} is pseudo-fired (Fig. 9(d));
- the end place (*p*6) of the LWF-net *PC* is marked by an uncertain marking. This means that through a pseudo firing sequence, the final marking of the process *PC* was reached without encountering a deadlock situation. Consequently, a recovery algorithm, presented in [38], is called to validate the sequence pseudo fired and to go back to a certain marking. In particular, this algorithm archives the pseudo-firing of the transition t_{p5} (Fig. 9(e)) finalizing the execution of the process;
- the transition t_{a9} of the LWF-net *AU* is enabled by an uncertain marking and its interpretation is true. This means that through a pseudo firing sequence the process *AU* reached a transition that is not responsible for the emptying of the Siphon and, consequently, for the deadlock situation in the Petri net

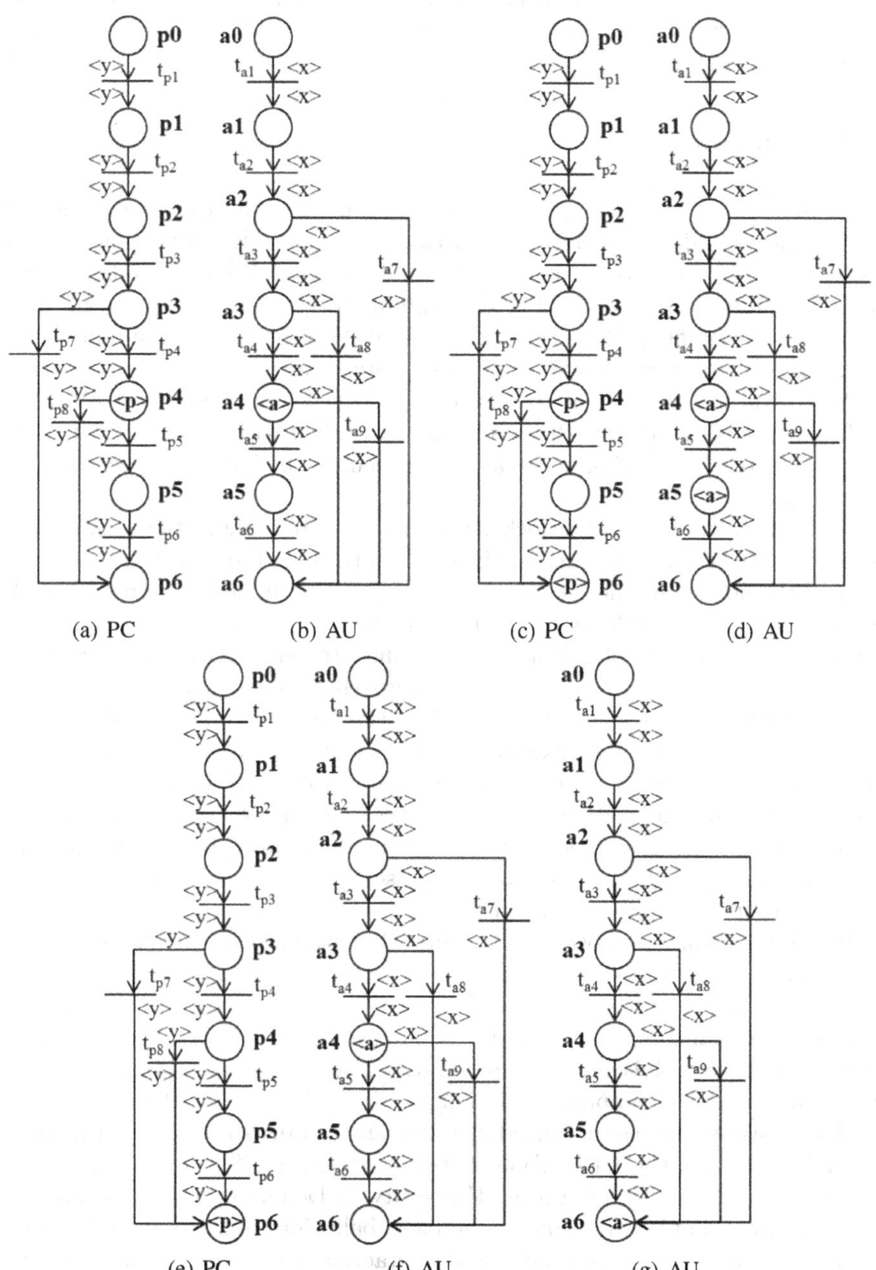

(a) PC (b) AU (c) PC (d) AU

(e) PC (f) AU (g) AU

Fig. 9. Simulation results of the scenario.

model of Fig. 1. Consequently, the recovery algorithm, presented in [38], is called to go back to a certain marking. In particular, this algorithm cancels the pseudo-firing of the transition t_{a5} (Fig. 9(f)) and fires with certainty the transition t_{a9} (Fig. 9(g)).

7 Conclusions

Taking into account that a significant part of industrial business process models is not in fact sound, which can lead, for example, to deadlock situations due to message ordering mismatches, in this article, an approach based on Siphon structures, possibilistic Petri nets and weak sound interorganizational WorkFlow nets is proposed. Combining the routing structure of WorkFlow nets, communication mechanisms of interorganizational processes, uncertain reasoning of possibilistic Petri nets and theoretical results on siphon theory, a kind of possibilistic WorkFlow net is obtained with the purpose of dealing with deadlock situations that can be reached during the real time execution in business processes not necessarily sound.

In the literature, the deadlock situations in interorganizational workflow processes are treated during the analysis phase through the modification of the design of the non sound model. Normally, the process's model is altered through the analysis of a reachable marking graph as in [3] or by adding a control place that forces the number of tokens in the Siphon to remain strictly positive as in [4]. Comparing these works with the approach presented in this paper, the main advantage is that it ensures the existence of at least one transition firing sequence during the real time execution of weak sound interorganizational workflow processes, enabling the completion of the process without encountering a deadlock situation and without modifying the control structure of the model. In addition, the presented method works for the weak sound interorganizational workflow processes, given that most processes in practice do not satisfy the soundness property as was shown in [7].

As a future work proposal, the quality of this approach should be explicitly validated through a kind of experimental approach that allows for the programming of transition pseudo firing. This means that its key aspects must be confirmed through practical examples. Taking into account that the proposed approach is based on IOWF-nets and on possibilistic Petri nets, simulation techniques can be used to support validation given that it is one of the most established analysis techniques supported by a vast array of tools [45–47]. Fortunately, it would seem that the CPN Tools software resources [48], developed by the computing science group of Aarhus University in Denmark, should be able to implement in a simple way some of the basic behaviors of a possibilistic token player given that they combine advanced interaction techniques into a consistent interface for editing, simulating, and analysing Coloured Petri Nets. Such implement should prove the gain in the overall process performance and the correct finalization of the process, i.e., the deadlock situations must not be encountered. In addition, it will be interesting to model and test, besides of simple cases, a larger business process using the CPN/Tools software through Monte Carlo simulation [49].

Acknowledgement. The authors would like to thank CAPES (Coordenação de Aperfeiçoamento de Pessoal de Nível Superior), FAPEMIG (Fundação de Amparo a Pesquisa do Estado de Minas Gerais) and CNPq (National Counsel of Technological and Scientific Development) for financial support.

References

1. van der Aalst, W., van Hee, K.: Workflow Management: Models, Methods, and Systems. MIT Press, Cambridge (2004)
2. Members, W.M.C.: Glossary - a workflow management coalition specification. Technical report, Coalition, Workflow Management (1994)
3. van der Aalst, W.M.P.: Modeling and analyzing interorganizational workflows. In: International Conference on Application of Concurrency to System Design, pp. 262–272 (1998)
4. Silva, L.d.F., Soares Passos, L.M., Soares, M.d.S., Julia, S.: Siphon-based deadlock prevention policy for interorganizational workflow net design. In: IEEE International Conference on Information Reuse and Integration, pp. 293–300 (2013)
5. van der Aalst, W.M.P.: The application of petri nets to workflow management. J. Circ. Syst. Comput. **8**, 21–66 (1998)
6. Soares Passos, L., Julia, S.: Qualitative analysis of workflow nets using linear logic: Soundness verification. In: IEEE International Conference on Systems, Man and Cybernetics, SMC 2009, pp. 2843–2847 (2009)
7. Fahland, D., Favre, C., Koehler, J., Lohmann, N., Völzer, H., Wolf, K.: Analysis on demand: Instantaneous soundness checking of industrial business process models. Data Knowl. Eng. **70**, 448–466 (2011)
8. van der Aalst, W.M.P.: Loosely coupled interorganizational workflows: modeling and analyzing workflows crossing organizational boundaries. Inf. Manage. **37**, 67–75 (2000)
9. Xiong, P., Zhou, M., Pu, C.: A petri net siphon based solution to protocol-level service composition mismatches. In: IEEE International Conference on Web Services, pp. 952–958 (2009)
10. Tang, F., You, I., Yu, S., Wang, C.L., Guo, M., Liu, W.: An efficient deadlock prevention approach for service oriented transaction processing. Comput. Math. Appl. **63**, 458–468 (2012)
11. Mohanty, M., Kumara, P.: Deadlock prevention in process control computer system. In: International Conference on Distributed Computing and Internet Technology, pp. 12–16 (2013)
12. Park, J., Reveliotis, S.: Deadlock avoidance in sequential resource allocation systems with multiple resource acquisitions and flexible routings. IEEE Trans. Autom. Control **46**, 1572–1583 (2001)
13. Kohler, M., Schaad, A.: Avoiding policy-based deadlocks in business processes. In: International Conference on Availability, Reliability and Security, pp. 709–716 (2008)
14. Gang, X., Ming, W.Z.: Systemic solutions to deadlock in FMS. Am. Control Conf. **6**, 5740–5745 (2004)

15. Ezpeleta, J., Colom, J.M., Martnez, J.: A petri net based deadlock prevention policy for flexible manufacturing systems. IEEE Trans. Robot. Autom. **11**, 173–184 (1995)
16. Huang, Y., Jeng, M., Xie, X., Chung, S.: Deadlock prevention policy based on petri nets and siphons. Int. J. Prod. Res. **39**, 283–305 (2001)
17. Li, Z., Zhou, M.: Elementary siphons of petri nets and their application to deadlock prevention in flexible manufacturing systems. IEEE Trans. Syst., Man, Cybern. **34**, 38–51 (2004)
18. Uzam, M., Zhou, M.: An iterative synthesis approach to petri net-based deadlock prevention policy for flexible manufacturing systems. IEEE Trans. Syst. Man Cybern. **37**, 362–371 (2007)
19. Ahmad, F., Huang, H., Wang, X.: Analysis of the petri net model of parallel manufacturing processes with shared resources. Inf. Sci. **181**, 5249–5266 (2011)
20. Chen, Y., Li, Z.: Design of a maximally permissive liveness-enforcing supervisor with a compressed supervisory structure for flexible manufacturing systems. Automatica **47**, 1028–1034 (2011)
21. Chen, Y., Li, Z., Zhou, M.: Behaviorally optimal and structurally simple liveness-enforcing supervisors of flexible manufacturing systems. IEEE Trans. Syst. Man Cybern. **42**, 615–629 (2012)
22. Huang, Y.S., Pan, Y.L., Zhou, M.: Computationally improved optimal deadlock control policy for flexible manufacturing systems. IEEE Trans. Syst. Man Cybern. **42**, 404–415 (2012)
23. Li, Z., Liu, G., Hanisch, H.M., Zhou, M.: Deadlock prevention based on structure reuse of petri net supervisors for flexible manufacturing systems. IEEE Trans. Syst. Man Cybern. **42**, 178–191 (2012)
24. Liu, G., Li, Z., Barkaoui, K., Al-Ahmari, A.: Robustness of deadlock control for a class of petri nets with unreliable resources. Inf. Sci. **235**, 259–279 (2013)
25. Murata, T.: Petri nets: Properties, analysis and applications. Proc. IEEE **77**, 541–580 (1989)
26. Boer, E., Murata, T.: Generating basis siphons and traps of petri nets using the sign incidence matrix. IEEE Trans. Circ. Syst. I: Fundam. Theor. Appl. **41**, 266–271 (1994)
27. Barkaoui, K., Abdallah, I.: Deadlock avoidance in FMS based on structural theory of petri nets. IEEE Symp. Emerg. Technol. Factory Autom. **2**, 499–510 (1995)
28. Chu, F., Xie, X.L.: Deadlock analysis of petri nets using siphons and mathematical programming. IEEE Trans. Robot. Autom. **13**, 793–804 (1997)
29. Maruta, T., Onoda, S., Ikkai, Y., Kobayashi, T., Komoda, N.: A deadlock detection algorithm for business processes workflow models. IEEE Int. Conf. Syst. Man Cybern. **1**, 611–616 (1998)
30. Sadiq, W., Orlowska, M.E.: Analyzing process models using graph reduction techniques. Inf. Syst. **25**, 117–134 (2000)
31. Iordache, M., Moody, J., Antsaklis, P.: Synthesis of deadlock prevention supervisors using petri nets. IEEE Trans. Robot. Autom. **18**, 59–68 (2002)
32. Awad, A., Puhlmann, F.: Structural detection of deadlocks in business process models. In: Abramowicz, W., Fensel, D. (eds.) Business Information Systems. Lecture Notes in Business Information Processing, vol. 7, pp. 239–250. Springer, Heidelberg (2008)
33. van der Aalst, W.M.P., van Hee, K.M., ter Hofstede, A.H.M., Sidorova, N., Verbeek, H.M.W., Voorhoeve, M., Wynn, M.T.: Soundness of workflow nets: Classification, decidability, and analysis. Form. Asp. Comput. **23**, 333–363 (2011)

34. Aalst, W.: Interorganizational workflows: an approach based on message sequence charts and petri nets. Syst. Analy. Model. Simul. **34**, 335–367 (1999)
35. Sibertin-Blanc, C.: High level petri nets with data structure. In: Jensen, K., (ed.) Proceedings of the 6th European Workshop on Application and Theory of Petri Nets, Espoo, Finland, pp. 141–170 (1985)
36. Sibertin-Blanc, C.: Cooperative objects: principles, use and implementation. In: Agha, G., De Cindio, F., Rozenberg, G. (eds.) APN 2001. LNCS, vol. 2001, pp. 216–246. Springer, Heidelberg (2001)
37. Cardoso, J.: Time fuzzy petri nets. In: Cardoso, J., Camargo, H. (eds.) Fuzziness in Petri Nets, vol. 22, pp. 115–145. Springer, New York (1999)
38. Cardoso, J., Valette, R., Dubois, D.: Petri nets with uncertain markings. In: Applications and Theory of Petri Nets, vol. 483, pp. 64–78 (1989)
39. Zhong, C., Li, Z.: Petri net based deadlock prevention approach for flexible manufacturing systems. In: Information Science Reference, pp. 416–433 (2011)
40. David, R., Alla, H.: Discrete, Continuous, and Hybrid Petri Nets, 2nd edn. Springer Publishing Company, Incorporated, Heidelberg (2010)
41. Hack, M.: Analysis production schemata by petri nets. Master's thesis, Massachusetts Institute of Technology (1972)
42. Karatkevich, A.: Analysis by solving logical equations - calculation of siphons and traps. In: Karatkevich, A. (ed.) Dynamic Analysis of Petri Net-Based Discrete Systems. Lecture Notes in Control and Information Sciences, vol. 356, pp. 87–93. Springer, Heidelberg (2007)
43. Ezpeleta, J., Couvreur, J., Silva, M.: A new technique for finding a generating family of siphons, traps and st-components. application to colored petri nets. In: Rozenberg, G. (ed.) APN 1993. LNCS, vol. 674, pp. 126–147. Springer, Heidelberg (1993)
44. Dingle, N.J., Knottenbelt, W.J., Suto, T.: Pipe2: A tool for the performance evaluation of generalised stochastic petri nets. SIGMETRICS Perform. Eval. Rev. **36**, 34–39 (2009)
45. Weske, M.: Business Process Management - Concepts, Languages Architectures. Springer, Heidelberg (2007)
46. van der Aalst, W.M.P.: Business process management: a comprehensive survey. ISRN Softw. Eng. **2013**, 1–37 (2013)
47. Rosemann, M., Vom Brocke, J.: The six core elements of business process management. In: Vom Brocke, J., Rosemann, M. (eds.) Handbook on Business Process Management 1, pp. 107–122. Springer, Heidelberg (2010)
48. Beaudouin-Lafon, M., Mackay, W.E., Jensen, M., Andersen, P., Janecek, P., Lassen, H.M., Lund, K., Mortensen, K.H., Munck, S., Ratzer, A., Ravn, K., Christensen, S., Jensen, K.: CPN/Tools: a tool for editing and simulating coloured petri nets ETAPS tool demonstration related to TACAS. In: Margaria, T., Yi, W. (eds.) TACAS 2001. LNCS, vol. 2031, pp. 574–577. Springer, Heidelberg (2001)
49. Rubinstein, R., Kroese, D.: Simulation and the Monte Carlo Method, 2nd edn. Wiley, New York (2008)

Generation of Economical Driving Plans Using Continuous Case-Based Planning

André P. Borges[1](✉), Osmar B. Dordal[2], Richardson Ribeiro[3], Bráulio C. Ávila[2], and Edson E. Scalabrin[2]

[1] Department of Informatics (DAINF), Federal University of Technology - Paraná (UTFPR), Av. Monteiro Lobato, s/n, Ponta Grossa, Paraná, Brazil
apborges@utfpr.edu.br

[2] Programa de Pós-Graduação em Informática, Pontifícia Universidade Católica do Paraná, Rua Imaculada Conceição, Curitiba, Paraná 1155, Brazil
{osmarbd,avila,scalabrin}@ppgia.pucpr.br

[3] Department of Informatics (DAINF), Federal University of Technology - Paraná (UTFPR), Via do Conhecimento, Km 1, Pato Branco, Paraná, Brazil
richardsonr@utfpr.edu.br

Abstract. This paper presents an approach for generate train driving plans using continuous Case-Based Planning (CBP). Each plan P is formed by a set of actions elaborated without human intervention which, when applied, can move a train in a stretch of railroad. The actions are planned due the reuse and sharing of past experiences, a complex due to the variations in the (i) weight, number of locomotives and railroad cars of the train, (ii) profiles of stretches travelled and (iii) environmental conditions. To overcome these difficulties, a driver a support system is provided to help in the conduction. Here, we distributed the main steps of the CBP among specialized agents with different roles: *Planner*, *Executor* and *Case-Manager*. Our approach was evaluated by different metrics: (i) accuracy of the case recovery task, (ii) efficiency of task adaptation and application of such cases in realistic scenarios and (iii) fuel consumption. We show that the inclusion of new experiences reduces the efforts of both the *Planner* and the *Executor* and the fuel consumption and allow the reuse of the obtained experiences in similar scenarios with low effort.

Keywords: Case-based planning · Driving plans · Train driving

1 Introduction

Nowadays, almost all sectors of the economy have been tested in relation to their innovation capabilities and competitiveness to do better what they already do well. In general, these capabilities aims to create new cash flows for a company. Thus, the use of informations is crucial for reduce costs without compromising

S. Hammoudi et al. (Eds.): ICEIS 2015, LNBIP 241, pp. 192–213, 2015.
DOI: 10.1007/978-3-319-29133-8_10

quality, resources and security. A comparative can be done with the railroad that, to be competitive, must minimize transportation costs and capitalize every available resource (e.g. railroad cars and locomotives).

Although the railroad is one of the most feasible modes for freight transportation, there is still latitude for cost reduction. The use of any technological resource that can reduce expenses, for example, fuel consumption, can represent significant cost reduction in one year of operation. For example, the United States of America railroads consumed 3.6 mi of gallons of fuel in 2012. This number represents 145.7 thousand gallons per locomotive - a cost $ 14.285 mi [1].

The establishment of general train driving policies that derive from important financial returns is difficult because of: (i) the need (or existence) of specialized training for drivers; (ii) variations in train features (e.g., number of locomotives, railroad cars); and (iii) influence of driving conditions (e.g., climate, constraints). Moreover, the train driver must possess significant knowledge regarding rules and regulations (e.g., driver cab controls, signalling systems, and track safety), traction knowledge (e.g., engine layout and safety systems) and route knowledge, in addition to several hours of practical driver skills. This set of requirements is necessary in order to achieve a feasible driving of several trains. To be considerate feasible, a driving must be safe, fast and use few resources as possible.

In this context, an approach for generating centralized driving plans that drive with static rules has a small possibility of producing significant results given variations in the use conditions of the track and diversification of the experiences gained. The approach proposed here includes the use of a distributed architecture to increase the experiences available and comprehensiveness of plans before and during a journey. Furthermore, the application of Case-Based Reasoning learning allows those involved to become increasingly specialized and autonomous. To achieve autonomy and specialization, the existence of some agents specialized in well-defined tasks is assumed: *Case-Manager*, *Planner* and *Executor*.

Case-Manager is responsible to maintain the experiences stored in the case-base. The *Planner* and *Executor* agents adapt and execute plans, respectively, against different driving conditions and strategies. For example, a given strategy can target specific goals, such as energy efficiency. The construction base of each strategy can be purely mathematical, algorithmic, or rule-based (e.g., ⟨IF-THEN⟩) [2]. These techniques offer few possibilities for adaptation without the intervention of an expert in this field during the plan generation. Such difficulty represents an important limitation when there is diversification of the profiles of the railroads and trains involved due the fact that the expert are not always available to help in the plan generation.

In this paper, the main motivation is to improve the performance of *Executor* agents when facing new situations, by exchanging experiences between agents, reducing the necessary efforts to apply a driving plan. The exchange of experiences occurs when the executed driving plans by human drivers, or another sources, is incorporated to the knowledge base of *Case-Manager* agent and is used by *Planner* agent to elaborate new driving plans.

The collaborative driving approach developed directly considered the experiences of human drivers (adjusting them if necessary), as well as the experiences of automatic driving systems. In this line, capitalizing the classical approach of case-based planning (CBP) seemed more natural to us. CBP is based on case-based reasoning [3,4], where the main idea is that, in order to solve a new problem, an entity (person or software), does not need to create an entirely new plan step by step. Instead, it remembers past similar situations and adapts according to the new situation [5]. The solution of the new problem extends the experience base. Such online incremental learning capability, even in unusual environments and facilitates the acquisition and maintenance of knowledge [6], unlike rule-based systems, for example, where the learning ability is not inherent and there is difficulty adapting to changes, because of the need for updating the rules by experts in this field. This makes a rule-based system complex and difficult to maintain.

CBP is divided in four main steps: *recover* the past case solutions that are similar to the new problem, *reuse* and reuse the most similar past solution retrieved, *revise* the proposed solution to guarantee its applicability and *retain* the solution of the new problem for future use. At first step, an Euclidian Distance is used by the *Case-Manager* agent to calculate the distance between the new problem and the stored cases. A set of most similar cases, normalized between $[0, 1]$, will be adapted using the Genetic Algorithm to optimize the new solution. The best adapted solution is revised according to domain specific knowledge, to guarantee the safety during the journey, avoiding situations that damage the train or the railroad, like slipping, lack of moving force or high speed. At end, the executed driving plans are stored by *Case-Manager* agent when it returns to the station.

The approach was evaluated by the accuracy of the case recovery task, and the efficiency of task adaptation and application of such cases in several scenarios. The applicability of the proposed solution is evaluated in terms of fuel consumption, comparing our best scenario against the fuel consumptions obtained for other approaches with the same configurations of train and railroad. We show that the inclusion of new experiences reduced the efforts of both the *Planner* and the *Executor* and reduces significantly the fuel consumption. In addition, the CBP approach allowed the reuse, with low effort, of the obtained experiences in similar scenarios.

The next section introduces some related works. Section 3 presents the developed system. Then, Sect. 4 shows some of the experiment results. Finally, the last section presents our conclusions.

2 Related Papers

Many researches have applied Case-based reasoning within various problem-solving domains. For example, like a recommender mechanism [7] or in autonomic systems to minimize human intervention and to enable a seamless self-adaptive behavior in the software systems [8].

Case-Based Reasoning was used successfully in collaborative systems whose missions were to assist people in various tasks, such as selecting the appropriate behavior for an unattended vehicle ride [9,10], optimizing industrial processes [11], urban freight transport [12], short term stock selection [13]. In these systems, the goal was to share plans as a way of enriching experiences by generating shared and interactive plans and execution.

Different from another papers, the collaborative driving approach of our application considered directly the experiences of human drivers (adjusting them if necessary), as well as the experiences of automatic driving systems. Also, our main difference lies in the independent execution of the plan. During the execution of a plan there is no interaction with the *Planner* located in the processing station. The *Executor* is embedded in the onboard computer of the main locomotive, without a dedicated communication channel with the agents of its origin station. There is no transmission of driving plans because of environmental restrictions, such as the lost of GPS signal in tunnels, distance of transmission towers.

In railroad, several works were developed over the years in order to optimize driving and use of the rail network. In [14] the focus was to determine the speeds practised during the trip, using non-linear programming to avoid abrupt actions from the driver agent. A similar focus was given by [15], but with the use of fuzzy neural networks to control actions. In [16] the authors present several approaches developed for re-scheduling problem in rails networks. In [17] the authors present a train control-system to optimize trips that requires the continuously profile update by GPS (Global Positioning System) to control the locomotives, however, due the presence of tunnels the GPS signal may fail and become unavailable. In [18] an agent, based on CBR, was created to prepare train-driving plans based on the recovery of a single action at a time. Also, the internal organization of the case base was proposed in the composition of the cases and specializations. The disadvantage of this approach is the time required to organized the case-base. Also, the paper resulted in lower percentages of success than those presented here. Furthermore, the planning of a single action at a time made the approach computationally costly.

3 Methodology

The developed system, referred to as the Intelligent Train Drive System (ITDS) utilizes the following resources: rail network, freight train, and software agent [19]. The rail network is viewed as a graph where the vertices represent physical or logical stations, and the edges have information from the track (i.e., profile). Each station hosts a *Case-Manager* agent and a container of agents *co* with a *Planner*, and one or more *Executors* for each stretch $St_{a,b,c}$, where a is the departure station, b is the arrival station and c the id of the way. This configuration is illustrated in Fig. 1.

The interaction between the different agents is well defined in time. *Planner* $PA1$ receives, from an external system, a demand d to drive the train on a stretch

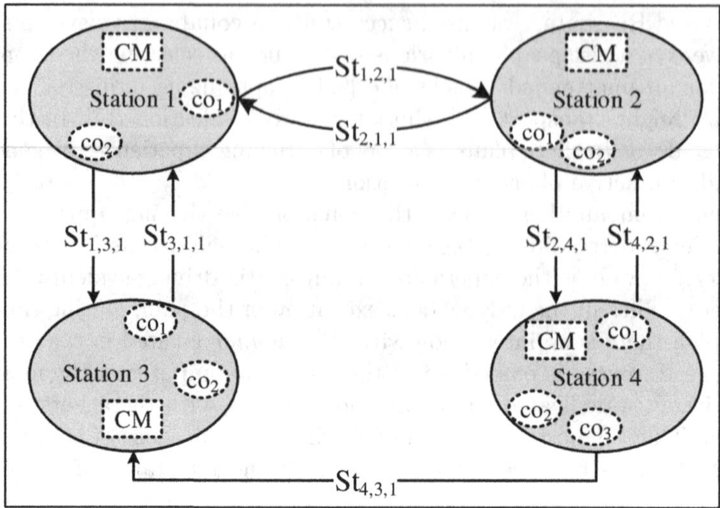

Fig. 1. Representation of 4 stations connected by different stretches St, where each station contains a *Case-Manager* CM and *Containers* of agents co.

S_i. $PA1$ then segments plan P of stretch St_i into n parts $p_1, ..., p_n$, according to the vertical profile of the stretch. Vertical profiles stores the percentage of ramp every 20 meters.

When the cycle starts, for each p_k, $PA1$ forwards to *Case-Manager* agent $CM1$ a request for plans applicable in p_k. $CM1$ collaboratively returns to $PA1$ a set of candidate plans $SP = sp_1, ..., sp_m$. $PA1$ reduces this set SP to a single feasible plan sp_k, adapting it to the current situation, and includes sp_k in plan P. Then, it selects p_{k+1} and repeats this cycle n times. At the end, P is forwarded to an $EA1$, which embarks on the train and applies it.

During the application of P, there is no communication between the agents, a differential aspect when compared to other approaches [14,15,17]. However, because the conditions for plan execution may change, it may be necessary to partially redo parts of plan P. The capacity of the *Executor* to redo parts of plan P ensures feasible and safe driving without the need to receive a new plan from $PA1$ - an important aspect for making the use of communication channels less relevant. Existing train-station communication is only used for monitoring and controlling the position of each train. Due this feature, our approach also helps to reduce the costs of freight transport and coupling across agents responsible for execute the tasks. These agents will be described in the next section.

3.1 Agents

The role of the Dispatcher is to globally manage the times and orders for the movement of trains in a rail network, rationally attempting to occupy the spaces and existing resources [20]. Dispatcher decides whether to stipulate the maximum allowable speed at certain points of the track, and to restrict or allow the passage of the train in a sector [20]. This information is sent to the *Planner* along with the dispatch order, trigger for planning.

The *Planner* generates a driving plan P to meet the demand of the Dispatcher, which is to move train T from end E_i to E_{i+1}. Each action of P can take one of the following behaviours: accelerate, maintain, or reduce the speed of train T. Each behaviour is adjusted according to a specified power. Accelerate and Reduce correspond, respectively, to increase and decrease acceleration points. In a locomotive, each acceleration point, typically from 1 to 8, generates a positive power capable of moving the train. Speed reduction can be accomplished by generating a power less than the sum of the resistances or by applying the brakes. Braking involves applying pressure in the brake pipe, measured in *psi* (pressure in pounds per square inch) and is represented here by acceleration point -1. To move the train, an appropriate acceleration point for a given position of the railroad stretch to be covered must be planned in order to avoid sliding and overcome the sum of resistances [21].

To ensure train movement in all points of the track, it is also necessary to know the minimum required power. This power is calculated by the Dispatcher and reported to the *Planner* in the dispatch order. The calculation considers the minimum tractive force of all the locomotives intended to move a train against the high resistance of the stretch to be covered. Moreover, the resulting set of actions should meet the objectives, which are in opposition in the first two at the base, of performing a quick trip, reducing fuel consumption, and complying with the security restrictions. Thus, one should plan speeds near the cruise speed, for example, 5 km/h below the maximum speed. Within this criterion, actions should reduce fuel consumption and travel time. The resulting set is the driving plan P for train T in a stretch St_i.

The *Executor* is responsible to apply plan P, received at end E_i, performing the following basic tasks: testing the applicability of a_k based on the current train conditions, adjusting the parameters of a_k (if necessary), and applying a_k. Until the complete execution of P, P may undergo several Δ adjustments. For example, in the case of non-applicability of an action a_k, the *Executor* may adjust a_k based on driving skills. Adverse conditions may represent, for example, a climate change (changes the friction coefficient), changes in the maximum allowable speed, and others. Such conditions perceived by various sensors are read in predetermined time intervals.

At least, *Case-Manager* has two basic functions: (i) providing the *Planner* with a set of plans applicable to each part of a given stretch and (ii) maintaining a base of plans in a dynamic memory structure [22]. Each *Case-Manager*, located in a station, maintains only the plans applied in the stretches from ends St_i to St_{i+1} and from St_i to St_{i-1}. Maintaining only the plans of the stretches connected to the station allows specialization in these stretches. Each plan executed $P + \Delta$ is returned to the *Case-Manager* of the origin end point to be integrated into the local base of the station plans. Such structure allows the inclusion of a new plan that can activate simple internal processes of plan reclassification and/or more sophisticated optimization of data structures and indexing of plan contents [22].

3.2 Plan Elaboration

The elaboration of a plan requires: information from the train (i.e., position, number of locomotives and railroad cars, and weight) and from the track stretch (i.e., maximum speeds, friction coefficients, and vertical profile). The vertical profile is critical for defining the relevant portions of a stretch $St = s_1, ..., s_n$ (see Fig. 2).

For each part s_i, a plan is prepared that corresponds to a new problem to be solved. Each part must become specialized. Figure 2 illustrates plan P with $p_1, ..., p_n$. Each p_i describes a set of actions with more predictable behaviours (maintain, accelerate, and reduce) for a vertical profile (rising, falling, and plain/plateau).

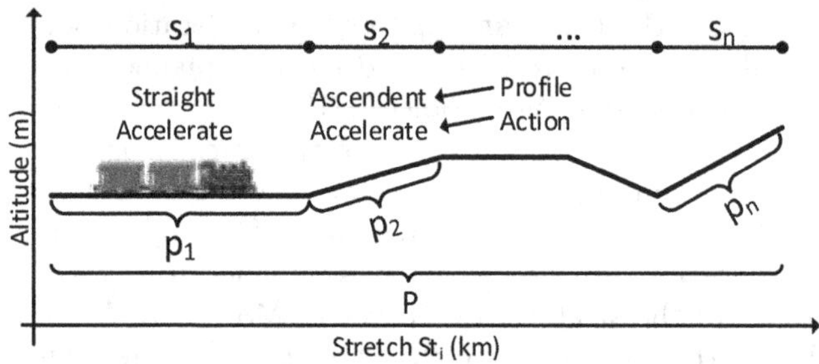

Fig. 2. Example of segmentation of a stretch St_i into parts $s_1, ..., s_n$ according to the vertical profile and a set of cases $p_1, p_2, ..., p_n$, which when ordered form a plan P for the movement of trains.

The behaviours that must be undertaken for proper driving are shown in Fig. 3. Such behaviours will vary depending on current speed s, initial speed s_i, cruise speed s_c, and maximum speed s_s [23]. Proper driving is obtained when the current speed is greater than the initial speed and less than the maximum speed, remaining close to the cruising speed. States indicate actions that must be performed to achieve proper driving. State I suggests ACCELERATING the train because the current speed is less than the initial speed. States II and III_1 suggest ACCELERATE or MAINTAIN speed. On the other hand, state III_2 must REDUCE the speed because of the proximity to the current speed with the maximum speed. In state IV, it must ACCELERATE to approximate the current speed to the speed regimen. The BRAKING action is recommended in state V because the train can exceed the maximum allowable speed.

Pragmatically, case C is a representation of a real-world object or episode in a particular representation scheme [5]. A case represents a finite set of n attribute/value pairs that is a snapshot of the situation executed by a train conductor during one trip.

Figure 4 shows an example of a case recovered in the form of pairs $\langle$*attribute*, *value*$\rangle$ formed by the following attributes: action performed (EAC), initial kilometre (KM), number of locomotives (NL), number of railroad cars (NW), initial

V
S_s
S_c
S_i
S_critical
III_1
III_2
II
IV
I_2
I_1

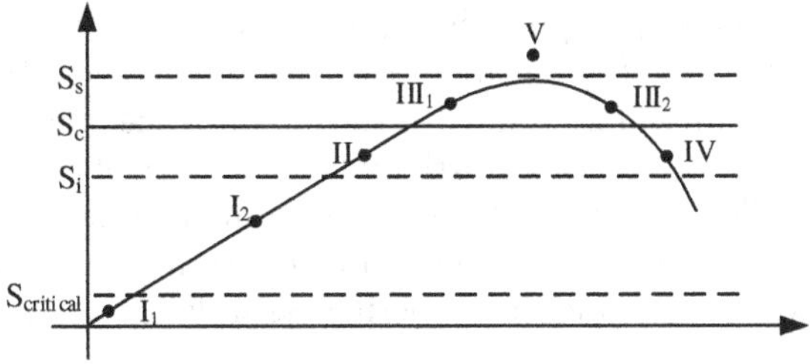

Fig. 3. Possible states of train driving [23].

speed (IS) in km/h, final speed (FS) in km/h, maximum speed (MS) in km/h, ramp percentage (%R), and total displacement (CL) in meters. Attribute values of IS, $Profile$, KM, $\%R$ are obtained from sensors, the values of NL and NW attributes are extracted from the dispatch order, and finally, the attribute values EAC, FS and CL are derived from specific calculations. Although such attributes are presented as an illustration, they represent the dominant features in the movement of a train.

c1 = <EAC, Maintain>, <KM, 339.495>, <NL, 3>, <NW, 58>, <IS, 20>, <FS, 28>, <MS, 40>, <%R, 0>, <CL, 520>, <J, <0,8><5,3><25,4><35,6><50,8>>

Fig. 4. Example of a past case with the solution applied.

A case also has a solution formed by a set $J = \langle m_1, AP_1\rangle, \langle m_2, AP_2\rangle, \langle m_j, AP_j\rangle$ of ordered pairs, where each pair contains an acceleration point (AP) and an application position (M) defined in meters. Figure 5 shows an instance of P, and an application of each AP, from left to right, must move from 0 Km to 60 km. The determination of each element of P should allow the *Executor* to move the train feasibly.

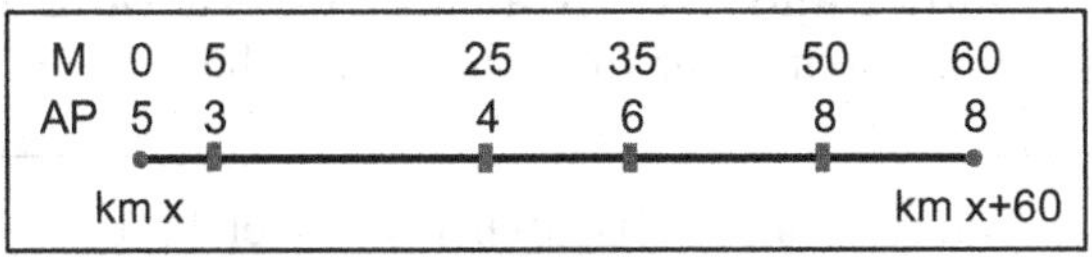

M 0 5 25 35 50 60
AP 5 3 4 6 8 8
km x
km x+60

Fig. 5. Example of the solution of an applicable case used to move a train from the kilometre (km) x to the kilometre $x + 60$.

It is expected that, as the *Case-Manager* agent has in its case base, a number of cases applied in stretches leaving the station where it resides, there are greater possibilities of recovering an applicable case. If the case is not fully applicable, it is believed that the adaptations are in reduced percentages. Table 1 shows the signature of cases organized according to the actions taken and the constituents of the track profile. Table 1 shows, partially the solutions of cases (m_1 and AP_i). This organization allows recovery of cases more similar to the stretch of the track in question and the action to be applied. Each descriptor element in each case has a weight, assigned via validated experiments in laboratory.

Table 1. Scheme partial storage cases and weights of the attributes of the signatures. In this example, the solution of the cases is omitted.

Case-base													
i	Action	Profile	Signature								Solution		
			KM	NL	NW	IS	FS	MS	%R	CL	m_1	AP_1	...
1	Accelerate	Straight	339414	3	58	9	10	40	0.28	0.009	0	5	...
2	Accelerate	Straight	339404	3	58	10	11	45	-0.41	0,403	0	6	...
3	Accelerate	Straight	277677	3	47	34	43	53	-0.03	0.915	0	4	...
4	Accelerate	Ascendant	302883	4	59	24	25	53	1.54	0.243	0	8	...
5	Accelerate	Descendant	335872	3	58	3	23	45	1.24	0.310	0	6	

3.3 Inter and Intra Agents Data Flow

Figure 6 shows the basic flow of inter and intra agent collaboration. In this figure, the Dispatcher has been omitted. The flow is started by the *Planner*, whose first activity is to receive the dispatch order generated by the Dispatcher and to generate a new problem. As a result, two collaboration cycles are established: the first interactively involves the *Planner* and the *Case-Manager* agent, and the second sequentially involves the *Planner*, *Executor*, and *Case-Manager*. Henceforth, $PA1$ is used to designate a *Planner*, $EA1$ an *Executor*, and $CM1$ a *Case-Manager* agent.

Planning Flow: Planner and Case-Manager Interaction. Planning starts when $PA1$ receives a dispatch order from the Dispatcher.

```
(inform :sender Dispatcher :receiver PA1
:content (locomotives=3, wagons=58, [...]))
```

Then, the perception of the environment is performed, resulting in a new case $c1$ to traverse stretch S_i. The instantiation of $c1$ is managed by a dedicated module that performs two basic functions: (i) read sensors for speed, position, traction, and others, of the train; (ii) calculate, in this case, the values for

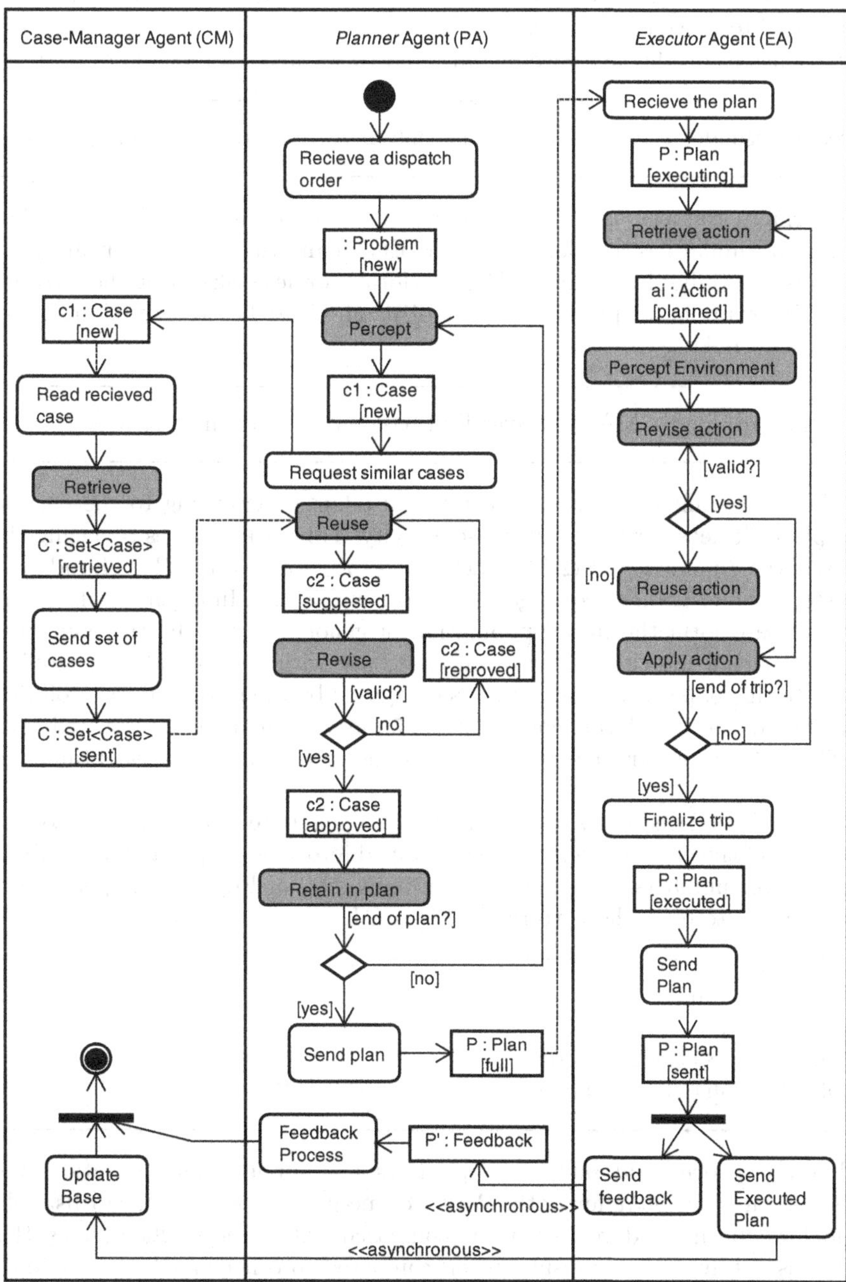

Fig. 6. Basic ITDS flow.

resistance, effective tractive force of the pulling locomotives, acceleration force, adherent tractive force, etc. The data set (perceived and derivatives) defines the values used to move the train [21].

$PA1$ passes on the new case instantiated by means of a request to MA1.

(request :sender PA1 :receiver MA1 :content (⟨attributes of the problem⟩))

Internally, the message is received and managed by the *Case-Manager*. The recovery of similar cases is done using the Euclidian distance. The advantage of this division of labor is to allow $PA1$ to perform another task during the recovery phase, for example, to process another dispatch order.The recovered cases are then sent to $PA1$.

(inform :sender MA1 :receiver PA1 :content (⟨set of similar cases⟩))

The most similar case c_i is selected and adapted according to the current perception (if necessary) by the Reuse activity. This task involves replacing the values of the J pairs (e.g., Fig. 5), which are, respectively, $\langle m_1, AP_i\rangle$. The adaptation step of the *Planner* used a genetic algorithm [24,25]. In a genetic algorithm the case base form the initial population of genotypes. Firstly, the algorithm retrieves partial matching cases from case base with specified design requirements. In this paper, each individual is composed by the recovered case solution J and the initial population consist of the 50 most similar cases recovered from the *Case-Manager* to represent the average number of similar cases obtained in retrieve step.

Next the retrieved cases are mapped into a genotype representation, so, the solution J of the each recovered case is mapped into a genotype of an individual, using integer numbers. For example, the individual of Fig. 5 is mapped as the frame bellow, to obey the pattern used by ECJ.

Individual Number: i0|
Evaluated: T
Fitness: f1138065562|427.0047|
i0|i5|i5|i3|i25|i4|i35|i6|i50|i8|i60|i8

Later crossover and mutation operators are applied. The mutation and crossover rates are 50 % for both. We used one-point crossover since this technique have been good results when compared with others [26] and as this mode has obtained better results when compared to other breeding techniques like travelling salesman problem, a classic problem of combinatorial optimization. Finally, newly generated genotypes are mapped into corresponding phenotypes/cases by inferring values for the attributes and adding the context of the new design.

Applying the genetic algorithm to case adaptation also requires the identification of a fitness function. In this paper, two of the main objectives are to reduce the fuel consumption and optimizing the speed practised by *Executor* agents. So, the fitness function $g(x)$, illustrated in Eq. 1, was defined to minimize such objectives, although they are opposites. These attributes have a great impact on the generation of individuals and will determine their utility in the population. Each attribute has a factor which represents his weight in the problem: fuel consumption ($flgtt$) and speed (fv), where $flgtt = 0.02$ e $fv = 0.01$. The values of fuel consumption ($lgtt$) and speed (v) are obtained by simulating the application of the individual in the problem. During the simulation, the following values are calculated for each action: consumption, travel time, resistance, force to drive the train, and others. Therefore, the fitness function considers calculations that result in the forces required to move the train considered [18].

$$g(x) = \sum_{j=0}^{J} \left(\frac{1}{(flgtt \times lgtt_j) + (fv \times v_j)} \right) \quad (1)$$

The values of $flgtt$ and fv were calculated by a genetic algorithm made specific for it, where the individuals are composed by pairs of $\langle flgtt, fv \rangle$. Each parameter can vary according the interval [0.01; 1.00], totalling 100 possible values for each factor, being this the value of each population generated by the algorithm. For each individual a journey was simulated, all with the same train and railroad configurations. The fuel consumption obtained in each journey was used as fitness function value. The crossover and mutation techniques used the same configuration developed for this paper. The stopping criteria was set to 100 generations, because there is a 10000 possible factor combinations.

During the fitness calculation, penalties are assigned to the situations which entail lack of security, damage to rail or train. The situations which are assigned maximum penalties for individuals out of place are: speed exceeding maximum speed; skating; displacement action greater than the maximum expected displacement; increasing the speed without sufficient acceleration force; speed reducing but with a positive acceleration force and projected speed bigger than maximum speed. These penalties are intended to prevent such individuals from spreading in the population. If any individual generated fall into any of these conditions, your fitness value is equal to $100/(geneSize/2)$. The value 100 is meaningful to the average values obtained by the fitness function.

Returning to the adaptation step of this paper, the crossover and mutation operations creates individuals that consists of solutions for the actual problem, called proposed solutions. Each solution generated by the genetic algorithm J is composed by acceleration points and places of its applications, according to Fig. 5. Each proposed solution J is simulated, applying the acceleration points at the positions specified in J. The resulting fuel consumption corresponds to the fitness of the individual. If the proposed solution is not applicable, because it results in slipping or lack of movement force, the individual is penalized with a high value for the fitness and this individual is discarded. The stopping criterion of the strategy was the number of generations, equal to 10, a satisfactory number in terms of fuel economy and greater speed in the adaptation of cases. At end, the individual with minor value of fitness will be chosen for the adapted case. The fitness function maximizes some value by default, so, to minimize the fuel consumption we convert the fitness function to $1/g(x)$.

The adapted case $c1'$ (corresponds to case $c1'$ in Fig. 7) is feasible if and only if all parts of J meet the following situations: (i) does not result in sliding, (ii) have sufficient force to move the train, and (iii) if the acceleration point can be reduced and continue to move the train, which indicates unnecessary fuel consumption of the action. If the case is not approved, the values of J are again submitted to the Reuse step, and this is repeated until a valid solution is found and the case is approved. A valid solution must comply with the criteria (i) and (ii) described in the previous paragraph, but not necessarily with criterion (iii), added only to reduce fuel consumption.

c1' = <EAC, Maintain>, <KM, 335>, <NL, 3>, <NW, 58>, <IS, 20>, <FS, 20>, <MS, 40>, <%R, 0>, <CL, 520>, <J, <0,8><5,3><25,3><35,7><50,8>>

Fig. 7. Adapted case.

After adding the valid adapted case in P, $PA1$ verifies whether the application of the plan results in the arrival at the destination. If not, the planning cycle is repeated for the next part of stretch s_i. If so, P is sent to $EA1$.

(execute :sender PA1 :receiver EA1 :content (the plan P))

$EA1$ is embedded in the onboard computer of the main locomotive and begins to command it. If later, another train passes through the same station, another *Executor* $EA2$ is created with a specific plan for the new train.

Flow of Execution of the Plan: Executor. The plan execution cycle is similar to the planning cycle. Each *Executor* starts its activities upon receiving the trip plan P. In possession of P, $EA1$ starts the trip. During the trip, $EA1$ Recovers an action a_k of P and evaluates its preconditions. For such, it perceives the environment through data read from the onboard computer of the lead locomotive (e.g., maximum speed, friction coefficient, and others). If no precondition is violated at the time of reading, the a_k action is applied, resulting in new information (i.e., speed, position, and others), which becomes the precondition for the next action a_{k+1}. On the other hand, if one or more preconditions are invalid, for example, because of some unforeseen event (e.g., rain, fog, or changing the speed limit), $EA1$ corrects the action of the plan based on its knowledge of driving (Reuse). Such adjustment is made by evaluating the reason for the failure, which can be: sliding, lack of force to move, or stopping unexpectedly. It is expected for each change (when required) to cause as insignificant an impact as possible, i.e., the shortest distance between the planned and the applied acceleration point, thus resulting in a reduced state space search.

Once the task of $EA1$ driving the train from end E_i to end E_{i+1} is complete, the Finalize trip activity is executed. In it, plan P and its Δ adjustments are processed, resulting in a plan P. P is returned to the origin station E_i by an *Executor* whose destination is E_i.

(inform :sender EA1 : receiver MA1 :content(an executed plan $P + \Delta$))

The transport of the modified plan to the origin by means of another train is assumed because, during the trip there is no communication channel dedicated to transmit the plans between the train and the station. If the stretch has only one direction, the plan is stored at the station and forwarded to the next station that has a connection with the plan origin station. Communication between train and origin station is limited to sending information related to the conditions of the railroad and the position of the train because of the cost of data transmission and limitations of the means of communication, most of the time, against geographical conditions.

Update Case Base: Case-Manager. *Case-Manager* agent MA1, upon receiving plan P, does the following: for each profile p_i of P, identify the action taken (accelerate, maintain, or reduce) based on the speed variation practised. Each separate and identified part of the plan is compared with other existing cases in the base. If it is already present, its reputation receives a backup. Otherwise, a new event is inserted. The reputation is a piece of information that allows management of the case base (if necessary, thus reducing the number of cases).

Sharing Plans: Sharing plans aims not, the planning cycle is repeated for the next of problems. In some cases, such as the first mission in a given section, the sis-theme has no plan excerpt in question. So one can use plans of other portions having the same station as the starting point. These other plans were made by other agents. The sharing of plans for a station is ensured by the *Case-Manager*. He has the knowledge of the station all residents planners on the same computer or station unit. It is hoped that the use of knowledge of other agents who plans tion leads generated can be better than planes formed without considering previous knowledge.

4 Experiments

The approach was evaluated by different metrics: (i) fuel consumption (*LGTT*), (ii) accuracy of the case recovery task, and (iii) efficiency of task adaptation and application of such cases in synthetic scenarios which were created inspired in real-world scenarios. The last two indicate the efficiency of the collaboration of the *Case-Manager* and *Planner*.

The experiments were conducted in a simulated driving environment, where all field equations of [21] was validated and implemented. The validation was performed by comparing data from a simulated trip with actual data from sensors with drivers travel histories; data were recorded without human intervention-in. The comparison was made after the implementation of the mathematical model. The speed at the real driving was confronted (Human Driver Speed) with the speed practised in the simulator (Speed), cf. Figure 8.

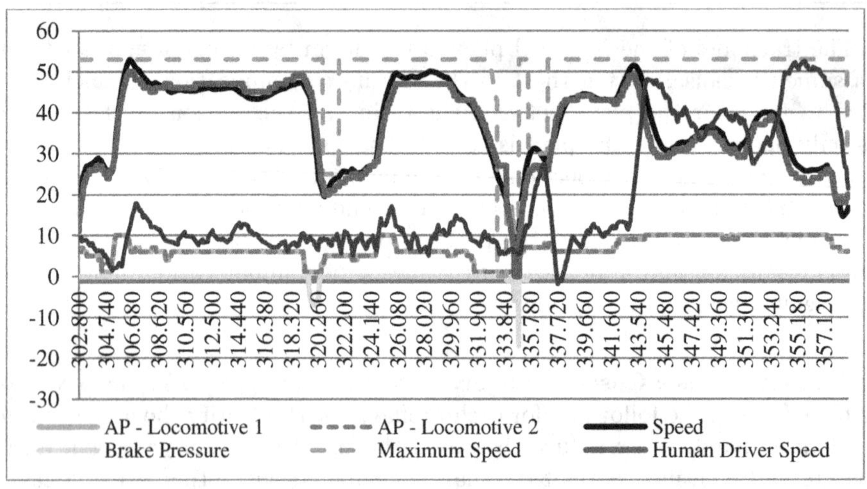

Fig. 8. Comparison between real and simulated data.

It was observed that, using the same acceleration points used by the driver, resulting in the same power, and the simulated and actual speed remained very close to each other. This equalization of speeds was made possible by the mathematical model used to calculate effort and train movement resistance that generated very close to those practised in actual travel results.

We also used a Java Evolutionary framework [27] to implement the Genetic Algorithm. Moreover, the profiles of the railroads, trains, and the initial case base are derived from real situations obtained from a railway company.

The train configurations used in the experiments are shown in Table 2. Two different stretches of real railroads were included: St_1 and St_2, both with the same length (approximately 64 km), but with different profiles vertical and horizontal and maximum speed restrictions.

To evaluate the learning curve of each agent and the performance of the collaboration in terms of sharing and reusing plans, four scenarios were defined (see Table 3).

The initial case base of the *Case-Manager* agent, in all tested scenarios, contains actual trip plans and trips executed in simulators [2].

Table 2. Train configuration used in the experiments.

Train	Locomotives	Railway cars	Weight (tons)
1	3	58	6278
2	4	100	6342
3	4	58	6541
4	2	31	3426
5	3	47	5199
6	2	31	3441
7	4	59	6579
8	2	28	3118

Table 3. Simulated scenarios in the experiments.

Scenario	Train (Table 1)	Reuse plans	Stretch
A	1	No	St_1
B	1	Yes	St_1
C	1	Yes	St_2
D	[1;8]	Yes	St_1

The scenarios are evaluated according to the efficiency (%) of the recovery and adaptation steps of the cases. This percentage indicates the success of recovery or adaptation of a case. For example, at any given time, the *Case-Manager* agent recovers, for the *Planner* agent, a case with a set of actions $A = \{\langle 0,6\rangle, \langle 10,6\rangle, \langle 30,8\rangle, \langle 60,8\rangle\}$. This set is adapted by the *Planner*, resulting in $A' = \{\langle 0,6\rangle, \langle 10,6\rangle, \langle 30,7\rangle, \langle 60,7\rangle\}$. Thus, the recovery task has an accuracy of 75 %. Then, A is passed to the *Executor* agent and applied without any changes, resulting in a 100 % fitting accuracy. Soon, the adaptation effort is 25 % and the execution effort, in terms of adaptation, is null.

In scenario A, the *Case-Manager* agent uses only the initial case base. Ten trips were planned and all of them for train 1 in stretch St_1. All plans were executed by an *Executor*. At the end of each trip, the new experiences (new plans) were not incorporated to the case base of the *Case-Manager*. Figure 9 presents the efficiency (%) of the recovery and adaptation steps of all the cases in the ten trips. It is observed that the recovery of cases is less effective than the adaptation of cases. In percentage, the difference between the recovery and adaptation task corresponds to the contribution of the adaptation task to make the plan applicable to a given case. The average of this difference is 8 %, with a standard deviation of 1 %. Compared to a method of satisfaction of constraints, the effort obtained is less in terms of memory used, execution time, and number of states. Regardless of the highest peaks of success of the recovery and adaptation task being 46 % and 51 %, respectively, the generated and executed plans are similar at 86 %. The similarity is calculated by the Cosine Distance.

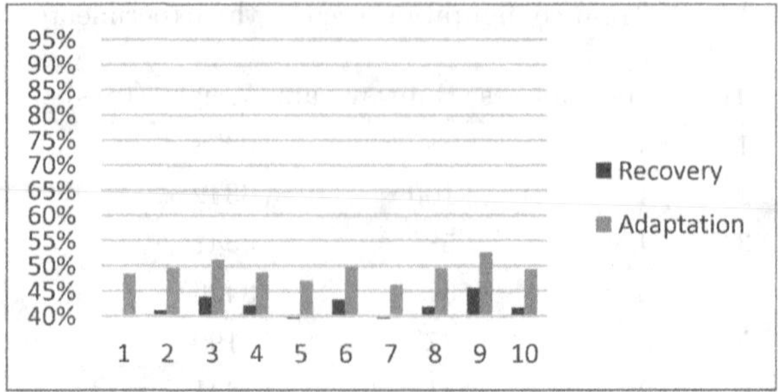

Fig. 9. Results of scenario A. Ten trips with the same train configuration (configuration 1), in stretch St_1 and without reusing plans.

In scenario B, the same train configuration and the same stretch from scenario A was used. However, at every trip made by the *Executor*, the applied plan was incorporated to the case base of the *Case-Manager*. Figure 10 shows that the inclusion of new plans in the case base of the *Case-Manager* increased by approximately 25 % the efficiency of the recovery and adaptation tasks. The similarity between what was planned and what was executed is on average 90 %. The addition of new cases to the experience base broadens the efficiency of the planning task. It is observed that between trips 1 and 3, there is an increasing linear trend of 20 %. Moreover, from trip 3, there is a slightly increasing stability, with average variation of 4 % for both tasks, and with standard deviation of 2 %. The variation is justified because the trips followed speeds similar to each other, but with differences in driving plans at certain times. This difference occurs because of adaptations made by the genetic algorithm, which in some places suggested different acceleration points. This results in variation in the power used, and consequently, variation of the practised speeds. This fact is inherent to the natural behaviour of the genetic approach (e.g., mutation).

In scenario C, as in scenario B, on each new trip made by the *Executor*, the applied plans are incorporated into the experience base of the *Case-Manager*, and thus reused by the *Planner* agent. The case base of the *Case-Manager* began with the experiences generated in scenario B. The steps for recovery and adaptation have an average efficiency of 80 % and 86 %, respectively (see Fig. 11).

In percentage, the difference between the recovery and adaptation task was 9 % at the beginning of the experiment, and then immediately fell to an average of 5 %, with a standard deviation of 1 %. Despite increased effort because of unfamiliarity with the environment, the results are significant. These results encourage the use of a collaborative approach between agents, located at different stations, to exchange plans.

Figure 12 shows the results of scenario D, where the trips always occur in the same track, but with eight different train formations. In this scenario, the *Case-Manager* agent initiates the experiences of scenario B. In terms of efficiency of recovery and adaptation tasks, the adaptation task proves superior. There is an expected drop in success because the train configurations are different for each trip. However, even in this scenario without repetition of train configuration, it is possible to note that, to the extent that new cases are included in the base, the overall efficiency improves. Hopefully, with a greater number of trips with similar configurations, efficiency rates move rapidly towards scenario B.

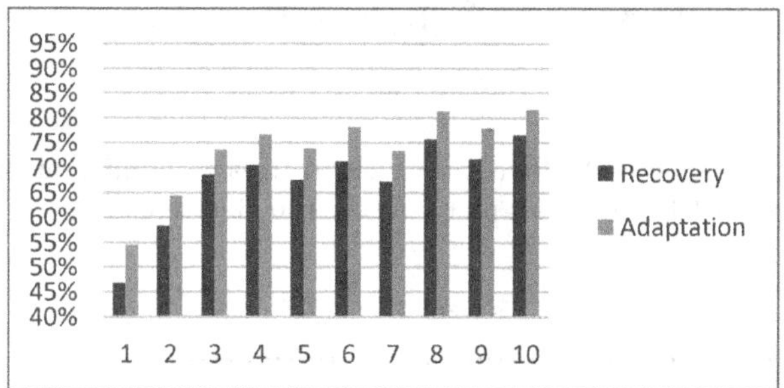

Fig. 10. Results of scenario B where was executed ten trips with the same train configuration (configuration 1), in stretch St_1 and reusing implemented plans.

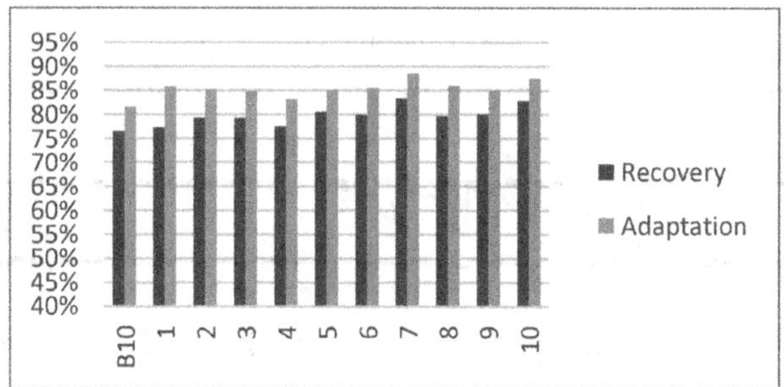

Fig. 11. Results of scenario C where was executed trips with same train configuration (configuration 1) and initial plans of scenario B, but in stretch St_2.

In the scenarios on which we worked, it can be observed that without reusing plans as past solutions, the average success rates in the recovery and adaptation tasks remain low, 42 % and 49 %, respectively. However, when we start to reuse the plans as past solutions, the average success rates of recovery and adaptation tasks increase to 64 % and 74 %, respectively. In terms of complexity, raising the efficiency of such tasks reduces the effort of searching for the problem solution. Finally, the contribution of the adaptation task, in the reuse of shared experiences of different stretches, remained at the same level of scenario B. This suggests that the accumulation of cases in a given scenario proves to be useful in another scenario.

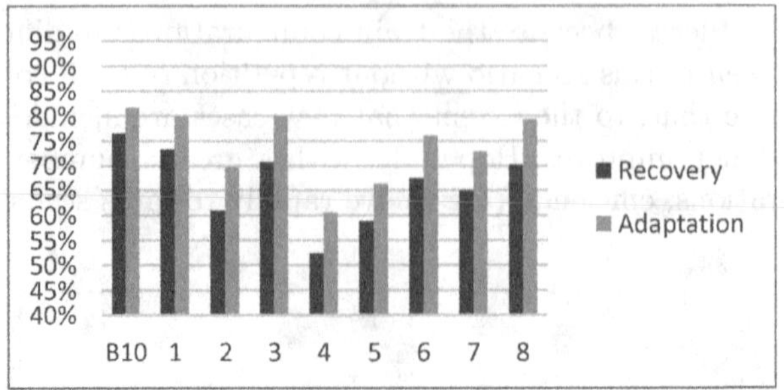

Fig. 12. Results of scenario D where was executed trips with different train configurations (configurations 1 to 8), initial plans of scenario B, stretch St_1.

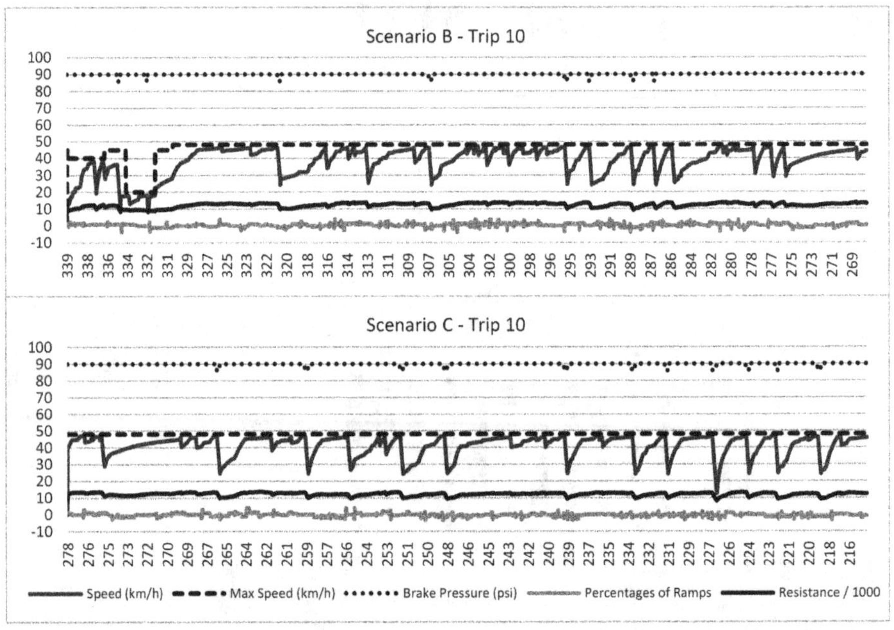

Fig. 13. Data of trips made for the same train configuration in different stretches.

Figure 13 shows graphically the execution of the ten trips for scenarios B and C. It can be noted that there is a significant difference for each profile. Such differences can be observed in the maximum speeds practised, percentages of ramps, and resistances. The evolution of the speeds shows a significant difference in driving style. The decrease in speeds is related to the applications of the brakes, and to reflections of the driving policy that attempts to maintain the speed of the train near the maximum allowable speed. Such heuristics are applied to attempt to reduce the duration of a trip. It should be indicated that the first application of the brake follows a default value and must heavily influence train speed.

In all observed situations the effort on adaptation is present, but efficient, and rises over time. For the field in question, as the trains and the environment change, the plans used in past situations are not easily applicable to others; this effectively requires an adaptive and efficient approach. This finding goes to the direction of what has classically been understood as an advantage of the CBP in view of a rule-based approach [5]. The latter approach requires explicit knowledge models regarding the application domain. This demand is difficult to execute in a complex environment. It also fails when there is no rule that can be applied in the field. Furthermore, if the environment changes, there is a need to update the rule base to be able to derive a solution. As in CBR, knowledge of the field is represented in the form of cases. It exempts an explicit representation of the application domain. This allows dynamically maintaining and learning new knowledge as new cases are incorporated into the case base.

Table 4 is a comparison table that contrasts the performance of human drivers (Actual column) driving a simulator where the actions applied are determined by a constraint satisfaction system (DCOP column) [2] and by the approach presented (Our column). DCOP column represents the best values obtained in this approach. It is emphasized that for all consumption values (measured in *LGTT*), our approach is higher than for the other competitors, except on a single opportunity (train 2), where the DCOP is higher by 5 %.

Table 4. Consumptions obtained in scenario C in *LGTT*.

Train	Consumption (LGTT)		Reduction		
	Actual (A)	DCOP (B)	Our (C)	C-A (%)	C-B (%)
1	6.19	4.16	3.36	50 %	26 %
2	5.68	4.18	4.22	30 %	-5 %
3	6.23	4.09	3.95	41 %	10 %
4	6.49	4.51	3.88	46 %	23 %
5	6.29	4.22	3.31	49 %	24 %
6	6.17	3.99	3.69	40 %	8 %
7	6.26	4.07	3.86	42 %	11 %
8	5.68	4.41	4.00	34 %	6 %

The feasibility of an automatic train driving system seems significantly important. For example, for a fuel consumption expenditure of approximately 250 million dollars per year, any cost savings above 6 % can have a significant impact on the competitiveness of the freight transport sector.

5 Conclusions

We presented an approach for sharing experiences in generating plans for driving trains with collaborative ability. Results obtained shows that the adopted approach can be generalized and deployed at various stations of a rail network and also shows that the efficiency of recovery and adaptation tasks increases as new cases are included in the case-base. Such efficiency generates a tendency to reduce efforts in planning and re-planning driving plans when different situations appear (e.g. new train features or new stretch of railroad). However, if conditions change significantly, planning efforts increase, at least initially.

In terms of domain application, two results are important: the generated driving plans can produce significant monetary gains; and in terms of reuse of experiences, the approach suggested that good drivers should be used to drive trains in several different stretches of a railroad, for a certain time, in order to generate experiences. Such experiments can then be used to generate good plans for less experienced drivers that not know the stretch to be covered. This helps rationalize the expertise capable for driving trains efficiently. Future work should follow the following directions: the use of multi objective approaches to adapt the retrieved cases and the expansion of the experiments in another railroads.

Acknowledegements. Our thanks to Brazilian Federal Agency for the Support and Evaluation of Graduate Education (CAPES) and Brazilian Innovation Agency (FINEP) to support this research.

References

1. U.S. Department of the Assistant Secretary for Research, and of Transportation (US DOT), T. O.-R. U. D., Table 4–17: Class i rail freight fuel consumption and travel, Eletronic (2014)
2. Sato, D. et al.: Lessons learned from a simulated environment for trains conduction. In: 2012 IEEE International Conference on Industrial Technology (ICIT), pp. 533–538 (2012)
3. Aamodt, A., Plaza, E.: AI Commun. **7**, 39 (1994)
4. Spalzzi, L.: Artif. Intell. Rev. **16**, 3 (2001)
5. Kolodner, J.: Case-based Reasoning. Morgan Kaufmann Publishers Inc., San Francisco (1993)
6. Smiti, A., Elouedi, Z.: Int. J. Comput. Appl. **32**, 49 (2011)
7. Wang, C.-S., Yang, H.-L.: Expert Syst. Appl. **39**, 4335 (2012)
8. Khan, M.J., Awais, M.M., Shamail, S., Awan, I.: Simul. Model. Pract. Theory **19**, 2256 (2011)
9. Rodríguez, S., Corchado, J.M., Bajo, J.: Intelligent guidance and suggestions using case-based planning. In: Weber, R.O., Richter, M.M. (eds.) ICCBR 2007. LNCS (LNAI), vol. 4626, pp. 389–403. Springer, Heidelberg (2007)
10. Vacek, S., Gindele, T., Zollner, J., Dillmann, R.: Using case-based reasoning for autonomous vehicle guidance. In: IEEE/RSJ International Conference on Intelligent Robots and Systems, 2007, IROS 2007, pp. 4271–4276 (2007)
11. Navarro, M., et al.: Expert Syst. Appl. **39**, 7887 (2012)

12. Bouhana, A., Zidi, A., Fekih, A., Chabchoub, H., Abed, M.: Exp. Syst. Appl. **42**, 3724 (2015)
13. Ince, H.: Appl. Soft Comput. **22**, 205 (2014)
14. Gu, Q., Cao, F., Tang, T.: Energy efficient driving strategy for trains in MRT systems. In: 2012 15th International IEEE Conference on Intelligent Transportation Systems (ITSC), pp. 427–432 (2012)
15. Hengyu, L., Hongze, X.: An integrated intelligent control algorithm for high-speed train ato systems based on running conditions. In: 2012 Third International Conference on Digital Manufacturing and Automation (ICDMA), pp. 202–205 (2012)
16. Fang, W., Sun, J., Wu, X., Yao, X.: Re-scheduling in railway networks. In: 2013 13th UK Workshop on Computational Intelligence (UKCI), pp. 342–352 (2013)
17. Eldredge, D., Houpt, P.: Trip optimizer for railroads. Technical report, IEEE Control Systems Society (2011)
18. Borges, A. et al.: An intelligent system for driving trains using case-based reasoning. In: 2012 IEEE International Conference on Systems, Man, and Cybernetics (SMC), pp. 1694–1699 (2012)
19. Wooldridge, M., Jennings, N.R.: Knowl. Eng. Re. **10**, 115 (1995)
20. Company, G.R.S.: Elements of railway signaling, General Railway Signal (1979)
21. Loumiet, J., Jungbauer, W., Abrams, B.: Train Accident Reconstruction and FELA and Railroad Litigation. Lawyers & Judges Publishing Company, Tucson (2005)
22. Schank, R.C.: Dynamic Memory: A Theory of Reminding and Learning in Computers and People. Cambridge University Press, New York (1983)
23. Pinto, B., Scheneebeli, H., Borba, J., Amaral, P., Ferreira, A.B.: Microcomputador de bordo para controle de potência de locomotivas em tração múltipla. II Congresso Nacional de Automação Industrial, vol. 1, pp. 125–129. São Paulo, SP, Brazil (1985)
24. Baeck, T., Fogel, D., Michalewicz, Z.: Evolutionary Computation 1: Basic Algorithms and Operators. Taylor & Francis, New York (2000)
25. Mitra, R., Basak, J.: Int. J. Intell. Syst. **20**, 627 (2005)
26. Mendes, Magalhães: J. WSEAS Trans. Comput. **12**, 164 (2013)
27. Luke, S., et al.: ECJ 23: A Java evolutionary computation library (2014). http://www.cs.gmu.edu/~eclab/projects/ecj/

Resource Allocation Mechanisms and Time Constraint Propagation Techniques in Fuzzy Workflow Nets

Joslaine Cristina Jeske de Freitas, Stéphane Julia, and Leiliane Pereira de Rezende(✉)

Computing Faculty, Federal University of Uberlândia, Uberlandia, MG, Brazil
joslaine@gmail.com, stephane@facom.ufu.br, leily_rezende@yahoo.com.br

Abstract. The main objective behind Workflow systems is to support the definition, execution and control of Workflow processes. A Workflow process defines a set of activities and the specific order in which they should be executed, in order to reach a common objective. Therefore, it is important to manage in the best possible way time and resources. The proposal of this work is to express in a more realistic way the resource allocation mechanisms when human behavior is considered in Workflow activities. In order to accomplish this, fuzzy sets delimited by possibility distributions will be associated with the Petri net models that represent human type resource allocation mechanisms. Additionally, the duration of activities that appear on the routes (control structure) of the Workflow process, will be represented by fuzzy time intervals. To define the execution of activities belongings to minimum and maximum intervals, a time constraint propagation mechanism is proposed. New firing rules based on a joint possibility distribution will then be defined.

Keywords: Petri net · Workflow net · Resource allocation · Fuzzy time · Possibility theory · Time constraints · Visibility intervals

1 Introduction

The purpose of Workflow Management Systems is to execute Workflow processes. Workflow processes represent the sequence of activities that have to be executed within an organization to treat specific cases and to reach a well-defined goal. Of all notations used for the modeling of Workflow processes, Petri nets are very suitable [1], as they represent basic routings. Moreover, Petri nets can be used for specifying the real time characteristics of Workflow Management Systems (in the time Petri net case) as well as complex resource allocation mechanisms. As a matter of fact, late deliveries in an organization are generally due to resources overload.

Many papers have already considered the Petri net theory as an efficient tool for the modeling and analysis of Workflow Management Systems. In [1],

L.P. de Rezende—Scholarship CAPES - Proc. $n°$ 99999.001925/2015-06.

S. Hammoudi et al. (Eds.): ICEIS 2015, LNBIP 241, pp. 214–235, 2015.
DOI: 10.1007/978-3-319-29133-8_11

Workflow nets, which are acyclic Petri net models used to represent Workflow process, are defined.

Workflow nets have been identified and widely used as a solid model of Workflow processes, for example in [2–5]. In [6], an extension of Workflow nets is presented. This model is called time Workflow net and associates time intervals with the transitions of the corresponding Petri net model. In [7], an extended Workflow Petri net model is defined. Such a model allows for the treatment of critical resources which have to be used for specific activities in real time. In [8], a resource-oriented Workflow net (ROWN) based on a two-transition task model was introduced for resource-constrained Workflow modeling and analysis. Considering the possibility of task failure during execution, in [5], a three-transition task model to specify a task start, end and failure was proposed. Additional research can be found in [9–12].

The majority of existing models put their focus on the process aspect and do not consider important characteristics of the Workflow Management System. In [2,3] for example, the resource allocation mechanisms are represented only in an informal way. In [5–7] and resource allocation mechanisms are represented by simple tokens in places as it is generally the case in production systems [13]. But a simple token in a place will not represent in a realistic way human employees who can treat simultaneously different cases in a single day, as it is usually the case in most Business processes.

A Workflow model should describe as well as analyse the time and the temporal behaviour of both resources and activities. In general, typical temporal phenomena include activity execution delays, limits to the occurrence of valid intervals over the activities, limit to valid intervals over resources (limits to resourse life cycle), limits to duration of process execution, time distance between two activities, etc.

Many Petri Net based time related Workflow models have been proposed. In [14], Time Workflow Nets (TWF-Nets), along with the extended WF-Nets were proposed. In TWF-Nets, each transition is attached to an interval, and the execution duration of the transition must be kept to within that interval. Based on TWF-Nets, in [15] an Extended Time Workflow Nets (XTWF-Net) was proposed. An XTWF-Net consists of several TWF-nets based on specific rules, which can describe concurrent time constraints in Workflows.

In the real world, due to dynamic features of resources and activities in business processes, most of time information is uncertain and cannot be precisely described. In this study, a Workflow net model incremented with minimum and maximum fuzzy intervals for describing the duration of activities and waiting times is then presented.

The proposal of this work is to express in a more realistic way resource allocation mechanisms when human behavior is considered. For that, fuzzy sets delimited by possibility distributions [16] will be associated with the Petri net models that represent human type resource allocation mechanisms and fuzzy time intervals will be associated to activity durations. To mark the minimum and maximum execution time intervals of the activities, a time constraint propagation mechanism is proposed. A firing mechanism using a joint possibility distribution will then be defined in order to associate through a single formalism explicit time constraints as well as resource availability information.

The remainder of this paper is as follows. Section 2 introduces the concepts of fuzzy sets and possibility measures. Section 3 shows Workflow modeling. Section 4 presents resource allocation mechanisms. Section 5 presents a fuzzy time constraint propagation mechanism. Section 6 defines new firing rules that consider fuzzy time constraints as well as fuzzy resource allocation mechanisms. Finally, Sect. 7 concludes the paper and provides references for additional works.

2 Fuzzy Sets and Possibility Measures

The notion of fuzzy set was introduced by [17] in order to represent the gradual nature of human knowledge. For example, the size of a man could be considered by the majority of a population as small, normal, tall, etc. A certain degree of belief can be attached to each possible interpretation of symbolic information and can simply be formalized by a fuzzy set F of a reference set X that can be defined by a membership function $\mu_F(x) \in [0,1]$. In particular, for a given element $x \in X$, $\mu_F(x) = 0$ denote that x is not a member of the set F, $\mu_F(x) = 1$ denotes that x is definitely a member of the set F, and intermediate values denote the fact that x is more or less an element of F. Normally, a fuzzy set is represented by a trapezoid where the smallest subset corresponding to the membership value equal to 1 is called the core, and the largest subset corresponding to the membership value greater than 0 is called the support.

There exist three particular cases of fuzzy sets that are generally considered, the triangular form where a2 = a3, the imprecise case where a1 = a2 and a3 = a4 and the precise case where a1 = a2 = a3 = a4.

When considering two distincts fuzzy sets A and B, the basic operations are as follows [18]:

- the fuzzy sum $A \oplus B$ defined as:
  $[a1, a2, a3, a4] \oplus [b1, b2, b3, b4] =$
  $[a1 + b1, a2 + b2, a3 + b3, a4 + b4]$,
- the fuzzy subtraction $A \ominus B$ defined as:
  $[a1, a2, a3, a4] \ominus [b1, b2, b3, b4] =$
  $[a1 - b4, a2 - b3, a3 - b2, a4 - b1]$,
- the fuzzy product $A \otimes B$ defined as:
  $[a1, a2, a3, a4] \otimes [b1, b2, b3, b4] =$
  $[a1.b1, a2.b2, a3.b3, a4.b4]$.

A fuzzy set F can be delimited by a possibility distribution Π_f, such as: $\forall x \in X$, $\Pi_f(x) = \mu_F(x)$ [16,19]. Given a possibility distribution $\Pi_a(x)$, the measure of possibility $\Pi(S)$ and necessity $N(S)$ that a data a belongs to a crisp set S of X is defined by $\Pi(S) = sup_{x \in S} \Pi_a(x)$ and $N(S) = inf_{x \notin S}(1 - \Pi_a(x)) = 1 - \Pi(\overline{S})$. If $\Pi(S) = 0$, it is impossible that a belongs to S. If $\Pi(S) = 1$, it is possible that a belongs to S, but it also depends on the value of $N(S)$. If $N(S) = 1$, it is certain that (the larger the value of $N(S)$, the more the proposition is believed in). In particular, there exists a duality relationship between the modalities of the possible and the necessary which postulates that an event is necessary when its contrary is impossible. Some practical examples of possibility and necessity measures are presented in [16].

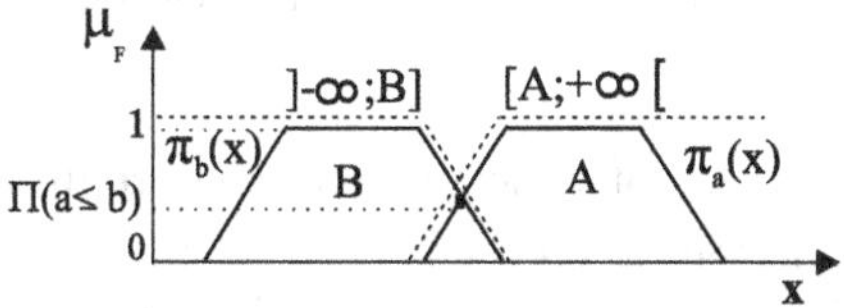

Fig. 1. Possibility measure.

Given two data a and b characterized by two fuzzy sets A and B as shown in Fig. 1, the measure of possibility and necessity of having $a \leq b$ are defined as:

$$\Pi(a \leq b) = sup_{x \leq y}(min(\Pi_a(x), min(\Pi_b(y))) = max([A, +\infty[\cap] - \infty, B]) \tag{1}$$

and

$$N(a \leq b) = 1 - sup_{x \leq y}(min(\Pi_a(x), min(\Pi_b(y))). \tag{2}$$

Given a normalized possibility distribution π_a, [20] defines the following fuzzy sets of the time point that are:

- possibly after a: $\mu_{[A,+\infty[}(x) = sup_{x \in X}\pi_a(s)$ (see Fig. 2);
- necessarily after a: $\mu_{]A,+\infty[}(x) = inf_{x \in X}(1 - \pi_a(s))$ (see Fig. 2);
- possibly before a: $\mu_{]-\infty,A]}(x) = sup_{x \in X}\pi_a(s)$ (see Fig. 3);
- necessarily before a: $\mu_{]-\infty,A[}(x) = inf_{x \in X}(1 - \pi_a(s))$ (see Fig. 3).

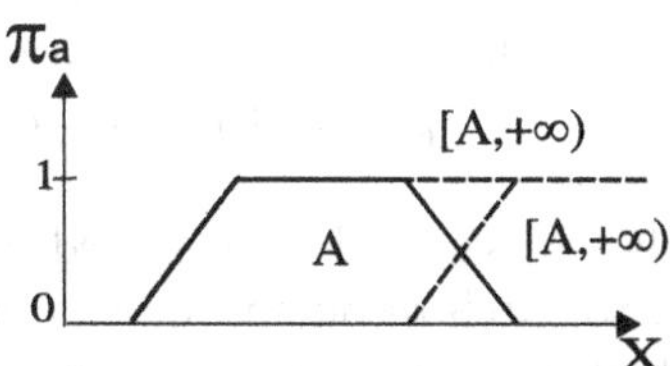

Fig. 2. Possibly/necessarily after a.

A visibility time interval $[a, b]$ is a period of time between two dates a and b. In the case where a and b are fuzzy dates A and B (delimited by π_a and π_b) respectively, the interval $[a, b]$ is represented by the the following pair of fuzzy sets:

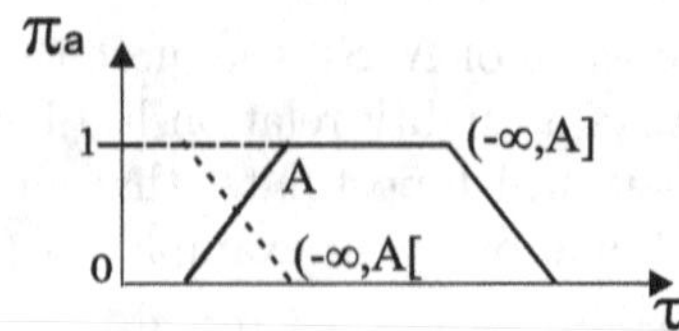

Fig. 3. Possibly/necessarily before a.

- $[A, B]$, the conjunctive set of time instants that represents the set of dates possibly after A and possibly before B;
- $]A, B[$, the conjunctive set of time instants that represents the set of dates necessarily after A and necessarily before B.

The joint possibility admits as upper bound in [16]:

$$\forall x \in X \quad \forall y \in Y \quad \pi(x, y) = min(\pi_X(x), \pi_Y(y)) \tag{3}$$

when the reference sets are non-interactive (the value of x in X has no influence on the value of y in Y, and vice versa).

3 Workflow Modeling

Modeling a Workflow process in terms of a Workflow net is rather straightforward: transitions are active components and models the tasks, places are passive components and model conditions (pre and post), and tokens model the cases to be treated [1].

To illustrate the mapping of a process into a Workflow net, the process for handling complaints, shown in [1] is considered: an incoming complaint is first recorded. Then the client who has complained along with the department affected by the complaint are contacted. The client is approached for more information. The department is informed of the complaint and may be asked for its initial reaction. These two tasks may be performed in parallel, i.e. simultaneously or in any order. After this, data is gathered and a decision is made. Depending upon the decision, either a compensation payment is made or a letter is sent. Finally, the complaint is filed.

As mentioned previously, a task can be associated to a transition in a Workflow net. However, in order to catch resources in use when a task is in execution and released them when the task is done, we use two sequential transitions plus a place to model a task. The first transition represents the beginning of the task, the place the task, and the second transition the end of the task [8].

As shown in Fig. 4, transition B represents the beginning of a task execution; E represents the end of the task execution. Place $A3$ represents the task in execution. From reachability analysis perspective, Fig. 4 can be reduced to a single transition which represents the entire task execution as a single logic unit.

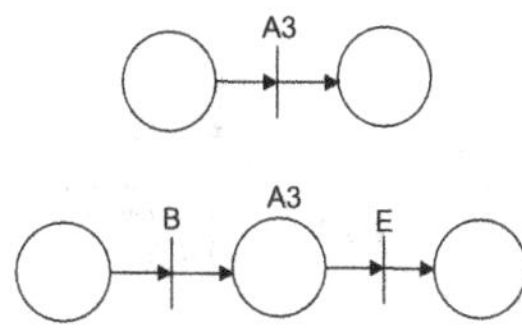

Fig. 4. Petri net model of a task.

4 Resource Allocation Mechanism

Resources in Workflow Management Systems are non-preemptive [1] ones: once a resource has been allocated to a specific activity, it cannot be free before ending the corresponding activity. There exists different kinds of resources in Workflow Processes. Some of them are discrete type and can be represented by a simple token. For example, a printer used to treat a specific class of documents will be represented as a non-preemptive resource and could be allocated to a single document at the same time. On the contrary, some other resources cannot be represented by a simple token. This is the case of most human type resources. As a matter of fact, it is not unusual for an employee who works in an administration to treat simultaneously several cases. For example, in an insurance company, one employee could treat normally several documents during a working day and not necessarily in a pure sequential way. In this case, a simple token could not model human behavior in a proper manner. The different kind of allocation mechanisms will be formalized in the following sections.

4.1 Discrete Resource Allocation Mechanism

A discrete resource allocation mechanism can be defined by the marked ordinary Petri net model [21]

$C_{DR} =< A_{DR}, T_{DR}, Pre_{DR}, Pos_{DR}, M_{DR} >$ with:

- $A_{DR} = \bigcup_{\alpha=1}^{N_{DR}} A_\alpha \cup \{R_D\}$ where R_D represents the discrete resource place, A_α an activity place and N_{DR} the number of activities which are connected to the discrete resource place R_D.
- $T_{DR} = \bigcup_{\alpha=1}^{N_{DR}} T_{in_\alpha} \cup \bigcup_{\alpha=1}^{N_{DR}} T_{out_\alpha}$ where T_{in_α} represents the input transition of the activity A_α and T_{out_α} represents the output transition of the activity A_α.
- $Pre_{DR} : A_{DR} \times T_{DR} \rightarrow \{0,1\}$ the input incidence application such as $Pre_{DR}(R_D, T_{in_\alpha}) = 1$ and $Pre_{DR}(A_\alpha, T_{out_\alpha}) = 1$ (other combinations of place/transition are equal to zero).
- $Pos_{DR} : A_{DR} \times T_{DR} \rightarrow \{0,1\}$ the output incidence application such as $Pos_{DR}(R_D, T_{out_\alpha}) = 1$ and $Pos_{DR}(A_\alpha, T_{in_\alpha}) = 1$ (other combinations of place/transition are equal to zero).
- $M_{DR} : R_D \rightarrow N$ the initial marking application such as $M_{DR}(R_D) = m_D$ the number of discrete resources of the same type.

If it is supposed that in the "Handle Complaint Process", presented in [22] an employee of the Complaint Department is used to treat the activities

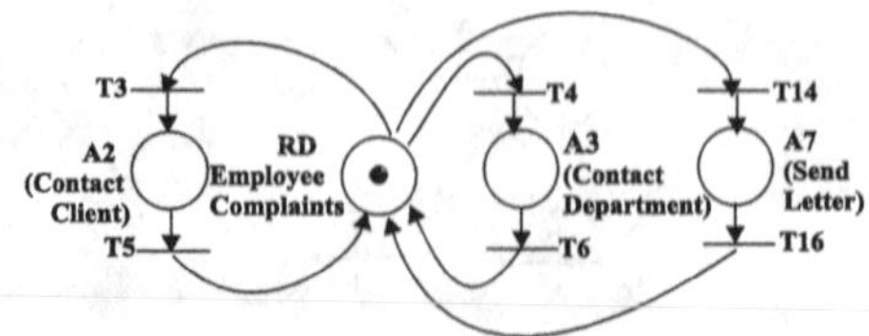

Fig. 5. Discrete allocation resource.

"Contact-Client", "Contact-Department" and "Send-Letter". The example of discrete resource allocation mechanism given in Fig. 5 is then obtained.

In this figure, it is clear that if the token in R_D is used to realize the activity A_2, then the activities A_3 and A_7 could only be initiated after the end of activity A_2. This means that resource R_D could only be used on a pure non-preemptive way. In particular, once the activity A_2 initiated, if the employee cannot enter in contact immediately with the client, he could not use his available time (waiting for an answer from the client) to initiate another activity, like sending a letter for example (activity A_7). It is evident that in practice, such a situation will not happen. If the client is not available at a given instant, the employee will use his available time to execute another task.

4.2 Continuous Resource Allocation Mechanism

A continuous allocation mechanism can be defined by the marked hybrid Petri net model [21]

$C_{CR} =< A_{CR}, T_{CR}, Pre_{CR}, Pos_{CR}, M_{CR} >$ with:

- $A_{CR} = \bigcup_{\alpha=1}^{N_{CR}} A_\alpha \cup \{R_C\}$ where R_C represents the continuous resource place, A_α an activity place and N_{CR} the number of activities which are connected to the continuous resource place R_C.
- $T_{CR} = \bigcup_{\alpha=1}^{N_{CR}} T_{in_\alpha} \cup \bigcup_{\alpha=1}^{N_{CR}} T_{out_\alpha}$ where T_{in_α} represents the discrete input transition of the activity A_α and T_{out_α} represents the discrete output transition of the activity A_α.
- $Pre_{CR} : A_{CR} \times T_{CR} \rightarrow R^+$ the input incidence application such as $Pre_{CR}(R_C, T_{in_\alpha}) = X_\alpha$ with $X_\alpha \in R^+$ and $Pre_{CR}(A_\alpha, T_{out_\alpha}) = 1$ (other combinations of place/transition are equal to zero).
- $Pos_{CR} : A_{CR} \times T_{CR} \rightarrow R^+$ the output incidence application such as $Pos_{CR}(R_C, T_{out_\alpha}) = X_\alpha$ and $Pos_{CR}(A_\alpha, T_{in_\alpha}) = 1$ (other combinations of place/transition are equal to zero).
- $M_{CR} : R_C \rightarrow R^+$ the initial marking application such as $M_{CR}(R_C) = m_C$ the availability (in percentage) of the continuous resource.

An example of continuous resource is given in Fig. 6. This figure shows that only 30 % of the employee availability is necessary to realize the activity "Contact-Client". It will be then possible for the employee to treat simultaneously more than one activity. For example, even after the beginning of the activity "Contact-Client", if the client is not immediately available for answering

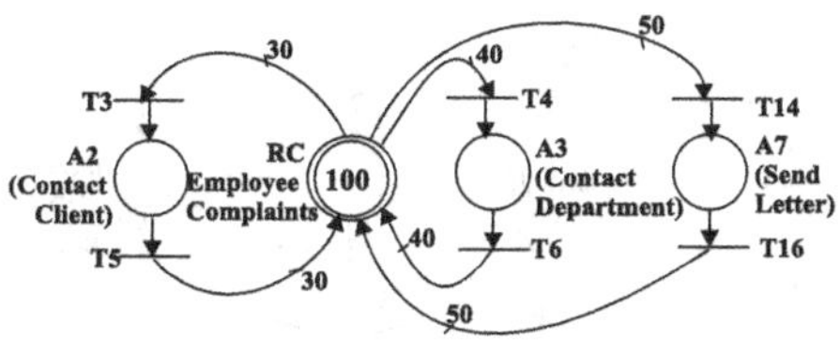

Fig. 6. Continuous allocation resource.

the questions of the employee, this last one could use his available time (waiting for an answer from the client) to initiate another activity, like sending a letter for example (activity A_7). As a matter of fact, 50 % of the employee availability is necessary for the activity "Send-Letter", and after the beginning of the activity "Contact-Client", the employee is still 70 % available.

The limitation of such a model is related with the fact that the representation of human behavior in term of availability in a practical situation will be known only as an uncertain value (a fuzzy percentage).

4.3 Fuzzy Continuous Resource Allocation Mechanism

A fuzzy continuous allocation mechanism can be defined by the marked fuzzy hybrid Petri net model

$C_{FCR} =< A_{FCR}, T_{FCR}, Pre_{FCR}, Pos_{FCR}, M_{FCR} >$ with:

- $A_{FCR} = \bigcup_{\alpha=1}^{N_{FCR}} A_\alpha \cup \{R_{FC}\}$ where R_{FC} represents the fuzzy continuous resource place, A_α an activity place and N_{FCR} the number of activities which are connected to the fuzzy continuous resource place R_{FC}.
- $T_{FCR} = \bigcup_{\alpha=1}^{N_{FCR}} T_{in_\alpha} \cup \bigcup_{\alpha=1}^{N_{FCR}} T_{out_\alpha}$ where T_{in_α} represents the discrete input transition of the activity A_α and T_{out_α} represents the discrete output transition of the activity A_α.
- $Pre_{FCR} : A_{FCR} \times T_{FCR} \rightarrow F$ the input incidence application such as $Pre_{FCR}(R_{FC}, T_{in_\alpha}) = [w1, w2, w3, w4]$ with w2 = w3 and $Pre_{FCR}(A_\alpha, T_{out_\alpha}) = [1, 1, 1, 1]$ (other combinations of place/transition are equal to zero) with F the set of fuzzy numbers of the triangular form.
- $Pos_{FCR} : A_{FCR} \times T_{FCR} \rightarrow F$ the output incidence application such as $Pos_{FCR}(R_{FC}, T_{out_\alpha}) = [w1, w2, w3, w4]$ with w2 = w3 and $Pos_{FCR}(A_\alpha, T_{in_\alpha}) = [1, 1, 1, 1]$ (other combinations of place/transition are equal to zero).
- $M_{FCR} : R_{FC} \rightarrow F$ the initial marking application such as $M_{FCR}(R_{FC}) = [m1, m2, m3, m4]$ the fuzzy availability (in percentage) of the fuzzy continuous resource.

An example of fuzzy continuous resource is given in Fig. 7. For example, this figure shows that 30 % ± 10 % of the resource availability R_{FC} is necessary to realize the activity A2 (Contact-Client).

The behavior of a fuzzy continuous resource allocation model can be defined through the concepts of "enabled transition" and "fundamental equation".

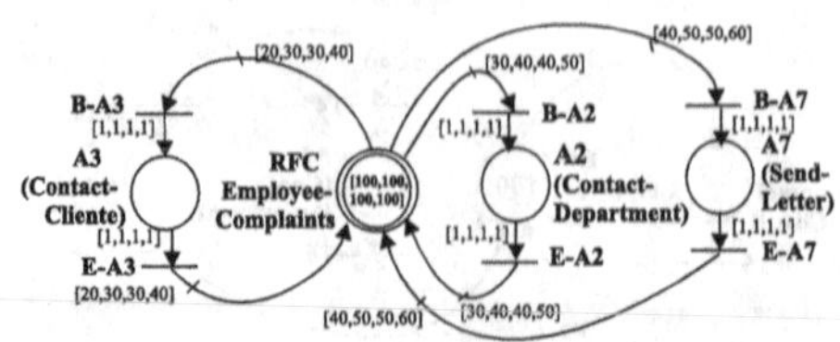

Fig. 7. Fuzzy allocation resource.

In an ordinary Petri net, a transition t is enabled if and only if for all the input places p of the transition, $M(p) \geq Pre(p,t)$, which means that the number of tokens in each input place is greater or equal to the weight associated to the arcs which connect the input places to the transition t. With a fuzzy continuous resource allocation mechanism, considering a transition t, the marking of an input place p and the weights associated to the arc which connects this place to the transition t are defined through different fuzzy sets. In this case, a transition t is enabled if and only if (for all the input places of the transition t):

$\Pi_t = \Pi(Pre_{FCR}(p,t) \leq M_{FCR}(p)) > 0$

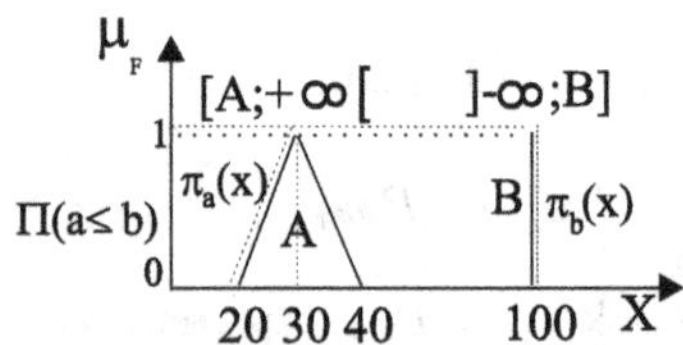

Fig. 8. Possibility measure of t3.

For example, the transition $t3$ in Fig. 8 is enabled because $\Pi_{t3} = \Pi(Pre_{FCR}(R_{FC}, t3) \leq M_{FCR}(R_{FC})) = 1 > 0$ as shown in Fig. 6 ($a = Pre_{FCR}(R_{FC}, t3)$ and $b = M_{FCR}(R_{FC})$).

For an ordinary Petri net, once a transition is enabled by a marking M, it can be fired and a new marking M' is obtained according to the fundamental equation:

$M'(p) = M(p) - Pre(p,t) + Pos(p,t)$

With a fuzzy continuous resource allocation model, the marking evolution is defined through the following fundamental equation:

$M'_{FCR}(p) = M_{FCR}(p) \ominus Pre_{FCR}(p,t) \boxplus Pos_{FCR}(p,t)$

The operation "$\ominus$" corresponds to the fuzzy substraction. The operation "$\boxplus$", when considering the sum of two fuzzy sets, is different from the one given in fuzzy logic and is defined as:

$[a1, a2, a3, a4] \boxplus [b1, b2, b3, b4] =$

$[a1 + b4, a2 + b3, a3 + b2, a4 + b1]$

This difference is due to the fact that the fuzzy operation "$\oplus$" does not maintain the marking of the fuzzy continuous resource allocation model invariant (the p-invariant property of the Petri net theory [23]). As a matter of fact, after realizing different activities, the resource's availability must go back to 100 %, even in the fuzzy case. To a certain extent, from the point of view of the fuzzy continuous resource allocation mechanism, the operation "$\boxplus$" can be seen as a kind of defuzzyfication operation. In particular, using this operation, it will be possible to find a linear expression of the fuzzy marking which will always be constant and which will correspond to the following expression:

$$M_{FCR}(R_{FC} \boxplus (w_1 \otimes M_{FCR}(A1)) \boxplus (w_2 \otimes M_{FCR}(A2)) \boxplus \cdots \boxplus (w_{N_{FCR}} \otimes M_{FCR}(A_{N_{FCR}})) = CONST$$

with $w_\alpha = Pre_{FCR}(R_{FC}, t_{in_\alpha}) = Pos_{FCR}(R_{FC}, t_{out_\alpha})$ for $\alpha = 1$ to N_{FCR}.

Example. To illustrate the fuzzy concepts of "enabled transition", "transition firing" and "invariant marking", the firing sequence $t_3 \rightarrow t_4 \rightarrow t_{14} \rightarrow t_5 \rightarrow t_6 \rightarrow t_{16}$ will be considered when considering the fuzzy resource allocation mechanism in Fig. 7.

- Firing of t_3: the possibility measure of t_3 is:
  $\Pi_{t3} = \Pi(Pre_{FCR}(R_{FC}, t3) \leq M_{FCR}(R_{FC})) = 1 > 0$ as shown in Fig. 8 (with $a = Pre_{FCR}(R_{FC}, t3)$ and $b = M_{FCR}(R_{FC})$).
  After the firing of t_3, the new markings of R_{FC} and A2 are:
  $M'_{FCR}(R_{FC}) = M_{FCR}(R_{FC}) \ominus Pre_{FCR}(R_{FC}, t3) = [100, 100, 100, 100] \ominus [20, 30, 30, 40] = [60, 70, 70, 80]$ and $M'_{FCR}(A2) = M_{FCR}(A2) \boxplus Pos_{FCR}(A2, t3) = [0, 0, 0, 0] \boxplus [1, 1, 1, 1] = [1, 1, 1, 1]$
  The invariant marking associated to the fuzzy continuous resource model is:
  $M_{FCR}(R_{FC}) \boxplus (Pre_{FCR}(R_{FC}, t3) \otimes M_{FCR}(A2)) \boxplus (Pre_{FCR}(R_{FC}, t4) \otimes M_{FCR}(A3)) \boxplus (Pre_{FCR}(R_{FC}, t14) \otimes M_{FCR}(A7)) = [60, 70, 70, 80] \boxplus ([20, 30, 30, 40] \otimes [1, 1, 1, 1]) \boxplus ([30, 40, 40, 50] \otimes [0, 0, 0, 0]) \boxplus ([40, 50, 50, 60] \otimes [0, 0, 0, 0]) = [60, 70, 70, 50] \boxplus [20, 30, 30, 40] = [100, 100, 100, 100]$
- Firing of t_4: the possibility measure of t_4 is:
  $\Pi_{t4} = \Pi(Pre_{FCR}(R_{FC}, t4) \leq M_{FCR}(R_{FC})) = 1 > 0$
  After the firing of t_4, the new markings of R_{FC} and A3 are:
  $M'_{FCR}(R_{FC}) = M_{FCR}(R_{FC}) \ominus Pre_{FCR}(R_{FC}, t4) = [60, 70, 70, 80] \ominus [30, 40, 40, 50] = [10, 30, 30, 50]$ and $M'_{FCR}(A3) = M_{FCR}(A3) \boxplus Pos_{FCR}(A3, t4) = [0, 0, 0, 0] \boxplus [1, 1, 1, 1] = [1, 1, 1, 1]$
  The invariant marking associated to the fuzzy continuous resource model is:
  $M_{FCR}(R_{FC}) \boxplus (Pre_{FCR}(R_{FC}, t3) \otimes M_{FCR}(A2)) \boxplus (Pre_{FCR}(R_{FC}, t4) \otimes M_{FCR}(A3)) \boxplus (Pre_{FCR}(R_{FC}, t14) \otimes M_{FCR}(A7)) = [10, 30, 30, 50] \boxplus ([20, 30, 30, 40] \otimes [1, 1, 1, 1]) \boxplus ([30, 40, 40, 50] \otimes [1, 1, 1, 1]) \boxplus ([40, 50, 50, 60] \otimes [0, 0, 0, 0]) = [10, 30, 30, 50] \boxplus [20, 30, 30, 40] \boxplus [30, 40, 40, 50] = [50, 60, 60, 70] \boxplus [30, 40, 40, 50] = [100, 100, 100, 100]$
- Firing of t_{14}: the possibility measure of t_{14} is:
  $\Pi_{t14} = \Pi(Pre_{FCR}(R_{FC}, t14) \leq M_{FCR}(R_{FC})) = 0,33 > 0$ as shown in Fig. 9 (with $a = Pre_{FCR}(R_{FC}, t14)$ and $b = M_{FCR}(R_{FC})$).

  After the firing of t_{14}, the new markings of R_{FC} and A7 are:
  $M'_{FCR}(R_{FC}) = M_{FCR}(R_{FC}) \ominus Pre_{FCR}(R_{FC}, t14) = [10, 30, 30, 50] \ominus [40, 50, 50, 60] = [-50, -20, -20, 10]$ and $M'_{FCR}(A7) = M_{FCR}(A7) \boxplus Pos_{FCR}(A7, t14) = [0, 0, 0, 0] \boxplus [1, 1, 1, 1] = [1, 1, 1, 1]$
  The invariant marking associated to the fuzzy continuous resource model is:

$M_{FCR}(R_{FC})\boxplus(Pre_{FCR}(R_{FC},t3)\otimes M_{FCR}(A2))\boxplus(Pre_{FCR}(R_{FC},t4)\otimes M_{FCR}(A3))\boxplus (Pre_{FCR}(R_{FC},t14)\otimes M_{FCR}(A7)) = [-50,-20,-20,10]\boxplus([20,30,30,40]\otimes[1,1,1,1]) \boxplus ([30,40,40,50]\otimes[1,1,1,1]) \boxplus ([40,50,50,60]\otimes[1,1,1,1]) = [-50,-20,-20,10]\boxplus [20,30,30,40]\boxplus[30,40,40,50]\boxplus[40,50,50,60] = [-10,10,10,30]\boxplus[30,40,40,50]\boxplus [40,50,50,60] = [40,50,50,60]\boxplus[40,50,50,60] = [100,100,100,100]$

- Firing of t_5: the possibility measure of t_5 is:
  $\Pi_{t5} = \Pi(Pre_{FCR}(A2,t5) \leq M_{FCR}(A2)) = 1 > 0$
  After the firing of t_5, the new markings of R_{FC} and A2 are:
  $M'_{FCR}(R_{FC}) = M_{FCR}(R_{FC}) \boxplus Pos_{FCR}(R_{FC},t5) = [-50,-20,-20,10]\boxplus [20,30,30,40] = [-10,10,10,30]$ and $M'_{FCR}(A2) = M_{FCR}(A2)\ominus Pre_{FCR}(A2,t5) = [1,1,1,1]\ominus[1,1,1,1] = [0,0,0,0]$
  The invariant marking associated to the fuzzy continuous resource model is:
  $M_{FCR}(R_{FC})\boxplus(Pre_{FCR}(R_{FC},t3)\otimes M_{FCR}(A2))\boxplus(Pre_{FCR}(R_{FC},t4)\otimes M_{FCR}(A3))\boxplus (Pre_{FCR}(R_{FC},t14)\otimes M_{FCR}(A7)) = [-10,10,10,30]\boxplus([20,30,30,40]\otimes[0,0,0,0])\boxplus ([30,40,40,50]\otimes[1,1,1,1])\boxplus([40,50,50,60]\otimes[1,1,1,1]) = [-10,10,10,30]\boxplus [30,40,40,50]\boxplus[40,50,50,60] = [40,50,50,60]\boxplus[40,50,50,60] = [100,100,100,100]$
- Firing of t_6: the possibility measure of t_6 is:
  $\Pi_{t6} = \Pi(Pre_{FCR}(A3,t6) \leq M_{FCR}(A3)) = 1 > 0$
  After the firing of t_6, the new markings of R_{FC} and A3 are:
  $M'_{FCR}(R_{FC}) = M_{FCR}(R_{FC}) \boxplus Pos_{FCR}(R_{FC},t6) = [-10,10,10,30]\boxplus [30,40,40,50] = [40,50,50,60]$ and $M'_{FCR}(A3) = M_{FCR}(A3)\ominus Pre_{FCR}(A3,t6) = [1,1,1,1]\ominus[1,1,1,1] = [0,0,0,0]$
  The invariant marking associated to the fuzzy continuous resource model is:
  $M_{FCR}(R_{FC})\boxplus(Pre_{FCR}(R_{FC},t3)\otimes M_{FCR}(A2))\boxplus(Pre_{FCR}(R_{FC},t4)\otimes M_{FCR}(A3))\boxplus (Pre_{FCR}(R_{FC},t14)\otimes M_{FCR}(A7)) = [40,50,50,60]\boxplus([20,30,30,40]\otimes[0,0,0,0])\boxplus ([30,40,40,50]\otimes[0,0,0,0])\boxplus([40,50,50,60]\otimes[1,1,1,1]) = [40,50,50,60]\boxplus [40,50,50,60] = [100,100,100,100]$
- Firing of t_{16}: the possibility measure of t_{16} is:
  $\Pi_{t16} = \Pi(Pre_{FCR}(A7,t16) \leq M_{FCR}(A7)) = 1 > 0$
  After the firing of t_{16}, the new marking of R_{FC} and A7 are:
  $M'_{FCR}(R_{FC}) = M_{FCR}(R_{FC})\boxplus Pos_{FCR}(R_{FC},t16) = [40,50,50,60]\boxplus[40,50,50,60] = [100,100,100,100]$ and $M'_{FCR}(A7) = M_{FCR}(A7)\ominus Pre_{FCR}(A7,t6) = [1,1,1,1]\ominus [1,1,1,1] = [0,0,0,0]$
  The invariant marking associated to the fuzzy continuous resource model is:
  $M_{FCR}(R_{FC})\boxplus(Pre_{FCR}(R_{FC},t3)\otimes M_{FCR}(A2))\boxplus(Pre_{FCR}(R_{FC},t4)\otimes M_{FCR}(A3))\boxplus (Pre_{FCR}(R_{FC},t14)\otimes M_{FCR}(A7)) = [100,100,100,100]\boxplus([20,30,30,40]\otimes [0,0,0,0])\boxplus([30,40,40,50]\otimes[0,0,0,0])\boxplus([40,50,50,60]\otimes[0,0,0,0]) = [100,100,100,100]$

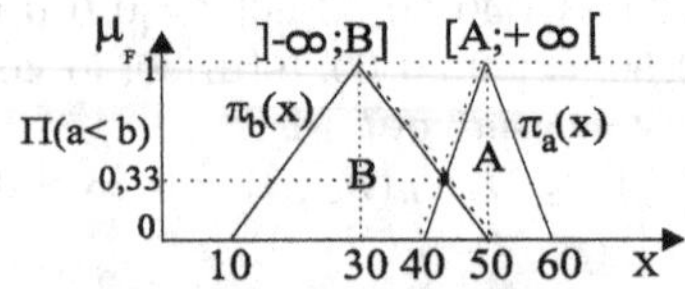

Fig. 9. Possibility measure of t3.

The negative part of the fuzzy marking of R_{FC} which appears after the firing of $t14$ simply shows the possibility of overloading the resource (the employee works above his normal capacity). It is important to underline that the negative part of the marking is not inconsistent with the Petri net theory. As a matter of fact, only the positive part of the fuzzy marking can be used to enable a transition of the fuzzy continuous resource model.

5 Time Constraint Propagation Mechanism

As the actual time required by an activity in a Workflow Management System is non-deterministic and not easily predictable, a fuzzy time interval can be assigned to every Workflow activity.

The fuzzy static interval represents the permanency duration (sojourn time) of a token in a non-available state for the firing of a transition. Before the duration a the token is in the non-available. After a and before b, the token is in the available state for the firing of a transition. After b, the token is again in the non-available state and cannot enable any transition anymore: it becomes a dead token. In a real time system case, the "death" of a token has to be seen as a time constraint that is not respected. A transition cannot be fired with dead tokens because it would correspond to an illegal act of behavior: a constraint violation.

A fuzzy visibility interval associated with a token defines the earliest fuzzy date when the token becomes available for the firing and the latest fuzzy date after which the token becomes non-available and cannot be used for the firing of any transition.

In a Workflow Management System, the visibility intervals depend on a global clock associated to the entire net which calculates the passage of time from date $\delta = 0$, which corresponds to the start of the systems operation. In particular, the existing waiting times between sequential activities can be represented by a visibility interval whose minimum and maximum fuzzy boundaries will depend on the earliest and latest delivery dates of the considered case (for each Client Complaint, there exists a specific case represented by a token in the Petri net model which represents the corresponding business process). Through correct knowledge of the beginning date and the maximum duration of a case, it is possible to calculate the estimated visibility intervals associated with the each token in each waiting place using constraint propagation techniques very similar to the ones used in scheduling problems based on activity-on-arc graphs without circuits [24]. The calculation of the visibility intervals associated with the tokens in the waiting places will be realized by considering the different kinds of routings that can exist in a Workflow process. In order to illustrate the constraint propagation technique proposed in this article, for each kind of routing, an example will be used to show how to calculate the minimum and the maximum fuzzy boundaries of visibility intervals. The following notations will appear in the proposed examples:

- minEY = minimum fuzzy boundary of the visibility interval associated with a case in the waiting place EY.
- maxEY = maximum fuzzy boundary of the visibility interval associated with a case in the waiting place EY.
- minAY = minimum fuzzy boundary of the static interval associated with the activity AY.
- maxAY = maximum fuzzy boundary of the static interval associated with the activity AY.

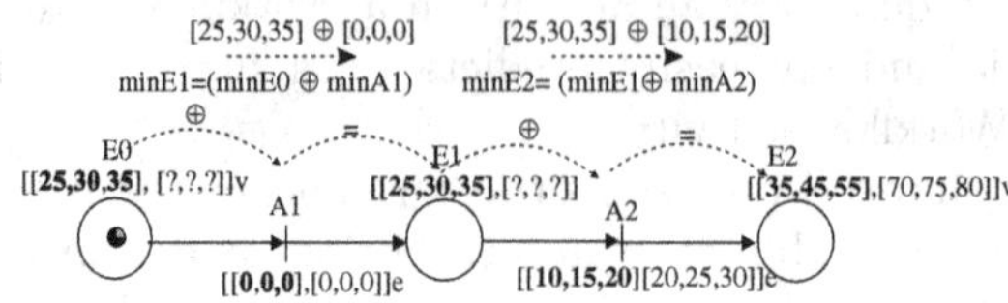

Fig. 10. Sequencial routing minimum fuzzy boundaries.

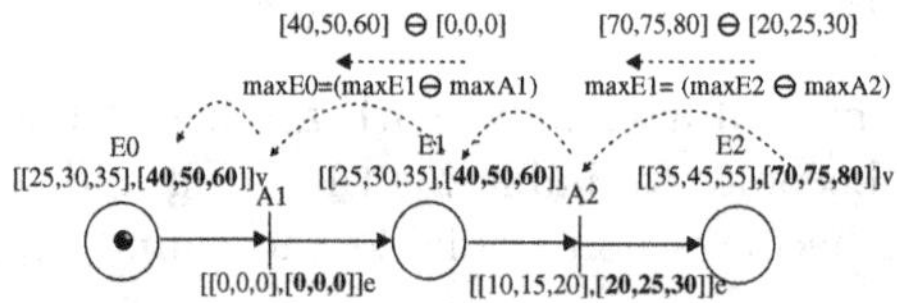

Fig. 11. Sequencial routing maximum fuzzy boundaries.

For instance, "$minE1 = minE0 \oplus minA1$" means that the minimum fuzzy boundary of the visibility interval associated with a specific case in place $E1$ is equal to the minimum fuzzy boundary of the visibility interval associated with the case in the place $E0$ plus the minimum fuzzy boundary of the static interval associated with the activity $A1$.

Figures 10 and 11 show how to calculate the minimum and maximum fuzzy boundaries, respectively, on a sequential routing. The case considered herein, represented by a token in place $E0$, can be initiated at fuzzy date [25, 30, 35] (minimum fuzzy boundary of the visibility interval associated with the case in $E0$). If the maximum duration allowed for the realization of this case is 45, then, the maximum fuzzy boundary of the visibility interval in place $E2$ will be [25, 30, 35] (minimum boundary associated with the case in $E0$) $\oplus$ [45, 45, 45] (maximum duration of the case) = [70, 75, 80]. In order to calculate all the other boundaries of the estimated visibility intervals associated with the waiting places of the sequential routing, the minimum and maximum fuzzy boundaries of the static intervals associated with the activity transition will be considered as shown in Figs. 10 and 11.

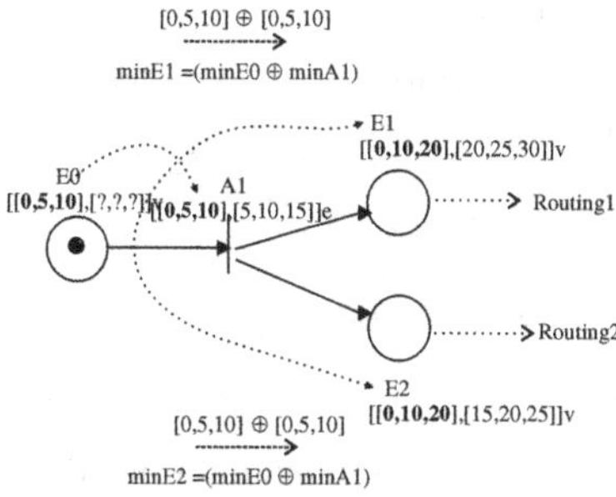

Fig. 12. Parallel routing minimum fuzzy boundaries.

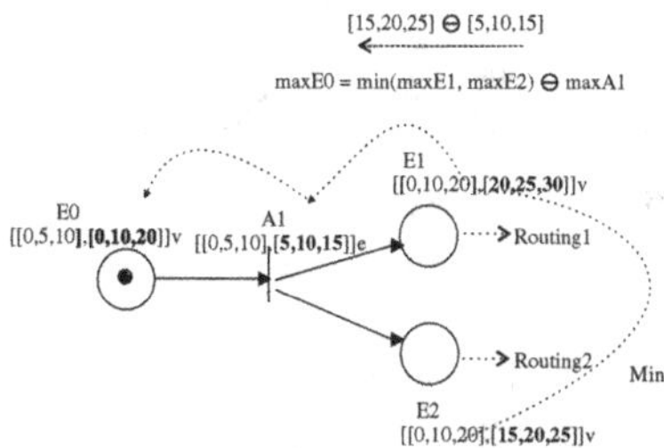

Fig. 13. Parallel routing maximum fuzzy boundaries.

Figures 12 and 13 show how to calculate the minimum and maximum fuzzy boundaries, respectively, on a parallel routing. The case considered herein, represented by a token in place $E0$, can be initiated at fuzzy date [0, 5, 10] (minimum fuzzy boundary of the visibility interval associated with the case in $E0$). The maximum duration of this case is 20 and 15 respectively. The maximum fuzzy boundaries in places $E1$ and $E2$ are [20, 25, 30] and [15, 20, 25] ((minimum boundary associated with the case in $E0$) $\oplus$ (maximum duration of the case)) respectively. The minimum fuzzy boundaries in places $E1$ and $E2$ will be calculated considering the minimal fuzzy boundary of the visibility interval in place E0 and the minimum fuzzy boundary of the static interval in A1 as shown in Fig. 12. The maximum fuzzy boundary of the visibility interval associated with the token in place E0 will be calculated considering the minimum value of the

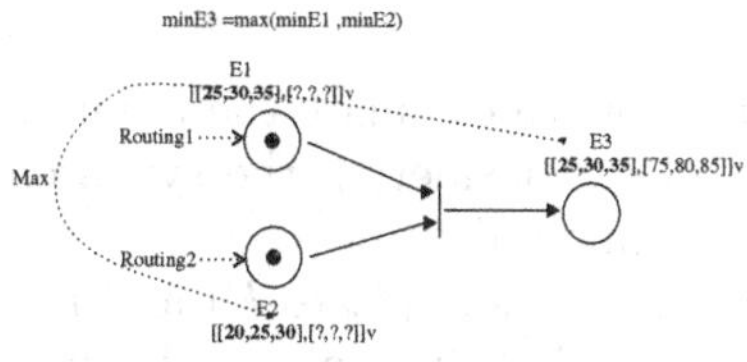

Fig. 14. Synchronization minimum fuzzy bounds.

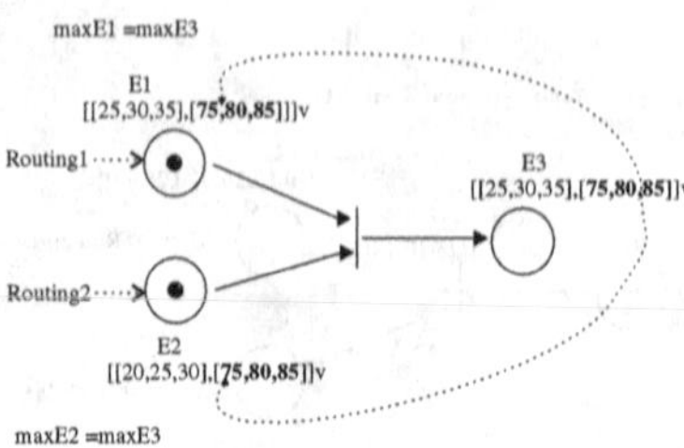

Fig. 15. Synchronization maximum fuzzy boundaries.

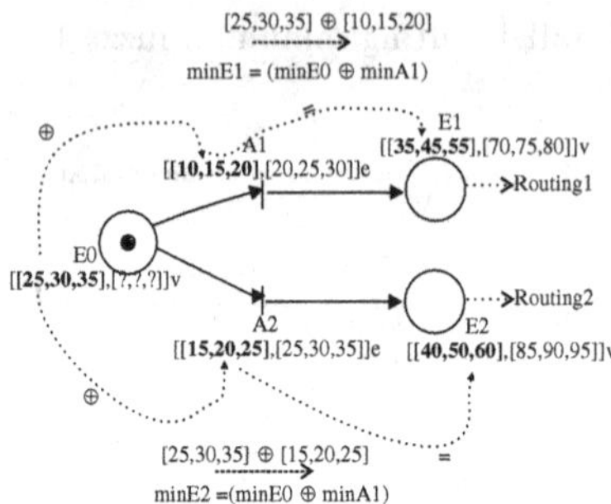

Fig. 16. Selective routing minimum fuzzy boundaries.

maximum fuzzy boundaries in places $E1$ and $E2$ (min(maxE0,maxE2)) and the maximum fuzzy boundary of the static interval associated with the activity $A1$ as shown in Fig. 13.

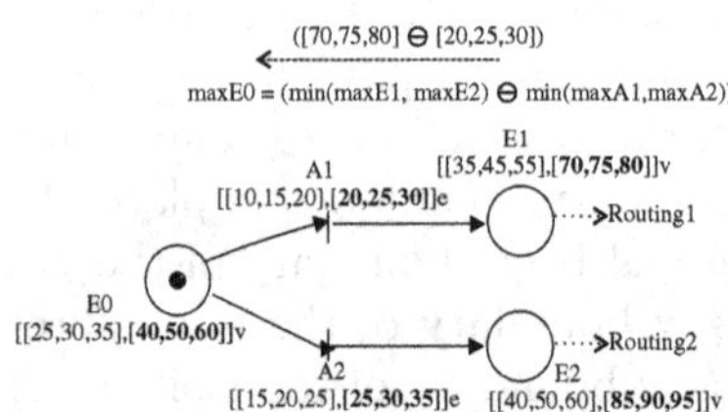

Fig. 17. Selective routing maximum fuzzy boundaries.

Figures 14 and 15 show how to calculate the minimum and maximum fuzzy boundaries, respectively, when considering the synchronization of two parallel routings. The minimum beginning date of the case is such that minimum fuzzy boundaries of the visibility intervals in places $E1$ and $E2$ (these places belong to different sequential routings and their minimum fuzzy boundaries do not have to be necessarily the same) are [20, 25, 30] and [25, 30, 35], respectively. The maximum duration of the considered case is 50 an, then, the maximum fuzzy boundary of the visibility interval in place $E3$ is [75, 80, 85] (maximum value of the minimum fuzzy boundaries of the visibility intervals in places $E1$ and $E2$ $\oplus$ maximum duration of the case). The minimum fuzzy boundary of the visibility interval in place $E3$ will be calculated considering the maximum value of the minimum fuzzy boundaries of the visibility intervals in places $E1$ and $E2$ (max(minE1; min E2)) as shown in Fig. 14. The maximum fuzzy boundaries of the visibility intervals associated with the token in place $E1$ and $E2$ will be equal to the maximum boundary of the visibility interval in place $E3$ (see Fig. 15). Due to the fact that places $E1$, $E2$ and $E3$ are waiting places, the boundaries of their visibility interval do not depend on activity durations.

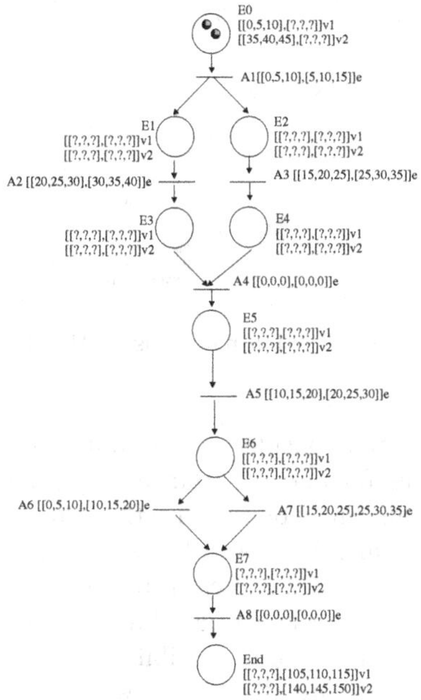

Fig. 18. Visibility intervals - "Handle Complaint Process".

Figures 16 and 17 show how to calculate the minimum and maximum fuzzy boundaries, respectively, on a selective routing. The case considered herein, represented by a token in place $E0$, can be initiated at fuzzy date [25, 30, 35]. The maximum duration of this case is such that the calculated maximum fuzzy boundaries in places $E1$ and $E2$ are [70, 75, 80] and [85, 90, 95], respectively. As a matter of fact, these places belong to different sequential routings (routing 1 and routing 2) and their maximum fuzzy boundaries do not have to be necessarily equal. The minimum boundaries in places $E1$ and $E2$ will be calculated, considering the minimum fuzzy boundary of the visibility interval in place $E0$ and the minimum boundary of the static interval in $A1$ as shown in Fig. 16. The maximum fuzzy boundary of the visibility interval associated with the token

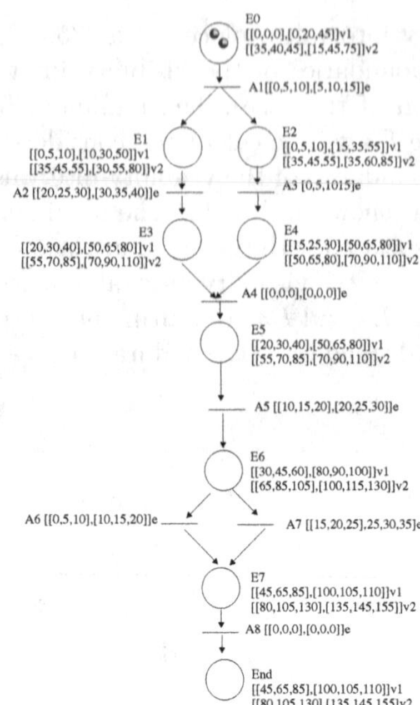

Fig. 19. Time constraint propagation mechanism "Handle Complaint Process".

in place $E0$ will be calculated considering the minimum value of the maximum fuzzy boundaries in places $E1$ and $E2$ (min(maxE1; maxE2)) minus the minimum value of the maximum fuzzy boundaries the static interval associated with activities $A1$ and $A2$ (min(maxA1; maxA2)) as shown in Fig. 17.

On the Workflow net in Fig. 18, two cases represented by two tokens in place $E0$ are considered. The first can be initiated at date [0, 5, 10], which is represented as the minimum boundary of the visibility interval v1 in $E0$. The second case can be initiated at fuzzy date [35, 40, 45], which is represented as the minimum fuzzy boundary of the visibility interval. It is considered that the maximum permitted duration of a case is equal to 105, and, as a consequence, the maximum fuzzy boundaries of the estimated visibility intervals attached to the last place End of the process are equal to $[0, 5, 10] \oplus [105, 105, 105] = [105, 110, 115]$ for the first case and $[35, 40, 45] \oplus [105, 105, 105] = [140, 145, 150]$ for the second case. In Fig. 19, the minimal fuzzy boundaries of the estimated visibility intervals attached to the waiting places are calculated applying the forward constraint propagation techniques to the different kinds of routings associated with the "Handle Complaint Process" and the maximum fuzzy bounds of the estimated visibility intervals attached to the waiting places are calculated by applying the backward constraint propagation techniques to the different kinds of routings.

In the knowledge that the time interval $[a, b]$ is a time period between two dates a and b, with a and b being fuzzy dates A and $B4$ (bounded by π_a, π_b) respectively,

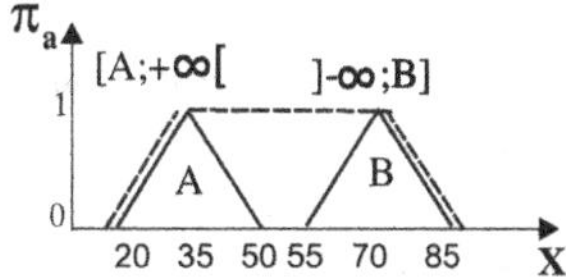

Fig. 20. Fuzzy interval.

the interval $[a, b]$ is represented by the conjunctive set of time instances, which represent the set of dates possibly after A and possibly before B. In this case, we will have each visibility interval defined by a unique fuzzy interval. For example, consider the fuzzy interval v1 of the place $E5$ $[[20, 35, 50], [55, 70, 85]]$. With the information at hand that the interval $[[20, 35, 50], [55, 70, 85]]$ is the conjunctive set of time instants that represents the set of dates possibly after A and possibly before B, then, we can obtain the single fuzzy interval $[20, 35, 70, 85]$. Figure 20 shows the intervals in schematic form. Through the use of this methodology, all visibility intervals will be transformed into a unique fuzzy intervals. In particular, based on such information, possibilities for the firing of the transitions of the Workflow net will be computed then.

6 Firing Rules with Fuzzy Time and Fuzzy Resource

If a transition has n input places and if each one of these places has several tokens in it, then the enabling time interval $[a1, a2, a3, a4]$ of this transition is obtained by choosing for each one of these n input places a token, the visibility interval associated with it. In this paper, there exists no time restriction on the resources (the static interval attached to the resource places is always $[0, \infty]s$ and, as a consequence, the enabling time interval of a transition will simply be equal to the visibility interval associated with the case to be treated by the corresponding transition. For example, knowing that the visibility interval attached to the case represented by a token in place $W1$ is equal to $[0, 10, 40, 60]v$, the enabling time interval of the transition B-$A2$ will be $[0, 10, 40, 60]v$ too.

For firing a transition, it is necessary that the arrival date of the token in the input place of the transition belongs to the fuzzy visibility interval associated with the input place of the transition ($\mu > 0$) and the resource availability (Eq. (1)) necessary to realize the activity initiated by the firing of the transition must be greater than 0 ($\Pi(a \leq b) > 0$). To evaluate the availability of resource and time simultaneously, the joint possibility presented in Eq. (3) must be calculated, where $\pi_X(x)$ corresponds to the resource availability and $\pi_Y(y)$ to the time possibility.

In order to understand the mechanism for transition firing in a Workflow net with fuzzy resources and fuzzy time, the authors consider a particular fragment of the "Handle Complaint Process", which is shown in Fig. 21.

(a) At the fuzzy date $[0, 5, 25, 50]$:

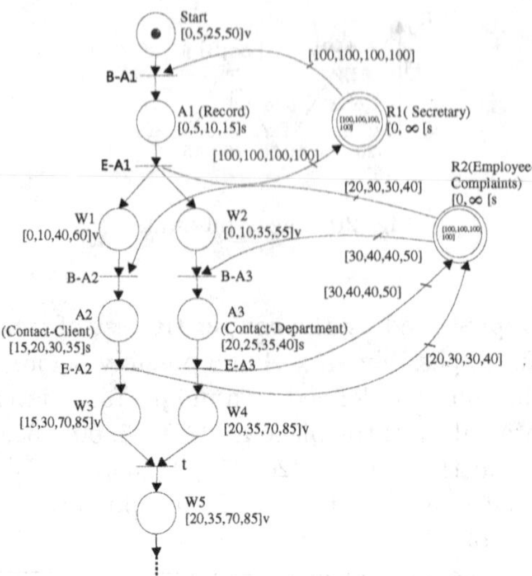

Fig. 21. Fragment of the workflow net - "Handle Complaint Process".

- the case in the *start* place becomes available to be treated by the resource in $R1$. We choose to fire the transition $B\text{-}A1$ at date 5 to reach the higher value possible (normal situation to treat the case) when considering the joint possibility $\pi_{(x,y)} = min(\pi_X(x), \pi_Y(y)) = 1$ with $\pi_X(x) = 1$ (time possibility equal to 1 when $x = 5$) and $\pi_Y(y) = \Pi(a \leq b) = 1$ (resource availability possibility). After the firing of the transition, a token is produced in place $A1$ with a visibility interval equal to $[5, 5, 5, 5]$ (firing of $B\text{-}A1$) $\oplus$ $[0, 5, 10, 15]s = [5, 10, 15, 20]v$.

(b) At the fuzzy date $[5, 10, 15, 20]$:

- if the activity $A1$ associated is finalized at date 10, the token becomes available in $A1$, the transition $E\text{-}A1$ is fired because the joint possibility $\pi(x, y) = min(\pi_X(x), \pi_Y(y)) = 1$ with $\pi_X(x) = 1$ (time possibility equal to 1 when $x = 10$) and $\pi_Y(y) = \Pi(a \leq b) = 1$ (resource availability possibility) and the resource is returned to $R1$. At the same time, tokens are produced in $W1$ and $W2$. To fire $B\text{-}A2$ and $B\text{-}A3$ it is necessary to evaluate the time and resource availability through Eq. (3). For $B\text{-}A2$, the joint possibility $\pi_{(x,y)} = min(\pi_X(x), \pi_Y(y)) = 1$ with $\pi_X(x) = 1$ (time possibility equal to 1 when $x = 10$) and $\pi_Y(y) = \Pi(a \leq b) = 1$ (resource availability possibility - see Fig. 22.) In the same manner, for $B\text{-}A3$, the joint possibility $\pi_{(x,y)} = min(\pi_X(x), \pi_Y(y)) = 1$ with $\pi_X(x) = 1$ (time possibility equal to 1 when $x = 10$) and $\pi_Y(y) = \Pi(a \leq b) = 1$ (resource availability possibility - see Fig. 23.) Thus, the transitions $B\text{-}A2$ and $B\text{-}A3$ are fired and a token is produced in $A2$ with a visibility interval of $[25, 30, 40, 45]v$ and another in $A3$ with a visibility interval of $[30, 35, 45, 50]v$. At this moment, $R2 = [10, 30, 30, 50]$.

(c) At the fuzzy date $[25, 30, 40, 45]$

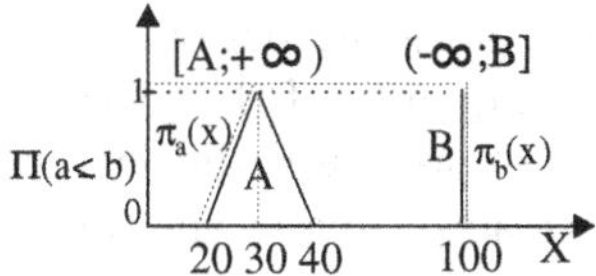

Fig. 22. The possibility measure associated with *B*-*A*2 (resource *R*2).

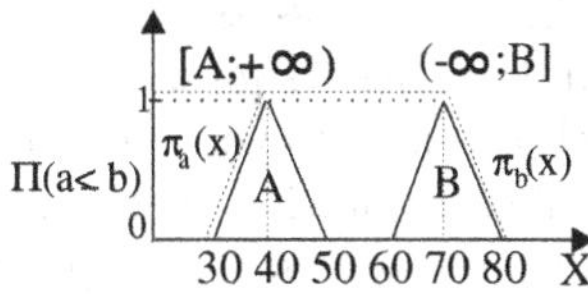

Fig. 23. The possibility measure associated with *B*-*A*3 (resource *R*2).

- if the activity for $A3$ is finalized at date 30, the token becomes available in $A3$, then transition E-$A3$ is fired ($\pi_(x, y) = min(\pi_X(x), \pi_Y(y)) = 1$ with $\pi_X(x) = 1$ (time possibility equal to 1 when $x = 30$) and $\pi_Y(y) = \Pi(a \leq b) = 1$ (resource availability possibility)) and the resource is returned to $R2$. At this moment, $R2 = [60, 70, 70, 80]$. A token is produced in $W4$;

(d) At the fuzzy date $[30, 35, 45, 50]$

- if the activity for $A2$ is finalized at date 35, the token becomes available in $A2$, then the E-$A2$ transition is fired ($\pi_(x, y) = min(\pi_X(x), \pi_Y(y)) = 1$ with $\pi_X(x) = 1$ (time possibility equal to 1 when $x = 35$) and $\pi_Y(y) = \Pi(a \leq b) = 1$ (resource availability possibility)) and the resource is returned to $R2$. At this moment, $R2 = [100, 100, 100, 100]$. A token is produced in $W3$. The transition t is fired and a token is produced in $W5$.

7 Conclusions

This article presented how to model fuzzy hybrid resources in Workflow nets with fuzzy time intervals associated to the activities. In order to mark the minimum and maximum intervals for the execution of activities, a propagation restriction mechanism was proposed. Besides this, through the definition as well as use of a joint possibility distribution, it was possible to define a transition firing definition. This definition takes into consideration the time constraints associated to the cases of the process as well as the availability of the resources used to execute the activities.

Some advantages of this approach can be cited. For example, the event log will show the possibilities of firing each activity and may lead to a type of process quality analysis: if the activities, most of the time, are working with a possibility equal to 1, then the work resulting from the process will be of good quality. On the other hand, if a large number of the activities are associated with possibilities near to 0, then the quality of the process will be of poor quality. In addition, during the execution of process activities, the management of activities could suffer a certain influence according to the semantics associated with a low firing possibility. Finally, in the case of transitions in conflict, the information concerning the firing possibility can be used to make a decision: for example if the possibility is low because of delayed activities, we will give priority to the transition in relation to another that possesses a higher firing possibility.

As a future work proposal, the authors intend to combine the time constraint propagation mechanisms with a token player algorithm as the one presented in [22,25], which will use a conflict resolution mechanism with the aim of calculating the activity sequence that respects the disjunctive constraints (resource allocation mechanisms) as well as the time constraints (date intervals). Besides this, it will be interesting to represent human behavior in a manner that is close to real life, a firing mechanism involving a conditional possibility, in such a way that the availability of the resource will be conditioned to time. Moreover, new firing rules based on a conditional possibility will then be defined and will be implemented at a business managing level through the use of a real time token player algorithm.

Acknowledgement. The authors would like to thank CAPES(Coordenação de Aperfei-çoamento de Pessoal de Nível Superior), FAPEMIG (Fundação de Amparo a Pesquisa do Estado de Minas Gerais) and CNPq (National Counsel of Technological and Scientific Development) for financial support.

References

1. Aalst, W.M.P., Hee, K.: Workflow Management: Models, Methods, and Systems. MIT Press, Cambridge (2004)
2. Aalst, W.M.P.: Verification of workflow nets. In: Azéma, P., Balbo, G. (eds.) ICATPN 1997. LNCS, vol. 1248, pp. 407–426. Springer, Heidelberg (1997)
3. Hee, K., Sidorova, N., Voorhoeve, M.: Fundam. Inf. **71**(2–3), 243–257 (2006)
4. Martos-Salgado, M., Rosa-Velardo, F.: Dynamic soundness in resource-constrained workflow nets. In: Bruni, R., Dingel, J. (eds.) FORTE 2011 and FMOODS 2011. LNCS, vol. 6722, pp. 259–273. Springer, Heidelberg (2011)
5. Wang, J., Li, D.: Resource oriented workflow nets and workflow resource requirement analysis. Int. J. Softw. Eng. Knowl. Eng. **23**(5), 677–694 (2013)
6. Ling, S., Schmidt, H.: Time petri nets for workflow modelling and analysis. In: 2000 IEEE International Conference on Systems, Man and Cybernetics, vol. 4, pp. 3039–3044. IEEE (2000)
7. Kotb, Y.T., Badreddin, E.: Synchronization among activities in a workflow using extended workflow petri nets. In: CEC, pp. 548–551. IEEE Computer Society (2005)
8. Wang, J., Tepfenhart, W.M., Rosca, D.: Emergency response workflow resource requirements modeling and analysis. IEEE Trans. Syst. Man Cybern. Part C **39**(3), 270–283 (2009)

9. Adogla, E.G., Collins, J.W.: Managing resource dependent workflows. US Patent 8,738,775, 27 May 2014
10. He, L., Chaudhary, N., Jarvis, S.A.: Developing security-aware resource management strategies for workflows. Future Gener. Comput. Syst. **38**, 61–68 (2014)
11. Deng, N., Zhu, X.D., Liu, Y.N., Li, Y.P., Chen, Y.: Time management model of workflow based on time axis. Appl. Mech. Mater. **442**, 458–465 (2014)
12. Guo, X., Ge, J., Zhou, Y., Hu, H., Yao, F., Li, C., Hu, H.: Dynamically predicting the deadlines in time-constrained workflows. In: Huang, Z., Liu, C., He, J., Huang, G. (eds.) WISE Workshops 2013. LNCS, vol. 8182, pp. 120–132. Springer, Heidelberg (2014)
13. Lee, D.Y., DiCesare, F.: Scheduling flexible manufacturing systems using petri nets and heuristic search. IEEE Trans. Robot. Autom. **10**(2), 123–132 (1994)
14. Ling, S., Schmidt, H.: Time petri nets for workflow modelling and analysis. In: 2000 IEEE International Conference on Systems, Man, and Cybernetics, vol. 4, pp. 3039–3044. IEEE (2000)
15. Zhu, D.S., Rong, T.J., Dong, L.G.: An extended time workflow model based on twf-net and its application. J. Comput. Res. Dev. **4**, 002 (2003)
16. Dubois, D., Prade, H.: Possibility Theory. Plenum Press, New York (1988)
17. Zadeh, L.A.: Fuzzy sets. Inf. Control **8**, 338–353 (1965)
18. Klir, G., Yuan, B.: Fuzzy Sets and Fuzzy Logic: Theory and Applications. Prentice-Hall Inc., Upper Saddle River (1995)
19. Cardoso, J., Valette, R., Dubois, D.: Possibilistic petri nets. IEEE Trans. Syst. Man Cybern. Part B **29**(5), 573–582 (1999)
20. Dubois, D., Prade, H.: Processing fuzzy temporal knowledge. IEEE Syst. Man Cybern. **19**, 729–744 (1989)
21. David, R., Alla, H.: Discrete, Continuous, and Hybrid Petri Nets, 2nd edn. Springer, Heidelberg (2010)
22. Julia, S., Oliveira, F.F., Valette, R.: Real time scheduling of workflow management systems based on a p-time petri net model with hybrid resources. Simul. Model. Pract. Theor. **16**(4), 462–482 (2008)
23. Murata, T.: Petri nets: properties, analysis and applications. Proc. IEEE **77**(4), 541–580 (1989)
24. Gondran, M., Minoux, M., Vajda, S.: Graphs and Algorithms. Wiley, New York (1984)
25. Julia, S., Valette, R.: Real time scheduling of batch systems. Simul. Pract. Theor. **8**(5), 307319 (2000)

Carpooling as Complement to Multi-modal Transportation

Kamel Aissat[1(✉)] and Sacha Varone[2,3]

[1] Lorraine Research Laboratory in Computer Science and its Applications, University of Lorraine, Nancy, France
kamel.aissat@loria.fr

[2] University of Applied Sciences and Arts Western Switzerland (HES-SO), Delemont, Switzerland
sacha.varone@hesge.ch

[3] HEG Genève, Carouge, Switzerland

Abstract. We propose a new aspect of mobility that combines in a same journey and in real time a carpooling service and a traditional multi-modal transportation. This mix allows to improve and complete both services. The main idea of our approach is based on the traditional multi-modal path, in which we try to sequentially substitute some sub-paths of traditional multi-modal transportation to carpooling, in order to decrease the rider's arrival time at his destination. For this purpose, we first define a closeness estimation between the user's itinerary and available drivers. This allows to select a subset of potential drivers. We then compute sets of driving quickest paths, and design a substitution process. Finally, among all admissible solutions, we select a best one based on the earliest arrival time. We provide numerical results using geographical maps, real data and public transportation timetabling. Our numerical results show the effectiveness of our system, which improves rider's arrival time compared to the traditional multi-modal path. The running time of our approach remains reasonable to use real-time transportation application.

Keywords: Carpooling · Multi-modal routing · Real-time · Public transportation · Geographical maps

1 Introduction

Sustainable mobility is at the heart of our global concerns for livable cities and regions, now and for the generations to come. Major efforts are needed in research and practice on both the invention and implementation of sustainable mobility solutions. Indeed, the public transport which is the backbone of the sustainable urban mobility system must be complemented and improved such as land-use planning, mobility management, combined mobility. One of the easiest ways to address these needs, without impacting the economic prosperity, social welfare and ecological viability is to jointly consider carpooling services with public transport.

S. Hammoudi et al. (Eds.): ICEIS 2015, LNBIP 241, pp. 236–255, 2015.
DOI: 10.1007/978-3-319-29133-8_12

Traditional multi-modal transportation networks include various modes of transportation, such as bus, trains, bicycles, etc. A path on such a network may be composed of subpaths, each covered by different modes of transportation, except carpooling mode. In this paper, we explain a methodology able to combine in a same journey from an origin to a destination, traditional multi-modal transportation and carpooling. This mix provides new aspects of the mobility, which combines fixed timetabling from public transportation and highly dynamic carpooling, and might also be an interesting transportation business.

We consider the following situation: a user, called a rider, wishes to travel from an origin to a destination at a given time. His goal is to reach his destination as quickly as possible, using either public transportation and walking, or carpooling. He might enter the system at any time, being considered as a request. Other users called drivers offer to share all or part(s) of their drive, even at the price of a (not too long) detour; they also have origins, destinations and starting times. The system first find a traditional multi-modal transportation path that satisfies the rider's request, and then tries to sequentially substitute part of the rider's path with carpooling. This paper extends and improves of the idea expressed in [1]. Compared to [1], the number of launched Dijkstra algorithms is reduced by focusing on the number of transit stops rather than the number of potential drivers. More precisely, instead of computing for each potential driver two Dijkstra algorithms, one from the driver's origin to potential pick-up stops and another from potential drop-off stops towards the driver's destination, we compute for each potential pick-up stop only one Dijkstra algorithm with backward search from the origins of potential drivers towards the stop. Similarly, for each potential drop-off location, we compute only one Dijkstra algorithm with forward search from each potential drop-off stops towards drivers' destinations.

2 Related Work

Technological progress plays a crucial role in transportation by making this service more accessible and easier to use. Specifically, the use of GPS-enabled smartphone has increased the possibilities to match riders and drivers, which is nowadays done in quasi real-time (see for example [2]). The concept of carpooling is close to the dynamic Dial A Ride Problem, in which rides' requests have to be fulfilled in real-time with one (or sometimes several) vehicle(s), starting from a depot. The latter problem is a special case of pick-up and delivery problems, in which requests have to be fulfilled for users instead of goods. The main difference is that in carpooling, there is no depot, but a list of Origin-Destination drives which might change to pick-up and drop-off some riders. A recent survey of the pick-up and delivery problem can be found in [3], and recent survey for dynamic carpooling problems has been done in [4]. The background of dynamic carpooling is the ability to compute shortest paths. This problem has been well studied by researchers and very efficient algorithms allow to solve this problem on continental size instances within a few milliseconds. Recent advances in route planning algorithms can be found in [5], which updates the survey of [6].

Multi-modal itinerary computation for carpooling does not only include shortest paths calculation, but also multi-criteria paths, transition or waiting times, etc. which is usually not taken into account in shortest paths on pure road networks. The authors in [7] use for example an objective with several features and consequently focus almost exclusively on the modal change node. They provide a two-step algorithm for the computation of multi-modal routes. In [8], an exact algorithm is given for a carpooling problem with arrivals and departures time-windows. Multi-criteria search has been proposed by [9] using genetic algorithm or by computing the Pareto set in [10].

Public transportation problems have received a lot of attention, solving earliest-arrival problems (EAP) knowing departure time and station, arrival station and timetable information. A review of this topic can be found in [11,12]. The two main multi-modal networks are described, namely, the time-expanded graph and the time-dependent graph. Our approach uses the time-dependent graph, since does not explode the number of nodes. Timetabling information and EAP solving is nowadays often available on-line, either via a web browser or via requests to a restful server. In some cases, timetables information might not be accurate and approximations based on probability distribution might be applied, as done in [13]. Our approach considers that such a service is available. The only study which considers the multi-modal transportation problem and the carpooling service is presented in [14]. Their approach, called "the two synchronization point shortest path problem (2SPSPP)" synchronizes two paths (driver's path and rider's path) at two points of the network so that the duration of the cumulated path is minimized. The two synchronized paths can be decomposed into 5 subpaths. Two convergent paths towards a first synchronization point, i.e. the meeting point, a shared path towards the second synchronization point, i.e., the drop-off point and two divergent paths from this drop-off point towards each destination. Their approach is based on the computation of several shortest paths in a multi-modal network. More specifically, the driver's network is the one for a personal vehicle, whereas the rider's network combines the public transportation network and the walking network. This network restriction is based on the use of a regular language which allows to model constraints on modes. It defines the regular language constrained shortest path problem (RegLCSP). The algorithm which allows to exclude some modes of transport or limit the number of transfers in a multi-modal network is presented in [15]. This can be seen as a generalization of the Dijkstra algorithm to determine valid paths, in accordance with the sequences set in advance by the user.
The exact approach described in [14] presents several limits, namely:

- The user must set the driver in advance before launching the process.
- The model does not take into account the driver's detour time constraint, i.e. the total time of the detour is not bounded.
- The quadratic complexity time of the approach prevents its use in a real-time context.

The remains of this paper is organized as follows: Sect. 3 explains the algorithmic process and its complexity, each step being illustrated with an example. Section 5 presents the performance of our approach and gives concluding remarks.

3 Solving Approach

A network, combining public transportation, walking and driving networks, is modelled as a directed graph $G(N, A)$, N being the set of nodes and A the set of arcs. Nodes represent intersections and arcs describe street segments. A non negative function, called a cost, is associated with each arc; it determines the driving duration between two nodes. A quickest path, which is also a shortest path in our network, is a path that minimizes the sum of its costs. A *stop* is defined as the location for which a transit or road node exists. Stops correspond to bus stops, subway stations, parkings, etc. We describe in this paper an algorithmic approach to the real-time multi-modal earliest-arrival problem (EAP) in urban network, using carpooling, walking and public transportation.

Our approach starts with the finding of a shortest path using traditional multi-modal transportation. As the different transit stops are given by the path so far discovered, pick-up and drop-off are only allowed around those stops in order to reduce the search space. Moreover, we also consider the *best offer selection problem*, i.e. for a given rider, we select the best driver that improves the rider's itinerary by setting the different transit stops as potential pick-up and drop-off locations, under driver's detour time and driver's waiting time constraints.

We define now the problem to be solved: a rider u wishes to go from an origin point O_u to a destination point D_u. He might use either public transportation, walking, carpooling or a combination of all. All public transportation timetabling are assumed to be known or at least accessible easily. In Switzerland, one might use the Swiss public transport API (Application Programming Interface)[1]; in France, a similar service is available[2]. The origin-destination (OD) couple of potential carpooling drivers are also detected and located in real-time.

Throughout this section, together with the described algorithmic process, we present an illustrative example in order to better understand the different steps that constitute our approach. The example represents the following situation: a user u requests to travel from an origin O_u to a destination D_u, starting at time t_u = 9:00. Public transportation allows him to go from a point x_2 to another point x_{nbs}, close to respectively points O_u and D_u, via points $x_2, x_3, \ldots, x_{nbs-1}$. In order to simplify the understanding, our illustrative example supposes that the origin O_u is already a bus stop, hence $O_u = x_1$. For simplicity again, only one driver k is considered (see Figs. 4, 5, 6, 7 and 8).

The traditional multi-modal transportation path is noted as $P = O_u, x_2, \ldots, x_{nbs}, D_u$, its successive points are called "stops". Note that "nbs" stands for number of stops.

[1] http://transport.opendata.ch.

[2] http://www.navitia.io.

Let's call OD the set of origin-destination couple of users. An element $O_k D_k \in OD$ is characterized by its origin O_k, its destination D_k and its starting time t_0^k for user k.
Table 1 lists the notations used throughout this paper.

Table 1. A list of notations.

Notation	Definition
$s \rightsquigarrow e$	driving quickest path between s and e
$\delta(s,e)$	duration of a quickest path between s and e
$d(s,e)$	distance as the crow flies between s and e
$\hat{\delta}(s,e)$	estimated smallest duration from s to e $\hat{\delta}(s,e) = \frac{d(s,e)}{v_{\max}}$, where $v_{\max}$ is the maximal speed
λ_k	detour coefficient of driver k, $\lambda_k \geq 1$
$\tau(x)_{ab}$	time required for moving from modality a to b at x
$t_a^u(x,m)$	arrival time at x using the m transport modality for user u
$t_d^u(x,m)$	departure time at x using the m transport modality for user u
$w_{\max}^k$	maximum waiting time for driver k at pick-up point
$LD_x^{\downarrow}$	list of potential drivers having x as potential pick-up stop
$LD_x^{\uparrow}$	list of potential drivers having x as potential drop-off stop
LP_k	list of potential sub-paths for driver k

We will further note as p the traditional multi-modal transportation modality, and as c the car modality. The traditional multi-modal transportation path retrieved by the API is projected on the road network. In this way, the specific multi-modal transport network is not necessary.

3.1 Substitution Process

We only consider feasible substitution sub-paths that do not increase the arrival time of the rider to his destination. For that purpose we introduce the notion of *reasonable substitution sub-path* with the following definition:

Definition 1 (Reasonable Substitution Sub-path). *An arc (x,y) forms a reasonable substitution sub-path for the driver k and the rider u if and only if the maximal waiting time $w_{\max}^k$ constraint for the driver k at a pick-up location (1), the maximum detour constraint (2) for the driver k, and the latest arrival time constraint (3) for the rider u are satisfied, i.e.,*

$$t_a^u(x,p) + \tau(x)_{pc} - t_a^k(x,c) \leq w_{\max}^k \qquad \textit{waiting} \qquad (1)$$

$$\delta(O_k,x) + \max\left\{t_a^u(x,p) + \tau(x)_{pc} - t_a^k(x,c), 0\right\} + \delta(x,y) + \delta(y,D_k) \leq \lambda_k \delta(O_k,D_k) \qquad \textit{detour} \qquad (2)$$

$$\max\left\{t_a^k(x,c), t_a^u(x,p)+\tau(x)_{pc}\right\}+\delta(x,y)\leq t_a^u(y,p) \qquad \textit{arrival} \qquad (3)$$

Constraints (1), (2) and (3) take into account time required for moving from traditional multi-modal transportation modality to carpooling modality.

The objective function that defines the best substitution sub-path is based on time-savings: among all *reasonable substitution sub-path*, we select the *best substitution sub-path* (x,y) that generates for the rider the most positive time-savings, if he uses carpooling with driver k from the pick-up stop x to the drop-off stop y rather than traditional multi-modal transportation modality.

3.2 Processing Initial Request Based on Traditional Multi-modal Path

As a ride request O_uD_u arrives in the system at time t_0, a shortest path using traditional multi-modal transportation is processed, as well as possible driving substitution sub-paths along the traditional multi-modal transportation path. This is the purpose of Algorithm 1.

Algorithm 1. Processing based on Traditional Multi-modal Path.

Require: Demand O_uD_u, starting time t_0
Ensure: Traditional multi-modal path P
List of potential sub-paths $PDrive$
Driving quickest sub-paths

1: Find path $P = O_u, x_1, \ldots, x_{nbs}, D_u$ using public transportation API, starting in O_u at time t_0, with its associated arrival times $t_a^u(x,p)$ and departure times $t_d^u(x,p)$, $x \in P$.
2: Compute driving quickest paths along P, with its associated arrival times $t_a^u(x,c)$, $x \in P$.
3: Set $PDrive := \emptyset$
4: **for all** $x, y \in P$, x before y **do**
5:    **if** $t_a^u(x,p)+\tau(x)_{pc}+\delta(x,y)\leq t_a^u(y,p)$ **then**
6:       $PDrive := PDrive \cup \{(x,y)\}$
7:    **end if**
8: **end for**

Step 1 gives the traditional multi-modal transportation path P using traditional multi-modal transportation, with its arrival time and departure time on each of its commute node between position O_u and destination D_u. Step 2 computes possible driving substitution paths along P. Only those whose arrival time at the drop-off stop is less than the arrival time using traditional multi-modal transportation are kept. The time at the potential pick-up stop plus the transshipment time plus the carpooling time until stop y, is compare to the arrival time at y without carpooling. If the gain in time for the user is not positive, then the considered carpooling (x,y) is not admissible. The admissible carpooling set is defined by $PDrive$.

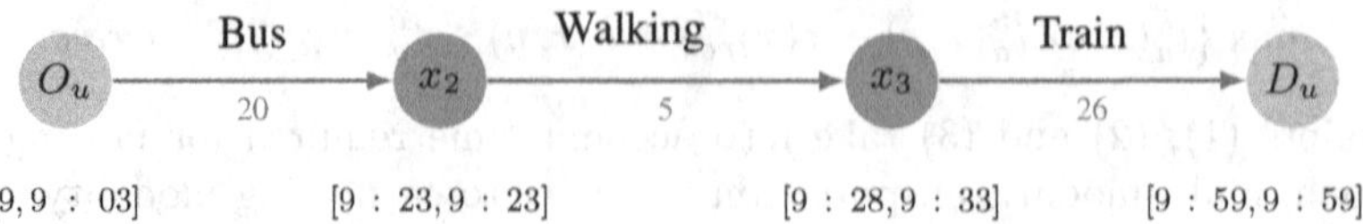

Fig. 1. Traditional multi-modal transportation path P using public transportation API.

Figure 1 illustrates an instance where a rider u travels at starting time t_u = 9:00 from his origin O_u, which is also the first stop x_1, to his destination D_u. Specifically, it represents the situation after step 1 of Algorithm 1. For each stop $x_i \in P$, we associate a time window $[t_a^u(x_i, p), t_d^u(x_i, p)]$ that represents the arrival time at the stop x_i and the departure times from stop x_i, respectively. The path found by the API is composed of three different modes. The rider waits at his origin 3 min before boarding the bus at 9:03, then he is dropped off at stop x_2, walks from stop x_2 to stop x_3 during 5 min, and finally waits 5 more minutes before taking the train to reach his final destination D_u (see Fig. 1).

Figure 2 represents step 2 of Algorithm 1, where all potential driving substitution sub-paths are computed.

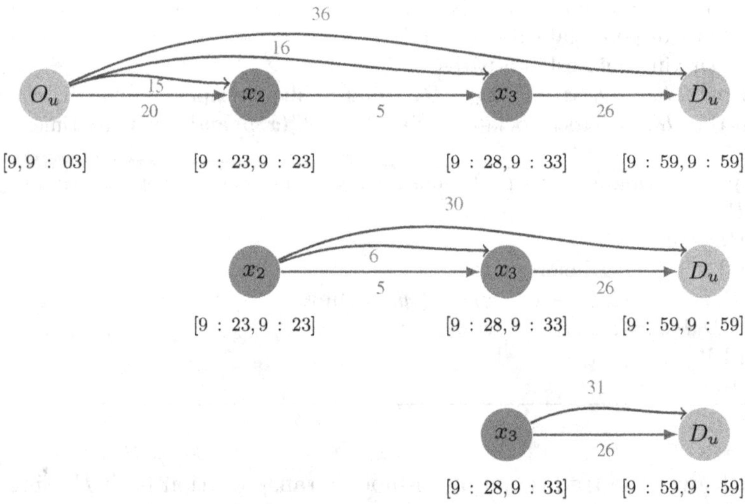

Fig. 2. Quickest driving paths for every pair (x_i, x_j) such that stop x_j is situated after stop x_i are shown as dashed blue line (Color figure online).

In Fig. 3 are shown the admissible potential substitution sub-paths, returned by Algorithm 1. The carpooling path (x_2, x_3) would results in an arrival time at x_3 later than that one if traditional multi-modal transportation is use, since it requires 6 min from x_2 to x_3, rather then 5 min. A similar situation occurs

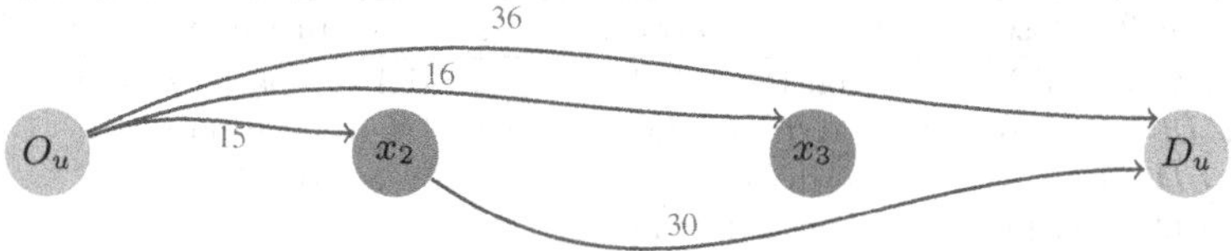

Fig. 3. Admissible driving substitution arcs.

for the carpooling path (x_3, D_u): 31 min of carpooling compared to 26 min by traditional multi-modal transportation. Therefore both sub-paths (x_2, x_3) and (x_3, D_u) are canceled.

3.3 Closeness Estimation Between a User's Itinerary and Available Drivers

We define an estimate on how close is a substitution driving path OD to a traditional multi-modal transportation sub-path of P. This estimated distance is defined as the minimal sum of the estimated distance from a vertex in OD to a vertex in P, and backward from P to OD. Four different points are used, so that only non-trivial substitution are allowed (i.e. no substitution of a single vertex). For that purpose, we estimate the distance between two points given by their latitude/longitude with the Haversine formula.

This formula uses a spherical model to estimate the distance between two points $x = (\lambda_1, \theta_1)$ and $y = (\lambda_2, \theta_2)$ on the earth surface.

$$a = sin(\frac{\theta_2 - \theta_1}{2})^2 + cos(\theta_1) * cos(\theta_2) * sin(\frac{\lambda_2 - \lambda_1}{2})^2$$

$$d(x, y) = R * 2 * atan2(\sqrt{a}, \sqrt{1-a})$$

where $\lambda_i, i = 1, 2$ are the latitudes, $\theta_i, i = 1, 2$ are the longitudes, $R \approx 6371$ [km] is the earth's radius. Thus, the estimated smallest duration from x to y is noted by $\hat{\delta}(x, y) = \frac{d(x,y)}{v_{max}}$, such that v_{max} is the maximal speed of a car in concerned area. This is a solution to the so called great-circle distance between two points problem (sometimes also called "orthodromic distance" problem).

Algorithm 2 restricts the list of potential drivers to those whose OD is close enough to P, and whose detour time is less than a threshold value. Step 1 initializes the lists of drivers, namely, $LDriver$, $LD_x^{\downarrow}$ and $LD_y^{\uparrow}$ as empty lists. Step 7 checks if the driver's time from his origin to destination including the detour via x and y is less than its maximal detour bound. This latter is based on estimated durations for each driver k from O_k to x (step 5) and from y to D_k (step 6). For each potential pick-up stop x, we keep in the list $LD_x^{\downarrow}$ only drivers satisfying the detour time constraint. The same reasoning is applied for each potential drop-off stop y in the list $LD_y^{\uparrow}$. The maximum detour time of a driver must not exceed 20 % of its quickest duration (i.e. $\lambda_k = 1.2$) in our experiments, since insurance companies limit their duties to a detour time under 20 %, in

---

Algorithm 2. Closeness estimation between the user's itinerary and available drivers.

Require: Classical Multi-modal Path P, list of potential sub-paths $PDrive$.
Ensure: $LD_x^{\downarrow}$: List of potential drivers having x as pick-up location
$LD_y^{\uparrow}$: List of potential drivers having y as drop-off location
$LDriver$: List of potential drivers
LP_k: List of potential sub-paths for driver k, $\forall k \in LDriver$
Update $PDriver$.

1: **Initialization :** $LDriver := \emptyset$,
$LD_x^{\downarrow} := \emptyset$, $LD_y^{\uparrow} := \emptyset$, $PDrive' = PDrive$.
2: **for each** driver in database **do**
3: $LP_k = \emptyset$
4: **for all** $(x, y) \in PDrive$ **do**
5: Estimate $\hat{\delta}(O_k, x)$ from O_k to x
6: Estimate $\hat{\delta}(y, D_k)$ from y to D_k
7: **if** $\hat{\delta}(O_k, x) + \delta(x, y) + \hat{\delta}(y, D_k) \leq \lambda_k \delta(O_k, D_k)$ **then**
8: $LD_x^{\downarrow} := LD_x^{\downarrow} \cup \{k\}$
9: $LD_y^{\uparrow} := LD_y^{\uparrow} \cup \{k\}$
10: $LP_k = LP_k \cup \{(x, y)\}$
11: $PDrive' = PDrive' \cup (x, y)$
12: **end if**
13: **end for**
14: **end for**
15: Update $PDrive$ to $PDrive'$ (i.e. remove from $PDrive$ all substitution paths (x, y) which are not detected by any potential driver)

---

case of a work accident. The latter is an accident that occurs during a mission of an employee. Step 2 scans the set of drivers in the system having the same departure date and the same geographic area. Figure 4 illustrates the situation of a driver k when the request of rider u arrives in the system.

Figure 5 shows the estimated durations using the Haversine formula (steps 5 and 6).

Figure 6 represents different tests performed on each potential substitution sub-paths from a driver's starting position to its destination. The numbers above

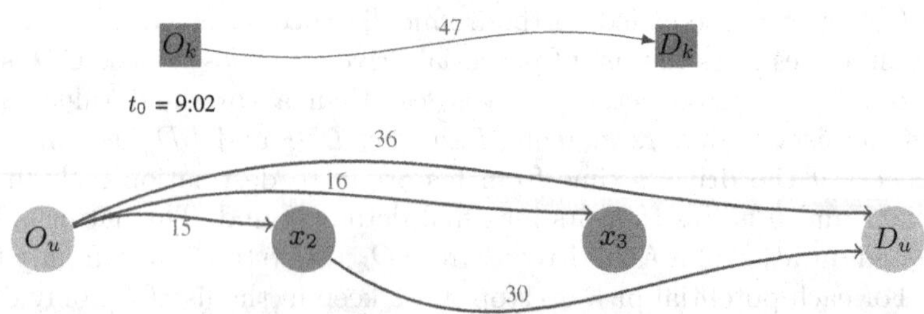

Fig. 4. Driver k drives from O_k to D_k, starting at time 9:02. Nodes in path P with potential carpooling sub-paths are shown in solid blue lines (Color figure online).

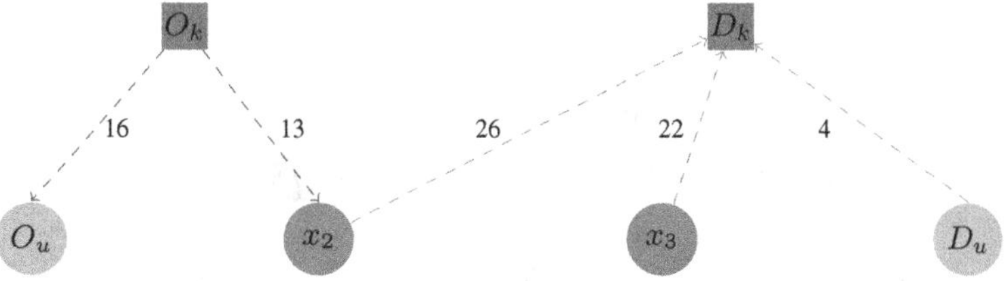

Fig. 5. Estimation of the duration to each potential pick-up nodes, and from each potential drop-off nodes, for driver k, using the Haversine formula. Each geographical position are supposed to be known.

dashed lines represent the estimated durations, while the numbers above solid lines (quickest driving path) represent the exact duration, as determined by Algorithm 1.

Figure 7 shows the result of Algorithm 2, where arc (O_u, x_2) has been removed since carpooling on this path would implies to drive during $16+15+26 = 57$ min, exceeding the detour limit of $1.2 \times 47 = 56.4$ min. Then, we remove the potential driving substitution arc (O_u, x_2) because the lower bound of driver's detour duration is not satisfied. This allows to restrict the list of potential pick-up and drop-off locations.

3.4 Shortest Paths Computation and Best Substitution Sub-Path

Once the list of potential drivers has been determined, Algorithm 3 computes all shortest paths, so that the admissibility of a solution can be verified. The three constraints are namely a *driver's detour time*, a *driver's waiting time at pick-up location* and the *rider's arrival time.* Two kinds of shortest path calculations are performed. A first one from the actual position of each driver to each potential pick-up stop (step 3). A second one from each potential drop-off stop to each destination of potential driver (step 9). These calculations are performed in two phases. A first phase determines the duration from their actual positions to potential pick-up stops. Based on these durations, we update $LD_y^{\uparrow}$ by removing drivers not respecting all three constraints: *driver's detour time*, *driver's waiting time at pick-up location* and *rider's arrival time.* Once all sets of $LD_y^{\uparrow}$ are updated, a second phase computes the exact duration from each drop-off stop y towards each driver contained in the list $LD_y^{\uparrow}$. Whenever the exact duration of a driver k is determined in this second phase, we scan its potential sub-paths LP_k by checking the exact admissibility of driver's detour time constraint. Finally, among all admissible sub-paths, we select one with greatest time-savings. Figure 8 shows the *admissibility* of potential sub-paths corresponding to our example.

Algorithm 4 describes the whole process. Step 7 is performed once the rider has reached a drop-off stop $y^{\star}$.

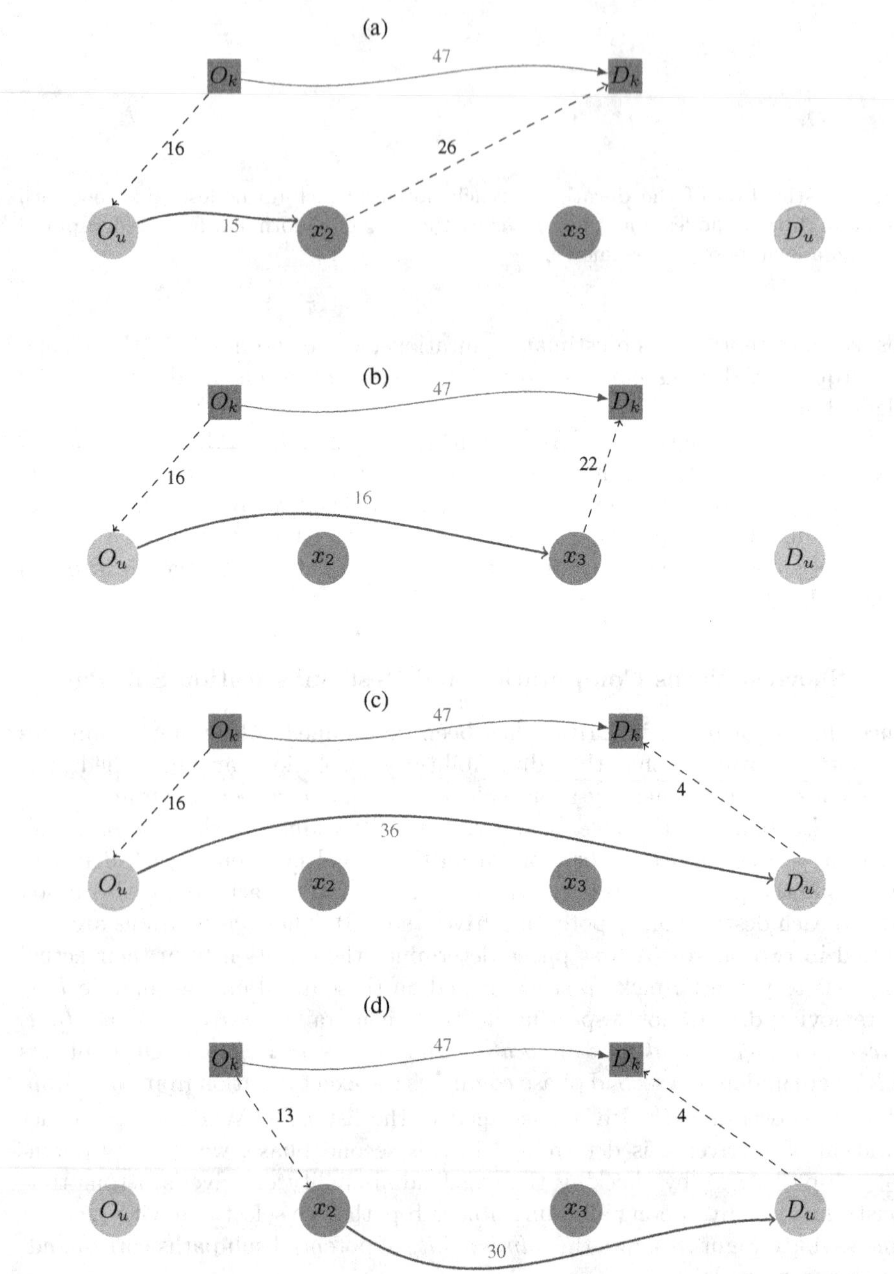

Fig. 6. All potential substitution sub-paths are evaluated against the detour constraint.

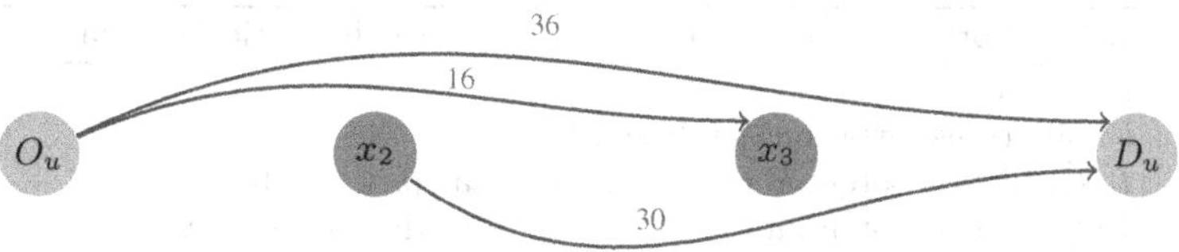

Fig. 7. Only potential substitution sub-paths that do not violate the detour constraint are kept.

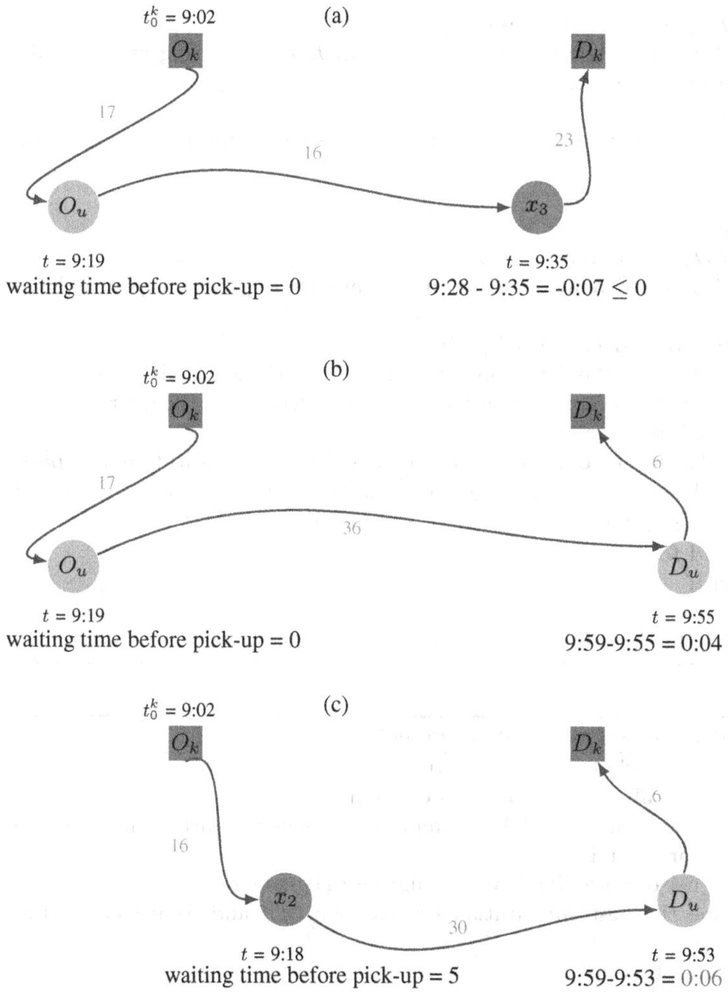

(a)

t_0^k = 9:02

O_k D_k

17 16 23

O_u x_3

t = 9:19
waiting time before pick-up = 0

t = 9:35
9:28 - 9:35 = -0:07 $\leq$ 0

(b)

t_0^k = 9:02

O_k D_k

17 36 6

O_u D_u

t = 9:19
waiting time before pick-up = 0

t = 9:55
9:59-9:55 = 0:04

(c)

t_0^k = 9:02

O_k D_k

16 6 30

x_2 D_u

t = 9:18
waiting time before pick-up = 5

t = 9:53
9:59-9:53 = 0:06

Fig. 8. Best substitution sub-path. Ride-sharing (O_u, x_3) increases the earliest arrival time at x_3; therefore it is canceled. Between carpooling (O_u, D_u) and (x_2, D_u), the last one better improves the arrival time at D_u; it is therefore the best substitution sub-path.

Algorithm 3. Shortest paths computation and best substitution sub-path.

Require: Demand $O_u D_u$,
Public transportation database (API)
$LD_x^{\downarrow}$: List of potential drivers having x as pick-up stop x
$LD_y^{\uparrow}$: List of potential drivers having x as drop-off stop y
LP_k: List of potential sub-paths for driver k
$PDriver$: List of potential drivers.
Ensure: Best driver $k^\star$
Best substitution sub-path $(x^\star, y^\star)$ or failure

1: **for all** $x \in P$ **do**
2: **if** $LD_x^{\downarrow}$ is not empty **then**
3: Compute driving quickest paths from $LD_x^{\downarrow}$ to x using reverse Dijkstra algorithm one-to-all.
4: **end if**
5: Update $LD_x^{\downarrow}$ taking into account the durations determined by the previous step 3.
6: **end for**
7: **for all** $y \in P$ **do**
8: **if** $LD_y^{\uparrow}$ is not empty **then**
9: Compute driving quickest paths from $LD_y^{\uparrow}$ to y using Dijkstra algorithm one-to-all.
10: **for all** driver k in $LD_y^{\uparrow}$ **do**
11: Retrieve the list of potential sub-path LP_k for the driver k
12: Check the admissibility between the driver k and the rider u for all potential sub-paths $x \rightarrow y, \forall x < y$.
13: Keep the best driver $k^\star$ as well as the substitution sub-path $(x^\star, y^\star)$ that generate the greatest time-savings, i.e. $\max_{k^\star, x^\star, y^\star} \{t_a^u(y^\star, p) - (\max\{t_a^{k^\star}(x^\star, c), t_a^u(x^\star, p) + \tau(x^\star)_{pc}\} + \delta(x^\star, y^\star))\}$
14: **end for**
15: **end if**
16: **end for**
17: Update the driver's route $O_{k^\star} \rightsquigarrow x^\star \rightsquigarrow y^\star \rightsquigarrow D_{k^\star}$.

Algorithm 4. Best substitution sub-path

Require: Demand $O_u D_u$, starting time t_0
Ensure: Best substitution sub-path or failure.
Find traditional multimodal path and its components starting at t_0 from O_u to D_u, using **Algorithm 1**
Find the list of potential drivers using **Algorithme 2**
Determine the best substitution sub-path $(x^\star, y^\star)$ and its driver $k^\star$ using **Algorithme 3**
if $y^\star \neq D_u$ **then**
$t_0' = \max\{t_a^{k^\star}(x^\star, c), t_a^u(x^\star, p) + \tau(x^\star)_{pc}\} + \delta(x^\star, y^\star)$
Update the rider's route $O_{u^\star} \rightsquigarrow x^\star \rightsquigarrow y^\star$.
Move to step 1 taking into account $y^\star$ as the new origin and t_0' as new departure time.
end if

Note that from a drop-off location, the rider's route have to be recomputed to take into account his new arrival time. In this example, the drop-off location corresponds to the destination of rider.

The new itinerary of the rider is represented in Fig. 9 and the new itinerary of the driver k will become $O_k \rightsquigarrow x_2 \rightsquigarrow D_u \rightsquigarrow D_k$.

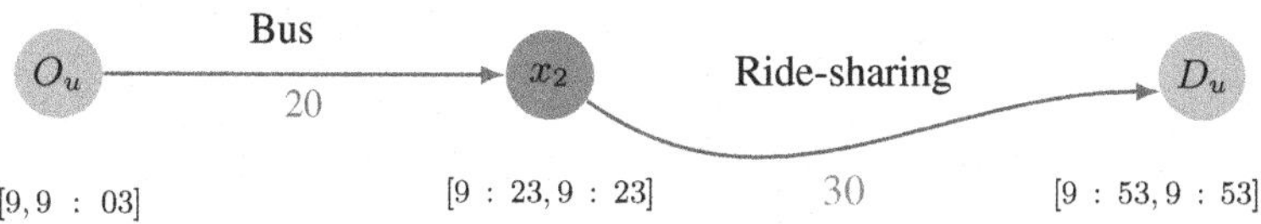

Fig. 9. New itinerary of the rider.

3.5 Complexity

We describe the complexity of the whole process in a worst case analysis. Algorithm 1 initializes the request processing in $O(\mathcal{D}_{road} \cdot (|P| - 1) + \mathcal{D}_{API})$-time, where $\mathcal{D}_{road}$ (resp. $\mathcal{D}_{API}$) is the complexity of the Dijkstra algorithm in a road (resp. multi-modal) network. Algorithm 2, which allows to estimate the closeness of the user's itinerary and available drivers, runs in $O(|LDrive| \cdot |PDrive|)$-time. Algorithm 3 checks the admissibility of drivers in terms of detour time constraint by determining also the best substitution sub-path. This latter is done in $O(|P^+| \cdot \mathcal{D}_{road} + |P^-| \cdot (\mathcal{D}_{road} + |PDrive|))$. Therefore, the complexity of the whole process described by Algorithm 4 is in $O\big(\mathcal{D}_{API} + (|P| + |P^+| + |P^-| - 1) \cdot \mathcal{D}_{road} + (|P^-| + |LDrive|) \cdot |PDrive|\big)$. Once the rider has reached a best drop-off stop $y^\star$, the process must be re-run taking into account its new arrival time.

4 Computational Experiments

In this section, we provide experimental results using the proposed method. This latter were implemented in C# Visual Studio 2010. The experiments were done on an Intel(R) Core(TM) i7-3520M 2.9 GHz processor, with 8 GB RAM memory. Our road network corresponds to the French Lorraine region which is derived from the publicly available data of OpenStreetMap[3]. Its consists of 797830 nodes and 2 394 002 directed edges. We use real data provided by Covivo company[4] corresponding to employees of Lorraine region traveling between their homes and their work places. In our experiments, we consider the trip from their homes to their workplaces. These data are composed of 537 offers of carpooling and 538 of ride requests. The smallest and the greatest trip's distances are respectively 2 Km and 130 km. The set of offers and demands are filtered such that we can

[3] http://www.openstreetmap.org.

[4] http://www.covivo.fr.

never find driver's offer and a rider's demand which have the same starting and ending locations. The departure time of each trip is fixed to 7:30 a.m. The detour time of the driver (rider) is fixed to at most 20 % of his initial trip duration.

In Fig. 10 we project some offers of carpooling. Red and blue points are the geocoded home and work locations, respectively.

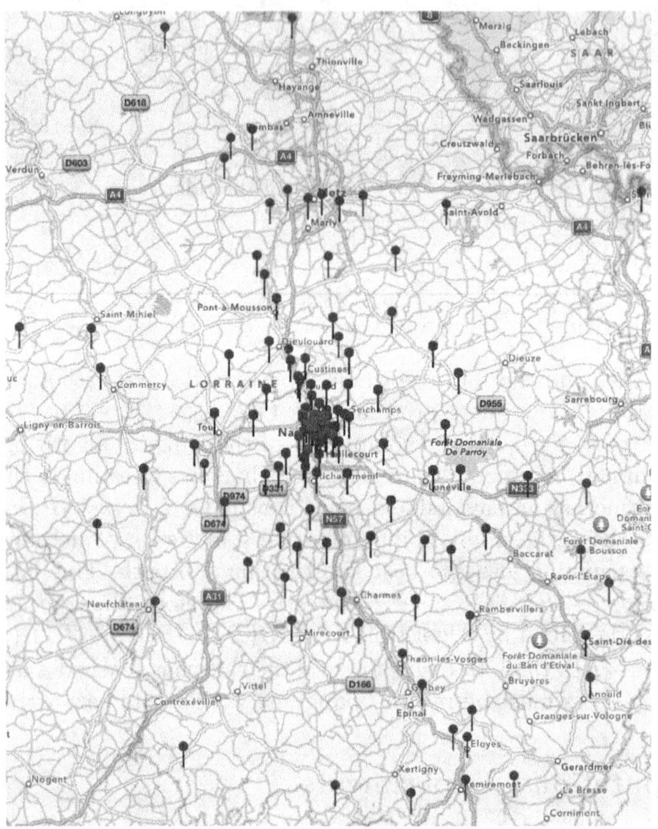

Fig. 10. Map visualization of offers (Color figure online).

Our scenario is the following; we scan each rider's request, and for each rider's request we consider all offers (537). We first evaluate the number of improved trips using our approach compared to the traditional multi-modal transportation path. For this, we split the instances into three groups:

- No ride: request satisfied only with traditional multi-modal transportation.
- Ride only: request satisfied only with ride-sharing.
- Both: requests satisfied with ride-sharing and traditional multi-modal transportation.

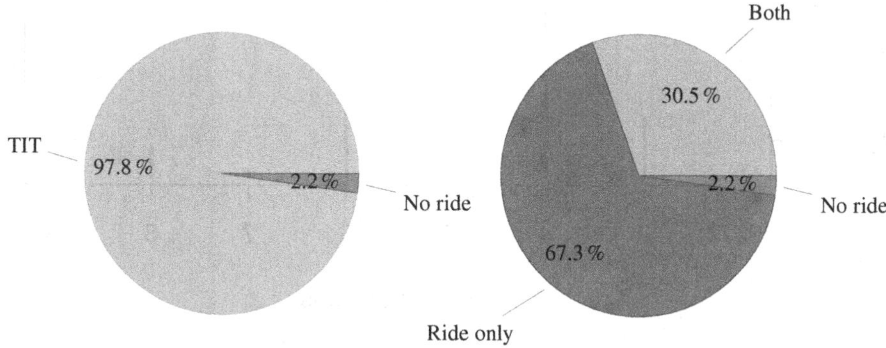

Fig. 11. Percentage of number of trips for each group, TIT(Total Improved Trips), No ride, Ride only and Both.

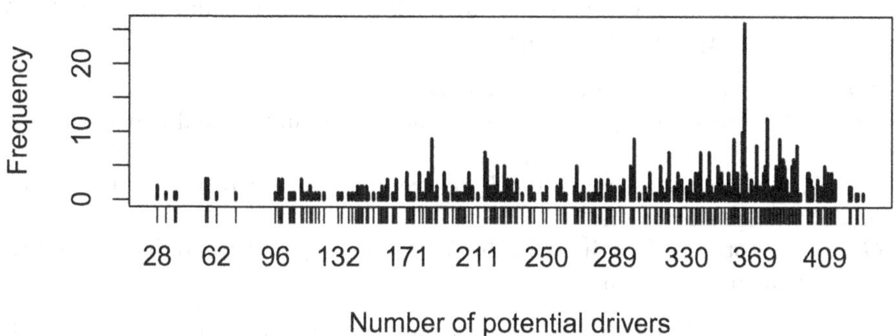

Fig. 12. Frequency of number of potential drivers.

Figure 11 indicates that compared to the initial trips returned by API, 97.8 % of the trips are improved. Among them, 67.3 % is composed only with ridesharing and 30.5 % combines ridesharing and traditional multi-modal transportation.

Figure 12 represents the frequency of the number of potential drivers for each instance. As shown in the Fig. 10, the offers are close to each other and so the number of potential drivers is high. The potential drivers correspond to the drivers who have been selected by the closeness estimation step.

Figure 13 represent the frequency of the number of stops, which varies between 2 and 9. A trip with two stops (origin and its destination) may occur when the trip is composed of only one mode (i.e. public transport or carpooling). The major part of trips are composed of four transit stops. We note that it is sometimes possible that the user might give an upper on the number of transit stops, when interacting with the public transportation API. In our approach, this number is not bounded since the objective function to be minimized is the earliest arrival time.

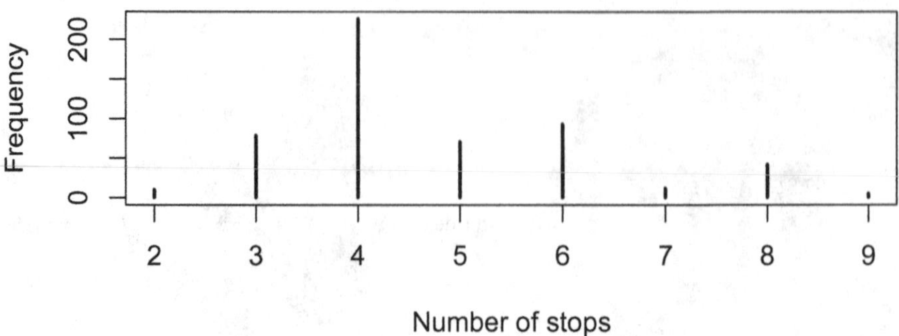

Fig. 13. Frequency of number of stops.

In this second part, we present the running time and time-savings that our approach generates compared to the traditional multi-modal transportation path. For this purpose, we note by:

- *Time*: CPU computation time [seconds]
- *Gain*: total time-savings compared to traditional multi-modal transportation only.
- $Gain_{Ride}$: total time-savings for *Ride* group compared to traditional multi-modal transportation only.
- $Gain_{Both}$: total time-savings for *Both* group compared to traditional multi-modal transportation only.

The gain is divided into two groups, the group which is composed of only carpooling ($Gain_{Ride}$) and the another group which combines the two services $Gain_{Both}$.

Table 2. Performance of our approach.

Median				
Gain (min)	$Gain_{Ride}$ (min)	$Gain_{Both}$ (min)	Trip duration (min)	*Time* (s)
52	55	24.43	84	52.85

The values in the Table 2 correspond to the median over all instances. The column "Trip duration" represents the median value of the initial trip's duration determined by the API. This duration includes the waiting times at the different transit stops. The generated time-savings is very significant that reaches approximatively one hour in the case where the frequency of buses is low. The running time is kept reasonable so that it allows its use in a commercial application context.

Figure 14 represents the running time according to the number of potential drivers for each different number of stop. We show that the running time

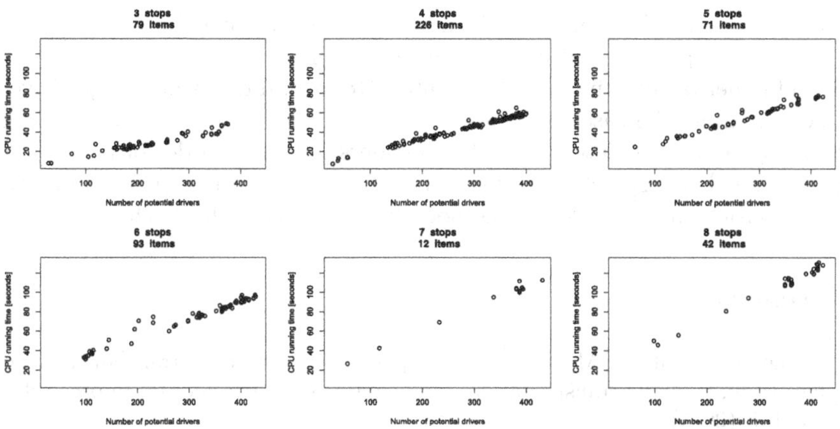

Fig. 14. Running time according to the number of stops and potential drivers.

increases with both the number of potential drivers and the number of stop. This increase is linear and depends also on the position of drivers that affect the running time of launched Dijkstra algorithm.

One of possible improvements is to limit the searches on the potential drivers by bounded the Dijkstra algorithms.

5 Conclusions

In this paper, we have proposed a new multi-modal transportation design. Extending traditional multi-modal systems, we consider the carpooling service in the rider's choice, while taking into account real life constraints like driver's detour time and driver's waiting time. Experimental results show the effectiveness of our approach compared to traditional multi-modal transport in terms of time-savings. Our approach reduces the driver's detour by offering to the rider the opportunity to use intermediate locations. It also improves the cost-saving for both drivers and riders compared to the traditional carpooling.

The particular interest of our work is in making the service of carpooling and public transportation more flexible and efficient. Specifically, in contrast to the traditional carpooling service, our approach allows to reduce the driver's detour by using intermediate pick-up and drop-off locations for the rider, and to increase the savings for both drivers and riders, compared to the traditional carpooling service. The carpooling service can be considered as a complement to transit for public transportation, i.e. the carpooling will improve transportation service in rural areas, difficult to serve by public transportation only. This is the main reason that will incite the public transport agencies to use carpooling to complement their services. Despite the relative importance of integrating carpooling into public transport services, as far as we know, no previous work exists that allows to deal with this problem in dynamic and real-time context.

One of the reasons could be the difficulty to define and combine in real-time the two services: carpooling and public transportation.

As a further perspective, we aim to integrate several riders in a single driver's car. For example, the case where a driver is ready to travel with several riders, then the system must determine a list of riders and their order of pick-up and drop off. Another research direction is to reduce the shortest paths'computing time by considering acceleration methods like contraction hierarchies.

References

1. Varone, S., Aissat, K.: Multi-modal transportation with public transport and ride-sharing multi-modal transportation using a path-based method. In: In proceedings of ICEIS (2015)
2. Chan, N.D., Shaheen, S.A.: Ridesharing in north america: past, present, and future. Transp. Rev. **32**(1), 93–112 (2012)
3. Berbeglia, G., Cordeau, J., Laporte, G.: Dynamic pickup and delivery problems. Eur. J. Oper. Res. **202**(1), 8–15 (2010)
4. Agatz, N.A.H., Erera, A.L., Savelsbergh, M.W.P., Wang, X.: Optimization for dynamic ride-sharing: a review. Eur. J. Oper. Res. **223**(2), 295–303 (2012)
5. Bast, H., Delling, D., Goldberg, A., Müller-Hannemann, M., Pajor, T., Sanders, P., Wagner, D., Werneck, R.: Route planning in transportation networks. MSR-TR-2014-4 8, Microsoft Research (2014)
6. Delling, D., Sanders, P., Schultes, D., Wagner, D.: Engineering route planning algorithms. In: Lerner, J., Wagner, D., Zweig, K.A. (eds.) Algorithmics of Large and Complex Networks. LNCS, vol. 5515, pp. 117–139. Springer, Heidelberg (2009)
7. Ambrosino, D., Sciomachen, A.: An algorithmic framework for computing shortest routes in urban multimodal networks with different criteria. Procedia - Soc. Behav. Sci. **108**, 139–152 (2014). Operational Research for Development, Sustainability and Local Economies
8. Liu, L., Yang, J., Mu, H., Li, X., Wu, F.: Exact algorithms for multi-criteria multi-modal shortest path with transfer delaying and arriving time-window in urban transit network. Appl. Math. Model. **38**(9–10), 2613–2629 (2014)
9. Herbawi, W., Weber, M.: The ridematching problem with time windows in dynamic ridesharing: a model and a genetic algorithm. In: Proceedings of the IEEE Congress on Evolutionary Computation, CEC 2012, 10–15 June 2012, pp, 1–8. IEEE, Brisbane, Australia (2012)
10. Wagner, D., Dibbelt, J., Delling, D., Werneck, R.F., Pajor, T.: Computing multimodal journeys in practice. In: Bonifaci, V., Demetrescu, C., Marchetti-Spaccamela, A. (eds.) SEA 2013. LNCS, vol. 7933, pp. 260–271. Springer, Heidelberg (2013)
11. Müller-Hannemann, M., Schulz, F., Zaroliagis, C.D., Wagner, D.: Timetable information: models and algorithms. In: Geraets, F., Kroon, L.G., Schoebel, A., Wagner, D., Zaroliagis, C.D. (eds.) Railway Optimization 2004. LNCS, vol. 4359, pp. 67–90. Springer, Heidelberg (2007)
12. Pyrga, E., Schulz, F., Wagner, D., Zaroliagis, C.: Efficient models for timetable information in public transportation systems. J. Exp. Algorithmics **12**, 2.4:1–2.4:39 (2008)

13. Murueta, P.O.P., García, E., de los Angeles Junco Rey, M.: Finding in multimodal networks without timetables. In: VEHICULAR 2014: The Third International Conference on Advances in Vehicular Systems, Technologies and Applications (2014)
14. Bit-Monnot, A., Artigues, C., Huguet, M.J., Killijian, M.O.: Carpooling: the 2 synchronization points shortest paths problem. In: 13th Workshop on Algorithmic Approaches for Transportation Modelling, Optimization, and Systems (ATMOS), France, Sophia Antipolis, vol. 13328, p. 12, September 2013
15. Barrett, C., Jacob, R., Marathe, M.: Formal-language-constrained path problems. SIAM J. Comput. **30**(3), 809–837 (2000)

A Simulated Annealing-Based Approach for the Optimization of Routine Maintenance Interventions

Francesco Longo, Andrea Rocco Lotronto(✉), Marco Scarpa, and Antonio Puliafito

Dipartimento di Ingegneria, Università degli Studi di Messina, Viale F. Stagno d'Alcontres, 31, 98166 Messina, ME, Italy
{flongo,alotronto,mscarpa,apuliafito}@unime.it

Abstract. Metaheuristics are often adopted to solve optimization problems where some requests need to be scheduled among a finite number of resources, i.e., the so called scheduling problems. Such techniques approach the optimization problems by taking inspiration from a certain physical phenomenon. Simulated annealing is a metaheuristic approach inspired to the controlled cooling of a material from a high temperature to a state in which internal defects of the crystals are minimized. In this paper, we use a simulated annealing-based approach to solve the problem of the scheduling of geographically distributed routine maintenance interventions. Each intervention has to be assigned to a maintenance team and the choice among the available teams and the order in which interventions are performed by each team are based on team skills, cost of overtime work, and cost of transportation. We compare our solution algorithm versus an exhaustive approach. First, we consider a real industrial use case and show several numerical results to analyze the effect of the parameters of the simulated annealing on the accuracy of the solution and on the execution time of the algorithm. Then, we provide results varying the parameters and dimension of the considered problem highlighting how they affect reliability and efficiency of our algorithm.

Keywords: Routine maintenance interventions · Metaheuristic approaches · Simulated annealing · Scheduling problems · Optimization problems

1 Introduction

The use of limited resources with utilization requests over time originates a class of problems called *scheduling problems* [1]. The contexts with this type of problems are multiple and, consequently, for each of such contexts the final objectives, the number and kind of the limited resources, and the number and kind of the utilization requests can be different. Moreover, the same problem could not exhibit a unique solution. Instead, a set of solutions that are all admissible

S. Hammoudi et al. (Eds.): ICEIS 2015, LNBIP 241, pp. 256–279, 2015.
DOI: 10.1007/978-3-319-29133-8_13

can be generated, differentiated by their cost. The nature of such a cost and the way it is evaluated and determined is of course different in different application contexts. However, even if the application context changes, the following property is usually satisfied: *making a minimal change to a particular solution of a scheduling problem can produce a substantial change in its cost.* This determines, in the general economy of any application context, the necessity to find a solution to a specific scheduling problem that is as less expensive as possible. Moreover, it makes such a task particularly difficult given that small perturbations can heavily influence the overall cost.

An algorithm exploited to solve this kind of problems usually tests if a given solution is admissible for the problem and, defining a *cost function* (usually depending on the aspects of the problem that is necessary to minimize/maximize), calculates its cost. Problems of this nature where the goal is to minimize/maximize a cost function are generally identified as *optimization problems.*

In this paper, we take into consideration the problem of scheduling a list of geographically distributed routine maintenance interventions among a set of maintenance teams, taking into account team skills, cost of overtime work, and cost of transportation. This kind of problems can present a set of admissible solutions that is too large to implement an algorithm that assesses all of them in order to determine the one with the minimum cost, in a finite time. Therefore, we follow a different approach exploiting a *metaheuristic technique* [2].

In particular, we exploit the *simulated annealing* (SA) [3] metaheuristic to solve our routine maintenance scheduling problem with the goal of optimizing the routes of the maintenance teams minimizing the cost and trying to maximize the number of maintenance operations actually performed in a given day. In order to show the effectiveness of our approach, we take into consideration a real industrial use case provided by Meridionale Impianti[1], a company active in the industrial and electrical plant design sector. We compare the solution obtained by our approach with the exact solution obtained by applying an exhaustive algorithm that comprehensively enumerates all the solutions finding the one that produces the minimal cost. We also perform a large set of experiments evaluating the impact of the different parameters of our SA approach to the accuracy of the solution and the efficiency of the algorithm in terms of execution time, with the aim of tuning the optimal values of such parameters for future execution of the same algorithm. Finally, we demonstrate the scalability of our approach with respect to the problem dimension.

2 Related Work

In this paper, we present an efficient and general method for solving routine maintenance scheduling problems based on SA metaheuristic. Several works in literature propose the use of SA for the solution of scheduling problems in the context of the maintenance of specific installations, especially power plants.

[1] http://www.merimp.com/en/.

In [4], authors address the problem of the periodic maintenance of electric generators by using SA. They aim at scheduling system maintenance operations along a planning horizon assuming that the time interval between maintenance actions for the same generator is fixed. In our approach, we do not take into consideration the time interval between maintenance actions but we deal with the scheduling of interventions that are supposed to be conducted in a certain working day accordingly to a predetermined business policy. As in [4,5] deals with the maintenance of generators in a power plant by using a hybrid approach based on a combination of genetic algorithms and SA. In [6], the tabu search metaheuristic is applied to the maintenance of generators in a power station with the aim of reducing the cost associated with the management of the maintenance operations and to increase the time interval between two maintenance operations for the same generator. In our case a pure SA approach is exploited mainly focusing on the overall cost of performing a set of geographically distributed maintenance operations during a working day taking into account transportation and overtime costs.

More generally, the SA metaheuristic and its variations are often used for the solution of optimization problems in several application fields spanning from ICT to biomedicine. In [7], SA, combined with additional momentum terms in order to improve cooling rate, is exploited to solve the problem of router node placement with service priority constraint to improve the performance of a wireless mesh network. In [8], the SA algorithm is adopted for creating maneuver plans for the guidance of a satellite cluster. In a gene expression data matrix, a bicluster is a submatrix of genes and condition. The problem of detecting the most significant bicluster has been shows to be NP-Complete. In [9], the authors present a biclustering technique based on SA to efficiently discover the more significant biclusters.

In this paper, we use SA to solve a maintenance operation scheduling problem. During problem formalization we do not take into consideration any specific application context. However, we show its application to a real industrial use case dealing with the maintenance of energy plants. We are interested in routine maintenance operations, i.e., maintenance operations that are not related to an actual failure of the considered system but are scheduled in advance. We start from the assumptions that a set of maintenance operations are scheduled to be conducted in a specific day and our goal is to optimize the maintenance team routes and maximize the number of interventions that are actually performed. Contrary to maintenance operations upon failures, such routine operations can be postponed if it is not possible to guarantee that all the operations that are supposed to be conducted in a day will be actually fulfilled. However, our algorithm is also able to deal with maintenance operations that need to be executed with a higher priority.

3 Reference Scenario

We take into consideration a company that needs to perform maintenance operations in a set of geographically distributed locations. We only deal with routine maintenance interventions, i.e., interventions that are scheduled in advance. However, our approach also takes into account that some higher priority interventions could be necessary, representing failures and/or specific situations that need immediate attention. We focus on the set of maintenance operations that need to be performed in a single day by a limited set of maintenance resources. The maintenance resources are represented by a number of teams, each composed of a set of company employees and one vehicle. The teams leave from the company principle headquarters in the morning, follow a specific route established in advance, perform all the maintenance interventions that they have been assigned to, and return to their starting point. This kind of problems falls under the class of scheduling problems.

The problem we need to solve is to assign the maintenance operations that are supposed to be conducted in the considered day to the teams. Constraints are present related to the nature of each maintenance intervention. In fact, all maintenance operations have specific characteristics in terms of both the location where the intervention needs to be conducted and the technical skills that are necessary to accomplish the intervention. Being each intervention team composed of one or more workers and one vehicle, accordingly to the technical skills that each worker presents and to the characteristics of the vehicle (that can reach a specific location or not), it is possible to understand which teams are able to perform a specific intervention (it may be a subset of all the teams).

Of course, maintenance activities represent a cost for the company. In our reference scenario, costs are related to the hourly wage of the workers and to the transportation expenses. A worker hourly wage increases if the worker needs to do overtime, so a solution algorithm assigning interventions to teams needs to minimize the possibility to go into overtime taking into consideration both the time that is needed to perform each maintenance intervention and the traveling time for a team to move from one intervention site to the following. Transportation expenses are mainly related to fuel and maintenance for all the vehicles used during the working day.

The main objective of this paper is to provide an algorithm that automatically assigns the maintenance interventions to the worker teams, taking into consideration the above reported constraints with the aim of minimizing the overall cost for the company.

4 Problem Formulation

This section provides a formalization of the scenario described in Sect. 3 unambiguously describing all the characteristics of the considered scheduling problem, together with all the constraints and the costs that need to be taken into account. Starting from our formalization, in Sect. 5, we will first provide the solution based on SA and then we will present an exhaustive algorithm that will be used as a reference for the solution of the problem.

Let $\mathcal{Q}$ indicate the set of available maintenance teams and let Q be the cardinality of such a set ($Q = |\mathcal{Q}|$), i.e., the total number of teams. Moreover, let $\mathcal{C}$ indicate the set of all the possible technical skills of the company workers, while C is the total number of skills ($C = |\mathcal{C}|$). We use $\mathcal{I}$ to indicate the set of all the possible kinds of maintenance operations and I to indicate their total number ($I = |\mathcal{I}|$). Finally, let $\mathcal{P}$ indicate the set of all the possible geographic locations for the maintenance interventions and let P be the cardinality of such a set ($P = |\mathcal{P}|$), i.e., the total number of sites where maintenance operations can be conducted.

Each day, a total number of L maintenance interventions need to be carried out by the Q teams. We indicate with $\mathcal{L}$ the list of such interventions, with $L = |\mathcal{L}|$. Each maintenance intervention $l \in \mathcal{L}$ is characterized by the following information:

- geographic location: the geographical coordinates of the site $p_l \in \mathcal{P}$ where the maintenance intervention l needs to be performed;
- maintenance operation: the maintenance operation $i_l \in \mathcal{I}$ that actually needs to be performed during intervention l;
- execution time: the time $t_l \in \mathbb{R}$ that is necessary to carry out the maintenance intervention l, once on site;
- priority: the level of priority $c_l \in \{normal, urgent\}$ assigned to intervention l.

The goal of the scheduling algorithm that we need to design is to determine:

- the optimal number of maintenance interventions that each team has to carry out (denoted with $L_q \leq L$ where $1 \leq q \leq Q$);
- the actual list $\mathcal{L}_q$ of maintenance operations each team has to perform among those in $\mathcal{L}$;
- the optimal order each team has to perform the maintenance operations, i.e., the optimal ordering of list $\mathcal{L}_q$.

Note that $L_q = |\mathcal{L}_q|$ and that the following constrains apply:

$$\sum_{q=1}^{Q} L_q \leq L, \tag{1}$$

$$\bigcup_{q=1}^{Q} \mathcal{L}_q \subseteq \mathcal{L}. \tag{2}$$

Eqs. (1) and (2) explicitly take into consideration the possibility that, in the considered working day, not all the scheduled maintenance interventions are actually performed (presence of $\leq$ and $\subseteq$ symbols). This could happen if an overtime is needed to exhaustively perform all the maintenance operations for some of the teams and if such a cost overcomes the cost associated with the missing interventions.

If there are maintenance operations that require specific skills, they necessarily have to be included in the list of one of the teams whose components have those skills. Let us define

$$F_{\mathcal{C}_q} : \mathcal{Q} \rightarrow 2^{\mathcal{C}} \tag{3}$$

associating to each maintenance team the set of skills they possess, and

$$F_{c_i} : \mathcal{I} \rightarrow 2^{\mathcal{C}} \tag{4}$$

that associates to each specific maintenance operation the set of skills that are necessary to carry it out. Then, a maintenance operation $l \in \mathcal{L}$ can be assigned to team $q \in \mathcal{Q}$ if and only if $F_{c_i}(l) \subseteq F_{c_q}(q)$.

Finally, if some of the maintenance interventions in $\mathcal{L}$ exhibit a *urgent* priority they need to be included in lists $\mathcal{L}_q$ in the top positions. In the following, we will indicate with $\mathcal{L}_q[i].priority$ the priority assigned to the ith intervention assigned to team q.

Let us denote the list of the geographical positions and the execution times of the maintenance operations assigned to team q as follows:

$$\mathcal{M}_q = \{(p_q^1, t_q^1), (p_q^2, t_q^2), \ldots, (p_q^i, t_q^i), \ldots, (p_q^{N_q}, t_q^{N_q})\}$$

where:

- $p_q^i \in \mathcal{P}$ is the position of the ith maintenance operation assigned to team q;
- $t_q^i \in \mathbb{R}$ is the execution time of the ith maintenance operation for team q.

with $1 \leq i \leq L_q$. In particular, let p_q^0 indicate the position of the location from where team q leaves at the beginning of the working day and let $p_q^{L_q+1}$ indicate the final position to where the team has to go back.

Let v_q^i define the travel time associated with the ith maintenance operation for the q team. Of course, v_q^i depends on p_q^{i-1} and p_q^i and can be obtained by applying a routing algorithm finding the best route from one geographical location to another. As an assumption, $v_q^{L_q+1}$ is the travel time that is necessary for the team to go back to the final position.

For each team q to which a list of maintenance operations $\mathcal{L}_q$ has been assigned, the duration of the working day D_q can be computed as follows:

$$D_q = \sum_{i=1}^{L_q+1} (v_q^i + t_q^i) \tag{5}$$

with $t_q^{L_q+1} = 0$.

Denoting with D the maximum duration of the working day, we want $D_q < D$ for each team. If it is not possible to perform all the maintenance operations L in the working day, we define $\bar{L}$ as the number of maintenance operations that can be carried out during the standard working hours. This $\bar{L}$ operations are associated with a normal cost, while we associate a cost of overtime for the remaining maintenance operations. For each travel of each team, we associate a cost CV_q^i that can be computed as a function of the total distance associated with the ith maintenance operation of team q also including vehicles wear out. It can be assumed that there is an additional cost for each team whose duration of the working day exceeds D. Therefore, if $D_q > D$, this generates a cost of overtime and we indicate it with CS_q.

All this assumed, the multi-objective optimization problem for our scenario can be formally defined as follows:

Problem 1: *Find* $\mathcal{L}_q$ *(with* $1 \leq q \leq Q$*) such that:*

(i) $\sum_{q=1}^{Q} \sum_{i=1}^{L_q} CV_q^i$ *is minimized;*
(ii) $\sum_{q=1}^{Q} CS_q$ *is minimized;*
(iii) $\bar{L}$ *is maximized;*
(iv) $\forall q, \forall i : F_{c_i}(i) \subseteq F_{c_q}(q)$;
(v) $\forall q, \forall i : \mathcal{L}_q[i].priority \leq \mathcal{L}_q[i+1].priority$.

5 Solution Algorithms

Simulated annealing (SA) is commonly considered to be the oldest meta-heuristic which explicitly applies a strategy to avoid getting stuck in local minimum, while searching the problem solution space [10]. The name and the inspiration of SA derive from the physical phenomenon known as *annealing*. The annealing process consists in firstly heating a material to high temperature and then cooling it in a controlled manner. This process increases the size of the material crystals, while reducing their internal defects.

The SA algorithm has been firstly introduced as an adaptation of the Metropolis-Hasting algorithm, a Montecarlo method to generate states of a thermodynamic system [11]. In such a work, the SA algorithm produces a sequence of material states. Starting from the system initial state, the next state of the sequence is generated by applying a perturbation mechanism. Such a mechanism randomly produces a new state which is close to the given one in terms of their amount of thermodynamic energy, with the aim of reaching the system state with the lower possible energy level. At each algorithm iteration, starting from a state s^i with energy E_{s^i}, the SA algorithm randomly generates a new state s^{i+1} with energy $E_{s^{i+1}}$. If the new state has an amount of energy such that $\Delta E = (E_{s^{i+1}} - E_{s^i}) \leq 0$, the new state is accepted as the current state, thus lowering the energy of the system. On the other hand, if $\Delta E > 0$, i.e., the energy of the system would be increased, the algorithm accepts the new state, even if it is worst than the previous one, accordingly to a probabilistic approach that depends on the actual temperature of the system. In fact, as in the physical annealing process, in the SA algorithm, starting from a state with a high temperature, the temperature is gradually lowered while advancing in the generation of new system states. When a newly generated state produces a difference in energy greater than zero ($\Delta E > 0$), the new state is accepted with a probability equal to $e^{(-\Delta E/T)}$, where T is the current temperature (so called *Metropolis* criterion [11]). This results in a high probability to accept new states, even if they are worst than the previous one, during the initial iterations of the algorithm. However, while lowering the temperature also the acceptance probability will decrease. This strategy allows SA not to get stuck in local minimum. Applying the SA meta-heuristic to a given optimization problem involves designing all its characteristic aspects adapting them to the specific context [12]. Specifically, it is necessary to: (i) properly define the solution space S; (ii) associate a cost function to the problem; (iii) design the mechanism to generate neighboring solutions; (iv) specify a cooling scheme for temperature decreasing; (v) define an acceptance rule for new solutions.

5.1 Formalization of a Solution

In order to show how SA has been exploited for the solution of our optimization problem, namely the problem of scheduling a list of geographically distributed routine maintenance interventions among a set of maintenance teams, taking into account team skills, cost of overtime work, and cost of transport, it is first necessary to define how a possible problem solution can be represented in a formal way.

With this aim, let us consider a specific case in which $L = 10$ maintenance interventions need to be scheduled among $Q = 4$ maintenance teams. A possible solution of such a problem consists in finding the four lists $\mathcal{L}_1$, $\mathcal{L}_2$, $\mathcal{L}_3$, and $\mathcal{L}_4$ associating to each team the interventions to perform in a specific order. An example is the following: $\mathcal{L}_1 = \{1, 8\}$, $\mathcal{L}_2 = \{2, 9, 10\}$, $\mathcal{L}_3 = \{4, 3\}$, $\mathcal{L}_4 = \{7, 6, 5\}$, i.e., the first team is scheduled to perform interventions number 1 and 8 in this order, the second team is scheduled to perform interventions number 2, 9, and 10 in this order, and so on. Such a problem solution can be formally represented in a matrix form as follows:

$$\begin{bmatrix} 1\,0\,0\,0\,0\,0\,0\,2\,0\,0 \\ 0\,1\,0\,0\,0\,0\,0\,0\,2\,3 \\ 0\,0\,2\,1\,0\,0\,0\,0\,0\,0 \\ 0\,0\,0\,0\,3\,2\,1\,0\,0\,0 \end{bmatrix}. \tag{6}$$

In such a matrix each row is associated with a maintenance team while each column refers to a maintenance intervention. The values of nonzero elements indicates the order in which each intervention is performed by the corresponding team. So, for example, the element belonging to the first row and to the eightth column is equal to 2 because intervention number 8 is scheduled to be performed by the first team as the second intervention in its list.

Generalizing such an example, a generic solution of a generic instance of our scheduling problem is given by a specific distribution of L maintenance interventions among Q maintenance teams. Thus, if we want to formally represent it in a matrix form, we need a $Q \times L$ matrix $\mathbf{A} = \{a_{i,j}\}$ such that $i \in [1, Q]$, $j \in [1, L]$, and $a_{i,j} \in [1, L]$:

$$\mathbf{A} = \begin{bmatrix} a_{1,1} & a_{1,2} & \cdots & a_{1,L} \\ \vdots & \vdots & \ddots & \\ a_{Q,1} & a_{Q,2} & \cdots & a_{Q,L} \end{bmatrix}. \tag{7}$$

In particular, being L the interventions to be performed, the matrix in Eq. (7) represents a solution of our optimization problem only if a maximum of L among its $Q \cdot L$ elements are nonzero: $nz(\mathbf{A}) \leq L$ where $nz : \mathbb{R} \times \mathbb{R} \rightarrow \mathbb{N}$ is a function that provides the number of nonzero elements in a given matrix. Moreover, given that each matrix column is associated with a specific intervention and given that each intervention can be assigned only to one team, it follows that in each column of matrix $\mathbf{A}$ only one element can be nonzero, indicating the team to which the corresponding intervention is assigned. Thus, indicating with $\mathbf{c}^j$ the jth column of matrix $\mathbf{A}$ with $j \in [1, L]$ (it is considered as a $Q \times 1$ matrix):

$$\mathbf{c}^1 = \begin{bmatrix} a_{1,1} \\ a_{2,1} \\ \vdots \\ a_{Q,1} \end{bmatrix}, \mathbf{c}^2 = \begin{bmatrix} a_{1,2} \\ a_{2,2} \\ \vdots \\ a_{Q,2} \end{bmatrix}, \cdots, \mathbf{c}^L = \begin{bmatrix} a_{1,L} \\ a_{2,L} \\ \vdots \\ a_{Q,L} \end{bmatrix} \quad (8)$$

then, $nz(\mathbf{c}^j) \leq 1, \forall j \in [1, L]$.

Finally, the value of the nonzero element of each column $\mathbf{c}^j$ has to represent the execution order of the maintenance intervention $j \in [1, L]$ within the list of interventions associated with the corresponding team. In formula, $a_{x,j} \neq 0 \Leftrightarrow \mathcal{L}_x[(a_{x,j})] = j$ with $x \in [1, Q]$ and $j \in [1, L]$ and x is the index associated with the team to which the intervention j is assigned.

5.2 Applying SA to Our Optimization Problem

In the case of our optimization problem, the characteristic aspects of the SA algorithm have been designed as follows.

Solution Space: Accordingly to what reported in Sect. 5.1, the solution space of our optimization problem can be formally represented as the set of all the possible $Q \times L$ matrices in the form of Eq. (7): $S = \{\mathbf{A}^i\}$ with Q and L depending on the specific problem and satisfying all the constraints previously discussed.

Cost Function: In our optimization problem, the cost function associates a cost to each possible matrix in S. Accordingly to the definition of Problem 1 and to what has been exposed in Sect. 4, our cost function is the following:

$$E_A = f(\mathbf{A}) = \sum_{q=1}^{Q} \sum_{j=1}^{L_q} CV_q^j + \sum_{q=1}^{Q} CS_q. \quad (9)$$

Generation Mechanism of the Neighboring Solutions: In our optimization problem, function $\Psi : S \times \{row, column\} \rightarrow S$ operates on a matrix in S returning another matrix that is close to the first one in terms of disposal of its elements: $\mathbf{A}^{i+1} = \Psi(\mathbf{A}^i, p)$ with $\mathbf{A}^{i+1}, \mathbf{A}^i \in S$, $p \in \{row, column\}$.

The parameter p is used to define two ways of modifying matrix $\mathbf{A}^i$ in terms of element disposal obtaining matrix $\mathbf{A}^{i+1}$. In particular:

- **Row Swapping:** If $p = row$, two elements in a row of the matrix are swapped. Specifically, we randomly select one of the matrix rows in which two or more nonzero elements with the same priority are present, i.e., we randomly select a team whose list of interventions contains two or more interventions with the same priority:

$$generate\ q \in [1, Q] : |\mathcal{L}_q^i| > 1.$$

Then, we randomly select two different nonzero elements, always with the same priority, in the row:

$$generate\ x, y \in [1, L] : a_{q,x}^i \neq a_{q,y}^i \neq 0$$

and we swap them, i.e., we invert the order in which two interventions, with the same priority, in the list are performed:

$$\begin{aligned} a_{q,x}^{i+1} &= a_{q,y}^i, \\ a_{q,y}^{i+1} &= a_{q,x}^i. \end{aligned} \tag{10}$$

- **Column Swapping:** If $p = column$, the nonzero element of a column of the matrix is moved from one row to another one, possibly modifying its value if necessary. In particular, we randomly select one of the matrix columns $\mathbf{c}^l$ in which a nonzero element is present, i.e., we select an intervention l that is already assigned to a team:

  $$generate\ l \in [1, L] : nz(\mathbf{c}^l) \neq 0,\ i.e.,\ l \in \bigcup_{q=1}^{Q} \mathcal{L}_q^i.$$

  Then, we randomly select one matrix row z in which the corresponding element $a_{z,l}^i$ of the matrix column $\mathbf{c}^l$ is equal to zero:

  $$generate\ z \in [1, Q] : a_{z,l}^i = 0.$$

  The value of the nonzero element in the column vector $\mathbf{c}^l$ is set to zero. Finally, if all the elements of the row z in matrix $\mathbf{A}^i$ are zero then element $a_{z,l}^{i+1}$ in matrix $\mathbf{A}^{i+1}$ is set to 1:

  $$a_{z,l}^{i+1} = 1 \tag{11}$$

  while, if in the row z in matrix $\mathbf{A}^i$ there are nonzero elements, we compute the maximum value among all the elements with the same priority equal to the $a_{z,l}^{i+1}$ element, and we assign this value to element $a_{z,l}^{i+1}$ in matrix $\mathbf{A}^{i+1}$ the value:

  $$a_{z,l}^{i+1} = max(z, \mathbf{A}^i) + 1, \tag{12}$$

  i.e., we take one intervention from one team and we give it to another one that will perform it as the last intervention with this priority.

Cooling Scheme: The aspects of the cooling scheme have been designed as follows:

- **(a)** initial temperature - An initial problem solution $\mathbf{A}^1$ is generated and the initial temperature is set to its cost: $T = E_{A^1}$;

- **(b)** temperature updating mechanism - We designed an updating mechanism based on a cooling factor $\alpha \in \mathbb{R}^+$ such that: $T = T - (\alpha \cdot T)$;
- **(c)** number of iterations for each temperature value - $n_t \in \mathbb{N}$ iterations are performed for each temperature value T by correspondingly generating n_t solutions: $A^1, A^2, \cdots, A^{n_t}$;
- **(d)** stop criterion - We designed a criterion which is based on both the value of the temperature and the progress of the SA algorithm itself. We defined a target temperature $T_{low} \in [0, T[$ at which the SA algorithm is terminated. Moreover, we use a vector $vectE$ to store the cost associated with the last $|vectE|$ solutions:

$$vectE = \{E_{A^y}, E_{A^{y+1}}, \cdots, E_{A^{y+|vectE|}}\} \tag{13}$$

If the cost associated with such solutions is exactly the same for a number of temperature levels equal to $|vectE|$ the algorithm is terminated:

$$E_{A^y_{(Q,L)}} = E_{A^{y+1}_{(Q,L)}} = \cdots = E_{A^{y+|vectE|}_{(Q,L)}} \tag{14}$$

Acceptance Rule: The solutions generated for each temperature value T are compared using *Metropolis* criterion. When solution $\mathbf{A}^{i+1}$ is generated its cost is computed by Eq. (9) and the cost variation with respect to solution $\mathbf{A}^i$ is computed: $\Delta E = f(\mathbf{A}^{i+1}) - f(\mathbf{A}^i)$. If $\Delta E \leq 0$ the new solution is accepted. Otherwise, if $\Delta E > 0$ the new solution is accepted only if $\xi < e^{(-\Delta E/T)}$ where ξ is a random number uniformly distributed over $[0, 1]$ and T is the current temperature. If $\xi > e^{(-\Delta E/T)}$ the new solution is discarded and current solution $\mathbf{A}^i$ is used to generate a new one.

Algorithm 1 (Table 1) reports all the steps of the SA algorithm as applied to our routine maintenance problem.

Specifically, in lines 1–7 all the necessary variables are declared: s and s' represent the current solution and the neighboring solution, respectively; vector $vectE$ of size d stores the cost of the last d solutions; α is the cooling factor; T contains the initial temperature of the system and the following temperature values while T_{low} is the minimum temperature to be reached; E and E' represent the cost of the current solution s and of the neighboring solution s', respectively; n_t is the number of iterations to be performed for each temperature value. In line 9 the initial solution is generated through *generate_initial_solution*() and in line 10 $f()$ returns its cost. Such a cost is used to set the temperature initial value in line 11. The SA algorithm itself consists of two nested loops. The outer loop (lines 12–29) is used for temperature cooling while the inner loop (lines 14–23) is used to perform the n_t iterations for each temperature value. In particular, in lines 24–27 functions *store_last_cost*() and *check_stop_criteria*() are used to check if the last $|vectE| = d$ solutions are exactly the same. In such a case the algorithm is stopped. Otherwise the algorithm stops as soon as temperature T_{low} is reached. In both cases, the current solution and its cost are returned (line 30).

Table 1. SA and exhaustive algorithms.

Algorithm 1. SA algorithm for the solution of the routine maintenance problem.

```
declare s, s';
declare d;
declare α;
declare vectE[d];
declare T, T_low;
declare E, E';
declare n_t;

s ← generate_initial_solution()
E ← f(s);
T ← E;
while T > T_low do
    i ← 1;
    while i < n_t do
        s' ← Ψ(s);
        E' ← f(s');
        ξ ← rand();
        if E' ≤ E or e^(-(E'-E)/T) > r then
            s ← s';
            E ← E';
        end if
        i ← i + 1;
    end while
    vectE ← store_last_cost(vectE, E);
    if check_stop_criteria(vectE, d) then
        break;
    end if
    T ← T − (α · T);
end while
return s, E;
```

Algorithm 2. Exhaustive algorithm for the solution of the routing maintenance problem.

```
declare VDist[0] ← 0
declare MDist[]
declare listOp
declare handySol
declare finalSol

for i ← 1 to Q^L do
    VDist[i] ← NextDist(VDist[i − 1], Q)
end for
for i ← 0 to Q^L do
    MDist[i] ←
  GetMatrixFromVector(VDist[i])
end for
for i ← 0 to Q^L do
    if CheckSkill(MDist[i]) then
        for j ← 0 to Q do
            listOp ← GetRow(MDist[i], j)
            handySol.setTeam(FindMinCost
         (listOp, j), j)
        end for
    end if
    if i = 0 AND handySol ≠ null then
        finalSol ← handySol
    else
        if handySol.cost < finalSol.cost then
            finalSol ← handySol
        end if
    end if
end for
return finalSol;
```

5.3 Exhaustive Algorithm

Through the use of the SA, we are not guaranteed that the found solution is the best solution for our optimization problem. It is therefore necessary to identify a reference value to evaluate the quality of the solutions found with the SA. To this purpose, we designed an exhaustive algorithm.

Exhaustive algorithm is composed of two parts. The first part has the role to find all the possible *distributions* of the L maintenance interventions to the Q maintenance teams. The *distribution* operation simply executes the division of the L maintenance interventions to the Q maintenance teams by creating Q unordered lists identified as $\mathcal{U}_q$:

$$\bigcup_{q=1}^{Q} \mathcal{U}_q \subseteq \mathcal{L} \tag{15}$$

where $U_q = |\mathcal{U}_q| : U_q \leq L$ and $\mathcal{U}_q[i] \in [1, Q] : i \in [1, L]$. To solve the *distribution* operation a method which use a vector with dimension L has been developed: $V_L = \{v_1, v_2, \cdots v_L\}$. Each elements of the V_L vector represents one of the maintenance interventions of the list $\mathcal{L}$: $v_i \in \mathcal{L}$. The value of each element of the vector V_L determines at which $\mathcal{U}_q$ unordered list is assigned, whereas the position in the vector determines the identifier of the maintenance operation:

$$\mathcal{U}_{v_i}[x] = i \quad : x \in [1, L] \tag{16}$$

The V_L vector allows us to implement and automate the generation of all the possible distributions of the L maintenance operations to the Q maintenance teams, using the V_L vector like a number in Q basis with L digits, it is possible to generate all the numbers in Q in the range $[0, Q^L]$ by defining the following function

$$V_L^i = next(V_L^{i-1}, b) \tag{17}$$

where $i \in [0, Q^L]$ and $V_L^0 = \{0\}$. The function (17) receives in input a number V_L^{i-1} expressed in array form, and its basis b. Therefore the function generates the next number of the input in basis b. This last number is always expressed in array form.

The second part of the exhaustive algorithm, using all vector form numbers found with function (17), computes all the possible solutions for our problem which are later evaluated to determine the best solution.

For each vector numbers all possible ***simple permutations*** of the $\mathcal{U}_q$ are evaluated. Therefore, for each $\mathcal{U}_q$ several solutions are generated for our problem, each evaluated to determine the best solution.

Algorithm 2 reports all the steps of the exhaustive algorithm, used to find the best solution to our routine maintenance problem.

Specially in lines 1–5 all the necessary variables are declared: *VDist[]* is a data structure with dimension Q^L that stores all vectors V_L calculated as numbers in basis Q, the first element of this data structure is a vector V_L with all elements equal to zero, *MDist[]* is another data structure with the same dimension of *VDist[]* used to store the $\mathcal{U}_q$ unordered lists obtained from each element of *VDist[]*; *handySol* and *finalSol* are two objects aiming to store solutions of the problem. In the lines 7–9 all possible V_L vectors are generated with the aid of the *NextDist()* function. *NextDist()* function implements the function (17) where the inputs are "*VDist[i-1]*" and Q. In lines 10–12 all the $\mathcal{U}_q$ unordered lists are generated with the aid of the *GetMatrixFromVector()* function. The *for* loop in line 13 is used to evaluate all $\mathcal{U}_q$ unordered list stored in *MDist[]*. The function *CheckSkill()* (line 14), checks if a specific $\mathcal{U}_q$ unordered list meets the constraints defined in Sect. 4 referred to the interventions skills. If *CheckSkill()* evaluates to *true*, the solution with minimal cost of the *i-th* element in *MDist[]* is computed by using the functions *GetRow()* and *FindMinCost()* (line 15–18). The function *GetRow()* return the $\mathcal{U}_j$ unordered list of the *i-th* V_L stored in *VDist[]*. The function *FindMinCost()* calculates all the simple permutations of the $\mathcal{U}_j$ then discard all the permutations that don't respect the priority order, and evaluates each cost to determine the specific simple permutation with minimum cost. Thinking to *handySol* and *finalSol* as two objects with their methods and attributes, the *setTeam* method is used to store the cost of the team with the ID j. The instructions in the lines 21–26 are used to compare and store the objects solutions produced in a single iteration.

6 Experimental Results

The use case, where the SA algorithm was applied, is related to a real Italian company, located in the north west of Sicily, with the responsibility of managing the maintenance related to electrical installations.

As mentioned in Sect. 1, to perform the maintenance operations the company needs to solve a scheduling problem to minimize the overall cost for maintenance. The solution of the optimization problem must be found respecting the formalization of the objectives and constraints specified in **Problem 1**.

In particular, the use case is related to a typical working day, where the company needs to schedule the daily maintenance operations to its maintenance teams. The maintenance operations occur in the electrical installations managed by the company. The geographical points of installations and company headquarters compose the all possible geographical locations P defined in Sect. 4 and listed in Table 2.

As introduced in Sect. 4, L maintenance services are provided in a typical working day; each of them is characterized by an execution time, a set of skills needed to perform the maintenance, and a location. We applied our optimization algorithm to a problem with variable dimensions; we solved a lot of cases where L varies from 4 to 20 maintenance services. A partial list of the maintenance interventions we used in our experimentation is reported in Table 3; each maintenance intervention is identified by an **intervention ID**, whereas the location where the maintenance has to be done is identified through the **Installation ID** of Table 2.

We assumed in our experimentation the company has four maintenance teams ($Q = 4$), composed of one or more workers and a single vehicle. Each of the teams is an element of the matrix $\mathcal{Q}$. Each worker is characterized by one or more skills, collected in $\mathcal{C}$. In our use case three possible skills have been identified ($C = 3$) and they have been associated to each worker as described in Table 4, where the cost per hour and the maintenance team have been specified.

The vehicles owned by the company are summarized in Table 5 together with the fuel type (petrol or diesel), the costs, and the maintenance team ID to which each vehicle is assigned.

Each maintenance team is characterized by both the skills of its workers and the characteristics of its vehicle. This means that each teams can perform only the maintenance services fitting adequate skills specified through Eqs. (3) and (4). In the specific case of the use case here considered, columns **Skills ID** and **Skills** of Table 3 represents the function of Eq. (4). It is easy to see that the monetary cost of each team depends on the workers hourly cost (Table 4) and on the travel cost (Table 5).

To completely define the optimization problem, we have to define the cost functions introduced in **Problem 1** (items *(i)* and *(ii)*). These functions depend on the working day duration D that is assumed to be eight hours long ($D = 8$) in our use case. Let C_q be the hourly cost by each maintenance team during the regular working time; C_q is computed by adding the hourly wage of each worker of the team shown in Table 4. In *(ii)* is defined the cost function to be

Table 2. Geographical points of installations.

Installation ID	Name	Latitude	Longitude
0	Palermo (company headquarter)	38.116667	13.366667
1	Kaggio	38.000000	13.283333
2	Bagheria	38.083333	13.500000
3	Balestrate	38.050000	13.000000
4	Terrasini	38.150000	13.083333
5	Misilmeri	38.033333	13.450000
6	Carini	38.131310	13.181360
7	Torretta	38.131450	13.235950
8	Capaci	38.171270	13.238690
9	Mondello	38.201360	13.325380
10	Termini Imerese	37.984250	13.695910
11	Scordia	37.294400	14.841670
12	Aci Trezza	37.561450	15.157520
13	Belpasso	37.589750	14.976080
14	Zafferana Etnea	37.690610	15.103620
15	Fontanarossa	37.451010	15.047830
16	Motta S. Anastasia	37.513400	14.969730
17	Barcellona P.G.	38.146570	15.212630
18	Milazzo	38.221450	15.238030
19	Villafranca	38.231840	15.436990
20	Santa Teresa	37.945880	15.366690
21	Taormina	37.851400	15.285240
22	Torre Faro	38.264700	15.642210
23	Tremestieri	38.141980	15.522220
24	Paternò	37.566890	14.903980
25	Acireale	37.607970	15.166620
26	Bronte	37.789700	14.831190
27	Ramacca	37.384880	14.693520
28	Fiumedinisi	38.026050	15.378790
29	Antillo	37.976340	15.246190
30	Pellegrino	38.141300	15.39321

applied after the first eight working hours. The cost CS_q defined in **Problem 1**, representing the cost during the extra working time, is defined as $CS_q = 2 * C_q$. The cost CV_q^i is computed using the data in Table 5 and fixed values for *diesel* and *petrol* cost that are \$1.746 for the petrol and \$1.627 for the diesel.

Table 3. Maintenance interventions.

Interventions ID	Priority	Duration	Installation ID	Skills ID	Skills
1	1	60	1	1	{2,3}
2	1	120	2	1	{2,3}
3	0	60	2	2	{1,3}
4	1	180	3	2	{1,2}
5	0	90	3	3	{2,3}
6	1	12	5	3	{2,3}
7	0	90	4	4	{1,2}
8	1	180	1	4	{2,3}
9	1	120	5	5	{1,2}
10	1	90	4	5	{1,2}

Table 4. Workers cost per hour and skills.

Worker ID	Cost ($/h)	Skills	Team ID
1	6.80	{1,3}	1
2	6.50	{2}	1
3	7.00	{2}	2
4	6.40	{1,2}	2
5	6.25	{2,3}	3
6	6.90	{1}	3
7	6.20	{1,3}	4
8	6.00	{2}	4

Table 5. Vehicles characteristics.

Vehicle ID	Fuel type	l/Km	Wear/Km($)	Team ID
1	Diesel	8.2	0.57	1
2	Diesel	8.2	0.57	2
3	Petrol	5.9	0.25	3
4	Petrol	5.9	0.25	4

6.1 Optimal Parameters

In the following, we will present the results obtained by applying the optimization Algorithm 1 to the problem defined above. In order to maintain the scenario as simple as possible, we assume that all maintenance intervention have the same priority, and we fix L to 10. The goal of this first experiment is to estimate the optimal value of internal parameters of the optimization algorithm for the specific case study we are dealing with.

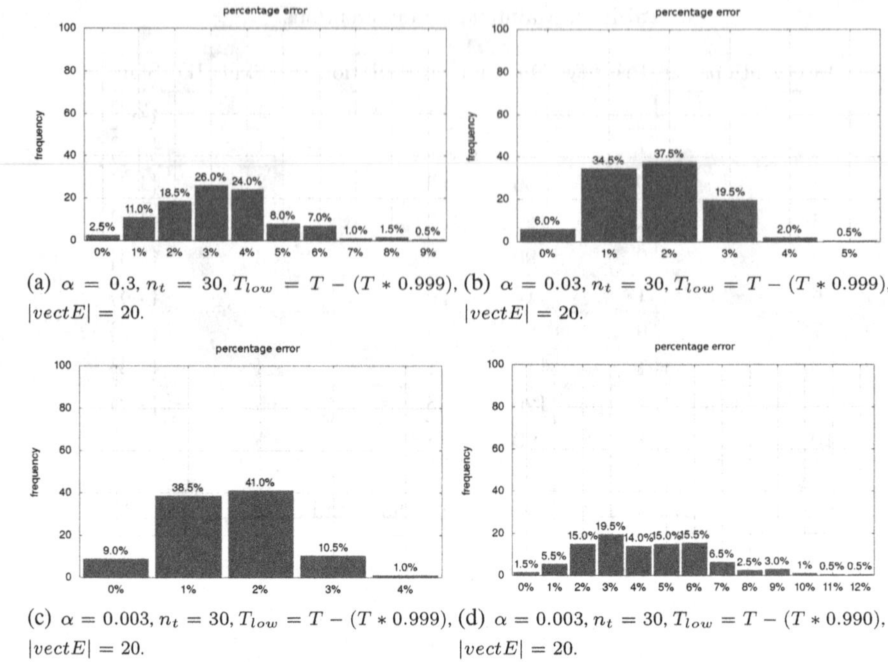

(a) $\alpha = 0.3$, $n_t = 30$, $T_{low} = T - (T * 0.999)$, $|vectE| = 20$.

(b) $\alpha = 0.03$, $n_t = 30$, $T_{low} = T - (T * 0.999)$, $|vectE| = 20$.

(c) $\alpha = 0.003$, $n_t = 30$, $T_{low} = T - (T * 0.999)$, $|vectE| = 20$.

(d) $\alpha = 0.003$, $n_t = 30$, $T_{low} = T - (T * 0.990)$, $|vectE| = 20$.

Fig. 1. Accuracy of the SA algorithm with respect to the exhaustive one varying α and the cooling scheme.

Since the SA is a based on a meta-heuristic approach, the obtained result is not the best optimized solution for sure, thus we compare the results with the real optimum computed through the exhaustive Algorithm 2 (see Sect. 5.3). The purpose of the comparison is twofold: (1) evaluate the quality of the solution, and (2) evaluate the time efficiency of the algorithm. During our experiments, we varied the SA parameters in order to show their impact on the final solution. We evaluated the SA behavior with respect to the parameters α and n_t, related to the cooling, and T_{low} and $|vectE|$, related to the stop criterion of Eq. (14).

Given a set of fixed parameters, we run the SA algorithm 200 times and we computed the distance of each obtained optimal solution with respect to that evaluated by the exhaustive algorithm; the percentage error has been estimated as $\frac{|E_o - E_A|}{E_o} \cdot 100$, where E_o and E_A are the value of the cost function $f()$ evaluated over the solutions given by Algorithms 1 and 2 respectively. The overall results are synthesized in Fig. 1(a), (b) and (c) by varying α and fixing n_t and T_{low}; each histogram depicts the error distribution. As an example Fig. 1(a) shows that the Algorithm 1 has a probability equal to 26 % to give an estimation of the optimum with an error equal to 3 %. The graphs show that decreasing the value of α the accuracy of the result decreases accordingly, the average error ranging from 3.275 %, with $\alpha = 0.3$, to 1.56 %, with $\alpha = 0.003$.

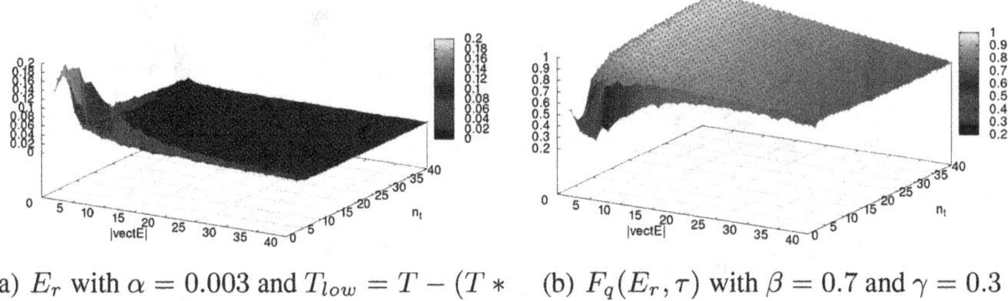

(a) E_r with $\alpha = 0.003$ and $T_{low} = T - (T *$ (b) $F_q(E_r, \tau)$ with $\beta = 0.7$ and $\gamma = 0.3$

Fig. 2. Accuracty and execution time of the SA algorithm varying n_t and $|vectE|$.

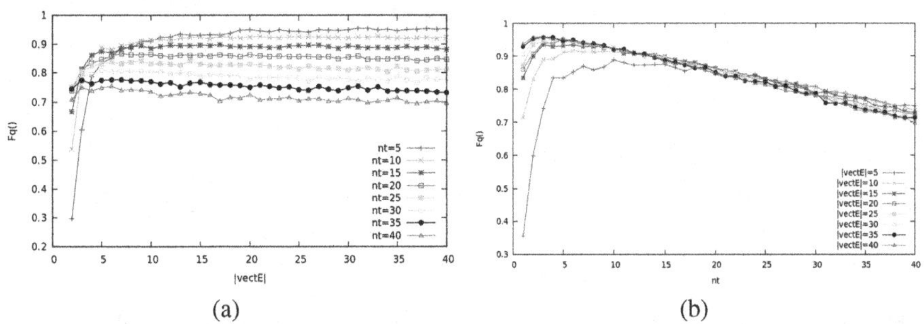

(a) (b)

Fig. 3. Accuracy and execution time of the SA algorithm with $\beta = 0.7$ and $\gamma = 0.3$.

Another set of experiments has been performed by fixing the value of α to 0.003 and varying the parameter T_{low} from $T_{low} = T - (T * 0.999)$ (Fig. 1(c)) to $T_{low} = T - (T * 0.990)$ (Fig. 1(d)), thus increasing the value of the target temperate. This change produces a sharp deterioration of the solutions found with Algorithm 1 to an average percentage error equal to 4.319, as shown in Fig. 1(d). This deterioration is justified by the fact that fewer iterations are performed with Algorithm 1 to search the solution of the optimization problem.

To evaluate how the parameters n_t and $|vectE|$ affect the Algorithm 1 in the search of the solution, we considered as a quality index the relative error E_r of the solution obtained by the exhaustive algorithm:

$$E_r = \frac{E_a}{x_m} \tag{18}$$

where $E_a = \frac{|x_m - V_a|}{2}$ is the mean absolute error affecting the solution, V_a is the result of exhaustive algorithm, and x_m is the average value of the solutions obtained from Algorithm 1.

Figure 2(a) depicts E_r versus both n_t and $|vectE|$. As can be seen in Fig. 2(a), E_r decreases when n_t and $|vectE|$ increase starting from 0 but its value does not substantially change when n_t and $|vectE|$ reach a certain threshold.

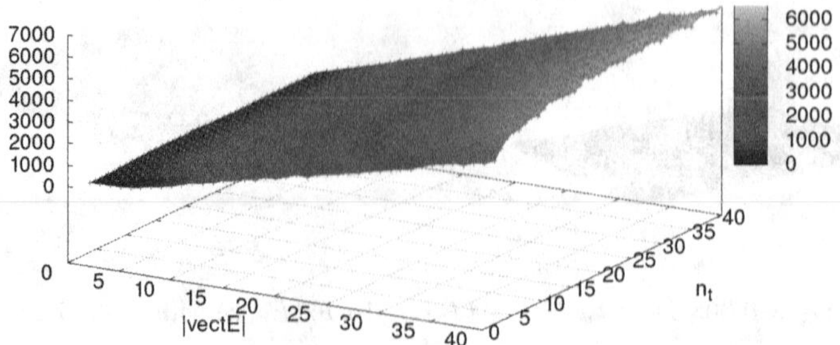

(a) Execution time of the SA algorithm varying n_t and $|vectE|$.

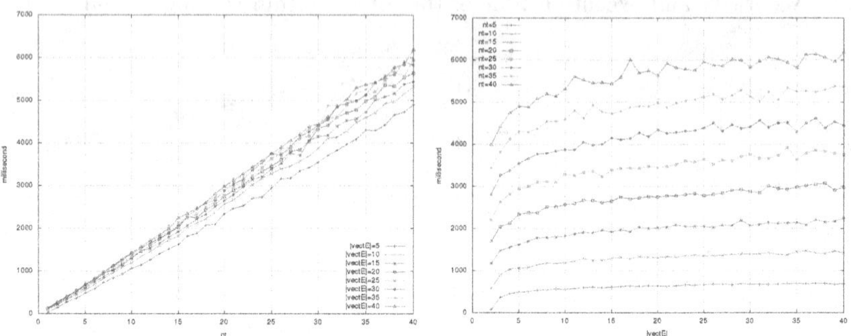

(b) Execution time of the SA algorithm varying n_t.

(c) Execution time of the SA algorithm varying $|vectE|$.

Fig. 4. Accuracy and execution time of the SA algorithm.

To better analyze the behavior of the SA algorithm, we also considered the execution time through the following function:

$$F_q(E_r, \tau) = 1 - \left[\left(\beta \cdot \frac{E_r - min_{E_r}}{\Delta_{Er}} \right) + \left(\gamma \cdot \frac{\tau - min_\tau}{\Delta_\tau} \right) \right] \tag{19}$$

The quantities used to define $F_q()$ are the following: $\Delta_{E_r} = max_{E_r} - min_{E_r}$, where max_{E_r} and min_{E_r} are the maximum and the minimum relative error obtained by varying n_t and $|vectE|$; τ is the measured execution time of the Algorithm 1; $\Delta\tau = max_\tau - min_\tau$, where max_τ and min_τ are the maximum and the minimum execution time obtained by varying the parameters n_t and $|vectE|$; the parameters β and γ, such that $\beta + \gamma = 1$, are two constants used to give a different weight to the quality of the solutions and to the execution time of the Algorithm 1 respectively. The graph in Fig. 2(b) shows the trend of function (19) computed with α and T_{low} set to the optimal values found in the first set of experiments ($\alpha = 0.003$ and $T_{low} = T - (T \cdot 0.999)$) and by varying n_t and $|vectE|$. The values of β and γ are fixed to $\beta = 0.7$ and $\gamma = 0.3$ in order to give more weight to the solution quality than to the execution speed of the Algorithm 1. The analysis of the graph reveals a maximum identifying the best

Table 6. Execution time Algorithm 1 and exhaustive algorithm.

Execution Time Algorithm 1 (ms)		
n_t	$\|vectE\|$	
5	5	485.0
5	10	556.2
5	20	639.4
5	35	697.4
10	5	1057.2
10	10	1186.8
10	20	1313.8
10	35	1442.4
20	5	2332.0
20	10	2569.4
20	20	2746.4
20	35	2977.2
35	5	4304.8
35	10	4597.0
35	20	4986.2
35	35	5259.0
Execution Time Algorithm 2 (ms)		
2100000		

pairs of parameters to optimize the behavior with respect either the precision and the execution time.

To better identify the value of the parameters, we depicted in Fig. 3(a) and (b) the 2-D versions of the graph in Fig. 2(b). In Fig. 3(a), each line corresponds to a single value of n_t (z axis in Fig. 2(b)) whereas in Fig. 3(b) each line corresponds to a single value of $|vectE|$ (x axis in Fig. 2(b)).

Parameters n_t and $|vectE|$ carry out a complementary role. Using hight values of $|vectE|$, we impose a stop criterion heavily based on temperature T; this configuration produces excellent results as long as n_t doesn't excessively increase otherwise a performances degradation is manifested. As well shown in Fig. 3(b), the graph has a maximum located around $n_t = 5$ and $|vectE| = 35$.

We also reported in Table 6 the execution times obtained by running Algorithm 1 with different sets of parameters and the execution time of the exhaustive algorithm. As can be observed, Algorithm 1 completes in some milliseconds, irrespective of the set of parameters, whereas the exhaustive algorithm needs a lot of minutes to find the final problem solution.

The time behavior of Algorithm 1 versus the configuration parameters variation is shown in Fig. 4. In Fig. 4(c), each line corresponds to a fixed value of n_t, whereas each graph of Fig. 4(b) is built by fixing a value of $|vectE|$. The graphs show that the execution time is linearly dependent on the value of $|vectE|$ (Fig. 4(b)) while it reaches a stable value when n_t increases (Fig. 4(c)).

6.2 Scalability Evaluation

In the following, we will present the results obtained by applying the optimization Algorithm 1 to different use cases, included the use case defined in Sect. 6.1. All the experiments have been performed by setting the optimal parameters for the optimization Algorithm 1 obtained by previous tests. We will analyze the

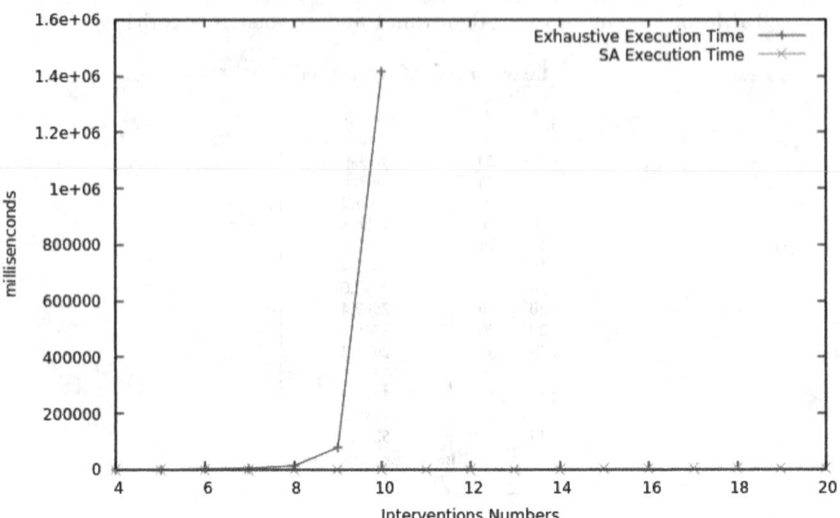

Fig. 5. Execution time of Algorithms 1 and 2 with small distance among interventions.

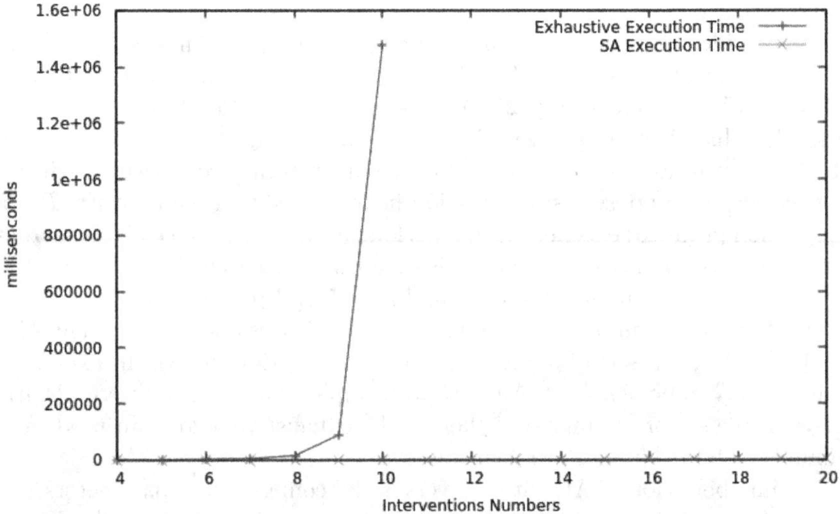

Fig. 6. Execution time of Algorithms 1 and 2 with medium distance among interventions.

behavior of the Algorithm 1 varying the number L of maintenance interventions and their relative distance, i.e. the elements of P.

To evaluate the scalability of the Simulated Annealing approach, we compared the execution time of the Algorithms 1 and 2; both of them are applied to three different scenarios, where we changed the order of magnitude of the distance among the geographical points where the maintenance interventions should

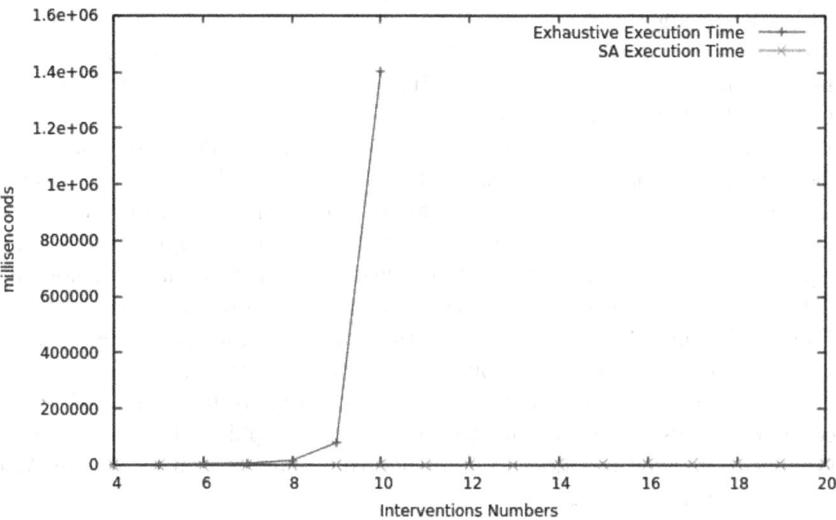

Fig. 7. Execution time of Algorithms 1 and 2 with large distance among interventions.

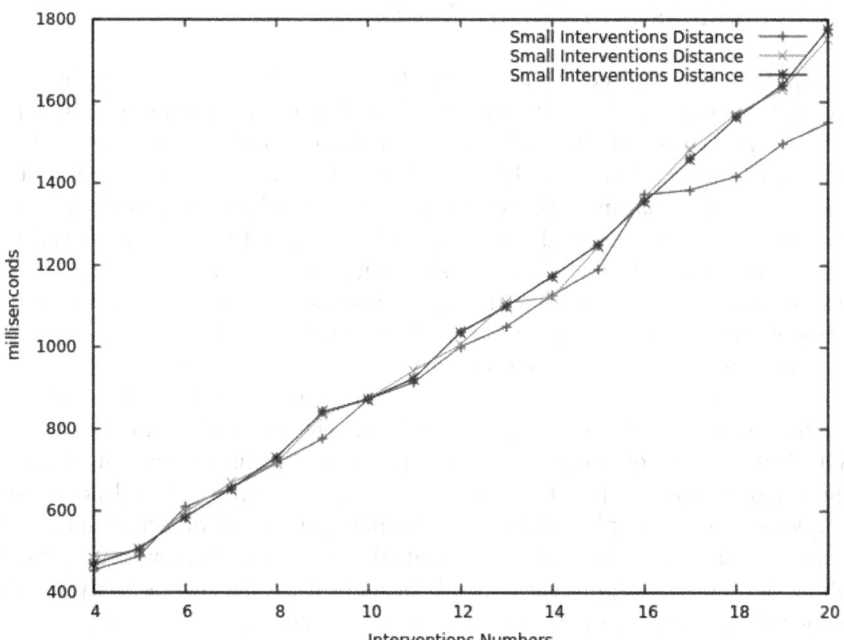

Fig. 8. Execution time of Algorithm 1 with small, medium and large interventions distance.

be performed. We considered from 4 to 20 points randomly chosen among that of Table 2 imposing the constrains about the geographical distance. Moreover, we also randomly assigned a priority to the different interventions. In this way, we analyzed how problem dimension influences the behavior of the Algorithm 1 with respect to that of the Algorithm 2.

The overall results are synthesized in Figs. 5, 6 and 7. The first remark that can be done is that no execution time of the Exhaustive Algorithm is available when problem dimension exceeds 10; this is due to the high level of memory usage such that central memory becomes saturated and the application is killed. This problem does not afflict the SA algorithm that can manage without any memory consumption problem irrespective on problem dimension.

The graphs show that the execution time of the Algorithm 1 (Fig. 8) grows linearly with the problem dimension; instead the Algorithm 2 (Figs. 5, 6 and 7) exhibits an exponential grow of the completion time when the number of maintenance interventions grows. At the opposite, the geographical distribution of the maintenance interventions doesn't influence the behavior neither of the Algorithm 1 nor the Algorithm 2.

We can also note the introduction of priorities does not improve enough the performance of Algorithm 2 even if a lot of possible solutions are discarded during the analysis.

7 Conclusions and Future Work

In this paper, we proposed the use of simulated annealing for the solution of the scheduling problem of a set of geographically distributed routine maintenance interventions. We based the choice of which team to pick among the available ones for each intervention and the order in which each team performs its interventions on several parameters, i.e., team skills, cost of overtime work, and cost of transportation. We applied the proposed algorithm to a real industrial use case provided by an electrical plant design company and we compared it versus an exhaustive approach. Several numerical results have been shown highlighting the effects of the parameters of the simulated annealing on the accuracy of the solution and on the execution time of the algorithm. Moreover, we also showed how the dimension of the considered problem affects the effectiveness of the proposed approach. We demonstrated that the execution time of our SA-based algorithm varies linearly with the problem dimension while in the case of the exhaustive algorithm it varies exponentially. Future work will be focused on implementing a complete tool for maintenance intervention scheduling, testing and stressing it on the ground of realistic use cases. Moreover, we plan to combine the proposed approach with advanced routing algorithms analyzing the influence of their efficiency on our solution technique.

Acknowledgement. The research leading to these results has received funding from the Italian National project "SIGMA - Integrated Cloud-Sensor System for Advanced Multirisk Management" under grant agreement PON01_00683.

References

1. Herroelen, W., Demeulemeester, E., De Reyck, B.: Metaheuristics in combinatorial optimization: overview and conceptual comparison. In: Weglarz, J. (ed.) Project Scheduling: Recent Models, Algorithms and Applications, p. 126. Kluwer Academic Publishers, Boston (1999)
2. Glover, F., Kochenberger, G. (eds.): Handbook of Metaheuristics. Kluwer Academic Publishers, New York (2003)
3. Fleischer, M.: Simulated annealing: past, present and future. In: Alexopoulos, C., Kang, K., Lilegdon, W., Goldsman, G. (eds.) Proceedings of the 1995 Winter Simulation Conference, pp. 155–161 (1995)
4. Saraiva, J.T., Pereira, M.L., Mendes, V.T., Sousa, J.C.: A simulated annealing based approach to solve the generator maintenance scheduling problem. Electr. Power Syst. Res. **81**(7), 1283–1291 (2011)
5. Keshav, K.P., Chakpitak, N.: Generator maintenance scheduling in power systems using metaheuristic-based hybrid approaches. Electr. Power Syst. Res. **77**(7), 771–779 (2007)
6. El-Amin, I., Duffuaa, S., Abbas, M.: A tabu search algorithm for maintenance scheduling of generating units. Electr. Power Syst. Res. **54**(2), 91–99 (2000)
7. Lin, C.-C., Shu, L., Deng, D.-J.: Router node placement with service priority in wireless mesh networks using simulated annealing with momentum terms. IEEE Syst. J. **PP**(99) (2014)
8. Brown, A.G., Ruschmann, M.C., Duffy, B., Ward, L., Hur-Diaz, S., Ferguson, E., Stewart, S.M.: Simulated annealing maneuver planner for clusterflight. In: 24th International Symposium on Space Flight Dynamics, Laurel, MD, April 2014
9. Bryan, K., Cunningham, P., Bolshakova, N.: Application of simulated annealing to the biclustering of gene expression data. IEEE Trans. Inf. Technol. Biomed. **10**(3), 519–525 (2006)
10. Blum, C., Roli, A.: Metaheuristics in combinatorial optimization: overview and conceptual comparison. ACM Comput. Surv. **35**(3), 268–308 (2003)
11. Metropolis, N., Rosenbluth, A.W., Rosenbluth, M.N., Teller, A.H., Teller, E.: Equation of statecalculations by fast computing machines. J. Chem. Phys. **21**(6), 1087–1092 (1953)
12. Pham, D.T., Karaboga, D.: Intelligent Optimisation Techniques: Genetic Algorithms, Tabu Search. Simulated Annealing and Neural Networks. Springer, London (2000)

Dimension Enrichment with Factual Data During the Design of Multidimensional Models: Application to Bird Biodiversity

Lucile Sautot[1(✉)], Sandro Bimonte[2], Ludovic Journaux[3], and Bruno Faivre[1]

[1] UMR Biogéosciences, Université de Bourgogne, Dijon, France
{lucile.sautot,bruno.faivre}@u-bourgogne.fr

[2] IRSTEA Centre de Clermont-Ferrand, Aubière, France
sandro.bimonte@irstea.fr

[3] UMR LE2I, Université de Bourgogne, Dijon, France
ludovic.journaux@agrosupdijon.fr

Abstract. Data warehouses (DW) and OLAP systems are technologies allowing the on-line analysis of huge volume of data according to decision-makers' needs. Designing DW involves taking into account functional requirements and data sources (mixed design methodology) [1]. But, for complex applications, existing automatic design methodologies seem inefficient. In some cases, decision-makers need querying, as a dimension, data which have been defined as facts by actual automatic mixed approachs. Therefore, in this paper, we offer a new mixed refinement methodology relevant to constellation multidimensional schema. The proposed methodolgy allows to decision-makers to enrich a dimension with factual data. In order to validate our theoretical proposals, we have implemented an enrichment tool and we have tested it on a real case study from bird biodiversity.

Keywords: Multidimensional design · Data warehouse · OLAP · Data mining

1 Introduction

Data warehouses (DW) and OLAP systems are business intelligence technologies allowing the on-line analysis of huge volume of data. Warehoused data is organized according to the multidimensional model that defines the concepts of dimensions and facts. Dimensions represent analysis axes and they are organized in hierarchies. Facts are the analysis subjects and they are described by numerical indicators called measures. Warehoused data are then explored and aggregated using OLAP operators (e.g. Roll-up, Slice, etc.) [2].

The success of DW projects essentially depends on the design phase where functional requirements meet data sources [1]. Three main methodologies have been developed: user-driven, datadriven and mixed [3]. User-driven approach puts decision-makers at the center of the design phase by providing them tools to

S. Hammoudi et al. (Eds.): ICEIS 2015, LNBIP 241, pp. 280–299, 2015.
DOI: 10.1007/978-3-319-29133-8_14

define the multidimensional model exclusively according to their analysis needs. Usually, data driven methodology proposals deduce the multidimensional model from structured and semistructured [4,5] data sources exploiting metadata (e.g. foreign keys) and some empirical values. Finally, mixed approaches fusion the two previous described methods.

Hierarchies are crucial structures in DW since they allow aggregation of measures in order to provide a global and general analytic view of warehoused data. For that reasons, some works investigate definition of hierarchies by means of Data Mining (DM) algorithms [6,7]. However, this design step is applied once the multidimensional model has been defined, and it takes into account only members of one dimension.

From our point of view, these methodologies present an important limitation since in real DW projects often those DM algorithms need data of different dimensions and facts. Thus, in this paper we present a framework for a mixed design of multidimensional models by integrating DM algorithms in a classical data driven-approach. This allows defining hierarchical structures, according to decisional users' requirements, that cannot be deduced by classical datadriven methods. This hierarchical organization of dimensional data is translated in a complex multi-factual multidimensional model in order to represent as well as possible semantic of data sources.

The paper is organized in the following way: Sect. 2 introduces related work; a retail case study and the motivation are presented in Sect. 3; our design method is detailed in Sect. 4 and its implementation is shown on Sect. 5.

2 Related Work

Three types of approaches can be used to design a data warehouse: (i) Methods based on user specifications, or demand-driven approaches; (ii) Methods based on available data, or data-driven approaches; (iii) Mixed methods, or hybrid approaches. For example, [8] is an iterative demand-driven method where at each iteration, the system searches for the best data corresponding with the information required by the user in terms of dimensions or facts. Moreover, several other have proposed systems based on hybrid approach such as [9] that propose to express functional requirements using SQL queries.

Relational data driven approaches deduce multidimensional structures (facts and dimensions) from conceptual [1] and/or logical models [5,10]. In particular some works investigate automatic discovering facts using some heuristics [10]. About dimensions some works propose using logical database metadata such as foreign keys [5] or some heuristics.

Other works use more complex algorithm to identify dimensions hierarchies. [11] propose a system to dynamically build hierarchies based on data from Twitter [11]. [12] present a new OLAP operator named OPAC that allows to aggregate facts that refer to complex objects, such as images. This operator is based on hierarchical clustering algorithm. [6] provide a framework for automatic defining hierarchies according to user rules. In order to personalize the multidimensional schema, [13] propose to create new levels in a hierarchy with the K-means algorithm. [14] propose to increase the OLAP cube exploration functionalities by providing the user data mining algorithms to analyze data. [15] use a hierarchical clustering to integrate continuous variables as dimensions in an OLAP schema. In the same line, [7] propose using Agglomerative Clustering for designing hierarchies, and the integration in a rapid prototyping methodology is presented in [16].

Concerning the multidimensional schema evolution issue, [17,18] offer an interesting litterature review.

However, all existing works define hierarchies using only either dimensional data (i.e. attributes of dimension members) or factual data (i.e. measures) (see Table 1). But, in a constellation schema, a dimension can be enriched with a hierarchy created by using other dimensions and facts. It means that the creation of a new hierarchy can involved a refinement of facts and dimensions in the entier constellation schema. We detail this issue in the following section, using a real application case from bird biodiversity.

Table 1. Summary of literature review related to automatic hierarchy building.

		Data sources		
		Star schema		Constellation schema
		Facts	One dimension	Facts and dimensions
Algorithm	K-means	[13]	[13]	
	Hierarchical classification	[7,15,16]	[12]	Our proposal
	Other	[6,11]	[14]	

3 Motivations from a Real Case Concerning Bird Biodiversity

3.1 Case Study

Temporal Monitoring of Nesting Birds Along a River. Our case study comes from the STORI (*Suivi Temporel des Oiseaux nicheurs en Rivière*: Temporal Monitoring of Nesting Birds along a River), financed by the French Ministery of Environment since 1990 and by the European Union (ERDF: European regional development fund) since 2000.

The STORI was created to inventory bird species along two French rivers (the Loire river and the Allier river). The STORI has three aims:

1. First, the STORI aims to understand relationships between bird species and environments, particularly the impact of landscapes (habitat diversity, land cover,...) on the bird species distribution along a river.

2. The second aim of the STORI is the bird species monitoring, i.e. the appreciation of temporal changes in bird communities over several years.
3. Finally, the STORI aims to elaborate a bio-indicator based on bird species.

The STORI's point of view is original compared to other works, which have similar aims. Classically, bio-indicators of river condition (fishes or insects) are not able to take into account the entire valley, because these bio-indicators are strongly dependant to the water [19]. Moreover, actual works are centered on one species whereas the STORI studies the entire bird community. Ecologically, studying communities is more relevant, in regards of the definition of an ecosystem.

In conclusion, the STORI is an original ecological study, which has produced an important data set on a long period (from 1989 to 2012) in a large spatial and biological area (the Loire river is 1000 Km long and harbores approximately 200 bird species).

Dataset Description. *Ornithological Data.* Our ornithological data were collected during the STORI. To inventory bird species, we use a protocole based on point counts with unlimited distance, named the IPA method [20,21]. The IPA method defines several precise "census points" (presented on Fig. 1), where each nesting bird is censused if it was detected by sight or by hearing (migratory birds and wintering birds are not censused). 198 census points have been defined along the Loire river. With the IPA method, we have obtained, at each census points, an semi-quantitative non-parametric index between 0 and 5. In conclusion, the ornithological data are a set of abundance index, censusing 213 bird species, in 198 census points, during four census campaigns (1990, 1996, 2002 et 2011).

Environmental Data. Our environmental data, describing the Loire river and the landscapes in the river valley, come from three main sources:

- Field surveys executed in the same time that the bird species census: these surveys describe locally the riverbed (altitude, valley width, flow velocity, riverbank type, substratum, etc.).
- Satellite images: they describe the river valley with attributes from image processing algorithms (percent of the area covered by forest, by grassland, connectance, cover land diversity, etc.).
- Geographical data bases, which describe precisely the catchment area of the Loire river in terms of water system, geological area, ecological area and land cover.

The environmental data have been collected for each census point along the Loire river.

Numerous environmental data are time dependent. On the one hand, some environmental data can vary in value over years. On the other hand, many environmental data are not available at each bird census campaign. For examples:

- The altitude of a census point is not a time dependent attribute, because we can easily assess that the altitude of a census point did not change between 1989 and 2012.
- The percent of the area covered by forest around a census point has probably changed between 1989 and 2012, thus this attribute is time dependent. This attribute has been collected on a satellite image in 2001. This attribute is consequently available only for the bird census campaign in 2002.

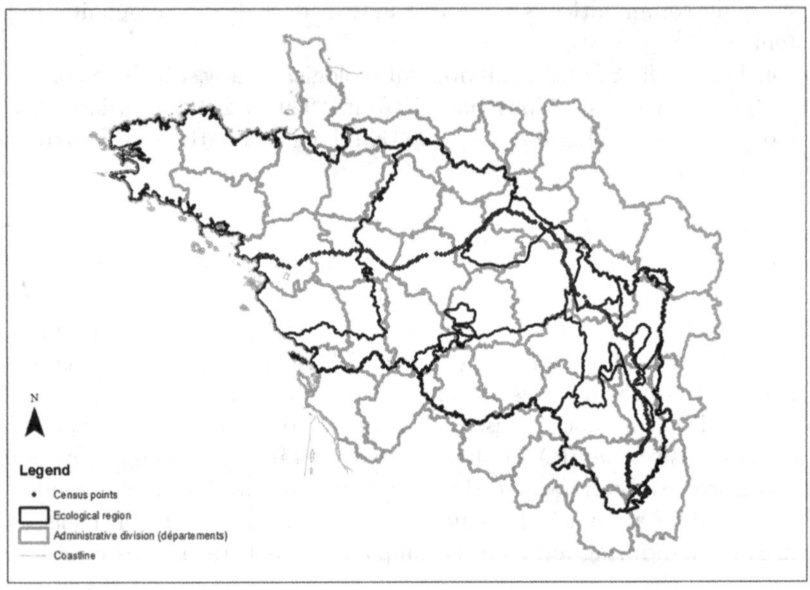

Fig. 1. Census points along the Loire river.

3.2 Motivation

In order to describe motivation of our new DW design methodology we present in this section a real case study concerning the bird biodiversity analysis [7]. This dataset has been collected to analyze spatio-temporal changes in bird populations along the Loire River (France) and to identify local and global environmental factors that can explain these changes. Data sources are stored in a relational database (PostGIS). Applying the data driven algorithm proposed in [9] we obtain the constellation schema depicted in Fig. 2, which presents two facts as described in the following. Abundances is one fact, and can be analyzed according to three dimensions (an instance is shown on Table 3): (i) the species dimension, which stores species names and attributes, (ii) the time dimension, which corresponds to the census years and (iii) the spatial dimension, which describes census points along the river. Using this model decision-maker can answer to queries like: *"What is the total of birds per year and census point?"* or *"What is the total of birds per year and altitude?"*. To complete bird census, the landscape and the river are described around each census point. Environment descriptions are represented by another fact, which is associated to the time dimension and the spatial dimension. With this model, it is possible to describe census points, for example a possible OLAP query is *"What is the percentage of forest per census point in 2012?"*.

Note that descriptions of census points that are not dependent from time, such as altitude and geology, are used as spatial dimension levels, while other attributes are represented as measures of another fact (e.g. percentage of forest). Unfortunately, abundances for a specie have not meaning if not related to environmental data of census points. In this situation a drill-across operation is not adequate since it will hide the species dimension. Indeed, with the drill-across operators facts are joined only on common dimensions. Moreover, the multidimensional model of Fig. 2 does not make possible to provide the decision-makers with OLAP queries aggregating abundance by classes of environmental variable (30 % of forest, 50 % of water, etc.), for example *"What is the total of birds per year and group of census point with 30 % of forest?"* or *"What is the total of birds per year and group of census point with 50 % of water?"*, since environmental parameters do not appear as levels, but as measures, prohibiting group-by queries.

Therefore, in our case study, decision-makers need for a new design method that group census points (dimensional data) by environmental parameters (factual data) and year (dimensional data).

Note that administrative division is not a spatial hierarchy which makes sense to study bird biodiversity. On the map presented on Fig. 1, boundaries of French departements and boundaries of large ecological areas do not match.

The multidimensional model allowing correct OLAP analysis should be the one shown on Fig. 3 [22]. This multidimensional schema presents only one fact and the spatial dimension is enriched with some levels representing group of environmental parameters for each year. Indeed, environmental parameters for census points in 2001 can be different from ones of 2002 implying that the same census point is not grouped in the same level on two different years as shown on Table 3.

For example, data describing agricultural activities around the census points, are available only for the 2002 census campaign. Therefore, it is important to take into this different classification when navigating on the temporal dimension during an OLAP analysis session. For example, the query *"What is the total of birds in 2002 and in census points with the same environmental parameters?"* has to use the environment type 2002 level, and *"What is the total of birds in 2011 and in census points with the same environmental parameters?"* has to use the environment type 2011 level. For example an OLAP query using the environment type 2002 level and the temporal member 2011 is not coherent since it associates the number of birds on 2011 in the past geographical-environmental configuration of 2002, leading to erroneous interpretation.

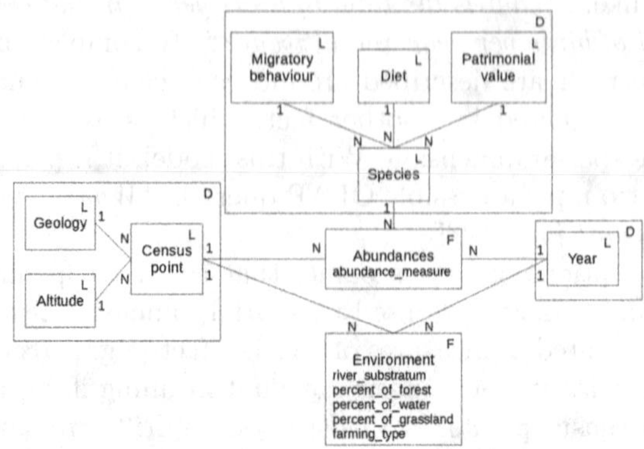

Fig. 2. Bird biodiversity case study: data-driven constellation schema.

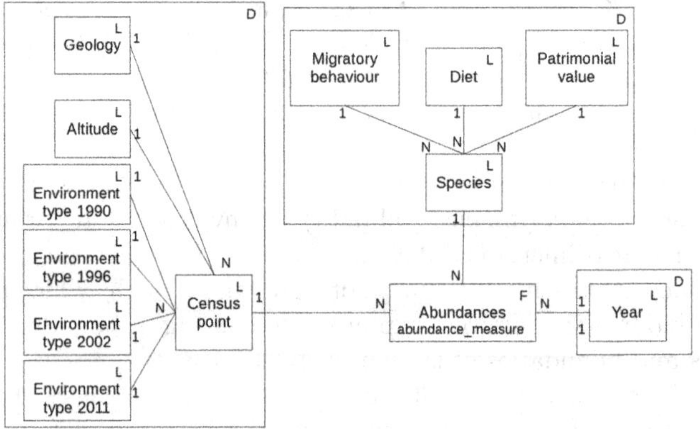

Fig. 3. Bird biodiversity case study: manually driven multi-version schema.

Table 2. Factual data of "Environments" node.

Years	Census points	Agencies	Percent of forest	Percent of grassland
2002	1	LE2I	0.176	0.250
2002	1	ONEMA	0.356	0.261
2002	2	LE2I	0.311	0.420
2002	2	ONEMA	0.255	0.574
2011	1	LE2I	0.189	0.278
2011	1	ONEMA	0.241	0.385
2011	2	LE2I	0.322	0.568
2011	2	ONEMA	0.257	0.575

Table 3. Factual data of "Abundances" node.

Years	Census points	Species	Abundance
2002	1	Yellowhammer	1.5
2002	1	Coal Tit	0.5
2002	2	Yellowhammer	1.5
2002	2	Coal Tit	0
2011	1	Yellowhammer	1
2011	1	Coal Tit	3
2011	2	Yellowhammer	1
2011	2	Coal Tit	2

4 Our Proposal

In this section we introduce our framework for the refinement of multidimensional in a mixed approach. The main idea of our proposal is using an existing data driven methodology in a first step. Then, in our new design step, we collect user needs about hierarchies that are not been deduced in the multidimensional schema by means of the functional dependencies. These users' needs are expressed in the form of facts existing in the constellation multidimensional model. In particular, the main idea is to provide an algorithm that transforms the constellation multidimensional schema by eliminating a fact node and integrating factual data in an associated dimension used for creating new levels.

To perform this algorithm, we translate the multidimensional model in a multidimensional graph.

In the following section we describe the multidimensional graph definitions (Sect. 4.1), the main algorithm is detailed in Sect. 4.2 and the calculation of new versioned hierarchies is explained in Sect. 4.3.

4.1 Preliminaries

In this subsection, we present some preliminary definitions.

We represent a multidimensional model using a graph.

Definition 1. **Multidimensional graph.** A multidimensional graph is a directed graph $M_G =< D, F, A >$ with:

$D = \{d_1, ..., d_m\}$, dimensional nodes, which represent dimensions.

$F = \{f_1, ..., f_n\}$, fact nodes representing facts.

$A = \{a_1, ..., a_p\} \mid \forall i \in [\![1, p]\!], a_i = (f_j, d_k)$, with $j \in [\![1, n]\!]$ and $k \in [\![1, m]\!]$, are arcs[1], meaning that arcs are only directed from a fact node to a dimensional node.

[1] In this paper, the notation (f_i, d_j) represents the arc from fact node f_i to dimensional node d_j.

Moreover, M_G contains no alone node, isolated of another node, but can contain possibly disconnected sets of nodes if each sub-graph must contain at least one fact node.

Example. An example of multidimensional graph is shown on Fig. 4. "Species" dimension, "Census points" dimension, "Years" dimension, "Abundances" fact and "Environments" fact are described in previous sections. "Sources" dimension represents agencies, which collect data. "Budget" fact represents the funds allowed by each agency for each year to collecting data.

In our approach decision-maker want to enrich a dimension with some new hierarchies using some factual data. That dimension is called Target dimension.

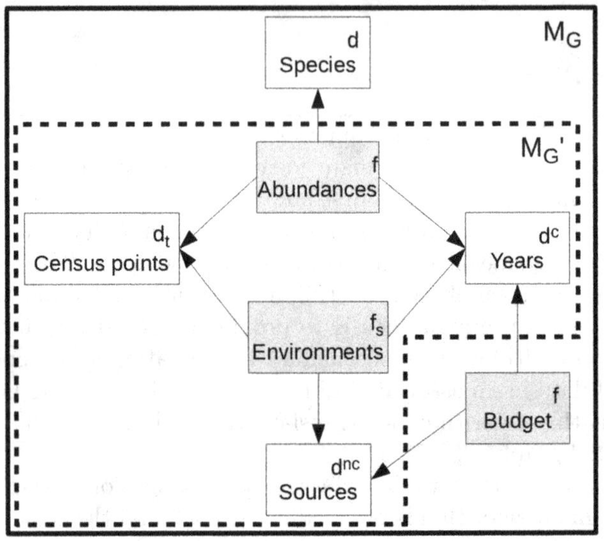

Fig. 4. Multidimensional graph M_G.

Definition 2. **Target dimension.** The target dimension d_t of a multidimensional graph M_G is a dimension such as:

This means that dt is associated at least to two facts since one has to be removed and used to create its new levels.

Example. An example of possible target dimension is the "census point" dimension (Fig. 4).

Let us now formalize the fact node that is used to create levels.

Definition 3. **Source node.** The source node of a M_G with a target dimension d_t is a fact node $f_s \in \{f_1, ..., f_u\}$.

Example. With "census point" dimension as target node, an example of possible source node is the fact node "Environments".

As we have said before our algorithm removes the source node from the graph. Therefore, a part of the structure of the graph is changed. Note that only nodes related to the source nodes are affected. We define this sub-graph in the following way

Definition 4. **Source-target multidimensional sub-graph.** Let M_G a multidimensional graph with a target dimension d_t and a source node f_s then the Source-target multidimensional sub-graph M'_G is a multidimensional graph such as: $M'_G =< D', F', A' >$ with:

$F' = \{f_i \in F \mid \exists(f_i, d_t)\}$
$D' = \{d_i \in D \mid \exists(f_s, d_i)\}$
$A' = \{(f_i, d_j) \mid f_i \in F', d_j \in D'\}$

M'_G contains thereby only fact nodes linked to d_t and dimensional nodes linked to f_s. In M'_G, all fact nodes are so linked to at least one dimensional node and all dimensional nodes are so linked to at least one fact node. There is no isolated node in this sub-graph. M'_G is so a well-formed multidimensional graph.

Example. An example of Source-target multidimensional sub-graph using the previous example is shown on Fig. 4.

In order to formalize inputs of the agglomerative hierarchical clustering algorithm used for the creation of levels of the target dimension, we formalize factual data aggregated to a set of dimensions levels using the definition of instance fact node.

Definition 5. **Instance fact node.** Let M_G a multidimensional graph. Let m_i a member of the dimension d_i. Then the instance fact node $I(f, d_1.m_1, ..., d_n.m_n)$ is the set of tuples representing facts of f aggregated to the dimensions members $d_1.m_1$, ..., $d_n.m_n$.

Example. Let, Table 2 representing the instance fact node for the node "Environments", then Table 4 represents facts aggregated to the All member of the "Agencies" dimension:

(I("Environments", "Agencies.ALL", "Years.1990", "Census_points.*"))[2]

4.2 Algorithm

In this section we provide details and formalize our approach.

Removing a fact node from the multidimensional graph implies its redefinition. Thus, the main idea is in a first step to work on the source-target multidimensional graph exclusively, transform this sub-graph adding levels to the target dimension and removing the source node, and then finally re-integrate the new sub-graph in the rest of original multidimensional graph.

Removing the source node implies to handle its associated dimensions. It is possible to distinguish three types of dimensions:

[2] '*' means 'all members of the dimension'.

- The target dimension that will rest in the transformed sub-graph,
- the Non Context dimensions D_{nc}, and
- the Context dimensions D_c.

The Non context dimensions D_{nc} are dimensions that are only associated to the source node fact. In order to remove one dimension it is possible to provide a classical Dice operator, which consists in aggregating fact data to the top dimension member. Let us note that in order to avoid summarazability problems (aggregation cannot be reused) [23], in our approach we allow using only distributive and algebraic aggregation functions for the Dice operator.

Example. An example of Non contextual dimension is the "Agencies" node. In Table 4 is shown an example of the Dice operator on the Agencies dimension, which is a Non contextual dimension.

Table 4. Factual data of "Environments" node aggregated on "Agencies".

Years	Census Points	Percent of Forest	Percent of grassland
2002	1	0.266	0.256
2002	2	0.283	0.497
2011	1	0.215	0.332
2011	2	0.290	0.572

Formally,

Definition 6. **Non contextual dimension.** Let Source-target multidimensional sub-graph $M'_G =< D', F', A' >$, then the set of non contextual dimension D_{nc} is

$$D_{nc} = \{d_1^{nc}, ..., d_v^{nc}\} \subset D' \mid \forall i \in [\![1, v]\!] \exists!(d_i^{nc}, f_j) \mid f_j \in F'$$

Note that in the previous formula, all dimensional nodes in D_{nc} are only linked to f_s. Indeed, all dimensional nodes in M'_G are linked to f_s and dimensional nodes in D_{nc} are linked to one (and only one) dimensional node.

The Context dimensions D_c are dimensions in M'_G that are associated to f_s and another fact node f. With the future refined graph, users analyze facts in f according to d_t. But, data used for calculating new hierarchies in d_t come from f_s and are thereby dependent of dimensions in D_c. Therefore, we need to ensure that data used to create the hierarchy are coherent with data consulted by the user during their OLAP analysis. With this in mind, we offer a system that calculates hierarchies according a context, this context defining with D_c.

Formally,

Definition 7. **Contextual dimension.** Let Source-target multidimensional sub-graph M'_G, then the set of contextual dimension D_c is

$$D_c \subset D' \mid D_c = D' - (D_{nc} \cup \{d_t\})$$

Example. An example of contextual dimension is the "Years" node. On Table 3, we present data from "Abundances" node: data are dependent of "Years" dimensional node.

Once we have defined non context and contex dimensions let us provide our algorithm supposing that we have only one context dimension.

The input of this algorithm is the multidimensional graph M_G presented on Fig. 4.

Begin of the Refinement Algorithm

1. *Identify the Source-target multidimensional sub-graph* M'_G.
2. *Calculate a hierarchy for each instance of each context. This part of the algorithm is detailed in particular in the* Sect. 4.3.
3. *Remove* f_s *from* M_G.
4. *Remove isolated nodes. The isolated nodes can be only dimensional nodes linked to* f_s. *Then* M_G *is well formed.*

End of the Refinement Algorithm

The output of this algorithm is a multidimensional graph, presented on Fig. 5. We note that f_s has been removed and there are new hierarchies in the "census points" node. Moreover, M_G remains a well-formed multidimensional graph and can be also implmented in a ROLAP architecture.

4.3 Automatic Creation of Hierarchies

In this section we describe how the is applied to create new levels of the target dimension.

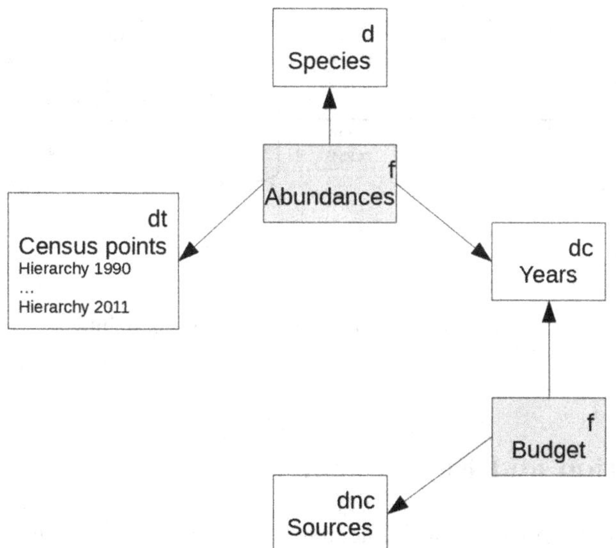

Fig. 5. Refined multidimensional graph M_G.

A complete methodology to create new hierarchies in a multidimensional model with Hierarchical Agglomerative Clustering is presented in [7]. The main idea of this methodology is to build a new hierarchy into a dimension by using data, which describe items at the lowest level of the hierarchy. In our case, items are census points and description data are factual data. We suggest to use the Hierarchical Agglomerative Clustering, due to the similarity between the output of the Hierarchical Agglomerative Clustering and a hierarchy into an OLAP dimension [12].

Main steps of this algorithm are: (1) Calculation of distances between individuals; (2) Choice of the two nearest individuals. (3) Aggregation of the two nearest individuals in a cluster. The cluster is considered an individual. (4) Go back to the step 1 and loop while there is more than one individual.

In our approach the clustering (AHC) takes as inputs the instance of the source node f_s evaluated on each member of the context dimension and dicing it non context dimensions.

Formally, the step 2 of our algorithm is the following:

Begin of the Hierarchy Builder Algorithm
for each $member_i$ *of* d_c
. *create a new hierarchy of* d_t
. $AHC(I(f_s, d_1^{nc}.ALL, \ldots, d_v^{nc}.ALL, d^c.member_i, d_t.*))$
End of the Hierarchy Builder Algorithm

An example is presented on Fig. 6. We note that two hierarchies for the spatial dimension have been created for years 2002 and 2011.

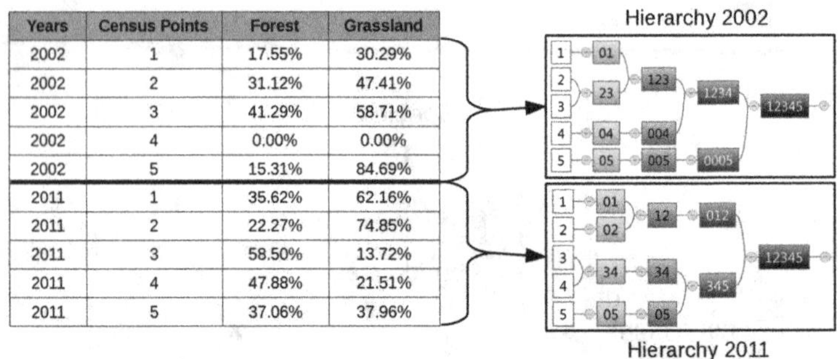

Years	Census Points	Forest	Grassland
2002	1	17.55%	30.29%
2002	2	31.12%	47.41%
2002	3	41.29%	58.71%
2002	4	0.00%	0.00%
2002	5	15.31%	84.69%
2011	1	35.62%	62.16%
2011	2	22.27%	74.85%
2011	3	58.50%	13.72%
2011	4	47.88%	21.51%
2011	5	37.06%	37.96%

Fig. 6. Contextual hierarchies of census points.

5 Validation and Experiments

In this section we present the implementation our proposal. Next, we present some calculated hierarchies. Finally, a semantic and performance evaluations are detailed in Sect. 5.3.

5.1 Implementation

The refinement tool implements our algorithm using Matlab[3]. It allows defining graph using a simple visual interface as shown on Fig. 7. The considered multi-dimensional graph is presented on the top part of the visual interface. On the bottom one, the algorithm ask inputs to users in a command window.

The data warehouse is implemented using PostgreSQL[4]. The OLAP server is Mondrian[5], and the OLAP client is Saiku[6].

5.2 Results

In this section, we present a comparison between two contextual hierarchies.

On Fig. 8, we provide the three main clusters of census points along the Loire river, using field survey data collected by the STORI in 1990. In contrast, the Fig. 9 provides the two main clusters of census points along the Loire river, using land cover data collected in a geographical information system[7] by French state agencies in 2011.

These two clustering results correspond to the top levels of the hierarchies calculated by the proposed refinement algorithm. The refinement algorithm

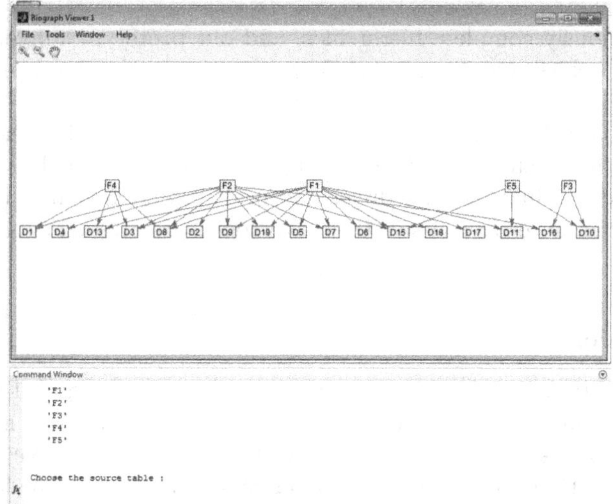

Fig. 7. Visual interface of the refinement tool.

[3] http://www.mathworks.com.
[4] http://www.postgresql.org.
[5] http://community.pentaho.com/projects/mondrian/.
[6] http://community.meteorite.bi/.
[7] http://www.sigloire.fr/.

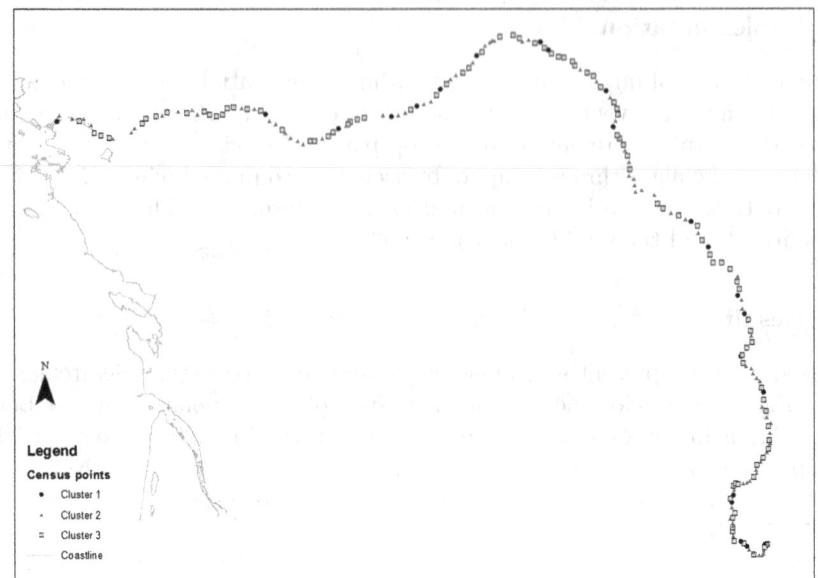

Fig. 8. Census point clusters obtained by AHC based on field surveys in 1990.

calculates obviously complete hierarchies, and our prototype implements these complete hierarchies. On Figs. 8 and 9, we provides only the top levels for a better reading.

If we compare the map in Figs. 1, 8 and 9, we can note that the typologies calculated by the refiement algorithm for 1990 and 2011 are not the same, and do not correspond to administrative division or ecological area defined in the catchment area of the Loire river. Thus, these typologies are original classifications of census points.

5.3 Validation

Semantic Evaluation. In this subsection, we describe the added-value of our methodology from a design point of view (i.e. does the refinement methodology corresponds to decision-makers needs?). For that goal two we have investigated two aspects: (1) Do dimensions and facts created using our methodology correspond to decision-makers analysis needs?; (2) Do hierarchies created using our methodology improve analysis capabilities?

Therefore have decided to compare the result of our methodology with one proposed in [22]. Indeed, [22] propose a manually method to obtain a multi-version multidimensional schema, and when the time dimension is chosen as the context dimension our approach results a multi-version multidimensional schema. The result of this validation shows that the multidimensional schema produced with the manual methodology and our automatic methodology are equal.

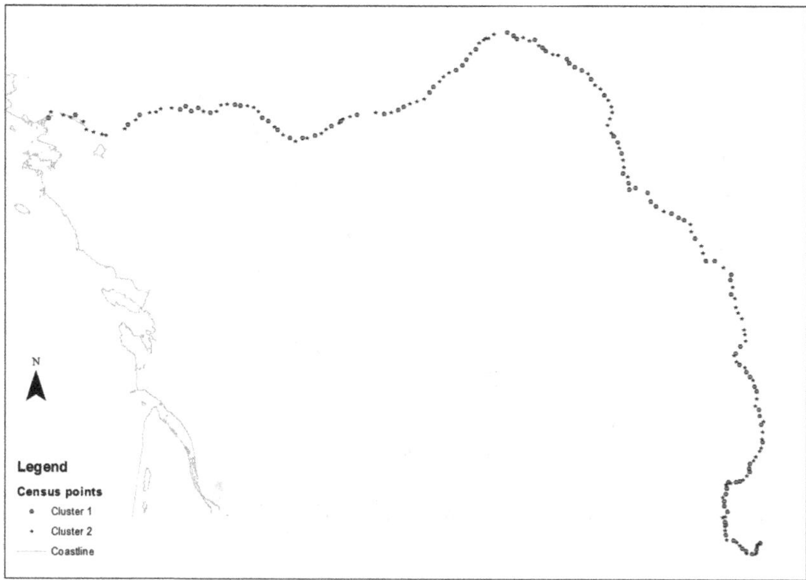

Fig. 9. Census point clusters obtained by AHC based on land cover in 2011.

Moreover, in order to validate the semantic correctness of using AHC for hierarchies definition, we have asked to ecologists of the project to choice between a spatial dimension with only one level, and a spatial dimension with a hierarchy created using AHC. When the number of created levels is not superior to 5, decision-makers prefer having hierarchies, since they can reveal interesting pattern such as agricultural profiles of census points. For example, data in the "Environments" fact table contains data that describe agriculture policies around each census point at each year. The data clustering according to these data can classify census points and allows decision-makers analyzing impact of agricultural practices on bird biodiversity. For example, decision-makers can analyze biodiversity according to agricultural forest and grassland parameters of census points, by using this simple OLAP query: "What is the biodiversity value per group of census points (first level of the hierarchy obtained with clustering) in 2002 and 2003?". This query can reveal that for the same year, for example 2002, biodiversity is very affected by agricultural parameters since the aggregated biodiversity value for each group of census point is different.

Performance Evaluation. In this subsection, we test time performance of our methodology in order to validate its feasibility from a project deployment process point of view.

In particular we study time performance related to: (1) refinement algorithm for facts and dimension design, and (2) hierarchy creation using AHC.

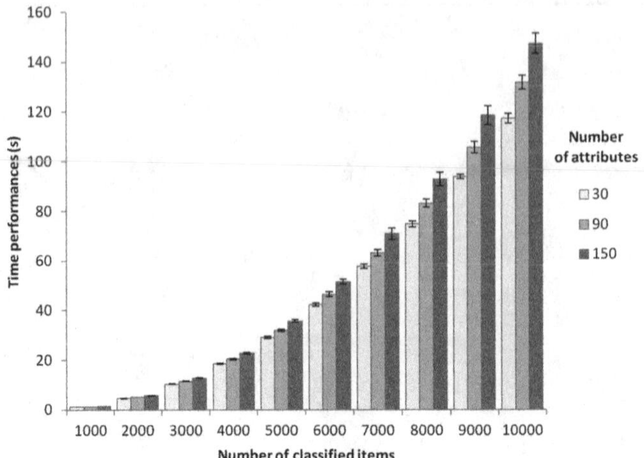

Fig. 10. Execution times according the number of attributes and classified items.

In order to test the first point, we have created a set of 200 simulated constellation schema using from 2 to 100 dimensions, since real usable multidimensional schema presents maximum between 3 and 10 dimensions [2]. Finally, the worst time execution is 15.23 s. The average execution time is equal to 11.7 s with a standard deviation equal to 1.17 s. These performances are satisfactory for are good for an off-line design phase.

In this paragraph, we study time performances of the AHC algorithm. In this paragraph, "classified items" are census points (which are members of the "census points" dimension, the target dimension) and "attributes" are aggregated facts from the "Environments" fact node (which is the source fact node). The AHC algorithm has been also implemented in Matlab and its performance has been also tested. Using our case study data, we perform 2090 tests, with a number of classified items (source node instances-Enverinments facts) between 10 and 190, and a number of attributes (source node attributes-Enverinments fact measures) between 10 and 100, and the average calculation time is equal to 0.072 s, with a standard deviation equal to 0.002 s. To complete our evaluation, we simulate a data set with 10,000 classified items and 150 attributes. In this case, the AHC calculates a hierarchy in 147.36 s, with a standard deviation equal to 4.03, with a maximal calculation time equal to 214 s. All time performances are shown on Fig. 10. This calculation time (approximately four minutes) is efficient for an off-line design phase.

6 Conclusion and Future Work

Design data warehouses system is a complex and crucial task depending on available data sources and decisional requirements. Existing work do not exploit the semantics of data to automatically create complex hierarchies. Thus in this paper, we present a mixed multidimensional refinement methodology, that transform constellation schema to define hierarchy level using a hierarchical clustering algorithm. Our refinement methodology enriches a dimension with factual data, and considers the context of factual data.

In our case, the context was the "Time" dimension. In this case, our work can be considered as a versionning methodology. But, the proposed prototype does not use temporal properties of the "Time" dimension. In other words, the proposed prototype is able to calculate new hierarchies for the spatial dimension depending on years, as well as new hierarchies for the temporal dimension depending on census points.

We present also the implementation of our method in a ROLAP architecture.

We perform the proposed methodology on a real application case from bird biodiversity. We have noted that actual automatic multidimensional design methodologies cannot produce a multidimensional schema, which covers all decision-maker needs due to the data complexity. Our methodology offers a solution to enrich dimensions with factual data and, by this way, to refine the multidimensional schema.

Our ongoing work is the extension of our methodology to simplify and reduce the number of created levels, using other DM algorithms such as SVM, etc., in order to provide decision-makers with easy OLAP exploration analysis and its implementation in a ROLAP architecture.

Moreover, we are also working to integrate our approach in the rapid prototyping methodology proposed in [16], and extending to help decision-makers and DW experts choose the right DM algorithms and parameters of the refinement algorithm (source node, contextual dimensions, etc.).

Future work concerns the usage of the formal evaluation framework Goal Question Metric [24] to evaluate our methodology.

Acknowledgements. Data acquisition received financial support from the FEDER Loire, Etablissement Public Loire, DREAL de Bassin Centre, the Région Bourgogne (PARI, Projet Agrale 5) and the French Ministry of Agriculture. We also thank heartily Pr. John Aldo Lee, from the Catholic University of Leuven, for his help.

References

1. Phipps, C., Davis, K.C.: Automating data warehouse conceptual schema design and evaluation. In: Proceedings of the 4th International Workshop on Design and Management of Data Warehouses (DMDW), vol. 2 (2002)
2. Kimball, R.: The Data Warehouse Toolkit: Practical Techniques for Building Dimensional Data Warehouses. Wiley, New York (1996)
3. Romero, O., Abello, A.: A survey of multidimensional modeling methodologies. Int. J. Data Warehouse. Min. **5**, 1–23 (2009)
4. Mahboubi, H., Ralaivao, J.C., Loudcher, S., Boussaïd, O., Bentayeb, F., Darmont, J., et al.: X-WACoDa: an XML-based approach for warehousing and analyzing complex data. In: Data Warehousing Design and Advanced Engineering Applications: Methods for Complex Construction, pp. 38–54 (2009)

5. Jensen, M.R., Holmgren, T., Pedersen, T.B.: Discovering multidimensional structure in relational data. In: Kambayashi, Y., Mohania, M., Wöß, W. (eds.) DaWaK 2004. LNCS, vol. 3181, pp. 138–148. Springer, Heidelberg (2004)
6. Favre, C., Bentayeb, F., Boussaid, O.: A knowledge-driven data warehouse model for analysis evolution. Frontiers Artif. Intell. Appl. **143**, 271 (2006)
7. Sautot, L., Faivre, B., Journaux, L., Molin, P.: The hierarchical agglomerative clustering with gower index: a methodology for automatic design of OLAP cube in ecological data processing context. Ecol. Inf. **26**, 217–230 (2014) (in Press)
8. Jovanovic, P., Romero, O., Simitsis, A., Abelló, A.: Ore: An iterative approach to the design and evolution of multi-dimensional schemas. In: Proceedings of the Fifteenth International Workshop on Data Warehousing and OLAP, DOLAP 2012, pp. 1–8. ACM, New York (2012)
9. Romero, O., Abello, A.: Automatic validation of requirements to support multidimensional design. Data Knowl. Eng. **69**, 917–942 (2010)
10. Carmè, A., Mazon, J.N., Rizzi, S.: A model-driven heuristic approach for detecting multidimensional facts in relational data sources. In: Bach Pedersen, T., Mohania, M.K., Tjoa, A.M. (eds.) DAWAK 2010. LNCS, vol. 6263, pp. 13–24. Springer, Heidelberg (2010)
11. Nguyen, T.B., Tjoa, A.M., Wagner, R.R.: An object oriented multidimensional data model for OLAP. In: Lu, H., Zhou, A. (eds.) WAIM 2000. LNCS, vol. 1846, pp. 69–82. Springer, Heidelberg (2000)
12. Messaoud, R.B., Boussaid, O., Rabaséda, S.: A new OLAP aggregation based on the AHC technique. In: DOLAP 2004, ACM Seventh International Workshop on Data Warehousing and OLAP, pp. 65–72 (2004)
13. Bentayeb, F.: K-means based approach for OLAP dimension updates. In: 10th International Conference on Enterprise Information Systems (ICEIS), pp. 531–534 (2008)
14. Leonhardi, B., Mitschang, B., Pulido, R., Sieb, C., Wurst, M.: Augmenting OLAP exploration with dynamic advanced analytics. In: 13th International Conference on Extending Database Technology (EDBT 2010) (2010)
15. Ceci, M., Cuzzocrea, A., Malerba, D.: OLAP over continuous domains via density-based hierarchical clustering. In: König, A., Dengel, A., Hinkelmann, K., Kise, K., Howlett, R.J., Jain, L.C. (eds.) KES 2011, Part II. LNCS, vol. 6882, pp. 559–570. Springer, Heidelberg (2011)
16. Sautot, L., Bimonte, S., Journaux, L., Faivre, B.: A methodology and tool for rapid prototyping of data warehouses using data mining: application to birds biodiversity. In: Ait Ameur, Y., Bellatreche, L., Papadopoulos, G.A. (eds.) MEDI 2014. LNCS, vol. 8748, pp. 250–257. Springer, Heidelberg (2014)
17. Arora, M., Gosain, A.: Schema evolution for data warehouse: a survey. Int. J. Comput. Appl. (0975–8887) **22**, 6–14 (2011)
18. Subotic, D., Poscic, P., Jovanovic, V.: Data warehouse schema evolution: state of the art. In: Proceedings of the Central European Conference on Information and Intelligent Systems, pp. 18–25 (2014)
19. Legube, B., Merlet, N.: Les indicateurs biologiques de la qualité de l'eau. In: L'analyse de l'eau. 9e edn., pp. 865–962. Dunod (2009)
20. Blondel, J., Ferry, C., Frochot, B.: Point counts with unlimited distance. In: Ralph, C.J., Scott, J.M. (eds.) Estimating Numbers of Terrestrial Birds. Studies in Avian Biology. vol. 6, pp. 414–420 (1981)
21. I.B.C.C.: Censuring breeding bird by the I.P.A. method. Pol. Ecol. Stud. **3**, 15–17 (1977)

22. Miquel, M., Bédard, Y., Brisebois, A., Pouliot, J., Marchand, P., Brodeur, J.: Modeling multi-dimensional spatio-temporal data werehouses in a context of evolving specifications. Int. Arch. Photogrammetry Remote Sens. Spat. Inf. Sci. **34**, 142–147 (2002)
23. Lenz, H.J., Thalheim, B.: A formal framework of aggregation for the OLAP-OLTP model. J. Univ. Comput. Sci. **15**, 273–303 (2009)
24. Briand, L.C., Morasca, S., Basili, V.R.: An operational process for goal-driven definition of measures. IEEE Trans. Softw. Eng. **28**, 1106–1125 (2002)

Information Systems Analysis and Specification

Validating a Software Engineering Framework Through Technical-Action-Research in Union with Case Studies

Miguel Morales-Trujillo[1(✉)], Hanna Oktaba[1], and Mario Piattini[2]

[1] KUALI-KAANS Research Group, National Autonomous University of Mexico, Mexico City, Mexico
{migmor,hanna.oktaba}@ciencias.unam.mx

[2] Alarcos Research Group, University of Castilla – La Mancha, Paseo de la Universidad 4, 13071 Ciudad Real, Spain
mario.piattini@uclm.es

Abstract. Software Engineering is an up-to-date discipline in constant development. It is continuingly enriched with new proposals from both industry and academy. Adequate validation of these proposals is a must if their real value for Software Engineering is to be determined. This paper demonstrates how a Software Engineering framework was validated with the help of Technical-Action-Research and Case Study methods, which were applied in several life cycles during a validation process of three years. Integration of these methodologies resulted in a solid research method with continuous feedback on and placement of the artifact in a real context. Using Technical-Action-Research together with Case Studies allowed to achieve research objectives and to meet the needs and goals of the organizations involved in the validation process, which emphasizes this method's advantages and usefulness for Software Engineering.

Keywords: TAR · SEMAT · OMG · Case studies · Evidence-based · Validation · Software engineering

1 Introduction

Software Engineering is one of the most knowledge intensive disciplines [1, 2]. However, this particular field contains many proposals or theories that have no theoretical rigorousness and have not been adequately validated in practice.

According to [3] most of these theories are not subject to serious academic discussion; they are not evaluated or compared as regards traditional criteria of theoretical quality such as consistency, correctness, comprehensiveness, and precision.

As [4] stated "Software Engineering is afflicted by a lack of credible experimental evaluation and validation". The behavior of the discipline is not that which is desired, thus motivating the need to transform it and to build theories around it, to understand it, and more importantly, generate proven knowledge.

The above fostered the origin of the Software Engineering Method and Theory (SEMAT) initiative in 2009, in the form of a call for action to refound Software Engineering. With the appearance of SEMAT the software engineering community sought

S. Hammoudi et al. (Eds.): ICEIS 2015, LNBIP 241, pp. 303–327, 2015.
DOI: 10.1007/978-3-319-29133-8_15

to formally address concerns of Software Engineering and generate theoretical basis for this branch of knowledge. SEMAT enjoys the collaboration of several experts in the field, and defines its primary goal as refounding Software Engineering upon new and solid fundamentals [5].

Other areas of concern identified by SEMAT are: definition of concepts for practices, definition of universals and a kernel language in order to describe them, construction and validation of theories, and laying down universal metrics to assess software related aspects [5]. Some members of this initiative also pertain to organizations that are part of the Object Management Group (OMG). This worldwide IT consortium endorsed SEMAT, launching it as the Foundation for the Agile Creation and Enactment of Software Engineering Methods Request for Proposals (FACESEM RFP) [6], thus making it even more formal and feasible.

Since the KUALI-KAANS research group actively participated from the beginning in SEMAT, it answered to the OMG RFP by undertaking the project of creating its own proposal, KUALI-BEH: Software Project Common Concepts [8]. The proposal was submitted to the OMG standardization process in 2011 and later joined the proposal ESSENCE – Kernel and Language for Software Engineering Methods [7]. This standardization process is described in detail and may be consulted in [9].

KUALI-BEH addresses important concerns of Software Engineering practitioners: how to structure their own ways of working and, as a consequence, how to control their work. It helps practitioners to create their own methods by defining work units and applying various operations to them. This framework brings together software projects common concepts and provides guidelines for methods authoring. It consists of a static and an operational views. The former gives practitioners necessary tools to manage the common concepts in order to define and assess their ways of working. The latter assists work teams in method enactment and in adapting practices to a specific project and/or stakeholder needs.

KUALI-BEH aims at creating and sharing knowledge related to Software Engineering; however, this knowledge produced by practitioners should be validated and agreed upon inside and outside the organization.

Certain attributes of methods and practices should be observed during the authoring process [8]. Preservation of properties of coherency, consistency and sufficiency in a set of practices brings about a well-formed method. This method is meant to be recycled in future projects; to increase its suitability, it can be adjusted to new contexts by applying adaptation operations of substitution, concatenation, combination and splitting.

In order to validate KUALI-BEH and evaluate its usefulness we have, over the last three years, developed a collaborative workshop and three case studies. The objective of this paper is to present the process applied to validate KUALI-BEH.

This paper is organized as follows: Sect. 2 presents a general background to the research methods in Software Engineering, focusing on those which are most relevant for the purpose of this paper. Section 3 describes the research strategy applied to create and validate KUALI-BEH. Sections 4 and 5 show the Collaborative Workshop and the Family of three Case Studies. The lessons learned are presented in Sect. 6, while the paper concludes in Sect. 7.

2 Research Methods in Software Engineering

Software Engineering requires both theoretical and empirical research. The former focuses on foundations and basic theories of software engineering, whilst the latter concentrates on fundamental principles, tools/environments, and best practices [10].

As mentioned by [11], Software Engineering should have strong foundations as a scientific and engineering discipline. This implies that validation processes must be sufficiently mature to provide evidence that will support its advances. One alternative that can be used to achieve this goal is that of empirical software engineering since, according to [12], this type of research provides the opportunity to build and verify its theories.

In Software Engineering, the validation must always involve scaling up to practice, which means that successive tests take place under increasingly realistic conditions [13]. No matter what its form, the essence of an empirical study is the attempt to learn something useful by comparing theory to reality and to improve our theories as a result [14].

According to [10, 15], the primary methods used for empirical studies in Software Engineering encompass: Experiments [16], Surveys [17], Case Studies [18, 19], Action-Research [20], Systematic Literature Reviews [21] and Standardization.

More than one method was considered for the validation of KUALI-BEH, and for the purposes of this paper, the most relevant research methods are therefore described in the following subsections.

2.1 Technical-Action-Research Method

Technical-Action-Research (TAR) is an approach that is used to validate new artifacts under conditions of practice [22]. In TAR the researcher uses an artifact in a real world project to help a client, or gives the artifact to others to use them in a real world project [23].

TAR can be seen as a research method that starts from the opposite side of traditional research methods. TAR starts with an artifact, and then tests it under conditions of practice by using it to solve concrete problems [22].

In this method the researcher first develops the artifact, then tests it in a hypothetical situation in a laboratory and later scales it to be tested in real world situations, from an idealized context to the real one.

In technical disciplines, prototypes of artifacts are first tested in the idealized conditions of the laboratory, and these conditions are gradually relaxed after each iteration until a realistic version of the artifact is tested in a realistic environment, thus allowing the technical scientist to develop knowledge about the behavior of artifacts in practice [22].

These iterations are called engineering cycles [22] or regulative cycles [24]. In the engineering cycle an improvement problem is investigated, a treatment with which to solve the problem is then designed and validated, its improved version is later implemented, and finally the experience with the implementation is evaluated and the cycle is executed again [22].

Each engineering cycle is composed of four steps:

1. **Problem Investigation:** during this step the stakeholders, their goals and the improvement problem are identified.
2. **Treatment Design:** during this step the researcher designs the artifact that will be used as a treatment in the problem context.
3. **Design Validation:** after the artifact has been designed, the researcher states the expected effects, expected value, trade-offs and sensitivity.
4. **Treatment Implementation and Evaluation:** this step involves the insertion of the artifact into the real world. The artifact has to be validated and the researcher has to evaluate the resulting effects.

TAR is based on the assumption that what the researcher learns in this particular case will provide lessons learned that will be usable in the next case [22]. The expected result from TAR is the validation of the proposed artifact in the specified context, thus satisfying the stakeholders' needs and giving it value.

2.2 Case Study Research Method

A case study is an intensive investigation and analysis of a particular technology, project, organization, or environment based on information obtained from a variety of sources such as interviews, surveys, documents, test or trial results, and archival records [10]. Wang establishes that case studies link a theory to practice, which allows conclusions to be drawn about the suitability of a given method for real world problems at industrial scales [10].

A case study is, according to [18] an empirical inquiry that investigates a contemporary phenomenon in depth and within its real-life context, especially when the boundaries between phenomenon and context are not clearly evident.

The essence of a case study, the central tendency among all types of case study, is that it tries to illuminate a decision or set of decisions: why they were taken, how they were implemented, and with what result [25].

Case studies may be used to validate a theory or method by means of empirical tests. They are also useful as regards providing a counter instance for a generally accepted principle. However, the drawback of case studies as an empirical method in Software Engineering is the difficulties of data collection and the generalization of findings via limited cases, particularly when they are positive but non-exhaustive [10].

According to [19] the differences between Software Engineering study objects rely on the fact that: (i) they are entities that develop software rather than using it; (ii) they are project-oriented rather than function oriented organizations; and (iii) the work studied is advanced rather than routine engineering. The generic phases of a case study described by [19] are:

1. **Case study Design:** objectives are defined and the case study is planned.
2. **Preparation for Data Collection:** procedures and protocols for data collection are defined.
3. **Collecting Evidence:** data collection procedures are executed on the studied case.

4. **Analysis of Collected Data:** data analysis procedures are applied to the data.
5. **Reporting:** the study and its conclusions are packaged in feasible formats for reporting.

3 Research Strategy Applied

The research strategy used to validate KUALI-BEH was guided by the integration of TAR and Case Study methods. The TAR method was applied as a framework in which the evaluation during engineering cycles was carried out by applying the Case Study method.

The research process consisted of five engineering cycles (see Fig. 1). The validation of these engineering cycles was carried out by means of case studies primarily developed in real world software development organizations. The artifact was also inserted in circles formed of practitioners and experts from academy and industry, such as a collaborative academy-industry workshop and the OMG Analysis and Design Task Force in charge of developing IT standards.

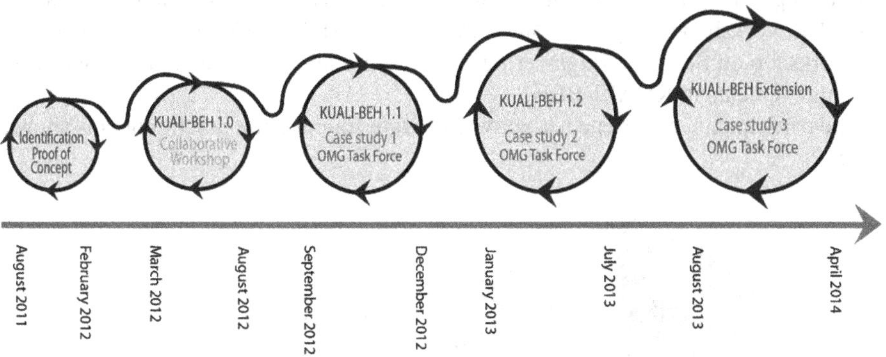

Fig. 1. Engineering cycles of the applied research process.

The first engineering cycle (from August 2011 through February 2012) consisted of identifying the common concepts used in the context of a software project and was carried out using a literature review.

During the second engineering cycle (from March through August 2012), an initial version of the artifact was released and validated by means of a collaborative workshop, whose participants were active Software Engineering practitioners, Master's degree students and researchers from the discipline.

The third engineering cycle was developed from September through December 2012. A first case study was carried out during these months in which an improved version of the artifact was validated in a Mexican enterprise in charge of software development and hardware construction. The artifact was also evaluated by the OMG task force.

During the fourth cycle (January through July 2013), improvements and lessons learned from the previous cycle were applied to the artifact. It was also used in a second case study, which took place in an entity that specializes in requirements specification and software projects design.

During the fifth and the last engineering cycle, which took place between August 2013 and April 2014, the artifact was enriched and an Authoring Extension was designed, which now belongs to the ESSENCE OMG formal specification. At that point the artifact was newly validated by the OMG task force, while a third case study was simultaneously carried out in a very small entity in charge of software development.

A detailed and in-depth description of the validation of the artifact is presented in Sects. 4 and 5.

4 Collaborative Workshop

KUALI-BEH was validated by means of a collaborative workshop attended by active practitioners from industry and academy. It was attended by 16 participants, practitioners and method engineers from 3 software industry organizations, in addition to 3 Master's students. The workshop methodology included on-site and virtual interactive sessions, together with activities and surveys that the participants had to carry out in order to apply the proposal in real life situations and analyze its usefulness, merits and flaws. The workshop took place from March till August 2012. Conducting a collaborative workshop on Software Engineering Methods brought about valuable feedback on and improvements to KUALI-BEH.

The participants' experience as active Software Engineering practitioners is shown in Fig. 2.

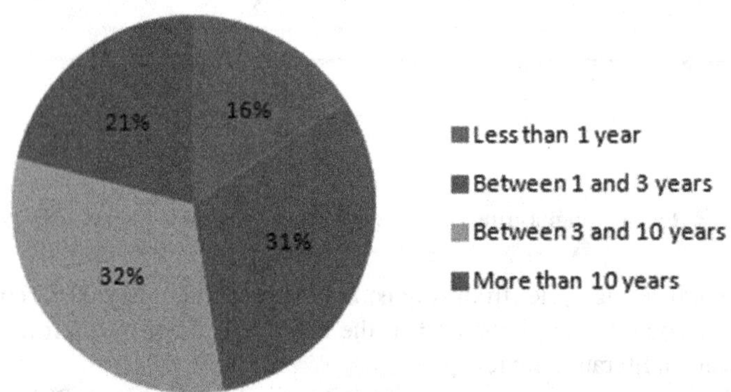

Fig. 2. Participants' experience in years.

The roles developed by practitioners in an organization are shown in Fig. 3.

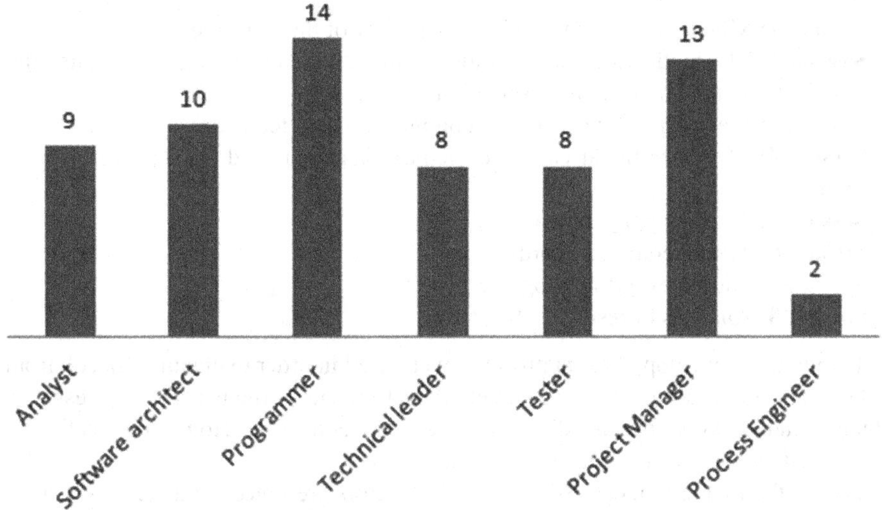

Fig. 3. Roles developed by the participants in their organizations.

This section presents a detailed description of this workshop.

4.1 Problem Investigation

The propositions of the study were focused on the pertinence, appropriateness and proficiency of the KUALI-BEH common concepts. These propositions were evaluated by asking the following questions:

- Are the common concepts pertinent?
- Are the definitions of the common concepts appropriate?
- Are the definitions of the common concepts similar to real world usage?
- Are the common concepts proficient?

These questions helped us to support the decisions made during the acceptance/ rejection process carried out during the identification phase.

4.2 Artifact Design

The artifact to be validated by means of the workshop was the first version of KUALI-BEH, which was the output of the Identification phase of this research, and corresponded to its first engineering cycle. This version was base lined on February 20th, 2012.

4.3 Design and Implementation

The workshop was divided into eight on-site and online sessions. The theoretical components of KUALI-BEH were presented as follows:

- **Session 1:** Motivation, background and overview of the framework.
- **Session 2:** The Static view, the definitions of its 20 common concepts and its relationships and the graphical representation.
- **Session 3:** Method properties and the common concept templates.
- **Session 4:** The Operational view, the Method Enactment and the Practice Instance Lifecycle.
- **Session 5:** The adaptation operations.
- **Session 6:** The Operational boards.
- **Session 7:** Putting everything together.
- **Session 8:** Analysis of results and closure.

During the workshop, three approaches were used in order to obtain feedback from participants: application of surveys, direct interaction with participants during sessions, which included Q&A runs, and direct observation of activities. "Homework" activities also helped analyze the understanding of the proposal.

During the first part of each session, the instructors presented the theoretical part of KUALI-BEH, and during the second part the participants took part in the following activities:

- **Activity 1:** Document a practice that you execute in your daily work using the practice template.
- **Activity 2:** Document a method and its respective practices that you execute in your daily work using the method template.
- **Activity 3:** Discuss the differences and similarities between real life and the proposed method enactment.
- **Activity 4:** Apply operations in order to adapt the previously documented method.
- **Activity 5:** Adapt the practice instance and method enactment boards to your daily work.
- **Activity 6:** Carry out the method in your organization.

After each session a survey was available online until the next session, during which the results of the most recent survey were analyzed.

- **Survey 1:** Similarity between the proposal and real life.
- **Survey 2:** Pertinence, appropriateness and proficiency of the common concepts.
- **Survey 3:** Pertinence and appropriateness of the method properties.
- **Survey 4:** Pertinence and appropriateness of the practice instance lifecycle and method enactment.
- **Survey 5:** Pertinence and appropriateness of the method adaptation and proficiency of the operations.
- **Survey 6:** Pertinence and appropriateness of the practice instance and method enactment boards.

4.4 Evaluation

The data collected during the workshop resulted in a set of suggestions that were analyzed and classified by the researchers. The suggestion review process consisted of 4 steps:

1. First, each of 93 suggestions was associated with its related KUALI-BEH element.
2. During the second step we determined which of them would be rejected, either because they did not apply or were duplicated, thus cutting the previous number to 32 suggestions.
3. The remaining suggestions were later divided into Change/Improvement or Out-of-Scope, thus making the cut 27.
4. Finally, after reviewing and analyzing the 27 suggestions, the KUALI-BEH team fully applied 16, while 11 were included with some modifications.

After this process, the main improvements made to KUALI-BEH concerned the following issues: (i) The definitions of terms were enhanced; (ii) New definitions and operations were added; and (iii) Operational rules were improved.

The main drawbacks mentioned by the practitioners or observed by the KUALI-BEH team were:

- The level of detail of the expressed way of workings varies among organizations, mainly among tasks and activity concepts.
- The definition of verification criteria and measures are mainly considered to be part of the project managers' responsibilities, and giving the control of these variables to practitioners was new and unusual for them.
- The need for a tool or set of tools that implements the templates and the boards during enactment is mandatory.

At the end of the workshop, benefits were identified and obtained by both parties. During interviews the software industry participants identified such benefits as:

- *"We organize our knowledge better though practices and methods"*.
- *"Now we can transmit our knowledge to other teammates and apply it in the organization"*.
- *"Using this structure, it is easy to effectively train new people in my organization"*.
- *"I find this approach with which to document my actual way of working attractive. That is to say, I document what I actually do and not what I am supposed to do"*.

4.5 Results

We developed a collaborative workshop to which organizations and active software engineers were invited. During the workshop we validated the first version of KUALI-BEH and we had the chance to try out its elements one by one.

The feedback received was extremely valuable input with which to improve KUALI-BEH and bridge the gap between theory and practice. We should also mention the participants' active contribution and involvement which helped establish a confident environment in which to share opinions and criticize KUALI-BEH.

This collaborative workshop was the closure to the second engineering cycle and the suggestions obtained served as a first step toward developing an improved version of KUALI-BEH.

5 Family of Case Studies

In order to prove the usefulness and sufficiency of the framework and its common concepts, KUALI-BEH was validated using three case studies.

During each case study the practitioners defined their actual ways of working using KUALI-BEH, which is referred to as an authoring project. This section provides a detailed description of the case studies and their respective results.

5.1 General Considerations

The research question for the case studies was defined as follows: *Is KUALI-BEH suitable as regards defining practitioners' ways of working during software projects?*

Two more questions also proved to be relevant for the research:

1. Is the effort of applying KUALI-BEH suitable when carrying out an authoring project?
2. What is the value obtained by the organization after having defined its own practices and method?

These questions were used as a basis to define the objectives (Os) that are common to the three case studies, as follows:

- **O1:** To demonstrate the sufficiency of the KUALI-BEH elements in describing practitioners' ways of working.
- **O2:** To measure the feasibility of using the concept of Practice to express practitioners' tacit practices.
- **O3:** To identify the value obtained by the organization as a consequence of defining its own method composed of its own practices.

In order to decide whether or not the objective had been achieved, the following indicators (Is) were collected

- **I1:** Associated with O1, which was collected applying two surveys to practitioners.
- **I2:** Associated with O2, which was obtained by measuring the effort required by practitioners to document their ways of working.
- **I3:** Associated with O3, which was obtained by means of an interview during the Feedback step, in which practitioners expressed the benefits and drawbacks of structuring their ways of working using KUALI-BEH.

Each of the case studies is described in more detail in the following subsections.

5.2 Case Study 1: InfoBLOCK

The first case study (CS1) was carried out at InfoBLOCK1[1], a Mexican organization founded in 1997. InfoBLOCK's main activities involve hardware construction and software development.

[1] InfoBLOCK, http://www.infoblock.mx/.

Two of InfoBLOCK's general managers and two programmers participated in this case study. The programmers had spent between 1 and 3 years as active practitioners and reported having played the roles of Analyst, Tester, Project Manager and Programmer.

Background. Despite the soundness and constant growth of the organization, its managers were concerned about controlling the progress of projects in a more detailed way, but they did not have a defined development process. The needs expressed by the organization were consequently:

- To define the actual software development process followed in the organization.
- To be aware of what is being done by the work team at a particular moment during the development process.

The artifact to be validated using CS1 was the second version of KUALI-BEH, which was the output of the second engineering cycle, and had passed through the Collaborative Workshop presented in Sect. 4.

Design and Execution. The case study was designed as a sequence of the following seven steps:

1. Presentation of the case study. The research team presented the objectives of the case study to the InfoBLOCK team, after which KUALI-BEH and its elements were explained. This step took 90 min.
2. Description of practitioners' way of working. This step was carried out in one work session, during which the researcher guided the practitioners as regards the documentation of their first practice using the KUALI-BEH Practice template.
   This also served to gain an insight into the organization and identify the individual goals and daily responsibilities of the practitioners involved in the case study.
   After ensuring that the practitioners understood how to describe their ways of working using the concept of practice, the researcher assigned them activities that they should perform independently during the next step. This step took 120 min.
3. Authoring of practices.
   The InfoBLOCK team began the authoring of practices and the running of an internal project simultaneously. Throughout this phase, the communication between the team and the researcher was carried out by videoconferencing and email.
   The team completed the following tasks:
   (a) The practitioners documented their way of working using the Practice template. This was done before they executed the practice in the internal project.
   (b) The researcher then checked aspects of consistency between the KUALI-BEH concepts and what the team interpreted.
   (c) The researcher later suggested improvements that could be made to the use of concepts but not the way of working itself.
   (d) Finally, the practitioners discussed the suggestions and then generated the 1.0 version of the practice.

4. Implementation of documented practices.
   Owing to the fact that the case study was developed alongside a real project, the practitioners performed the practices almost immediately after documenting them. This resulted in adjustments being made to the initial version of the practices, which were carried out by following the same tasks developed in the previous step. During the three weeks of the project, 13 practices were identified, documented, implemented and adjusted by practitioners.
5. Composition of a method.
   After the practices had been documented, executed and adapted, the practitioners proceeded to compose a method that represented their actual way of working using the 13 practices created.
   The resulting method was then modified to achieve properties of coherency, consistency and sufficiency, thus attaining a well-formed method.
   The practitioners used the method template and the graphical representation of KUALI-BEH to complete this step.
6. Presentation of results and Feedback interview.
   This step consisted of a session in which the documented practices and the composed method were presented to the organization's members.
   During this meeting the researchers collected and registered orally-expressed lessons learned from this particular case study, such as suggestions for improvement, and the benefits and drawbacks of KUALI-BEH. The InfoBLOCK team also had the opportunity to think about their actual way of working and the improvements to be made in future projects.
7. Closure.
   At the phase of closure, the products eventually generated and the case study report were delivered to the InfoBLOCK team.

Analysis. At the end of this case study a method composed of 13 practices using KUALI-BEH was documented. According to the initial objectives of this case study the following results were obtained:

- O1. Based on the data collected by means of surveys and practitioners opinions, it was concluded that the elements of which KUALI-BEH consists were sufficient to describe the InfoBLOCK practitioners' way of working during the real project selected.
  Moreover, it was possible to observe that the common concepts were everyday concepts for practitioners, who used them in a natural and straightforward manner.
- O2. After considering the time and effort required by practitioners to understand KUALI-BEH, we were able to conclude that making practitioners' ways of working explicit in a short period of time was feasible. Except for the first practice, which required the researcher's support in documenting it, 12 more practices were expressed by the practitioners themselves without having to rethink the common concepts.
  The total effort required was 10 h, resulting in an average of less than 50 min per practice. It was also observed that a practice contained an average of between 3 and 4 activities.

Finally, documenting their way of working allowed the practitioners to identify work products that were generated during the project. A total of 28 work products were identified and grouped into 9 categories.

- O3. The organization obtained the first version of its actual software development method, allowed its managers to share it with others, and also planned to use it as the means to train new employees. More importantly, the managers now have a means to manage progress and control the projects using the authored practices, thus making it easier to distribute and measure the work.

Feedback and Improvements. The most important improvement made to the KUALI-BEH proposal was the adjustment of the practice template in order to make it more legible, and these changes were focused on the visual organization of its elements.

During the feedback meeting, InfoBLOCK's members expressed several beneficial aspects to the organization, highlighting the fact that they formalized their way of working. The points mentioned by them were:

- *"As a first result now there is clarity on how practitioners work, and they defined it by themselves."*
- *"Having the method defined, now it is possible to distribute it, among other members of the organization, and ask for improvements and unification of the working way".*
- *"With this (the method), that actually belongs to the organization, we will be able to teach and train in-house our new entrants".*
- *"KUALI- BEH brings order to disorder".*
- *"These (the practices) are guidelines that must be implemented in the organization".*
- *"The value of the case study rests with the practitioners themselves".*
- *"This allow us to reassess various aspects and things that are important for practitioners".*
- *"Using three levels, method– practice– activity, it was sufficient to express and control the work done in the project".*

The results of the case study, expressed by the organization's practitioners and heads during a feedback interview, were:

- *"KUALI-BEH is easy to understand and apply by practitioners" (four hours training and 6 h work to define a 13-practice method in a four week project).*
- *"Now we have explicit documentation of what we actually do, (which) means value for us (organization managers); these practices can be used to train new employees".*
- *"For us, KUALI-BEH (common) concepts are sufficient to express and model our different ways of working as methods composed by practices".*

Table 1 shows the summary of the case study.

Table 1. Summary of case study 1.

	InfoBLOCK
Size of project team	2 programmers
	2 directors
Previously adopted method or process	No
Organization core business process	Software development
Number of expressed practices	13
Total authoring effort (in hours)	**10**

5.3 Case Study 2: Entia

The second case study (CS2) was developed at Entia[2], a Mexican IT company that has been present in the industry since 2003 and has 20 employees. With the motivation to increase its projects' success rate, Entia developed ActiveAction, a game-centered intensive workshop which allows the organization to carry out the inception phase of its projects.

The general manager and a coach from Entia and two assistants from the research team took part in this case study.

Background. The game nature of ActiveAction and the constant on-the-fly adaptations had led to a rapid evolution of the workshop, one of whose consequences was the lack of documentation related to the workshop, while all the knowledge and techniques belonged to the people in charge and not to the organization.

The objective defined by the Entia general manager was therefore:

- To document each step of the workshop activities. The artifact to be validated using CS2 was the third version of KUALI-BEH, the output of the third engineering cycle, which involved CS1.

Design and Execution. The generic design of the family of case studies steps was adapted according to Entia's context. This case study was therefore divided into the following six steps:

1. On-site observation of the workshop.
   An on-site observation was conducted in order to understand the new game-based technique, its purpose and execution.
   It is important to mention that an ActiveAction workshop takes between 10 and 12 h, signifying that this step took 720 min.
2. Presentation of the case study.

[2] Entia, http://www.entia.com.mx/.

The objectives of the case study and KUALI-BEH were explained to the participants. This step took 60 min.

3. Description of practitioners' way of working.
   This step was identical to that in CS1, with the difference that the researcher, the general manager and the two assistants participated in it. This step took 60 min.
4. Authoring and adaptation of practices.
   During this phase the assistants identified the practices involved in the workshop, completing the same tasks defined in Step 3 of CS1, with the only difference that the assistants presented the practices to the general manager, who suggested modifications, which were applied and then generated using the 1.0 version of the practice. During the three months of the project, 19 practices were expressed by the assistants and were agreed upon by the game expert.
   The challenge of this step was to identify the inputs and results of each practice, since Entia used to manage all of them as one work product: a mind map.
5. Composition of a method.
   Having documented the practices, the method composition step was a relatively easy task, because it resulted in the practices being ordered one after another, like a waterfall approach.
6. Presentation of results and Closure.
   This step consisted of a session in which the documented practices and the composed method were presented to the Entia general manager.
   The main result of this case study was the "unusual" method and its practices, which was presented as a research paper [26] during the 9th International Conference on Evaluation of Novel Approaches to Software Engineering 2014 (ENASE'14) which took place in Lisbon, Portugal.

Analysis. At the end of this case study a method composed of 19 practices was documented using KUALI-BEH. According to the initial objectives the following results were obtained:

- O1. The data collected by means of the surveys and the assistants' opinions allowed the researchers to conclude that the elements of which KUALI-BEH is composed were sufficient to describe the game-based method.
- O2. In this case study the required authoring effort was 26 h, resulting in an average of 82 min per practice. It was concluded that expressing the workshop practices in a short period of time was feasible.
- O3. The only objective defined by Entia's general manager was that of documenting each step of the workshop activities, and this was fully achieved.
  Moreover, documenting the method reduced the possibility of variation and allowed Entia to identify ways in which to improve it and, more importantly, replicate it in affiliates.

Feedback and Improvements. On the one hand, this case study benefited Entia and allowed it to achieve important business goals in order to remain competitive. By publishing the paper at ENASE'14 Entia became more visible.

On the other hand, the KUALI-BEH proposal was improved and its usefulness was demonstrated in a context in which software development was not the main purpose.

Table 2 shows the summary of the case study.

Table 2. Summary of case study 2.

	Entia
Size of project team	1 director
	1 coach
	2 assistants
Previously adopted method or process	No
Organization core business process	Software projects design
Number of expressed practices	19
Authoring effort (in hours)	**26**

5.4 Case Study 3: Tic-Tac

The third case study (CS3) was developed at San Luis Potosi Superior Tech Institute (ITSSLP) in a software development entity called Tic-Tac. Tic-Tac was part of the Tech business incubator program. Two professors and two recently graduated systems engineers participated in this case study.

Background. The software development entity was carrying out projects without having a defined method or process that could be followed. The objectives defined by the professors in charge of coordinating the entity were therefore:

- To document their software development process.
- To train new work team members using the process defined.

The artifact to be validated using CS3 was the KUALI-BEH Authoring Extension, which was base lined on November 12th, 2012.

Design and Execution. In order to satisfy the needs defined by the ITSSLP team, this case study added another objective to the three previously defined in Sect. 5.1. The new objective was established as follows:

- **O4:** To measure the effort required to train a new work team member using the method defined.

The indicator that would demonstrate whether or not the objective had been achieved was the following:

- **I4:** Associated with O4, which was obtained by measuring the effort required by the practitioners to train a new work team member.

1. Presentation of the case study.
   The objectives of the case study and KUALI-BEH were explained. This step took 60 min.
2. Description of practitioners' way of working.
   The researcher and the ITSSLP team documented its first practice, as had occurred in CS1 and CS2. This step took 60 min.
3. Authoring of practices.
   The ITSSLP team carried out this step in the same way as that defined in CS1. This step resulted in 23 documented practices.
4. Composition of a method.
   After the practices had been documented, executed and adapted, the Tic-Tac method was composed. It will be noted that, unlike the other case studies, the ITSSLP proposed that their method be divided into phases.
5. Adaptation of the method.
   In order improve and adjust the method, some adaptation operations were applied. The ITSSLP team adjusted its method using the concatenation and combination operations defined in KUALI-BEH.
6. Presentation of results and Feedback interview.
   During this step, the documented practices and the composed method were presented to the ITSSLP authorities.
   The researchers used a videoconference to collect and register orally-expressed lessons learned from this particular case study, such as suggestions for improvement, along with the benefits and drawbacks of KUALI-BEH.
   Another result of this case study was the lessons learned by Tic-Tac, which were reported as a research paper [27] during the International Conference on Software Engineering Innovation and Research 2015 (CONISOFT'15) that took place in San Luis Potosí, Mexico.
7. Closure.
   The products generated and the report of the case study were delivered to the ITSSLP team.

Analysis. At the end of this case study a method that represented the ITSSLP software development entity's way of working was composed. The 23 authored practices and a list of required work products was also generated. According to the objectives of this case study, the following results were obtained:

- O1. The sufficiency of KUALI-BEH elements as regards describing the practitioners' way of working was confirmed. The results collected by the surveys demonstrated that it was possible and appropriate for practitioners to express their tacit practices using KUALI-BEH, and that its elements are understandable and useful.
- O2. In this case study the required effort was 44 h, resulting in an average of 115 min per practice. The professors in charge of the entity expressed satisfaction with the effort made.
- O3. A software development method was documented and served as basis for the execution of the new software projects carried out by the entity. At that moment, two

new projects were successfully developed and two new members were trained and integrated into the team.

- O4. The ITSSLP followed a seven-step strategy in order to incorporate two new members, and the time investment was 7 h. According to the professors, the strategy's success was primarily related to the participants' knowledge and skills.

Feedback and Improvements. This case study experience allowed us to improve KUALI-BEH and its Authoring Extension, and it more specifically permitted us to better define the states and transitions of the Practice Authoring and Method Authoring Alphas.

We additionally confirmed that two of the adaptation operations are suitable and have real meaning for practitioners, although it is still necessary to verify their usefulness in other projects.

The results of the case study, expressed by the work team and professors during the feedback interview, were:

- *"We were able to organize our way of working".*
- *"It allows us to complete a project properly, it was an important improvement when the team distributed tasks".*
- *"We also think that KUALI-BEH guides the practitioner and causes his/her better participation in a project".*
- *"In addition, it will serve to generate a repository of available methods and practices for different projects".*
- *"Team members can think and rethink about how they do things".*
- *"We observed that working with this methodology requires a culture of collaborative work".*

Table 3 shows the summary of the case study.

Table 3. Summary of case study 3.

	Tic-Tac
Size of project team	2 professors
	2 developers
Previously adopted method or process	No
Organization core business process	Software development
Number of expressed practices	23
Authoring effort (in hours)	**44**

5.5 Results

Conducting the case studies allowed us to learn many lessons, thus permitting us to improve KUALI-BEH and its validation process. The main lessons learned from these three case studies and the collaborative workshop concern the following issues:

A Tool is Required to Support the Practice-Authoring Process. The use of the Track changes function of the word processor permitted the come-and-go of authored practices between practitioners and researchers to become a valuable learning process. However, managing the control version strategy of each practice, making adaptations and sharing practices became more difficult processes. At this point the need for a tool that would automate this process became essential.

Support from Managers and Commitment from Practitioners is Necessary. The validation process is a process that involves many variables that must be controlled. On the one hand, it requires the organization's interest in the proposal and an understanding of how it will deal with its particular needs. On the other hand, the people in charge of applying the proposal must see benefits reflected in their daily work if bias and reluctance are to be avoided. A two-level support from managers and practitioners is therefore mandatory, and if either of these levels is not committed, the case study will not be possible.

Finding Suitable Projects in Order to Validate the Proposal. It is clear that support and enthusiasm are not the only ingredients needed to carry out a case study. The proposal needs to be validated in a real context and in a suitable project. While the research team is almost always available and open to the idea of conducting case studies, the organization needs to estimate the time, effort and risks of being involved

Table 4. Effort by step in each case study.

	CS1	CS2	CS3
On-site observation	–	720	–
Presentation of the CS	90	60	60
Way of working description	120	60	60
Authoring of practices	390	600	2520
Implementation of practices		–	
Composition of a method		120	
Training new members	–	–	420
Results and Feedback	60	60	60
Closure	30	30	30
Total effort (in hours)	**11.5**	**27.5**	**52.5**
Practices authored	13	19	23
Authoring effort (in hours)	**10**	**26**	**44**
Average effort per practice	46.2	82.1	114.8

beforehand, which may lead to time matching problems between the researcher and the organization's project.

Identifying Improvements and Adjustments to Artifact. The case studies have allowed us to improve many aspects of KUALI-BEH, thus making it a solid and accepted proposal that now belongs to an international standard.

We were also able to establish that the effort made (see Table 4) permitted a high ROI for both parties: practitioners and researchers.

5.6 Threats to Validity and Limitations

In order to avoid threats to validity, various factors were considered in the collaborative workshop and the three case studies.

Construct Validity. Multiple data sources were used in order to provide evidence and respond to the research question. The sources used were interviews, direct observations, surveys and work artifacts, thus covering the three degrees defined by [19].

Moreover, the validity of the construct (or artifact) was ensured since it was created following the mandatory requirements requested by the OMG in the FACESEM RFP. It was also validated many times by the OMG Analysis and Design Task Force.

Internal Validity. The case studies' results demonstrated that the objective for which KUALI-BEH was created was achieved, thus allowing us to accomplish our goals and the participants' needs.

Different causal relations were examined:

- The surveys' trustworthiness. The data collected with surveys is closely related to the practitioners' experience. In these case studies, the participants' experience covered the "juniors" through "seniors" classification.
- The number of participants. Although the number of participants is not large, we can state that the sample is representative of the profile of practitioners working in small software organizations.
- The participants' age, education and experience. These factors could have affected whether they were in favor or against KUALI-BEH. However, the sample of participants was diverse.

After having analyzed these factors, all of them were disallowed, and as a result we have been able to determine that the implementation of KUALI-BEH in the case studies allowed us to achieve the case studies' objectives.

External Validity. In spite of the limited number of organizations that participated in the case studies, we can state that each organization can be categorized as a typical software developer entity. The three participating organizations shared the main characteristics of very small entities in charge of software development endeavors, which is the target audience of the KUALI-BEH proposal.

The selection of the participants was not intentional: the organizations that participated in the case studies expressed their interest in participating.

It is important to highlight that the methods that were expressed using KUALI-BEH were the actual ways of working of active practitioners involved in real projects.

We consequently believe that the sample and the context of this research were representative. What is more, thanks to the scopes of OMG and SEMAT, the results obtained were contrasted with researchers and practitioners from other countries who backed it up.

We therefore conclude that the results obtained make it possible to generalize about the subject being researched.

Reliability. The case studies were carried out by two researchers and the results were constantly triangulated to third parties, such as colleagues and members of the research group. The participants were additionally informed of the results and lessons learned, which were and extensively disseminated in each of the case study reports delivered to them.

A detailed plan that served as guidance for the case studies is also available, thus making its replication possible.

In order to improve the validity of the case studies, it was compared with the checklists provided by [19].

The following approaches were also taken into account:

- The prolonged involvement, mainly in CS2 and CS3 (3 and 6 months respectively), which allowed us to develop a trusting relationship with the participants, thus making the collection of data an unobstructed process and, in general, to develop the case studies in a pleasant atmosphere.
- During CS2 we had two assistants who participated in the data collection process, thus allowing us to analyze different data sources, such as interviews, surveys and direct observations. This circumstance made triangulation possible.
- Peer debriefing took place in all three case studies, owing to the fact that the case studies were carried out by two researchers. In addition, the findings and results were periodically discussed with the other members of the research group.
- The work products and documents generated during each case study were given to the participants so that they could review them. This took place at minimum after the finalization of each step of the study, but the member checking action was carried out at any moment if deemed to be necessary.
- A version control strategy was defined from the very beginning of each case study. Given the technological background of all the participants, the audit trail mechanism was easy to follow and its application was very successful.

Finally, the limitations of the case studies can be summarized in two points:

- The sample size is small, which therefore limits the power of generalization. It is necessary to replicate the case studies with bigger populations.
- Bias in the case studies could have occurred and been related to the participants' feeling of being observed and evaluated. This may have led to an alteration in their actual way of working.

6 Lessons Learned

After three years of continuous work, we can conclude that the TAR is a valuable research method for the purposes of this research. Its application, in combination with case studies, allowed us to validate and improve KUALI-BEH after each engineering cycle.

The iterative approach of TAR allowed us to obtain continuous feedback about and validation of the artifact in a real context and these are, in our opinion, the main advantages of the TAR.

As researchers we had the opportunity to develop the three roles identified by Wieringa: Designer, Helper and Researcher. Starting as designers, we created an artifact whose objective was to resolve a type of problems present in the industry. During the engineering cycles we inserted the artifact into organizations which were affected by this type of problem. In order to apply the proposed treatment, and so acting as helpers, we used the artifact and assessed its functioning.

As researchers we later took advantage of the lessons learned and analyzed the resulting effects, the value achieved and the trade-offs obtained with the objective of adjusting and improving the artifact.

Validating the artifact in a real context allowed us to gain experience and generate knowledge through the lessons learned which, according to [28] are the principal means of obtaining knowledge in the Software Engineering discipline.

TAR also provided the organizations involved in this research with benefits. At the end of the case studies we were able to establish that:

- Each organization had achieved the stated objectives.
- The practitioners had been trained in a new technology, in this case KUALI-BEH, at no "extra" cost.
- The case study results were used to achieve business goals, signifying that the artifact was useful and applicable to their particular contexts.
- Collaboration and partnership ties were promoted between the university and organizations.

Finally, we can define TAR as a research method which gives researchers a valuable opportunity to learn and obtain knowledge by applying theories in practice in order to solve real problems by solving real problems.

7 Conclusions

This paper presented an innovative research strategy that is a combination of TAR and Case Study methods. The case studies were integrated into the engineering cycles of TAR. Following these engineering cycles gave the present research a solid inner structure and continuity. Besides, it brought about a valuable validation of the artifact in the real context.

Additionally, taking this research strategy as a guide had a positive side effect on minimizing the disadvantages of a full empirical study, which according to [11] can be disruptive and time-consuming for the companies involved.

The cyclic nature of this combined method helped to improve the artifact: critical reviews, by theoreticians and practitioners from OMG, SEMAT and other research groups, provided fruitful feedback that was applied during the treatment design phase of each next engineering cycle. Moreover, being involved in the OMG standardization process resulted to be a valuable experience which is reported in [9].

The real context case studies helped to establish the artifact's sensitivity and to assess its expected value for stakeholders. Having a theoretically-proved artifact immersed into a real world scenario is an advantage of collaboration between academy and industry, which is an ideal way of generating new knowledge.

This research strategy benefited the involved companies as well. They obtained a clearer vision of their processes and were able to manage them more efficiently. Also, training of new members became possible in fewer hours. Consequently, more maturity and more profits are perceptible, which specially the case with CS2.

Thus, this research strategy allowed us to generate the KUALI-BEH framework in the first place, to enrich it and take it through a validation process later on, and to achieve the objective and goals set for this research as a whole.

In conclusion, we affirm that combining TAR and Case Studies was a successful experience applied to the Software Engineering context, and it is a feasible resource for bridging the gap between academy and industry.

Acknowledgements. This work has been funded by GEODAS-BC project (Ministerio de Economía y Competitividad and FEDER, TIN2012-37493-C03-01); GLOBALIA project (Consejería de Educación, Ciencia y Cultura (Junta de Comunidades de Castilla La Mancha) and FEDER, PEII11-0291-5274); SDGear project (TSI-100104-2014-4), framed under the ITEA 2 Call 7, and co-funded by "Ministerio de Industria, Energía y Turismo (Plan Nacional de Investigación Científica, Desarrollo e Innovación Tecnológica 2013-2016) and FEDER"; the Graduate Science and Engineering Computing (UNAM) and CONACYT (México).

References

1. Edwards, J.S.: Managing software engineers and their knowledge. In: Aurum, A., Jeffery, R., Wohlin, C., Handzic, M. (eds.) Managing Software Engineering Knowledge, pp. 5–27. Springer, Heidelberg (2003)
2. Bjørnson, F.O., Dingsøyr, T.: Knowledge management in software engineering: a systematic review of studied concepts, findings and research methods used. Inf. Softw. Technol. **50**(11), 1055–1068 (2008)
3. Johnson, P., Ekstedt, M., Jacobson, I.: Where's the theory for software engineering? IEEE Softw. **29**(5), 96 (2012)
4. Jacobson, I., Ng, P.-W., McMahon, P., Spence, I., Lidman, S.: The essence of software engineering: the SEMAT kernel. Queue **10**(10), 40–51 (2012)
5. Jacobson, I., Meyer, B., Soley, R.: The SEMAT initiative: A call for action (2009)
6. A foundation for the agile creation and enactment of software engineering methods RFP. Technical report, Object Management Group, Needham, USA (2011)

7. ESSENCE– Kernel and language for software engineering methods. Technical report, Object Management Group, Needham, USA (2013)
8. KUALI-BEH– Software project common concepts. Technical report, Object Management Group, Needham, USA (2012)
9. Morales-Trujillo, M., Oktaba, H., Piattini, M.: The making-of an OMG standard. Comput. Stand. Interfaces **42**, 84–94 (2015)
10. Wang, Y.: Software Engineering Foundations: A Software Science Perspective, 1st edn. Auerbach Publications, Boston (2007)
11. Harrison, R., Badoo, N., Barry, E., Biffl, S., Parra, A., Winter, B., Wst, J.: Directions and methodologies for empirical software engineering research. Empirical Softw. Eng. **4**(4), 405–410 (1999)
12. Belady, L., Lehman, M.: A model of large program development. IBM Syst. J. **15**(3), 225–252 (1976)
13. Wieringa, R.: Empirical research methods for technology validation: Scaling up to practice. J. Syst. Softw. **95**, 19–31 (2014)
14. Perry, D., Porter, A., Votta, L.: Empirical studies of software engineering: a roadmap. In Proceedings of the ICSE 2000, pp. 345–355. ACM (2000)
15. Genero, M., Cruz-Lemus, J., Piattini, M.: Métodos de Investigación en Ingeniería del Software. RA-MA Editorial (2014)
16. Wohlin, C., Runeson, P., Höst, M., Ohlsson, M.C., Regnell, B., Wesslén, A.: Experimentation in Software Engineering: An Introduction. Springer-Verlag, Heidelberg (2012)
17. Kitchenham, B., Pfleeger, S.: Personal opinion surveys. In: Shull, F., Singer, J., Sjberg, D. (eds.) Guide to Advanced Empirical Software Engineering, pp. 63–92. Springer, London (2008)
18. Yin, R.: Case Study Research: Design and Methods. Applied Social Research Methods, 4th edn. SAGE Publications, Thousand Oaks (2009)
19. Runeson, P., Host, M., Rainer, A., Regnell, B.: Case Study Research in Software Engineering: Guidelines and Examples. Wiley, Hoboken (2012)
20. Medeiros, P., Horta-Travassos, G.: Action research can swing the balance in experimental software engineering. Adv. Comput. **83**, 205–276 (2011)
21. Kitchenham, B., Charters, S.: Guidelines for performing systematic literature reviews in software engineering. Technical report, EBSE-2007-01 (2007)
22. Wieringa, R., Moralı, A.: Technical action research as a validation method in information systems design science. In: Peffers, K., Rothenberger, M., Kuechler, B. (eds.) DESRIST 2012. LNCS, vol. 7286, pp. 220–238. Springer, Heidelberg (2012)
23. Engelsman, W., Wieringa, R.: Goal-oriented requirements engineering and enterprise architecture: two case studies and some lessons learned. In: Regnell, B., Damian, D. (eds.) REFSQ 2011. LNCS, vol. 7195, pp. 306–320. Springer, Heidelberg (2012)
24. Van Strien, P.: Towards a methodology of psychological practice the regulative cycle. Theor. Psychol. **7**(5), 683–700 (1997)
25. Schramm, W.: Notes on Case Studies of Instructional Media Projects [microform]/Wilbur Schramm. ERIC Clearinghouse (1971)
26. Morales-Trujillo, M., Oktaba, H., González, J.: Improving software projects inception phase using games: ActiveAction Workshop. In Proceedings of the ENASE 2014, pp. 180–187 (2014)

27. Arroyo-López, E., Ríos-Silva, T., Morales-Trujillo, M., Rico-Martínez, A., Oktaba, H.: Expresando Nuestra Manera de Trabajo con KUALI-BEH: Lecciones Aprendidas por Tic-Tac-S. Congreso Internacional de Investigación e Innovación en Ingeniería de Software (CONISOFT'15), Editorial UABC, pp. 25–32 (2015). ISBN: 978-0-692-43292-1
28. Endres, A., Rombach, D.: A Handbook of Software and Systems Engineering: Empirical Observations, Laws and Theories. Fraunhofer IESE Series on Software Engineering. Pearson/Addison Wesley (2003)

Taking Contextual Parameters into Account and Using RDF Patterns for the Semantic Web Image Annotation

Rim Teyeb Jaouachi[1,2(✉)], Mouna Torjmen Khemakhem[1], Maher Ben Jemaa[1], Ollivier Haemmerle[2], and Nathalie Hernandez[2]

[1] ReDCAD Laboratory, National School of Engineers of Sfax, University of Sfax, Sfax, Tunisia
{rima.teyeb,maher.benjemaa}@gmail.com, mouna.torjmen@redcad.org
[2] IRIT, University of Toulouse - Jean Jaures, Toulouse, France
{ollivier.haemmerle,nathalie.hernandez}@univ-tlse2.fr

Abstract. Semantic annotation of web resources presents a solution to pass from traditional web to future semantic web. Indeed, it is a process which allows to formalize extracted interpretations from web resources. In this paper, we present a new method allowing the semantic annotation of web extracted from the web. The originality of our approach lies in two points. The first point is the use of several contextual factors surrounding the image to annotate it. The second point is the construction and the instantiation of RDF (Resource Description Framework) patterns. Each pattern presents a group of information related to threaten domain. In our experimentations,we are interesting to cinema domain.

Keywords: Semantic annotation · RDF patterns · Information retrieval · Domain ontology

1 Introduction

According to Tim Berners-Lee, the original creator of the World Wide Web, "The Semantic Web is an extension of the current Web in which information receives a well-defined meaning, improving opportunities for collaborative works between computers and people" [1]. The main idea behind this kind of web is to weave a web that not only links documents to each other but also that recognises the meaning of the information in those documents. The aim of Tim Berners-Lee was to transform the current web from a set of interconnected data by simples links semantically isolated into a huge mass of information linked in a semantic manner.

In other words, the semantic web consists in adding formal semantics to the web content in order to allow a more efficient access and management. This is possible thanks to the improvement of the capability of computers to manipulate data meaningfully by providing meaning into web resources[1]. In doing so,

[1] A web resource is an entity that can be described on the web. Each resource is identified by a unique URI (Uniform Resource Identifier).

S. Hammoudi et al. (Eds.): ICEIS 2015, LNBIP 241, pp. 328–344, 2015.
DOI: 10.1007/978-3-319-29133-8_16

external software agents have to carry out complex tasks on behalf of a human user and to improve the degree of cooperation between humans and computers.

However, the transformation from traditional web to semantic web depends on the presence of a critical mass of metadata [2] corresponding to web resources. The acquisition of these metadata is a major challenge for the semantic web community. As a solution, many manual tools [3–6], semi-automatic tools [1,7,8] and automatic tools [9,10] for semantic annotation have been developed.

In our case, we are interested in the semantic annotation of web images. With the presence of a huge number of web images, many approaches were developed. There are many approaches based on the image content (color, texture, etc.) in order to produce annotations and only a few works using the contextual factors of the image to annotate it without human intervention.

Our goal is to obtain a fully automatic approach for web images annotation based on contextual factors such as image caption, document title and surrounding text. The main idea is to generate an RDF[2] graph from each contextual factor. The elementary RDF graph (concerning one contextual factor) is composed of concepts and instances of concepts linked between them by semantic relations. After the generation of all elementary RDF graphs from all the contextual factors, the next step consists in combining them into a global RDF graph which is considered as an image annotation.

The originality of our work is the use of a set of RDF patterns and a domain ontology in order to guide the step of annotation.

This paper is organised as follows: Sect. 2 reviews the related works. Section 3 details the approach we propose for the image annotation. Section 4 finally demonstrates the obtained results.

2 Related Works

2.1 Approaches for Images Annotation

We can classify the existing approaches into two categories: (1) Content-Based Image Annotation; and (2) Context-based Image Annotation.

Several works have studied Content-Based Image Annotation. Among these approaches, we find [11–15]. The main idea of this type of approaches is to associate a semantic description with the image in totality or to describe a specific region of the image. [16] shows a good classification of these different approaches. Using the content of the image for annotation purpose resolves, partially, the Semantic Gap Problem defined by [17].

Only a few works use contextual factors of the image in order to annotate it. Among these approaches, we find [18]. This approach was proposed in the project Esperonto. It was based on natural language techniques, ontologies and other knowledge bases.

The approach proposed in [19] used two contextual factors associated with web images. It exploited the caption and keywords associated with the image in order to construct a graph representing its semantics.

[2] http://www.w3.org/tr/2004/rec-rdf-primer-20040210/.

2.2 Approaches of Semantic Relations Extraction

In order to determinate semantic relations between concepts, various approaches are proposed. Among these approaches, we find approaches that use statistical techniques as the approach of [20] which exploits the cooccurrence terms. Besides the statistical methods, we found approaches that are based on syntax such as approaches in [21–23]. The approach presented in [22] aims to annotate medical entities and identify semantic relations between them. MeatAnnot [23] proposes the MeatAnnot plateform. This approach uses UMLS [24], a meta-thesaurus biomedical.

The approach of Daniel Gerber et al. [25] is among new approaches interested to semantic relations extraction. This approach aims to extract RDF triples from unstructured text. It is based on the use of bootstrapping system datA the web (BOA) System.

ReVerb[3] is another example of tools that automatically identifies and extracts binary relationships from English sentences. It is designed for web-scale information extraction.

2.3 SPARQL Query Generation Using Patterns

Our work is inspired by the SWIP system presented in [26]. This system allows the translation of natural language queris into formal ones, expressed in SPARQL. The translation process is done thanks to the use of query patterns, each pattern representing a family of typical queries. After the selection of the pattern which is the best match to the natural language query, that pattern is modified in order to build the SPARQL query corresponding to the natural query. The formal definition of a pattern is given in [27]. An extension of that work has been presented in [28]. It allows the generation of SPARQL queries based on different ontologies of a same domain, thanks to ontology alignments.

Even if our goal is to annotate documents instead of querying them, we propose to use patterns in our work. These patterns are deeply inspired by the patterns defined in [27], but they are used for multimedia document annotation purpose. The patterns are adapted in order to take into account the notions related to images. The details of our approach is presented in Sect. 3.

3 Our Approach for Semantic Annotation of Images

In this section, we present our approach aiming at annotating web images. Our idea is to use RDF patterns in order to guide the extraction of relevant information from contextual factors surrounding the image to be annotated.

Among these factors, we cite (1) the image caption; (2) the paragraph title; (3) the text around the image; (4) the hyperlinks between documents containing images (if they exist); (5) the image name (if it is significant) and (6) the table content if the images are grouped in this structure.

[3] http://reverb.cs.washington.edu.

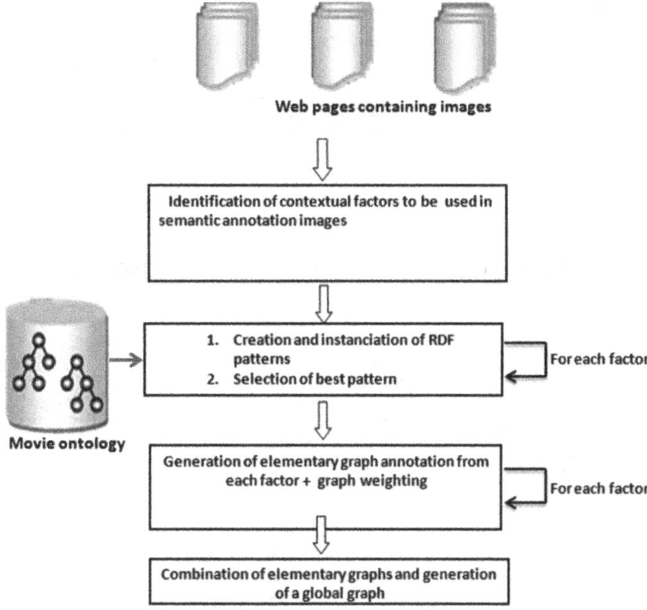

Fig. 1. General approach overview.

After the choice of the factors to be used, the next step is to apply, for each factor, a set of processings. The goal of this step is to instantiate the RDF patterns and to select the best instantiated pattern. More details about our approach can be found in [29]. Figure 1 shows an overview of the proposed approach.

In this paper, we will focus on the step of the definition, the creation, the instantiation and the selection of RDF patterns.

3.1 Definition of RDF Patterns

Our definition of a pattern is inspired from [26].

A pattern p is composed of 5 elements (G, Q, SP, Img, S):

- G is a connected RDF graph which describes the general structure of the pattern to be instantiated. Such a graph is composed of triples according to the structure presented in Fig. 2. This structure is formed by a subject (which can be a concept or an instance of a concept), a predicate and an object (which can be a concept or an instance of a concept or an image);
- Q is a subset of elements of G, these elements are considered to be characteristics of the pattern. Such an element can be a class or an object property or an image of G;
- SP is the set of sub-patterns sp of p;
- Img is the set of distinct images called qualifying images present in the pattern. An image can illustrate an element of the pattern;
- S is a description of the meaning of the pattern in natural language.

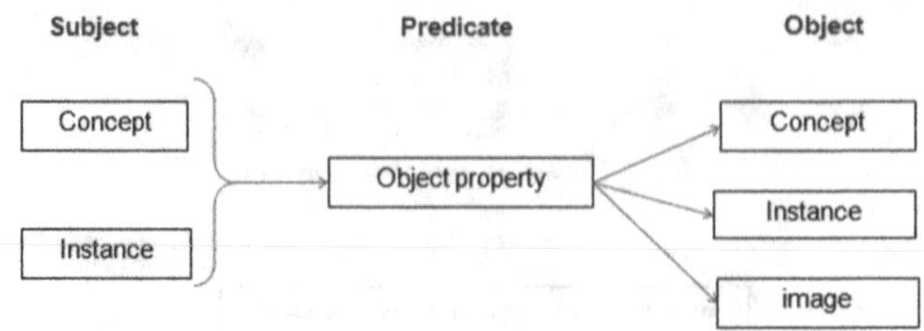

Fig. 2. Triples constituting the graph patterns.

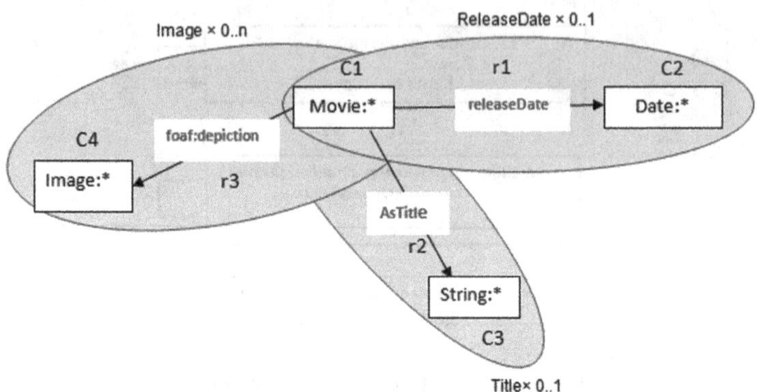

Fig. 3. Example of a pattern used for the annotation.

Example. Figure 3 shows an example of an RDF pattern used for the step of annotation. It is composed of three sub-patterns which are [Movie, releaseDate,Date], [Movie,AsTitle,String] and [Movie,foaf:depection,Image]. All of them are optional because they can remain uninstantiated.

Sub-patterns [Movie,releaseDate,Date] and [Movie,AsTitle,String] are not repeatable and have as cardinalities *ReleaseDate*0..1* and *Title*0..1* respectively with 0 is the minimal cardinality and 1 is the maximum cardinality. Indeed, a movie has one title and one release date.

However, the sub-pattern [Movie,foaf:depiction,Image] is repeatable and has as cardinality *image*0..n*, n being the maximum cardinality.

3.2 Creation of RDF Patterns

In order to annotate web images, we define some RDF patterns. Each pattern represents a prototype of a group of information related to the domain studied. In our case, we used six patterns considered as important by the experts of the domain. Each pattern is centered around a vertex which is the Movie concept and formed by a set of sub-patterns.

A sub-pattern can be defined as a simple triple with the subject which is an instance of the Movie concept (eg. triple [Movie:*,hasSoundmix,Sound-Mix:*] with Movie:* is a vertex of the pattern) or a set of triples whith one of them which is linked at the vertex of the pattern (eg. triples [Movie:*,

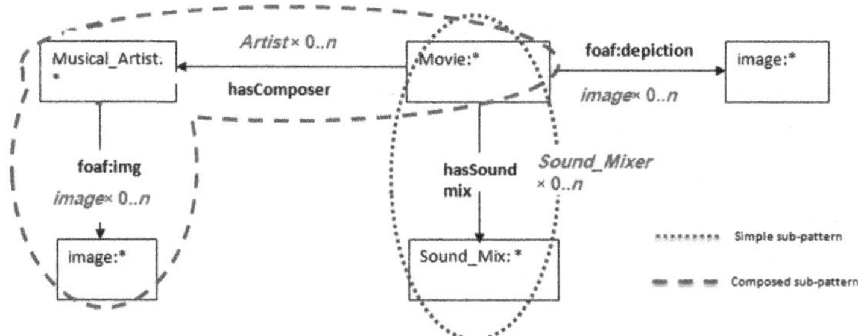

Fig. 4. Examples of sub-patterns.

hasComposer,Musical_Artist:*] and [Musical_Artist:*,foaf:img,image:*]). The Fig. 4 reinforces the two definitions.
In order to define formally a pattern, we need three type of vocabularies:

- The first vocabulary allows the description of the patterns in general. Indeed, we use the *patters ontology*[4] proposed in [26]. This ontology defines the grammar allowing the representation of patterns.
- The second vocabulary is the vocabulary of the domain addressed in the context of the image. It is necessary to associate each element or relationship of a pattern with a concept or a relationship belonging to the domain ontology used for the evaluation. In our case, we use the domain ontology named Movie ontology which will be presented in Sect. 4.1. We use properties of this ontology to link the various properties used in the construction of the RDF patterns. For example, we have exploited the properties ***releaseDate*** from the Movie ontology to specify the predicate between Movie concept and Date concept and consequently to construct a sub-pattern of the pattern shown in Fig. 3.
- The third vocabulary is necessary to describe all the elements of the RDF patterns in relation to images. Indeed, by this vocabulary, we link an image to the appropriate element of the pattern. In our case, we use two properties from the foaf project: *foaf:depiction* and *foaf:img*. The first property represents a relationship between a thing and an image that depicts it, and the second property relates a Person to an image that represents him/her.
  To conclude, this step allows us to obtain several patterns that have to be instantiated based on any document related to the domain (cinema in our case).

Example. Figure 5 shows an example of RDF pattern according to the formal definition and uses the three vocabularies mentioned above.

This pattern is composed of two sub-patterns: location and country. The three numbers after the name of each sub-pattern are respectively: the minimal cardinality, the maximal cardinality and the identifying of the element in order to instantiate the concerned pattern.

[4] http://swip.univ-tlse2.fr/SwipWebClient/welcome.html.

```
prefixes
    www:                "http://www.movieontology.org/2009/11/09/"
    movieontology:      "http://www.movieontology.org/2009/10/01/movieontology.owl#"
    page:               "http://dbpedia.org/page/"
    ontology:           "http://dbpedia.org/ontology/"
    foaf:               "http://xmlns.com/foaf/0.1/"
end prefixes

pattern movie_location_country

        [ 1_www:Movie     2_movieontology:hasFilmLocation
3_page:Place;
        3                 4_foaf:depiction                        5_foaf:Image;
    ]location:0..1/5
        [ 1               6_movieontology:hasReleasingCountry
7_ontology:Country;
        3                 8_foaf:depiction                        9_foaf:Image;
    ]country:0..1/9

    sentence
        -1- -location-[" located in "-3-" which has picture "-5-] -country-["
released in "-7-" which has picture "-9-]
    end sentence
end pattern
```

Fig. 5. Examples of pattern presented in formal definition.

3.3 Instanciation of RDF Patterns

The purpose of defining and using RDF patterns is to guide the annotation procedure. We are not willing to extract all the pieces of information contained in a document but only to extract the pieces of information which allow the instantiation of the patterns.

For example, by using the pattern shown in Fig. 3, we want to extract triples from a document that can be instance of one of the three sub-patterns. In other words, we look for the date of the Movie, its title and its images.

This is possible by the following steps that will be repeated as many times as the number of sub-patterns:

- The first step consists in identifying the predicate of the sub-pattern. This step is based on the application of extraction rules that will be described in Sect. 4.2.
- Once found, the second step consists in identifying the subject and the predicate related by the identified relationship. This step is based on the identification of instances forming two approximates of the identified relationship.
- The third step consists in linking the web image to the appropriate element of the pattern. This step is based on the analysis of the image caption, if there is any indication in the text describing the instance of the concept concerned by the image.

We present in Fig. 6 the instantiation of the pattern shown in Fig. 3 by using the text and the image.

3.4 Selecting the Best Instantiated Patterns to Represent the Text

The purpose of using patterns is to generate an RDF annotation for the web document containing the image. Our strategy is to instantiate patterns and then to choose the best instantiated pattern.

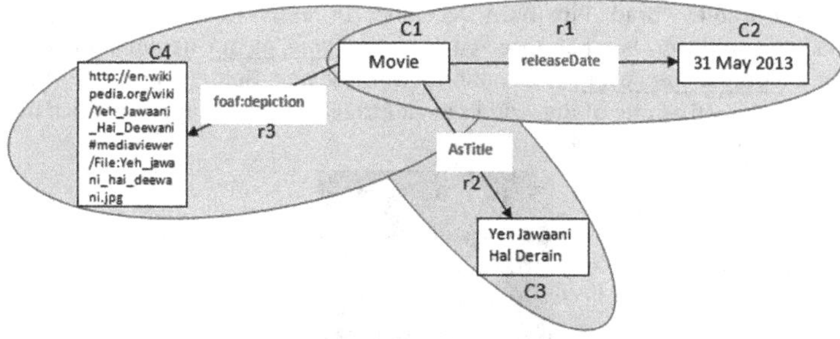

Fig. 6. Instantiation of the pattern presented in Fig. 3.

```
Rule:isAwardedwith
(
( (
 {Token.stem == "receiv"})


 ({Lookup.majorType == number} {SpaceToken})?
 ({Token.category == NP} {SpaceToken})?
 ({Token.category == NP}{SpaceToken})?

 ({Token.stem == "award"})?
)
|
(
  {Token.lemma == "win"}
 )

(
  {Token.lemma == "earn"}
 )
)

:is_Awarded_with -->
:is_Awarded_with.RelationShip = {kind = "is_Awarded_with", rule=isAwardedwith}
```

Fig. 7. Rule example of JAPE grammar.

In order to rank the instantiated patterns, we focus on a set of criteria such as recall, precision, number of correct extracted triples, number of automatic extracted triples. It is possible to use the three first criteria only if we have a manual annotation as reference. However the last criteria is independent of manual annotation.

In this paper, we present the results based on the number of automatic extracted triples. The results using this criteria are presented in Sect. 4. As a reference, we will compare the results obtained by using our approach with manual ranking.

4 Experimentations and Evaluation

4.1 The Movie Ontology

Like in most research domains, there are ontologies which are used in order to represent, share and reuse knowledge. Ontologies contain an effective structure

William Bradley "Brad" Pitt (born December 18, 1963) is an American actor and film producer. Pitt has received four Academy Award nominations and five Golden Globe Award nominations, winning one Golden Globe. He has been described as one of the world's most attractive men, a label for which he has received substantial media attention.

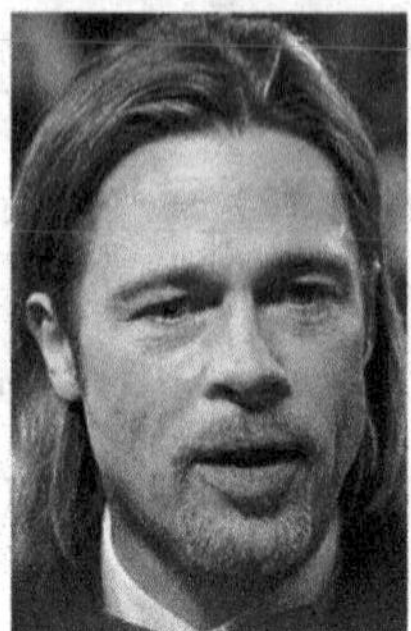

Fig. 8. Example of web image with surrounding text.

of the domain knowledge which improves the efficiency of the retrieval system. The semantic web techniques and technologies provide a manner to construct and use web resources by attaching semantic information to them.

In our work, we are interested in improving the management of multimedia information by means of knowledge representation, indexing and retrieval. Among the multimedia entertainment, cinema stands a good position so that we are interested, especially, in the cinema domain.

In the literature, there is an ontology of the cinema field which describes movie scenes. It is called "Movie ontology"[5] and it is developed by the Department of Informatics at the University of Zurich. This ontology contains concept hierarchies for movie categorisation, instances of concepts and relations between concepts.

It contains distinct concepts like Award, Certification, Film, Person (Actor, Actress, Writer, Producer, etc.).

4.2 Extraction Rules for Semantic Relation Detection

In order to instantiate the RDF patterns, we use the NLP (Natural Language Processing) tools, GATE platform [1], Porter stemmer [30] and our own extensions dedicated to determinate the semantic relations for different patterns.

In this step, we used JAPE language [1]. It is a language based on regular expressions. Using extraction rules, we try to detect an instance of the Movie ontology relations (adapted as a predicate for RDF pattern) and to detect instances of concepts linked by this relationship.

[5] http://www.movieontology.org/.

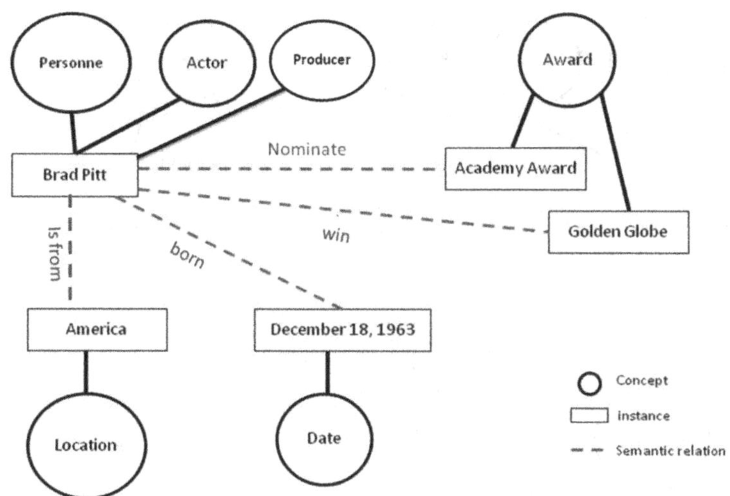

Fig. 9. The manual RDF graph of Fig. 4.

Such a rule represents a set of phases, each of which consists of a set of pattern/action rules. It has always two sides: Left (LHS: Left-Hand Side) and Right (RHS:Rigth-Hand Side). The LHS of the rule contains the identified annotation pattern that may contain regular expressions and the RHS outlines the action to be taken on the detected pattern and consists of annotation manipulation statements. The example below (Fig. 7) shows a grammar which allows the detection of instances of the semantic relation "isAwardedWith".

In the Fig. 7, we find an example of a rule that is labeled **isAwardedWith**. "Token.stem" corresponds to the lemmatised form of the word, "Token.category" corresponds to the grammatical category of the word, "Token.Kind" design the kind of word. It means the word represents a number or a simple word or a punctuation. "Lookup.majortype" means that the word is considered as the default concept. "Lookup.minortype" corresponds to the specific categories of the word. `''|''` means that there are many alternatives. `''-->''` is the boundary of the LHS rule.

Our relation will be part of the annotation properties that can be seen in GATE. This is possible using: is_Awarded_with.RelationShip = kind = "is_Awarded_with", rule= isAwardedwith.

4.3 Efficacy of Using Extraction Rules for Semantic Relation Detection

In this section, we present reasons on which we are based for using extraction rules and Domain ontology to extract semantics relations and later in the creation of RDF patterns instead of using simple grammatical functions.

We present a comparison between a previous work based on the treatment of grammatical functions exploiting the Gate Predicate-Argument Extractor (PAX) [2,29] and our actual work based on extraction rules.

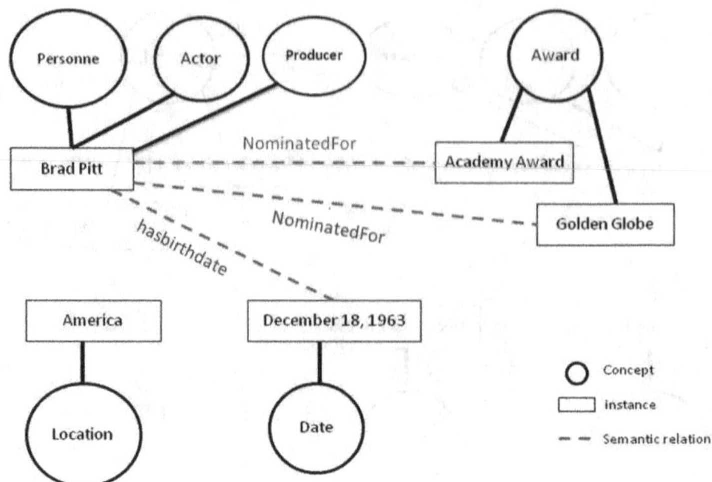

Fig. 10. The automatic RDF graph of Fig. 4 generated using extraction patterns.

We used, for this purpose, a corpus composed of 50 wikipedia pages related to cinema domain and. In this experiments, we have used only surrounding text of images to construct the RDF graph.

As a reference, we annotate the corpus manually and we generated RDF graph corresponding to semantic annotation of each image. Figure 9 shows an example of manual annotation graph associated to Fig. 8.

Figure 10 illustrates the automatic annotation of the image shown in Fig. 4 using extraction patterns written in JAPE language.

To make a comparison, we divided our corpus into two parts. The first part is devoted into learning phase (consisting of 40 documents in our corpus = 80 % from our corpus) and the second part is reserved for testing and determination of results (consisting of 40 documents in our corpus = 10 % from our corpus).

The application of the cross validation in our corpus generates five learning corpus and five test corpus. For each test documents, we use the appropriate corpus for the learning phase in order to determinate the suitable extraction patterns.

Results obtained for this step is regrouped in the Table 1.

Table 1. Obtained results using extraction patterns.

Test corpus	MRs	Aut.Ex.R	C.Ex.R	%P	%R
Test corpus 1	90	43	41	0,87	0,53
Test corpus 2	75	20	17	0.82	0,24
Test corpus 3	75	28	27	0.87	0,35
Test corpus 4	51	37	34	0,93	0,74
Test corpus 5	70	36	34	0,96	0,49

Table 2. Generated results using patterns and PAX component.

Manual relations	370	Manual relations	370
PAX extracted relations	219	Extracted relations using patterns	219
PAX correct relations	145	Correct relations using patterns	153
% Precision using PAX	0.59	Precision using patterns	0.9
% Recall using PAX	0.39	Recall using patterns	0.47

Table 2 shows a comparison between obtained results using domain ontology and extraction patterns and results using PAX component.

We can see that results generated by PAX requires more improvement. This is due to the use of grammatical functions only. Indeed, PAX can handle sentences and use the grammatical function of each word to generate annotations which explains the large number of extracted relations. Relative to Recall measure, we can notice that the rate is a low. This rate is explained by the inability of PAX to extract semantic relationships from complex sentences.

Unlike the method based on PAX, the method using patterns has a smaller number of extracted relationship but better quality. This result is explained by the guided research via cinema ontology relations.

For these reasons, we choose to work with extraction rules and domain ontology in order to determinate semantic relations and the creation of RDF patterns in the rest of our experiments.

4.4 Results using RDF Patterns

In order to validate our proposition, we used a corpus composed of 10 Wikipedia pages related to the cinema domain, written in English language and containing images. The choice of these pages was arbitrary. In our experiments, we have used only the surrounding text of images in order to instantiate six patterns.

As a reference, we annotated the corpus manually and we generated the RDF graph corresponding to the semantic annotation of each image. Figure 11 shows an example of a web image and its surrounding text.

In order to choose the best pattern to be considered as the basis for the annotation of the image, we did a ranking according to the number of extracted triples.

Tables 3 and 4 present the results for the image shown in Fig. 11 using our approach firstly, and the result of the manual classification secondly.

We note that for this document, we obtained the same best rated pattern (pattern 2 is the highest rated pattern obtained by our approach and by a manual approach).

We note that the number of triples in a pattern can influence the final ranking. Indeed, the pattern 2 (the best ranked pattern) contains the highest number of triples. In addition, the presence of the generic triples having a maximum cardinality equal to n, can affect scheduling. For example, we can instantiate the

Krrish 3

From Wikipedia, the free encyclopedia

Krrish 3 ([ˈkrɪʃ 3]) is a 2013 Bollywood superhero science fiction film produced and directed by Rakesh Roshan.[5] It is the third film in the Krrish series following *Koi... Mil Gaya* (2003) and *Krrish* (2006).[6] The film stars Hrithik Roshan, Vivek Oberoi, Priyanka Chopra, and Kangna Ranaut in the lead roles. The story follows the life of Rohit Mehra, a scientist, and Krishna Mehra a.k.a. Krrish, his superhero son, who face an elaborate conspiracy orchestrated by the evil genius Kaal and his female henchman Kaya. In the process, Krishna's pregnant wife Priya is kidnapped by Kaal and the form-changing Kaya takes her place at the Mehra home and eventually falls in love with Krishna.

Fig. 11. Example of image used for the evaluation.

Table 3. Automatic ranking of patterns corresponding to image 11.

Rank	Patterns ranking	Number of automatic triple
1	Pattern 2	7
2	Pattern 4	6
3	Pattern 1, pattern 6	4
4	Pattern 3, pattern 5	0

Table 4. Manual RDF patterns classification.

Rank	Patterns ranking	Number of manual triple
1	Pattern 2	6
2	Pattern 6	4
3	Pattern1	3
4	Pattern 3, pattern 4	1

generic triple [Movie: * hasActor, Actor *] repeatedly since a film can have the participation of several actors.

We repeated the same work for the ten web documents used for the evaluation.

In order to evaluate the quality of the annotation for the test collection, we used the following measure:

$$QA = \frac{Nr.\ of\ well\ annotated\ documents}{Total\ number\ of\ documents} \qquad (1)$$

with QA is the quality of the annotation.

We consider a well-annotated document if it is annotated by P_i ($i \in [1..6]$ with 6 is the number of pattern used) having the first place automatically and the first place manually (the same P_i).

We also calculate QA where P_i obtains the second rank automatically.

Table 5 presents the results on the entire collection.

Table 5. Quality of annotation.

Automatic rank of P_i	QA
1	0.44
2	0.55

Obtained results are encouraging. Indeed, having high rates for the two best patterns (compared to manual annotation) shows the importance of our work.

We succeeded to associate eighteen images to different elements of patterns that can be illustrated by a picture.

The success of these association shows the interest of our approach to annotate text and image at a time.

Choosing the number of extracted triples as criterion of classification is not arbitrary. In fact, it is impossible to use precision and recall as criterion of selection because it is not possible to obtain manual annotation for every test.

However, we note that the use of this criterion (number of extracted triples) has the disadvantage of promoting the pattern with the greatest number of sub-patterns or with a maximum cardinality greater than 1 (repeatable sub-patterns).

To overcome this problem, we plan to propose a new ranking function in our future work.

5 Conclusion

The potential of the semantic web to resolve information retrieval problems is tremendous. Based on semantic annotation technique, adding formal semantics to the web content is vital in order to improve information indexing and retrieval. In our case, our goal is to ameliorate web images research. To achieve this aim, we propose an automatic approach to semantically annotate images through their context. Indeed, we use contextual factors such caption of image, surrounding text, etc. to generate elementary RDF graph and to combine them into a global RDF graph.

In this respect, we detected concepts, instances of concepts linked by semantic relations and we created RDF patterns.

In this paper, we are focusing in the determination and the improvement of results finding in our previous work based on linguistic treatment and we focused on the process of creation and instantiation of RDF patterns.

As a solution, we used a domain ontology. This ontology is interested in cinema domain. It aims to provide a controlled vocabulary to semantically describe movie related concepts such concept Actor, genre, movies. By using this ontology, and specially different relations between concepts and distinct learning corpus, we defined our patterns of relations extraction. Different patterns were written in JAPE language.

Using relations existing in the domain ontology, we obtain an increase in precision and recall measures compared to results obtained by the exploitation of PAX element. So, we can conclude that the guided search, through the use of ontology relationships, is more efficient that the simple use of linguistic and grammatical functions.

Based on this result, we construct and instantiated RDF patterns using a domain ontology and patterns of extraction written in Jape language and the exploitation of instantiated patterns in order to choose the suitable annotation.

Results are encouraged to exploit all relationships present at the ontology and use a bigger cinema corpus. This corpus can be formed by Wikipedia pages speaking about different concepts like movies and genre.

As a future work, Working with all contextual factor represents our next step. The aim of this step is to generate elementary RDF graph from all factors and to generate a global annotation.

Furthermore, we plan to study how weights should be assigned for each factor and how generate a weighted global graph in order to improve indexation and research web images process.

References

1. Cunningham, H., Maynard, D., Bontcheva, K., Tablan, V.: GATE: a framework and graphical development environment for robust NLP tools and applications. In: The 40th Anniversary Meeting of the Association for Computational Linguistics, ACL 2002 (2002)
2. Krestel, R., Witte, R., Bergler, S.: Predicate-Argument EXtractor (PAX). In: Proceedings of the First Workshop on New Challenges for NLP Frameworks (2010)
3. Kahan, J., Koivunen, M.R.: Annotea: an open RDF infrastructure for shared web annotations. In: Proceedings of the 10th International Conference on World Wide Web, New York, pp. 623–632. ACM (2001)
4. Vlasseva, S., Etzioni, O., Gribble, S.D., McDowell, L.K., Halevy, A.Y., Levy, H., Pentney, W.R., Verma, D.: Mangrove: enticing ordinary people onto the semantic web via instant gratification. In: Fensel, D., Sycara, K., Mylopoulos, J. (eds.) ISWC 2003. LNCS, vol. 2870, pp. 754–770. Springer, Heidelberg (2003)
5. Handschuh, S., Staab, S., Maedche, A.: Cream: creating relational metadata with a component-based, ontology-driven annotation framework. In: Proceedings of the First International Conference on Knwoledge Capture (K-CAP), pp. 76–83 (2001)
6. Bechhofer, S., Goble, C.: Towards annotation using daml+oil. In: Workshop on Knowledge Markup and Semantic Annotation, Victoria (2001)
7. Laclavik, M., Hluchý, L., Seleng, M., Ciglan, M.: Ontea: platform for pattern based automated semantic annotation. Comput. Inform. **28**(4), 555–579 (2009)
8. Vargas-Vera, M., Motta, E., Domingue, J., Lanzoni, M., Stutt, A., Ciravegna, F.: MnM: ontology driven semi-automatic and automatic support for semantic markup. In: Gómez-Pérez, A., Benjamins, V.R. (eds.) EKAW 2002. LNCS (LNAI), vol. 2473, pp. 379–391. Springer, Heidelberg (2002)

9. Popov, B., Kiryakov, A., Kirilov, A., Manov, D., Ognyanoff, D., Goranov, M.: Kim semantic annotation platform. J. Nat. Lang. Eng. **10**(3–4), 375–392 (2004)
10. Kogut, P., Holmes, W.: Aerodaml: applying information extraction to generate daml annotations from web pages. In: First International Conference on Knowledge Capture (K-CAP 2001), Workshop on Knowledge Markup and Semantic Annotation (2001)
11. Li, J., Wang, J.Z.: Automatic linguistic indexing of pictures by a statistical modeling approach. IEEE Trans. Pattern Anal. Mach. Intell. **25**(9), 1075–1088 (2003)
12. Cusano, C., Ciocca, G., Schettini, R.: Image annotation using SVM. Proc. SPIE **5304**, 330–338 (2004)
13. Halaschek-wiener, C., Golbeck, J., Schain, A., Parsia, B., Hendler, J.: Annotation and provenance tracking in semantic web photo libraries. In: International Provenance and Annotation Workshop. Chicago, pp. 82–89 (2006)
14. Bellini, P., Bruno, I., Nesi, P.: Exploiting intelligent content via AXMEDIS/MPEG-21 for modelling and distributing news. Int. J. Softw. Eng. Knowl. Eng. **21**(1), 3–32 (2011)
15. Arndt, R., Vacura, M., Staab, S., Hardman, L., Troncy, R.: COMM: designing a well-founded multimedia ontology for the web. In: Aberer, K., et al. (eds.) ASWC 2007 and ISWC 2007. LNCS, vol. 4825, pp. 30–43. Springer, Heidelberg (2007)
16. Wang, C., Jing, F., Zhang, L., Zhang, H.J.: Content-based image annotation refinement. In: IEEE Conference on Computer Vision and Pattern Recognition, CVPR 2007, June 2007, pp. 1–8 (2007)
17. Smeulders, A.W.M., Worring, M., Santini, S., Gupta, A., Jain, R.: Content-based image retrieval at the end of the early years. IEEE Trans. Pattern Anal. Mach. Intell. **22**(12), 1349–1380 (2000)
18. Declerck, T., Crispi, C., Contreras, J., Corcho, O.: Text-based semantic annotation servicefor multimedia content in the esperonto project. In: Knowledge-Based Media Analysis for Self-Adaptive and Agile Multi-Media, Proceedings of the European Workshop for the Integration of Knwoledge, Semantics and Digital Media Technology, EWIMT 2004, 25–26 November, 2004, London, UK (2004)
19. Nguyen, M.T.: Vers une plate-forme d'annotations sémantiques automatiques partir de documents multimédias (2007)
20. Garofalakis, M., Gionis, A., Rastogi, R., Seshadri, S., Shim, K.: Xtract: a system for extracting document type descriptors from XML documents. SIGMOD Rec. **29**(2), 165–176 (2000)
21. Bourigault, D.: Lexter: a terminology extraction software for knowledge acquisition from texts. In: Proceedings of the 9th Knowledge Acquisition for Knowledge Based System Workshop (1995)
22. Abacha, A.B., Zweigenbaum, P.: Annotation et interrogation sémantiques de textes médicaux. In: Atelier Web Sémantique Médical 2010 (2010)
23. Khelif, K., Kefi-Khelif, L., Corby, O.: Une approche pour la gnration dannotations smantiquespartir de textes biomdicaux (2009)
24. Humphreys, B.L., Lindberg, D.A.: The UMLS project: making the conceptual connection between users and the information they need. Bull. Med. Libr. Assoc. **8**(2), 170 (1993)
25. Gerber, D., Ngomo, A.-C.N.: Extracting multilingual natural-language patterns for RDF predicates. In: ten Teije, A., Völker, J., Handschuh, S., Stuckenschmidt, H., d'Acquin, M., Nikolov, A., Aussenac-Gilles, N., Hernandez, N. (eds.) EKAW 2012. LNCS, vol. 7603, pp. 87–96. Springer, Heidelberg (2012)

26. Pradel, C., Haemmerlé, O., Hernandez, N.: Natural language query translation into SPARQL using patterns. In: Fourth International Workshop on Consuming Linked Data-COLD (2013)
27. Pradel, C., Haemmerl'e, O., Hernandez, N.: Des patrons modulaires de requtes SPARQL dansle systme SWIP. In: 23eme Journes Francophones dIngnierie des Connaissances (2012)
28. Gillet, P.: Gnration de patrons de requtes partir dalignements dontologies: application unsystme dinterrogation du web smantique fond sur les patrons (2013)
29. Jaouachi, R.T., Khemakhem, M.T., Jemaa, M.B., Hernandez, N., Haemmerle, O.: Multi-factor RDF graph based image annotation -application in cinema domain-. In: Fifth International Conference on Web and Information Technologies, ICWIT 2013 (2013)
30. Porter, M.F.: Readings in Information Retrieval. Morgan Kaufmann Publishers Inc., San Francisco (1997)

Characteristics of High Performance Software Development Teams

Alessandra C.S. Dutra[1(✉)], Rafael Prikladnicki[1], and Tayana Conte[2]

[1] Faculdade de Informática, Pontifícia Universidade Católica (PUCRS), Porto Alegre, Rio Grande do Sul, Brazil
{alessandra.dutra,rafaelp}@pucrs.br

[2] Department of Computing, Universidade Federal do Amazonas (UFAM), Manaus, Amazonas, Brazil
tayana@icomp.ufam.edu.br

Abstract. A high performance team is one that exceeds all reasonable expectations and produces extraordinary results. In this work, we are interested in understanding contexts and conditions in which software engineering teams are likely to achieve this status. To this end, we are carrying out a systematic literature review to identify what are the known factors that booster or hinder the performance of software engineering teams and an ad hoc literature review about training approaches in Software Engineering. This paper presents a discussion in relation to current training approaches to software development and their relation to high performance team formation. Based on what was found we reflect on the challenges of high performance teams for software development projects. This work constitutes a key preliminary result towards the design of more elaborate models and theories to predict and explain the performance of software engineering teams.

Keywords: Software Engineering · High performance teams · Training · Education · Systematic literature review

1 Introduction

The software development market operates in a global environment, with rapid changes, and needs to respond to these new opportunities and new markets with agility [24].

A study performed in 2010 by Standish Group [26] with a sample of 10,000 projects around the world produced a report called "Chaos Manifesto 2011", which revealed that the Information Technology (IT) industry faces several challenges; although 37 % of the IT projects have been successful, being delivered before the deadline and within the estimated cost; 42 % of the IT projects were delivered after the deadline and more expensive than the original plan; and 21 % of the IT projects were total failures, being cancelled before the delivered time, or were delivered but never used.

Faraj and Sambamurthy [8] say that improving the productivity and quality of projects are important. Initial approaches were focused on discovering better methodologies and tools, but there is an increasing perception that the projects also face several

S. Hammoudi et al. (Eds.): ICEIS 2015, LNBIP 241, pp. 345–363, 2015.
DOI: 10.1007/978-3-319-29133-8_17

challenges related to communication, coordination, learning, negotiation, diversity and on how to form high performance teams for software development projects.

This context indicates that the qualified education and training of professionals is more necessary in the society in which we live in. Beckman *et al.* [34] say that, among other factors, the quality of the professional is directly related to the quality of the education he/she received.

The quality of Software Engineering (SE) training can contribute meaningfully to improvements in the state of the art of software development and aid in solving some traditional problems and crises related to software industry practices [37]. Nowadays, training and capacity-building to prepare a software professional must include not only basic knowledge of the Computer Science field, but also the teaching of concepts, processes and techniques for the definition, development and maintenance of software [36].

As a result, the education process in Software Development has begun to question the methods used in training activities [34]. Recent studies observe that these methods involve traditional teaching strategies such as theory presentation, expositive classes and complementary reading, with which the students find in the industry a different scenario than what is taught in academia [29]. At the same time, software development projects have required high performance team training, and professionals with strong technical, behavioural, and business skills which current educational programs are not able to supply [32]. One of the reasons could be the fact that such programs concentrate on basic education focused on the traditional approaches for software development, instead of preparing the professional to act as a part of a software development team, which requires multifunctional competencies and a multidisciplinary environment.

Thus, the goal of this paper is to develop a reflection on how the current existing SE training approaches cover the various high performance team characteristics. We first conducted an ad-hoc literature study about the existing training approaches in SE and then a systematic literature review (SLR) about high performance teams characteristics. At the end, we reflected on how the existing training approaches help in forming high performance software development teams.

This paper is divided into six sections. In Sect. 2 we present the theoretical foundations. In Sect. 3, we report on existing training approaches. Section 4 provides a systematic literature review of high performance teams of software engineering. In Sect. 5 there is a discussion on training versus high performance teams characteristics. Finally in Sect. 6 the conclusions and future work are addressed.

2 Background

2.1 Software Engineering Training

Software Engineering is concerned with theory application, knowledge and practice for the effective and efficient software development of systems that satisfies users requirements [35]. SE began to be discussed as a discipline in 1968 [34] and currently is part of the curriculum of several courses such as Computer Science, Computer Engineering, Information Systems, Automation Control Engineering and Software Engineering.

Software Engineering is related with all software production aspects, from the initial stage to its maintenance, involving not only technical development processes, but also project management activities and tools, methods and theories that support its production [24]. Therefore, SE goes beyond programming code creation; it tries to discipline development and brings to software development principles, techniques and knowledge to discuss quality questions, deadlines and economic factors [35].

The professionals who conclude their undergraduate course, according to curricular recommendations, are able to, among other aspects, master knowledge and abilities that are part of the SE area; work individually or as part of a team to develop software artifacts with quality; design solutions using appropriate SE approaches that integrate ethical, social, legal and economic questions; know how to apply current theories, models and techniques that provide a baseline for identifying and analyzing problems, software design, development, implementation, verification and documentation; demonstrate understanding and appreciation of the importance of negotiation, efficient work habits, leadership, and good communication with stakeholders; and learn new models, techniques and technologies as soon as they emerge [35].

By analyzing the curricular recommendation listed, we have identified that there are several required competencies for an SE professional. The SE curriculum [35, 36] points to the necessity of education apart from expositive class formats, and one of the ways to increase education quality involves innovative strategies and didactics. According to Beckman [34], educational quality is one of the important factors that influence the quality of the professionals. Thus, some of the challenges for improving SE education are: to make SE courses more attractive to students; to focus appropriately on SE education, understanding its dimensions; to present industry practices to the students; provide education to industry professionals; to make education in SE evidence-based; to ensure that SE educators have the necessary experience and knowledge to this assignment; and to increase the research prestige and quality of the educational SE [24].

According to Conn [33], the SE professionals are dissatisfied with the lack of training of the university students that enter the job market, which means that the industry must complement their education with training that gives them necessary knowledge in order to make up for this deficiency. This training can involve professionals or teams, including high performance teams.

2.2 High Performance Teams

A high performance team is a group that brings together members committed to the mutual growth and personal success [17]. According to Chiavenato [4], the main high performance teams attributes are: participation, accountability, clarity, interaction, flexibility, focalization, creativity and quickness. The participation in a team increases the commitment and the fidelity of the people, resulting in delivery of high quality work [5].

A high performance team, besides all the requirements of a team, must have its members to be committed to the personal growth and success of each team member. Such a team will exceed the performance of all the other teams and achieve results above expectations [17].

Katzenbach and Smith [13], present some characteristics of high performance teams: "Deeply personal commitments of each one to the growth and the success of the others is what distinguish high performance teams from the majority of the existing teams. Energized by this extra sense of commitment, the high performance team typically reflects a vigorous amplification of the fundamental teams characteristics: deeper sense of purpose, more ambitious performance targets, a more complete approach, more fullness in mutual accountability, knowledge interchangeably and complementarity."

Boyett and Boyett [3] mention some companies that have achieved great results with high performance teams. The AT&T Credit Corporation has used high performance interfunctional teams in order to improve its efficiency and service to the client.

Roda [21] presents a model of three levels for self-organizing teams: creating, practicing and transcending. The high performance teams are at the last level and are characterized by technical and behavioral excellence, practicing and experimenting challenges continuously. A high performance team must have autonomy, attitude and more productivity than a traditional team and usually have great satisfaction in the work they do.

According to Raj [19], there is a major difficulty for an organization in disseminating high performance team practices, such as work reorganization, professional involvement in decision making processes and improvement in workers' skills, despite the evidence that organizations invest in these as practices to achieve greater productivity and efficiency.

3 Training Approaches in SE

Training in SE should prepare the students in both theory and effective participation in a collaborative and interdisciplinary environment. In this regard, it is important to consider the variation in training techniques.

Traditional approaches in SE training are considered to be [28]:

1. Dialogued expositive classes: This is a content exposition, with active participation by the students, whose previous knowledge must be considered and can be taken as a foundation.
2. Text Study: This is an exploration of an author's idea from the critical study of a text and/or information research and the author's ideas exploration.
3. Directed Study: This is study under guidance and direction by the professor, aiming to solve specific difficulties.
4. Use of a Discussion List: This is an opportunity for a group of people to be able to debate, at a distance, a theme in which they are experts or have done a previous study.
5. Verbalization and Observation Groups (VG/OG): This is an analysis of theme/ problem under a professor's coordination that divides the students in two groups: one for verbalization (VG) and the other for observation (OG).
6. Seminar: This is a space where a group discusses or debate themes or problems.
7. Case Study: This is the detailed and objective analysis of a real situation that needs to be investigated and that is challenge for the people that are involved.
8. Workshop: This is the gathering of a small number of people with common interests, which aims to study and work for the knowledge and deepening of a theme, under expert orientation.

These alternative approaches can help students learn more effectively. Alternative approaches are considered to be [29–32]:

1. Group Activities, distance education and practice activities: By using this approach, interaction with the students is emphasized through icebreakers that explore specific subjects. The characteristics are: diversification in the techniques for group activities; practical classes in laboratories; the planning of the student work; and part-time classes: 20 % of the discipline is done through distance education.
2. Capstone projects and practices activities: a Capstone project is an approach where a student group plans and executes a software project from the beginning to the end during one whole semester.
3. Playgroup and games: For this strategy, related content is first presented to the class. In the end, in order to consolidate comprehension, a playgroup is performed using LEGO®. The game makes it possible to design, from the defined requirements, a product to be built that is similar to the software development.
4. Games and educational simulators: Because of the need for training students in the SE process, one of the alternatives is the use of games to fill the gap between theoretical and practical aspects. From the reports found in the literature [32], it was noticed that the majority of the proposals developed are associated with simulator games.

The approaches that are more focused on the students and that promote their further active participation on the classes, for example with games and simulators [31, 32], have the potential to increase the students interest, motivate them and improve learning at level of concept application.

4 Systematic Literature Review Protocol

The purpose of the SLR was to select the main studies in the literature that report from high performance software development teams and identify its characteristics.

A SLR, according Kitchenham [14], is a secondary study that aims to identify, analyze, evaluate and interpret as broadly as possible the existing scientific evidence from a specific research question, subject area, or phenomenon of interest.

4.1 Research Question and Context

The research reported in this article was guided by three research questions: (1) *What is the concept of high performance teams in software development?* (2) *How are high performance teams characterized?* (3) *How are the software development environments where high performance teams work?*

This article is actually part of a broader research project that aims to generate a deep understanding of high performance teams in software engineering, by revisiting the definition of high performance teams, and identifying contextual conditions in which teams are likely to flourish. Thus, answering this research question is a cornerstone towards the development of comprehensive models for training and developing effective software engineering teams.

4.2 SLR Protocol

Inclusion and Exclusion Criteria. The papers included in the search were related to high performance teams training, characteristics and environments. We searched for papers available on the web, with the complete text in electronic format for reading as well published in a conference or a journal in the Computer Science field.

We have excluded papers that did not involve software development process and software engineering, did not deal with training of software development teams, and were not written in Portuguese or English.

The Search String. We were interested in retrieving studies published in conferences or journals in the Computer Science field, related to high performance teams training, characteristics and environments. Thus, we conducted an automatic search in a scientific data-basis.

Similar to the Salleh study [22], the database used as the research reference selected was SCOPUS because to its reputation and the greater numbers of abstracts and citations. The search string used was formed with the following composition:

1. *"high performance team"* OR *"high performance teams"*
2. *"performance teams"* OR *"team performance"*
3. *"teams performance"* OR *"high productivity team"*
4. *"high productivity teams"* OR *"good team"* OR *"best team"* OR *"team productivity"*
5. *"limitation"* OR *"practice"* OR *"characteristics"* OR *"environment"* OR *"organization"* OR *"concept"* OR *"productivity"*
6. *"software development"* OR *"software engineering"*

The final string received the following combination: 1 OR 2 OR 3 OR 4 AND 5 AND 6.

Data Analysis and Synthesis. The data extraction form was developed with the following fields: Paper, Year, Author; Conference (where published); Type (Journal, Conference); Objective; Context (Education, Practice, Tools); Contributing, evidences; Research methodology; Status (Relevant or not relevant); Justification (status regarding); Answers Question 1 (Yes or No?); Answers Question 2 (Yes or No?).

Regarding the context in which the studies were conducted, we sorted them in three categories:

- *Education:* Studies that assessed an educational tool for teaching.
- *Practice:* studies on the practice in software development.
- *Tools, Models, Frameworks:* Studies describing models, frameworks and support tools. Some reviews of these studies have been proposed which, for example, studies using experimental tools have proposed tool.

Regarding the research methods, in order to avoid interpretation biases and improve the reproducibility of this study, we noted the research methods based on what had been said by the authors, instead of based on what was actually done. Thus, we classified studies in Literature Review, Experiment, Survey, and Case Study, Simulation, Verbal Protocol, as there were no other methods reported.

In the extraction form, we also indicated whether the study fulfilled all the selection and exclusion criteria or not. For those excluded papers, we noted the reasons for which the paper was excluded in another field.

5 SLR Execution and Results

After we defined the research protocol, the review was executed. The initial search was made in phase 1 and returned only 3 papers. Because of this small quantity of papers, we decided to search for synonyms that match the research question, so for phase 2, we selected 112 papers. The synonyms were: productivity, productivity teams, high productivity, team performance, best team, good team, organization and concept. In phase 3, the 112 papers were classified as relevant or irrelevant, based on reading the title and abstract, and 61 papers were relevant.

In the final phase, all the papers selected in the previous phase were downloaded from the web, fully read and added to a read form implemented with MS Excel according to the protocol. In phase 4, after the reading, only 61 papers were selected; 20 papers did not answer the research question of this review and were removed, so that finished with 41 papers.

To serve as a starting point for future researches, we put the list of 41 references in the Appendix A.

5.1 General View of the Papers

Figure 1 shows there has been stability in the number of papers published every year addressing factors that influence the performance of software engineering teams. Over the last ten years, in particular, this stability has been evident. Among the published papers, a balanced number has been published by Journals (22/41) and Conferences (19/41).

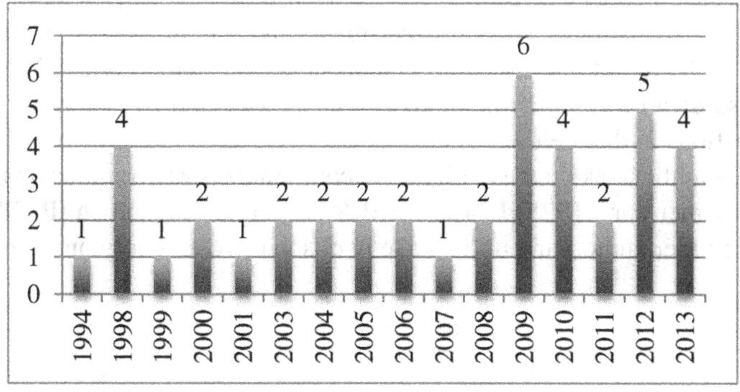

Fig. 1. Number of papers by year.

As shown in Fig. 2, studies are more frequently carried out with practitioners, and, secondly, with students. Regarding the research methods, as shown in Fig. 3, Surveys (19 papers) represent half of the studies, followed by Case Studies (17 papers).

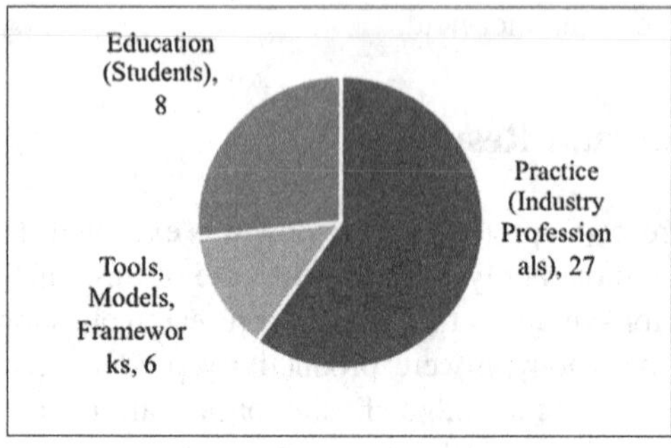

Fig. 2. Studied contexts.

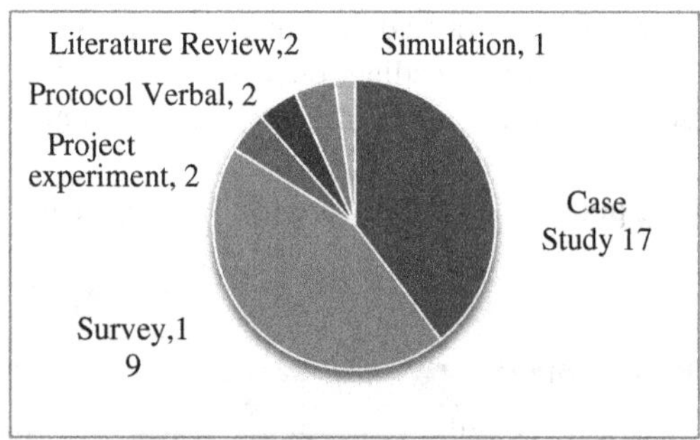

Fig. 3. Research methods.

Rather than expected, by crossing methods with contexts as shown in Table 1, it is possible to reveal that there are three equally frequent types of studies: surveys with practitioners, case studies with practitioners, and case studies with students. The lack of intervention research studies, such as experiments and action-research, is justifiable by the fact that such type of research with human subjects is naturally challenging. Additionally, these data on research methods reveal the exploratory nature of our current research questions in this field.

Among the authors, as shown in Fig. 4, we could find only two authors that published four papers: Samer Faraj [P25][P34][P38][P39], and Patricia Guinan [P37][P38][P39] [P41]. All the other authors in our list have published two and only one paper.

Table 1. Methods versus subjects and contexts.

	Case Study	Survey	Verbal Protocol	Simulation	Experiment	Literature Review
Practice (Industry professionnals)	P3, P8, P15, P16, P20, P23, P28, P32, P33, P34	P1, P2, P4, P5, P9, P14 P17,P18 P19,P26 P30,P37 P39, P38, P41	P29	P12	P10	
Education (Students)	P6, P7, P19, P27, P31, P35, P40,	P21				
Tools, Models, Frame-works		P13, P24 P25	P22		P36	P11

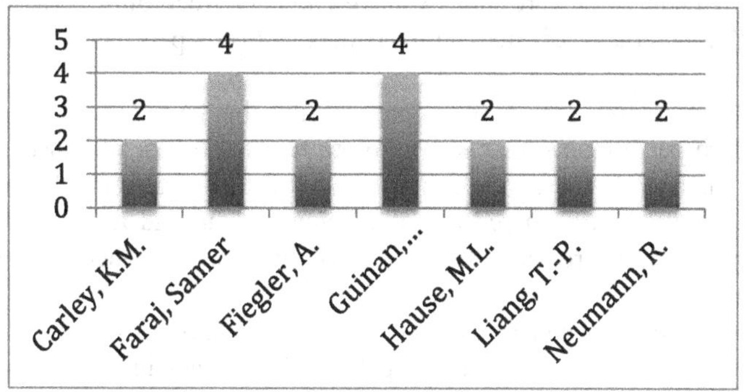

Fig. 4. Software Development Context.

Question 1: What is the concept of high performance teams in software development? In the papers searched on the SLR, we found studies that present high performance team characteristics that focus on how to increase their productivity. Staples and Cameron [25], describes how team performance is associated with characteristics such as: appropriate interpersonal skills, low team turnover, appropriate team size, so that the resources are enough to complete the tasks, showing strong team spirit, and creation of innovative ways to coordinate the team, helping to carry out their tasks.

In our research, we identified some characteristics that high performance teams must have for software development. We identified organizational, behavioral and technique characteristics. Those most cited are presented in Table 2 and are mainly behavioral characteristics.

Table 2. Characteristics most cited in the studies.

Characteristics most cited	Papers
Efficient Communication	[P2][P6][P7][P27][P13][P28]
Coordination	[P5][P6][P23][P28]
Team Work	[P2][P6][P7][P28]
Team Diversity	[P15][P17]
Leadership	[P2][P27]
Team Cohesion	[P2][P19]
Motivation	[P10][P13]

Thus, we can suggest that the high performance teams (1) have an effective communication, (2) present a diversity that stimulates learning and innovation, (3) have cohesion, motivation, leadership and coordination, in order to achieve their goals.

Question 2: How are High Performance Teams characterized? For this research question, 48 characteristics were cited by the researchers. According to Table 2, Efficient Communication was the most cited, with 6 papers, with 4 papers, was Coordination and Team Work.

Hause [10] in the final results of his paper writes that he found the following characteristics: High performance teams were more focused on specific tasks, were more organized in their work, thus, they communicated less, had to make fewer decisions, hence worked fewer hours, shared better information and had fewer conflicts; had a leadership style more appropriate for team work; and had a balance between communication, participation and work division.

According to Klimoski and Zukin [15], the growth in knowledge, abilities, and skills needed to solve the tasks that create competitive advantages in today's organizations makes it impossible for individuals to work independently of teams.

In his systematic review of empirical studies on agile software development, Dyba and Dingsøyr [7] cite Robinson and Sharp [20] who characterized the agile development teams as a team that has faith in its own abilities and shows respect and responsibility that establishes the truth and that preserves quality of life at work.

Regarding communication, its importance to team work is evident, according to related studies on this issue [6, 9–12, 25]. One must highlight Hause's research [11], explain that the difference between high and low performance groups is measured by the amount of produced communication, with low performance groups producing more communication. Still, the analysis of their work process suggests that is not the quantity, but the quality of communication that is important in the determination of performance.

The characteristics of the teams were classified, based on Capability Maturity Model Integration CMMI [23], where technical competencies are the abilities to use tools, data and required process by a project or process. Organizational abilities, meaning the behavior regarding organizational structure, roles and responsibilities; and Contextual Abilities, which are abilities in self-management, communication and inter-relationship. Table 3 presents all the characteristics we found for high performance teams.

Table 3. Characteristics classified for high performance teams.

High performance teams' characteristics					
Organizational characteristics		Contextual characteristics		Technical characteristics	
Team diversity [P15][P17] [P2]	Team work [P2] [P6][P7][P28] [P3]	Communication [P2][P6][P7] [P27][P31][P28]	Motivation [P10] [P13]	Coordination [P5][P6] [P23][P28]	Managerial involvement [38]
Team size [P23] [P28]	Team Leadership [P2] [P27]	Team Cohesion [P2][P19]	Unexpected Challenges [P1]	Professional Orientation [P13]	Restriction of External Influence [P38]
Team's autonomy [P15][P28]	Personality [P13]	Improvisation [P1]	Attitude [P13]	Teamwork Orientation [P13]	Performance Evaluation [P38]
Work less hours [P27]	Organization [P27]	Respect [P11]	Passion to Teach [P11]	Focus on Specific Tasks [P27]	Competencies of Management [P13]
Organizational Commitment [P5]	Comprehension [P4]	Empathy [P4]	Better sharing Information [P27]	Experience in Propagation [P38]	Usage of Resources [P6]
Life quality at work [P11]	Accountability [P11]	Emotional Intelligence [P4]	Believe on the own abilities [P11]	Knowledge [P13]	
Low Turnover [P28]	Flexibility [P4]	Cognitive Work/Abilities [P13]	Tasks Participation [P27]	Less Decision Made [P27] [P31]	
	Intelligence [P10]	Less tendency to conflicts [P27]	Confidence [P11]	Work Tasks Division [P27]	
	Analytic [P11]	Socialization [P10]	Awareness [P10]	Goals Fixing [P32]	

Question 3: How are the Software Development Environments Where High Performance Teams Work? For this research question, five characteristics about software development environments were cited. According to Table 4, Distributed teams were the most cited with 11 papers, with 5 papers, was Use Agile approaches, and with 2 papers Environments with changes.

Eleven studies addressed distributed teams ([P1][P7][P8][P12][P14][P18][P19][P21][P23][P28][P31]), five use agile approaches ([P2][P3][P11][P15][P30]), and two addressed Environments with changes ([P1][P15]). According to De Melo [16], agile methods such as Extreme Programming [1] and Scrum [2] were developed as approaches to simplify the software development process, potentially leading to better productivity. The author explains that agile methods shorten development time and inevitable changes resulting from market dynamics. On the other hand, Da Silva [6] comments on the team building criteria in software projects, and mentions that the difference between the project results with agile and traditional approaches are relevant in practice, although it still requires further studies to produce empirical evidence.

Dyba and Dingsøyr [7], in his systematic review of empirical studies about agile software development, shows four studies comparing the productivity of agile teams with the productivity of teams that use traditional development methods and, in general, the results showed an increase of 42 % in productivity of the agile team.

According to Magni's studies [27], several characteristics of environments were mentioned, including the issue of distributed environments, of environments in constant changes and of interdependent tasks. Interesting to note the author's research about the environments in constant changes and about the interdependent tasks.

Table 4. Software development environments.

Characteristics most cited	Papers
Work With Distributed teams	[P1][P7][P8][P12][P14][P18][P19][P21][P23][P28][P31]
Use Agile Approaches	[P2][P3][P11][P15][P30]
Environments with changes	[P1][P15]
Environments with Interdependent Tasks	[P1]
Great volume of business	[P3]

In those, there is a challenge to respond to the changing customer expectations during the project development, while in these the software development is a complex task that involves many interdependencies.

We also identified in this systematic review that the issue of research on the characteristics of the software development environment in which high performance teams operate was answered by bringing as answer: (1) that most of the environments in which these teams operate are distributed environments; that some of these environments (2) use agile approaches, (3) are inconstant changes, (4) have interdependent tasks, and (5) have great volume of business.

6 Discussion

The reflection on existing training approach and high performance team characteristics for software development led to a necessity and an opportunity. There is a necessity for adopting alternative approaches for forming high performance teams in SE, and an opportunity to use them in undergraduate and graduate classes at Universities.

Considering the high performance team characteristics most cited, we can identify that the majority of the alternative training approaches have focus on the improvement of these characteristics such as teamwork, communication, leadership and motivation [29].

We also identified, that at an organizational level, little relation is seen between high performance team characteristics and training approaches. From a behavioural viewpoint, characteristics such as leadership, communication, teamwork, motivation, cohesion, and flexibility are characteristics that can be associated to some of the training approaches found. The characteristic related to technical competencies are easier to be worked with current training approaches, given that technical competencies are the aspect most worked on with current training. Therefore, in an initial reflection, we understand that it is important to map training approaches in relation to the high performance team characteristics in software development.

By analyzing some of the approaches in relation to high performance teams characteristics, we can observe that: (1) Verbalization Groups (VG) and Observations Groups (OG), workshops and alternatives approaches, have the goal of developing skills such as teamwork and communication; (2) group activity approaches, distance education and practical activities [29], enable the student to work with characteristics such as teamwork, communication, and responsibility, as well as students' motivation in relation to the work done, (3) expositive classes focus more on the content.

Although the professor asks the students questions, and they interpret and discuss the study object, this approach does not work on team, leadership and communication aspects; Capstone projects and practical activities, icebreakers and educational simulators can benefit the training on communication, teamwork, leadership and organization, along with team activities.

In that regard, and considering this reflection, we have some evidence that: (1) it is important to understand what high performance teams are in terms of software development and their characteristics, (2) it is necessary to define the training approaches based on what one wants to teach, and not only from the approaches that one already know how to teach. In terms of research opportunities, we also identify: (1) the need for mapping between training approaches and high performance team characteristics. Such a study would facilitate the approaches professors choose in relation to the teams characteristics that he/she wishes to work on, in this case a focus on high performance, (2) the opportunity to propose a methodological approach that is aimed at educating high performance teams in SE.

We also identified the following challenges: (1) to be able to identify, in a software development team, the characteristics that one wishes to train; (2) to work on training of professors in order to, through innovative approaches, better prepare them and their students to form high performance software development teams.

7 Conclusion

In this paper we presented a reflection about the relation between current training approaches and the characteristics of high performance teams in software engineering. The development of this reflection was done in two steps. First, a study was performed on the existing training approaches in SE; and second, a systematic literature review (SLR) was performed with the goal of evaluating, synthesizing studies on high performance team in software development, seeking research opportunities and a theoretical foundation for future researches. We discussed how these two themes could complement each other with a view to improving the quality of SE education and training.

As any other empirical study, this study has some limitations. The first is related to researcher bias during the paper analysis process. For this reason, two researchers were involved in the systematic literature review execution, both in paper selection and data extraction. The study on existing training approaches also had research bias during the study process as a limitation.

As a next step we intend to execute of a viability study to deepen the analysis on the characteristics of high performance teams, identifying their practices as well as training approaches used, aiming at proposing ways for developing such practices, involving existing or new training approaches, and thus contributing to the formation of high performance teams for software development.

Appendix A

The list of all 41 references of the SLR.

[P1] Magni, M., Maruping, L.M., Hoegl, M., Proserpio, L., Managing the unexpected across space: Improvisation, dispersion, and performance in NPD teams. In: Journal of Product Innovation Management, 2013.

[P2] Da Silva, F.Q.B., França, A.C.C., Suassuna, M., De Sousa Mariz, L.M.R., Rossiley, I., De Miranda, R.C.G., Gouveia, T.B., Monteiro, C.V.F., Lucena, E., Cardozo, E.S.F., Espindola, E., Team building criteria in software projects: A mix-method replicated study. In: Journal Information and Software Technology, 2013.

[P3] De Melo, C.O., S. Cruzes, D., Kon, F., Conradi, R., Interpretative case studies on agile team productivity and management. In: Journal of Information and Software Technology, 2013.

[P4] Günsel, A., Açikgöz, A.., The Effects of Team Flexibility and Emotional Intelligence on Software Development Performance. In: Journal of Group Decision and Negotiation, 2013.

[P5] Chen, P.-C., Chern, C.-C., Chen, C.-Y., Software project team characteristics and team performance: Team motivation as a moderator. In: Proceedings - Asia-Pacific Software Engineering Conference, APSEC, 2012.

[P6] Jiang, L., Carley, K.M., Eberlein, A., Assessing team performance from a socio-technical congruence perspective. In: International Conference on Software and System Process, ICSSP 2012 – Proceedings, 2012.

[P7] Fernández-Sanz, L., Misra, S., Analysis of cultural and gender influences on teamwork performance for software requirements analysis in multinational environments. In: Journal of IET Software, 2012.

[P8] Staats, B.R., Unpacking team familiarity: The effects of geographic location and hierarchical role. In: Journal of Production and Operations Management, 2012.

[P9] Maheshwari, M., Kumar, U., Kumar, V., Alignment between social and technical capability in software development teams: An empirical study. In: Journal of Team Performance Management, 2012.

[P10] Georgieva, K., Neumann, R., Fiegler, A., Dumke, R.R., Validation of the model for prediction of the human performance. In: Proceedings - Joint Conference of the 21st International Workshop on Software Measurement, IWSM 2011 and the 6th International Conference on Software Process and Product Measurement, MENSURA 2011.

[P11] Dybå, T., Dingsøyr, T., 2008. Empirical studies of agile software development: A systematic review. In: Journal of Science Direct.

[P12] Czekster, R.M., Fernandes, P., Sales, A., Webber, T., Analytical modeling of software development teams in globally distributed projects. In: Proceedings - 5th International Conference on Global Software Engineering, ICGSE 2010.

[P13] Siau, K., Tan, X., Sheng, H., Important characteristics of software development team members: An empirical investigation using Repertory Grid. In: Journal of Information Systems Journal, 2010.

[P14] Ganesh, M.P., Gupta, M., Impact of virtualness and task interdependence on extra-role performance in software development teams. In: Team Performance Management, 2010.

[P15] Lee, G., Xia, W., Toward agile: An integrated analysis of quantitative and qualitative field data on software development agility. In: MIS Quarterly: Management Information Systems, 2010.

[P16] Soares, F.S.F., Júnior, G.S.D.A., Meira, S.R.D.L., Incentive systems in software organizations. In: 4th International Conference on Software Engineering Advances, ICSEA 2009, Includes SEDES 2009: Simpósio para Estudantes de Doutoramento em Engenharia de Software, 2009.

[P17] Chen, D.-N., Shie, Y.-J., Liang, T.-P., The impact of knowledge diversity on software project team's performance. In: ACM International Conference Proceeding Series, 2009.

[P18] Avritzer, A., Lima, A., An empirical approach for the assessment of scheduling risk in a large globally distributed industrial software project. In: Proceedings - 2009 4th IEEE International Conference on Global Software Engineering, ICGSE 2009.

[P19] Swigger, K., Alpaslan, F.N., Lopez, V., Brazile, R., Dafoulas, G., Serce, F.C., Structural factors that affect global software development learning team performance. In: SIGMIS CPR'09 - Proceedings of the 2009 ACM SIGMIS Computer Personnel Research Conference, 2009.

[P20] Au, Y.A., Carpenter, D., Chen, X., Clark, J.G., Virtual organizational learning in open source software development projects. In: Journal of Information and Management, 2009.

[P21] Zhang, S., Tremaine, M., Egan, R., Milewski, A., O'sullivan, P., Fjermestad, J., Occurrence and effects of leader delegation in virtual software teams. In: International Journal of e-Collaboration, 2009.

[P22] Vaccare Braga, R.T., Chan, A., Peony: A Web environment to support pattern-based development. In: Proceedings - 8th International Conference on Web Engineering, ICWE 2008.

[P23] Å mite, D., Moe, N.B., Torkar, R., Pitfalls in remote team coordination: Lessons learned from a case study. In: Lecture Notes in Computer Science (including subseries Lecture Notes in Artificial Intelligence and Lecture Notes in Bioinformatics), 2008.

[P24] Liang, T.-P., Liu, C.-C., Lin, T.-M., Lin, B., Effect of team diversity on software project performance. In: Journal of Industrial Management and Data Systems, 2007.

[P25] Faraj, S., Sambamurthy, V., Leadership of information systems development projects. In: IEEE Transactions on Engineering Management, 2006.

[P26] Ashworth, M.J., Carley, K.M., Who you know vs. what you know: The impact of social position and knowledge on team performance. In: Journal of Mathematical Sociology, 2006.

[P27] Hause, M.L., Distributed team performance in software development. In: Proceedings of the 10th Annual SIGCSE Conference on Innovation and Technology in Computer Science Education, 2005.

[P28] Staples, D.S., Cameron, A.F., The effect of task design, team characteristics, organizational context and team processes on the performance and attitudes of virtual team members. In: Proceedings of the Annual Hawaii International Conference on System Sciences, 2005.

[P29] Teleki, S., A practical approach to predictable software development performance in small to medium size software development organizations. In: 2004 IEEE/UT EngineeringManagement Conference, 2004.

[P30] Williams, L., Shukla, A., Antón, A.I., An initial exploration of the relationship between pair programming and Brooks' law. In: Proceedings of the Agile Development Conference, ADC 2004, 2004.

[P31] Hause, M., Petre, M., Woodroffe, M., Performance in international computer science collaboration between distributed student teams. In: Proceedings - Frontiers in Education Conference, 2003.

[P32] Hoegl, M., Parboteeah, K.P., Goal setting and team performance in innovative projects: On the moderating role of teamwork quality. In: Journal of Small Group Research, 2003.

[P33] Hoegl, M., Gemuenden, H.G., Teamwork Quality and the Success of Innovative Projects: A Theoretical Concept and Empirical Evidence. In: Journal of Organization Science, 2001.

[P34] Faraj, S., Sproull, L., Coordinating expertise in software development teams. In: Journal of Management Science, 2000.

[P35] Feldgen, Maria, Clua, Osvaldo, Hardware dissection in Computer Science as a tool to improve teamwork. In: Proceedings - Frontiers in Education Conference, 2000.

[P36] Kraus, D., Gramopadhye, A.K., Team training: role of computers in the aircraft maintenance environment. In: Journal of Computers and Industrial Engineering, 1999.

[P37] Sawyer, S., Guinan, P.J., Software development: Processes and performance. In: IBM Systems Journal, 1998.

[P38] Guinan, P.J., Cooprider, J.G., Faraj, S., Enabling Software Development Team Performance during Requirements Definition: A Behavioral Versus Technical Approach. In: Information Systems Research, 1998.

[P39] Guinan, Patricia J., Faraj, Samer, Reducing work related uncertainty: The role of communication and control in software development. In: Proceedings of the Hawaii International Conference on System Sciences, 1998.

[P40] Becker, Shirley A., Proposed learning environment for goal-specific improvements. In: Proceedings of the Hawaii International Conference on System Sciences, 1998.

[P41] Chung, Woo Young, Guinan, Patricia, Effects of participative management. In: Proceedings of the ACM SIGCPR Conference, 1994.

References

1. Beck, K., Andres, C.: Extreme Programming Explained: Embrace Change, 2nd edn. Addison-Wesley Professional, Reading (2004)
2. Beck, K., Beedle, M., van Bennekum, A., Cockburn, A., Cunningham, W., Fowler, M., Grenning, J., Highsmith, J., Hunt A., Jeffries, R., Kern, J., Marick, B., Martin, R.C., Mellor, S., Schwaber, K., Sutherland, J., Thomas, D.: Manifesto for agile software development (2001). http://agilemanifesto.org/
3. Boyett, J.H., Boyett, J.T.: The Guru Guide-the Best Ideas of the Top Management Thinkers. Wiley, New York (1998)
4. Chiavenato, I.: People Management: the New Role of Human Resources in Organizations, 3a edn. Elsevier, Rio de Janeiro (2008). (in Portuguese)
5. Cleland, D.I., Ireland, R.L.: Project Manager's Portable Handbook, pp. 1–257. McGraw-Hill, New York (2000)
6. Da Silva, F.Q.B., França, A.C.C., Suassuna, M., De Sousa Mariz, L.M.R., Rossiley, I., De Miranda, R.C.G., Gouveia, T.B., Monteiro, C.V.F., Lucena, E., Cardozo, E.S.F., Espindola, E.: Team building criteria in software projects: a mix-method replicated study. J. Inf. Softw. Technol. **55**, 1316–1340 (2013)
7. Dybå, T., Dingsøyr, T.: Empirical studies of agile software development: a systematic review. J. Sci. Dir. **50**, 833–859 (2008)
8. Faraj, S., Sambamurthy, V.: Leadership of information systems development projects. IEEE Trans. Eng. Manag. **53**, 238–249 (2006)
9. Fernández-Sanz, L., Misra, S.: Analysis of cultural and gender influences on teamwork performance for software requirements analysis in multinational environments. J. IET Softw. **6**, 167–175 (2012)
10. Hause, M.L.: Distributed team performance in software development. In: Proceedings of the 10th Annual SIGCSE Conference on Innovation and Technology in Computer Science Education (2005)
11. Hause, M., Petre, M., Woodroffe, M.: Performance in international computer science collaboration between distributed student teams. In: Proceedings - Frontiers in Education Conference (2003)

12. Jiang, L., Carley, K.M., Eberlein, A.: Assessing team performance from a socio-technical congruence perspective. In: International Conference on Software and System Process, ICSSP 2012 – Proceedings (2012)
13. Katzenbach, J.R., Smith, D.K.: The Wisdom of Teams. Summarized by permission of Harvard Business School Press Copyright by McKinsey and Company, Inc. 275p. (1993)
14. Kitchenham, B.: Guidelines for performing systematic literature reviews in software engineering. EBSE technical report (2007)
15. Klimoski, R., Zukin, L.N.: Selection and staffing for team effectiveness. In: Sundstrom, E. (ed.) Supporting Work Team Effectiveness, pp. 63–91. Jossey-Bass, San Francisco (1999)
16. De Melo, C.O., Cruzes, D.S., Kon, F., Conradi, R.: Interpretative case studies on agile team productivity and management. J. Inf. Softw. Technol. **55**, 412–427 (2013)
17. Moscovici, F.: Teams Work Right: Multiplication of Human Talent, 8a edn. José Olympio, Rio de Janeiro (2003). (in Portuguese)
18. Hackman, R.J.: Why Teams Don't Work Theory and Research on Small Groups. Plenum Press, New York (1998). Chapter 12, edited by R. Scott Tindale et al.
19. Raj, P.P., Baumotte A.C.T., Fonseca D.P.D., Silva, L.H.C.M.: Project human resource management. Editora FGV – Fundação Getúlio Vargas, Rio de Janeiro, 180p. (2006). (in Portuguese)
20. Robinson, H., Sharp, H.: The characteristics of XP teams. In: Eckstein, J., Baumeister, H. (eds.) XP 2004. LNCS, vol. 3092, pp. 139–147. Springer, Heidelberg (2004)
21. Roda, R.: Self-organizing agile teams: a grounded theory. Tese de Doutorado, Victoria University of Wellington (2011)
22. Salleh, N., Mendes, E., Grundy, J.: Empirical studies of pair programming for CS/SE teaching in higher education: a systematic literature review. IEEE Trans. Softw. Eng. **37**(4), 509–525 (2001)
23. SEI: CMMI® for Development, Version 1.2. CMU/SEI-2006-TR-008 ESC-TR-2006-008, p. 561. PA Software Engineering Institute-SEI, Carnegie Mellon University, Pittsburgh
24. Sommerville, I.: Software Engineering, 9a edn. Pearson Prentice Hall, Englewood Cliffs (2006)
25. Staples, D.S., Cameron, A.F.: The effect of task design, team characteristics, organizational context and team processes on the performance and attitudes of virtual team members. In: Proceedings of the Annual Hawaii International Conference on System Sciences (2005)
26. The Standish Group, "Chaos". http://www.versionone.com/assets/img/files/CHAOSManifesto2013.pdf
27. Magni, M., Maruping, L.M., Hoegl, M., Proserpio, L.: Managing the unexpected across space: improvisation, dispersion, and performance in NPD teams. J. Prod. Innov. Manag. **30**, 1009–1026 (2013)
28. Anastasiou, L.G.C., Alves, L.P:. Teaching strategies. In: Proceedings of Education at the University. Strategies Work in the Classroom (3rd edn.), pp. 67–100. Univille, Joinville (2004). (in Portuguese)
29. Prikladnicki, R., Albuquerque, A., Wangenheim, C., Cabral, R.: Teaching software engineering: challenges, teaching strategies and lessons learned in FEES - education forum in software engineering (2009). (in Portuguese)
30. Gresse, V.W.C., Shull, F.: To game or not to game? IEEE Softw. **26**(2), 92–94 (2009)
31. Halma, A.: Robomind.net – Welcome to Robomind.net, the new way to learn programming (2009). http://www.robomind.net
32. Monsalve, E., Werneck, V., Leite, J.: Teaching software engineering with SimulES-W. In: Conference on Software Engineering Education and Training (CSEE&T) (2011)
33. Conn, R.: Developing software engineers at the C-130 J software factory. IEEE Softw., Los Alamitos **19**(5), 25–29 (2002)

34. Beckman, K., Coulter, N., Khajenouri, S., Mead, N.: Collaborations: closing the industry–academia gap. IEEE Softw. **14**(6), 49–57 (1997)
35. ACM/IEEE: Software Engineering Curriculum. Guidelines for Undergraduate Degree Programs in Software Engineering (2004)
36. ACM/IEEE: Computer Science Curriculum, Guidelines for Undergraduate Degree Programs in Software Engineering (2008)
37. Gibbs, W.: Software's chronic crisis. Sci. Am. **271**(3), 86–95 (1994)

Planning of Composite Logistics Services: Model-Driven Engineering and Evaluation

Michael Glöckner[1(✉)], Stefan Mutke[1], Christoph Augenstein[1], and André Ludwig[2]

[1] Leipzig University, Grimmaische Straße 12, 04109 Leipzig, Germany
{gloeckner,mutke,augenstein}@wifa.uni-leipzig.de
[2] Kühne Logistics University, Großer Grasbrook 17, 20457 Hamburg, Germany
andre.ludwig@the-klu.org

Abstract. Tactical planning of composite services in heterogeneous logistics networks is facing two major problems. First, existing planning methods lack in concreteness as they instruct to compare different alternatives of possible composite services in order to find the best solution, but they do not state how to develop and engineer those alternatives. Second, the planning and evaluation of composite services via simulation is difficult, because services are offered and processed by different logistics service providers of the network and thus are based on different information sources and different kind of models. In this paper both issues are addressed with a comprehensive method. Engineering is supported by the service map that is an electronic catalog and construction system for services to create alternatives of process models from composite services automatically. Evaluation is assisted by an automated transformation of process models to simulation models. Information exchange between both concepts is realized with a model-driven integration approach.

Keywords: Logistics · Planning · Model-driven · Process alternatives · Engineering · Evaluation

1 Introduction

Logistics focuses on planning, operating and monitoring systems that comprise material flow as well as the related information flow [1]. Resulting from the common paradigms of division of labor and outsourcing, a high number of participants within logistics systems arises. Each of them maintains a wide range of IT-systems as well as a wide range of services with differing provider-specific descriptions [2]. This complexity is difficult to handle, e.g. see [3,4], in order to negotiate and fulfill specific and individual logistics contracts. Especially, the planning phase of a logistics system forms the basis of all future operations and system's results. This fact implicates a challenging issue that arises from the high amount of stakeholders, services, their descriptions and possible combinations.

Planning is generally differentiated into the commonly accepted classification of strategic (long-term), tactical (mid-term) and operational (short-term)

S. Hammoudi et al. (Eds.): ICEIS 2015, LNBIP 241, pp. 364–384, 2015.
DOI: 10.1007/978-3-319-29133-8_18

planning [5]. Tactical planning in logistics is typically situated in the competence area of central logistics departments [5], which could also be outsourced to and represented by a central logistics integrator (e.g. fourth party logistics service provider [6,7] or lead logistics provider), while actual operation and physical movement of goods is carried out by subsidiary logistics service providers (LSP) [8,9]. Tactical planning in logistics addresses the flexibility of processes (volume, delivery and preconditions of operation) as well as supply chain design, relationships and inter-organizational information systems [4,10,11]. The term flexibility means the ability to be easily modified by maintaining and analyzing a variety of alternatives in order to choose the best for a specific task under current conditions [12]. In summary, tactical planning in logistics focuses on the *engineering* of available process alternatives and their *evaluation* [10].

When analyzing the applied methods of tactical planning in logistics, literature provides a wide range of publications addressing this specific topic, see e.g. [1,10,13,14]. Consensus of all approaches is a planning procedure subdivided into several distinct phases, whereas there are different numbers of phases and aspects to be considered in each approach. Further consensus could be found in a non-linear phase-sequence as iterative loops are allowed and encouraged in order to develop appropriate solutions. Another important similarity - as already pointed out - is the development of distinct planning alternatives and the subsequently evaluation of each in order to either approximate the current solution towards an optimum or to find the best solution to a given task. However, a common shortcoming of planning methods is an inadequacy in a specific description on how to create and evaluate process alternatives.

Especially, tactical planning - as the foundation of flexibility - in the field of transport and distribution is underrepresented in research [10]. Further, the related adaptable IT is important for inter-organizational information linkage [4,12]. This leads to additional difficulties as a variety of annotations and modeling methods exists next to the variety of IT-systems of the LSP. Hence, the paper focuses on fostering tactical planning issues on IT-level. Since tactical planning lacks in a concrete method for the development of different alternatives and this issue is an essential aspect for flexibility, an approach is needed that supports the finding and subsequent evaluation of alternatives. A comprehensive overview for logistics integrators of currently available alternatives of services and processes in the network is needed to develop a wide range of potential solutions. Due to a high number of participants and their diverse approaches for service description within an open logistics network [2,9], a suitable solution for engineering and evaluation of composite services and the resulting processes within the heterogeneous LSP-landscape (and their related service descriptions and IT-systems) could be found in a model-driven approach.

The paper's contribution is a method for linking engineering and evaluation of process alternatives to support logistics integrators. After presenting the basic concepts in Sect. 2, a model-driven approach is introduced in Sect. 3 that focuses on their combination using a common metamodel. The developed method for engineering and evaluation in Sect. 4 and a summary with future research prospects in Sect. 5 conclude the paper.

2 Basic Concepts

With the issues in mind (engineering and evaluation of alternatives), the following section first introduces an approach of a combined catalog and construction system (the logistics service map) for engineering and afterward focuses on simulation in logistics as an approach for the evaluation of composite service alternatives.

2.1 Logistics Service Map

The challenge of retrieving appropriate services with heterogeneous descriptions from different IT-systems [2] that arise from a complex logistics network with numerous participants demands a solution that is commonly accepted by all network participants. Those challenges create the requirement of presenting the services of a network in a common way (catalog function) and combining them in order to form composite services (modular service construction system function). This issue can be solved by the concept of the service map (SM).

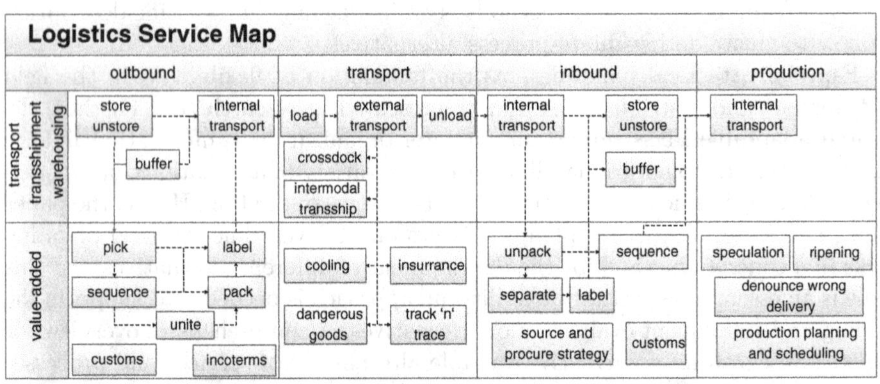

Fig. 1. Exemplary catalog-part of the SM with two dimensions: 'classic logistics function vs. value-added' and 'stage-specific'. Dashed arrows mark compatible services for composition.

The concept of the SM addresses the challenges by combining these two functions [15]. On the one hand, a catalog of all available services and process activities is provided. Every network participant has to subscribe its services to this catalog in order to have a commonly used single point of truth. With these characteristics the SM covers the conceptual functionality of a service repository. Though, to increase usability, the overview could be categorized by the user's needs in different abstraction layers. As shown in Fig. 1, a graphical representation with two spatial dimensions for the user-chosen categories simplifies the interaction for users when searching for services or process activities. In that way, service retrieval is enhanced and can be done in an intuitive way. Besides the intuitive manual usage, the catalog function also fosters a systematic categorization for (semi-)automated retrieval of atomic services. On the other hand, the concept includes a modular service construction system in order to combine atomic services to composite services. Through combination, service descriptions of the composite services are derived so that they could be transformed into process models later on for, e.g. collaborative planning in networks, simulation or mediation. With this approach, the network participants are supported in retrieving services in different use cases. (1) Adding a new service provider to the network and matching its offered services to the existing set of services in a logistics network by adding the new service provider to the provider list of the particular existing services. (2) Developing a new composite service to meet a specific customer's need by selecting and composing appropriate services from the SM. Service-specific information and attributes can be displayed when changing the selected granularity to a more detailed level to foster engineering and management. Moreover, the unique standard of the used set of services within a network and the visualization foster a precise mediation and communication between all stakeholders during the whole service life-cycle. (3) Finding compensational service or provider when realizing the urgency for re-planning or elimination of errors because of unpredictable disturbances in the network or an insufficiency in solving a given task. By analyzing the category of a distinct service that is to be replaced, a similar service with similar capabilities can be found automatically. Summarizing, the SM is capable of representing and creating planning alternatives.

Literature provides a wide variety concerning the SM concept. Either (a) the term 'service map' is used and also the functionality meets partly the requirements mentioned above, e.g. [16–19], or (b) the term is used but a different substantial functionality is addressed, e.g. [20] or (c) the term is not used but the described concept partly includes functionality for the mentioned purpose, e.g. [21,22]. Collectively, none of the approaches comprise both functionalities of catalog and construction system. As the SM concept comprises both, its functionality enables the engineering of services for a later combination to more complex processes. Hence, the creation of composite service alternatives could be realized with the use of this concept.

2.2 Simulation in Logistics

The planning of composite logistics services is performed using several different models (e.g. process model, service profile, and simulation model). A rough plan, including each sub-service and their temporal dependencies, is represented by a process model. Based on this, dynamic aspects of logistics systems can be analyzed using simulation. The main task of simulation in logistics is studying the behavior of composite logistics services (e.g. lead times, transport volumes and capacities) to ensure that customers' requirements can be met. Thus, it is possible to analyze the flow of goods through the logistics system with regard to the capacity to identify bottlenecks at an early planning stage. As a result, simulation models of logistics networks can be used to evaluate different composite service alternatives or process alternatives, respectively and consequently can improve the decision-making process in tactical logistics planning. Especially, discrete-event simulation (DES) is appropriate to enhance decision support in the planning process by analyzing several system configurations, which differ in structure and behavior [23]. However, the use of simulation also leads to a number of problems.

As mentioned previously, different models (process model, provider models and simulation model) are used within the planning process. This is a major problem because each time a model is slightly modified, any of the other related models must also be revised. As already outlined in the introduction, the modeled information itself could also differ from one provider to another whereby a wide range of descriptions and used annotations arises within a network with a high number of participants. This increases the modeling effort. Further, building simulation models requires special training and experience in order to avoid errors. It is a methodology that is learned over time. Consequently, the creation and analysis of simulation models could be expensive while consuming an enormous amount of time. This can lead to a non-profitable use of simulation [24]. As a consequence, the effort for the development of simulation models has to be reduced. In terms of planning logistics systems several models are used. These models build upon one another and show dependencies among each other. A change in a model also implicates and claims changes in subsequent models. To ensure the interaction between simulation and other models, simulation techniques have to be well-integrated in the planning process [25]. It is necessary that the created process models within the planning process, based on a separate description of each logistics service, can be transformed automatically into a simulation model. Accordingly, an approach to combine different heterogeneous planning models in order to force the reuse of already modeled information is needed. This requirement aims to minimize the planning effort of a logistics integrator by reusing already modeled information. In addition, manual errors in the creation of a simulation model are avoided. Furthermore, the need for special training and special experience in simulation model building is reduced.

In this section an approach is presented to transform process models into simulation models in order to reuse already modeled information and thus reduce modeling effort. Related work is presented by describing different simulation approaches that have influenced the development. Simulation is widely used in the field of logistics in order to plan logistics systems. Ingalls discusses the benefits of simulation as a method of studying the behavior of logistics networks [26]. Additionally, advantages and disadvantages are illustrated for the analysis of supply chains with the use of simulation. A concrete simulation approach is not provided. In [27], a commonly applicable simulation framework for modeling supply chains is presented. Contrary to [26], they focus on a more technical perspective as they show an overview of event-discrete simulation environments in terms of domains of applicability, types of libraries, input-output functionalities, animation functionalities, etc. Cimino et al. also show how and when to use certain programming languages as a viable alternative for such environments. A modeling approach and a simulation model for supporting supply chain management are presented by Longo and Mirabelli in [28]. They also provide a decision making tool for supply chain management and, therefore, develop a discrete event simulation tool for supply chain simulation. All these approaches are relevant for developing an integrated planning and simulation approach. However, all these approaches satisfy the logistics integrator's specific requirements [25] only partially. The development of simulation models based on process models is insufficiently considered.

In addition, we make use of transformation approaches for defining transformation models as a mediator between process and simulation models. In both approaches of [29,30] a transformation model is used in an additional step in order to derive a simulation model from an already existing process model. Both approaches take the fact that process models are independently defined from simulation requirements. In practice, process models serve to foster transparency or documentation and to analyze the requirements for the introduction or implementation of new information systems. However, both approaches assume that a process model is defined using Event-driven Process Chain. Cetinkaya proposes a comprehensive theoretical framework for model driven development in the field of modeling and simulation (M&S) for the efficient development of reliable, error-free and maintainable simulation models (MDD4MS framework) [31]. In a case example it is shown that MDD4MS framework is applicable in the Discrete Event System Specification (DEVS)-based discrete event simulation domain. The transformation of the Business Process Model and Notation (BPMN) elements into DEVS components has provided an effective way to easily model and simulate business processes. However, the MDD4MS framework currently provides only model transformation method from BPMN process model (conceptual modeling language) to DEVS (platform-independent simulation model) and from DEVS to Java (platform-specific simulation models). Furthermore, the required parameters for simulation were added directly to the Java code and thus can be performed by simulation experts only. Huang describes another interesting approach for Automated Simulation Model Generation [32]. The proposed method can use existing data to automatically generate simulation models. Therefore, a domain meta-model and the model component library have to be designed before the existing data can be used to provide the information about the model structure and parameterization. However, in contrast to our research the use of existing process models as source models are not considered. Nevertheless, the use of existing data for the parameterization of simulation models shows similarities to our research.

The added value of the simulation approach presented in this paper is the automatic transformation of existing process models to simulation models, as described in the following. A process model, e.g. BPMN or Event-driven Process

Chain (EPC), is simulation independent, i.e. the model does not contain any information regarding to the dynamic aspects such as arrival times, processing times or capacities. The process model is transferred into a transformation model and enriched with information required to run a simulation. However, the transformation model is platform independent and therefore cannot be executed in a specific simulation tool. The specific simulation models (e.g. Enterprise Dynamics (ED), Arena) are generated from the transformation model. The structure of the transformation model is described in more detail in [33]. Figure 2 illustrates this approach.

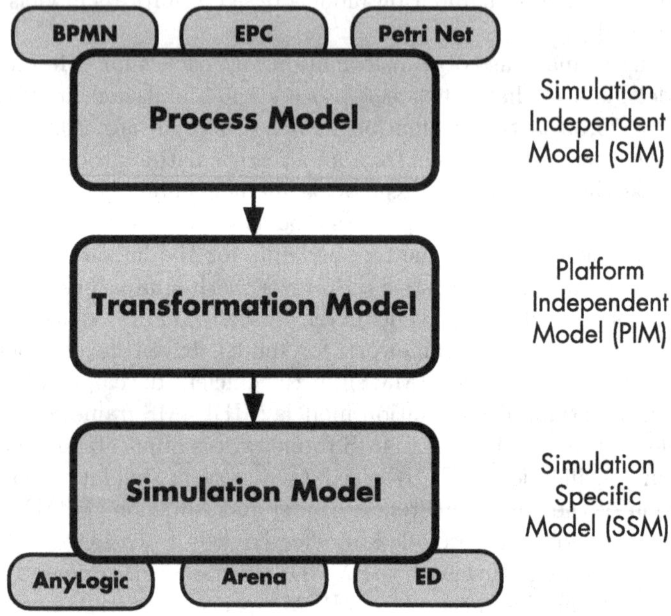

Fig. 2. Transformation approach from process models to simulation models.

Even though, simulation provides a possibility to evaluate composite service alternatives, the main problem in the current context is a dependency on process models that need to be existent before the transformation is done, in order to conduct their evaluation via simulation models afterward. Accordingly, a combination with the former presented SM concept appears to be a suitable approach for an integrated engineering and evaluation of composite service alternatives. The connection of both concepts is presented in the following section.

3 Model-Driven Connection of Concepts

The combination of these presented concepts for engineering and evaluation of process alternatives is realized by a model-driven approach. General information about and a foundation of model-driven development and metamodeling can be found in [34]. The basic idea of this approach is to create metamodels of these introduced concepts that conform to a common metametamodel. As models are derived from those metamodels and thus conform to them as well, interconnection and data-consistency can be ensured between models with a (transitive) common metametamodel. In the beginning the general approach is introduced as well as the distinct metamodels of both concepts and at the end of the section their connection is described.

3.1 Model Integration

Models used for planning composite logistics services are designed to maintain specific information of involved services. Each planning tool has therefore a distinct metamodel as a formal base. In order to model the process of such a composite service we use, for instance, BPMN, but there is no explicit limitation in the choice of a process modeling language. Thus, during the whole process of defining a composite service, such a service is comprehensively described using various models. Dependant on the distinct modeled aspect the resulting models might then contain either disjoint or overlapping information in a sense that the same information is contained in multiple models. Since many stakeholders are involved in modeling, this situation can even get worse, when the same aspect is modeled differently by different stakeholders (e.g. using homonyms or synonyms). At the same time, we have to ensure that new modeling/planning tools can be integrated and that the overall planning, monitoring and controlling process for composite services is kept efficient. So, in our approach we foster the reuse of already modeled information and with this we are also able to avoid modeling the same aspect in different manners.

To overcome the above mentioned situation, the Service Modeling Framework (SMF) and its components [35–37] serve as a mediator and are crucial for model and information management. In SMF services are defined using a variety of models which represent certain aspects, for instance an interface or a process description, a service level agreement specification or specific characteristics in terms of runtime performance. The SMF is responsible for coping with these models, for integrating and for storing them in order to ensure consistent engineering and evaluation and thus, enables a standardized handling of service descriptions and service models. The main purpose of SMF is to interconnect all involved models on metamodel level in a such way that contained information can be extracted and reused. Each model is seen as a projection of a virtual comprehensive model within the framework. Applied to the concepts in this article, SMF is responsible for interconnecting models in the planning phase for engineering and evaluation of composite services in order to transfer information from the engineering of alternatives of composite service models to the evaluation of simulation models. SMF thus supports development of a proper simulation model from a initially developed composite service model.

3.2 Service Map Metamodel

The SM supports the categorization and development of services. Instances of the SM can be derived by the logistics integrator from the metamodel to describe specific distinct service catalogs of a network or of different networks. The advantage of a metamodeling approach is a high abstraction that provides a high reusability in a wide range of cases and a simple interaction between several instances. The SM metamodel follows the restrictions of the service modeling framework (SMF) [36], i.e. based on the EMOF (Essential Meta Object Facility) compatible Ecore metametamodel of the Eclipse Foundation. Figure 3 shows the current version of the SM metamodel [38].

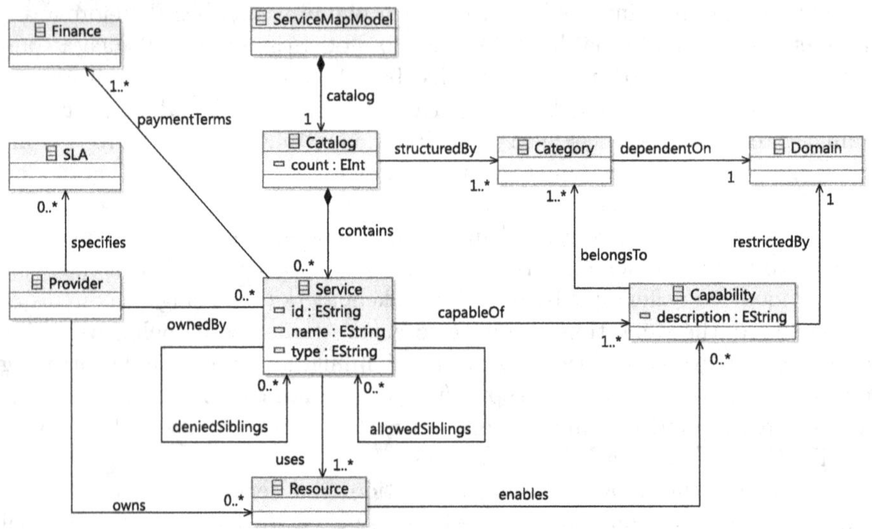

Fig. 3. Service map metamodel [38].

The following aspects are determined through the presented metamodel. Each instance of the SM metamodel consists of exactly one catalog containing services available within the network. This catalog is structured using categories that depend on a specific domain (i.e. logistics in our case). Thus, the catalog represents a structured overview of services, each capable of one or more capabilities. These capabilities belong to specific categories and are restricted by the concrete domain. On a high level, for instance, capabilities represent the ability to transport, store or to fulfill more complex composite and value adding services. In order to provide capabilities in terms of services, a provider owns specific resources like trucks or warehouses which are consumed during service execution but typically are available again afterward. Each provider is also allowed to specify zero or more service level agreements (SLA) for its services in which it specifies service level constraints and service provisioning in terms of payment. Finally, services can either depend on other services or are restricted not to work with other services. Exemplary, restrictions for the transportation of dangerous goods could be mentioned, see [39]. Therefore, each service contains references to others which are either available for the creation of a composite service (allowedSiblings) or not (deniedSiblings).

An instance of a logistics SM thus represents a complete list of capabilities (represented by services) of the provider network, including services the integrator can provide on its own. Hence, the service map serves as a catalog of available services. Moreover, during the creation of a composite logistics service for a customer, the service map also serves as a unique point of information and as a reference for searching appropriate services and providers. This becomes apparent in the development phase in particular. During rough planning of a logistics service, the composite service has to be constructed by choosing suitable services. According to customers' requirements, appropriate providers have to be chosen for each task in the composite service. Therefore, the service map is used to identify providers who offer the needed service type and SLA. Because the logistics SM follows a metamodel-based approach, an integrator also has the ability to manage multiple provider networks independently, for instance in automotive industry. Requirements of OEMs (Original Equipment Manufacturer) are very strict as they often demand secure supply chains. Providers are not allowed to use distinct resources in different contracts. For instance, an integrator responsible for warehouses with vendor managed inventory (VMI) for multiple OEMs at nearby production sites is liable to provide warehouse resources to each of the OEM exclusively, i.e. separate infrastructure and employees, in order to keep business secrets. With this in mind, an integrator is still able to optimally allocate resources if he partitions its complete network into independent parts and manages each of them separately. Though, same services are in different catalogs, the integrator is aware of the total resources available and can create an efficient supply chain for each customer.

With the metamodel the contained information itself as well as the existing connections and attributes between several classes are structured and thus facilitate retrieval processes and allow an information based connection to other types of models or between different instances of SMs.

3.3 Generic Simulation Metamodel

The generic simulation metamodel also follows the approach of the service modeling framework (SMF) [36], i.e. based on the EMOF compatible Ecore metametamodel of the Eclipse Foundation.

In the following, the approach is described in more detail and it is shown how the generic simulation metamodel (platform independent) was created by considering the basic concepts of DES and the specific requirements from the perspective of a logistics integrator. Process models describe functional or structural aspects that are relevant for a process. Depending on the used process model notation, these functional aspects (e.g. Task in BPMN, Function in EPC, Transitions in Petri Net) represent the different partial atomic services as parts

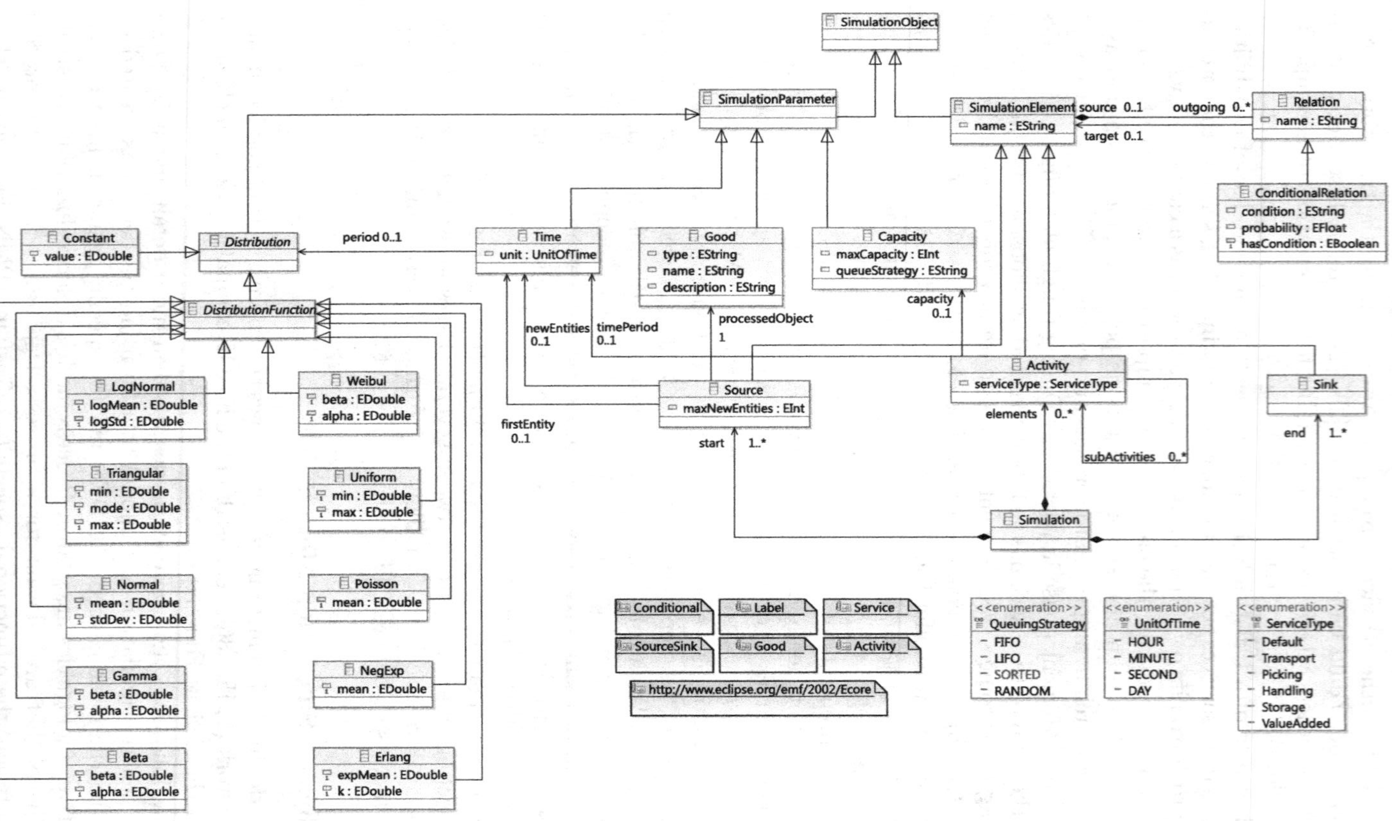

Fig. 4. Generic simulation metamodel [40].

of the composite services and processes in the scope of a logistics integrator's planning process. In [41] an approach for formal and semantic description of services in the logistics domain using concepts of service orientation and semantic web technologies is presented. The approach also categorizes and describes modular logistics services such as transport, handling, storage, value-added services, etc. using a logistics ontology. Concepts of this ontology are used in this research paper to refer to the description of specific logistics services from the functional aspects depending on the used process model language (Task, Function or Transition). Thus, each functional aspect is assigned to a specific logistics service type. Consequently, the result is a process model including all atomic services necessary to meet customers' requirements. Despite having a process model and using this model as the basis for creating a simulation model, for simulation additional information as to the pure visualization of the processes is necessary. Therefore, literature was analyzed concerning information that is additionally required to create a simulation model and relating basic concepts were derived (Entities, Events, Attributes, Activities and Delays) [40]. In addition to these basic concepts of DES, a simulation also has logistics-specific properties. Therefore, two simulation tools using an application-oriented modeling concept (ED and Arena) have been used to create different examples of simulation models in order to study transport volumes and capacities. These tool-dependent models have been analyzed and compared in terms of used modeling concepts and the required data. The common concepts of these tool-dependent models and the basic concepts of DES were used to create the metamodel shown in Fig. 4.

The generic simulation metamodel basically consists of SimulationElements, SimulationParameters and Relations. A Source generates goods at predefined time periods and they leave the model at the Sink. The purpose of an Activity is to manipulate goods in some ways, e.g. to store or to transport them. Therefore, Goods enter an activity and remain there for a certain time period. Moreover, an activity is assigned to a certain ServiceType which defines the specific functionality of this activity. These three main concepts are subsumed under SimulationElements. All Time periods can also be specified more precisely with the help of DistributionFunctions. Regarding the service type, a Capacity is an additional characteristic of an activity. For instance, an activity with the service type "warehouse service" is restricted by a maximum capacity and has a certain queuing strategy. Time, capacity, goods and distribution are subsumed under SimulationParameters. The connecting elements between the activities are represented by two different kinds of Relations. On the one hand, relations can be simple, i.e. without specific characteristics. On the other hand, a connection between activities can be represented by ConditionalRelations with additional, specific characteristics (conditions, probabilities). Depending on values of these characteristics, in a simulation either one or the other path is used. With this metamodel, it is possible to create simulation-tool-independent models, which contain all information necessary to perform a simulation. Further, a structure is built between several information aspects and thus fosters a parameter specific evaluation and improvement of processes or composite services, respectively.

3.4 Interconnecting the Models

Especially, for an efficient engineering and evaluation, services and their descriptions have to be handy in terms of analyzing and processing. The SMF editor component provides a flexible way of interconnecting models and model elements so that appropriate information is picked from the individual models and merged into a more complex service definition. To provide a basis for interconnection of service models, SMF contains a metamodel called Common Service Model (CSM, [35]). The CSM serves as a basic structure for the SMF as essential concepts in general are defined and connected to each other. It also introduces specialized elements, namely ServiceAspect and ServiceDescriptionElement, in order to connect models and their elements respectively. The CSM is also point of origin for a set of artifacts, like the SMF editor. In contrast to automated model transformation approaches, SMF relies on a descriptive, informal interconnection. Existing approaches for a model-to-model transformation connect elements from different models on metamodel level and then perform a semi-automated transformation on model level. This isn't appropriate for our approach because of the following reasons: on the one hand, transformations are realized directly and only on metamodel level. If we then wanted to add a new model type we would have to define multiple transformations for each already existing metamodel. On the other hand, transformations can only be implemented in an automated fashion by comparing the abstract syntax of a language. Very often, however, manual steps have to be added in order to make sure that the transformation is correct and complete (e.g. see the definition of extensional connections in [42] or see the definition of intermodel-correspondences in [43]). Model transformations are valuable and easy to perform if both models (source and sink) cope with the same issue (e.g. transformation of a BPMN-model into a BPEL-model). Within the SMF we, however, have to cope with models which are entirely different in scope and functionality. On a conceptual as well as technical level we use a modified version of the CSM within the editor and thus are able to model only valid relationships (in matters of SMF) between different services and their models respectively. Because the CSM is the metamodel of the editor the resulting model is thus a version of the comprehensive service model for a certain service. Later on, we can also extend this version if new service models are added to the service or if requirements changed and dependencies between models have to be updated. The comprehensive model is then used as input for an information extraction step which takes the contained models and their elements respectively and sees to transfer information into the appropriate places.

In the following it is presented by whom and how the SMF editor should be used. SMF components in general are designed for the usage at the logistics integrator's site. Participating partners like customers or LSPs are not confronted with these concepts as they are not directly involved in tasks like network management or building complex supply chains. Instead, the editor is intended for usage by logistics domain experts. They are able to analyze logistics processes and descriptions from subsidiary providers, to model information in logistics service models and therefore have deep knowledge about different model types.

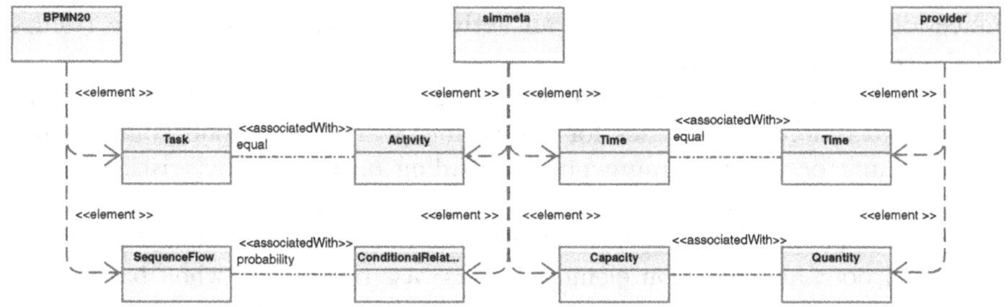

Fig. 5. SMF editor modeling (excerpt) [36].

Logistics domain experts use the SMF editor in order to identify and mark model elements of different models which contain equal or similar information.

Services and models can be dragged from a repository component into the editor and relationships can be defined as depicted in Fig. 5. Information has to be integrated from a process model ("BPMN2.0") - derived from the composite service - and from different "provider" models into a simulation model ("simmeta"). The process model is derived from the composite service built with the service map and thus conforms the service map metamodel. Simmeta equals the generic simulation metamodel. Thus, we look for elements in the source as well as in the sink models which contain equal or similar information with respect to conceptual identity. A task in a process, is e.g. semantically equal to an activity in the simulation model. Further, information from modeled sequence flows can be used in simulation. Defining such connections is repeated for each used model and the resulting service model is used as input for the extraction component of SMF which in turn is responsible for creating and updating models.

The two presented metamodels are kept simple and only consist of a few essential elements and their relationships. As both follow the SMF of [36] it is possible to interconnect elements from different models with the common service model (CSM) [35]. The CSM contains a metamodel for integration and transformation of differing models. Both models are defined through the same modeling language on metamodel-level, i.e. Ecore metametamodel. Hence, we are able to reuse information contained in these models and to easily interweave them. The metamodels are defined in Ecore but could be easily implemented in other frameworks as well. The Service is the central element of the SM metamodel. As services implicate a kind of input and output connected to a certain capability and can contain sub-services, a connection to the Activity element of the generic simulation metamodel is suggested. Hence, an interchange of information and an automated workflow can be implemented to combine engineering and evaluation of process alternatives.

4 Method Engineering

In this section a method for semi-automated engineering and evaluation is developed. The leading approach is a process model for method engineering. After connection of the basic approaches an activity diagram illustrates the results and the contribution of this paper.

The process model for method engineering presented by Ralyté and Roland outlines two different strategies for assembling so called method components, method chunk or method fragments. Depending on the characteristics, either an *association* strategy or an *integration* strategy is proposed for assembling method components [44]. The first strategy is recommended for method components without any common elements. This case occurs e.g. when basic components are working in a serial manner, i.e. the output of one component is used as the input for another component. Thus, by associating the two initial components a method can be created that provides a larger coverage than any of the basic ones. Hence, the objective of this assembling process strategy is to *retrieve connection points* and build a bridge between them. In contrary, the latter strategy concentrates on merging overlapping elements in two components that focus on similar tasks but with e.g. different solving strategies. The range of possible results remains similar but functionality is enhanced. The focus of this assembling process strategy is the retrieval of overlapping elements in order to merge them. Consequently, the *association strategy* is suitable for the purpose of the current paper. Engineering and evaluation are two different method components that focus each on solving different tasks. Further, the output of the engineering, i.e. one or more composite service alternatives and the related process models, constitutes the input for the subsequent evaluation. The non-existence of common elements, which is to be recognized when comparing the presented metamodels, underlines the decision for the association strategy as well as the serial characteristic of the designated final functionality of the two initial components.

The figuring out of connection points for the association of the basic components is also based on the approach of Ralyté and Roland, taking [45,46] into account. Mainly, the original approach focuses on detecting semantical and structural similarities between the elements of the two components that are to be connected. By evaluating their common properties and links, several similarity measures are calculated to conduct the assembly later on. However, an adapted and, for the purpose of this paper, simplified argumentative-deductive version is used. As already outlined, the element *Activity* of the simulation metamodel comprises an input-output relation for a specific object. Further, there is the possibility of dividing activities into sub-activities and they are always restricted by a certain capacity. This complies with the element *Service* of the SM metamodel. A service also focuses on taking an input object in order to releasing a modified output object. The division into subservices or combination to composite services also complies with the activity-pendant. Finally, as a service always depends on a certain resource and those resources have inherent distinct capacities, a similarity can be detected between those aspects. As the original purposes of the two metamodels strongly differ, no other similarities can be figured out. In summary, the analysis of the both metamodels shows that the suggested possible connection point of the Activity and the Service element can be confirmed and implemented in the SMF editor.

Following [44], the "specification of method requirements" is outlined in the introduction in Sect. 1 and the "construction of the basic method components" is conducted through the cited literature of Sects. 2 and 3. Subsequently, the paper now proceeds with the "assembly" by determining the order of the components, identifying the connection point, i.e. the product of the first component that constitutes the source for the second one, and merging both. The engineering of an alternative before evaluating it implies the order of the components. Moreover, an iterative loop is obligatory until all possible alternatives are calculated. Connection point between the two components is the process model of the composite service that is the output of the construction system, as it is simultaneously the input for the transformation model for the later simulation. Information can be interchanged via the CSM. The final result is shown in Fig. 6.

The final method starts with the determination of customer requirements and the selection of the process or composite service from the repository that is to be (re-)planned. After selecting the process steps or sub-services, which are to be alternated and analyzed, the loop iteration starts. When no alternatives are available, an empty list of alternatives is presented to the user. As long as alternatives are still available, for every chosen (sub-)service all available alternatives from its category in the catalog are selected to create a new composite service in the construction system. With the derived description of the composite service, the engineering of the process alternative is conducted and a process model is created as the output of the first method component. The process model as the source of the generic simulation approach, is transformed into the transformation model, enriched with necessary simulation parameters, which could be analyzed and inserted from former operation statistics (like service profiles of [47]) to fully automate the method. Subsequently, the simulation is conducted in order to evaluate the composite service alternative. If the customer's requirements are met by the current alternative, it is added to the list that will be shown to the user later on. If not, the procedure continues without saving. If all available possibilities within one category for a specific sub-service are evaluated, the next sub-service is chosen to be alternated. After all sub-services have been alternated and all possible process alternatives have been evaluated, the final list with all alternatives, which meet the given customers requirements, is presented to the user. Sorted by its preferences (e.g. SLA, lead time, costs), the user could choose its favored alternative that is to be implemented afterward.

A simple use case could be a customer that is unsatisfied with the current performance of its supply chain that was planned by the logistics integrator. By analyzing the current performance parameters the lack in a certain transportation and a packing services is revealed. Hence, the integrator selects those services within the supply chain that are to be alternated and the resulting alternatives that are to be evaluated regarding the customers required performance parameters. Another use case could be a disturbance within a supply chain through an insolvency of

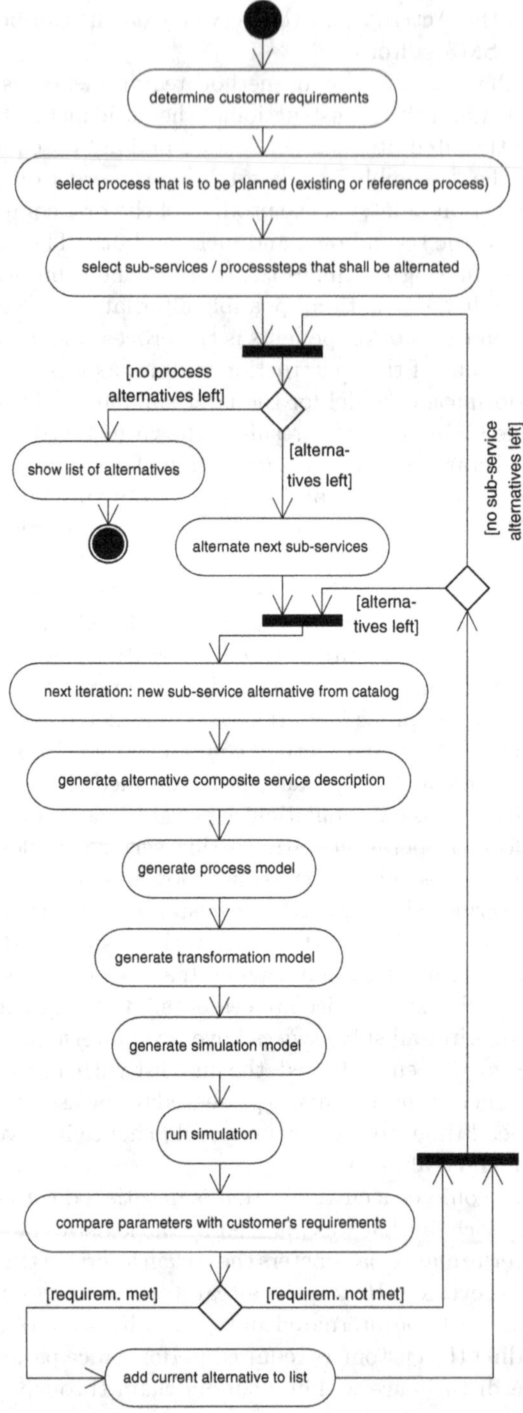

Fig. 6. Activity diagram of the resulting method.

one LSP within the network. Hence, cheap and/or reliable alternative LSPs are to be found for the affected supply chain processes.

5 Conclusion

Tactical planning of composite services in logistics networks is a challenging task because of the ongoing outsourcing trend. This results in the combination of logistics services from different LSP with heterogeneous service descriptions. This task is further complicated by the distribution of essential information to distinct models. Planning thus depends strongly on the combination of information from several sources. As current planning approaches in literature lack in a specific description on how to create process alternatives that are evaluated afterward, this paper presented a new method for automated engineering and evaluation of process alternatives in tactical logistics planning. Further, the challenging task of combining the required information from different models is solved. The method consists of two basic concepts, the *service map* as a combined catalog and construction approach for service engineering and a *generic simulation approach* for evaluation. Both concepts are designed especially for working in an environment of heterogeneous service descriptions and process models. By combining both concepts through a *model-driven approach*, the basis for interweaving the contained information is ensured. With the process model of [44] for assembling methods from sub-components, an associated method for combined engineering and evaluation of composite service is finally developed.

Academic implication of the current article is a first method towards automated and integrated engineering and evaluation of composite services alternatives or process alternatives in the heterogeneous field of logistics. Current literature about planning in logistics does only propose to create several alternatives and to evaluate them, but does not provide explicit methods on *how* to do so. Hence, the current paper also aims at motivating further research by the community in the field of IT-enabled support of planning activities in complex service networks.

Managerial implications cover the development of interest in (semi-)automated planning support and the creation of sensibility for benefits in terms of time and quality resulting from a possible automation. Further, cited references could be used to gain deeper understanding in particular fields of interest.

Limitations of our approach can be found in the focus on one specific modeling framework, i.e. the Ecore metametamodel. However, it is based on the EMOF constraints and thus, it is transferable to other modeling frameworks as well.

With this in mind, future work could cover a transfer to other platforms. Further, a refinement and the development of differing approaches of the automated engineering of process alternatives appears to be an interesting field of research. An evaluation with sample data from real life case studies is an urgent topic for upcoming research.

Acknowledgements. The work presented in this paper was funded by the German Federal Ministry of Education and Research under the project LSEM (BMBF 03IPT504X).

References

1. Gudehus, T., Kotzab, H.: Comprehensive Logistics. Springer, Heidelberg (2012)
2. Arnold, U., Oberländer, J., Schwarzbach, B.: LOGICAL - development of cloud computing platforms and tools for logistics hubs and communities. In: Proceedings of the Federated Conference on Computer Science and Information Systems (FedCSIS 2012), Wroclaw, Poland, 9–12 September 2012, pp. 1083–1090. IEEE (2012)
3. Faber, N., de Koster, R.B.M., van de Velde, S.L.: Linking warehouse complexity to warehouse planning and control structure: an exploratory study of the use of warehouse management information systems. Int. J. Phys. Distrib. Logistics Manag. **32**(5), 381–395 (2002)
4. Stevenson, M., Spring, M.: Flexibility from a supply chain perspective: definition and review. Int. J. Oper. Prod. Manag. **27**(7), 685–713 (2007)
5. Stadtler, H., Fleischmann, B., Grunow, M., Meyr, H., Sèurie, C.: Advanced Planning in Supply Chains: Illustrating the Concepts Using an SAP® APO Case Study. Springer, New York (2011)
6. 4flow AG: 4flow supply chain services (2014). http://www.4flow.de/
7. 4PL Central Station Deutschland GmbH: 4pl central station deutschland - leading provider in europe for fourth party logistics services (2014). http://4plcs.com/
8. Handfield, R., Straube, F., Pfohl, H.C., Wieland, A.: Trends and Strategies in Logistics and Supply Chain Management: Embracing Global Logistics Complexity to Drive Market Advantage. Bundesvereinigung Logistik, Hamburg (2013)
9. Langley, J., Long, M.: 2015 third-party logistics study: the state of logistics outsourcing: the 19th annual study (2015)
10. Esmaeilikia, M., Fahimnia, B., Sarkis, J., Govindan, K., Kumar, A., Mo, J.: Tactical supply chain planning models with inherent flexibility: definition and review. Ann. Oper. Res., 1–21 (2014). doi:10.1007/s10479-014-1544-3
11. Schütz, P., Tomasgard, A.: The impact of flexibility on operational supply chain planning. Int. J. Prod. Econ. **134**(2), 300–311 (2011)
12. Bibhushan, Prakash, A., Wadhwa, B.: Supply chain flexibility: some perceptions. In: Sushil, Stohr, E.A. (eds.) The Flexible Enterprise. Flexible Systems Management, pp. 321–331. Springer, New Delhi (2014)
13. Rushton, A., Croucher, P., Baker, P.: The Handbook of Logistics and Distribution Management: Understanding the Supply Chain. Kogan Page, London (2014)
14. ten Hompel, M., Schmidt, T., Nagel, L.: Materialflusssysteme: Förder- und Lagertechnik, 3rd edn. Springer, Heidelberg (2007)
15. Glöckner, M., Ludwig, A.: Towards a logistics service map: support for logistics service engineering and management. In: Blecker, T., Kersten, W., Ringle, C. (eds.) Pioneering Solutions in Supply Chain Performance Management: Proceedings of the Hamburg International Conference of Logistics (HICL 2013). Reihe: Supply chain, logistics and operations management, vol. 17, pp. 309–324. Eul (2013)
16. Kohlmann, F., Alt, R.: Aligning service maps - a methodological approach from the financial industry. In: Sprague, R.H. (ed.) Proceedings of the 42nd Annual Hawaii International Conference on System Sciences, pp. 1–10. IEEE Computer Society Press (2009)

17. Kim, J., Lee, S., Park, Y.: User-centric service map for identifying new service opportunities from potential needs: a case of app store applications. Creativity Innov. Manag. **22**(3), 241–264 (2013)
18. Vaddi, S., Mohanty, H., Shyamasundar, R.: Service maps in XML. In: Potdar, V. (ed.) Proceedings of the CUBE International Information Technology Conference, pp. 635–640. ACM (2012)
19. Kutscher, D., Ott, J.: Service maps for heterogeneous network environments. In: MDM 2006, Japan. IEEE Computer Society (2006)
20. Ryu, M.S., Park, H.S., Shin, S.C.: QoS class mapping over heterogeneous networks using application service map. In: Networking, International Conference on Systems and International Conference on Mobile Communications and Learning Technologies. ICN (2006)
21. Kohlborn, T., Fielt, E., Korthaus, A., Rosemann, M.: Towards a service portfolio management framework. In: ACIS 2009 - Australian Conference on Information Systems, pp. 861–870 (2009)
22. Fleischer, J., Herm, M., Homann, U., Peter, K., Sternemann, K.H.: Business capabilities als basis fähigkeitsorientiertel konfigurationen. ZWF - Zeitschrift für wirtschaftlichen Fabrikbetrieb **100**(10), 553–557 (2005)
23. VDI-Richtlinie: 3633, blatt 1: Simulation von logistik-, materialfluß- und produktionssystemen (2010)
24. Banks, J.: Handbook of Simulation Principles, Methodology, Advances, Applications, and Practice. Wiley, New York (1998). Co-published by Engineering & Management Press
25. Mutke, S., Klinkmüller, C., Ludwig, A., Franczyk, B.: Towards an integrated simulation approach for planning logistics service systems. In: Daniel, F., Barkaoui, K., Dustdar, S. (eds.) BPM 2011. Lecture Notes in Business Information Processing, vol. 1, pp. 306–317. Springer, Berlin (2012)
26. Ingalls, R.G.: The value of simulation in modeling supply chains. In: Medeiros, D.J., Watson, E.F., Carson, J.S., Manivannan, M. (eds.) Proceedings of the 30th Conference on Winter Simulation, pp. 1371–1376. IEEE Computer Society Press (1998)
27. Cimino, A., Longo, F., Mirabelli, G.: A general simulation framework for supply chain modeling: state of the art and case study. Int. J. Comput. Sci. Issues **7**(2), 1–9 (2010)
28. Longo, F., Mirabelli, G.: An advanced supply chain management tool based on modeling and simulation. Comput. Ind. Eng. **54**(3), 570–588 (2008)
29. Petsch, M., Schorcht, H., Nissen, V., Himmelreich, K.: Ein transformationsmodell zur überführung von prozessmodellen in eine simulationsumgebung. In: Loos, P., Nüttgens, M., Turowski, K., Werth, D. (eds.) Modellierung betrieblicher Informationssysteme - Modellierung zwischen SOA und Compliance Management, pp. 209–219 (2008)
30. Kloos, O., Schorcht, H., Petsch, M., Nissen, V.: Dienstleistungsmodellierung als Grundlage für eine Simulation. In: Thomas, O., Nüttgens, M. (eds.) Dienstleistungsmodellierung 2010, vol. 5, pp. 86–106. Physica-Verlag HD, Heidelberg (2010)
31. Cetinkaya, D.: Model driven development of simulation models: defining and transforming conceptual models into simulation models by using metamodels and model transformation. Ph.D. thesis (2013)
32. Huang, Y.: Automated simulation model generation. Ph.D. thesis (2013)
33. Mutke, S., Augenstein, C., Ludwig, A.: Model-based integrated planning for logistics service contracts. In: Bagheri, E., Gasevic, D., Hatala, M., Motahari Nezhad,

H.R., Reichert, M. (eds.) 17th IEEE International Enterprise Distributed Object Computing Conference, vol. 1, pp. 219–228. IEEE Computer Society (2013)
34. Atkinson, C., Kuhne, T.: Model-driven development: a metamodeling foundation. IEEE Softw. **20**(5), 36–41 (2003)
35. Augenstein, C., Ludwig, A., Franczyk, B.: Integration of service models-preliminary results for consistent logistics service management. In: 2012 Annual SRII Global Conference (SRII), pp. 100–109. IEEE (2012)
36. Augenstein, C., Ludwig, A.: The service meta modeling editor – bottom-up integration of service models. In: vom Brocke, J., Hekkala, R., Ram, S., Rossi, M. (eds.) DESRIST 2013. LNCS, vol. 7939, pp. 386–393. Springer, Heidelberg (2013)
37. Augenstein, C., Ludwig, A.: Interconnected service models - emergence of a comprehensive logistics service model. In: Bagheri, E., Gasevic, D., Halle, S., Hatala, M., Nezhad, H.R.M., Reichert, M. (eds.) 17th IEEE Enterprise Distributed Object Computing Conference Workshops (EDOCW 2013), pp. 239–245. IEEE, Vancouver (2013)
38. Glöckner, M., Ludwig, A., Augenstein, C.: Metamodel of a logistics service map. In: Abramowicz, W., Kokkinaki, A. (eds.) BIS 2014. LNBIP, vol. 176, pp. 185–196. Springer, Heidelberg (2014)
39. ADR: European Agreement Concerning the International Carriage of Dangerous Goods by Road. United Nations, New York (2012). Accessed 15 June 2015
40. Mutke, S., Roth, M., Ludwig, A., Franczyk, B.: Towards real-time data acquisition for simulation of logistics service systems. In: Pacino, D., Voß, S., Jensen, R.M. (eds.) ICCL 2013. LNCS, vol. 8197, pp. 242–256. Springer, Heidelberg (2013)
41. Hoxha, J., Scheuermann, A., Bloehdorn, S.: An approach to formal and semantic representation of logistics services. In: Schill, K., Scholz-Reiter, B., Frommberger, L. (eds.) Workshop on Artificial Intelligence and Logistics (AILog), pp. 73–78 (2010)
42. Romero, J.R., Jan, J.I., Vallecillo, A.: Realizing correspondences in multi-viewpoint specifications. In: IEEE International Enterprise Distributed Object Computing Conference, pp. 163–172. IEEE (2009)
43. Selonen, P., Kettunen, M.: Metamodel-based inference of inter-model correspondence. In: Krikhaar, R., Verhoef, C., Di Lucca, G.A. (eds.) 11th European Conference on Software Maintenance and Reengineering, pp. 71–80. IEEE (2007)
44. Ralyté, J., Rolland, C.: An assembly process model for method engineering. In: Dittrich, K.R., Geppert, A., Norrie, M. (eds.) CAiSE 2001. LNCS, vol. 2068, pp. 267–283. Springer, Heidelberg (2001)
45. Castano, S., De Antonellis, V.: A constructive approach to reuse of conceptual components. In: Proceedings of the Advances in Software Reuse (1993)
46. Jilani, L.L., Mili, R., Mili, A.: Approximate component retrieval: an academic exercise or a practical concern. In: Proceedings of the 8th Workshop on Istitutionalising Software Reuse, Columbus, Ohio (1997)
47. Klarmann, A., Franczyk, B., Mutke, S., Roth, M., Ludwig, A.: Continuous quality improvement in logistics service provisioning. In: Abramowicz, W., Kokkinaki, A. (eds.) BIS 2014. LNBIP, vol. 176, pp. 253–264. Springer, Heidelberg (2014)

CrossCutting Concerns Identification Supported by Ontologies: A Preliminary Study

Paulo Afonso Parreira Jr.[1,2(✉)] and Rosângela Dellosso Penteado[1]

[1] Department of Computer Science, Federal University of São Carlos, Sao Carlos, Brazil
paulojunior@jatai.ufg.br, rosangela@dc.ufscar.br
[2] Computer Science Course, Federal University of Goiás, Jatai, Goias, Brazil

Abstract. **Contextualization**: CrossCutting Concerns (CCC) or Early-Aspects consist of software concerns that are spread and/or tangled with requirements of other concerns and can be treated by Aspect-Oriented Requirements Engineering (AORE). **Problem**: several AORE approaches have been proposed, however, some experimental studies have found problems regarding to the accuracy of these approaches. According to the authors of these studies these problems occur, due to: (i) the lack of knowledge presented by the users of these approaches about the crosscutting nature of CCC; and (ii) the lack of resources to support users of these approaches during the CCC identification. **Goal**: this work aims to improve the CCC identification accuracy from the support of domain ontologies. Hence, an ontology for the CCC domain was proposed and the *Theme/Doc* AORE approach was extended aiming to make it suitable for the usage of this ontology. As results, a preliminary experimental study showed a significant increasing of the recall of the extended approach, without negative effects on the precision and execution time of it.

Keywords: Aspect-Oriented Requirements Engineering · Ontologies · Early-Aspects · CrossCutting Concerns

1 Introduction

The increasing of the software complexity and its applicability in several areas require that Requirements Engineering (RE) be performed in a comprehensive and complete way, in order to: (i) accomplish the needs of the stakeholders; and (ii) allow the Software Engineers and the stakeholders to get a full understanding of the software functionality, services and constraints. In the RE context, a set of software requirements related to the same goal/purpose is defined as a "concern" [9]. For example, a security concern can address several requirements regarding to the following goal: "make sure that the software is safe".

In an ideal scenario of software development, each concern should be allocated in a specific module, which achieves its goals [13]. When it occurs, the software is called well-modularized, because all their concerns are clearly separated. However, there are some kinds of concerns for which this clear allocation into modules is not possible using only the usual abstractions of software engineering, such as use cases, view-points,

S. Hammoudi et al. (Eds.): ICEIS 2015, LNBIP 241, pp. 385–407, 2015.
DOI: 10.1007/978-3-319-29133-8_19

goals, scenarios among others [33]. For instance, a security concern may contain requirements related to the encryption and/or authorization. An encryption requirement, in its turn, may affect some requirements related to orders management concern.

The previous example describes a well-known problem, called "concern tangling", that occurs when requirements of one concern affect requirements of other distinct concern(s); this problem may make hard the software understanding and evolution [36]. Aspect-Oriented Requirements Engineering (AORE) [4, 5, 18, 33] is the field that joins efforts on the development of methods, techniques and tools for dealing with this problem from the initial phases of the software development cycle. This is done in order to promote the Separation of Concerns, *i.e.*, the identification and modularization of pieces of the software that are relevant for a particular purpose.

In a recent systematic mapping performed by the authors of this paper [31], there were thirty-eight different AORE approaches published in the literature. This study states that most of the existing AORE approaches include the **Concern Identification and Classification** activity, which is responsible for identifying the software concerns, as well as classifying them as base, *i.e.*, concerns that do not affect requirements of other concerns, or as crosscutting ones. Some experimental studies, conducted on the main AORE approaches [22, 34], have pointed out the concern identification and classification as a bottleneck activity in the AORE approaches. The authors state that identifying CCC is harder than identifying base concerns. Some of the possible reasons for this are [22, 34]:

Base concerns are better known and understood by the scientific community than the CCC ones and many approaches are based only on the experience of software engineers who apply them. Some approaches support the software engineers during the concern identification and classification through guidelines, such as catalogues, but these guidelines generally are complex to be read and understood by humans and they are not prepared for automated semantic processing [27]. Moreover, most of these approaches does not present a process that instruct the software engineer on how to use the proposed guidelines; and

Some CCC are not explicitly mentioned in the requirements document, *i.e.*, they emerge from other concerns and some AORE approaches are based only on searching for keywords in the requirements document, what may affect the identification of implicit concerns. For instance, if the software requires a good performance to persist its data, a possible strategy is using concurrency mechanisms, such as connection pooling. Hence, the "Concurrency" concern is observed from the existence of two other CCC: "Persistence" and "Performance" [34].

Theme/Doc [5, 11] is an AORE approach that has been used, evolved and evaluated in several recent studies [3, 22, 24, 32]. This approach proposes that concern identification and classification activity be performed using a set of keywords identified by the software engineer from the software requirements. This strategy makes *Theme/Doc* highly depended on the software engineers' experience, what may lead to low levels of recall and precision, as stated in some experimental studies [22].

The main goal of this work is increasing the recall and precision provided by the *Theme/Doc* approach, regarding to the concern identification and classification. To do this, an ontology for CCC (*OntoCCC)* and an extension of the *Theme/Doc*

(*OnTheme/Doc*), in which the concern identification and classification activity is supported by the usage of *OntoCCC* instances, are proposed.

An ontology defines a specific vocabulary that captures the concepts and relationships of a domain and a set of explicit decisions (axioms), which describe the meaning of this vocabulary [15, 19]. Hence, the purpose of the *OntoCCC* ontology is capturing the specific concepts and relationships of crosscutting concerns domain, which have been documented in several AORE approaches in the literature [1, 3, 6–8, 26, 29, 30, 35–37, 39].

In this work, we consider that the usage of *OntoCCC* ontology may improve the recall and precision provided by the *Theme/Doc* approach as follows:

- **Regarding to the Dependence of Software Engineers' Experience:** the knowledge base of the *OntoCCC* ontology may be used for the definition of better keywords, aiming to minimize the dependence of the professionals' experience; and
- **Regarding to the Implicit CCC:** the mutual influence among different CCC may be documented in the *OntoCCC* ontology, aiming to allow the identification of CCC that are not explicitly described in the requirements document.

It is important to state that the usage of ontologies in the context of requirements engineering has been widely explored [27]. However, according to a recent systematic mapping of the literature [13], the usage of ontologies for concern identification and classification has not been fully exploited yet.

To verify the goal proposed in this paper, an experimental study involving undergraduate and graduate students in Computer Science from two Federal Universities in Brazil was conducted. The study was planning and implemented according to the procedure proposed by Wohlin *et al.* [38]. As results, it was observed that, with 99.9 % of significance level, the values of recall provided by the *OnTheme/Doc* approach is higher than those provided by *Theme/Doc*, regarding to the CCC identification. Besides, it was observed no significant differences with regard to the precision provided by both approaches, neither for the time spent by the participants of the experiment during the application of these approaches.

The main contributions of the paper are threefold: (i) the proposed ontology can help software engineers to better understand the main concepts and relationships of CCC; (ii) the proposed ontology can allow software engineers to perform automatic processing on it, what it is not easy to do with other kinds of approaches, like catalogues, vocabularies, thesaurus, among others; and (iii) the proposed approach presents how to use ontologies in the context of CCC identification and gives indications that this usage can improve the accuracy of this activity.

This paper is organized as follows: (i) Sect. 2 presents the main concepts about domain ontologies and the *Theme/Doc* approach; (ii) Sect. 3 describes the *OnTheme/Doc* approach, as well as the *OntoCCC* ontology; (iii) in Sect. 4, the planning, execution, results and threats to validity of the experimental study performed in this work are presented; (iv) Sect. 5 discusses the main works related to the proposal of this paper; and (v) finally, Sect. 6 presents the final remarks of this work and some proposals for future works.

2 Background

2.1 Ontologies

A domain ontology can be defined as a simplified and abstract view of a domain that includes the concepts of some area of interest and the relationships among them [16, 17]. One important feature of an ontology is its must be shared, *i.e.*, the knowledge captured by an ontology must be consensual, not limited to a specific individual. This section presents the three main concepts of domain ontologies: **Classes**, **Properties** and **Individuals** [21, 23, 25]. To illustrate these concepts, parts of the *OntoCCC* ontology (Sect. 3) are presented.

Classes are concrete representations of a concept. In practical terms, classes are interpreted as sets that contain individuals [23]. For example, the *CCC* class (represent by an oval shape in Fig. 1) represents all individuals that are crosscutting concerns. Classes can be arranged in superclass-subclass hierarchies. In Fig. 1, the *FunctionalCCC* and *NonFunctionalCCC* classes are subclasses of *CCC* (described by the "is-a" relationship), what means that all functional and non-functional CCC also are crosscutting concerns.

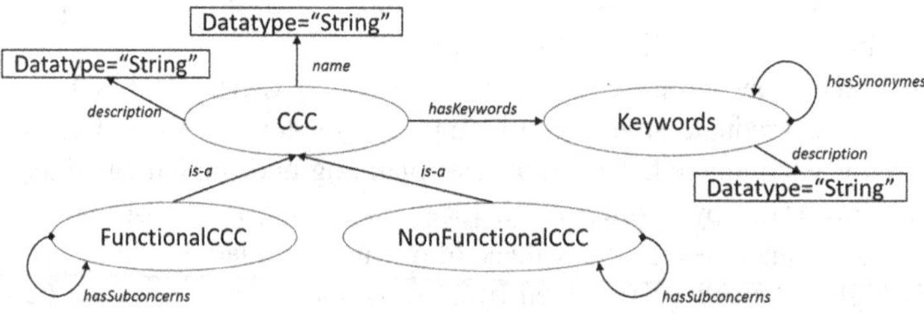

Fig. 1. Part of the *OntoCCC* ontology.

Properties are binary relationships that connect two individuals, two classes, an individual and a value or a class and a value. There are two main kinds of properties: "Object Properties" and "DataType Properties". The **"Object Properties"** are used to define relationships among classes. For example, the *hasKeywords* property (Fig. 1) connects the *CCC* class to the *Keywords* class. This property defines that a crosscutting concern, functional or non-functional, may contain a set of keywords that can be used to identify it. The *hasSubconcerns* property indicates that a CCC can be decomposed into sub-concerns, which also are CCC. Similarly, the *hasSynonymes* property recursively connects the *Keywords* class to itself, representing that a keyword may contain synonyms.

A **"DataType Property"** connects a class to a primitive value (*e.g.* an integer or a string value). For example, the *CCC* class has the *name* and *description* properties (Fig. 1), which can be connected to strings values; these properties specify, respectively, the name of a particular CCC and its description.

It is possible to enhance the meaning of the properties through the usage of attributes, such as "transitivity", "symmetry", among others. Accorded to Horrige *et al.* [23], if a property *P* is symmetric, and this property relates individual *A* to individual *B* then individual *B* is also related to individual *A* via property *P*. For instance, if *Matthew* is related to *Gemma* via the *hasSibling* property, then we can infer that *Gemma* must also be related to *Matthew* via the *hasSibling* property as well. If a property *P* is asymmetric, and it relates individual *A* to individual *B* then individual *B* cannot be related to individual *A* via property *P*.

A property *P* is said to be reflexive when the property must relate individual *A* to itself Horrige *et al.* [23]. Using the property *knows*, an individual *George* must have a relationship to itself using the property *knows*. In other words, *George* must *know* himself. If a property *P* is irreflexive, it can be described as a property that relates an individual *A* to individual *B*, where individual *A* and *B* are not the same. If a property *P* is transitive, and *P* relates individual *A* to individual *B*, and also individual *B* to individual *C*, then we can infer that individual *A* is related to individual *C* via property *P*. An example of transitive property is *hasAncestor*. If the individual *Matthew* has an *ancestor* that is *Peter*, and *Peter* has an *ancestor* that is *William*, then we can infer that *Matthew* has an *ancestor* that is *William*.

Accorded to the previous explanation, it is possible to notice that *hasSubconcerns* and *hasSynonymes* properties can be classified as irreflexive, asymmetric and transitive. This means that if the *A* keyword has a synonym *B* and *B* has a synonym *C*, so *C* is a synonym of *A* as well. A similar explanation can be derived for the *hasSubconcerns* property. The *hasKeywords* property, in turn, is irreflexive, asymmetric and intransitive.

Individuals, also known as "instances" or "class instances", represent objects of the domain of interest. In the *OntoCCC* ontology, examples of individuals are instances of CCC already identified and well-known by the scientific community (for example, security, logging, among others).

An example with six individuals is illustrated in Fig. 2: four individuals are instances of the *NonFunctionalCCC* class and two of the *Keywords* class (classes are highlighted in gray and individuals, in white). In this example, the non-functional CCC are "Logging", "Persistence", "Connection" and "Transaction"; "Connection" and

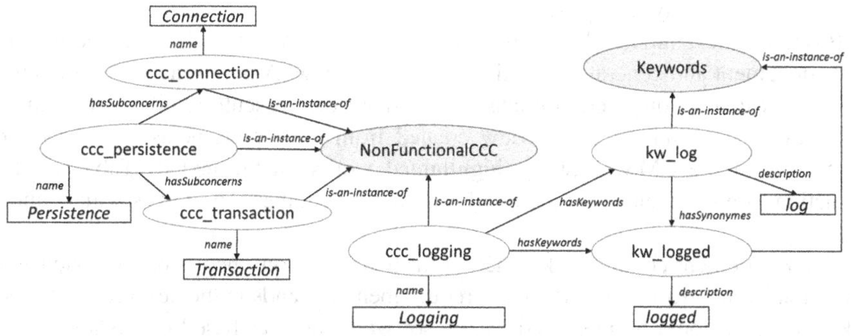

Fig. 2. Instantiation of the *OntoCCC* ontology.

"Transaction" are sub-concerns of "Persistence". In addition, the "Logging" concern is related to two keywords, called "logged" and "log", which are synonymous.

2.2 Theme/Doc Approach

The *Theme* approach [5, 11] supports the AORE field in two levels. At requirements level, the approach is called *Theme/Doc* and allows the software engineers to: (i) identify the software concerns from a set of keywords and software requirements; and (ii) refine the views provided by the approach to reveal which concerns are base and which are crosscutting ones. At design level, the approach is called *Theme/UML* and allows the software engineers to model, through specific notations, base and crosscutting concerns and specify how they can be combined.

To illustrate the main features of the *Theme/Doc* approach, an example of a Course Management Software – CMS [5], whose requirements are outlined in Table 1, is used.

Table 1. Requirements description of a course management software [5].

#	Requirements description
R1	Students can **register** for courses
R2	Students can **unregister** for courses
R3	When a student registers then it must be **logged** in their record
R4	When a student unregisters it must also be logged
R5	Professors can unregister students
R6	When a professor unregisters a student it must be logged
R7	Professors can **give** marks for courses
R8	When a professor gives a mark this must be logged in the record

Theme/Doc follows the process described in Fig. 3. To identify concerns, *Theme/Doc* offers a visualization resource, called "action-view". Two inputs are required for performing the **"Building an action-view"** activity of this approach: (i) a list of key-actions, which consists of verbs identified by the software engineer from the software requirements, during the execution of the **"Identifying key-actions"** activity; and (ii) a set of software requirements. The **"Classifying actions as base or crosscutting ones"** activity is explained later in this paper.

Based on these inputs, the software engineer performs an analysis of the requirements document and generates a preliminary action-view. A preliminary action-view is a view in which actions were not classified as base or crosscutting ones yet. Figure 4 illustrates the preliminary action-view created from the requirements and the list of key-actions of the CMS software (highlighted words, in the text of Table 1). The key-actions are represented by diamonds and the requirements by boxes with rounded edges.

If a requirement contains a key-action in its description, then it is associated with this action by an arrow that starts in the requirement and ends in the key-action. The set of key-actions should be identified by the software engineer based on his/her experience with regard to the domain for which the software is being developed.

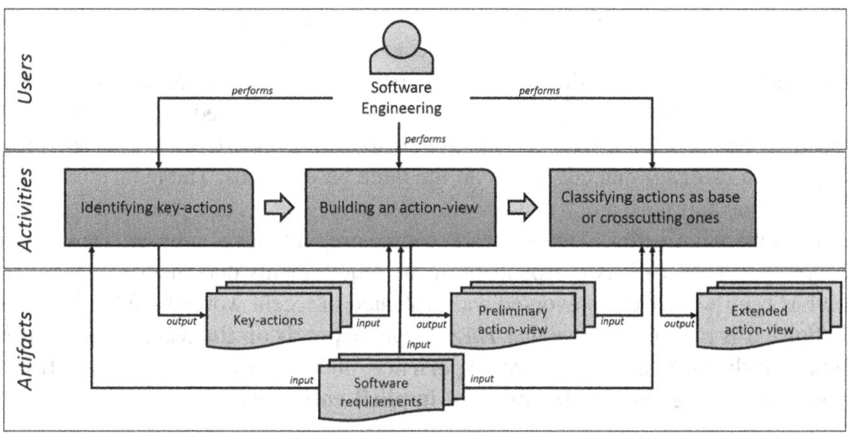

Fig. 3. *Theme/Doc* process.

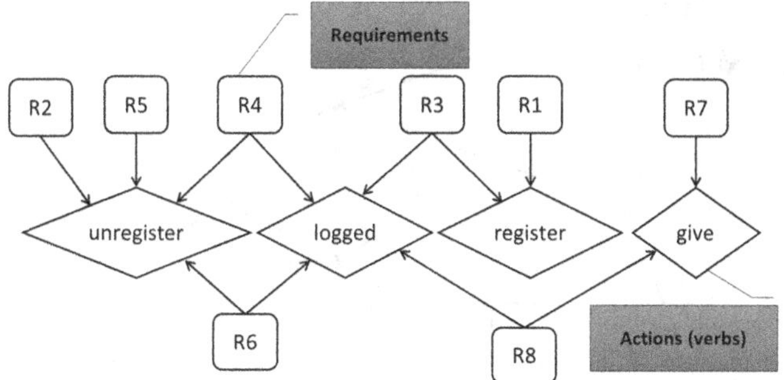

Fig. 4. Preliminary action-view.

There are situations where a requirement may refer to more than one key-action. For instance, the requirement "R3" (Fig. 4) refers to *register* and *logged* actions. In *Theme/Doc* approach, CCC are identified by analyzing such requirements.

The classification of actions as base or crosscutting ones may be performed by executing **"Classifying actions as base or crosscutting ones"** activity that requires as input the preliminary action-view and the set of software requirements. The software engineer initially must examine the requirements that refer to more than one action and determine what is the primary action (more important action) of these requirements. In the case of requirement "R3", the primary action is *logged*, since the requirement was written to specify the implementation of logging behavior. As the *register* action is not the primary action of this requirement, we say that this action is being affected by the behavior of the *logged* action. Hence, the *logged* action is classified as a crosscutting action and *register*, as a base action. To represent this kind of information, an arrow with a point at one of its ends is drawn from the *logged* action to the *register*, indicating that *logged* affects the *register* action.

The software engineer should examine all requirements that share the *logged* action and decide if they also are affected by its behavior. In addition, the software engineer should keep on examining the other requirements that share more than one action. Finally, after analyzing all requirements and actions, an extended action-view is generated (Fig. 5), with three base actions (*unregister*, *give* and *register*) and one crosscutting action (*logged*) that cut-across all the three base actions. The main strengths of the *Theme/Doc* approach are: (i) it uses visualization resources as a strategy for concern identification, what allows the software engineering to have a better view of the software concerns; (ii) it is independent of the requirements document language; and (iii) it has been widely used, evolved and evaluated in recent works [3, 22, 24, 32]. As limitations, it is possible to note that *Theme/Doc*: **depends on the usage of keywords; depends on the software engineers' experience;** and **does not support the software engineering during the identification of implicit concerns**.

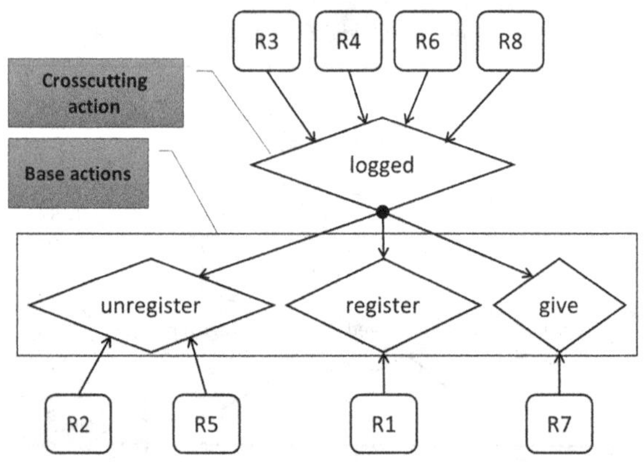

Fig. 5. Extended action-view.

Section 3 of this paper presents an extension of the *Theme/Doc* approach, called *OnTheme/Doc*, as well as an ontology for CCC, called *OntoCCC*. The main goal of the *OnTheme/Doc* and *OntoCCC* is to minimize the weaknesses of *Theme/Doc* and, hence, to improve the values of recall and precision provide by this approach.

3 OnTheme/Doc Approach

As described in Sect. 2, *Theme/Doc* requires that the software engineer works using only his/her prior knowledge about the problem domain and the concepts of concern identification and classification. This makes the approach highly dependent on the experience of its users. According to the extension proposed in this paper, besides his/her prior experience, the software engineer has the support of the knowledge represented in one or more instances of the *OntoCCC* ontology.

It is important to note that although *Theme/Doc* supports the identification of base and crosscutting concerns, this paper is worried only with the CCC identification, because, as already stated in this paper, this has been the bottleneck in the AORE process [22, 34].

3.1 OntoCCC Ontology

OntoCCC ontology is responsible for representing well-known and already published concepts and relationships on CCC. The concepts and relationships of the *OntoCCC* ontology describes the main features of a CCC, such as the name commonly used to identify it in the scientific community, its description, if it is a functional or non-functional CCC, as well as its possible relationships with other concerns.

To build the *OntoCCC* ontology, several studies that addressed the concern identification and classification subject were analyzed [1, 3, 6–8, 26, 29, 30, 35–37, 39].

In a systematic mapping conducted by the authors of this paper [31], thirty-eight AORE approaches were identified. Among these, ten included the concern identification and classification activity and proposed the usage of guidelines to support the software engineers during the execution of this activity. The main features of these guidelines were used to construct the *OntoCCC* ontology; this was performed to guarantee that the *OntoCCC* captures a consensual knowledge. For each concept/relationship defined in *OntoCCC*, we describe what work served as inspiration for it. The full version of *OntoCCC* ontology is presented in Fig. 6.

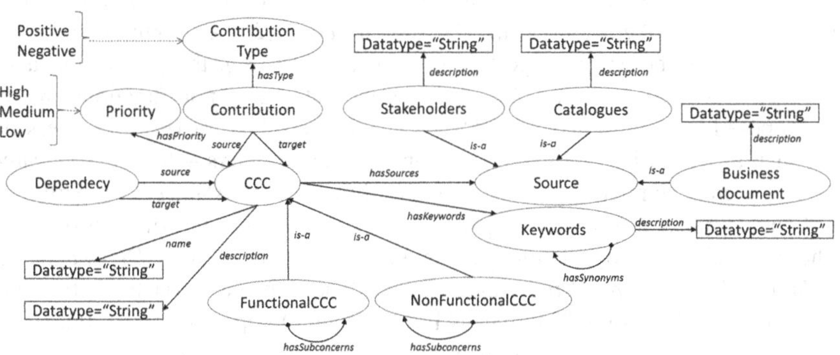

Fig. 6. *OntoCCC* ontology.

The concepts represented by *CCC, FunctionalCCC, NonFunctionalCCC* and *Keywords* classes, as well as the *name, description, hasSubconcerns, hasKeywords* and *hasSynomymes* properties were briefly commented in Sect. 2.1.

The *CCC* and *NonFunctionalCCC* concepts are well-known in AORE community and are reported in all analyzed studies. The *FunctionalCCC* concept, however, was taken from work of Moreira *et al.* [29], which was the first study to report that functional requirements also can cut-across other software requirements. Hence, the *FunctionalCCC* class represents the concerns related to functional features of the software that cut-across requirements of other concerns, for example, "Orders Management" and "Virtual Shopping Cart".

The concept of keywords appears in several AORE approaches [1, 8, 35], including the *Theme/Doc* [5, 11]. However, only the proposal of Agostinho *et al.* [1] presented a template to store the keywords used for identifying specific concerns. It is important because these keywords contain knowledge about these concerns that can be reused for concern identification in future projects.

The *Keywords* class was designed to store the keywords (and its synonyms) commonly used to identify a particular CCC. The *hasSynonyms* property can be useful when the software engineer wants to know how many distinct words (not synonymous) are present in the requirements document. We believe the more distinct keywords about a CCC presented in a requirements document, the stronger the indications of the presence of this CCC in the software.

The idea of decomposing concerns into sub-concerns, represented by the *hasSubconcerns* property, is new one and was not found in the analyzed studies. This property was considered important, since a given concern may be too large and complex that may complicate the reasoning of the software engineer. Hence, by decreasing the granularity of these concerns, treating them as sub-concerns, it is possible to know what kinds of concerns really are in the software and what are the most appropriate strategies to modularize them.

The concept represented by the *Source* class appears in some AORE approaches, such as proposed by Agostinho *et al.* [1], Moreira *et al.* [29] and Whittle and Araújo [37]. A source can be: (i) a suggestion of a stakeholder, *e.g.* the project manager – *Stakeholder* class; (ii) a catalog, for instance, the catalog of non-functional requirements proposed by Chung and Leite [10] – *Catalogues* class; or (iii) a business document, such as a security protocol of a company, among others – *Business Document* class. A CCC may be related to several sources through the *hasSources* property. Each kind of source has a *description* property that may store more information on it.

The two main types of relationships among CCC are defined by *Dependency* and *Contribution* classes. *Dependency* class defines a dependency relationship between two CCC: a source and a target. This means if “A” (source) depends on “B” (target) and “A” appears in the software requirements document, then “B” need to be there too. This type of information is important because: (i) it allows the software engineer to explore other CCC, before unrecognized by him/her, *i.e.*, by saying that “A” depends on “B”, he/she should also look for keywords related to “B” concern in the requirements document; and (ii) it allows the software engineer to verify inconsistencies in the requirements document, because, if a CCC “A” depends on “B” and “B” is not described in the software requirements and is not an implicit concern, then the requirements document may be inconsistent.

Another important concept about CCC is represented by the *Contribution* class. It represents a mutual influence among different CCC. This kind of influence is reported in the catalog Chung and Leite [10], but only for non-functional requirements. In AORE field, Moreira *et al.* [29] address this type of influence on their work. To do this, the authors proposed a “contribution matrix”, which is created by the software engineer, based on his/her experience and on some catalogues of non-functional requirements. In this matrix, it is possible to visualize the kind of contributions (negative or positive) among different CCC of the software. However, the knowledge about the contribution is limited to the project under analysis and there are no clearly defined mechanisms to reuse it in later projects.

A contribution can be *Negative* or *Positive* as defined by the *ContributionType* class and the *hasType* property. For example, the "Information Retrieval" and "Mobility" concerns are related as follows [29]: the higher the mobility, the greater the difficulties of retrieving information. This means that "Mobility" negatively contributes to "Information Retrieval". The inverse contribution is also negative, since the more complex is the information to be retrieved, the less mobile the software can be, since some wireless networks have limited bandwidth size. Another example is the case of the "Concurrency", "Performance" and "Cost" concerns. The implementation of concurrency mechanisms in the software can positively contribute to the software performance, but not to the cost of the project.

The knowledge presented in both previous examples can be represented in the *OntoCCC* ontology by means of *Contribution, ContributionType* and *CCC* classes and *hasType, source* and *target* properties. Figure 7 presents an instance of the *OntoCCC* ontology, in which the contribution among "Concurrency", "Performance" and "Cost" concerns is presented.

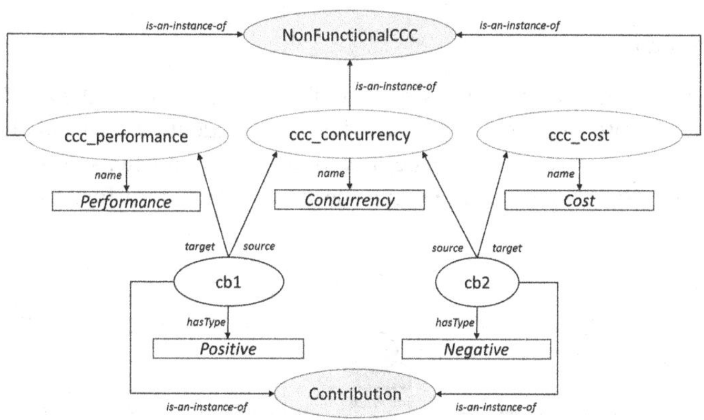

Fig. 7. Contributions among different *CCC*.

Finally, each CCC has a *hasPriority* property that relates a CCC to an instance of the *Priority* class. The priority can be defined by stakeholders or experts in CCC and may assume the following values: "High", "Medium" or "Low". This information is important when one specific CCC "A" is negatively influenced by other two different CCC "B" and "C", or when one specific CCC "A" exerts negative and positive influences on two different CCC "B" and "C"; in these cases, the software engineer must decide on what concern will be addressed and he/she need to know what are the impacts of his/her decision.

In the example of "Concurrency", "Performance" and "Cost" concerns, the software engineer will have to decide between prioritizing cost or performance; the *Priority* class and the *hasPriority* property may provide more information for the software engineer to make his/her decision. Priority is a concept discussed in the work of

Moreira *et al.* [29], but it is used only in the conflict detection and resolution activity – one of the last activities in the AORE process. We believe that treating this issue in the beginning of the AORE process is important, because it can reduce the rework, as well as the propagation of errors throughout this process.

Accorded to the property classification, provided in Sect. 2.1, *hasSources, source, target* and *hasPriority* can be classified as irreflexive, asymmetric and intransitive properties.

Using the concepts and relationships of *OntoCCC* ontology, commented above, it is possible to store the existing knowledge about specific types of CCC, creating instances of this ontology. Small examples of *OntoCCC* instances for the "Persistence", "Connection", "Transaction", "Logging", "Concurrency", "Performance" and "Cost" concerns were described in Fig. 2 and Fig. 7.

Instances of *OntoCCC* ontology can be created from: (i) catalogues of crosscutting concerns; (ii) other kind of catalogues, *e.g.*, the catalogue of non-functional requirements, such as those proposed by Cysneiros [12] and Chung and Leite [10]; (iii) the knowledge of experts on AORE; or (iv) historical data of previous projects, among others.

3.2 OnTheme/Doc

We believe that the knowledge represented by the instances of the *OntoCCC* ontology may help the software engineers to perform the concern identification and classification activity in a more effective way. Hence, it was proposed an extension of *Theme/Doc* approach, called *OnTheme/Doc*, following the process shown in Fig. 8.

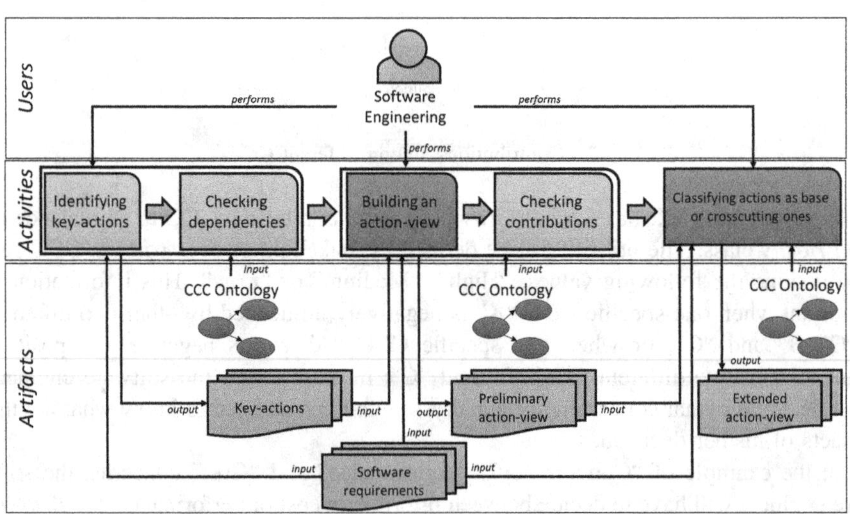

Fig. 8. *OnTheme/Doc* process (Color figure online).

The execution of *OnTheme/Doc* approach follows the same flow of the *Theme/Doc*. However, there are two new activities to be performed by the software engineers ("Checking Dependencies" and "Checking Contributions"), and the procedure for key-actions identification, described by the "Identifying key-actions" activity, was redefined. These three adapted/new activities are highlighted in blue in Fig. 8.

- **"Identifying Key-actions" Activity:** the software engineer should analyze each CCC defined in the *OntoCCC* instance, searching for the keywords presented in this instance in the requirements document.
- **"Checking Dependencies" Activity:** for each identified CCC, the software engineer should verify the relationships of it with other CCC, in order to detect possible dependencies among them. If there are dependencies between a CCC "A" with "B" e "C", the software engineer should also consider the keywords of "B" and "C". If there are no keywords related to "B" and "C" in the requirements, they may be implicit concerns and should be analyzed in the "Checking Contributions" activity, or the requirements document is inconsistent; and
- **"Checking Contributions" Activity:** after building an action-view, the software engineer should analyze the CCC ontology again looking for possible contributions of a CCC over other ones. In this activity, new CCC, before unidentified, may appear due to the mutual influence among different CCC. In addition, it may be necessary to resolve conflicts among different CCC. For this, the value of the priority property of each conflicting CCC must be observed. If the conflict persists (for example, when the priority levels of two CCC are the same), meetings with stakeholders may be necessary.

4 Experimental Study

The evaluation goal of this work is: "**To analyze:** the *OnTheme/Doc* approach. **In order to:** evaluate. **With respect to:** recall and precision provided by this approach. **From the point of view of:** software engineers. **In the context of:** a group of undergraduates and graduate in Computer Science.".

4.1 Planning

The planning of this experimental study was defined according to the Wohlin's proposal [38] and involves the following steps: (i) context selection; (ii) hypotheses formulation; (iii) variables selection; (iv) participants selection; and (v) design and execution of the experimental study.

(a) Context Selection. This experimental study was conducted with fourteen undergraduate and graduate students in Computer Science from two Federal Universities in Brazil.

An information system that aims to record complaints in health area, called *Health Watcher* [20], was used in this study. It is a well-known application in the AORE field and was chosen because it has a suitable requirements document for CCC identification. Its requirements document presents several CCC, such as security, persistence, concurrency, among others. In addition, all CCC of this application have already been identified and cataloged by experts [20], serving as an oracle to verify the answers given by the participants of this experimental study.

(b) Hypotheses Formulation. An important part of an experimental study is to specify the metrics that will be used. Based on these metrics, the researcher may establish hypotheses and draw conclusions from the results of the experiment.

In this work, three metrics were used, whose formulas and description are presented in Table 2: recall, precision and f-Measure (a harmonized average of the recall and precision).

These metrics are commonly used for measuring the effectiveness of products and processes in several research areas, such as information retrieval, natural language processing, among others. They also are widely used at works on concern identification and classification [22, 34]. In this work, the interpretation of these metrics is very trivial, the higher the value of recall, precision and f-Measure, the better the effectiveness of the approach. Based on these metrics, six hypotheses were developed for this study, two related to the recall metric, two for precision and two for f-Measure (Table 3).

(c) Variables and Participants Selection. Independent variables are those manipulated and controlled during the experimental study. In this study, the independent variable is related to the approaches for concern identification and classification. The dependent variables are those under evaluation and whose variations must be observed. In this experiment the recall, precision and f-Measure metrics are considered as dependent variables. The participants of this study were selected through non-probability for convenience sampling.

(d) Design and Execution of the Experimental Study. The distribution of the participants was performed aiming to form two homogeneous groups, with regard to the participants' experience and the amount of available participants in each group. Each group had seven participants and the participants' experience was verified by the application of a profile characterization questionnaire. It takes into account the knowledge of the participants about AORE and *Theme/Doc* approach. In addition, the experimental study was planned in phases (training and execution) to minimize the effect of participants' knowledge of the dependent variables.

Before starting the execution of the experimental study, a training was conducted, in order to homogenize the knowledge of participants on AORE and *Theme/Doc* and *OnTheme/Doc* approaches. During the training, it was not informed to the participants what approach was developed by the authors of this paper.

In the execution phase, the participants had to identify the CCC existing in the requirements document of the *Health Watcher* application. To do this, the Group 1 used the *Theme/Doc* approach and the Group 2, the *OnTheme/Doc*. The part of the requirements document analyzed by the participants had seven types of non-functional CCC: "Security", "Concurrency", "Usability", "Performance", "Distribution", "Availability" and "Persistence". "Distribution" and "Competition" were implicit concerns, *i.e.*, there were not keywords in the requirements document with regard to them.

Table 2. Metrics of the experimental study.

Metrics		
Recall (Re)	**Precision (Pr)**	**f-Measure (fM)**
$Re = \left(\frac{CIC}{EC}\right) * 100$	$Pr = \left(\frac{CIC}{TIC}\right) * 100$	$fM = 2 * \left(\frac{Re * Pr}{Re + Pr}\right)$
Description		
CIC (*Correctly Identified Concerns*): amount of correctly identified concerns, *i.e.*, without the false positives. **Re (Recall)**: percentage of correctly identified concerns, regarding to the amount of existing concerns. **EC (*Existing Concerns*)**: amount of existing concerns. **TIC (*Total of Identified Concerns*)**: amount of identified concern, *i.e.*, including the false positives. **Pr (Precision)**: percentage of correctly identified concerns, regarding to the amount of identified concerns. **fM (f-Measure)**: a harmonized average of the recall and precision values.		

Table 3. Hypotheses of the experimental study.

Hypotheses for Recall
H_{0Re}: there is no difference of using *OnTheme/Doc* or *Theme/Doc*, regarding to the recall. H_{0Re}: $Re_{OnThD} = Re_{ThD}$. H_{1Re}: there is difference of using *OnTheme/Doc* or *Theme/Doc*, regarding to the recall. H_{1Re}: $Re_{OnThD} \neq Re_{ThD}$.
Hypotheses for Precision
H_{0Pr}: there is no difference of using *OnTheme/Doc* or *Theme/Doc*, regarding to the precision. H_{0Pr}: $Pr_{OnThD} = Pr_{ThD}$. H_{1Pr}: there is difference of using *OnTheme/Doc* or *Theme/Doc*, regarding to the precision. H_{1Pr}: $Pr_{OnThD} \neq Pr_{ThD}$.
Hypotheses for f-Measure
H_{0fM}: there is no difference of using *OnTheme/Doc* or *Theme/Doc*, regarding to the f-Measure metric. H_{0fM}: $fM_{OnThD} = fM_{ThD}$ H_{1fM}: there is difference of using *OnTheme/Doc* or *Theme/Doc*, regarding to the f-Measure metric. H_{1fM}: $fM_{OnThD} \neq fM_{ThD}$.
Legend
X_{OnThD}, where X is a metric, means: the value of X obtained by a specific participant using the *OnTheme/Doc* approach. X_{ThD}, where X is a metric, means: the value of X obtained by a specific participant using the *Theme/Doc* approach.

To calculate the values of the recall, precision and f-Measure metrics, it was considered the amount of CCC identified by each participant, individually.

The participants of the Group 2 also received an instance of the *OntoCCC* ontology, created by the authors of this paper, from the catalogs of Moreira *et al.* [29], Chung and Leite [10] and Cysneiros [12]. A piece of the ontology presented to the participants as well as the Health Watcher requirements document are presented in Fig. 9 and Table 4, respectively. The complete version of the ontology and the

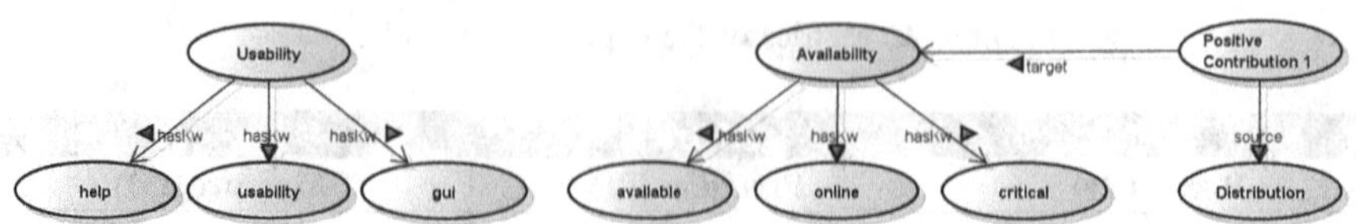

Fig. 9. Piece of *OntoCCC* instance.

Table 4. Piece of Health Watcher requirements document (Health Watcher).

#	Requirements description
R1	The system should have an easy to use GUI, as any person who has access to the internet should be able to use the system. The system should have an **on-line** HELP to be consulted by any person that uses it
R2	The system should be **available** 24 h a day, 7 days a week. The nature of the system not being a **critical** system, the system might stay off until any fault is fixed
R3	The system must be capable to handle 20 simultaneous users. The response time must not exceed 5 s

requirements document were omitted of this paper due to the limitation of space, but can be found at https://db.tt/Wqx2xWh3.

In Fig. 9 it is possible to notice the existence of some keywords that can help the software engineers while performing the CCC identification in the requirements document presented in Table 4. For instance, the "online", "available" and "critical" words appear in the description of some requirements (words highlighted in Table 4). Furthermore, the "Positive Contribution 1" relationship (Fig. 9) may give more information for the software engineer about the mutual influence between the "Availability" and "Distribution" concerns.

4.2 Results

Table 5 presents the results of this experimental study. The first (left) and the second (right) parts of this table, respectively, present the results for the *Theme/Doc* and *OnTheme/Doc* approaches. The first column of each part of this table presents the codes that identify each participant; the second, third and fourth columns refer to the values of recall, precision and f-Measure; the last column of this table shows the time (in minutes) that each participant took to finalize the CCC identification.

The values for the recall, precision and f-Measure metrics emphasize a statement made by Sampaio *et al.* [34] in their experimental study on AORE approaches: "Generally the AORE approaches do have good precision (…). However, the majority of these approaches do have limitations when considering recall". This means that there is little incidence of false positives, but the amount of correctly identified concerns is low. The precision values of both groups were higher than the recall values.

Taking into account the values for recall, participants who used the *OnTheme/Doc* approach had, on average, more promising results than those who used the *Theme/Doc*.

Table 5. Experimental results.

Approach *Theme/Doc*				
Part.	**Re (%)**	**Pr (%)**	**fM (%)**	**Time (min)**
P1	42,85	80,00	55,80	43
P2	42,85	100,00	59,99	48
P3	42,85	100,00	59,99	49
P4	28,57	80,00	41,48	48
P5	57,14	80,00	66,66	36
P6	42,85	100,00	59,99	31
P7	28,57	100,00	44,44	34
Avg	**40,81**	**91,42**	**55,48**	**41**

Approach: *OnTheme/Doc*				
Part.	**Re (%)**	**Pr (%)**	**fM (%)**	**Time (min)**
P8	71,42	80,00	75,47	62
P9	85,71	100,00	92,30	39
P10	85,71	100,00	92,30	54
P11	71,42	100,00	83,32	37
P12	57,14	80,00	66,66	43
P13	71,42	80,00	75,47	42
P14	71,42	100,00	83,32	42
Avg	**73,46**	**91,42**	**81,26**	**45**

Table 6. Concerns identified by each participant.

#	**Participants *Theme/Doc***							%	**Participants *OnTheme/Doc***							%
	1	**2**	**3**	**4**	**5**	**6**	**7**		**8**	**9**	**10**	**11**	**12**	**13**	**14**	
1	X	X						28	X	X	X	X	X			57
2	X	X	X	X	X	X	X	100	X	X	X	X	X	X	X	100
3		X						14		X	X	X		X	X	71
4			X	X	X	X		57	X	X	X	X		X	X	85
5					X	X	X	43	X	X	X			X	X	71
6	X		X		X			43	X	X	X	X	X			71
7								0					X	X	X	43
Average								**41**	**Average**							**71**
Legend: (1) Persistence; (2) Security; (3) Concurrency; (4) Usability; (5) Performance; (6) Availability; (7) Distribution																

To improve the discussion about the recall values, Table 6 presents: (i) the list of CCC of the *Health Watcher* application - first column; (ii) the CCC identified by each participant who used the *Theme/Doc* approach - from second to eighth columns; (iii) the percentage of participants who identified each CCC - ninth column; and (iv) the same information previously described to the *OnTheme/Doc* approach – from tenth to the eighteenth columns.

Based on this table, it is possible to note that only one of the participants who used the *Theme/Doc* approach was able to identify the "Concurrency" concern and none of them has identified the "Distribution" concern; "Concurrency" and "Distribution" were implicit concerns. Regarding to the participants who used *OnTheme/Doc* approach, just one participant did not identify the two implicit concerns. For all concerns, the percentage of participants who identified them is always greater for *OnTheme/Doc* approach than for the *Theme/Doc*. Consequently, on average, the percentage of participants who identified any concern using *OnTheme/Doc* approach (71 %) is higher than that one who used *Theme/Doc* (41 %).

Finally, it is important to note that even using ontologies, the percentage of participants who identified the "Distribution" concern is not satisfactory (43 %). This indicates that the strategy used to represent the mutual influence among different concerns must be reviewed.

Based on Table 5 again, it is possible to note that there is no difference between the two approaches with regard to the precision. This means that there was not a high incidence of false positives during the CCC identification for both approaches.

Regarding to f-Measure metric (Table 5), the average value obtained by the participants who used *OnTheme/Doc* was higher than that one obtained to the *Theme/Doc* approach. This occurs, because the precision provided by the two approaches is similar and the recall provided by *OnTheme/Doc* approach is higher than that one provided by *Theme/Doc*.

Table 5 still presents that the average time for execution of *OnTheme/Doc* (45 min) was higher than that one provided by *Theme/Doc* approach (41 min). This is due to the participants who used the *OnTheme/Doc* approach had another artefact to analyzed, *i.e.*, the instance of the *OntoCCC* ontology, as well as two new activities to be performed: "Checking Dependencies" and "Checking Contributions". However, we noted that the difference (4 min) is not significant. Although the participants who used the *OnTheme/Doc* approach had to perform additional tasks, the usage of the ontology and the proposed process may have led the participants to perform the concern identification activity in a more focused way. This may have minimized the impact on the time of execution of the *OnTheme/Doc* approach.

4.3 Hypothesis Tests

Although the values presented in Sect. 4.2 indicate that the usage of *OnTheme/Doc* approach provides good recall and f-Measure values with regard to CCC identification, it is necessary to perform statistical analyses by means of hypothesis tests, in order to ensure the reliability to the statements expressed in this paper. The hypotheses related to the precision metric was not tested, since the two analyzed samples did not show differences with regard to the values of this metric.

The purpose of a hypothesis test is to verify if the null hypothesis (H_0) may be rejected, with some significance level; when H_0 is rejected, the alternative hypothesis H_1 may be accepted. Before applying a hypothesis test, it is necessary to know in what type of probability distribution the data collected in the study is organized. This occurs because many hypothesis tests, such as the t-test [28], have as a prerequisite the need that data be normally distributed.

To verify if the data is normally distributed, we have applied a test known as Shapiro-Wilk test [28] and the values for recall, f-Measure and time metrics were considered normalized with a significance level of 99.9 %.

To verify the hypotheses defined in Table 3, the t-test was applied. Comparing the average values for recall provided by the approaches *Theme/Doc* (average = 40.81) and *OnTheme/Doc* (average = 73.46), the H_{0Re} null hypothesis can be rejected with significance level of 99.9 % (*p-value* = *0.0004*). This means that, with 99.9 % of confidence, we can say that the recall provided by *OnTheme/Doc* approach is higher than that one provided by *Theme/Doc*.

Similarly, comparing the average values of f-Measure metric of both approaches - *Theme/Doc* (average = 55.48) and *OnTheme/Doc* (average = 81.26) - the null hypothesis H_{0fM} can be rejected with significance level of 99.9 % ($p = 0.0002$).

Regarding to the average time spent by the participants to perform the activities in the *Theme/Doc* (average = 41 min) and in the *OnTheme/Doc* (average = 45 min), it was not possible to obtain statistical evidences, with significance level equal or higher than 95 %, to say that these values are different.

In summary, hypothesis tests have revealed that there are significant differences between the values for recall and f-Measure metrics measured for the two approaches in analysis, and the *OnTheme/Doc* approach presented better results. However, it is not possible to say that there are significant differences between the values for precision provided by both approaches, as well as for the time required to perform their activities.

4.4 Threats to Validity

Wohlin *et al.* [38] state that an experimental study may face situations that threaten the validity of its results. The main threats addressed in this study are:

(1) Conclusion Validity. This kind of threat refers to issues that affect the ability to draw correct conclusions about the experimental results. An example of this kind of threat is the choice of appropriate statistical methods for data analysis. In the case of this study, one of the statistical tests used was the t-test, which requires normally distributed data. To verify the normality of the data and minimize this threat, the Shapiro-Wilk test was applied and the result was positive for the samples.

(2) Internal Validity. It refers to issues that may affect the ability to ensure that the results were, in fact, obtained from the treatments (*i.e.* the AORE approaches: *OnTheme/Doc* and *Theme/Doc*) and not by coincidence. A threat of this kind can be related to the strategy used to select and group the participants of the experimental study. To mitigate this threat, we did not demonstrate expectations for any approach during the training phase. In addition, the participants were grouped according to their levels of experience.

(3) External Validity. This kind of threat refers to issues that affect the ability to generalize the results of an experiment to a wider context. In this case, the relevant factors that could have influenced the results of this study are: (i) the application used in the study, *i.e.*, *Health Watcher*; (ii) the quality of the resources (the CCC ontology and the requirements document) presented to the participants; (iii) the amount of participants of the study; and (iv) the use of undergraduate and graduate students in Computer Science. In order to mitigate these potential threats, we intend to replicate this experiment with other groups of participants and different applications.

5 Related Works

Several AORE approaches have been proposed in last years; among them, many approaches address the concern identification and classification activity. In a systematic mapping (SM), conducted by the authors of this work [31], it was noted that until 2014, there were thirty-eight different AORE approaches and twenty-two of them were related to this activity. Among these, ten provided resources to support software engineers during this activity [1, 3, 6–8, 26, 29, 30, 35–37, 39].

These approaches aimed to support the software engineer during the concern identification and classification through guidelines, such as catalogues of Non-Functional Requirements (NFR) [10, 12] or catalogues of CCC that were extensions of NFR catalogs [29]. Some problems with regard to the usage of these catalogs are [27]: (i) they are complex to be read and understood by humans; and (ii) they are not prepared for automated semantic processing. In addition, most of these approaches does not present a process that helps the software engineer on how to use the guidelines.

Another problem that was noted from the systematic mapping is that only five of these ten AORE approaches [6, 7, 29, 35, 36] were evaluated with some kind of experimental study. Hence, there is no way of knowing on the effectiveness of these approaches.

In another recent SM conducted by the authors of this study, it was found that several ontology-based approaches have been proposed for the requirements engineering field, however, none of them is specific to the context of AORE. Maybe, one of the closest works, related to this paper, is that one proposed by López *et al.* [27]. In this work, the authors presented an ontology for sharing and reusing NFR and design decisions. The proposed ontology aims to store the knowledge related to the NFR and design decisions, based on the description of NFR catalogues. The researcher can create instances, from this ontology, that address the NFR and design decisions of interest.

The proposal of López *et al.* [27] differs from that one proposed in this paper as following: (i) their work is not related to the AORE field, therefore, it does not address specific features of CCC, such as the classification of a CCC as non-functional or functional one, the relationships among CCC and keywords, the decomposition of concerns into sub-concerns, among others; (ii) their work does not present a process or a set of guidelines that helps the software engineer on how to use the proposed ontology; and (iii) the work does not present any kind of an experimental study on the proposal.

6 Final Remarks

Based on the problems mentioned in this paper and reported in related works [22, 34], it is possible to notice that the concern identification and classification activity from requirements documents is a relevant and challenging research subject yet.

This paper presented an extension of a well-known AORE approach (*Theme/Doc*), called *OnTheme/Doc*; its goal is improving the *Theme/Doc* recall and precision regarding to the crosscutting concern identification. One way of moving forward in the AORE field is initially understand the nature of the CCC domain. In this context, this paper presented an ontology for the domain of CCC, called *OntoCCC*. The main innovation of *OnTheme/Doc* approach is the usage of the ontology *OntoCCC* to support the software engineers during the CCC identification. An experimental study conducted on *OnTheme/Doc* showed that the usage of ontologies may improve the values for recall, without negatively impact on the execution time and precision of the approach. For instance, the recall provided by *OnTheme/Doc* approach was 1.8 times higher than that one provided by *Theme/Doc*. On the other hand, the precision values were the same for both approaches and the execution time of *OnTheme/Doc* was just 4 min higher than that one.

As future work proposals, we intend to: (i) register other kinds of concerns as instances of the *OntoCCC* ontology; (ii) create a computational tool for concern identification, based on instances of the *OntoCCC* ontology; and (iii) extend the *OntoCCC* ontology to include the concepts and relationship of base concerns (non-crosscutting concerns).

References

1. Agostinho, S., et al.: A metadata-driven approach for aspect-oriented requirements analysis. In: 10th International Conference on Enterprise Information Systems, Barcelona, Spain, pp. 129–136 (2008)
2. Alencar, F., et al.: Towards modular i* models. In: ACM Symposium on Applied Computing, pp. 292–297 (2010)
3. Ali, B.S., Kasirun, Z.M.D.: An approach for crosscutting concern identification at requirements level using NLP. Int. J. Phys. Sci. **6**(11), 2718–2730 (2011)
4. Araújo, J., Whittle, J., Kim, D.K.: Modeling and composing scenario-based requirements with aspects. In: Requirements Engineering Conference, Washington, USA (2004)
5. Baniassad, E., Clarke, S.: Theme: an approach for aspect-oriented analysis and design. In: 26th International Conference on Software Engineering, USA (2004)
6. Brito, I., Moreira, A.: Towards a composition process for aspect-oriented requirements. In: EA Workshop, Boston, USA (2003)
7. Chernak, Y.: Requirements composition table explained. In: 20th IEEE International Requirements Engineering Conference, Chicago, Illinois, USA, pp. 273–278 (2012)
8. Chitchyan, R., Sampaio, A., Rashid, A., Rayson, P.: A tool suite for aspect-oriented requirements engineering. In: International Workshop on Early Aspects at ICSE, pp. 19–26 (2006)
9. Chitchyan, R., et al.: Report synthesizing state-of-the-art in aspect-oriented requirements engineering, architectures and design. Technical report, Lancaster University, pp. 1–259 (2005)
10. Chung, L., Leite, J.S.P.: Non-Functional Requirements in Software Engineering, pp. 1–441. Springer, Heidelberg (2000)
11. Clarke, S., Baniassad, E.: Aspect-Oriented Analysis and Design: The Theme Approach. Addison-Wesley, Boston (2005)
12. Cysneiros, L.M.: Catalogues on non-functional requirements. http://www.math.yorku.ca/~cysneiro/nfrs/nfrs.htm. Accessed November 2014
13. Dermeval, D., et al.: Applications of ontologies in requirements engineering: a systematic review of the literature. Requirements Engineering, pp. 1–33. Springer, London (2015)
14. Dijkstra, E.W.: A Discipline of Programming, pp. 1–217. Pearson Prentice Hall, Upper Saddle River (1976)
15. Falbo, R.A., et al.: Um Processo de Engenharia de Requisitos Baseado em Reutilização de Ontologias e Padrões de Análise. In: Jornada Iberoamericana de Eng. del Soft. e Engeniería del Conocimiento, Lima, Perú (2007). (in Portuguese)

16. Fensel, D.: Ontologies: Silver Bullet for Knowledge Management and Electronic Commerce, pp. 1–138. Springer, Heidelberg (2001)
17. Gruber, T.R.: Towards principles for the design of ontologies used for knowledge sharing. Int. J. Hum.-Comput. Stud. **43**(5–6), 907–928 (1995)
18. Grundy, J. Aspect-oriented requirements engineering for component-based software systems. In: 4th IEEE International Symposium on Requirements Engineering Limerick, Ireland, pp. 84–91 (1999)
19. Guarino, N.: Formal ontology in information system. In: 1st International Conference on Formal Ontology in Information Systems, Italy, pp. 3–15 (1998)
20. Health Watcher. http://www.cin.ufpe.br/~scbs/testbed/requirements/aore/. Accessed November 2014
21. Hernandes, E.C.M.: Um processo automatizado para tratamento de dados e conceituação de ontologias com o apoio de visualização. Master dissertation, UFSCar (2009). (in Portuguese)
22. Herrera, J., et al.: Revealing CCC in textual requirements documents: an exploratory study with industry systems. In: Brazilian Symposium on Software Engineering, Natal, Brazil (2012)
23. Horrige, M., et al.: A practical guide to building OWL ontologies using Protégé 4 and CO-ODE tools. Tutorial. University of Manchester, Manchester (2011)
24. Kit, L.K., Man, C.K., Baniassad, E.: Isolating and relating concerns in requirements using latent semantic analysis. ACM SIGPLAN Not. **41**(10), 383–396 (2006)
25. Lima, J.C., Carvalho, C.L.: Ontologias - OWL. Technical report, Federal University of Goiás, Brazil (2005)
26. Liu, X., Liu, S., Zheng, X.: Adapting the NFR framework to aspectual use-case driven approach. In: International Conference on Software Engineering Research, Management and Applications, Hainan Island, China (2009)
27. López, C., Cysneiros, L.M., Astudillo, H.: NDR ontology: sharing and reusing NFR and design rationale knowledge. In: International Workshop on Managing Requirements Knowledge, USA, pp. 1–10 (2008)
28. Montgomery, D.C.: Design and Analysis of Experiments, 5th edn. Wiley, Hoboken (2000)
29. Moreira, A., Rashid, A., Araújo, J.: Multi-dimensional separation of concerns in requirements engineering. In: 13th International Conference on Requirements Engineering, Paris, France, pp. 285–296 (2005)
30. Mussbacher, G., Amyot, D., Araújo, J., Moreira, A.: Requirements modeling with the aspect-oriented user requirements notation (AoURN): a case study. In: Katz, Shmuel, Mezini, Mira, Kienzle, Jörg (eds.) Transactions on Aspect-Oriented Software Development VII. LNCS, vol. 6210, pp. 23–68. Springer, Heidelberg (2010)
31. Parreira Jr., P.A., Penteado, R.A.D.: Aspect-oriented requirements engineering: a systematic mapping. In: XVI International Conference on Enterprise Information Systems, 2014, Lisboa, Portugal (2014)
32. Penim, A.S., Araújo, J., Identifying and modeling aspectual scenarios with theme and MATA. In: ACM Symposium on Applied Computing, Switzerland, pp. 287–291 (2010)
33. Rashid, A., Moreira, A., Araújo, J.: Modularisation and composition of aspectual requirements. In: 2nd International Conference on Aspect-Oriented Software Development, New York, USA (2003)
34. Sampaio, A., Greenwood, P., Garcia, A.F., Rashid, A.: A comparative study of aspect-oriented requirements engineering approaches. In: International Symposium on Empirical Software Engineering and Measurement, Madrid, Spain, pp. 166–175 (2007)
35. Sampaio, A., Chitchyan, R., Rashid, A., Rayson, P.: EA-Miner: a tool for automating aspect-oriented requirements identification. In: International Conference on Automated Software Engineering California, USA, pp. 353–355 (2005)

36. Soeiro, E., Brito, I.S., Moreira, A.: An XML-based language for specification and composition of aspectual concerns. In: 8th International Conference on Enterprise Information Systems, Paphos, Cyprus (2006)
37. Whittle, J., Araújo, J.: Scenario modeling with aspects. IEEE Softw. **151**(4), 157–172 (2004)
38. Wohlin, C., et al.: Experimentation in Software Engineering: An Introduction, pp. 1–249. Springer, Heidelberg (2012)
39. Zheng, X., Liu, X., Liu, S.: Use case and non-functional scenario template-based approach to identify aspects. In: 2nd International Conference on Computer Engineering and Applications, Indonesia, pp. 89–93 (2010)

JOPA: Stay Object-Oriented When Persisting Ontologies

Martin Ledvinka(✉) and Petr Křemen

Czech Technical University in Prague, Technická 2, Prague, Czech Republic
{martin.ledvinka,petr.kremen}@fel.cvut.cz

Abstract. Accessing OWL ontologies from IT systems can bring many problems unfamiliar to developers used to the more common relational storage approach. These problems stem from the dynamic nature of ontologies, their open-world character and expressiveness. In this paper, we present the Java OWL Persistence API (JOPA), a persistence layer allowing object-oriented access to semantic web ontologies. It supports features like caching, transactional processing and a semantically clear contract between the ontology and the object model. In addition, we present the OntoDriver, a software layer decoupling storage access from the object-ontological mapping. We provide an in-depth theoretical complexity analysis of our approach in connection with an analysis and practical evaluation of the performance of ontological storage with regards to application access scenario.

Keywords: Ontology · Persistence · Application access · Complexity

1 Introduction

Large expressive ontologies are a powerful tool for knowledge modelling. However, their complexity requires proper design and development of end-user information systems. During information system design, its creators face the challenge of choosing an appropriate software library that is reasonably easy to use and maintain, but that allows exploiting the ontology in its complexity [1].

On one side, information systems, that accept closed-world assumption by their nature, have to deal with distributed and open-world knowledge represented in ontologies. On the other hand, ontological changes often do not affect the information system data model assumptions and thus can be smoothly applied without information system recompilation and redeployment (e.g. taxonomy/metadata extension). Furthermore, expressive power of semantic web ontologies is significantly higher than that of relational databases.

For example, an ontology specifies that each *Person* has a *name*. Due to the open world assumption, the ontology is consistent even if a particular *Person* does not have recorded his/her *name*. However, a genealogical application accessing the ontology needs the *name* to be known, which causes the application to crash whenever it receives (consistent, but application–incompatible) data from an ontological source, specifying a *Person* without a *name*.

S. Hammoudi et al. (Eds.): ICEIS 2015, LNBIP 241, pp. 408–428, 2015.
DOI: 10.1007/978-3-319-29133-8_20

This paper presents a solution for these issues – the Java OWL Persistence API (JOPA), see [2], a persistence layer that allows using the object-oriented paradigm for accessing semantic web ontologies. Comparing to other approaches, it supports validation of the ontological assumptions on the object level ([1,3]), advanced caching, transactions, unification and optimization of repository access through the OntoDriver component, as well as accessing multiple repository contexts at the same time. Additionally, we present a complexity analysis of OntoDriver operations that allows optimizing object-oriented access performance for underlying storage mechanisms. Next, we compare our solution to low level Sesame API in terms of efficiency. Last, we discuss several challenges of ontology access stemming from our experience in real-world application design.

Section 2 shows the relationship of our work to the state-of-art research. Section 3 introduces design and implementation of a prototype system for ontology-based information system access. Section 4 analyses complexity of operations defined in the API for storage access. In Sect. 5 we discuss the practical usage of both JOPA and OntoDriver. We further examine our experience from using JOPA in real-life application and the lessons we learned in Sect. 6. The paper is concluded in Sect. 7.

2 Related Work

Some object-oriented solutions try to approximate ontological OWL reasoning [4] by means of procedural code, like [5], or [6]. However, this significantly limits the expressive power of the ontology and is memory-consuming on the information system side.

There is another research direction, not compromising reasoning completeness, while maintaining its scalability – simplifying programmatic access to semantic web ontologies stored in optimized transactional ontology storages. This is also where our solution lies. Two main existing approaches are presented in the next sections.

2.1 Domain-Independent APIs

Many APIs for programmatic access to ontologies make no assumptions about the particular ontology schema. This paradigm is exploited in frameworks like OWL API [7], Sesame [8] or Jena [9]. These systems are generic, allowing to exploit full range of ontological expressiveness, trading it for verbosity and poor maintainability of the resulting code. Furthermore, using these tools requires software designers to hold deep knowledge of the underlying ontological structures. Comparing to these systems, our solution provides object-ontological mapping that helps software designers in keeping the design readable, consistent and short, see Sect. 5.1.

2.2 Domain-Specific APIs

There are already several established solutions, where the ontology schema is compiled directly into the object model. This paradigm makes use of an object-ontological Mapping (OOM). Representatives of this paradigm are e.g. Empire [10] or AliBaba[1]. Comparing to the former, these systems actually access ontologies in a frame-based (or object-oriented) manner. Object-ontology mappings bind the information system tightly to the particular ontology. This significantly simplifies programmatic access and is less demanding on the developer expertise in semantic web ontologies. However, it also discards most of the benefits of ontologies. The object model becomes as rigid as the model of applications based on relational databases, no difference is made between inferred and asserted knowledge and the application looses access to knowledge not captured in the domain model.

A thorough discussion of these architectures can be found in [2,3]. JOPA, introduced in Sect. 3, aims at taking the best of both types, as can be seen in Fig. 1. It provides compiled object-based mapping of the ontology schema similar to the domain-specific approaches described above, while also enabling access to the dynamically changing aspects of the ontology (see Sect. 3).

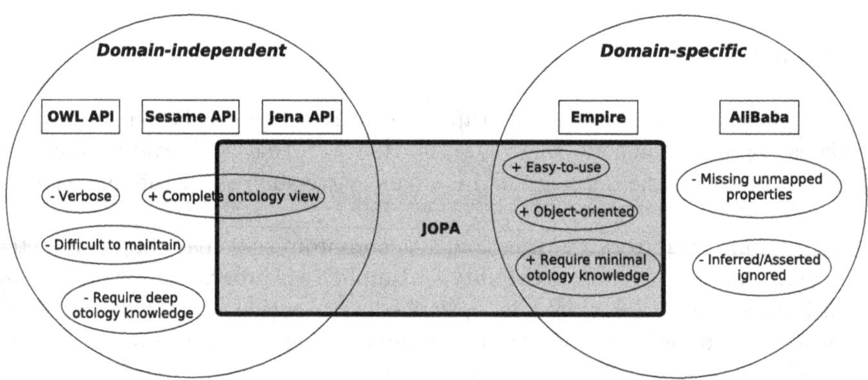

Fig. 1. JOPA compared to domain-independent and domain-specific approaches. The *complete ontology view* is included only partially in JOPA, because although it supports unmapped properties, accessing concepts not mapped by the object-model is limited in JOPA. It would require defining an entity mapping the *owl:Thing* concept, which would bring problems with object identity, as will be discussed in Sect. 6.1.

3 JOPA

JOPA stands for Java OWL Persistence API. It is in essence an API for efficient access to ontologies in Java, designed to resemble its relational-world counterpart Java Persistence API [11].

In this section, we introduce the architecture of JOPA.

[1] https://bitbucket.org/openrdf/alibaba, Accessed 04-08-2015.

Architecture. From the architectural point of view, JOPA is divided into two main parts:

OOM, realizes the object-ontological mapping and works as a persistence provider for the user application. The API resembles JPA 2 [11], but provides additional features specific to ontologies.

OntoDriver, provides access to the underlying storage optimized for the purposes of object-oriented applications. OntoDriver has a generic API which decouples the underlying storage API from JOPA.

Figure 2 shows a possible configuration of an information system using JOPA, together with some insight into the architecture of JOPA. The application object model is defined by means of a set of integrity constraints which guard that the ontological data are usable for the application and vice versa. Thanks to the well-defined API between the OOM part of JOPA and OntoDriver, there can be various implementations of OntoDriver and the user can switch between them (and between the underlying storages) without having to modify the actual application code.

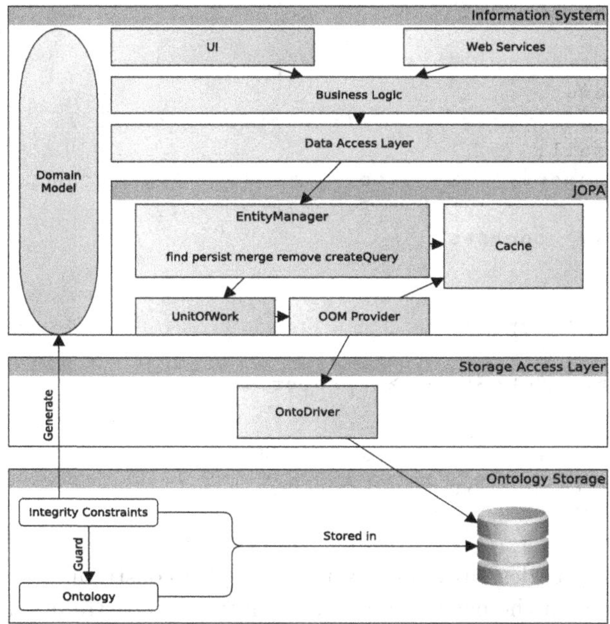

Fig. 2. JOPA Architecture. There are clear borders between the application, storage access layer and the storage itself. It is also visible that the domain model objects can be used throughout the application. Integrity constraints restrict the ontology so that it corresponds to the application's needs and annotations corresponding to these constraints are used to specify the domain model entity classes.

3.1 JOPA OOM

Let us now briefly describe the main features of the object-ontological mapping layer of JOPA.

The OOM layer is mainly represented by the **EntityManager** interface, which corresponds to its JPA 2 counterpart [11] to a large extent. It contains CRUD[2] operations: *find*, *persist*, *merge* and *remove*, but it enhances them with versions supporting context descriptors [2]. It also contains operations for transaction management and cache access.

Mapping. Object-ontological mapping is a mechanism of transforming ontological data, represented by concepts, properties and individuals, into classes, attributes and instances of the object-oriented paradigm and vice versa. This mapping enables one to define and use simple classes (called *entities*) as business objects in the application, a mechanism with which developers are familiar. Such an entity can be seen for example in Listing 1.1.

```
@OWLClass(iri="http://example.org/Student")
class Student {
  @Id(generated = true)
  URI id;
  @DataProperty(iri="http://example.org/name")
  String name;
  @DataProperty(iri="http://example.org/email")
  String email;
  @ObjectProperty(iri="http://example.org/course",
                  fetch = FetchType.LAZY)
  Set<Course> courses;
  @Inferred
  @Types
  Set<String> types;
  @Properties
  Map<String, Set<String>> properties;
}
```

Listing 1.1. Example of a business entity class declaration with JOPA annotations representing the object-ontological mapping.

The mapping is described by a set of integrity constraints, represented as Java annotations in the entity classes. Such integrity constraints define a clear contract between the object model and the ontology. The class declaration in Listing 1.1 reveals the simplicity of the description of the mapping. A class represents an ontological concept, data properties are attributes of primitive types (*String*, *Integer* etc.) and object properties are references to instances of other classes. The **types** field in the example then represents a set of concepts to which an individual mapped to an instance of this class belongs.

[2] Create, Retrieve, Update, Delete.

An ontological individual is fully identified by its IRI[3]. However, this is not the case in object oriented world, where the identity of each instance is tightly coupled with the class it belongs to. Therefore, JOPA places a constraint to the identity of individuals represented in it by requiring them to be explicitly stated to be of the specified ontology concept.

JOPA currently does not support blank nodes and anonymous individuals.

Unmapped Properties. One of the key features that differentiates JOPA from other ontology persistence frameworks like Empire and AliBaba is its ability to provide access to properties not captured by the object model. Such property values are represented by a map where the keys are property IRIs and values are sets of property values. The map is annotated with the `@Properties` annotation. This way the application has, although limited, access to the dynamic part of ontological data without having to adjust the domain model. See the `properties` attribute in Listing 1.1.

Inferred Attributes. Ontologies contain two types of information:

- *Explicit (asserted)*,
- *Implicit (inferred)*.

Inferred information cannot be changed, as it is derived from the asserted knowledge by a *reasoner* and can change only by modification of the explicitly stated information. As a consequence, it is necessary to prevent modification of inferred data. JOPA supports both asserted (in read/write mode) and inferred (read-only) attributes. This support is realized by means of the `@Inferred` and `@Asserted` annotations. The `@Asserted` annotation is optional. Every field not annotated with `@Inferred` is considered asserted and allowed to be modified.

Contexts. Another feature of JOPA is its ability to work with ontologies distributed in several contexts (graphs). When the underlying storage supports this feature, the application is able to specify not only in which context an instance should be searched for, but also contexts for individual attributes of the instance. If the context is not specified, the default one is used.

Transactions and Caching. JOPA supports transactional processing of the ontological data. However, the mechanism is different from standard relational-based persistence, because reasoning makes it more difficult to reflect pending changes to the transaction that produced them. For example, when a property value is changed during a transaction T_1, only T_1 has to be able to see effects of that change even before commit. JOPA itself does not employ any reasoning and offloads this burden to the underlying OntoDriver implementation. The OntoDriver is free to choose any strategy for keeping track of transactional changes. When a business transaction commits, JOPA tells the OntoDriver to make the pending changes persistent in the storage.

[3] Internationalized Resource Identifier.

Since applications often manipulate the same data, it is reasonable to use cache to reduce the necessity to query the storage. JOPA contains a *second-level cache* [11], which is shared between all open persistence contexts and enables quick entity lookup. Another performance improving feature is the support for lazily loaded attributes[4].

3.2 OntoDriver

OntoDriver is a software layer designed to decouple the object-ontological mapping done by JOPA from the actual access to the underlying storage. The goal for such decoupling is on the one hand the ability to switch between different storages without having to modify the application code. On the other hand, such layer enables vendor-specific optimizations of the storage access.

The concept of OntoDriver is similar to a JDBC[5] driver known from the relational world. But in contrast to JDBC, where all operations are done using SQL[6] statements, OntoDriver provides dedicated CRUD operations, which give the implementations more opportunity for optimizations, since they know beforehand what operation is executed.

However, the OntoDriver API does not eliminate the possibility of using SPARQL [12] queries for information retrieval and SPARQL Update [13] statements for data manipulation.

OntoDriver API. The key idea behind OntoDriver is a unified API providing access to ontology storages. To formally describe the API, let us first define basic ontological terminology:

Theoretical Background. We consider programmatic access to OWL 2 DL ontologies, corresponding in expressiveness to the description logic $\mathcal{SROIQ}(\mathcal{D})$[7]. In the next sections, consider an OWL 2 DL ontology $\mathcal{O} = (\mathcal{T}, \mathcal{A})$, consisting of a TBox $\mathcal{T} = \{\tau_I\}$ and an ABox $\mathcal{A} = \{\alpha_I\}$, where α_I is either of the form $C(i)$ (class assertion), or $P(i, j)$ (object property assertion), where $i, j \in N_i$ are OWL named individuals, $C \in N_c$ is a *named concept*, $P \in N_r$ is a *named object property*. Other axiom types belong to $\mathcal{T}$. W.l.o.g. we do not consider $C(i)$ and $P(i, j)$ for complex C and P here. We do not consider anonymous individuals either. See full definition of OWL 2 DL [4] and $\mathcal{SROIQ}(\mathcal{D})$ [14].

In addition to ontological (open-world) knowledge, a *set* $\mathcal{S}_C = \{\gamma_i\}$ *of integrity constraints* is used to capture the contract between an ontology and an information system object model. Each integrity constraint γ_i has the form of an OWL axiom with closed-world semantic, as defined in [15].

---

4 Lazily loaded attribute values are retrieved from the data source only upon application request.

5 Java Database Connectivity.

6 Standard Query Language.

7 For the sake of compactness, we neglect datatypes and literals ($\mathcal{D}$) and use description logic notation.

By *multi-context ontology* we denote a tuple $\mathcal{M} = (\mathcal{O}_d, \mathcal{O}_1, \ldots, \mathcal{O}_n)$, where each $\mathcal{O}_I$ is an ontology identified by a unique IRI and is called *context*, $\mathcal{O}_d$ denotes the *default ontology (default context)* which is used when no other context is specified. This structure basically corresponds to an RDF dataset with named graphs [16]. An *ontology store* is a software layer that provides access to $\mathcal{M}$.

An *axiom descriptor* δ_a is a tuple $(i, \{(r_1, b_1) \ldots (r_k, b_k)\})$, where $i \in N_i$, $r_m \in N_r$, $b_m \in \{0,1\}$ and $m \in 1 \ldots k$. The b_ms specify whether inferred values for the given role should be included as well. The axiom descriptor is used to specify for which information the OntoDriver is queried.

An *axiom value descriptor* δ_v is a tuple $(i, \{(r_1, v_1) \ldots (r_k, v_k)\})$, where $i \in N_i$, $r_m \in N_r$, $v_m \in N_i$ and $m \in 1 \ldots k$. The v_ms represent property assertion values for the given individual and property. The axiom value descriptor specifies information which shall be inserted into the storage.

Please note that for the sake of readability we have omitted context information from the formal definitions. In reality, a context can be specified for the whole descriptor and for each role.

OntoDriver API. The core operations of the OntoDriver API are as follows:

- *find*$(\mathcal{M}, \delta_a)$: $2^{\mathcal{M}} \times N_i \times N_r^k \times \{0,1\}^k \rightarrow 2^{N_i \times N_r \times N_i}$, where δ_a is an axiom descriptor,
  - Given an individual, load values for the specified properties,
  - Used by `EntityManager.find()` in OOM,
- *persist*$(\mathcal{M}, \delta_v) = \mathcal{O}_d \cup \{\alpha_1 \ldots \alpha_s\}$, where $\alpha_1 \ldots \alpha_s$ are property assertion axioms created from role-value pairs in δ_v,
  - Persist axioms representing entity attribute values,
  - Used by `EntityManager.persist()` in OOM,
- *remove*$(\mathcal{M}, \delta_a) = \mathcal{O}_d \setminus \{\alpha'_1 \ldots \alpha'_t\}$, where $\alpha'_1 \ldots \alpha'_t$ are property assertion axioms for the roles specified in δ_a,
  - Remove axioms representing entity attribute values,
  - Used by `EntityManager.remove()` in OOM,
- *update*$(\mathcal{M}, \delta_v) = (\mathcal{O}_d \setminus \{\alpha'_1 \ldots \alpha'_t\}) \cup \{\alpha_1 \ldots \alpha_s\}$, where $\alpha'_1 \ldots \alpha'_t$ are original property assertion axioms for the roles $r_1 \ldots r_k$ defined in δ_v and $\alpha_1 \ldots \alpha_s$ are new property assertion axioms created for role-value pairs in δ_v,
  - Remove old and assert new values for entity attributes,
  - Used by `EntityManager.merge()` or on attribute change during transaction in OOM,
- *getTypes*$(\mathcal{M}, i, b)$: $2^{\mathcal{M}} \times N_i \times \{0,1\} \rightarrow 2^{N_c}$, where the resulting axioms represent types of the specified individual i, b specifies whether inferred types should be included as well,
  - Get types of the specified named individual,
  - Used by `EntityManager.find()` in OOM,
- *updateTypes*$(\mathcal{M}, i, \{c_1 \ldots c_k\}) = (\mathcal{O}_d \setminus \{\alpha'_1 \ldots \alpha'_t\}) \cup \{\alpha_1 \ldots \alpha_k\}$, where $c_m \in N_c$, the α'_m are original class assertion axioms and the α_o are the new class assertion axioms for the given individual i,
  - Updates class assertion axioms for the given individual by removing obsolete types and adding new ones,

- Used by `EntityManager.persist()`, `EntityManager.merge()` or on attribute change during transaction in OOM,

– *validateIC*$(\mathcal{M}, \{\gamma_1 \dots \gamma_k\}) : 2^{\mathcal{M}} \times 2^{N_i \times N_r \times N_i} \times \mathcal{S}_c \rightarrow \{0, 1\}$, where $\gamma_m \in \mathcal{S}_c$ and $m \in 1 \dots k$,

- Validate the specified integrity constraints, verifying *reasoning-time* integrity constraints which cannot be validated at runtime [1],
- Called on transaction commit in OOM.

The actual programming interface written in Java contains, besides methods representing the above operations, also methods for issuing statements (presumably SPARQL and SPARQL Update) and transaction managing methods. We omit these here for the sake of brevity.

Prototype of OntoDriver. To evaluate our design of OntoDriver, we have created a prototypical implementation. For this prototype, we have chosen to use Sesame API. One of the main reasons for such decision was that there exist Sesame API connectors for some of the most advanced ontology repositories including GraphDB (successor of OWLIM, see [17]) and Virtuoso [18]. The implementation can thus be used to access a variety of storages. More optimized implementations of OntoDriver which would exploit specific features of the underlying storages can be created, but the prototype was intended as a general proof of concept for the layered design of JOPA.

The Sesame OntoDriver uses neither SPARQL nor the SeRQL [8] language to perform data manipulation. We use the Sesame filtering API, which filters statements according to subject, predicate and object (i.e. it basically corresponds to triple pattern matching in a SPARQL query). On the one hand, this requires for example asking for each property of an individual separately (or asking for all of them by making the property unbound). On the other hand a SPARQL query that would correspond to the *find* operation (see above) would be a union of triple patterns. In addition, we have a more fine-grained control over the operation itself, because we are able to specify whether inferred statements should or should not be included in the query result. This is an important feature of JOPA and can generally not be done in standard SPARQL statements.

Another important point is how the Sesame OntoDriver deals with transactions. As was mentioned in Sect. 3.1, JOPA transfers the burden of making changes done in a transaction visible to the transaction itself to the OntoDriver. The prototype handles this task by creating local graphs of added and removed statements. When the store is queried for some knowledge, the added and removed transactional snapshots are used to enhance the results returned by the storage to reflect the transactional changes. These local graphs are of course unique to every transaction on the OntoDriver level. Currently, this approach is handicapped by the fact that such local graphs do not provide any reasoning support, so they represent only explicit assertions. A solution to this drawback would be for example using an in-memory reasoner, e.g. Pellet [19], for the local graphs.

We are also considering another possible solution for keeping the transactional changes. This solution would require temporary contexts created by the store, which would hold the transactional changes kept currently in the local graphs. This would enable us to transfer the reasoning task over to the underlying storage. This solution remains as an idea for the future development.

4 Operation Complexity Analysis

The OntoDriver API enables us to examine the complexity of operations it consists of. In this section we consider this complexity with regards to several selected ontology storages. A careful reader may have noticed that some of the operations in the API could share the same implementation, for instance $update(\mathcal{M}, \delta_v)$ can be implemented using $remove(\mathcal{M}, \delta_a)$ and $persist(\mathcal{M}, \delta_v)$. Thus, we concentrate the analysis on the following operations:

- $find(\mathcal{M}, \delta_a)$,
- $persist(\mathcal{M}, \delta_v)$,
- $remove(\mathcal{M}, \delta_a)$.

When done with theoretical complexity analysis, we will proceed to experimental evaluation of our theoretical assumptions.

4.1 Complexity Analysis

For the theoretical complexity analysis, we have selected two well known storages, each representing a different approach to reasoning – one performing total materialization on data insertion, the other reasoning at query time and doing no materialization (the difference being similar to forward and backward chaining strategies in rule systems):

GraphDB, formerly known as OWLIM [17], is a Sesame SAIL[8] with rule-based reasoner using forward chaining,

Stardog,[9] performs real-time model checking with no materialization.

Each of these strategies has its pros and cons. Total materialization is fast in querying, as there is no reasoning performed at query execution time. On the other hand, statement removal and insertion are slow. In addition it is necessary to specify reasoning expressiveness before any data is inserted. Total materialization can also cause significant inflation of the dataset size. Real-time reasoning keeps the dataset compact and it is fast on insertion, however performing reasoning at query time can be time consuming.

[8] Storage And Inference Layer.

[9] http://www.stardog.com, Accessed 02-12-2014.

A Note on Indexes. The most important part of every ontology storage is its index – it determines how quickly the data can be accessed. Ontology repositories follow the trend of data storages from other domains and use B-trees [20]. GraphDB uses a modified version of B-trees – a B+ tree [21]. There is not much information about the indexing strategies of Stardog, but we were able to determine that it also uses a B+ tree from a post in Stardog forum[10].

To efficiently access data which are statements consisting of three parts – *subject* (S), *predicate* (P) and *object* (O), the storages usually contain multiple indexes. Since there exist six combinations of the three statement parts, there could be up to six different indexes. With increasing number of indexes the space required to store the data and the indexes obviously grows. Another problem of multiple indexes is their updating when the data is modified. Given the fact that most storages also support contexts, the number of possible indexes grows even more.

Therefore, storages usually restrict themselves to only a few indexes, based on the structure of the most frequent queries. It is often the case that property is bound in such queries. Thus, storages mostly use PSO and POS indexes, with others optionally available. The PSO index searches statements first by *predicate*, then by *subject* and last by *object*. The POS index is similar, only switching object and subject. Although the indexes are designed for generic RDF statements, they are adequate in our setup, as the ontological axioms manipulated by OntoDriver have the form of atomic class assertions, or atomic property assertions, both being serialized as single RDF triples. The PSO and POS indexes are also the default ones used by GraphDB [22] and Stardog [23].

Analysing Complexity of Typical Operations. In the following paragraphs we will examine time complexity of each of the operations enumerated at the beginning of this section with regards to the selected storages, with a short comment on possible implementations of these operations in OntoDriver.

Table 1. Asymptotic time complexity of the selected operations for GraphDB and Stardog. b is branching factor of the index B+ tree, n is the size of the dataset. The complexity of processing B+ trees is described in [20]. C_R is the reasoning cost, which depends on the selected language expressiveness and m is the number of reasoning cycles performed in materialization of statements inserted into GraphDB.

Storage	T_{find}	$T_{persist}$	T_{remove}
GraphDB	$O(log_b n)$	$O(\sum_{i=0}^{m} C_{Ri} \times log_b n)$	$O(\sum_{i=0}^{m} C_{Ri} \times log_b n)$
Stardog	$O(C_R) + O(log_b n)$	$O(log_b n)$	$O(log_b n)$

$find(\mathcal{M}, \delta_a)$ Multiple strategies can be employed to realize the *find* operation, but in essence they all perform a search for property assertion axioms where the

[10] The post is available at http://tinyurl.com/ke4ozf7, accessed 25-01-2015.

individual and property are bound. Therefore, the PSO index will be triggered. However, while GraphDB will proceed directly to finding the corresponding data, Stardog must first perform reasoning and rewrite the query according to the schema semantics. The complexity can be seen in Table 1.

We would like to stress here that the *find* operation is theoretically very favourable in terms of possible performance, because it does not require any joins, as it is supposed to return a simple union of property values for a single individual. Therefore it is straightforwardly mappable to the PSO index.

$persist(\mathcal{M}, \delta_v)$. Persisting assertion values specified in δ_v requires insertion of the corresponding statements into the storage's indexes (in our case the PSO and POS indexes).

In addition, in GraphDB, a materialization of statements inferred from the inserted knowledge is performed. Thus, from a set of statements K_E, inserted into the database, a new set K_I^0 of statements is derived, K_I^0 being in turn inserted into the dataset, triggering more materialization, until a set K_I^m is inserted, from which no additional knowledge can be deduced. This, of course, makes the *persist* operation in GraphDB more complex than in Stardog. Again, the theoretical complexity is shown in Table 1.

$remove(\mathcal{M}, \delta_a)$. Doing *remove* in an ontology requires knowledge of what exactly should be removed. Thus, JOPA performs *epistemic remove*, i.e. only values of properties mapped in the object model are removed. Therefore if the dataset contains property values which are not mapped by the object model managed by JOPA, these values are retained. In case the entity contains a field gathering unmapped asserted properties (see Sect. 3.1), the unmapped values are contained in this attribute and, to be consistent with the epistemic remove, JOPA deletes all statements where the removed individual is the subject.

remove in Stardog is again relatively straightforward. Since JOPA does allow only removal of explicit statements, there is no reasoning required. The procedure thus consists of finding the relevant statements and removing them from the index.

The situation is more interesting in GraphDB, because with the removal of explicit statements, some inferred knowledge may become irrelevant. GraphDB resolves the operation with a combination of forward and backward chaining [17]. In short, all possible inferred data is found from the removed statements first (this is the forward chaining part). From the results, backward chaining is performed to determine whether the implicit knowledge is backed by explicit knowledge other than that being removed. If not, the inferred statements are removed as well. Asymptotically, the complexity of *remove* in GraphDB is the same as *persist*, see Table 1.

The asymptotic complexities suggest that GraphDB is more suitable for read-oriented applications, especially when the expressiveness of reasoning increases. In these cases the cost of inference in GraphDB is paid when the dataset is loaded and at the actual runtime the queries will presumably be much faster. On the other hand, applications performing a lot of data modifications can benefit from the non-materializing approach of Stardog.

4.2 Experimental Complexity Evaluation

The theoretical complexity analysis provides information about asymptotic behaviour of the operations in the selected storages. However, there are hidden constants not visible in the formulas which may play a significant role for working with real-world data volumes. These hidden constants are mostly connected with the internal implementation of the storages. Hence, we decided to verify our conclusions with measurement.

Existing Storage Benchmarks. There exist several benchmarks for ontology storages. The key differences between them is expressiveness of their ontology and the queries. The Berlin SPARQL Benchmark (BSBM) [24] is purely RDF-oriented and used for testing of SPARQL endpoints. The well known Lehigh University Benchmark (LUBM) [25] contains basic OWL constructs, however, its schema is still missing more expressive features like nominals or number restrictions. The University Ontology Benchmark (UOBM) [26] is built upon LUBM, but adds more expressiveness, including transitive and equivalent properties or cardinality restrictions.

However, the queries used in the aforementioned benchmarks are general-purpose queries and they are not suitable for the object-oriented access scenario, which we primarily want to explore. Indeed, the operations required by JOPA (or any other OOM-supporting framework) are, as the reader already knows from Sect. 3.2, relatively straightforward and are focused on working with properties of a single individual. Therefore, we decided to create our own benchmark.

Object-UOBM. The benchmark we created exploits the existing schema and dataset generator of the UOBM benchmark. But instead of the generic queries of UOBM, it contains a set of eight queries tailored to the application access scenario. The queries are written in SPARQL and SPARQL Update in order to be interoperable for different storages, but they capture the essence of operations defined in the OntoDriver API.

We used this benchmark to evaluate performance of GraphDB and Stardog storages in order to verify our theoretical results.

Object-UOBM Results. Complete results of the experiments we conducted and a detailed description of Object-UOBM can be found in [27], we give just a brief overview here. The first observation that can be made from the results is that the price of real-time reasoning in Stardog is very high. The performance of a query representing the *find* operation with reasoning in Stardog is less than one query per second, while without reasoning it is able to answer nearly one thousand queries per second (see Fig. 3). A more surprising result is that SPARQL Update queries representing the *persist* and *update* were performing better in GraphDB than Stardog, although GraphDB has to perform materialization on insertion. Only for a DELETE query (representing the *remove*

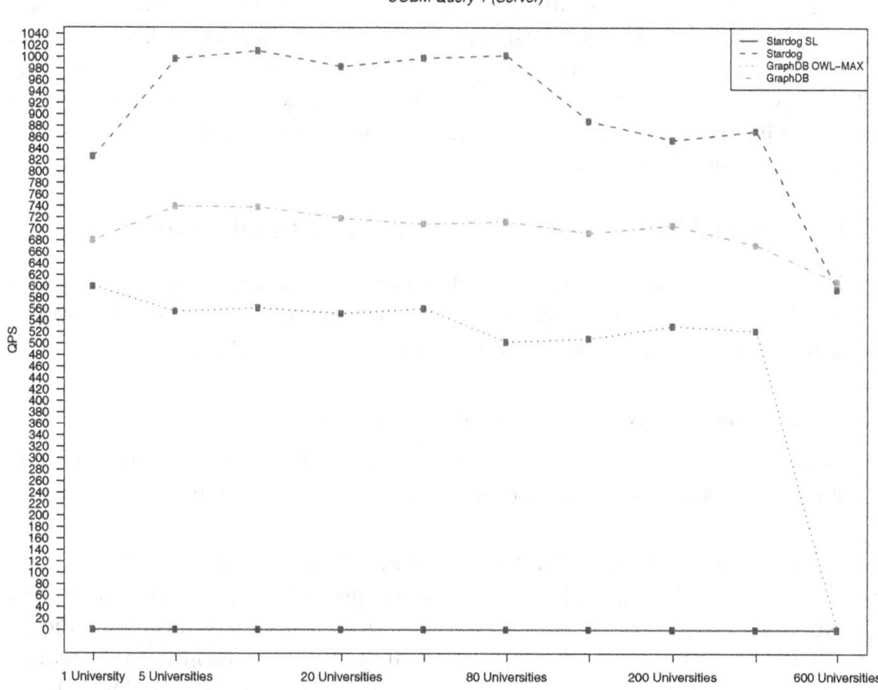

Fig. 3. Performance of Stardog and GraphDB for a SELECT query representing the *find* operation. Both storages were evaluated with reasoning (the Stardog SL and GraphDB OWL-Max lines, see [27] for explanation of the reasoning levels) and without it. GraphDB failed to answer the query for the largest dataset when using reasoning. One can cleary see the performance penalty of real-time reasoning in Stardog.

operation) the combination of forward and backward chaining made GraphDB slower than Stardog.

Another interesting result of the benchmark is that when loading an entity, it appears to be more efficient to filter the statements only by subject without specifying the properties to load. We had three variations of the same loading query, the first using unbound property and value, the second using a UNION of triple patterns specifying properties to load and the third doing the same, but using OPTIONAL. While the query using OPTIONAL performed decidedly worst, the query with unbound property performed the best, although it was loading unnecessary values of properties which were not mapped in the object model. Despite the fact that this situation could change in cases where the object model would map only a small portion of properties and values related to an individual, it seems to be more reasonable to use the unbound property strategy rather than specifying the properties to load explicitly.

Overall, it appears that GraphDB is more suitable for application access than Stardog. One has only to accept the fact that bulk loading is significantly faster in Stardog and that he has to specify repository expressiveness when creating it. The application-specific performance of GraphDB, which consists of querying and modifying existing data and inserting relatively small portions of new data, is better than that of Stardog.

5 Practical Evaluation of JOPA and OntoDriver

In this section we first evaluate the performance of OntoDriver when compared to a low-level approach represented by the Sesame API. Then we discuss our experience from developing a real-life IT system using JOPA.

5.1 Performance and Code Metrics Evaluation

In this section we briefly evaluate the performance of OntoDriver and compare it to approaches which directly use the native API of the underlying storage.

Performance of JOPA with OntoDriver. While we have already examined the theoretical complexity of operations present in the OntoDriver API and experimentally verified them on existing storages, we also need to validate that our implementation is efficient. The goal of this evaluation is to determine performance differences between ontology access using JOPA and OntoDriver and using Sesame API directly. Since the OntoDriver prototype internally uses Sesame API, we hardly expect JOPA to outperform pure Sesame API solution, instead we will concentrate on the possible performance penalties stemming from the additional logic that JOPA has to do. The test machine setup is as follows:

- Linux Mint 17 (64-bit)
- Java 8 update 31 (HotSpot), -Xms6g -Xmx6g
- Sesame API 2.7.14, GraphDB 6.0 RC6
- Intel i5 2.67 GHz
- 8 GB RAM

A class diagram of the benchmark schema is shown in Fig. 4. The application model is rather small, but sufficient to exercise a large part of the features supported by JOPA. The application model and the datasets are based on the UOBM benchmark [26], which we already used in our storage benchmark [27], and the datasets were generated using a generator application [28].

Results of the benchmark are shown in Table 2. The *find* operation was loading approximately 450 instances of `UndergraduateStudent`. Each of them was connected to three courses in average. Thus, the total number of loaded individuals with properties was more than 1800, representing over 5000 statements. The *persist* test inserted 500 new instances of `UndergraduateStudent`, connected to four existing courses and a new paper, into the ontology. The *update* evaluation updated the name and telephone of each of the previously persisted student, removed reference to one of his courses and added another one instead. Finally, the *remove* benchmark removed the 500 persisted undergraduate students.

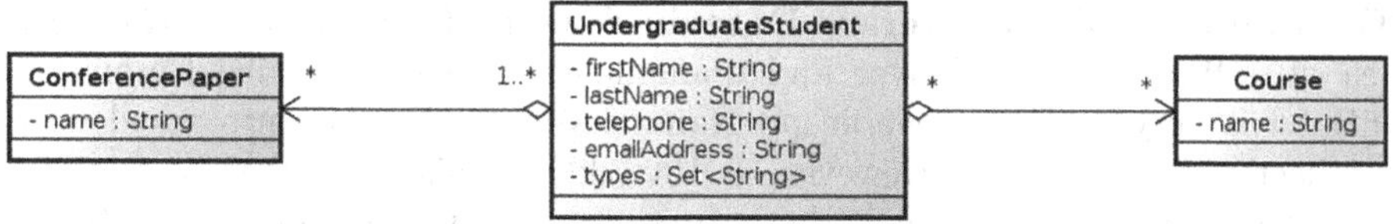

Fig. 4. Benchmark application model. Although small in size, it exercises most of the concepts supported by JOPA, including inferred entity types and data and object properties with lazy loading.

Table 2. Benchmark results. The times are average from 100 runs of the benchmark.

Dataset	$T_{persist}/s$		T_{find}/s		T_{update}/s		T_{remove}/s	
	JOPA	Sesame	JOPA	Sesame	JOPA	Sesame	JOPA	Sesame
UOBM 1	4.158	2.209	13.738	13.353	32.28	9.571	36.456	2.740
UOBM 5	4.245	2.252	13.830	13.366	32.461	9.993	36.718	2.918
UOBM 10	4.255	2.260	13.840	13.293	32.625	10.077	36.433	3.024

Benchmark Results Discussion. The benchmark results show that JOPA performs comparably when loading and persisting entities. It is important to point out that to mimic the behaviour of JOPA on entity loading, the Sesame API runner was verifying that the object property values were of the correct type. However, there is a significant performance gap between Sesame API and JOPA in *update* and *remove*. Major part in this gap is given by the fact that JOPA first has to load the entities before updating or removing them. For Sesame API, we simply removed (and inserted) the required statements without loading them first. Of course, the benchmark is skewed in this regard, because a real world application would most likely require the entity loading anyway. Also, JOPA currently does not support the `getReference` method [11], which would be suitable for the *update* and *remove* scenarios. Still, there is a large margin for improvement in JOPA for these operations.

In the future, we would like to try comparing different strategies of implementing OntoDriver.

JOPA and OntoDriver versus Sesame API. One of the most important advantages of using JOPA with OntoDriver is the ability to treat ontological individuals with their properties as coherent objects with attributes and possibly add behaviour to those objects, thus increasing readability and maintainability of the application. Such task cannot be accomplished using domain-independent APIs like Sesame API or OWL API without writing a large amount of boilerplate code. This difference is very similar to what the developer gains when using JPA instead of pure JDBC. Consider the example in Fig. 5. The difference in the amount of code written is clear, and the Sesame code does not even make any checks for correct types (for instance that a property value is another individual and not a literal) or integrity constraints.

JOPA and OntoDriver versus Domain-Specific Frameworks. The basic idea of JOPA and OntoDriver and domain-specific solutions like Empire or AliBaba is very similar – enable programmers to work with ontological data in object-oriented fashion. However, JOPA adds to this basic concept features which enable the user to exploit the nature of ontologies to more extent. JOPA supports working with unmapped properties, types and explicit distinction between inferred and asserted knowledge. In addition, the OntoDriver and its API enables JOPA to supports a wide range of ontological storages. AliBaba, on the other hand, is tied to storages supporting the Sesame API. Empire does have support for custom storage connectors, which are used by the framework via dependency injection. JOPA also offers better isolation of transactions and more advanced caching.

```
public Student find(URI pk) {
    return em.find(Student.class, pk);
}
```

```
private Map<String, Object> findPerson(URI pk, Map<URI, Map<String, Object>> knownPeople)
        throws RepositoryException {
    final Map<String, Object> values = new HashMap<>();
    RepositoryResult<Statement> r = connection.getStatements(pk, RDF.TYPE, null, false);
    final Set<String> types = new HashSet<>();
    boolean found = false;
    while (r.hasNext()) {
        final Statement s = r.next();
        if (s.getObject().stringValue().equals(personType)) {
            found = true;
        } else {
            types.add(s.getObject().stringValue());
        }
    }
    assert found;
    values.put("types", types);
    knownPeople.put(pk, values);
    r = connection.getStatements(pk, vf.createURI(firstName), null, false);
    Object value = getValue(r, Literal.class);
    values.put("firstName", value);
    ...
    final Set<Map<String, Object>> friends = new HashSet<>();
    r = connection.getStatements(pk, vf.createURI(friendOf), null, false);
    while (r.hasNext()) {
        final Statement s = r.next();
        if (!(s.getObject() instanceof URI)) {
            continue;
        }
        final URI friend = (URI) s.getObject();
        if (knownPeople.containsKey(friend)) {
            friends.add(knownPeople.get(friend));
        } else {
            friends.add(findPerson(friend, knownPeople));
        }
    }
    values.put("friends", friends);
    return values;
}

private Object getValue(RepositoryResult<Statement> values, Class<?> cls) throws RepositoryException {
    Object value = values.hasNext() ? values.next().getObject() : null;
    if (value != null && !cls.isAssignableFrom(value.getClass())) {
        throw new IllegalArgumentException();
    }
    return value;
}
```

Fig. 5. Find an entity. On the left hand side using JOPA. Entity definition is omitted, but it corresponds to the one shown in Listing 1.1. On the right hand side using Sesame API. The difference in the amount of code is clear.

6 Experience Using JOPA and OntoDriver

We have had an opportunity to use JOPA in a real-world application. This application is used to create reports about safety occurrences in aviation and is developed as part of the INBAS project [11]. We will now briefly summarize our experience.

[11] http://www.inbas.cz, Accessed on 07-08-2015.

Positives. One of the main positives of using JOPA stems from the frame-based approach and has already been discussed in great detail – it is the fact that the application works with coherent and logically defined objects. The objects can be, in addition to having behaviour of their own, easily passed over system boundaries, so for example we use the same domain objects when communicating with a JavaScript-based front end via REST web services, where they are serialized into JSON and deserialized back.

The support for operation cascading further reduces the amount of code by automatically carrying out the operation over relationships marked for cascading.

Another benefit of using JOPA and OntoDriver is the clear separation of storage access. Thus, we are able to use fast in-memory storage in tests and during development and switch to server based GraphDB solution when running in production. The only change that has to be made is modifying repository URL in a configuration file.

Deficiencies. The code imprint could be further reduced by integration with application frameworks like Spring. With that integration, transactions could be marked declaratively using annotations, persistence context injected automatically by the container and capabilities like Spring repositories used to minimize the data layer code that has to be written.

A feature that is missing in JOPA is the support for bidirectional relationships. Unless the relationship is explicitly defined using an inverse object property, there is currently no way of specifying a backwards reference to another object.

However, the greatest deficiency of JOPA and other domain-specific frameworks like Empire or AliBaba is the lack of support for ontology concept subsumption. Ontologies rely heavily on class hierarchies and it is very cumbersome to work around the lack of their support in persistence frameworks. For instance, in our application, we have a concept called *RunwayIncursion*, which describes an event when an object intrudes on a runway. This intruding object can be of the following types: *Aircraft*, *Vehicle* or *Person*. In ontology, this can modelled using the following hierarchy:

$$
\begin{aligned}
\mathcal{T} = \{&Aircraft \sqsubseteq AerodromeAgent,\\
&Vehicle \sqsubseteq AerodromeAgent,\\
&Person \sqsubseteq AerodromeAgent,\\
RunwayIncursion &\equiv \forall hasIntruder.AerodromeAgent\}
\end{aligned}
$$

It would be very convenient to be able to map such hierarchy to the domain model shown in Fig. 6. However, due to the lack of support for concept subsumption, this cannot be achieved in JOPA and we have to model such structure using an entity with fields of types *Aircraft*, *Vehicle* or *Person*, where only one of the fields can be non-null.

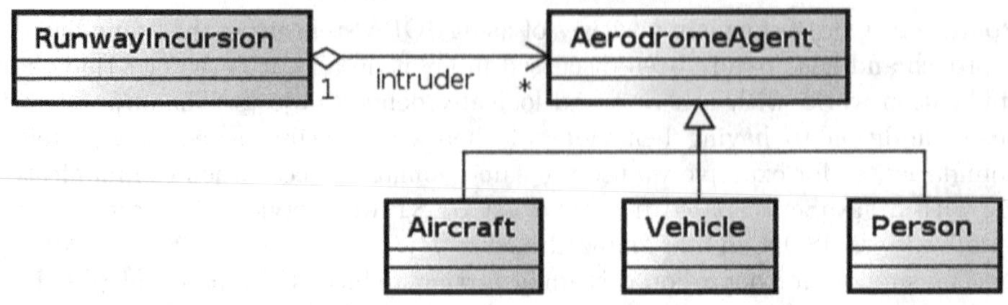

Fig. 6. Domain model, which would model an ontological concept hierarchy and range restriction.

6.1 Ontology Concept Subsumption

Let us now describe why it is difficult to represent concept subsumption in object-ontological mapping frameworks. Concept subsumption [29] is used to create hierarchies of classes[12] and can be used to model the *is a* relationship between the subsumed class and its subsumer (parent). Individuals of the subsumed class are also instances of the parent class, inheriting all of its properties. Unfortunately, such model cannot be straightforwardly transformed into the object-oriented paradigm. The *is a* relationship is realized through class *inheritance* in object-oriented languages. One problem with the Java language, in which most of the frameworks for working with ontologies are written, is that is supports only single-parent inheritance. However, ontological classes can be subsumed by multiple other classes.

A more crucial problem with ontological class hierarchies is the identity of the individuals. Consider the concept hierarchy described above and an individual *John* which belongs to the *Person* concept.

$$\mathcal{A} = \{Person(John)\}$$

Because *John* is an instance of *Person*, he is also an instance of *AerodromeAgent*. Now consider the object model in Fig. 6, which reflects the aforementioned concept hierarchy in object-oriented paradigm. If we load our individual *Adam* first as an *AerodromeAgent* and then as a *Person*, they will be two completely separate objects with the same IRI. However, it is still the same individual in the ontology.

This identity mismatch can lead to situations where for example the application changes the affiliation of the *AerodromeAgent* instance of *John* and at the same time changes the affiliation of the *Person* instance of *John*, but in the ontology, whichever modification comes first will be overwritten by the latter.

[12] *Class* is a term used in the OWL 2 language specification [4] and it corresponds to the term *concept*, used in description logics underlying the OWL language. We will use the terms interchangeably, unless a disambiguation between ontological classes and object-oriented paradigm classes is necessary.

As the astute reader may have noticed, the concept subsumption problem is not restricted to situations when the corresponding domain classes are related via inheritance. The same problem would occur if *AerodromeAgent* and *Person* were unrelated.

7 Conclusions

We have introduced JOPA as a solution for application access to ontologies, along with the OntoDriver, which separates the object-ontological mapping layer from the actual storage access, providing more opportunities for storage-specific optimizations and preventing vendor lock-in. We have examined the theoretical complexity of the operations defined in the OntoDriver API and tested two of the most advanced ontology storages for their suitability for application access.

We have also discussed our experience with JOPA as persistence provider in a real-world application, its benefits and deficiencies. We paid particular attention to the lack of support for class subsumption, which is a problem not specific to JOPA, but to all frameworks providing any form of object-ontological mapping.

In the future, we plan to thoroughly research the possibility of supporting some form of concept subsumption and domain class inheritance respectively in object-ontological mapping frameworks. We would also like to study possible optimizations of operations required by ontology-based applications.

Acknowledgements. This work was supported by the grant No. SGS13/204/OHK3/3T/13 Effective solving of engineering problems using semantic technologies of the Czech Technical University in Prague and No. TA04030465 Research and development of progressive methods for measuring aviation organizations safety performance of the Technology Agency of the Czech Republic.

References

1. Křemen, P., Kouba, Z.: Ontology-driven information system design. IEEE Trans. Syst. Man Cybern. Part C **42**, 334–344 (2012)
2. Ledvinka, M., Křemen, P.: JOPA: developing ontology-based information systems. In: Proceedings of the 13th Annual Conference Znalosti 2014 (2014)
3. Křemen, P.: Building ontology-based information systems. Ph.D. thesis, Czech Technical University, Prague (2012)
4. Motik, B., Parsia, B., Patel-Schneider, P.F.: OWL 2 web ontology language structural specification and functional-style syntax. In: W3C Recommendation, W3C (2009)
5. Meditskos, G., Bassiliades, N.: A rule-based object-oriented OWL reasoner. IEEE Trans. Knowl. Data Eng. **20**, 397–410 (2008)
6. Poggi, A.: Developing ontology based applications with O3L. WSEAS Trans. Comput. **8**(8) August 2009
7. Horridge, M., Bechhofer, S.: The OWL API: a Java API for OWL ontologies. In: Semantic Web - Interoperability, Usability, Applicability (2011)

8. Broekstra, J., Kampman, A., van Harmelen, F.: Sesame: a generic architecture for storing and querying RDF and RDF schema. In: Horrocks, I., Hendler, J. (eds.) ISWC 2002. LNCS, vol. 2342, pp. 54–68. Springer, Heidelberg (2002)
9. Carroll, J.J., Dickinson, I., Dollin, C., Reynolds, D., Seaborne, A., Wilkinson, K.: Jena: implementing the semantic web recommendations. In: Proceedings of the 13th International World Wide Web Conference (Alternate Track Papers & Posters), pp. 74–83 (2004)
10. Grove, M.: Empire: RDF & SPARQL Meet JPA. semanticweb.com (2010)
11. JCP: JSR 317: Java^{TM} Persistence API, Version 2.0 (2009)
12. Harris, S., Seaborne, A.: SPARQL 1.1 Query Language. Technical report, W3C (2013)
13. Gearon, P., Passant, A., Polleres, A.: SPARQL 1.1 Update. Technical report, W3C (2013)
14. Horrocks, I., Kutz, O., Sattler, U.: The even more irresistible SROIQ. In: Proceedings of the 10th International Conference on Principles of Knowledge Representation and Reasoning (KR 2006), pp. 57–67 (2006)
15. Tao, J., Sirin, E., Bao, J., McGuinness, D.L.: Integrity constraints in OWL. In: Fox, M., Poole, D. (eds.): AAAI. AAAI Press (2010)
16. Cyganiak, R., Wood, D., Lanthaler, M.: RDF 1.1 concepts and abstract syntax. Technical report, W3C (2014)
17. Bishop, B., Kiryakov, A., Ognyanoff, D., Peikov, I., Tashev, Z., Velkov, R.: OWLIM: a family of scalable semantic repositories. In: Semantic Web - Interoperability, Usability, Applicability (2010)
18. Erling, O.: Virtuoso, a hybrid RDBMS/graph column store. IEEE Data Eng. Bull. **35**, 3–8 (2012)
19. Sirin, E., Parsia, B., Grau, B.C., Kalyanpur, A., Katz, Y.: Pellet: a practical OWL-DL reasoner. Web Semant. Sci. Serv. Agents World Wide Web **5**, 51–53 (2007)
20. Comer, D.: The Ubiquitous B-Tree. Comput. Surv. **11**, 121–137 (1979)
21. Hepp, M., de Leenheer, P., de Moor, A., Sure, Y.: Ontology Management: Semantic Web, Semantic Web Services, and Business Applications. Springer, New York (2007)
22. Ontotext: GraphDB-SE-GraphDB6-Ontotext Wiki (2014) http://owlim.ontotext.com/display/GraphDB6/GraphDB-SE+Indexing+Specifics
23. Stardog: Stardog Docs (2014). http://docs.stardog.com/
24. Bizer, C., Schultz, A.: The Berlin SPARQL benchmark. Int. J. Seman. Web Inf. Syst. **5**(2), 1–24 (2009)
25. Guo, Y., Pan, Z., Heflin, J.: LUBM: A benchmark for OWL knowledge base systems. J. Web Semant. **3**, 158–182 (2005)
26. Qiu, Z., Liu, S., Pan, Y., Ma, L., Xie, G.T., Yang, Y.: Towards a complete OWL ontology benchmark. In: Sure, Y., Domingue, J. (eds.) ESWC 2006. LNCS, vol. 4011, pp. 125–139. Springer, Heidelberg (2006)
27. Ledvinka, M., Křemen, P.: Object-UOBM: an ontological benchmark for object-oriented access. In: Klinov, P., Mouromtsev, D. (eds.) KESW 2015. CCIS, vol. 518, pp. 132–146. Springer, Heidelberg (2015)
28. Zhou, Y., Grau, B.C., Horrocks, I., Wu, Z., Banerjee, J.: Making the most of your triple store: query answering in OWL 2 using an RL reasoner. In: Proceedings of the 22nd International Conference on World Wide Web (2013)
29. Baader, F., Calvanese, D., McGuinness, D.L., Nardi, D., Patel-Schneider, P.F. (eds.): The Description Logic Handbook: Theory, Implementation, and Applications. Cambridge University Press, New York (2003)

The Development of Information Models and Methods of University Scientific Knowledge Management

Gulnaz Zhomartkyzy(✉) and Tatyana Balova

D. Serikbayev East Kazakhstan State Technical University, 69 Protozanov A.K, Ust-Kamenogorsk, Kazakhstan
zhomartkyzyg@gmail.com, tbalova@ektu.kz

Abstract. The main aim of this paper is to develop some methods and technologies of information support for university scientific knowledge management. It examines the concept of knowledge management and life-cycle processes of university scientific knowledge. On-To-Knowledge methodology is used as the basis for the university knowledge management. Text Mining and Semantic Web technologies are used to develop the ontological information model and to process information resources. Some models and methods are explored to carry out the monitoring of university research schools development. The model of a specialist which reflects the level of research activity productivity and overall scientific activity evaluation has been described. The ontology based information model is used to form a specialist's professional competence in different areas. The approach to university scientific school identification based on the university academic community clustering by their common interests and the concept of university scientific knowledge semantic portal have been presented.

Keywords: Knowledge management system · Intellectual capital · Monitoring of scientific schools · The model of a specialist · Scientific community · Clustering · Semantic portal

1 Introduction

A large amount of accumulated information resources and the high speed of new information arrival impose increasingly high requirements to modern systems designed to provide information support to university scientific processes.

The intellectual capital or intangible assets of the university are the source of new scientific knowledge. At the level of organization scientific knowledge or intellectual resources is a complex category which combines intellectual capital, people, and various forms of intangible assets which concentrate knowledge and professional skills [1]. Knowledge as the intellectual capital is gradually becoming one of the most important factors in the development of economy and society.

The processes of creation, accumulation, use and dissemination of knowledge are becoming key factors which ensure training of competitive specialists for any modern institution of higher education as an open social and economic self-organizing system.

S. Hammoudi et al. (Eds.): ICEIS 2015, LNBIP 241, pp. 429–451, 2015.
DOI: 10.1007/978-3-319-29133-8_21

Russell Akkof, one of the classics of Operational Research, proposed the following hierarchy of knowledge: data - information - knowledge - understanding - wisdom [2]. There are different approaches to the classification of knowledge in organizations. The most common is the division of knowledge into explicit and tacit knowledge. The transformation of knowledge in an organization occurs through explicit and tacit knowledge interaction. The knowledge conversion or transformation results in its qualitative and quantitative increase.

The notion of knowledge management in an organization is determined by the authors in [3] as the strategy and the transformation of knowledge.

The main focus in knowledge-intensive organizations is on the creation, transfer and development of knowledge, so effective knowledge management is the matter of survival for such organizations [4, 5].

There arises a need in processes, infrastructure and organizational procedures at a higher education institution that would allow its employees to use its corporate knowledge base.

Section 2 describes the structure of university scientific knowledge management system. Section 3 presents the information model of university scientific activities. Section 4 describes the procedure of information resource processing and scientific profile formation. Sections 5–7 describe the monitoring of university scientific schools. Section 8 presents the development of scientific knowledge semantic portal. Section 9 is the conclusion.

2 The Structure of University Scientific Knowledge Management System

In this paper the university's scientific knowledge management system (SKMS) is considered as an aggregate of information, software, technical means, and organizational solutions aimed at efficient management of the university's available intellectual resources and training specialists who meet the modern requirements.

The purpose of university SKMS is the formation of a unique ontology-based integrated intellectual environment to improve the competitiveness of the university's science and education. The university SKMS is the technological component of the university SKM, which provides the creation, organization and dissemination of scientific knowledge among the university staff.

There are following approaches to knowledge management: organizational and technological [6]. The technological approach puts the application of IT-technologies in line with the organizational measures.

The process-oriented On-To-Knowledge methodology is used as the basis for university scientific knowledge management [7]. The methodology of KMS development and support is based on the process and metaprocess of working with knowledge (KnowledgeMetaProcess and KnowledgeProcess). The basis of the metaprocess of working with knowledge (KnowledgeMetaProcess) is the development of an ontology, which consists of the following steps: a feasibility study, the beginning, clarification, evaluation, support and evolution.

The ontology is the link/(linking element) of knowledge objects and a connecting bridge between different steps of knowledge transformation processes (KnowledgeProcesses). The development of the ontology is the important aspect of knowledge management solution support. The development and deployment of applications of knowledge management takes into account the requirements of "KnowledgeProcess" and considers such processes/issues as:

- metaprocess of working with knowledge (KnowledgeMetaProcess);
- software engineering (software development and design– Software engineering);
- the corporate culture of the organization.

The process of working with knowledge (Knowledge Process) focuses on the use of KM-solutions, i.e. after KM-application are fully realized and implemented in the organization, the cycle of knowledge transformation is performed. The knowledge transformation cycle consists of the following steps: creation, storage, search and access, use.

The developed model of technological approach to knowledge management based on the methodology described above is shown in Fig. 1.

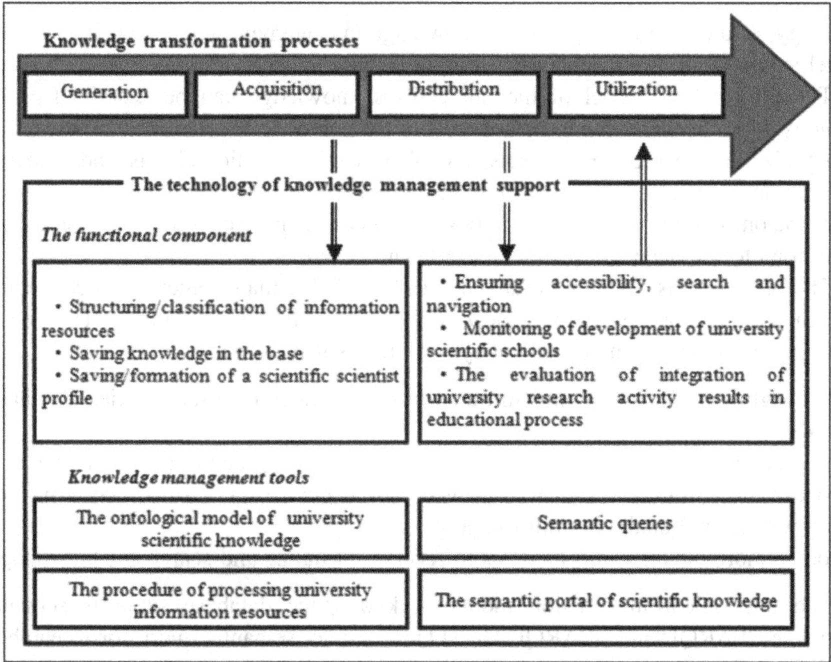

Fig. 1. Technological approach to university scientific knowledge management.

The proposed technological approach integrates a functional component and knowledge management tools.

The functional component and knowledge management tools. The functional component includes:

- classification of information resources,
- a scientist's/a specialist's scientific profile formation and saving;
- identification of university scientific schools and research directions;
- ensuring the availability, search and navigation.

Knowledge management tools are:

- the ontology based university scientific knowledge model,
- the procedure of university information resources processing,
- semantic queries,
- semantic Portal of university scientific knowledge.

The information model of university scientific activities is described further in the paper.

3 The Information Model of the University Scientific Activities

Ontology, as a common language in knowledge management, is a conceptual domain model as a system of concepts, their properties and relations [8].

The information model of the university's knowledge can be described as the ontology which includes the basic concepts of the university's scientific activities, such as organizational structure, subjects, the objects of scientific schools and research, information resources, other subdisciplines, etc. [9].

In the ontology of scientific activities the subclasses in "Scientific directions" class correspond to the headings of VINITI [10] knowledge areas classifier.

The ontology, as a common language in knowledge management, is a conceptual domain model as a system of concepts, their properties and relations. The use of ontology in knowledge management system makes it possible:

- to integrate the information distributed in various document repositories, databases and knowledge;
- to generalize and systematize the available information, acting as a metamodel;
- to use the automated logical conclusion for better search results, acquiring new knowledge and analyzing information;
- to use more effective mechanisms to receive, visualize and search for knowledge.

The ontological information model of knowledge database supports semantic queries in SPARQL and SPARQL-DL [11]. Example: semantic query for researchers and information resources in scientific directions can be written as follows:

Example 1:

```
Person and (peopleHasPublicationIR some (PublHasDivis some TopicsSolidStatePhysics))
```

Example 2:

```
Article and (PublHasDivis some TopicsSolidStatePhysics)
```

Navigation in scientific knowledge and information resources is done by the use of semantic links between the classes of the ontology.

4 The Procedure of the University Information Resources Processing with the Purpose to Form Scientific Profiles

The main stages of the information resources processing are given below:

1. Extraction of terminological collocations. Pearson criterion is used to detect collocations [12];
2. Feature selection. Mmutual Information method is used as a method for evaluating the importance of terms (Mmutual Information) [13];
3. Classification of texts according to scientific areas. The method of k nearest neighbour (kNN) is used for text classification [13, 14];
4. Working with the text files in the corpus with the purpose to perform statistical calculations requires the following preliminary steps:
5. To pre-translate to .txt format the files of different formats (pdf, doc, docx) in the corpus;
6. To delete all hyphenation beforehand;
7. To perform lemmatization of all the text files in the corpus, to delete all punctuation marks, to change all uppercase letters to lowercase letters.

A detailed description of processing stages is given in the following sections.

4.1 Collocation Extraction and Feature Selection for the Classification of Scientific Texts

A collocation is regarded as a non-random combination of two or more lexical items common to most scientific texts in a particular scientific field. The set of terminological collocations generated by the specified collection of scientific texts describes a narrow subject area (topics and subtopics) of this collection.

For automatic extraction of terminology collocations from scientific texts a freely distributable Java-library LingPipe interface is used [12]. The array of obtained collocations is ranked in order of importance, where the sequence of lexical tokens is dependent. The significance of the collocations is calculated based on the collocation the Pearson independence statistics. The higher the value of the significance of the collocation, the less the likelihood that the sequence of tokens is independent.

The general scheme of the formation of a software dictionary is shown in Fig. 2.

The main modification of the method based on the static approach includes the preliminary use of morphological templates of filters [15, 16]:

To obtain the list of dominant terms using the x^2 it is necessary to solve the following tasks:

- the extraction of collocations with the calculated coefficient of significance;
- the determination of the morphological characteristics of each word in the n-gram;

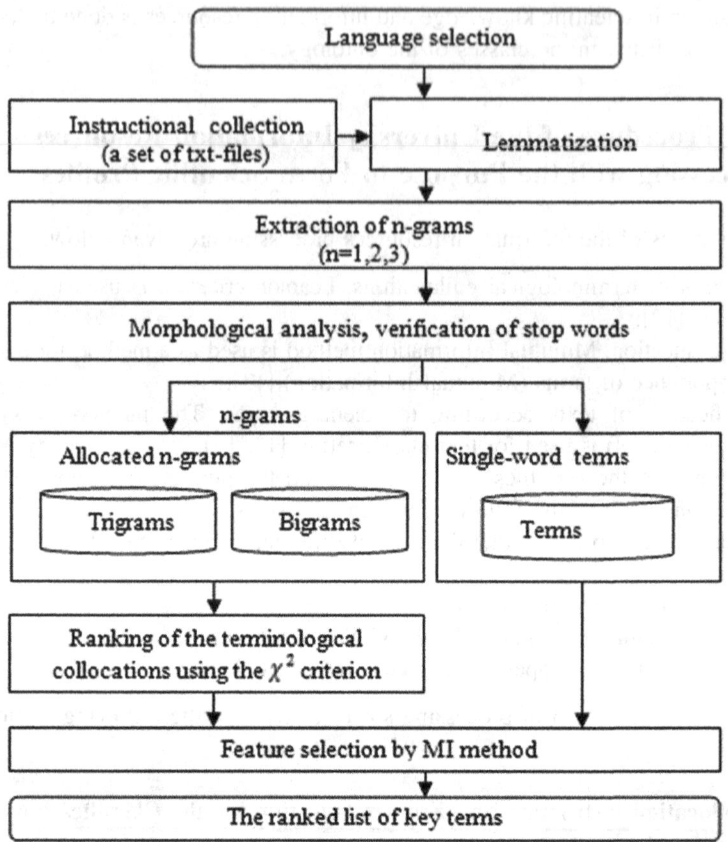

Fig. 2. The extraction and selection of domain terms.

- the removal of stop words and the selection of phrases that match the templates;
- the saving of collocations in a database table.

The following restrictions were set for a bigram and a trigram: the minimum frequency bigram equal to 10, the minimum frequency of trigrams equal to 15.

The thus obtained term-candidates form a list of n-grams (bigrams, trigrams).

Table 1 presents the results of the developed module for extraction and separation of terms according to domains. Table 1 shows some uninformative words with high critical value of χ^2, as well as some informative words with a lower value χ^2 (a superconducting property, a superconducting parameter).

Single-word terms are extracted based on a combination of frequency and the inverse document frequency of the term. The weight of a single-word term is calculated by the formula [13]:

$$Tf - Idf_{t,c} = tf_{t,c} \times \log \frac{N}{df_t} \tag{1}$$

Table 1. The comparison of mutual information values and χ^2 of terms.

Terms	Critical value χ^2	Value MI
okonchatel'nyy redaktsiya (окончательный редакция)	40462.68	0.093
tochka zreniye (точка зрение)	23093.13	0.100
sverkhprovodyashchiy granula (сверхпроводящий гранула)	15534.01	1.000
mezhkristallitnyy granitsa (межкристаллитный граница)	14328.13	1.000
pervyy ochered (первый очередь)	13659.12	0.212
vysokotemperaturnyy sverkhprovodnik (высокотемпературный сверхпроводник)	11518.91	1.000
sverkhprovodyashchiy perekhod (сверхпроводящий переход)	6566.12	1.000
fazovyy prevrashcheniye (фазовый превращение)	4703.25	1.000
obyekt issledovaniye (объект исследование)	4413.52	0.415
obyemnyy dolya (объемный доля)	3584.50	0.263
obsuzhdeniye rezultat (обсуждение результат)	3196.66	0.553
nastoyashchiy vremya (настоящий время)	3175.12	0.263
troynoy splav (тройной сплав)	2434.56	1.000
metallicheskiy provodimost (металлический проводимость)	2288.77	1.000
ukazannyy vyshe (указанный выше)	2243.87	0.652
amorfnyy plenka (аморфный пленка)	1910.57	1.000
maksimalnyy znacheniye (максимальный значение)	1832.25	0.049
sistema uravneniye (система уравнение)	744.95	0.000
sverkhprovodyashchiy sostoyaniye (сверхпроводящий состояние)	665.31	1.000
elektronnyy spektr (электронный спектр)	460.36	1.000
sverkhprovodyashchiy svoystvo (сверхпроводящий свойство)	256.72	1.000
sverkhprovodyashchiy parametr (сверхпроводящий параметр)	144.78	1.000

where $tf_{t,c}$ is term frequency in the collection of the c class; df_t is the number of documents in the collection of the c class which contain the term; N is the number of documents in the collection.

The generated list of terms with weights $Tf - Idf_{t,c}$ is ranked by a certain threshold value, a number of terms are selected which are further recorded in the database table.

The further stage of the vocabulary formation is the selection of features to eliminate noise-terms. Feature selection enhances the effectiveness of training the classifier by reducing the size of the vocabulary and the classification accuracy.

The measure of utility $A(t, c)$ of each term in the lexicon is calculated for each class c, and N terms with the largest value of $A(t, c)$ are selected. All other terms are discarded and are not involved in the classification.

To remove non-informative terms the method of mutual information was chosen [13]. The measure of mutual information estimates how much information about a class in information-theoretic sense the term includes. The measure the usefulness $\mathrm{MI}(\mathrm{t_k}, \mathrm{c})$ is calculated, and k terms with the highest values of this measure are selected. To select k terms $\mathrm{t}_1, \ldots, \mathrm{t_k}$ for a given class, the following formula is used:

$$MI(t_k, c) = \log_2 \frac{A \times Q}{(A+C) \times (A+B)} \quad (2)$$

where: A is the number of documents which belong to category c and contain term t; B is the number of documents, which do not belong to category c and contain term t; C is the number of documents which belong to category c and do not contain term t; Q is the instructional the training set of documents.

The results of applying the mutual information method for the selection of features obtained in the previous step are shown in Table 1.

As illustrated in Table 1, some terms with low rates of χ^2 have a high value of MI. At this stage it is necessary to perform a selection of informative terms weighted by their mutual information MI, which are selected in the domain vocabulary and then used for the text classification.

4.2 Classifications of Information Resources in Scientific Domains

For the classification of scientific resources *kNN* - classification is used. The classification task in machine learning is a task to assign an object to one of the predefined classes based on its formal characteristics. *kNN* method (*k* method of nearest neighbor) is a vector classification model. *kNN* classifier assigns the document to the prevailing class of nearest neighbors (Fig. 3), where *k* is the method parameter.

The *k* parameter in *kNN* method is often selected on the basis of experience or knowledge about the classification task at hand.

The classification results are *k*-nearest neighbors ranked classes, the parameter k is equal to 5. The classifier is written in Java, such tool sets as LingPipe, Apache Lucene (free Java library for text processing and high-speed full-text search) are used for further text processing.

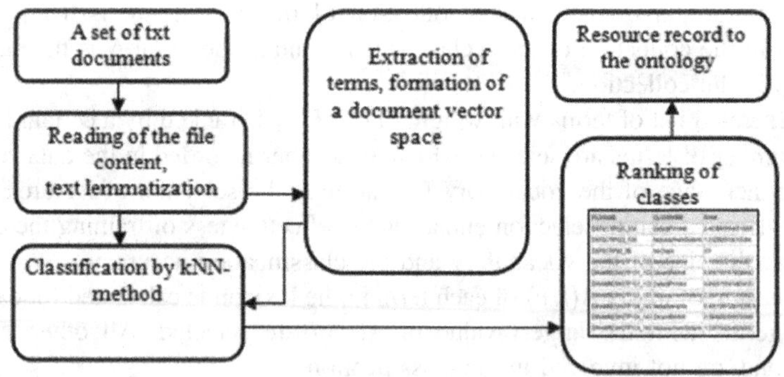

Fig. 3. The scheme of classification algorithm.

4.3 The Obtained Results and Conclusions

Checking the quality of the proposed classification procedure was performed on document collections in four sections of different scientific knowledge areas: "Green Economy", "Metals. Superconductors, "Semiconductors. Dielectrics" and "Physics of Plasma". All the documents are presented in pdf., doc. and docx. formats. The corpus of documents for processing was compiled from:

- articles published in "Physics of the Solid State" journal founded by the Russian Academy of Sciences, the Department of General Physics and Astronomy, Ioffe Physical Technical Institute, RAS (Science journal "Solid State Physics, 2013) [17];
- scientific electronic library eLIBRARY.RU.
- as well as various articles in electronic journals and publications on G-GLOBAL platform.

Measures F_1 and $MacroF_1$ with values ranging from 0 to 1 recommended in literature were used to evaluate the performance of classifiers. The measure F_1 assesses the balance between completeness and accuracy of the i-th classifier and is calculated as follows:

$$F_{1i} = \frac{2rp}{r+p} \tag{3}$$

where r is the classification completeness or the proportion of documents belonging to the class found by the classifier with regard to all documents of this class in the data selection; p is the classification accuracy within a class, or proportion of documents really belonging to this class with regard to all the documents which the classifier assigned to this class.

The macro-averaged measure Macro F_1 is calculated for all F_{1i} calculated by (3), it is an aggregate index and is calculated as the average of the measures:

$$Macro\,F_1 = \frac{1}{m}\sum\nolimits_{i=1}^{m} F_{1i} \tag{4}$$

The experimental results of kNN- classifier are shown in Table 2.

Table 2. Classification quality evaluation.

Knowledge area (classes)	Collection size (MB)	Accuracy, p	Completeness, r	F-measure
Green economy	4.41	0.97	0.83	0.89
Metals, Superconductors	4.51	0.89	0.96	0.92
Semiconductors, Dielectrics	9.00	0.88	0.89	0.89
Physics of plasma	12.8	0.86	0.92	0.89
$MacroF_1$				0.90

As it is seen in Table 2 the macro averaged measure calculated by (4) for all classes is 0.90, which indicates the acceptable results of the qualifiers.

The thematic classification of documents based on the developed processing procedure of information resources has allowed the researchers to build profiles and to implement a personalized search engine of the university semantic portal.

4.4 Forming Document Profiles Based on Information Resources Classification

As a result of the university scientific resources processing the document profiles are formed [18]. The profile of a document is determined as the vector of all its relevant classes:

$$PD = \left(R^d_{1,\ldots,} R^d_c\right) \tag{5}$$

where: R^d_c – are relevant topics c of document d.

The final step of the text classification is the formation of the document's semantic profile by creating the individuals of "Information resources" class in the ontology of scientific research activity.

The task of monitoring the university scientific schools development which is one of the functional components of university SKMS is considered in the next section.

5 Monitoring the Development of University Scientific Schools

The priority task of integrating research and education is the development of scientific schools which must be the main result of fundamental science and education interaction. Introduction to the research undertaken by scientists of scientific schools is the best school for young people.

Scientific schools provide constant growth of qualification of their participants; the presence of several generations in bundles of "teacher-student" ensures the continuity of generations [19]. The development of scientific schools and scientific and pedagogical teams is the basis for the development of fundamental scientific research and training quality improvement of research and educational personnel.

Scientific schools form that dynamic unit of science which ensures the continuity of scientific knowledge and creates optimal conditions for its development. Scientific school is the key element of collective preservation and multiplication of knowledge, one of the conditions to maintain the quality of research, and hence the quality of training scientific personnel. Scientific school is a clearly defined direction of scientific research carried out in the framework of specific scientific specialties [20].

Identification of scientific schools is becoming increasingly important in recent years in connection with the development of mechanisms for organization effectiveness assessment in tenders for financing projects, their certification and accreditation.

The availability of scientific schools is one of the most important criteria for foreign scientific funds which conclude contracts on joint research and grants as well as the criteria taken into account in establishing the rating of organizations.

One of the qualitative characteristics of a particular scientific direction's overall development and potential is the state of scientific schools. The creation, reorganization and coordination of scientific schools are regulated by universities. Monitoring the development of scientific schools remains a major issue in university scientific and innovation activity management. Thus, identification, recording, development, and monitoring the development of scientific schools is one of the priorities of science and education.

We have studied and developed a model of scientific community and the method of its intelligent processing to implement the functions of monitoring. The overall structure of monitoring the development of university scientific schools is presented in Fig. 4.

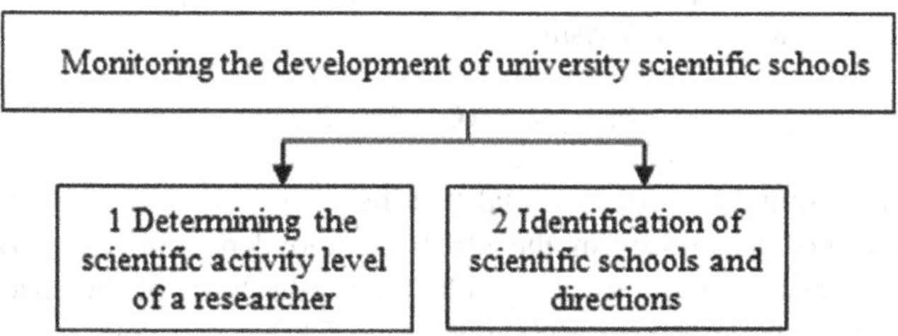

Fig. 4. The main functions of monitoring the development of university scientific schools.

The scheme of monitoring shows the following functions: determining the researcher's competence level, identification of scientific schools and research directions.

The following sections describe the model of a specialist which reflects the level of scientific activity productivity based on the calculation of entropy and overall scientific activity evaluation; as well as the approach to the university scientific school identification based on clustering the university scientific community for common interests (university scientific schools).

6 The Development of a University Researcher Model

One approach to human capital management is to develop a model of a university researcher (the model of a specialist).

Currently, there are two ways to create and support the model of a researcher: by a survey (qualification audit in an organization) and by monitoring their work in the knowledge management system (scientific papers, projects) [21]. The paper supports the definition given in [21], where the model of a researcher refers to a sound set of interrelated properties of a specialist, which can be formally described and used to support the efficient work with implicit knowledge.

In the scientific knowledge ontology the model of a specialist has the following formal description which includes a set of contextual and content metadata:

$$\mathrm{M_s} = \{\mathrm{M_{context}}, \mathrm{M_{content}}\} \tag{6}$$

where: $\mathrm{M_{context}}$ – is contextual metadata of a specialist description; $\mathrm{M_{content}}$ – is content metadata, which describe the specialist's competence.

Contextual metadata $M_{context}$ of a specialist include such parameters as:

- identification (a name, a photo, the date of birth, the place of birth, a login, a password);
- contact information (postal and email addresses, a personal web page, phone numbers;
- education (diplomas, certificates, etc.);
- professional achievements (prizes in competitions, awards, medals, etc.).

Content metadata $\mathrm{M_{content}}$ provide the description of the specialist's competence as a set of his competence characteristics:

$$\mathrm{M_{content}} = \{\mathrm{C_{sa}}, \mathrm{C_{cs}}, C_{oe}\} \tag{7}$$

where: C_{sa} – the competence of a specialist in fields of knowledge relevant to rubrics which are described as classes in the scientific knowledge ontology O_{SK}. C_{cs} – a measure of specialist's scientific activity efficiency (the level of the specialist's competence dispersion); C_{oe} - the overall assessment of scientific work.

The model of an individual researcher's scientific activity is determined by the factors of scientific activity (Fig. 5).

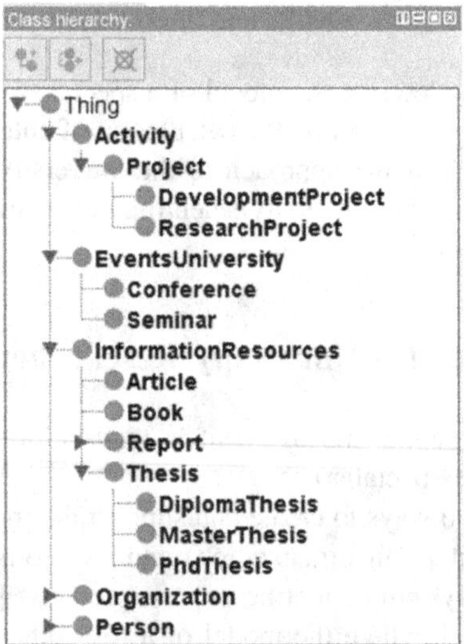

Fig. 5. Classes of the information model used to simulate a university researcher's activities.

In ontological information model these factors are grouped into the following classes: Event, Project, Publication.

6.1 A Specialist's Competence in Areas of Knowledge Based on the Classifications of Information Resources

Automatic processing of scientific electronic resources by the methods of Text Mining text processing are required to implement the described above model.

A specialist's competence in areas of knowledge C_{sa} is formed on the basis of the specialist's scientific profile. The specialist's scientific profile is based on the classification factors of his scientific activity (publications) by scientific areas. Accordingly, the specialist's competence in areas of knowledge C_{sa}, relevant to the specialist's scientific profile is determined as the profile of all his publications.

$$\mathrm{C_{sa}} = (PD_1, \ldots, PD_i) \tag{8}$$

where PD_i are all the author's documents.

6.2 The Calculation of the University Specialist's Scientific Activity Efficiency

To assess the university specialist's scientific activities efficiency we suggest using the level of dispersion of his competence.

The model of an individual researcher's scientific activities is determined by the factors of scientific activities. These factors are grouped into ontology classes in the model of ontology. The connection between the Person class and the class factor of scientific activities is shown below:

$$P_i \equiv P \cap \exists PersonHasIR.IR$$

$$IR_i \equiv IR \cap \forall \mathrm{publHasDivis}.FC_i$$

where, P is persons, IR is information resources, FC_i is the field of knowledge.

Each researcher works in at least one field of knowledge (VINITI rubricator, VINITI - All-Russian Institute of Scientific and Technical Information). Therefore, the classification of scientific activity factors is carried out by means of the VINITI rubricator of fields of knowledge up to level 3.

Cybernetics → Artificial Intelligence → Knowledge engineering

Cybernetics → Artificial Intelligence → Expert systems

Cybernetics → Theory of modeling → Mathematic modeling

This paper proposes the method for calculating the efficiency index of a specialist's scientific activities $\mathrm{C_{cs}}$ to analyze the competence of employees in a particular field. A specialist's scientific activity efficiency $\mathrm{C_{cs}}$ is calculated using the entropy.

The more papers of a specialist (researcher) are grouped by a certain category, the lower entropy and the higher the specialist's scientific activity efficiency [22, 23].

A specialist who has a high entropy works, as a rule, in several fields of knowledge, i.e., the specialist has a lower scientific activity efficiency (scientific competence):

$$C_{cs} = -\sum_{i}^{N} P_c \times \log_2(P_c) \tag{9}$$

$$P_c = \frac{P_i}{P} \tag{10}$$

P_i – is the number of the researcher's papers by heading $i = \overline{1, N}$;
P - the total number of the researcher's papers.

An example of calculations using formula 9 is shown in Table 3.

Table 3. A specialist's scientific activity efficiency calculation.

A researcher	Fields of knowledge	The number of scientific resources	The efficiency index of a specialist's scientific activities (C_{cs})
specialist$_1$.	Physics of Atom and Molecule	1	1.68
	General Physics	3	
	Solid State Physics (nano-sized objects, the structure of solids, general issues of Solid State Physics)	5	
	Physics of Gases and Liquids	1	
specialist$_2$	Solid State Physics	5	0
specialist$_3$	General Physics	6	0
specialist$_4$	Nuclear Physics	1	0.91
	General Physics	2	
specialist$_5$	General Physics	7	0.54
	Physics of Gases and Liquids	1	

Threshold values of the specialist's scientific activity efficiency C_{cs} were determined empirically:

$0 < C_{cs} < 1$ - a high level;
$1 \leq C_{cs} < 2$ - a medium level;
$C_{cs} \geq 2$ - a low level.

The analysis of results of personal calculation C_{cs} for leading university scientists by knowledge areas "General Physics", "Physics of Solids", "Physics of Atoms and

Molecules," "Physics of Gases and Liquids" and "Nuclear Physics" confirms the applicability of the formula for calculating the entropy of the researcher's scientific competence.

6.3 The Calculation of Total Assessment of the University's Specialist's Scientific Activity

The specialist's scientific activity efficiency is a quantitative indicator of knowledge, skills and abilities in a scientific field of a corresponding specialty.

The qualitative analysis, i.e. the definition of a specialist's professional competence, is also needed for making management decisions in the context of the university's different departments.

Each researcher has a trajectory of educational and scientific activities (Fig. 6): scientific activities, educational activities, participation in competitions and grant projects, international mobility.

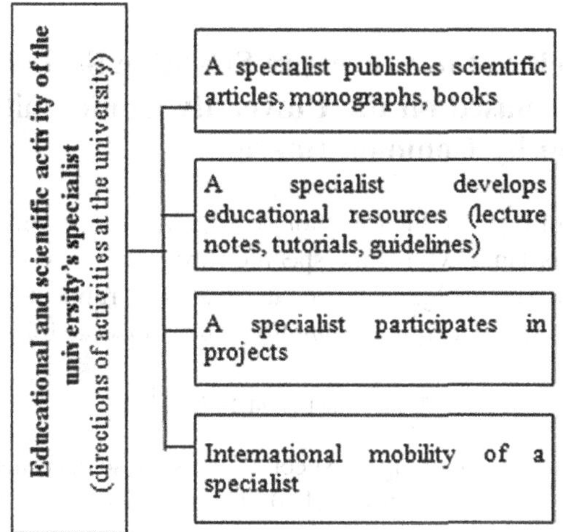

Fig. 6. Directions of scientific activities at the university.

This scheme allows us to calculate the qualitative characteristics of the overall assessment of the specialist's scientific activity.

The calculation of a specialist's overall scientific activity evaluation $-C_{oe}$ can be shown schematically as follows (Fig. 7).

A university specialist with a high overall assessment of scientific activity:

- Works in all areas of scientific activities;
- Has a high index of scientific competence C_{cs}.

A university specialist with a medium overall assessment of scientific activity:

- Only develops educational courses or is only involved in projects;

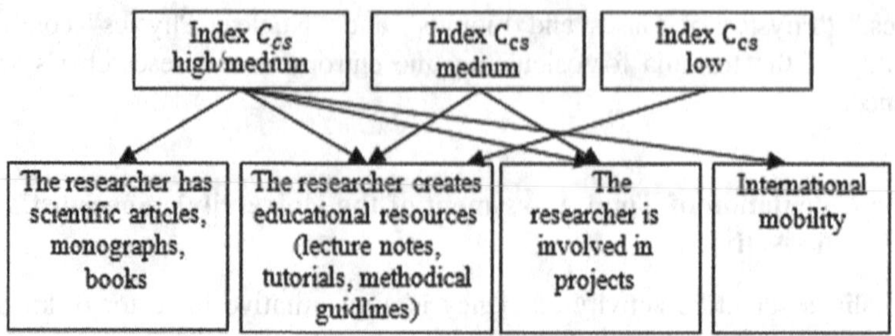

Fig. 7. The scheme of the calculation of a specialist's overall scientific activity evaluation.

- Has a medium index of scientific competence.

A university specialist with a low overall assessment of scientific activity:

- Only develops educational courses;
- Has a low index of scientific competence C_{cs}.

7 The Approach to the University Scientific School Identification Based on the University Community Clusterization by Common Interests

Each scientific school or scientific direction forms a scientific community by interests and develops in accordance with some specific rubrics of knowledge areas [24]. The VINITIrubricator of knowledge areas is used as the rubricator. In the proposed approach, a *model of the scientific community* is described as follows:

$$M_{SC} = \{r_{1.1},\ r_{1.2},\ r_{2.3},\} \tag{11}$$

where r_i are rubrics corresponding to specific areas of science and technology (one subrubric may be in several scientific fields). The model of a scientific community is shown in Fig. 8.

The proposed approach requires to carry out the university *scientific community* clustering based on its members' common interests to identify scientific schools and research directions.

To identify scientific schools and research directions DBSCAN clustering method is used in the scientific community model.

The principal advantages of this method served as the basis of the choice of DBSCAN density clustering method:

- Identification of the number of clusters (based on the notion of point density);
- The clustering algorithm is able to detect clusters of different shapes;
- Resistance to noise objects.

The idea underlying the algorithm is that within each cluster there is a typical dot density (of objects), which is significantly higher than the density outside the cluster

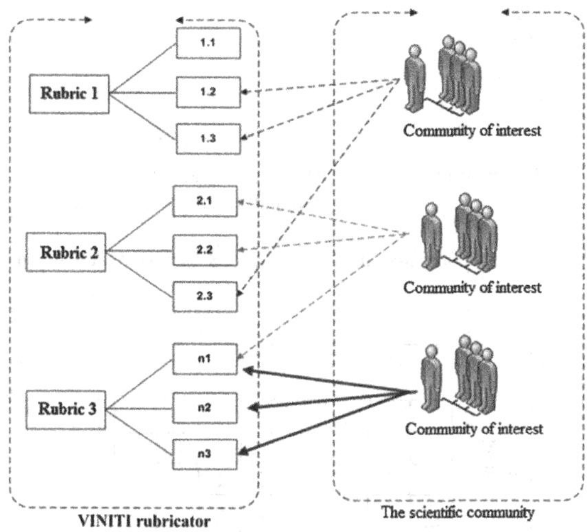

Fig. 8. A university scientific community by interests.

(Fig. 9). The density in the areas with noise is lower than the density of any of the clusters. For each dot of the cluster its neighborhood of a given radius must be at least a certain number of points, this number of dots is specified by a threshold value [25, 26].

In Fig. 9 A is a core point. B, C are border points. Cluster C_j is not the empty subset of objects satisfying the following conditions, at given *Eps* and *MinPt*, where Eps is the maximum distance between adjacent points, MinPt is the minimum number of neighboring points:

- $\forall p, q$: if $p \in C_j$ *and* q is density-connected from p, then $q \in C_j$, at given Eps and MinPt;
- $\forall p,\, q \in C_j : p$ is density connected from p, at given Eps, MinPt.

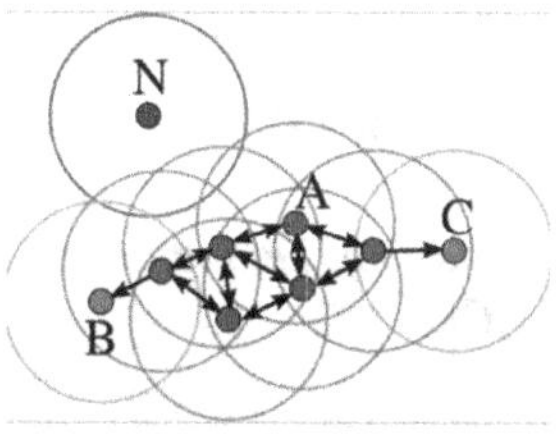

Fig. 9. Example of a cluster of arbitrary shape.

Figure 10 is given below for detailed description of the points.

Thus, a cluster is a set of closely-related points. Each cluster contains at least *MinPt* of documents. To perform clustering the model of a scientific community is translated into a binary matrix (Fig. 11). The values of matrix elements correspond to the presence or absence of work on the appropriate rubric.

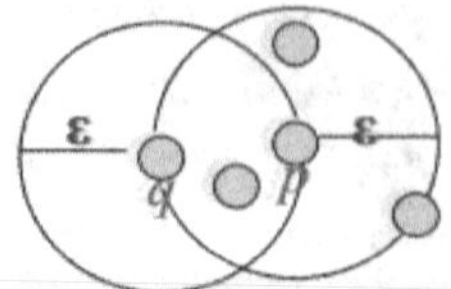

a) density-reachable points.

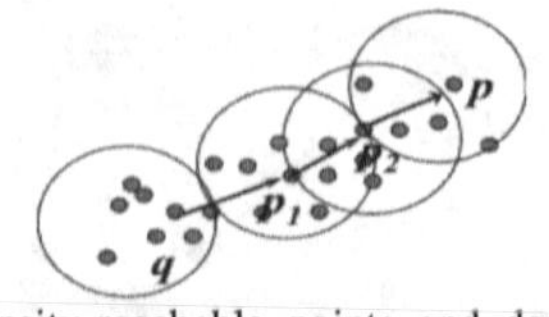

b) density-reachable points and density-connected points of the class.

Fig. 10. Types of points that form classes in DBSCAN algorithm.

Members of the scientific community	Rubrics								
	0	0	0	0	0	1	0	0	1
	1	0	0	0	0	1	0	0	1
	1	0	0	0	0	1	0	0	1
	1	0	1	0	0	0	1	0	1
	1	0	0	0	0	1	0	1	1
	0	0	0	0	0	1	0	0	1
	1	0	0	0	0	1	0	0	1

Fig. 11. The matrix of the scientific community model description.

The clustering algorithm based on the density of points is described below [25].

Input: a set of objects Q, parameters - Eps (the distance between the objects of the class), MinPt.

1. Determination of directly density-reachable points:

$$p \in N_{eps}(q),\ \ |N_{eps}(p)| \geq MinPt$$

where, q is a core point, p is a border point. Point p is directly density-reachable from point q,

2. Determination of all density-reachable, density-connected points of the current class:

$$p \leftarrow p_{(i+1)} \leftarrow p_i \leftarrow q$$

$$p \in N_{eps}(p_k),\ \ |N_{eps}(p_k)| \geq MinPt$$

Output: a set of clusters

Noise is a subset of objects that do not belong to any cluster,

$$p \in Q | \forall j \notin C, j = 1, |C|.$$

The value of *Eps* is determined as the distance between the researchers' profiles. A researcher's profile consists of all its relevant rubrics and is presented as a vector. VINITI rubricator of knowledge areas is used as a rubricator. The set of vectors forms a matrix of researchers's profiles . To calculate the distance a cosine measure of adjacency is used. The value *MinPt* is the minimum number of the subjects of scientific school, i.e. the subjects of "the communities of interest" in the model of a scientific community.

For approbation of the proposed approach we chose scientific communities of D. Serikbayev EKSTU and Ioffe Physical-Technical Institute of the Russian Academy of

Science (Ioffe Institute). Papers and research a directions of their scientific communities were examined. The results of numerical experiments confirmed the efficiency of the clustering algorithm used.

8 The Semantic Portal of University Scientific Knowledge

Previously considered models and methods formed the basis for the semantic portal of the university's scientific knowledge. Research in the field of semantic web portals began in the 2000s. A number of decisions for semantic portals have been published in scientific articles describing SEAL (SEmanticportAL) and Semantic Community Portal approaches [27].

The portal is viewed as an information system that organizes the unified access to target information space. The corporate portal of knowledge is generally understood as a single means of access to corporate information which allows employees to interact with each other, to communicate information to the collective understanding, values and experiences.

The problem of increasing the efficiency of information processes management for large volumes of information is particularly acute. One approach to solving this problem is to move on the semantic level in collection, processing, accumulation, storage, retrieval and dissemination of information. Portals that use semantic technologies to carry out their functions are called semantic portals. The following properties of the semantic portal of the university scientific knowledge can be identified as the main ones:

- It contributes to the collection, structuring and transfer of information from various internal and external sources and systems;
- allows the university employees to interact in scientific directions;
- displays the presence of scientific schools and directions by results of the university scientific activities;
- relates the information to the collective understanding, values and experiences, contributes to the emergence of new knowledge at the university.

The use of semantic technologies is considered as a means of improving the quality, adaptability and functionality of portals [28].

The main components of the semantic portal of the e-university's scientific knowledge are: the ontology of scientific knowledge, the ontology editor, the module of information resources classification and indexing, the module of navigation and search through the portal content, the database of ontological information. Figure 12 shows the semantic portal component connection.

To ensure the systematization of scientific knowledge and information resources the university's semantic portal supports the following functions:

- the software for navigation through the ontology of the university's scientific knowledge;
- the organization of search queries on the ontology concepts and relations;

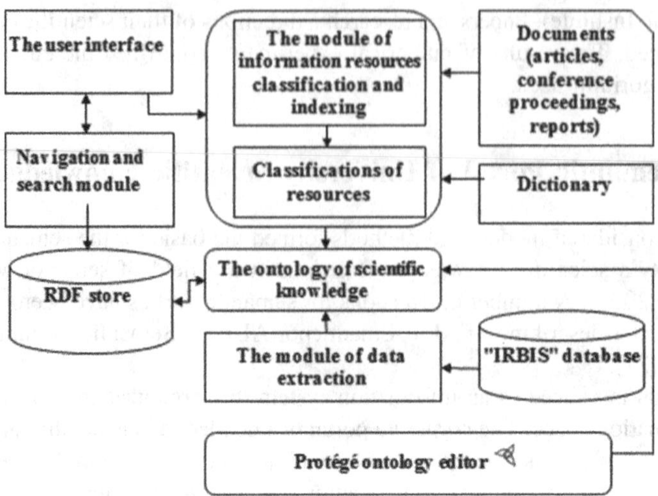

Fig. 12. The semantic portal's functional components.

- the classification of information resources to determine the development of the university's scientific schools and directions.

To create the ontology and the framework for building knowledge bases we chose a free and open resource Protégé (http://protege.stanford.edu/) as a visual environment. The technological framework is based on the Java programming language in the JavaVM environment. For faster data it was decided to load the ontology schema into an intermediate RDF-store of TDB built into Jena solution which supports all the features of work with JenaAPI, including preparation of SPARQL queries.

The RDF-store contains the description of scientific knowledge ontology in the form of RDF-triples. This description corresponds to the graph which nodes are the subjects and objects of RDF-predicates, and the ribs are the RDF-predicate itself.

Jena is a server for query processing in SPARQL language which stores the data as RDF-triples.

User queries are handled by the server applications which are associated with the semantic components. Remote clients work with the portal in all modern browsers using HTTP protocol. Queries are sent to the web application server. In the JavaVM (Virtual Machine) run-time environment stream starts query processing. The portal's architectural components provide the user with a transparent semantic access to the necessary data.

9 Conclusions

This paper solves the problem of developing a technological approach model for university scientific knowledge management and its support tools which provide a competitive advantage in education and the development of intellectual capital.

The paper contains the analysis of information resources description models for metadata formation, knowledge accumulation and distribution methods and techniques, standard architecture development, approaches and technologies to program implementation of knowledge management systems.

The models and methods described herein are functional components of the knowledge management system and university scientific knowledge information model.

The key scientific and practical results of this paper include:

- The ontology based information model of scientific knowledge has been developed on the basis of which semantic methods of data processing are implemented;
- The procedure for university information resources processing has been developed to form a scientific knowledge base of the university, which involves extracting terminological collocations based on the Pearson's X^2 method and morphological filter patterns; the formation of scientific profiles based on information resources classification by research areas;
- The model of a university researcher has been proposed as well as the approach to the identification of university scientific schools and their use in the knowledge management system.

The model of the university researcher reflects the level of productivity of scientific activities on the basis of the calculation of entropy and an overall assessment of research activities. The approach to the identification of university scientific schools is based on the clustering of academic community by common interests. The architecture of the university scientific knowledge portal prototype has been designed and its program implementation has been developed.

The next step of this work is the solution of the "University scientific activities assessment and the degree of its integration with the educational process" problem.

The work was performed under grant "The development of an e-university's ontological knowledge base", state registration number 0213RK00305.

References

1. Klimov, S.M.: Intellectual resources of society. St. Petersburg: IVESEP, Knowledge, (2002). Климов С. М. Интеллектуальные ресурсы общества. – СПб.: ИВЭСЭП, Знание (2002)
2. Ackoff, R.L.: From data to wisdom. J. Appl. Syst. Anal. **16**, 3–9 (1989)
3. Zaim, H.: Performance of knowledge management practices: a causal analysis. Knowl. Manag. **11**(6), 54–67 (2007). doi:10.1108/13673270710832163
4. Miles, I.: Knowledge intensive business services: prospects and policies. Foresight **7**(6), 39–63 (2005). doi:10.1108/14636680510630939. Emerald Group Publishing Limited
5. Scarso, E., Bolisani, E.: Knowledge-based strategies for knowledge intensive business services: a multiple case-study of computer service companies. Electron. J. Knowl. Manag. **8** (1), 151–160 (2010). http://www.ejkm.com

6. Tuzovskiy, A.F.: The development of knowledge management systems based on a single ontological knowledge base. Bull. Tomsk Polytech. Univ. **2**(310), 182–185 (2007). Тузовский А.Ф. Разработка систем управления знаниями на основе единой онтологической базы знаний. Известия Томского политехнического университета. 2 (310), 182–185 (2007)
7. Staab, S., Schunurr, H.-P., Studer, R., Sure, Y.: Knowledge processes and ontologies. IEEE Intell. Syst. Spec. Issue Knowl. Manag. **16**(1), 26–34 (2001)
8. Allemang, D., Hendler, J.: Semantic Web for the Working Ontologist. Morgan Kaufmann Publisher, Burlington (2011)
9. Zagorulko, Y., Borovikova, O.I.: Information model of scientific knowledge portal. Inf. Technol. **12**, 2–7 (2009)
10. All-Russian Institute of Scientific and Technical Information (10 June 2014). http://scs.viniti.ru/rubtree/main.aspx?tree=RV
11. SPARQL and SPARQL-DL. https://jena.apache.org/
12. Alias LingPipe. http://alias-i.com/lingpipe
13. Manning, C.D., Raghavan, P., Schütze, H.: Introduction to Information Retrieval. Cambridge University Press, Cambridge (2009)
14. Altınçay, H., Erenel, Z.: Analytical evaluation of term weighting schemes for text categorization. Proc. Pattern Recogn. Lett. **1**, 1310–1323 (2010)
15. Multiword Recognition and Extraction. http://www.ilc.cnr.it/EAGLES96/rep2/node38.html
16. Novikov, D.S.: Automatic allocation of the terms of the texts subject areas and linkages between them. In: Information and Telecommunication Technologies and Mathematical Modeling of High-tech Systems in 2012, RUDN, Russia. http://conf.sci.pfu.edu.ru/index.php/ittmm/2012/paper/view/245
17. Science journal "Solid State Physics". http://journals.ioffe.ru/ftt/. Accessed September 2013
18. Kryukov, K.V., Kuznetsov, O.P., Suhoverov, V.S.: On the notion of formal competence researchers. In: Proceedings of the III International Scientific and Technical Conference - OSTIS-2013, Minsk, pp. 143–146 (2013)
19. NC STI RK. Scientific schools and priorities for the development of the country. http://exclusive.kz/bez-rubriki/22068
20. Trubina, I.O., Zabelina, I.N.: Creating personnel's positive motivation in higher education institutions in the process of education and development of scientific schools. Creative Econ. **1**(49), 30–36 (2011)
21. Tuzovskiy, A.F.: Creating and using a knowledge base of specialists' competence profiles at organizations. Bull. Tomsk Polytech. Univ. **310**(2), 186–189 (2007)
22. Adamic, L., Zhang, J., Bakshy, E., Ackerman, M.S.: Knowledge sharing and yahoo answers: everyone knows something. In: Proceedings of the 17th International Conference on World Wide Web, pp. 21–25 (2008)
23. Baesso, P.T., Wolfgand, M.S., Cristina Vasconcelos de Andrade, L.: Finding reliable people in online communities of questions and answers.-analysis of metrics and scope reduction. In: Proceedings of the 16th International Conference on Enterprise Information Systems, pp. 526–535 (2014). doi:10.5220/0004954005260535
24. Cantador, I., Castells, P.: Extracting multilayered Communities of Interest from semantic user profiles: application to group modeling and hybrid recommendations. Comput. Hum. Behav. **27**(4), 1321–1336 (2011)
25. Bolshakova, E.I., Klyshinsky, E.S., Lande, D.V., Noskov, A.A,. Peskova, O.V., Yagunova, E.V.: Automatic processing of natural language texts and computational linguistics: Textbooks. MIEM (2011)
26. Marmanis, H., Babenko, D.: Algorithms of intellectual internet. Best practices for collecting, analyzing and processing data. Trans. from English. - SPb .: Symbol-Plus (2011)

27. Maedche, A., Staab, S., Stojanovic, N., Studer, R., Sure, Y.: SEAL – a framework for developing SEmantic web PortALs. In: Read, B. (ed.) BNCOD 2001. LNCS, vol. 2097, pp. 1–22. Springer, Heidelberg (2001)
28. Şah, M., Hall, W.: Building and managing personalized semantic portals. In: Proceedings of the 16th International World Wide Web Conference, Alberta, Canada, pp. 1227–1228 (2007)

Software Agents
and Internet Computing

Locality-Sensitive Hashing for Distributed Privacy-Preserving Collaborative Filtering: An Approach and System Architecture

Alexander Smirnov[1,2(✉)] and Andrew Ponomarev[1]

[1] St. Petersburg Institute for Informatics and Automation of the RAS, 14th line, 39, St. Petersburg, Russia
{smir, ponomarev}@iias.spb.su
[2] ITMO University, Kronverksky, 49, St. Petersburg, Russia

Abstract. Recommendation systems are currently widely used in domains where abundance of choice is conjoined with its subjective nature (books, movies, trips, etc.). Most of the modern recommendation systems are centralized. Although the centralized recommendation system design has some significant advantages, it also bears two primary disadvantages: the necessity for users to share their preferences and a single point of failure. This paper follows user-centric approach to distributed recommendation system design, and proposes an architecture of a collaborative peer-to-peer recommendation system with limited preferences' disclosure. Privacy in the proposed design is provided by the fact that exact user preferences are never shared together with the user identity. To achieve that, the proposed architecture employs a locality-sensitive hashing of user preferences and an anonymized distributed hash table approach to peer-to-peer design.

Keywords: Recommendation systems · Distributed collaborative filtering · Locality-sensitive hashing · Peer-to-peer · Anonymization · Privacy

1 Introduction

Recommendation systems play an important role in modern e-commerce systems by helping users to make their ways through the abundant variety of goods and services offers. From an architectural point of view, most of the widely used recommendation systems have a centralized design. It means that a system collects user's preferences and feedback (in the form of "likes", ratings, or some other), stores them in its inner database, and uses this database for making recommendations. An advantage of this design is that it allows employing a broad spectrum of user preference models to predict user's attitude to new items. Indeed, many recommendation methods and techniques are derived from machine learning and data mining [1], therefore the presence of representative data sets is crucial. Centralization also puts all the relevant user information under control of the recommendation system maintainer allowing to perform various research activities on this information besides providing online recommendations to users (see, e.g., Netflix Prize [19]).

S. Hammoudi et al. (Eds.): ICEIS 2015, LNBIP 241, pp. 455–475, 2015.
DOI: 10.1007/978-3-319-29133-8_22

However, the centralized approach has several drawbacks. First, it introduces a quandary about privacy and, in a wider perspective, about rights on the preferences data collected about users. As a rule, a user is not aware of what information the system collects about his/her behaviour and cannot extract this information from the centralized system. Moreover, if a recommendation system's maintainer abandons it, all the collected user profiles may be lost. Second, the centralization usually results in some kind of preferences partitioning. A user may communicate with several recommendation systems, sharing with each system some part of his/her preferences; therefore, all user's preferences become spread over several recommendation systems with no chance of being united. This is not desirable, as a complete preferences profile can potentially lead to recommendations that are more accurate. Third, any centralization usually leads to a single point of failure, however, in modern computer systems, this drawback is usually alleviated by multilevel duplication and replication.

Decentralization of recommendation systems brings two main advantages:

- a decentralized system may improve the users' privacy, as there exists no central entity owning the users' private information (however, this topic is subtle due to the inherent security issues of peer-to-peer systems);
- data-processing and recommendation functions can be distributed among all users, thus, removing the need for a costly central server and enhancing scalability.

There are several approaches to recommendation system decentralization. In this paper, a user-centric approach is examined. According to this approach the user holds all his/her preferences on his/her own system. This entirely removes the quandary about rights – the user fully controls his/her preferences storage. This can also remove the preferences' partitioning as all the user preferences become centralized in a device controlled by the user. When recommendations are needed, the users' device sends recommendation requests to other devices.

Albeit all the enumerated issues of the centralized recommendation systems design are circumvented by the user-centric decentralized recommendation system design, it poses several new issues. The main problem that is addressed in this paper is how to make recommendations based on collaborative filtering approach respecting user privacy by not sharing complete profiles among members of distributed recommendations network. Collaborative filtering is one of two main approaches to recommendation system; in collaborative filtering systems, in contrast to the other approach – content-based systems, recommendations are based solely on users' attitude to items (usually expressed as ratings), but not on explicit features of items. The focus of this paper is on collaborative filtering approach, because it is more universal, allowing to build recommendation system without creating a domain-specific item model. Decentralization of content-based systems, on the other hand, is generally simpler and does not bear principal difficulties.

In this paper, the recommendation system architecture that follows the user-centric approach is proposed. It is based on a structured peer-to-peer (P2P) network, where each peer corresponds to one user and holds his/her preferences. Recommendations are made by means of anonymized communication between peers. The proposed architecture enforces privacy by providing limited preferences disclosure. It means that there is no way to reliably match ratings and a user's network address without having global control over the entire P2P network. The proposed architecture is a hybrid P2P as it uses one special node for the data-driven coordination that, however, is not used directly in the recommendation process.

The rest of the paper is structured as follows. Section 2 presents an overview of existing P2P recommendation systems and approaches. In Sect. 3, the locality-sensitive hashing approach to recommendations is discussed. Section 4 contains the description of the proposed recommendation system's architecture. Section 5 contains an experimental evaluation of the proposed ideas. Main results are summarized in the conclusion.

2 Related Work

Peer-to-peer recommendation systems design is already addressed in literature.

In Draidi et al. in [8, 9] propose P2Prec system. The idea of this system is to recommend high quality documents related to query topics and content hold by useful friends (or friends of friends) of the users, by exploring friendship networks. To disseminate information about relevant peers, it relies on gossip algorithms. For publishing and discovering services a distributed hash table is used.

The authors of P2Prec employ two-level Latent Dirichlet Allocation to automatically model topics. At the global level performed by a bootstrap server a sample of documents is collected from peers and a set of topics is inferred. Then at the local level performed by each peer the local documents are analysed with respect to common topics. Each user maintains the friendship network. A user enlarges the friendship network by accretion of new friends relevant to queries and overlapping with this users' friendship network.

To establish friendship P2Prec use gossip protocols. Keyword queries are routed recursively through friends networks, based on user trust and usefulness.

In a number of methods described in literature, an overlay network structure based on a similarity between nodes is built and recommendation algorithm is defined on this network (e.g., [8, 22]). Recommendations are searched for among neighbours up to certain depth or certain similarity threshold.

One of the algorithms of an aligning network structure to peer similarities is T-Man [14]. T-Man relies on the ability of a peer to measure how it «likes» peers. Having defined this relation, T-Man algorithm aligns the structure of the overlay network to juxtapose peers that «like» each other.

The similarity-based overlay network structure is extensively studied in [20] where authors showed that overlay topologies defined by node similarity have highly unbalanced degree distributions to be taken into account when load-balancing the P2P recommendation network. They also proposed algorithms with favourable convergence of speed and prediction accuracy taking load balancing into account, considering collaborative filtering system where similarity of users is measured as cosine similarity.

In the proposed architecture, the exact ratings are not exposed together with a node identity, so there is no way to say how similar the two nodes are. Using the locality-sensitive hash values one can possibly say whether they are likely to be close enough or not.

Another approach is to rely on random walk search for similar nodes in the ordinary P2P network using some form of the flooding technique [26]. Similarly, Bakker et al. in [2] show that it is enough to take a random sample of the network and use the closest elements of that sample to make recommendations.

In [15], the random walks approach to collaborative filtering recommendations is examined in the context of P2P systems. The authors argue that the effect of random walk in decentralized environment is different than the centralized one. They also propose a system where epidemic protocols (gossip protocols) are used to disseminate the user similarity information. They start from a random set of peers and then in series of random exchanges compare their local-view with the local view of the remote node, leaving only the most similar peers in the local view (clustering gossip protocol). This process converges to form some overlay based on the peers' similarity. Then peers that are not farther than two hops from the given one are used to make recommendations.

In epidemic protocols, peers have access to a Random Peer Sampling service (RPS) providing them with a continuously changing random subset of the network peers. Each peer maintains a view of the network, which is initialized at random through RPS when a peer joins the network. Gossip protocols are fully decentralized, can handle high churn rates, and require no specific protocol to recover from massive failures.

There also published research papers where structured P2P networks are used. For example, in [10, 11], distributed hash tables are used to store ratings. The proposed approach stands close to this way except the point that ratings are not stored in a distributed hash table, instead a fast lookup capability provided by this kind of P2P architecture is employed for searching similar peers.

Most of the approaches involve sharing the rating data between nodes, while in the proposed architecture it is avoided.

Privacy concerns are directly addressed in [23]. The authors propose a file sharing network where users exchange their data only with their friends and the recommendation system on the top of it. They propose a privacy-conserving distributed collaborative filtering approach that is based on exchanges of anonymized items' relevance ranks between peers. Their approach, however, allows only unary ratings (initially, the fact of owning a specific file).

Distributed recommendation systems are also analysed in quite different context, seeking for efficient parallel implementations of centralized recommendation techniques. This research direction is entirely beyond the scope of this paper.

3 Locality-Sensitive Hashing for Recommendations

Locality-sensitive hashing (LSH) is a method widely used for a probabilistic solution of k-NN (k Nearest Neighbours) problem. The idea of this method is to hash multidimensional objects in such a way that similar objects (w.r.t. some distance measure defined on them) are likely to have the same hash value.

3.1 The Idea of LSH

Let $d_1 < d_2$ be two distances according to some distance measure d. A family F of functions is said to be (d_1, d_2, p_1, p_2)-sensitive if for every f in F and two arbitrary objects x and y [24]:

- If $d(x, y) \leq d_1$, then probability that $f(a) = f(b)$ is at least p_1.
- If $d(x, y) \geq d_2$ then probability that $f(a) = f(b)$ is at most p_2.

An important concept in the locality-sensitive hashing theory is an amplification. Given a (d_1, d_2, p_1, p_2)-sensitive family F, a new family F' can be constructed by either AND-construction or OR-construction.

AND-construction of F' is defined as follows. Each member of F' consists of r members of F for some fixed r. If f is in F' and f is constructed from the set $\{f_1, f_2, \ldots, f_r\}$ of members of F, $f(x) = f(y)$ iff $f_i(x) = f_i(y)$ for all $i \in \{1, \ldots, r\}$. As members of F' are independently chosen from F, F' is an (d_1, d_2, p_1^r, p_2^r)-sensitive family [24].

OR-construction of F' is defined as follows. Each member of F' consists of b members of F for some fixed b. If f is in F', and f is constructed from the set $\{f_1, f_2, \ldots, f_b\}$ of members of F, $f(x) = f(y)$ iff there exists $i \in \{1, \ldots, b\}$, such that $f_i(x) = f_i(y)$. Similarly, F' is an $(d_1, d_2, 1 - (1 - p_1)^b, 1 - (1 - p_2)^b)$ -sensitive family.

Generally, it is desirable that p_1 be as large as possible and p_2 be as small as possible. If $p_1 < 1$, then there exists some possibility that similar objects will have different hash values. On the other hand, if $p_2 > 0$, some possibility exists that distant objects will have similar hash values. Therefore, family F is chosen in such a way that p_1 is large (close to 1) and p_2 is small (close to 0). There is a finite set of well-studied locality-sensitive function families and the desired levels of p_1 and p_2 cannot always be achieved with one "pure" family, and here the amplification comes into play.

If family F^{Ar} is obtained as AND-construction of r functions from family F, and G is then obtained as OR-construction of b functions from family F^{Ar}, then G is a $(d_1, d_2, 1 - (1 - p_1^r)^b, 1 - (1 - p_2^r)^b)$-sensitive family. Informally, AND-construction mostly lowers the initially low p_2 probability and subsequent OR-construction raises the initially high p_1 probability.

The idea of the nearest neighbours search based on LSH is described in many papers (e.g., [24, 25]). First, a hash family F (to be discussed in detail later) is chosen and b ordinary hash tables are arranged. For each hash table a hash function f_i^{Ar}, $i = 1, \ldots, b$ is defined an AND-construction of r random functions from F. Every object x is stored into each of the b hash tables. Key is the $f_i^{Ar}(x)$ and value is either some identity of x or x itself. It is natural that several objects can fall into one hash table bucket.

When searching for the nearest neighbours of an object y, first, $f_i^{Ar}(y)$, $i = 1, \ldots, b$ is calculated and then all values from the corresponding hash tables are retrieved resulting in a set of the nearest neighbour candidates. Precise distance to each of the candidates is then assessed and false positives are removed.

Particular choice of the hash function family depends on data representation and distance function d. For Hamming distance a bit sampling locality sensitive hash was proposed in [13], for cosine distance a random projections method was proposed in [3], a well-performing hash function for Euclidean distance is proposed in [6].

In the proposed architecture random projections method is used, i.e. each function f from F corresponds to one random hyperplane and can have value of one if an object being hashed is above the hyperplane, and value of zero if an object is below it. An object is usually represented as an n-dimensional vector ($x \in \Re^n$), and a hyperplane in that vector space is also denoted by its normal n-dimensional vector ($v(f) \in \Re^n$). Relative position of an object and a hyperplane can be found as a sign of a dot product of these two vectors:

$$f(x) \equiv \begin{cases} 1, v(f) \circ x > 0 \\ 0, v(f) \circ x \leq 0 \end{cases} \tag{1}$$

Functions $f_i^{Ar}(x)$ used to calculate hash table keys consist each of r functions from F (and therefore r hyperplanes), and the results of application of these functions are r-dimensional vectors of ones and zeroes. Formally, if $f_i^{Ar}(x) = (f_{i,1}, f_{i,2}, \ldots, f_{i,r})$, then:

$$f_i^{Ar}(x) \equiv (f_{i,1}(x), f_{i,2}(x), \ldots, f_{i,r}(x)) \tag{2}$$

3.2 Recommendations Generation

The problem of finding the nearest neighbours is closely related to the recommendation systems research area, namely neighbourhood-based methods in collaborative filtering systems (see, e.g., [7]). These methods of recommendation are based on an assumption that users that had similar preferences in the past are likely to have similar preferences now (and in the future). Therefore, to make recommendations, users with similar preferences should be found. To do this, user preferences are typically represented as numerical vectors and some measure is introduced in that vector space corresponding to preference similarity. In this setting, the problem of finding similar users translates into the nearest neighbours search. This subsection provides a formal description of collaborative filtering recommendation method based on the locality-sensitive hashing.

User-based collaborative filtering system is the recommendation system that infers recommendations from the similarity of users measured by the degree known user ratings coincide.

More formally, let r_{uj} be the rating assigned to the item j by the user u, which corresponds to how user u liked item j, or what was the subjective utility of j for u. Let U be the set of all users, I – the set of all items, I_u – the set of items rated by user u, and I_{uv} – the set of items rated by both user u and user v. Usually, a user has ratings for relatively small number of items, $|I_u| << |I|$. Neighbourhood methods of user-based collaborative filtering employ some similarity measure between users which is calculated based on common ratings ($sim(u, v) = f_s(\{r_{uj}, r_{vj} \mid j \in I_{uv}\})$) and estimate unknown rating r^*_{uj} based on known ratings r_{vj} and estimated similarities $sim(u, v)$.

In the recommendation systems research several user similarity measures were introduced [1]: Pearson and Spearman correlation coefficients, Jaccard similarity, Hamming distance, cosine similarity. In this paper, cosine similarity is employed as the similarity measure between users. It is defined as:

$$sim(u,v) = \frac{\sum_{I_{uv}} r_{uj} r_{vj}}{\sqrt{\sum_{I_u} r_{uj}^2} \sqrt{\sum_{I_v} r_{vj}^2}}. \quad (3)$$

The similarity measure choice is caused mostly by the fact that there exists a known way to approximate this measure by a set of locality-sensitive hash functions [3], which is not the case for other wide-spread similarity measures (e.g., Pearson correlation coefficient). It is also supported by the evidence that cosine similarity works well in many recommendation system settings [1].

User ratings are normalized in such a way that $r_{uj} > 0$ corresponds to positive attitude of user u to item j, $r_{uj} < 0$ corresponds to negative attitude, and zero corresponds to neutral. Absolute value shows strength of the attitude. Probably, the simplest way of such kind of normalization is mean-centring of ratings.

A profile of user u in a pure collaborative filtering system can be understood as a set of r_{uj}, where $j \in I_u$. In some cases, it is also convenient to represent user's profile as a vector $p_u \in \mathfrak{R}^{|I|}$, constructed in the following way:

$$p_{u,j} \equiv \begin{cases} r_{uj}, j \in I_u \\ 0, j \notin I_u \end{cases} \quad (4)$$

It does not mean that user's profile should be stored in this way, it would not be efficient, as most of p_u components equal to zero, rather this representation makes some mathematical formulas more intuitive.

Prediction of an unknown rating r^*_{uj} requires the search of users v that are similar to u, or the nearest neighbours of u according to cosine similarity measure. This is where LSH comes into play. The original algorithm for LSH-based recommendations (e.g., [24]), consists of the following steps:

- Preparation. Several hash tables HT_i are organized, and corresponding number of locality-sensitive functions f_i are generated. Then, each user's identifier is put into each table, and its bucket in HT_i is determined by value of function $f_i(p_u)$, where p_u is the vector representation of users' profile.
- Recommendation. When searching for recommendations for user u, hash values of his/her profile are calculated and looked up in respective hash tables. Lookups result in a set $C = \{v \mid \exists i\ f_i(p_v) = f_i(p_u)\}$ of user identifiers that have at least one hash function value in common with the user u (and whose interests are likely, due to hash function properties, to be similar with u's). Then, exact similarities are calculated between user u and members of C and predictions are generated.

However, the recommendation step of the original algorithm does not allow to fulfil the goal, pursued in this paper. Namely, it requires calculation of exact similarity of users in C, which is impossible without sending complete profiles to the side that performs this calculation. This paper proposes a modification of the original algorithm that does not require exact similarity computation and thus allows to avoid profile sharing.

To obviate the need for profile sharing, an approximate similarity measure $s'(u,v)$ is introduced. It is defined as the number of locality-sensitive hash functions whose values are equal for users u and v:

$$s'(u,v) \equiv |\{i | f_i(u) = f_i(v)\}|. \tag{5}$$

The calculation of $s'(u,v)$ can be easily integrated into the modified recommendation step of the algorithm. More specifically, instead of the set C in the original algorithm a multiset C^*_u can be used. If $C^*_u = (U, m_U)$ is a multiset of user identifiers retrieved from hash tables using locality-sensitive hash functions on the user u's profile, then:

$$s'(u,v) = m_U(v), \tag{6}$$

where $m_u(v)$ is a multiplicity function of C^*_u. The proposed recommendation algorithm, at first, retrieves all approximate neighbours $Q_u = \{v \mid m_U(v) > 0\}$ of user u from hash tables and computes $s'(u, v)$ (where $v \in Q_u$). Then, each of the approximate neighbours $v \in Q_u$ is asked for the recommended items R_v. The proposed algorithm and the system as a whole do not predict ratings, instead it ranks all items that were recommended by approximate neighbours with respect to attractiveness estimate $\tilde{a}_{ui}$ of item i for user u defined by the following expression:

$$\tilde{a}_{ui} = \sum_{v \in Q_u} s'(u,v) P^R_{vi}. \tag{7}$$

Here P^R_{vi} is an indicator function that checks if item i is in the list of items recommended by user v:

$$P^R_{vi} = \begin{cases} 1, i \in R_v \\ 0, i \notin R_v \end{cases}. \tag{8}$$

In other words, the attractiveness estimate $\tilde{a}_{ui}$ is the sum of approximate similarities between user u and neighbours that "recommended" item i to user u.

To sum it up, in the proposed system architecture, a profile of user u is a set of pairs (i, r_{ui}), where i are item identifiers. To compute the hash function, a profile is normalized and transformed into a vector p_u (Eq. 4). Each of b locality-sensitive hash functions is represented by r vectors, whose dimensionality equals to the number of the known items ($|I|$). Finding a hash of a profile vector corresponds to computing inner products of the profile vector and hash functions vectors (Eq. 2). After application of all these hash functions, b r-dimensional binary vectors are obtained and stored into hash table. When looking for recommendations, b lookups are performed, and then each found approximate neighbour is queried for recommended items and the list of recommended items is sorted according to $\tilde{a}_{ui}$ value.

```
Algorithm 1 (Preparation)
Input:
|I| – the number of items;
p_u, u ∈ U – normalized user profiles in vector form, p_u ∈ ℜ^|I|;
b – the number of hash tables;
r – length of hash value, or the number of hyperplanes used.
begin
  // First, form the set of b hash functions
  fv ← Matrix(b, r, |I|) // hash functions' parameters array
  foreach i ∈ {1,…,b} do
    foreach j ∈ {1,…,r} do
      foreach k ∈ {1,…,|I|} do
        fv_i,j,k ← pick_random({-1, 1})
  // Then, initialize and fill hash tables
  foreach i ∈ {1,...,b} do
    HT_i ← HashTable()
  foreach u ∈ U do begin
    foreach i ∈ {1,…,b} do begin
      h ← []
      foreach j ∈ {1,…,r} do
        if fv_i,j ∘ p_u > 0 then h ← append(h, 1) else h ← append(h, 0)
      HT_i[h] ← append(HT_i[h], u)
    end
  end
end
Algorithm 2 (Recommendation)
Input:
u* ∈ U – user to look recommendations for;
|I| – the number of items;
p_u, u ∈ U – normalized user profiles in vector form, p_u ∈ ℜ^|I|;
b – the number of hash tables;
r – length of hash value, or the number of hyperplanes used;
θ – threshold, minimum normalized rating to recommend an item;
fv – matrix of functions' coefficients (b × r × |I|);
HT_i, i ∈ {1,…,b} – hash tables.
begin
  // Find neighbours
  nb ← Multiset(U, m_U)  // m_U will be the multiplicity function of the multiset
  foreach i ∈ {1,…,b} do begin
    h ← []
    foreach j ∈ {1,…,r} do
      if fv_i,j ∘ p_u* > 0 then h ← append(h, 1) else h ← append(h, 0)
    nb ← nb + HT_i[h]
  // Generate recommendations
  a_i ← Vector(|I|)     // estimated attractiveness, initialized with zeros
  foreach v ∈ nb do  // for each approximate neighbour
    foreach i ∈ {p_v,i > θ | i ∈ {1,…,|I|} do // highly rated items of user v
      a_i ← a_i + m_U(v)
  Pick required number of items i for which a_i is highest
end
```

Algorithms 1 and 2 are provided here without taking into account their distributed implementation, which is one of the aims of this paper. However, the analysis of their inputs reveals some challenges that have to be addressed by recommendation system's architecture. One of these challenges is connected to the fact that it should be possible to initiate recommendation algorithm (Algorithm 2) from any node of the peer-to-peer recommendation network. Therefore, each node should have *fv* matrix filled with the same values as a node that used this matrix to calculate hash value when inserted an item into HT_i had, and that leads to a problem of maintaining some shared state of a distributed network. Parameter θ controls what items should be considered as "recommended" and can be set for each user individually, usually in the range of [0.3, 1]. Parameters b and r affect selectivity of neighbours and quality of recommendations; their impact on recommendations quality is assessed in Sect. 5.

4 System Architecture

The proposed hybrid architecture enables the personalized recommendations exchange with the limited user preferences disclosure. In this section, target use cases are discussed, as well as components of the proposed system and scenarios that implement the target use cases.

4.1 Use Cases

Recommendation systems may provide for somewhat different end-user features. Specifically, in this paper the following recommendation use cases are considered: (a) attractiveness estimation of a given item (or set of items); (b) recommendations query; (c) rating an item.

Attractiveness estimation of a given item (or a set of items) is involved when a user encounters some item and wants to check if it is potentially interesting or useful for him/her. In this case, the user passes this item (item identity) to recommendation system and the recommendation system should return an expected attitude of this user to this item. Certainly, the user is not required to perform this request intentionally by hand; some other program or GUI element acting on behalf of the user can mediate this action. Attractiveness estimation request may contain several items. Though estimation for multiple items can always be implemented as a series of single item estimations, it is interpreted here as a use case extension, because in some circumstances the estimation for multiple items is potentially more efficient than multiple separate single item requests.

Recommendations query is initiated when a user wants to receive some recommendations – a list of new, previously unseen items matching his/her preferences.

Rating an item is initiated when a user encounters some new item and expresses his/her attitude to it.

Use cases are summarized in UML use case diagram (Fig. 1). It also can be seen that both recommendation use cases (attractiveness estimation and recommendation query) available to users involve finding of neighbours and sending requests to them.

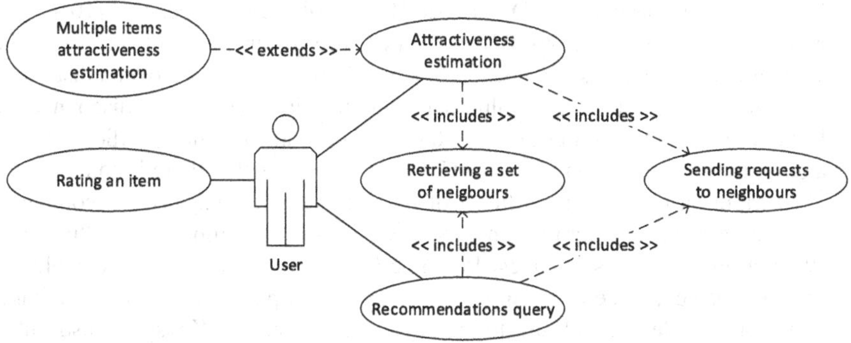

Fig. 1. Recommendation system's UML use case diagram.

4.2 Components

In the proposed architecture, the recommendation system is split into two parts: Peer-to-Peer (P2P) recommendations network and the Master node (Fig. 2). The presence of the Master node violates the conceptual purity of the P2P design, making it a hybrid P2P system. However, the Master node does not directly participate in primary use cases (attractiveness estimation and recommendations query) which are implemented solely by P2P network. The Master node is responsible for synchronizing supplementary information between peers.

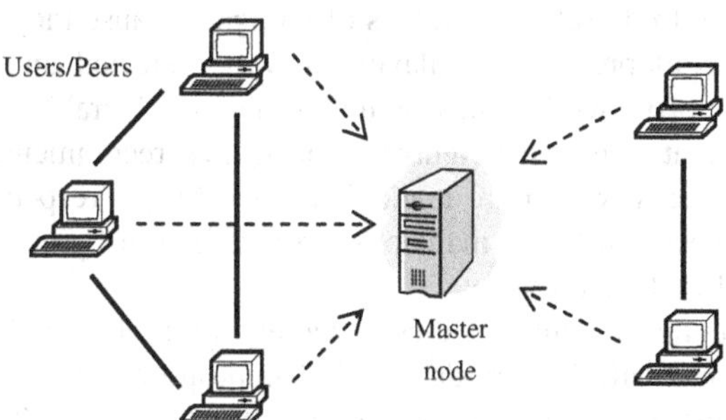

Fig. 2. Connections between nodes in the proposed architecture.

In Fig. 2, two types of connection between nodes are shown: connections between similar peers used to get recommendations are shown by solid lines, and occasional connections of peers to the Master node for retrieving the supplementary information are depicted by dashed lines.

(1) Peer-to-Peer recommendations network: In the proposed architecture, each user corresponds to exactly one node (or peer – these terms are used here interchangeably). That node holds all the information about one user's preferences, ratings, browsing history, but does not share this information with the other nodes, instead it shares only the locality-sensitive hash values of this information in order to find similar users to query for recommendations.

P2P network is based on the Distributed Hash Table (DHT) (see, e.g., [16]) model widely employed in various P2P networks. The general idea of DHT is rather straightforward. It holds a collection of key/value pairs scattered over a distributed set of nodes, supporting key/value pair migration in case of node disconnection. DHT usually refers to a class of systems rather than to some specific system or algorithm. Common point of all DHT-based systems is that there is some scheme of distribution of a keyspace (a set of possible keys) among peers accompanied with some regular pattern of links between nodes (sometimes called "fingers"). When a node receives a request for some key it checks if it is "responsible" for holding this key, and either responds with a value, or passes the request to a linked node that has identifier closest to the key being looked for. Keyspace distribution and link pattern ensure that distributed table lookups can be accomplished by no more than $O(\log n)$ nodes.

Original DHT has some security and privacy vulnerabilities. For example, in original DHT implementations a lookup request contains information about the node that initiated it, and therefore makes this information available for any malicious node that happen to redirect this lookup request or process it. In the context of recommendation systems, it means, for example, that a malicious node could be able to associate a value of locality-sensitive hash function of preferences profile (a key in the lookup) with a node (user). It does not reveal exact ratings, however narrows uncertainty distribution from uniform. Moreover, if P2P network contains several malicious nodes, then they are able to collect several hash values of one user's profile and uncertainty becomes even less. Even in this case, it is impossible to detect exact values of ratings, because they are not let out of a node, but overall preferences "flavor" may be detected and associated with a physical node of network, which is undesirable. Vulnerability that is even more important is that potential neighbor node makes recommendations by sending identifiers of items, which are marked as good by the respective user, therefore allowing its peer (probably malicious) to match some presumably high ratings with physical node address.

To overcome these vulnerabilities a variety of secure and anonymous DHT lookup implementations were designed. The proposed architecture relies on one of these anonymized implementations, namely Octopus [27]. The idea behind most of secured DHT implementations is that all the DHT lookups are made through other nodes accessible by anonymous paths through anonymization relays. Each node in the anonymization path knows only the neighbour nodes and does not know whether some request originated in the neighbour node, or was passed over from some other node.

DHT in the proposed system is used as a set of hash tables to perform nearest neighbour search, as described in Sect. 3. Each key/value pair stored in DHT holds information about one locality-sensitive hash value and the list of nodes corresponding to that hash value (potential neighbours). As it was discussed in the respective section, several (b) hash tables are needed to perform the nearest neighbour search. Each of the b tables uses its own locality-sensitive hash function. In the proposed architecture, all of these b hash tables are stored in one

DHT. In order to achieve this, key of the DHT pair includes a unique identifier of the locality-sensitive hash function and the value of that function. Keyspace of most DHT implementations consists of 160-bit values. In the proposed implementation, concatenation of unique identifier of function and its value are processed by SHA-1 algorithm to provide equable distribution of used keys in the keyspace.

Each node of the P2P network has its unique identifier taken from the same keyspace. It is produced by applying SHA-1 to the network address of the node. Before a starts to advertise itself in DHT it creates an anonymized path and uses the endpoint specification of this path as an address it shares with other nodes. These anonymized paths are created each time when the node connects network, resulting in different public identifiers of the same node.

As user preferences expressed in ratings are not changing very fast, it is reasonable for each node to locate other nodes with the similar profiles through DHT and store links to them. Therefore, a new overlay network of similar users is formed over the P2P network. It is important to differentiate between the three employed connection layers (Fig. 3). The first layer is the underlying network, that provides a physical connection between P2P nodes. The second layer is DHT connection layer that provides DHT key search, key redistribution etc. This layer is formed by links to adjacent nodes in structured P2P, the so-called "fingers". The third layer is formed by connections between similar nodes, where the similarity is interpreted like an equality of locality-sensitive hashes.

It is important to note, that links to neighbour nodes in the third layer are not exactly identifiers of nodes in P2P network, they are entrances to anonymized paths to these nodes.

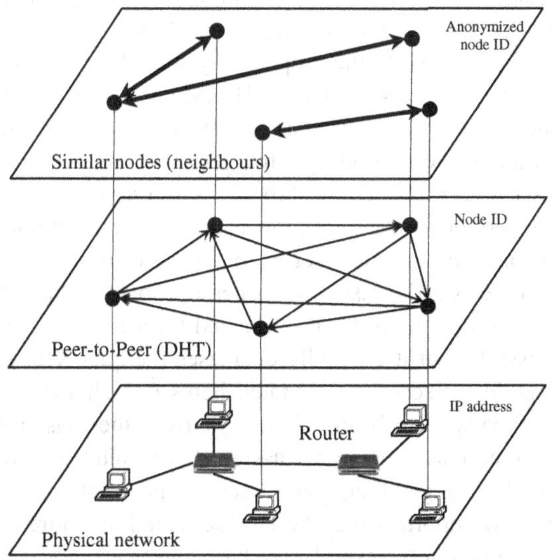

Fig. 3. Peer-to-peer layers.

(2) The Master node: The distributed nature of the proposed system causes one hindrance. LSH-based nearest neighbour search implies that when searching for the neighbours of object x, all the locality-sensitive hash functions that were used to hash other objects and fill hash tables are applied to x. In the proposed architecture, an object being hashed is a vector of normalized ratings assigned by the user to different items of interest and hashing functions family is represented by random hyperplane projections. Both to represent a user profile in the vector form, and to define a hyperplane to be used to calculate locality-sensitive hash value, the number of items (and their ordering) should be known. It is later referred to as *item space dimensionality*, or just dimensionality. In some cases, for instance, when the rating storage is centralized and/or all possible items are known in advance, knowing dimensionality is not a problem. However, in case of distributed rating storage when each node holds only ratings of one user, overall item space dimensionality can be found out only though communication between nodes. For example, let initially a system contains two nodes (of user Alice and user Bob) and no ratings. Then, Alice encounters three movies (items): *Forrest Gump*, *Scary Movie*, and *Sleepless in Seattle* and rates them 4, 3, 5 respectively. As Alice's node does not have information about other movies, vector representation of normalized Alice's preferences could be: (0, −1, 1). At the same time, Bob encounters the same three movies, but in different order: *Forrest Gump*, *Sleepless in Seattle*, and *Scary Movie* and rates them 4, 5, 3 respectively. Under the same considerations, vector representation of Bob's preferences could be (0, 1, −1). Then hash values of users's preferences using hyperplane (0, 1, 0) would be −1 for Alice and 1 for Bob, and as signs differ, the profiles are considered to be different, although ratings match perfectly.

Hence, it is needed to synchronize item space characteristics and random projection hyperplanes across all nodes. The problem of maintaining a global shared state in the P2P network is rather complex, and there are numerous papers dedicated to it, e.g. [4, 12, 21]. In the proposed system, this problem is addressed in a way similar to the one presented in [17] and sacrificing the P2P-purity of the system. It is the Master node that, first, collects all new items discovered and rated by peers, maintains their ordering and generates new locality-sensitive hash functions. So, each peer must connect to the Master node in two situations: first, to notify about some previously unknown item (which should become a new dimension), second, to get a new set of locality-sensitive hash functions. It must be noted, that there is no necessity in generation of new hash functions after an assessment of each new item. Using outdated hash functions with lower dimensions is still possible, but it gradually decreases the quality of recommendations. So, each user node collects the new rated items (which were not assigned identifiers yet) and then sends a batch of these items to the Master node. The Master node, in turn, accumulates new items, assigns them unique ordered identifiers, and when their number is great enough, issues a new set locality sensitive hash functions. It is also important that the new set is not an entire replacement of the previous, but contains only several new hash functions.

4.3 Scenarios

This subsection describes how main scenarios of the recommendation system are implemented by means of the proposed architecture. These scenarios can be split into two groups. The first group consists of scenarios implementing use cases listed in Sect. 4.1: rating an item, attractiveness estimation for a given item, recommendations query. The second group includes some supplementary scenarios that are needed to enable those of the first group: refreshing hash functions, and the search for similar peers.

(1) Attractiveness estimation of a given item: attractiveness estimation on a node is possible only after the integration of this node into the P2P network: receiving a set of hash functions from Master node and locating the nodes of the users with similar ratings (hereinafter these nodes are referred to as neighbour nodes). Let the neighbour nodes for the given one be stored in the *Neighbours* list. Then attractiveness estimation for the item is performed by sending requests to each node from the *Neighbours* list passing the item identifier over. Each neighbour node answers with a binary value meaning if it can recommend this item to others or not. Attractiveness estimation for the set of items is done mostly in the same way, except that the requester node passes the list of item identifiers instead one identifier and the answer contains a list of pairs (*itemId*, *recommend_flag*) for all items that the neighbour node is able to recommend from the requested set.
Informally, attractiveness estimation scenario can be interpreted as asking an advice from co-minded people. In centralized systems it is performed in some conceptual way, in the proposed hybrid P2P system it is performed literally sending requests to the respective nodes. When answering attractiveness estimation request, a node can base the response on the rating that is stored for the given item, or infer the rating from some other information. This is an extension point of the proposed system architecture.
These requests are sent and answered through anonymization relays, so the node does not expose both its identity and an exact rating for any item.

(2) Recommendations query: In this case, node that needs recommendations just sends requests to each of the neighbour nodes. The request contains additional information about what kind of recommendations the node is looking for, e.g., any high-rated objects, or new objects (encountered and rated after specified time) only. Each neighbour node answers with a list of (item, rating) pairs. Unlike the previous scenario, here the neighbour node needs to send not just identifiers of the recommended items, but their contents, something that the receiver side can use directly.
Anonymization relays make sure that the recommendations provider does not expose both ratings and its identity.

(3) Rating an item: The main issue of rating items is the generation of new locality-sensitive hash functions that must follow it. To address this issue each node has two lists: *Known* and *New*. The *Known* list holds all the items the Master node is aware of. This list is received from the *Master* node during the bootstrap process or periodical synchronization process. The order of items in this list is also

important as it corresponds to the order of dimensions of locality-sensitive hash functions. The *New* list, on the other hand, holds the items that are discovered by this node and are not yet approved by the Master node. When the user rates an item, the rating is saved and then, if the item is neither in *Known*, nor in *New* lists it is added to the *New* list.

When *New* list exceeds some predefined size or once in a predefined period of time (whatever happens first), the node sends its *New* list to the Master node and retrieves the global shared state from the Master node. Global shared state from the Master node includes up-to-date version of the *Known* list. Each node augments its *Known* list according to the one received from the Master node and removes from *New* list items that are present in *Known* list.

(4) Refreshing hash functions (supplementary scenario): Each node periodically queries the Master node for the global shared state. As it was described earlier, there are b functions, and each hash function is a vector of r $|I|$-dimensional random vectors (representing random hyperplanes). To reduce the amount of information exchange and load of the Master node, each hash function posted by the Master node is represented by three integers: function unique identifier (*funcId*), random seed and current number of items $|I|$ (i.e. item space dimensionality). When a node gets this information it generates random hyperplanes constituting each of the b locality-sensitive hash function as a sequence of $r*|I|$ ($|I|$ dimensions for each of r hyperplanes) random numbers from the specified seed using Mersenne twister [18].

(5) The search for similar peers (supplementary scenario): The search for similar, or neighbour, peers is initiated when a node is registered in the P2P network. Then this search is performed regularly. Before searching for neighbours a node have to refresh item list and hash functions from the Master node. Then each function from an up-to-date set of hash functions is applied to this node ratings vector. The results are merged into pairs (*funcId*, *value*) and these pairs are used as keys to look up in DHT. DHT look up returns a list of node identifiers similar to this one according to the respective locality-sensitive function. These lists are then merged and stored as the *Neighbours* list.

5 Experimental Study

Experimental study of the proposed approach was performed with the MovieLens 100 k dataset shared by GroupLens research lab. This dataset fits well with e-commerce scenarios (specifically, media streaming services), as it contains 100,000 real-life ratings assigned by 943 users to 1682 movies.

The purpose of the experimental study was twofold. First, to gain some insights into the internal quantitative characteristics of the proposed approach and to estimate time and spatial complexity of the DHT-based LSH recommendation system. Second, to evaluate the quality of recommendations with respect to some well-known baselines.

Ratings are normalized by centring over the user's mean rating.

5.1 Time, Space and Network Load

It was already noted that *b* (the number of hash functions) and *r* (the number of hyperplanes in each hash function) are parameters of the LSH-based recommender. Values of these parameters have significant impact both system performance and accuracy.

As each node puts itself into DHT *b* times, the size of the DHT is *n***b* it means that on the average only *b* records of the DHT are located on each node. In most cases, this burden is negligible. More important is the fact that the search for the neighbour nodes takes *b* lookups which is O(*b* log(*n*)) of internode communications. Even more important is the number of neighbours, as this number corresponds to the number of network queries performed to obtain recommendations, and it is desirable to keep the number of these queries as small as possible.

Figure 4 shows the dependency between *b* and *r* parameters of recommender and the average number of neighbours found through hash table look up. It can be seen that the number of neighbours increases with the growth of *b*, and the speed of growth significantly depends on the dimensionality of hash functions. It is expected behaviour, as small dimensionality of hash functions and large number of "alternative" hash functions make neighbour search procedure indiscriminative.

In this experiment, we assume that the reasonable number of hash functions is under 100 and the reasonable number of neighbours is under 50. The numbers are different as neighbours search is one-time action (and, therefore, can bear more overhead) and queries to neighbours happen more often.

The number of neighbours was also analysed, see Fig. 5. For fixed dimensionality (*r*) different values of *b* were tried and the average number of neighbours and the respective recall were evaluated. It can be seen, that when the number of neighbours is

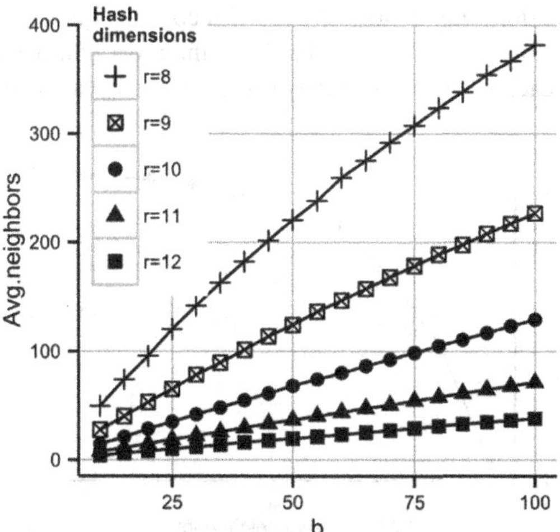

Fig. 4. Average number of neighbours depending on the number of hash functions (*b*) and their dimensionality (*r*).

less than approximately 50, the quality of recommendations is growing fast, whereas for bigger values of the number of neighbours it reaches a plateau.

Having this in mind, three configurations were selected to examine recommendations quality: ($r = 12$, $b = 100$), ($r = 10$, $b = 35$), ($r = 8$, $b = 10$). These configurations were selected because each of them gives on the average approximately 50 neighbours for a user in the explored dataset (see Fig. 4).

5.2 Recommendations Quality

As the proposed recommendation system does not predict item ratings, the conventional root mean square error metric for measuring recommendations quality is irrelevant. Instead, recall is used as a quality metric better tailored to top-n recommendation systems. The authors follow the approach described in [5]. Ratings dataset is split into two subsets: training set and testing set in 80/20 proportion. Training set is used to fill the hash table. Then, for each high rating (4 or 5) from the testing set a check is performed whether this item is in top n recommended items for that user. The outcome of this check may be either 1 (if it is in the top n) or 0 (if it is not). These outcomes are summed for all high ratings of the testing set to produce N_p value. Recall is calculated according to formula:

$$R@n = \frac{N_p}{N_H}, \quad (4)$$

where N_H is the number of high ratings. In other words, this value can be interpreted as a probability that a randomly taken high rated item is in fact recommended by the algorithm.

Recall of the proposed recommendation method was compared with two baseline non-personalized recommenders. First, a random recommender (Random) which recommends just n random items to any user, second, popular items recommender (PopRec) which recommends the items that have the most number of ratings. Figure 6 shows the recall of each of the recommenders at different values of n.

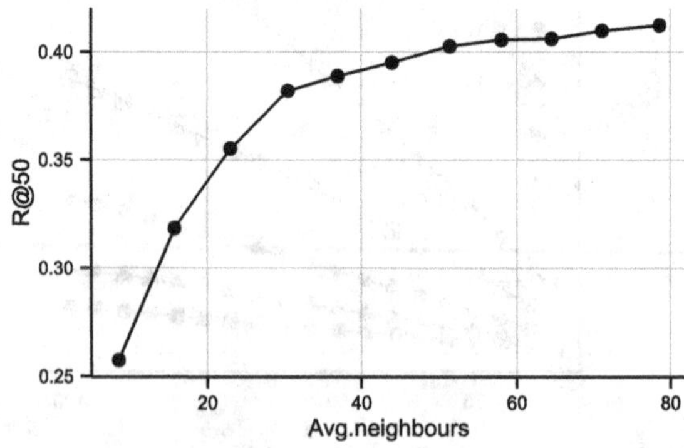

Fig. 5. R@50 depending on the number of nearest neighbours for LSH with $r = 10$ and b varying from 5 to 55.

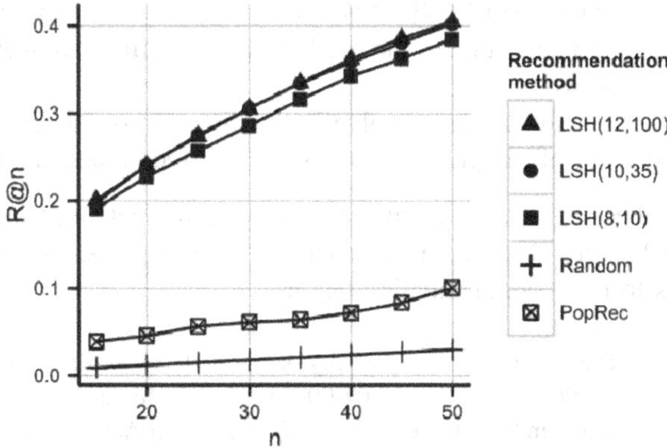

Fig. 6. Comparison of R@n for different recommendation methods.

All the tested variants of LSH recommendation method give similar results. It may be explained by the fact that in all of the tested variants there are nearly the same number of neighbour nodes (about 50, see Fig. 4). It can also be seen that the proposed recommendation algorithm significantly outperforms the non-personalized recommendation algorithms in terms of recall.

6 Conclusions

This paper proposes the architecture of a user-centric hybrid peer-to-peer recommendation system based on locality-sensitive hashing. One of the main distinguishing features of the proposed system is that exact ratings that a user assigns to items are never shared together with the user's identity (and network address), which provides privacy. This is achieved by employing locality-sensitive hashing technique and building an anonymized overlay in a P2P network.

The paper describes use cases of the recommendation system and shows how these use cases can be implemented via communication of nodes in P2P network and communication of nodes with the Master node responsible for data-driven coordination and holding a shared state of the distributed system.

The proposed approach was evaluated on a widely used dataset from an e-commerce scenario (movie ratings) and it was shown that the estimated recall of the proposed recommendation system is sufficiently higher than that of the trivial baselines. However, some limitations of this approach can also be enumerated:

- a principal limitation of a user-centric recommendation system is that a user can receive recommendations from only those other users that are online and connected to P2P network. It can be alleviated by using some virtual proxies ("avatars") that are always online, but using these "avatars" blurs difference between centralized and decentralized systems and needs further thorough examination;
- due to DHT limitations, the proposed approach is not applicable to the P2P networks with high churn;

- the proposed approach most likely does not fit highly dynamical domains, such as news recommendation, because of the need for sharing information about all objects all over the P2P network;
- modern recommendation systems evolve in the direction of context awareness, but context is totally out of the picture in the proposed recommendation technique.

In the future, the authors are planning to consider alternative solutions of sharing the global set of locality-sensitive hash functions among peers, as well as add contextual awareness to the recommendation engine.

Acknowledgements. The research was partially supported by projects funded by grants # 13-07-00271, # 13-07-00039, and # 14-07-00345 of the Russian Foundation for Basic Research, project 213 (program 8) of the Presidium of the Russian Academy of Sciences, project # 2.2 of the basic research program "Intelligent information technologies, system analysis and automation" of the Nanotechnology and Information technology Department of the Russian Academy of Sciences. This work was partially financially supported by the Government of the Russian Federation, Grant 074-U01.

References

1. Amatriain, X., Jaimes, A., Oliver, N., Pujol, J.M.: Data mining methods for recommender systems. In: Ricci, F., Rokach, L., Shapira, B., Kantor, P. (eds.) Recommender Systems Handbook. Springer, Heidelberg (2011)
2. Bakker, A., Ogston, E., van Steen, M.: Collaborative filtering using random neighbours in peer-to-peer networks. In: Workshop on Complex Networks in Information and Knowledge Management, pp. 67–75 (2009)
3. Charikar, M.S.: Similarity estimation techniques from rounding algorithms. In: STOC 2002 Proceedings of the 34th Annual ACM Symposium on Theory of Computing, pp. 380–388 (2002)
4. Chen, X., et al.: SCOPE: scalable consistency maintenance in structured P2P systems. In: Proceedings of IEEE INFOCOM 2005, pp. 1502–1513 (2005)
5. Cremonesi, P., Koren, Y., Turrin, R.: Performance of recommender algorithms on top-n recommendation tasks. In: Proceedings of the Fourth ACM Conference on Recommender Systems (RecSys 2010), pp. 39–46. ACM, New York, NY, USA (2010)
6. Datar, M., et al.: Locality-sensitive hashing scheme based on p-Stable distributions. In: SCG 2004 Proceedings of the 20th Annual Symposium on Computational Geometry, pp. 253–262 (2004)
7. Desrosiers, C., Karypis, G.: A comprehensive survey of neighborhood-based recommendation methods. In: Ricci, F., Rokach, L., Shapira, B., Kantor, P. (eds.) Recommender Systems Handbook. Springer, Heidelberg (2011)
8. Draidi, F., Pacitti, E., Kemme, B.: P2Prec: a P2P recommendation system for large-scale data sharing. J. Trans. Large-Scale Data Knowl.-Centered Syst. (TLDKS) **3**, 87–116 (2011)
9. Draidi, F., et al.: P2Prec: a social-based P2P recommendation system. In: Proceedings of the 20th ACM International Conference on Information and Knowledge Management, pp. 2593–2596 (2011)
10. Han, P., et al.: A scalable P2P recommendation system based on distributed collaborative filtering. Expert Syst. Appl. **27**(2), 203–210 (2004)

11. Hecht, F., et al.: Radiommendation: P2P on-line radio with a distributed recommendation system. In: Proceedings of the IEEE 12th International Conference on Peer-to-Peer Computing, pp. 73–74 (2012)
12. Hu, Y., Bhuyan, L.N., Feng, M.: Maintaining data consistency in structured P2P systems. IEEE Trans. Parallel Distrib. Syst. **23**(11), 2125–2137 (2012)
13. Indyk, P., Motwani, R.: Approximate nearest neighbors: towards removing the curse of dimensionality. In: STOC 1998 Proceedings of the 30th Symposium on Theory of Computing, pp. 604–613 (1998)
14. Jelasity, M., Montresor, A., Babaoglu, O.: T-Man: gossip-based fast overlay topology construction. Comput. Netw. **53**(13), 2321–2339 (2009)
15. Kermarrec, A.-M., et al.: Application of random walks to decentralized recommendation systems. In: Proceeding of the 14th International Conference on Principles of Distributed Systems, pp. 48–63 (2010)
16. Korzun, D., Gurtov, A.: Structured Peer-to-Peer Systems. Fundamentals of Hierarchical Organization, Routing, Scaling and Security. Springer, Heidelberg (2013)
17. Mastroianni, C., Pirro, G., Talia, D.: Data consistency and peer synchronization in cooperative P2P environments. Technical report (2008, unpublished)
18. Matsumoto, M., Nishimura, T.: Mersenne twister: a 623-dimensionally equidistributed uniform pseudo-random number generator. ACM Trans. Model. Comput. Simul. **8**(1), 3–30 (1998)
19. Netflix Prize. http://www.netflixprize.com/
20. Jelasity, M., Hegedűs, I., Ormándi, R.: Overlay management for fully distributed user-based collaborative filtering. In: D'Ambra, P., Guarracino, M., Talia, D. (eds.) Euro-Par 2010, Part I. LNCS, vol. 6271, pp. 446–457. Springer, Heidelberg (2010)
21. Oster, G., et al.: Data consistency for P2P collaborative editing. In: Proceedings of the 20th Anniversary Conference on Computer Supported Cooperative Work, pp. 259–268 (2006)
22. Pitsilis, G., Marshall, L.: A trust-enabled P2P recommendation system. In: Proceedings of 15th IEEE International Workshops on Enabling Technologies: Infrastructure for Collaborative Enterprises, pp. 59–64 (2006)
23. Pussep, K., et al.: A peer-to-peer recommendation system with privacy constraints. In: CISIS: IEEE Computer Society, pp. 409–414 (2009)
24. Rajaraman, A., Ullman, J.: Mining of Massive Datasets. Cambridge University Press, Cambridge (2012)
25. Slanley, M., Casey, M.: Locality-sensitive hashing for finding nearest neighbors. IEEE Signal Process. Mag. **25**(2), 128–131 (2008)
26. Tveit, A.: Peer-to-peer based recommendations for mobile commerce. In: Proceedings of 1st International Workshop on Mobile Commerce (WMC 2001), pp. 26–29. ACM (2001)
27. Wang, Q., Borisov, N.: Octopus: a secure and anonymous DHT lookup. In: Proceedings of the IEEE 32nd International Conference on Distributed Computing Systems, pp. 325–334 (2012)

An Approach to a Laser-Touchscreen System

Jeremiah Aizeboje and Taoxin Peng[(✉)]

School of Computing, Edinburgh Napier University,
10 Colinton Road, Edinburgh EH10 5DT, UK
Jeromino2009@gmail.com, t.peng@napier.ac.uk

Abstract. As modern day technologies advance, so have different methods in which users can interact with computers. Computers are currently being used in combination with devices like projectors for teaching and presentations, in which the mouse and the USB wireless presenter are two of the main presentation devices. However, such devices like the USB wireless presenter, is limited and cannot fully encapsulate what it aspires to simulate, a computer mouse. This device fails to simulate the movement of a mouse but may only simulate the actions of a right and left arrow key. This paper proposes a novel approach to allowing users to interact with a computer from a distance without the need of a mouse, but instead using a laser pointing device, a projector and a web camera, by developing a novel laser-touchscreen system. The test results confirmed the laser pointer could be used to simulate the movement of the mouse as well as mouse clicks with very high accuracy. It could also be potentially used in a gaming environment, especially in first person shooter games.

Keywords: Image recognition · Blob detection · Edge detection · Corner detection · Quadrilateral transformation

1 Introduction

As modern day technologies advance, so have different methods in which users can interact with computers. Throughout the years, teaching and presenting devices have progressed from chalk board to white-board and now the use of projectors. Furthermore, the mouse and the USB wireless presenter are two of the main presentation devices used in combination with a projector. However, such devices like the USB wireless presenter, is limited and cannot fully encapsulate what it aspires to simulate, a computer mouse. This device fails to simulate the movement of a mouse but may only simulate the actions of a right and left arrow key. In such an environment, a camera can be used to capture the projected screen along with the laser dot. The projected screen can be seen as a "laser-touchscreen" because the laser pointer device would act as a mouse; the cursor would move to the position of the laser in relation to the projected screen. However, the USB wireless presenter, usually a laser pointer, cannot simulate the movement of a mouse but only simulate the actions of right and left arrow keys.

The aim of this work is to improve and extend the functionalities of modern day USB wireless presenters to behave more like a computer mouse. The goal of this system would give the user more flexibility and more control over the targeted computer over any distance the laser pointer light can travel. The controller or presenter

S. Hammoudi et al. (Eds.): ICEIS 2015, LNBIP 241, pp. 476–495, 2015.
DOI: 10.1007/978-3-319-29133-8_23

using the laser-touchscreen system would be free to move amongst the audience with confidence knowing that they don't have to rush back to the front of the audience where the computer is located, in order to do a simple mouse interaction with it i.e. clicking the play button of a video embedded within a presentation slide.

This paper proposes a novel approach to allowing users to interact with a computer from a distance without the need of a mouse, but instead using a laser pointing device, a projector and a web camera, by developing a novel screen detection method (based on a simple pattern recognition technique), a laser detection method, and an accuracy algorithm to control the accuracy of the movement of the mouse cursor. The test results confirmed the laser pointer could be used to simulate the movement of the mouse as well as mouse clicks with very high accuracy. It could also be potentially used in a gaming environment.

The rest of this paper is structured as follows. Related works are described in next section. Section 3 introduces image recognition techniques that will be used to develop the application. The main contribution of this work is presented in Sect. 4, which introduces the novel approach, the design and implementation of the application. The testing and evaluation are discussed in Sect. 5. Finally, this paper is concluded and future work pointed out in Sect. 6.

2 Related Work

Beauchemin [1] compared and analysed different image thresholding techniques and proposed an image based thresholding based on semivariance analysis. This method "measures the spatial variability of a variable at different scales". Semivariance thresholding proved to be highly competitive from the results gained when compared against other popular thresholding methods. Regardless of the positive results gained, the semivariance method fails when the images' background is outshined by intermittent spatial patterns.

A rectangle shape recognition algorithm was developed by Rajesh [2]. The algorithm proposes the use of a one-dimensional array to examine the rectangular shape. The algorithm requires the image to be in binary mode. Afterwards, the image would need to be rotated to a standard X – Y axis before the rectangle testing algorithm can be run. The algorithm has been tested for three sample applications; 'Rice Sorting', 'Rectangle Shaped Biscuits Sorting' and 'Square Shaped Biscuits Sorting' as well as 'Raw Shape Sorting'. Rajesh proves the algorithm to be fast and accurate based on these applications. However, since only a one dimension array is used, only limited information can be stored. The algorithm doesn't produce accurate positions for corners, especially for unequal quadrilaterals.

Moon et al. [3] proposed a method, through the use of blob detection, to help computers detect tumours in automated ultrasound images. This computer-aided detection (CADe) method was proposed to revolutionise the way hand held ultrasound images are carried out since the results are dependent on the user. Blob detection has made it possible for an efficiently detailed and automated ultrasound to be proposed. However, before this method can be used in a clinical environment, further work needs to be done to reduce its frames per second as well as its execution time.

There are also two existing commercial systems like electronic whiteboard and USB wireless presenter.

Electronic Whiteboard (E.W.): The accuracy of this device is reliable when it has been calibrated. On the other hand it is quite costly and is not financially feasible for some commercial uses. This device works like a touchscreen; built with functionalities like mouse clicks and movement of the mouse cursor [4].

USB Wireless Presenter (USB W.P.): This device can be relied on when used within range of its receiver. It is built with an average range of 15 meters. It is also quite cheap and easily acquired. Its functionalities are merely pre-programmed buttons that simulates some keyboard buttons i.e. arrow keys. The USB receiver cannot work with any other pointer than the one that was built for it [5].

3 Image Processing Techniques

This section discusses image recognition techniques that will be used in this application.

3.1 Image Processing

Image processing can be defined as running a list of mathematical operations on an image in order to achieve the desired result. It has been in existence since the 1920s. The earliest record of a machine based image processing system was first recorded in 1952. As the development and improvement of computers grew so did this field as it became a widespread area [6].

Image processing has been used to solve several problems identified but it still has not solved some sensitive issues gathered in 1993, [7] such as:

Compression: Image compression is a technique for reducing the amount of digitized information needed to store a visual image electronically. Images are compressed to speed up transmission time from one place to another. This process causes the image to loose quality. If image processing could be used to compress a 1.2 Mbps video stream to a desirable 1 Kbps video stream without degrading in quality then "compression" would not be a problem in image processing.

Enhancement: Image enhancement is a method used to improve the quality of an image. Attributes such as hue, contrast, brightness, sharpness, etc. of an image may cause the need for an image to need enhancement. These could be seen as "degradations". The main problem of enhancement in image processing is how to remove these degradations without affecting the intended outcome of the image. Though many algorithms have been implemented but they still do not fully solve this problem.

Recognition: Image recognition is the identification of objects within an image. This area is widely used in computer vision. Such a system should be able to recognize objects from its input parameters (analysis of the image retrieved). The difficult task would be, being able to identify different classes of objects i.e. chairs, table, etc. How can one develop a general purpose system such as this? This is a question yet to be answered.

Even though all these problems and more exist, different algorithms and techniques have been developed in an attempt to address these issues. It can be argued to what extent the developed methods help in a quest for a solution.

3.2 Blob Detection

"Blob tracking is a method by which computers can identify and trace the movements of objects within images" [8]. A computer can find a blobs position in successive frames using this method. The idea is to track a group of pixels with similar colour or light values.

Apart from using blob detection for colour detection, Hinz [9] explains how blobs can be categorized by its geometric values:

- Blob area
- Geometric moments: centre points, and higher order moments
- Boundary length
- Parameters of a robustly fitted ellipse like:
  - Length
  - Width
  - Orientation

In any case, for a specific end goal in blob tracking to be viable, blob tracking calculations need to conquer the challenges revealed by high blob interaction, for example frequent uniting and disuniting of blobs [10].

3.3 The Canny Edge Detector

When analysing an image, one of the popular operations carried out is edge detection. The cause of its popularity is that edges form the outline of an object, in the generic sense. An edge outlines the perimeter of an object from another object or background. Edge detection is essentially needed for accuracy in identifying various objects in images [11].

The Canny Edge Detector is a very popular and effective edge feature detector that is used as a pre-processing step in many computer vision algorithms. In 1986, John Canny characterized a set of objectives for an edge identifier and portrayed an optimal strategy for attaining them [11].

Canny also stated three problems that an edge detecting system must overcome. These are:

- Error rate — the edge detector should respond only to edges, and should find all of them; no edges should be missed.
- Localization — the distance between the edge pixels as found by the edge detector and the actual edge should be as small as possible.
- Response — the edge detector should not identify multiple edge pixels where only a single edge exists.

The Canny edge detector is a multi-step detector which performs smoothing and filtering, non-maxima suppression, followed by a connected-component analysis stage to detect 'true' edges, while suppressing 'false' non-edge filter responses [12].

3.4 Thresholding

"Thresholding is a non-linear operation that converts a gray-scale image into a binary image where the two levels are assigned to pixels that are below or above the specified threshold value" [13]. Thresholding is a simple method used in segmenting images. It can be used to partition out different areas of an image. This partition is dependent upon the strength of the difference between the object pixels and the background pixels [14]. Before thresholding is applied, the image is normally converted to a grey scale image. Assuming an 8-bit grey scale image conversion was used, each pixel would have a value between 0 and 255; where 0 is black and 255 is white.

Figure 1 illustrated thresholding applied to the grey scale image on the left. The result produced on the right only contains two colours. The black colour could be classified as '0' and the non-black colour could be classified as '1' in terms of binary. When thresholding is being applied, it compares each pixel with the threshold value. If the compared pixel is less than the threshold value, that pixel is converted to 0 (black). But if the compared pixel is greater than the threshold value, that pixel would normally be converted to a non-black value (the user defines this value; between 0–255). This can also work in reverse as there are different forms of thresholding. The main goal of thresholding is to clearly separate or compress the wanted pixels from the unwanted pixels.

Fig. 1. Threshold ing applied on image [14].

4 The Approach

This section describes the proposed approach to allowing users to interact with a computer from a distance by using a laser pointing device, rather than a mouse.

4.1 Introduction

The implementation of this system is defined by its requirements. The functional requirement of this system is basically being able to use a laser pointing device to interact with a computer through the help of a web camera and a projected screen. The interaction here means the mouse must move when the laser pointing dot is moved within the projected screen and a click must be simulated when the laser pointer is turned off and on.

The accuracy of the movement is one of the main challenges. To achieve this objective, the system should answer the following two questions which are its non-functional requirements:

- How accurately are the four corners of the screen recognized?
- Is the position of the laser dot translated with great accuracy?

4.2 Screen Detection

This section proposes a method that can be used to detect the screen. When detecting the screen, the aim is to retrieve and store the coordinate of the four corners of the screen. When this coordinates have been stored, there would be no need to keep on detecting the screen. This would be costly and useless if the screen is being detected at every frame alongside with detecting the laser dot. Since the screen is inanimate and only going to be at one place, there is no need to keep on tracking so the detecting operation is carried out once. If the projector moves or is being readjusted, this method would need to be run again.

In order to detect the edges of the screen, the Canny edge detecting method was implemented as seen below.

The low threshold value applied varies but is reasonably high since we are aiming to detect the most intense pixels in the image (thanks to the light from the projected screen). Figure 2 shows a black background with a white quadrilateral. This quadrilateral reveals the edges of the screen would hardly be a perfect square or rectangle.

Retrieving the four corners would require some pattern matching technique. Below are samples of patterns retrieved from a live test.

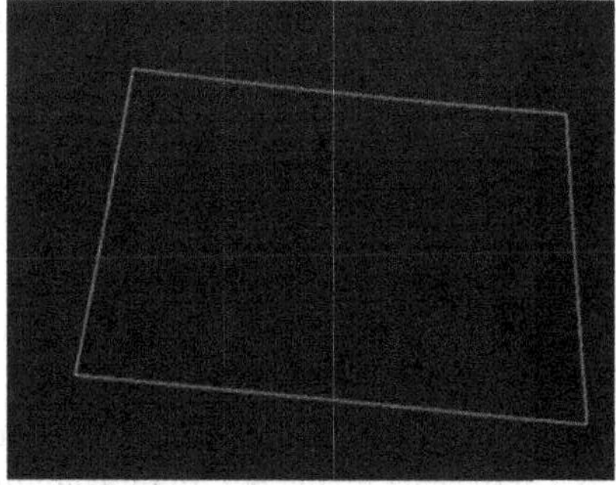

Fig. 2. Canny edge applied to detect screen.

Then 2D arrays (3 × 3) to represent the corners of the binary images in Fig. 3 can be generated. Table 1 shows an example array for the top left corner of the image in Fig. 3.

In order to recognise the left top corner of the screen where S is the current pixel in question; if S = 1 and the surrounding pixels have the values shown in Table 1 then the top left corner of the screen has been found. The main goal is to check all the 8 pixels around a visible pixel for the pattern and if found, the S value is stored as a recognised corner.

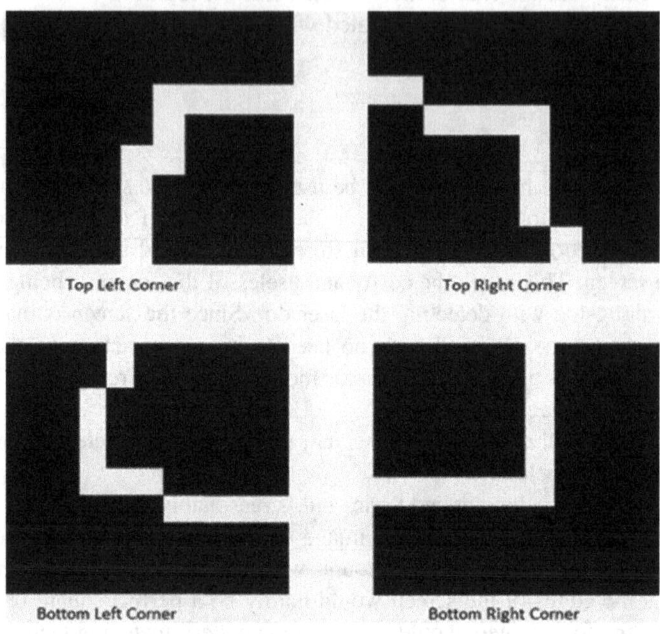

Fig. 3. Patterns of screen corners.

Table 1. A 2D array (3 × 3) representing the top left corner.

0	0	0
0	S	1
0	1	0

4.3 Laser Detection

This detection method implemented the thresholding technique. Each frame received was first of all converted to a grey scale image before thresholding was applied because a grey scale image has only one channel to work with while the original colour (RGB) image would have three channels to work with. Thresholding requires one channel and the grey scale image provides just that.

Then blob detection is applied to the retrieved binary image. The tracked feature would be the intensity of the image.

The following method is adopted from the OpenCV library which is used to find a blob within a binary image:

```
cvLabel(grey, displayFrame, blobs)
```

In the above implementation, cvLabel takes in three parameters. The first parameter (grey) passes in a grey scale image array (IplImage). The second parameter (displayFrame) passes by reference an empty image array (IplImage) to be filled on completion of the method run. The third parameter (blobs) passes by reference an object (cvBlobs) to store the blob details found.

The centroid values (x and y) of the blob found represents the CP values used in the accuracy algorithm, proposed in next section.

4.4 The Accuracy Algorithm

This novel algorithm is designed specifically for this laser-touchscreen system. The accuracy algorithm can be seen as an automated screen calibration system, which is designed to answer the two questions stated in Sect. 4.1.

To help to describe the accuracy algorithm, Figs. 4, 5 and 6, and relevant variables are introduced first.

Variables used for describing the algorithm are described in Tables 2, 3 and 4. These tables in conjunction with Figs. 4, 5 and 6 help to visualise the equations that would be introduced later in this chapter. The labelled figures help to illustrate the projected screen and how certain variables were chosen.

The algorithm translates the location of the laser dot on the projected screen to the expected mouse position on the computer.

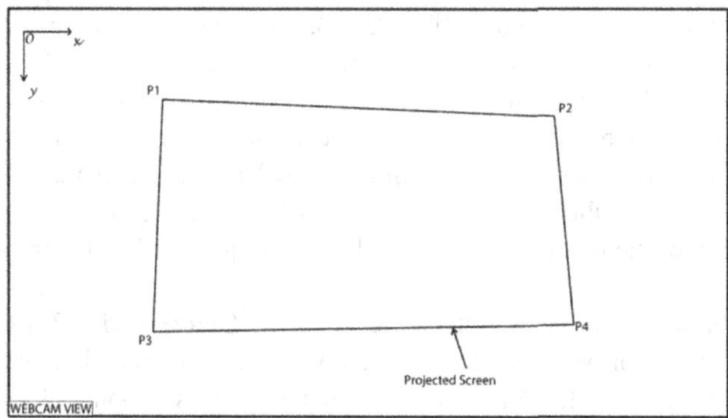

Fig. 4. Sketch of the projected screen on a wall.

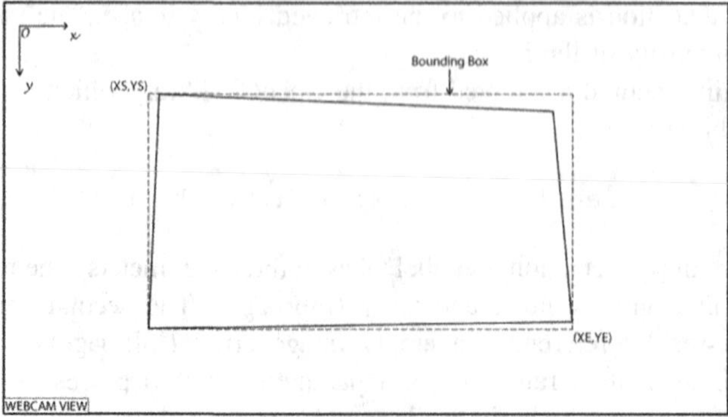

Fig. 5. Sketch of a bounding box around the projected screen.

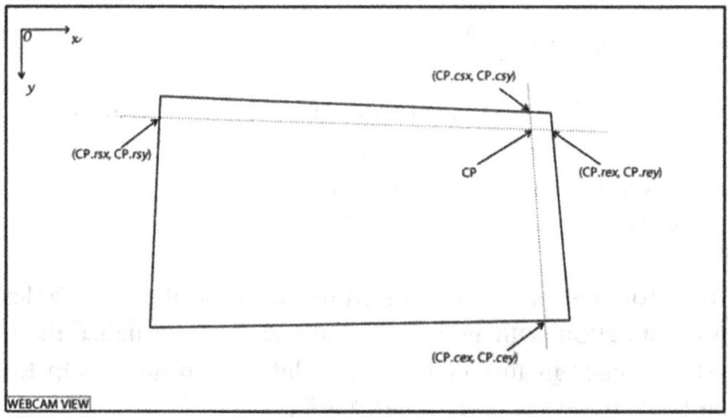

Fig. 6. Sketch of a laser pointer dot (CP) within the projected screen.

A simple application would represent the screen as the bounding box. This would mean the only accurate point given would be the centre (XE/2, YE/2) of the screen. If the perimeter of the projected screen (P1, P2, P3, P4) were to be the same as that of the bounding box then that technique would work, but it may be quite difficult to achieve this depending on where the camera is placed and how the projected screen is set up.

For a single pixel row and column on the projected screen, its starting X*r* and Y*r* value would likely differ with its ending X*r* and Y*r* value. This means that in order to accurately determine the position of any pixel in question, the starting and ending values (X*r* & Y*r*) of the pixel would need to be known to calculate the translated values (T*x*, T*y*).

Without obtaining the values of CP.*rsx,* CP.*rex,* CP.*csy* and CP.*cey*, the T*x* and T*y* values of CP cannot be calculated accurately. In order to calculate these value, the bounding box ((XS, YS) to (XE, XY)) would be used as a point of reference. The bounding box is to be used as a point of reference because each of its corners has a 90 degrees angle and none of its edges have a gradient. This would help keep the

Table 2. Variables about the project screen.

Variable	Meaning
P1.*x*	Top left corner X coordinate value of the screen
P1.*y*	Top left corner Y coordinate value of the screen
P2.*x*	Top right corner X coordinate value of the screen
P2.*y*	Top right corner Y coordinate value of the screen
P3.*x*	Bottom left corner X coordinate value of the screen
P3.*y*	Bottom left corner Y coordinate value of the screen
P4.*x*	Bottom right corner X coordinate value of the screen
P4.*y*	Bottom right corner Y coordinate value of the screen
R*w*	The *width* value of the resolution of the projected screen
R*h*	The *height value* of the resolution of the projected screen
DT.*x*	The *top* difference of the X axis of P2.*x* – P1.*x*
DT.*y*	The *top* difference of the Y axis of P1.*y* – P2.*y*
DL.*x*	The *left* difference of the X axis of P1.*x* – P3.*x*
DL.*y*	The *left* difference of the Y axis of P3.*y* – P1.*y*
DR.*x*	The *right* difference of the X axis of P4.*x* – P2.*x*
DR.*y*	The *right* difference of the Y axis of P4.*y* – P2.*y*
DB.*x*	The *bottom* difference of the X axis of P4.*x* – P3.*x*
DB.*y*	The *bottom* difference of the Y axis of P4.*y* – P3.*y*

Table 3. Variables about a bounding box around the projected screen.

Variable	Meaning
XS	The minimum value on the X axis between the P1.*x* and P3.*x*
XE	The maximum value on the X axis between the P2.*x* and P4.*x*
YS	The minimum value on the Y axis between the P1.*y* and P2.*y*
YE	The maximum value on the Y axis between the P3.*y* and P4.*y*
Y*r*	The correct value of a pixel on the Y axis i.e. where (P1.*x*, P1.*y*) is seen as (1, 1)
X*r*	The correct value of a pixel on the X axis i.e. where (P1.*x*, P1.*y*) is seen as (1, 1)
Y*p*	The bounding box value of a pixel on the Y axis i.e. where (XS, YS) is seen as (1, 1)
X*p*	The bounding box value of a pixel on the X axis i.e. where (XS, YS) is seen as (1, 1)
CP	A pixel (X*p*, Y*p*) within the bounding box i.e. between (XS, YS) and (XE, YE)

calculations simpler; not needing to take its gradient values into account. The *top* and *left* edges would be used in this case.

The idea is to make calculations based on the idea of having DT.*y* and DL.*x* to have a value of zero. Which would mean (P1.*x*, P1.*y*) would be equal to (XS, YS) and

Table 4. Variables about a laser pointer dot (CP) within the projected screen.

Variable	Meaning
CP.*rsx*	The *left* value of X*r* on single row of pixels
CP.*rsy*	The *left* value of Y*p* on single row of pixels
CP.*rex*	The *right* value of X*r* on single row of pixels
CP.*rey*	The *right* value of Y*p* on single row of pixels
CP.*csx*	The *top* value of X*p* on single column of pixels
CP.*csy*	The *top* value of Y*r* on single column of pixels
CP.*cex*	The *bottom* value of X*p* on single column of pixels
CP.*cey*	The *bottom* value of Y*r* on single column of pixels
O*t*	The *top* offset for CP
O*l*	The *left* offset for CP
O*b*	The *bottom* offset for CP
T*x*	The translated X-axis value of CP
T*y*	The translated Y-axis value of CP

(P4.*x*, P4.*y*) would be equal to (XE, YE). The calculations made would need to use the absolute values of DT.*y* and DL.*x* to calculate their offset values.

The calculation of O*l*:

$$
\begin{gathered}
Z = \begin{cases} P1.y, & \text{if } P1.y > P2.y \\ 0, & \text{if } P1.y \leq P2.y \end{cases} \\
W = (\mathrm{CP}.y - \mathrm{Z})/\mathrm{DL}.y \\
G = \begin{cases} 1 - W, & \text{if } P1.y > P2.y \\ W, & \text{if } P1.y \leq P2.y \end{cases} \\
Ol = G * \mathrm{DL}.x
\end{gathered}
\tag{1}
$$

The calculation of O*t*:

$$
\begin{gathered}
Z = \begin{cases} P1.x, & \text{if } P1.x > P3.x \\ 0, & \text{if } P1.x \leq P3.x \end{cases} \\
\mathrm{W} = (\mathrm{CP}.x - \mathrm{Z})/\mathrm{DT}.x \\
G = \begin{cases} 1 - W, & \text{if } P1.x > P3.x \\ W, & \text{if } P1.x \leq P3.x \end{cases} \\
Ol = G * \mathrm{DT}.y
\end{gathered}
\tag{2}
$$

The calculation of O*r*:

$$
\begin{gathered}
Z = \begin{cases} P2.y, & \text{if } P2.y > P1.y \\ 0, & \text{if } P2.y \leq P1.y \end{cases} \\
\mathrm{W} = (\mathrm{CP}.y - \mathrm{Z})/\mathrm{DR}.y \\
G = \begin{cases} 1 - W, & \text{if } P2.y > P1.y \\ W, & \text{if } P2.y \leq P1.y \end{cases} \\
Or = G * \mathrm{DR}.x
\end{gathered}
\tag{3}
$$

The calculation of O*b*:

$$\begin{aligned} Z &= \begin{cases} P1.x, & \text{if } P3.x > P1.x \\ 0, & \text{if } P3.x \leq P1.x \end{cases} \\ \mathrm{W} &= (\mathrm{CP}.x - Z)/DB.x \\ G &= \begin{cases} 1 - W, & \text{if } P3.x > P1.x \\ W, & \text{if } P3.x \leq P1.x \end{cases} \\ Ob &= G * \mathrm{DB}.y \end{aligned} \tag{4}$$

The four sets of equations above calculate the offsets values for each edge. The offset value is the space between the edge of the bounding box and the edge of the projected screen. Including the offset in the accuracy algorithm would go a long way in improving the systems accuracy.

Now that all offsets have been calculated:

$$\begin{aligned} \mathrm{CP}.rsx &= \mathrm{XS} + \mathrm{O}l \\ \mathrm{CP}.rex &= \mathrm{XE} - \mathrm{O}r \\ \mathrm{CP}.csy &= \mathrm{YS} + \mathrm{O}t \\ \mathrm{CP}.cey &= \mathrm{YE} - \mathrm{O}b \end{aligned} \tag{5}$$

Since each CP may have a different column height (CP.*cey* – CP.*csy*) and/or row width (CP.*rex* – CP.*rsx*) from other pixels, the above equations would be used to calculate its height and width with an end goal of solving its T*x* and T*y* values.

Once all values related to CP have been found, the translated position of a single pixel can now be calculated. The calculation of the translated X-axis value of a pixel (Q) on the projected screen:

$$\mathrm{T}x = (\mathrm{CP}.rsx/(\mathrm{CP}.rex{-}\mathrm{CP}.rsx)) * \mathrm{CP}.x \tag{6}$$

The calculation of the translated Y-axis value of CP on the projected screen:

$$\mathrm{T}y = (\mathrm{CP}.csy/(\mathrm{CP}.cey{-}\mathrm{CP}.csy)) * \mathrm{CP}.y \tag{7}$$

Translating the values of CP to (T*x*, T*y*) is basically what this algorithm does. The mouse cursor would be sent to the translated values of CP (T*x*, T*y*).

In conclusion, the accuracy formula wouldn't have been this accurate without adding the offsets to the edges and realising that each column of a single can have a various height values and each row of a single pixel can have a various width values. This algorithm can potentially be tweaked to triangulate a signal location when the signal is emitted anywhere within 4 receivers.

The pseudocode of the accuracy algorithm is outlined as below:

```
lu = top left corner coordinate
ld = bottom left corner coordinate
ru = right top corner coordinate
rd = right down corner coordinate
width = max_x_value(ru,rd) - min_x_value(lu, ld)
height = max_y_value(ld,rd) - min_y_value(lu, ru)
portXcoordinate = 2d array of width by height
portYcoordinate = 2d array of width by height
FOR currentX = 1 to width
  FOR currentY = 1 to width
    start_x = get_min_x_value_for_row(currentY)
    end_x = get_max_x_value_for_row(currentY)
    start_y = get_min_y_value_for_column(currentX)
    end_y = get_max_y_value_for_column(currentX)
    Xpercent = (currentY - start_y)/(end_y - start_y)
    Ypercent = (currentX - start_x)/(end_x - start_x)
    set current position in portXcoordinate to Xpercent
    set current position in portYcoordinate to Ypercent
 END FOR
END FOR
```

The pseudocode simulates, pre-calculates and stores every possible translated value of the laser dot (CP) in 2 different 2D arrays. This pseudocode assumes that the position of the projected screen would remain the same during the runtime of the application. Hence, there would be no need for always recalculating the same pixel multiple times if it would always return the same value.

4.5 Evaluation of the Accuracy Algorithm

In order to test how effective the accuracy algorithm is, an evaluating method is proposed in this section.

Figure 7 represents a projected screen with a green laser dot and a mouse cursor. It illustrates an inaccurate system for a better explanation on how the accuracy of this system is going to be evaluated.

To evaluate the accuracy of results, the following is designed:

$$S_{accuracy} = (1 - ((D_x + D_y)/(C_w + C_h))) * 100 \tag{8}$$

The formula calculates how close the position of the x and y coordinates of the laser dot is to the position of the x and y coordinates of the mouse on the screen.

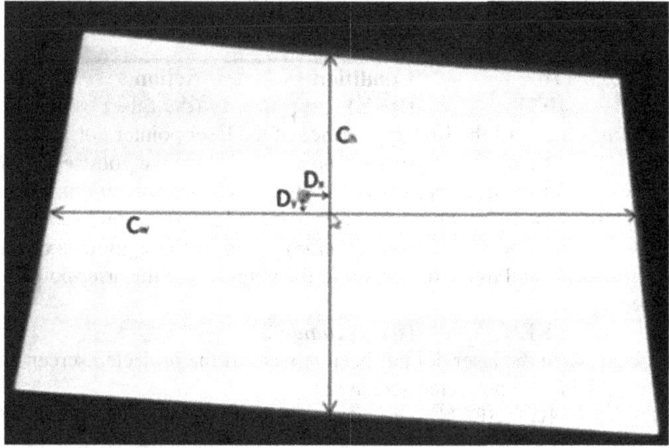

Fig. 7. A projected screen; Explanation of formula used to test applications accuracy.

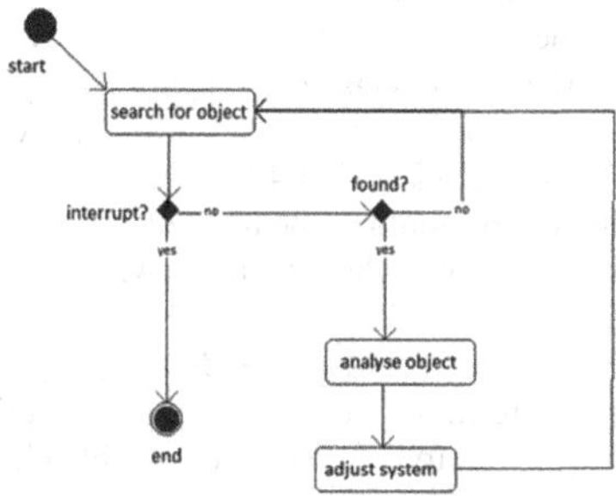

Fig. 8. Flow chart for detecting an object (projected screen and laser light dot).

4.6 Activity Design

The diagram shown in Fig. 8 summarises the flow of the program. The 'search for object' process searches for either the projected screen (when setting up the program) or the laser dot (when main aspect of the program is running). When an object has been found the program analyses the object. If the laser pointer dot is detected the 'analyse object' process checks for its position (coordinates) from the camera frame and then adjusts the system by moving the mouse to its designated position. If the user sends an interrupt command (press of the Esc key) the program terminates.

4.7 Event Design

This section elaborates on the 'adjust system' process from Fig. 8. Table 5 explains the possible states and actions carried out by the program during this process.

States, variables and functions that are involved in the 'adjust system' process are defined as follows:

Table 5. All possible laser triggered events at runtime.

ID	From	To	Condition	Action
0	**INIT**	**INIT**	**(!*seen*)**	**(dc=false)**
	Stays in the *init* state until the first appearance of the laser pointer dot.			
1	**INIT**	**SEEN**	**(*seen, range*)**	**(move_mouse(xNew, yNew))**
	Set state to *seen* after the laser pointer has spotting the laser pointer dot for the first time. Move the mouse to the point where the laser pointer dot is currently seen.			
2	**SEEN**	**SEEN**	**(*seen, range*)**	**(move_mouse(xNew, yNew))**
	Remain in *seen* state and move the cursor to the point where the laser pointer dot is currently seen.			
3	**SEEN**	**SEEN**	**(*seen* , !*range*)**	**-**
	This will occur when the laser dot has been moved off the projected screen area or has been spotted outside the projected screen area.			
4	**SEEN**	**NOT_SEEN**	**(!*seen, range, !dc*)**	**(determine_click_timer(), dc = true, nsc = 0, last_x = x, last_y=y)**
	When the laser pointer dot is not visible and was last spotted in range, set the state as *not_seen* and since *dc* is false, the *determine_click_timer()* function can be called. Then set *dc* to true and *nsc* to 1. The program needs to know if the user is attempting to click on something so it stores the *x* and *y* coordinates of the current position.			
5	**NOT_SEEN**	**NOT_SEEN**	**(!*seen,dc*)**	**-**
	Remain in the *not_seen* state. The timer called by event 4 is currently running. If the elapsed time from the previous click (event 4 or event 7) to now is currently greater that the *click_interval* then the timer would come to a halt, *dc* will be set to false, *nsc* to zero. This prevents fake clicks (situations when the user switches off the laser pointer or wants to cancel a click).			
6	**NOT_SEEN**	**SEEN**	**(*seen, range, dc*)**	**-**
	Since we are still trying to determine if user is attempting a click, we do nothing. After this event, event 7 is likely to run to simulate a left double click or a right click. If the elapsed time from the previous click (event 4 or event 7) till now is currently greater that the *click_interval* then event 8 will run.			
7	**SEEN**	**NOT_SEEN**	**(!*seen*, dc)**	**(nsc++)**
	The laser pointer dot is now in the *not_seen* state when *dc* is true. Since it is currently trying to determine if the user is clicking, *nsc* value should be incremented by 1. No need to move mouse. Event 6 will need to be run again when the user has finished clicking. Restart the *determine_click_timer().*			
8	**SEEN**	**SEEN**	**(*range*,!dc,nsc>0, nsc<4)**	**(mouse_click(nsc), nsc=0, dc=false)**
	The *determine_click_timer()*has run its course. The *mouse_click(type)* function can be called with the *nsc* variable passed to it. This is to determine what kind of click is called. Reset *nsc* to zero afterwards.			

States:

- INIT – when the program is run for the first time.
- SEEN – when the laser pointer dot is seen by the camera
- NOT_SEEN – when the laser pointer dot is not seen by the camera

Variables:

- seen – set to true if the laser dot has been seen or else false;
- dc – set to true if the 'determine_click_timer()' function is called and running.
- nsc – this is a counter. Counts how many times there was a SEEN to NOT_SEEN state when dc is true.
- range – set to true if laser dot is within the projected screen range or else false
- last_x – stores the last x-coordinate value seen.
- last_y – stores the last y-coordinate value seen.
- click_interval – number of seconds to wait after a single click to determine if the user has finished clicking (500 ms or 1 s; user defined).

Functions:

- move_mouse(x, y) – This moves the mouse cursor to coordinate (x, y) on the screen.
- determine_click_timer() – This starts a timer.
- mouse_click(type) – This simulates a mouse click. When type is:
  - 1: single left click
  - 2: double left click
  - 3: single right click

5 Experiments and Evaluation

The main focus of the following experiment is to evaluate if the proposed approach is feasible as an interactive system.

The tests carried out on the application were inspired by the developed functional and non-functional requirements stated in Sect. 4.1. Due to the facts that there are no benchmark scenarios for this kind of testing, a classic class room scenario was chosen where the device is used in a lecture room and the light/brightness of the room fails to affect the visual input of the camera e.g. the screen and the laser pointer dot. Though the presented results in this chapter had a few irregular classroom setting; the camera was placed right above (on) the projector with a slight angle. The distance from the right bottom corner of the projected screen to the centre of the projector's bulb was measured as 132 cm while the distance from the left bottom corner of the projected screen to the centre of the projector's bulb was measured as 151 cm. The goal of the following test is to see how well the system works in a bad setup since it already worked perfectly fine in a good setup.

5.1 Accuracy Test

Once the accuracy algorithm has been run, its results can be evaluated using the method proposed in Sect. 4.5 to evaluate how accurate the accuracy algorithm is in a real world environment.

For this test, the screen resolutions that would be used are 800 × 600, 1024 × 768, 1280 × 1024, and the camera resolutions used are 640 × 480 and 320 × 240. These resolutions are commonly found or supported by most projectors. Testing results are shown in Tables 6, 7 and 8:

Table 6. Results from an 800 × 600 display resolution.

Camera resolution	Best accuracy achieved	Worst accuracy achieved
640 × 480	99.99 %	97.02 %
320 × 240	99.99 %	96.88 %

Table 7. Results from a 1024 × 768 display resolution.

Camera resolution	Best accuracy achieved	Worst accuracy achieved
640 × 480	99.99 %	97.33 %
320 × 240	99.99 %	96.51 %

Table 8. Results from a 1024 × 1024 display resolution.

Camera resolution	Best Accuracy achieved	Worst accuracy achieved
640 × 480	99.99 %	97.23 %
320 × 240	99.99 %	96.58 %

The 640 × 480 camera resolution was able to process an average of 15 frames per second while the 320 × 240 camera resolution was able to process an average of 28 frames per second. Doubling the camera resolution halved the frames per seconds obtained.

The best accuracy was always achieved at the four corners of the projected screen. The reason could be because the accuracy algorithm used these points to define the screen boundaries.

On average the system can be said to be over 98 % accurate. The testing results confirm the proposed accuracy algorithm provides a perfect answer to the two questions in Sect. 4.1.

5.2 Clicking Test

The purpose of the clicking test evaluates how well the system simulates the clicking action by using laser pointer instead of the mouse.

There are 3 click actions involved; a left click, a double left click and a right click. A left click action is done by turning off and on the laser pointer, simulating the left click of a mouse. A double left click action is done by turning off and on the laser pointer device twice within a space of 1 s. A right click action is done by turning off and on the laser pointer thrice within a space of 1 s, simulating a right click of a mouse.

The testing results show that the approach worked perfectly on PowerPoint slides.

The application was also tested on DirectX game applications but it didn't work. Further research into a solution resulted in the need of using the DirectX API to simulate a mouse which remains as future work.

5.3 Evaluation

Comparing the developed screen detection method (Sect. 4.2), against Rajeshs' [2] rectangle shape recognition algorithm, the image does not need to be rotated to detect the quadrilateral screen. Rajeshs' binary segmentation algorithm wouldn't have been able to separate the screen from the background because it requires the background colour to be known. Since this application is being developed to be used in unknown environments the Canny detector (Sect. 3.3) proved to be superior.

The Laser-touchscreen system (L.T.S) developed in this project can be said to be accurate based on the results from the accuracy test carried out. The camera and the laser pointer used cost less than $100 which is relatively cheap. The interaction range of this system is dependent on the range of the laser light. The laser pointer used has a range 3 miles [15]. This system can simulate three mouse actions and also move the mouse cursor to the position of the laser dot. Different laser pointer devices can be used – its parts are interchangeable (P.I.).

Comparing this project with two interactive commercial devices described in Sect. 2, E.W. and USB P.W. would help to prove the usefulness of this project.

Table 9 shows that the developed prototype (the Laser-touchscreen system (**L.T.S**)) can easily replace the use of an electronic whiteboard and a USB wireless presenter.

Table 9. Comparing similar devices.

	E.W.	USB W.P.	L.T.S
Reliable	Yes	Yes	Yes
Cost	Expensive	Cheap	Cheap
Range	Short	Medium	Long
Accurate	Yes	N/A	Yes
P.I.	N/A	No	Yes

The test results illustrate that using a higher camera resolution could improve the accuracy but at the same time reduce the number of frames that can be processed in a second. It all comes down to sacrificing the application's speed against its quality (accuracy).

6 Conclusions and Future Work

This paper has presented a novel approach to a laser-touchscreen system, by using a laser pointer as a mouse with a web camera installed. The aim is to fully encapsulate what it aspires to simulate a computer mouse. Also the economic camera used makes the implementation of this system more attractive to potential users and perhaps financially feasible. To achieve this approach, a novel screen detection method (based on a simple pattern recognition technique), a laser detection method, and an accuracy algorithm were developed, which were successfully used to create the laser-touchscreen system. Experimental comparative studies show that in several environments with different device settings of screen resolutions and camera resolutions, on average the new system can achieve over 98 % accuracy. The result from the testing and evaluation proves the use of a laser pointer as a mouse to be achievable.

Although promising, much can be done to further improve the potential of this work. For future development, further investigation and research is required to determine the best course of action on how to improve the developed accuracy algorithm so it works better under terrible setups, either by improving the existing prototype or by creating a new standalone project for the sole purpose of improving its accuracy.

Another particular interest to the authors is to extend the application to gaming, by implementing the DirectX API into the system. It is believed that it would be very user friendly when a USB device, such as a laser pointer is used in playing games, especially in first person shooter games or games where the user is required to aim at a particular area on the screen to achieve a goal.

Finally, it is worth noting that, once a more improved accuracy algorithm has been developed, image processing chips could be looked into and how it could be integrated into a projector alongside with a good quality camera. It would be beneficial to both the gaming industry and users if all the external components utilised in this project can be integrated into a single device, which would ensure a proper and easy setup.

References

1. Bailey, D.G.: Design for Embedded Image Processing on FPGAs. Wiley, Singapore (2011)
2. Beauchemin, M.: Image thresholding based on semivariance. Int. Assoc. Pattern Recogn. **34**(5), 456–462 (2013)
3. DIGIFLEX, TRIXES 5in1 Green Laser Pointer Pen with 5 Patterned Projection Caps. http://www.digiflex.co.uk
4. Hinz, S.: Fast and subpixel precise blob detection and attribution. IEEE Int. Conf. Image Process. **3**, 11–15 (2005)
5. Huang, T.S., Aizawa, K.: Image processing: some challenging problems. Proc. Natl. Acad. Sci. U.S.A. **90**(21), 9766–9769 (1993)
6. Luo, Y., Duraiswami, R.: Canny edge detection on NVIDIA CUDA. In: IEEE Computer Society Conference on Computer Vision and Pattern Recognition Workshops, Anchorage, Alaska, USA, pp. 1–8 (2008)
7. Moon, W.K., Shen, Y., Bae, M.S., Huang, C., Chen, J., Chang, R.: Computer-aided tumor detection based on multi-scale blob detection algorithm in automated breast ultrasound images. IEEE Trans. Med. Imaging **32**(7), 1191–1200 (2013)
8. OpenCV: Basic thresholding operations. http://docs.opencv.org
9. Parker, J.R.: Algorithms for Image Processing and Computer Vision, 2nd edn. Wiley, Indiana (2010)
10. Rajesh, F.: Rectangle shape recognition using one-dimensional array. In: IEEE International Conference on Computational Intelligence and Computing Research (2010)

11. SANOXY: RF wireless remote control USB PowerPoint PPT presenter laser pointer PenSmart. http://sanoxy.com
12. Sharma, V.: A blob representation for tracking robust to merging and fragmentation. In: IEEE Workshop on Applications of Computer Vision, Colorado, USA, pp. 161–168 (2012)
13. SMART: SMART Board 8000 Series. http://smarttech.com
14. WaveMetrics: Image threshold. http://www.wavemetrics.com
15. Yao, N., Liu, Z., Qian, F., Sun, Z.: Target tracking method based on image patches exemplars. J. Comput. Inf. Syst. **9**(21), 8561–8570 (2013)

MiCATS: Middleware for Context-Aware Transactional Services

Widad Ettazi[1(✉)], Hatim Hafiddi[1,2], Mahmoud Nassar[1], and Sophie Ebersold[3]

[1] IMS Team, SIME Laboratory, ENSIAS, Mohammed V University, Rabat, Morocco
widad.ettazi@um5s.net.ma, hatim.hafiddi@gmail.com,
nassar@ensias.ma

[2] ISL Team, STRS Laboratory, INPT, Rabat, Morocco

[3] MACAO Team, IRIT Laboratory, University Toulouse 2-Le Mirail, Toulouse, France
ebersold@univ-tlse2.fr

Abstract. In context-aware service-based environments, fulfilling user's recommendations bring about several challenges that are mainly due to the dynamic nature and limited underlying resources of these environments. In this paper, we mainly focus on the transactional aspects of context-aware services. To cope with the aforementioned issues, we opt for a middleware-based solution (MiCATS). We therefore present our novel approach for managing context-aware transactions which allows for adaptation to the requirements of applications and mobile context in terms of transactional properties. Then, we introduce our context-aware transactional service model (CATSM) and a context-aware architecture based on adaptation policies. The proposed contributions are implemented within a middleware platform.

Keywords: Context-Awareness · ACID properties · Transactional service · Adaptation · Transaction model · ECA

1 Introduction

Since its appearance in database management systems, the notion of transactions has taken considerable growth insofar as transactions are now employed at all applications levels from operating systems to E-Commerce and B2B applications. The proliferation of these applications has led to an evolving subject area known as pervasive computing. The latter is an intuitive evolution of computing paradigms driven by the wide adoption of mobile devices and wireless networks. Systems are now expected to adjust to user's requirements and customize their services to user's needs. Nevertheless, supporting user's tasks from a functional point of view is not enough to gain his satisfaction. In context-aware environments, transactions must be able to adjust to systems that are not necessarily in a perfect environment, for example, that don't require a lock of their resources and do not care if transactions run for short periods of time or longer periods. These systems will operate in a flexible, dynamic environment, but less reliable and that presents contextual requirements (i.e., requirements and preferences expressed or implied by the user, connectivity, bandwidth, etc.) that hinder the transactions execution.

S. Hammoudi et al. (Eds.): ICEIS 2015, LNBIP 241, pp. 496–512, 2015.
DOI: 10.1007/978-3-319-29133-8_24

This paper investigates into the issue of context-awareness and transactional aspects exigencies in service-oriented platforms and surveys how applying context-awareness to transactional services can help to improve data consistency, transactions execution and quality of service.

Despite the multitude of research works on transaction management in service-oriented systems, the notion of context-awareness in the management of these transactions is not yet addressed. Let's consider, for example, a simple transaction that books a room in a hotel. Current approaches will simply commit the transaction if the required room is available in the hotel. They do not take into account the context information such as a room should be booked in a hotel which is located nearby. To meet the variables requirements of transactional services, the need to relax the classical ACID (Atomicity, Consistency, Isolation and Durability) properties has been proposed in many researches since the early 90s. There was a great effort on extended transaction models [1, 2]. This effort has been continued more recently in the context of mobile computing to satisfy the constraints of the execution environment [3]. Researches have led to different notions of atomicity (strict, relaxed and semantic atomicity), consistency (strict or weak), and isolation (strict or relaxed allowing a flexible interleaving between transactions and a controlled sharing of intermediate results) [4]. Several standards specifications have been proposed, including WS-Transaction specification [5] and Business Transaction Protocol [6]. However, they don't take into account the context information. Many transactional models and techniques have been proposed [7–9] but they have limitations, namely, a non-consideration of the context information and the conception of advanced models with transactional properties that differ from one application to another.

This article is organized as follows. The next section will be devoted to review some basic concepts. Section 3 summarizes related work. We introduce in Sect. 4 the proposed model for managing CATS. Section 5 describes the adaptation approach. Section 6 gives an overview of the architecture of MiCATS and highlights the interaction between the different components. We illustrate in Sect. 7 the application of our proposal with an e-tourism scenario. Section 8 concludes the paper with plans for the future.

2 Basic Concepts

We present in this part some backgrounds related to context-awareness and ACID properties.

2.1 Context Awareness

Context-aware computing appeared since the 90s driven by the work of [10]. This term refers to systems capable of perceiving a set of conditions of use in order to adjust their behavior in terms of providing information and services. According to [11], the definitions ascribed to a context-aware system do not include all types of context-aware systems. Indeed, under these definitions, a system that simply collects the context in order to provide it to an application is not considered a context-aware system. Thus, the authors believe that "a system is context-aware if it uses context to provide relevant information and services to the user, where relevance depends on the task requested by the user".

Indeed, in environments where communicating objects are pervasive, recognized and automatically located without a special user's action, the major challenge is to capture and model the user's intention and to resolve ambiguities. However, transactional models and existing protocols do not take into account the context information. Therefore, it is imperative to consider the context information in the management of transactions in service-oriented architectures.

2.2 Acid Properties

To control the adverse effects of concurrent modifications in a data system, the transaction defines four properties identified by the acronym ACID (Atomicity, Consistency, Isolation and Durability). The transaction model generally associated with ACID properties is the flat transaction model [12]. This one is particularly suited to transactions running in parallel, short and with a limited data handling.

However, the diversity of current application contexts requires to define new transactional models to support transactions of long duration (hours, days, weeks), which handle potentially large and structured data, and for which a degree of cooperation between participants may be required to perform a complex task. Therefore, ACID properties have limitations. Thus, they must be released because the property of atomicity is a major constraint for long-running transactions. Indeed, the risk of aborting the transaction increases in proportion to its length. In addition, the cost of aborted transactions also increases with the duration and complexity of the implemented process.

3 Literature Review

Several models for mobile transactions have been proposed, in which context requirements are handled differently. Even though these models allow flexibility according to mobile behavior, they do not provide the necessary flexibility with respect to transactional properties.

In [13] a new model for context-aware transactions in the context of mobile services is developed. This model provides a relaxed set of transaction correctness criteria called SACReD (Semantic Atomicity, Consistency, Resiliency, Durability) and a protocol for enforcing them. Unlike ACID criteria, SACReD does not impose isolation policy thus enabling transactions to be partially committed. Resiliency property allows for alternative services wherein a given service fails or if it does not meet the required context. However, the proposed model is not generic and does not allow its extension to other degree of atomicity. In addition, the implemented protocol leads to failure when no available alternative service is found. Authors in [14] present an approach for selecting and composing web services according to their transactional requirements, QoS characteristics and to the end-user preferences. The approach is not completely context-aware, since it doesn't include all context parameters. Moreover, the approach simply leads to a process failure when no suitable service is found. A Model-Driven Engineering approach is developed in [15] to achieve the context-aware service independently of platforms and application domains. Thus, the basic service focuses solely on the business logic and all adaptations of the Context Views will be defined separately as Aspects called Adaptation Aspects. However, transactional requirements of context-aware services have not been addressed by this work. [16] introduce the Adaptable Model Transaction (AMT) according to multiple execution models on fixed and mobile hosts. The AMT model allows programmers to define transactional alternatives for an application task depending on context changes. Even though the approach is interesting, transactional service properties are not taken into consideration. [17] propose an approach for modeling adaptation in web service compositions to ensure a guaranteed quality of service for the whole composite service. A special adaptation mechanism is the rebinding of single services while the process is executed if the services fail or could not reach the needed QoS level. The approach supports rebinding in BPEL processes and is based restrictively on QoS metrics. Other contextual parameters such as user's requirements are not included in the design process. [18] develop a middleware solution called mConnect: a Context aware real time Mobile Transaction Middleware which handles the multiplicity of devices and provides a context agnostic view to the Transaction (back end) server. Nevertheless, the middleware is restricted to the computational resources available with the handheld devices. [19] propose CATE: a component-based architecture that is based on the Two-Phase-Commit (2PC) protocol and on a context-aware transaction service. The adaptation of CATE is achieved by components reconfiguration to select the most appropriate protocol with respect to the execution context. The adaptation approach is based on the selection of a suitable commitment protocol among 2PC derivatives and hence, is limited to the classical commit protocols and does not take into account the context information such as location and time. Authors in [20] propose a context-aware transaction model and a context-driven coordination algorithm based on the acceptable final states concept. The transaction model and coordination algorithm can dynamically adapt to the context, significantly improving the success rate of MUC (Mobile Ubiquitous Computing) transactions. However, the transactional model is limited to the compensatable transactions.

The proposed approaches for context-aware service adaptation are based primarily on creating customized services by specific development of the context-awareness code. Other works propose techniques for selecting the service that suits the user's request depending on the context of use, or adaptation by service rebinding and dynamic weaving of aspects that separates the implementation of non-functional requirements from the functional ones. However, this adaptation work has not focused on the transactional aspects of context-aware services.

4 The Proposed Model

In this section, we introduce and design our context-aware transactional service model.

4.1 CATS Model

In our approach, we propose a new model for context-aware transactional services called Context-Aware Transactional Service Model (CATSM). This approach enables the implementation of context-aware services based on nested transactions models [21]. A transactional service according to CATSM is hierarchical and is based on the transaction model shown in Fig. 1. In CATSM, the global transaction can be decomposed into a set of sub-transactions TSi, for example, a travel planning service can be represented as a global transaction, while its operations flight booking, hotel, restaurant and car rental reservations can be represented by sub-transactions.

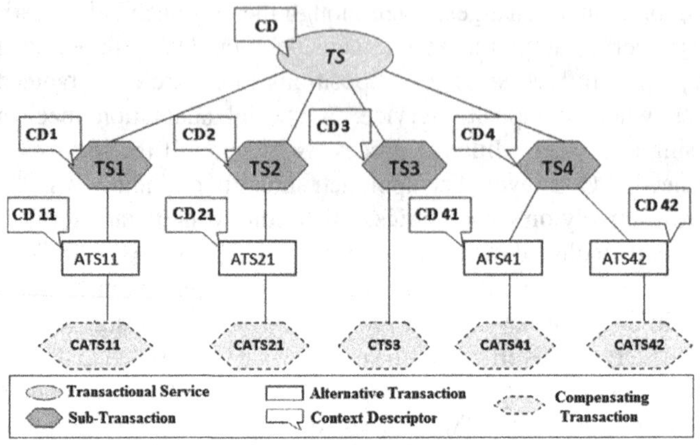

Fig. 1. Structure of context aware transactional service.

To cope with the context-awareness aspect, we associate to the global transaction a Context Descriptor (CD), which refers to the resources state and conditions of service execution environment (see Table 1). Context Descriptor is mainly representing the following sub-contexts: transactional service, user, device, environment and wireless network contexts.

a. Device sub-context: operating system, navigator type, supported type of data, screen size, battery level, available memory, computing capacity, etc.
b. User sub-context: profile, requirements, purpose, etc.
c. Environment sub-context: location, time, weather, etc.
d. Transactional service sub-context: time interval, response time, availability, response rate, etc.
e. Wireless network sub-context: connectivity, bandwidth, cost, stability, etc.

Table 1. Example of context descriptor for device sub-context.

Context parameter	State(s)
Battery level	High, moderate, low
Screen size	Large, average, small
Available memory	Available, saturated

For more flexibility and resistance to failures, a sub-transaction may be associated to alternative transactions ATSij, for example, in case of failure of the hotel booking, it is possible to book another hotel. We note that according to the context descriptor CDij of each ATSij, only one alternative will be invoked if the transaction to which it is associated has failed. In case the alternative context descriptor matches the current context, ATSij is initiated instead of the main transaction. A compensation mechanism is also invoked by adding to each sub-transaction TSi and each alternative

ATSi a compensating transaction CATSi and CTSi respectively, for example, payment transactions are compensated in case of failure. Figure 1 shows the general structure of the proposed model.

The execution mode of the global transaction, which is a combination of a set of sub-transactions, is defined according to context changes. In CATSM, we associate to each transaction a property type, namely, replayable, replaceable, compensatable and critical. These properties determine the behavioral profile of each transaction.

a. Replaceable transaction: A transaction is said to be replaceable if it may be replaced by an alternative transaction which will be invoked depending on the context descriptor.
b. Replayable transaction: A transaction is said to be replayable if it can be retried one or more times after its failure. For example, the operation of sending the reservation document can be rerun.
c. Compensatable transaction: A transaction is defined as compensatable if it provides mechanisms to undo its effects. The system must allow canceling the payment operation in case of abort of the overall transaction.
d. Critical transaction: A transaction is said to be critical if it requires the abort of the global transaction after its failure. For example, the flight reservation is a critical transaction.

Our model offers support to ensure multiple execution models that meets different levels of atomicity:

- Strict Atomicity requires that all sub-transactions vote to commit before the validation of the global transaction. This must consist only of critical and non-compensatable sub-transactions.
- Semantic Atomicity requires that the global transaction consists of critical sub-transactions, some of which can be compensatable. Compensatable sub-transactions can be committed before the completion of the global transaction. In case the latter is aborted, compensating transactions must be executed to semantically undo the effects of transactions that have been unilaterally committed.
- Relaxed Atomicity is obtained in case the global transaction consists of any combination of critical or non-critical sub-transactions, compensatable or not. If one or more non-critical sub-transactions are aborted, the overall transaction can still be committed.

4.2 CATS Definition

In our context-aware transactional service model, transaction execution and context-awareness are combined. The resulting complexity of CATS requires them to be designed prior to being implemented. Disregarding the context-awareness aspect, during the design process of transactional services, results in systems with low accommodation and inappropriate behaviors. We therefore design our CATS as follows:

$$\text{CATS} = \{(\text{TSi, TPi, CDi, CTSi, ATSi}), \text{i} \geq 1\}. \quad (1)$$

$$\text{TPi} = \{(\text{p1, p2, p3, p4})\}. \quad (2)$$

$$\text{p1} \in \{\text{Compensatable, non-Compensatable}\}. \quad (3)$$

$$\text{p2} \in \{\text{Replaceable, non-Replaceable}\}. \quad (4)$$

$$\text{p3} \in \{\text{Replayable, non-Replayable}\}. \quad (5)$$

$$\text{p4} \in \{\text{Critical, non-Critical}\}. \quad (6)$$

$$\text{CDi} = \{\text{ContextParameter} = \{\text{States}\}\}. \quad (7)$$

$$\text{ATSi} = \{(\text{ATSik, CDk, CATSik}), \text{k} \geq 1\}. \quad (8)$$

- TSi represents the sub-transaction.
- TPi is the set of transactional properties that TSi supports. It defines the behavioral profile of each transaction.
- CDi corresponds to the context descriptor. In CATS model, every transaction is associated with its context descriptor which defines the required contextual conditions of execution. For example: Battery level = {high, medium, low}.
- CTSi is the compensating transaction of TSi in case TPi contains the {compensatable} element.
- ATSi represents the list of alternative transactions that can substitute the main transaction TSi:
- ATSik is the kth alternative of TSi.
- CATSik is the compensating transaction of ATSik if it is compensatable.
- CDk is the context descriptor of ATSik.

5 CATS Adaptation Approach

Our adaptation approach is based on four main phases (see Fig. 2):

- *Capturing User's Requirements:* Our approach starts from the assumption that users submit their requests via a graphical user interface provided by our middleware platform which is installed on their devices. Each request comprehends functional requirements and user's preferences (e.g., critical tasks, execution order, recommendations, etc.). The desired degree of atomicity is semantically deducted. For instance,

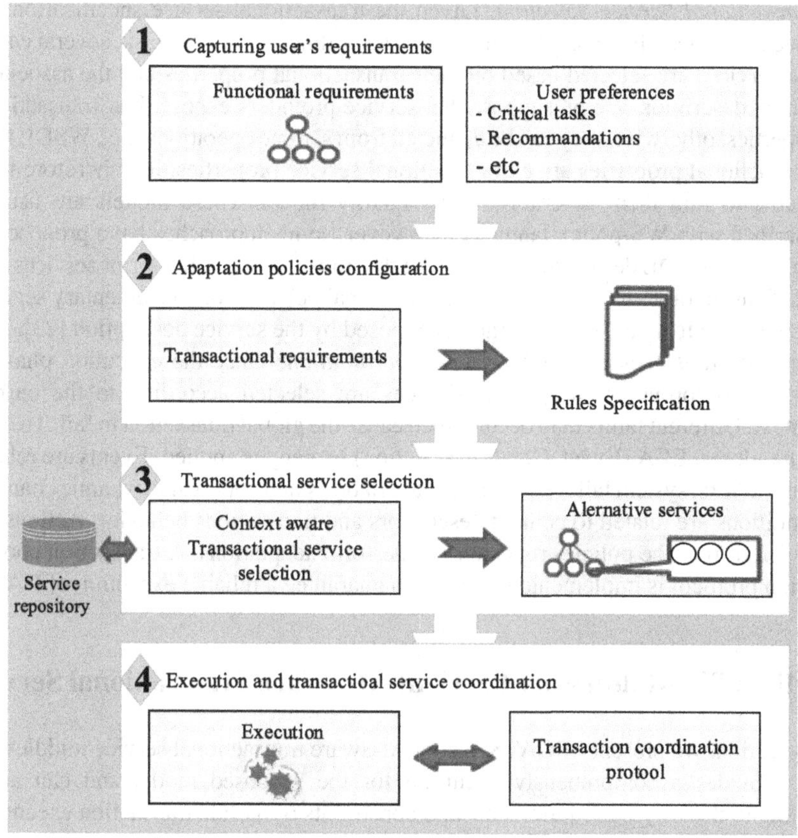

Fig. 2. Context-aware transactional service adaptation approach.

if the user prefers to book a flight, a hotel room and a table at a specific restaurant for three different persons at the same time, the atomicity degree - in this case - is strict. If the user specifies that restaurant reservation is not crucial to him, then the atomicity degree is relaxed.

– *Adaptation Policies Configuration:* Context-aware systems are generally associated with the specification of policies and rules that determine a system's behavior in response to a context state [22]. Once user's requirements are captured, we proceed to build the transactional service rules specification accordingly. Given various alternatives for a user task, it is possible to construct multiple execution plans depending on the context. Adaptation policies are described in Extensible Markup Language (XML) files. The use of XML provides a hierarchical representation of data. These structures can be easily checked, browsed and distributed. In addition, the language level of formalism remains affordable by users. Our rules specification describes (i) transactional properties and the desired degree of atomicity, (ii) CATSM structure, namely, the sub-transactions and their types, their compensating transactions, their alternatives and the associated context descriptors.

- *Transactional Service Selection:* Given the transactional service specification, we proceed to select the transactional services accordingly. For each task, several candidate services are selected based on their transactional properties and the associated context descriptor. We presuppose that service providers expose their transactional properties; otherwise, they can be deducted from service operations (i.e., WSDL file). Transactional properties are extra-functional service properties; it is therefore foreseeable to find them as criteria of its quality model. These models are usually described with WS-policy language. However, some approaches have proposed to extend the WSDL description to describe the transactional behavior of services [23, 24]. Thus, in order to determine the transactional behavior of an elementary service, it is possible to analyze the operations exposed by the service description [23].
- *Execution and Transactional Service Coordination:* Once the execution phase is started, appropriate transactional services are selected according to the current context. Different faults may occur which cause the global transaction to fail. To cope with failures, ECA (Event, Condition, Action) strategy is applied. Events are related to user errors, system failures, resources availability and contextual dynamic changes. Conditions are related to context descriptors and transactions behavior. Actions are triggered from the policies repository to perform adaptations. A transaction coordination protocol is implemented in order to guarantee a reliable execution of CATS.

6 MiCATS: Middleware for Context-Aware Transactional Service

In this section, we present MiCATS, a context-aware transactional service middleware which provides a comprehensive solution for the proposed model and can adapt according to the varying requirements and constraints of mobile transaction execution.

6.1 MiCATS Architecture

Our middleware comprehends the following components: User Request Manager, Policy Generator, Transactional Service Selector, Transaction Composition Generator, Context Manager, Adaptation Policy Manager, Decision Engine, Transaction Manager and Execution Engine. Figure 3 illustrates succinctly the middleware architecture.

- *User Request Manager:* Is responsible for parsing the user request and providing information related to the activities forming the user task and his requirements in terms of preferences and transactional properties (e.g., critical tasks, desired degree of atomicity, etc.). The component receives the user's task specification and determines its underlying activities with respect to user's preferences and the set of transactional properties imposed by the global task.
- *Policy Generator:* Once the user request manager parses the user's request, the policy generator splits the user's specification into elementary requests and interprets them to generate the appropriate policy accordingly. The desired degree of atomicity can be explicitly expressed by the user or implicitly deducted from the policy generator component according to user's recommendations. Policies describes (i) user's and

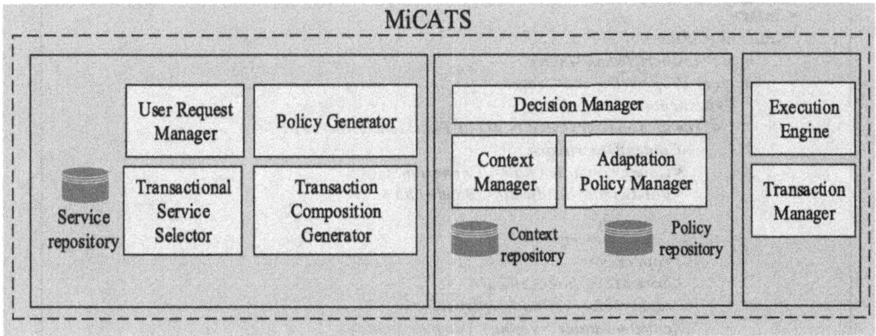

Fig. 3. MiCATS architecture.

application requirements in terms of transactional properties by specifying the desired degree of atomicity and (ii) the activities associated with the different tasks, their context descriptorsand their transactional properties. If the activity is replayable we specify the time between two attempts and the number of allowed attempts. If it is replaceable we identify a list of alternatives associated with a context descriptor which refers to the qualified context of execution in case of service substitution. Figure 4 shows the general structure of the policy specification.

- *Transactional Service Selector:* Is responsible for selecting transactional services able to fulfill the user task according to functional and non-fonctional (i.e., transactional semantics and context-awareness) points of view. The selection is based on the policy specification generated by the policy generator.
- *Transaction Composition Generator:* Produces an executable transactional service composition based on the user task specification and the selected services by the transactional service selector. Compared to policy specification where abstract user tasks are listed, the executed composition provides information needed to bind a service for each abstract activity.
- *Context Manager:* Is responsible for processing raw context data retrieved from sensors. It provides context information and the mechanisms to collect and update data in case of context changes. Context is related to the transactional service, user, device, environment and wireless network sub-contexts (Cf Sect. 4.1 CATS Model). Each activity is associated with its environment descriptor which defines the required environment conditions of execution. An *Environment Descriptor* aggregates a list of *Context Descriptor.* A Context Descriptor aggregates a list of *Context Parameter*. Figure 5 sketches the context metamodel.
- *Adaptation Policy Manager:* Is responsible for parsing the policy (XML document) and converting the adaptation rules into a data format that can be used by the decision engine. The policy is loaded at any time to support dynamic policies reconfiguration. Adaptation rules can be adjusted dynamically during the execution time taking into account user's requirements and application semantics, but also to optionally expand the required context.
- *Decision Engine:* Based on ECA strategy, the decision engine interprets the adaptation policy based on the context state information provided by the context manager

```
<Rules>
 <Rule id ="Rule-ID ">
   <name>PropertyName</name>
   <degree>PropertyDegree</degree>
     <TransactionalServiceList>
       <TransactionalService id ="ID-of-TransactionalService1 ">
         <ContextDescriptor>
           <ConnexionState>state</ConnexionState>
           <Bandwidth>bandwidth</Bandwidth>
           .........
         </ContextDescriptor>
         <Properties>
           <critical>yes/no</critical>
           <replayable> yes/no</replayable>
           <compensatable> yes/no</compensatable>
           <replaceable> yes/no</ replaceable >
          </Properties>
        <replay>
         <ActivationNumber>NumberOfAttempts</ ActivationNumber >
         <ActivationPeriod>PeriodBetweenAttempts</ ActivationPeriod >
           <replay>
           <replaceBy>
             <AlternativeList>
               <Alternative id ="ID-of-Alternative1 ">
                 <ContextDescriptor>
                   <ConnexionState>state</ConnexionState>
                   <Bandwidth>bandwidth</Bandwidth>
                     ............
                 </ContextDescriptor>
                <Compensation id ="ID-of-compensating-Alternative ">
                 </Compensation>
               </Alternative>
               <Alternative id ="ID-of-Alternative2 ">
                 <ContextDescriptor>
                   <ConnexionState>state</ConnexionState>
                   <Bandwidth>bandwidth</Bandwidth>
                     ............
                 </ContextDescriptor>
               </Alternative>
             </AlternativeList>
           </replaceBy>
           <Compensation id ="ID-of-compensating-Transaction">
           </Compensation>
        </TransactionalService>
        <TransactionalService id ="ID-of-TransactionalService2 ">
              <ContextDescriptor>
                 ............
              </ContextDescriptor>
          ..........
             </TransactionalService>
     </TransactionalServiceList>
   </Rule>
     </Rules>
```

Fig. 4. CATS rules specification.

and the inspecting result of the policy manager to trigger the execution of the appropriate adaptation. The rule processing is performed at the time of loading, time of the transaction initiation or its failure (e.g., to be either rerun or to run an alternative) and when a change in the context state occurs. Based on the context state and the data retrieved from the rule, the module decides which strategy will be triggered (e.g., identify the alternative transaction to run).

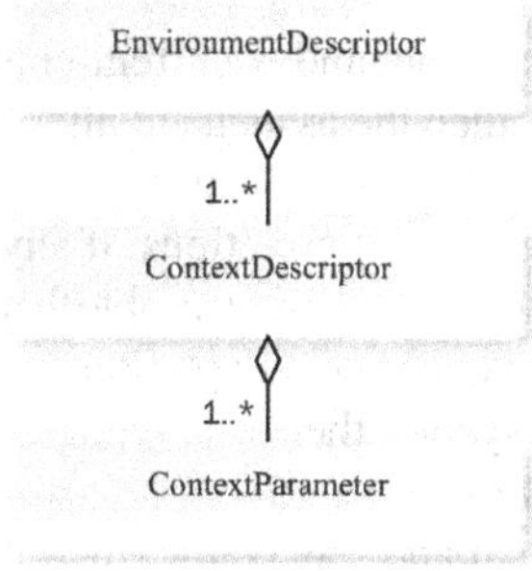

Fig. 5. Context meta-model.

- *Execution Engine:* Is responsible for running transactional service composition with respect to the decision engine instructions and substituting the failed services of a running composition according to the adaptation policy strategy.
- *Transaction Manager (Coordinator):* Once the execution engine starts running the transactional service composition, the main coordinator TSC handles the processing of the global transaction TS, then it submits the sub-transactions to the sub-coordinators TSCi, which are associated with the different TSi services. Each TSCi is running its TSi service and exchanges messages with the main coordinator.

In order to increase transaction commit rate, the transation execution protocol is based on two main phases:

a. Verification of the required context: The main coordinator TSC sends a message to each sub-Coordinator TSCi to check the required context for execution. If the current context is qualified, TSCi sends a 'yes' message to the TSC telling that the transaction can be normally executed. If not, TSCi sends a 'no' message to the TSC. The following program is designed to verify the qualified context:

Program 1. Procedure for verifying the required context.

```
      Input: TS={TSi, i>=1}
      Input: CC[] Current context
      Outputs: Result[]  result array
Procedure verify-context( TS, CC)
    Begin
       For each sub-coordinator TSCi
        loop
          If ( CC is qualified )
                Result[i]= 'yes';
          Else
                Result[i]= 'no';
        End loop;
        Return result;
    End;
```

b. Commit phase: In the previous phase, if one of the sub-coordinators TSCi responds that the current context is not qualified, the decision will be as follows:

- If the transaction is replaceable and if current context corresponds to the alternative context descriptor then the associated alternative is executed.
- If the transaction is critical then the main transaction is aborted (in case of failure). In this situation, the committed transactions, if any, will be compensated.
- If the transaction is neither critical nor replaceable then the transaction is just ignored.

In case the current context is qualified, adaptation actions are as expressed below:

- If the transaction is replayable, then it is replayed according to the number of attempts (in case of failure).
- If the transaction is critical and replayable, then it is replayed according to the number of attempts and re-execution parameters are updated (in case of failure).

Figure 6 illustrates the commit phase. To simplify the process, we deemed useful to describe the state diagram in the case of one sub-coordinator TSCi.

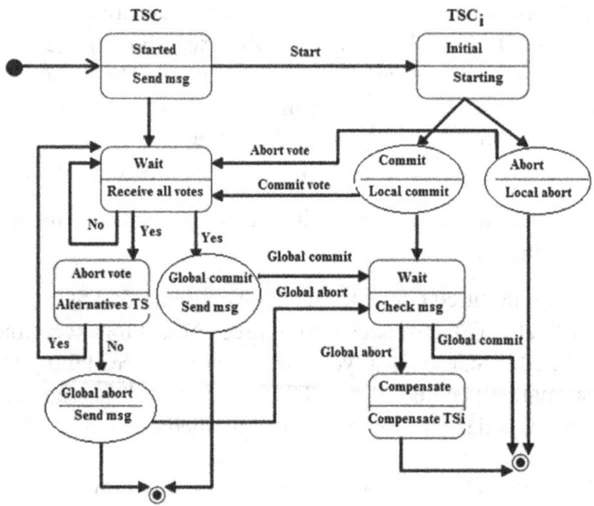

Fig. 6. State diagram of the proposed protocol.

The TSC stores information about the overall transaction in log files and sends a "Start" message to TSCi to initiate the sub-transactions TSi. The TSC goes to "wait" state while waiting for TSCi messages. TSCi records information about TSi transaction in the log file. The TSi execution result (commit or abort) is recorded in the log file (Local commit or Local abort) and sent to TSC to make the decision. TSC receives the votes of all TSCi. If all TSCi vote to commit, the TSC forces the commit of the global transaction (Global commit) and sends the message to the sub-coordinators. In case one of the sub-transactions is not committed, if it is replaceable, the corresponding TSCi initiates the alternative transaction and sends the result to the TSC. If it is not replaceable but critical, the overall transaction will be aborted (Global abort). If TSCi receives an abort message from TSC for the global transaction, compensating transactions will be executed. All execution results are recorded in the log files.

7 Illustrative Scenario

Let's consider a travel planning system. Mr John plans to attend an art show scheduled in Marrakech. For this, he intends to book a flight, a hotel room, a restaurant table, and a place in the art show. Reservations are not of equal importance, and the restaurant table reservation can for example be omitted from the transaction. In case of the abort of the overall transaction, the partial validated results require the execution of compensating transactions. We should note that each reservation consists of three operations,

```
<Rules>
 <Rule id ="Rule-ID">
   <name>PropertyName</name>
   <degree>PropertyDegree</degree>
     <TransactionalServiceList>
       <TransactionalService id ="ID-of-TransactionalService1">
          <ContextDescriptor>
            <ConnexionState>state</ConnexionState>
            <Bandwidth>bandwidth</Bandwidth>
             ............
          </ContextDescriptor>
          <Properties>
            <critical>yes/no</critical>
            <replayable> yes/no</replayable>
            <compensatable> yes/no</compensatable>
            <replaceable> yes/no</ replaceable >
           </Properties>
          <replay>
           <ActivationNumber>NumberOfAttempts</ ActivationNumber >
           <ActivationPeriod>PeriodBetweenAttempts</ ActivationPeriod >
            <replay>
            <replaceBy>
              <AlternativeList>
                <Alternative id ="ID-of-Alternative1">
                   <ContextDescriptor>
                      <ConnexionState>state</ConnexionState>
                      <Bandwidth>bandwidth</Bandwidth>
                        ...............
                   </ContextDescriptor>
                  <Compensation id ="ID-of-compensating-Alternative">
                   </Compensation>
                </Alternative>
                <Alternative id ="ID-of-Alternative2">
                   <ContextDescriptor>
                      <ConnexionState>state</ConnexionState>
                      <Bandwidth>bandwidth</Bandwidth>
                        ...............
                   </ContextDescriptor>
                </Alternative>
              </AlternativeList>
            </replaceBy>
            <Compensation id ="ID-of-compensating-Transaction">
            </Compensation>
          </TransactionalService>
          <TransactionalService id ="ID-of-TransactionalService2">
                 <ContextDescriptor>
                   ...............
                 </ContextDescriptor>
            ...............
              </TransactionalService>
      </TransactionalServiceList>
   </Rule>
      </Rules>
```

Fig. 7. Example of CATS rules specification.

namely, the booking operation, the payment transaction, and the sending of a specific document for every reservation.

This system is a well-known scenario of a long-running transaction that requires extra ACID properties. The compliance with the rules imposed by the ACID model is no longer recommended in such a situation since a simple change of context (e.g., low battery or a change in the connection state) can induce the abort of the overall transaction. Thus, it is desirable in the transaction management, that a transaction can respond to contextual information and adapt its behavior to the context changes.

Figure 7 illustrates an example of rules specification:

As shown in Fig. 7, the flight reservation is a critical transaction. In other words, this sub-transaction is a crucial task for the travel planning application. Let's imagine that a change in the context occurs during the flight reservation transaction due to a disconnection event. According to CATS specification displayed below, flight reservation is a replaceable transaction that may be replaced by an alternative transaction which corresponds to the required execution context. In this case, the adaptation strategy is to execute *FlightReservationAgencyA* on local device and synchronize once reconnected (i.e., adaptation action) whenever the transaction is *replaceable*, *connection state* is disconnected, *memory* is available to store data and *bandwidth* is medium (i.e., adaptation condition).

8 Conclusion

The latest decades have been marked by the rapid development of distributed information systems, and particularly by the extraordinary increase of mobile Internet-enabled devices. Many transactional models were developed to overcome the constraints induced by the evolution of distributed systems towards wireless and cellular data networks.

In this paper, we propose a solution to the problems of transactional applications flexibility in order to allow adaptation to different types of transactional execution models according to the environment characteristics which are described in context descriptors and the application semantics. This adaptation is based on the specification of policies that provide the ability to replay, the choice of alternative transactions and compensation actions depending on the context. For this, we propose a flexible and adaptable support for context-aware transactional services introducing the "CATS" model. This model allows the specification of the transactional service and is the basis for all techniques that will be developed. A context-aware middleware "MiCATS" for the support of the adaptability is also designed. The main contributions of this middleware are (i) a transaction model that provides shared qualification of context and transactional behaviors in service-oriented environments, (ii) a context-aware transactional service design approach allowing to build the transactional service structure able to fulfill the user functional and non-functional requirements, and (iii) a policy-driven adaptation approach to cope with context fluctuations during the execution of transactions.

In order to improve the actual state of our middleware, we mainly focus on validating our policy-driven adaptation approach experimentally. We are interested in studying the response time of our ECA based algorithm with respect to timeliness requirements in context-aware environments.

References

1. Elmagarmid, A.K.: Database Transaction Models for Advanced Applications. Morgan-Kaufmann, San Francisco (1992)
2. Chrysanthis, P.K., Ramamrithan, K.: Synthesis of extended transaction models using ACTA. ACM Trans. Database Syst. (TODS). **19**(3), 450–491 (1994)
3. Segun, K., Hurson, A.R., Spink, A.: A transaction processing model for the mobile data access system. In: Malyshkin, V.E. (ed.) PaCT 2001. LNCS, vol. 2127, pp. 112–127. Springer, Heidelberg (2001)
4. Radu, V.: Application. In: Radu, V. (ed.) Stochastic Modeling of Thermal Fatigue Crack Growth. ACM, vol. 1, pp. 63–70. Springer, Heidelberg (2015)
5. Sun, C., Hammer, D., Biemolt, G., Groefsema, H.: Web service transactions: an evaluation of description and management standards and languages. Version: 1.0, Technical report, July 2006
6. OASIS Committee specifications: Business Transaction Protocol, version 1.0 (2002)
7. Schafer, M., Dolog, P., Nejdl, W.: An environment for flexible advanced compensations of web service transactions. ACM Trans. Web TWEB **2**(2), 1–36 (2008)
8. Lakhal, N., Kobayashi, T., Toyota, H.: FENECIA: failure endurable nested-transaction based execution of composite web services with incorporated state analysis. VLDB J. **1**, 1–56 (2009)
9. Choi, S., Kim, H., Jang, H., Kim, J., Kim, S.M., Song, J., Lee, Y.: A framework for ensuring consistency of web services transactions. Inf. Softw. Technol. J. **50**, 684–696 (2008)
10. Schilit, B., Theimer, M.: Disseminating active map information to mobile hosts. IEEE Netw. **8**(5), 22–32 (1994)
11. Dey, A., Abowd, G., Salber, D.: Conceptual framework and a toolkit for supporting the rapid prototyping of context-aware applications. Hum. Comput. Interact. **16**(2), 97–166 (2001)
12. Gray, J., Reuter, A.: Transaction Processing: Concepts and Techniques Series in Data Management Systems. Morgan Kaufmann, San Francisco (1993)
13. Younas, M., Mostefaoui, S.K.: Context-aware mobile services transactions. In: 24th IEEE International Conference on Advanced Information Networking and Applications, AINA 2010, Perth, Australia, pp. 705–712 (2010)
14. El Haddad, J., Manouvrier, M., Ramirez, G., Rukoz, M.: QoS-driven selection of web services for transactional composition. In: IEEE International Conference on Web Services, ICWS 2008, pp. 653–660 (2008)
15. Hafiddi, H., Baidouri, H., Nassar, M., ElAsri, B., Kriouile, A.: A Context-aware service centric approach for service oriented architectures. In: 13th International Conference on Enterprise Information Systems, ICEIS 2011, vol. 3, pp. 8–11, Beijing, China (2011)
16. Serrano-Alvarado, P., Roncancio, C., Adiba, M., Labbé, C.: Context aware mobile transactions. In: IEEE International Conference on Mobile Data Management (2004)
17. Strunk, A., Reichert, S., Schill, A.: An infrastructure for supporting rebinding in BPEL processes. In: 13th IEEE Enterprise Distributed Object Computing Conference Workshops, EDOCW 2009, pp. 230–237 (2009)

18. Muralidharan, K., Karthik, G.V., Gupta, P., Chowdhury, A.R.: mConnect: a context aware mobile transaction middleware. In: 3rd International Conference on Communication Systems Software and Middleware and Workshops, COMSWARE 2008, Bangalore, India, pp. 381–386 (2008)
19. Merle, P., Serrano-Alvarado, P., Rouvoy, R.: Towards context-aware transaction services. In: Eliassen, F., Montresor, A. (eds.) DAIS 2006. LNCS, vol. 4025, pp. 272–288. Springer, Heidelberg (2006)
20. Tang, F., Guo, M., Li, M.: An adaptative context aware transaction model for mobile and ubiquitous computing. Comput. Inform. **27**(5), 785–798 (2008)
21. Moss, J.E.B., Hosking, A.L.: Nested transactional memory: model and architecture sketches. Sci. Comput. Program. **632**, 186–201 (2006)
22. Baldauf, M., Dustdar, S.: A survey on context-aware systems. Int. J. Ad Hoc Ubiquit. Comput. **2**(4), 263–277 (2007)
23. Micalsen, T., Tai, S., Ravellou, I.: Transactional attitudes: reliable compositions of autonomous web services. In: Workshop on Dependable Middleware Based Systems, March 2002
24. Pires, P.F., Benevides, M.R., Mattoso, M.: Building reliable web services compositions. In: Chaudhri, A.B., Jeckle, M., Rahm, E., Unland, R. (eds.) NODe-WS 2002. LNCS, vol. 2593, pp. 59–72. Springer, Heidelberg (2003)

Human-Computer Interaction

A Wearable Face Recognition System Built into a Smartwatch and the Blind and Low Vision Users

Laurindo de Sousa Britto Neto[1,2(✉)], Vanessa Regina Margareth Lima Maike[2], Fernando Luiz Koch[3], Maria Cecília Calani Baranauskas[2], Anderson de Rezende Rocha[2], and Siome Klein Goldenstein[2]

[1] Department of Computing, Federal University of Piauí (UFPI), Teresina, Brazil
laurindoneto@ufpi.edu.br

[2] Institute of Computing, University of Campinas (UNICAMP), Campinas, Brazil
vanessa.maike@gmail.com, {cecilia,rocha,siome}@ic.unicamp.br

[3] Samsung Research Institute, Campinas, Brazil
fernando.koch@samsung.com

Abstract. Assistive technologies need to be affordable, ergonomic and easy to use. In this work we argue that smartwatches could be assistive devices for the visually impaired, if they have the potential to run complex applications. Hence, in this paper we propose a face recognition system to show that it's technically possible to develop a real-time computer vision system in a wearable device with limited hardware, since such systems generally require powerful hardware. A case study is presented using the first generation Samsung Galaxy Gear smartwatch. The system runs only on the watch's hardware and consists in a face detection and recognition software that emits an audio feedback so that visually impaired users know who is around them. The case study includes an evaluation of the proposal with users. Results are shown and discussed validating the technological aspects of the proposal and pointing out room for improving the aspects of interaction.

Keywords: Human-Computer interaction · Assistive technology · Computer vision · Accessibility · Wearable device · Wearable system

1 Introduction

In 2013, the World Health Organization estimated that 285 million people worldwide have visual disabilities, of which 39 million are blind and 246 million have low vision [32]. Daily tasks such as walking, reading and recognizing objects or people may be very difficult or even impossible for those who are blind or have low vision. Technology can assist the visually impaired in some of these tasks, providing them more autonomy and social inclusion. In particular, the field of Computer Vision has a lot to contribute to Assistive Technologies [18], since, in a way, it allows a machine to replace the user's lost sight. In this paper, we focus on the twofold challenge of running a facial recognition in a wearable device to assist visually impaired users in recognizing people who are in their surroundings. One part of the challenge lies in the technological aspects of the

S. Hammoudi et al. (Eds.): ICEIS 2015, LNBIP 241, pp. 515–528, 2015.
DOI: 10.1007/978-3-319-29133-8_25

proposal, and the other part lies in the socio-technical aspects, i.e., the interaction between the user, the technology and everything else in the context of use.

For instance, imagine a scenario in which a visually impaired person walks into an environment where silence and discretion are required, such as a work meeting or a library. Under usual circumstances she would have to disrupt the silence to know who are the other people present in the environment. However, with the use of a face recognition system embedded into a wearable device, the user could accomplish the task with the required discretion. For this to be possible, it would be necessary, on the technological end, to have efficient facial recognition algorithms installed into a hardware that has compatible processing power and that is small enough to be wearable. On the socio-technical end, the feedbacks provided by the system to the user would have to be easily understandable, efficient and discrete; the camera present in the device could not invade the privacy of the people surrounding the user or make them uncomfortable; finally, the way in which the user would wear the devices could not cause embarrassment.

The described system may seem impossible to accomplish, but in the next few sections, we will present a proof of concept that shows how it is technically possible to develop a simple, yet quite effective, real-time face recognition system, running in a wearable device with low processing power. We will also present initial user tests that show the interaction between people and the proposed system, investigating the potential gains users can have from the system. The wearable platform we use here is the first generation Samsung Galaxy Gear smartwatch. As this model is not the newest, it has less powerful hardware than the later ones, and it is assumed that if the system works well in the limited device, it should work better in the more advanced ones. The Galaxy Gear wristwatch features a 1.9 Megapixel camera on the wrist band, which is good enough for the system we propose. Additionally, having the camera attached to the wrist allows the smartwatch to be used in hands-free operations.

Our prototype uses a library of known subjects that need to be registered prior to recognition – we do not use Internet or social-media searches to find potential matches. The smartwatch constantly acquires images, analyzes them in search of a person's face, and then gives audio feedback of that analysis. In the case of an unknown face, the system allows the registration of a new instance of an existing person, or of a new individual. Since the first generation of the Galaxy Gear runs the Android OS, the system also ran even better on a Samsung Galaxy Note 3 smartphone.

This paper is organized as follows: Sect. 2 describes the literature in the face recognition area focusing on wearable devices in the aid of the visually impaired, with a variety of different approaches; Sect. 3 describes the device used in our case study; Sect. 4 describes the developed system; Sect. 5 describes the dataset used and the experiments performed as a preliminary evaluation of the system; and Sect. 6 concludes this work and points out further work.

2 Related Work

We have performed a search on digital libraries looking for papers that approach the problem of using wearable devices to aid the visually impaired. In this section we present an overview of the works we found, in order to characterize the current state of the art of the problem we are trying to solve.

Pun et al. (2007) [22] present a survey on assistive devices for sight-handicapped people. The survey covers works that use video processing for converting visual data into an alternative rendering modality, such as auditory or haptic. Most of these studies focuses on daily tasks such as navigation and object detection, but not on people recognition.

We can see an extensive literature review on face recognition for biometrics in [26] and [35] – the literature focusing on accessibility is more scarce. Krishna et al. (2005) [15] developed a pair of sunglasses with a pinhole camera, which uses the Principal Component Analysis (PCA) algorithm [13] for face recognition. The idea is to be able to later evolve the system from face to emotion, gesture and facial expressions recognition. The sunglasses system was validated with a highly controlled dataset, which uses a precisely calibrated mechanism to provide robust face recognition.

Kramer et al. (2010) [14] present a smartphone that provides audible feedback whenever a face from a database enters or exits the scene. Their detection algorithm runs in a server that uses the VeriLook face technology [20]. In contrast, in our system, the face recognition algorithms are running within the wearable device itself.

Astler et al. (2011) [2] used a camera atop a standard white cane to perform face recognition using the Luxand FaceSDK [17], and to identify six kinds of facials expressions using the Seeing Machines FaceAPI[1].

Tanveer et al. (2012) [25] developed a system called FEPS, which uses Constrained Local Model algorithm for facial expressions recognition providing audible feedback, and Fusco et al. (2012) [9] proposed a method which combines face matching and identity verification modules in feedback.

As we see in the survey [22], there are several studies conducted to create more assistive devices for the blind and low-vision people. Few reports are presented on systems that make use of smartwatch. The first is the FreevoxTouch [8], a smartwatch created for the visually impaired that runs on an Android platform. Currently, it has the following functions: speaking watch, memorecorder, music player and a stopwatch/countdown. The smartwatch is entirely controlled through a touch screen, and all clock functions can be set to have an audio feedback.

Porzi et al. (2013) [21] developed a gesture recognition system for a smartwatch that increases its usability and accessibility to assist people with visual disabilities. The user presses the smartwatch's display to start the gesture input. Then, the user performs a gesture and the signals generated by the smartwatch's integrated accelerometers are sent via Bluetooth to a smartphone. These signals are processed and then the system recognizes the gesture and activates the corresponding function. When the task is completed, the user receives vibration feedback. Moreover, the system has two modules: one for identifying wet floor signs and one for automatic recognition of predefined logos. A downside of it is that the smartwatch cannot be directly programmed.

Watanabe et al. (2014) [29] proposed an activity and context recognition method in which the user carries a neck-worn receiver comprising a microphone, and small

[1] http://www.seeingmachines.com/.

speakers on his wrists that generate ultrasounds. The system uses the volume of the received sound and the Doppler effect to recognize gestures. The system recognizes the place where the user is in and the nearby people by ID signals generated by speakers placed in rooms and on people. The authors presented the device and considered that the proposed method can be used with the Samsung Galaxy Gear smartwatch.

2.1 Face Recognition

In order to succeed, real face-recognition systems have to perform, really well, a series of complex tasks. Usually they have to detect faces, normalize them, extract descriptors, and then perform the recognition. Not all steps are present in every system, and in some methods the extraction of descriptors and the face-recognition are done together.

The most commonly used face detector is the presented by Viola and Jones (2004) [28]. Introduced first in the 2001 Conference on Computer Vision and Pattern Recognition CVPR, it presents a real-time robust algorithm for face detection and face tracking that uses Haar functions, integral images, and boosting on weak classifiers, ultimately offering efficiency and requiring less computational complexity.

Dalal and Trigg (2005) [7] developed a descriptor named Histogram of Oriented Gradients (HOG), used to describe characteristics of objects of interest based on image gradients and borders. Other descriptors that use spatio-temporal information are the Local Binary Pattern (LBP) [1] and its variations, such as the Volume Local Binary Pattern (VLBP) [34], and the Extended VLBP (EVLBP) [11].

There are several classic face recognition methods, such as the Eigenfaces [27] and the Fisherfaces [4] based in PCA. They were not used in our proposal because they would add complexity to the processes of adding new people to the database and of determining the distance threshold for recognition. An initial analysis showed that the trade-off between this complexity and the possible performance gains did not pay off.

Li et al. (2013) [16] proposed a complex framework that used a multi-modal sparse coding approach to utilize depth information for face recognition. Other approaches using infrared images [5, 30] and 3D depth maps [10] were also explored to achieve face recognition. Research about the possibility of analyzing face images by modelling local facial features [31] were performed.

3 Case Study

Our case study is based on a face recognition system we built into the Samsung Galaxy Gear (GEAR – Fig. 1). The GEAR is a smart device shaped wristwatch (smartwatch) equipped with a 800 MHz processor, 512 MB RAM, 4 GB internal memory, the Android 4.2.2 operating system, two microphones, a speaker, Bluetooth and a 1.9 Megapixel camera on the wristband. It was developed to be used together with the Samsung Galaxy Note 3 smartphone, so the user can perform smartphone tasks through the smartwatch, such as make calls or send text messages. The two devices communicate by Bluetooth, and every audio feedback can be heard through their sound outputs or through a stereo Bluetooth headset. This wearable device also comes with the Samsung S Voice application installed, a software that allows the user to issue voice commands, making it an interesting tool for visually impaired users.

Moreover, the GEAR has accelerometer and gyroscope sensors, making possible the use of a gesture recognition system like in [21]. This is especially useful in situations where the interaction through voice commands may not be used (such as during a meeting), or when they may not work properly (such as crowded scenarios or noisy environments).

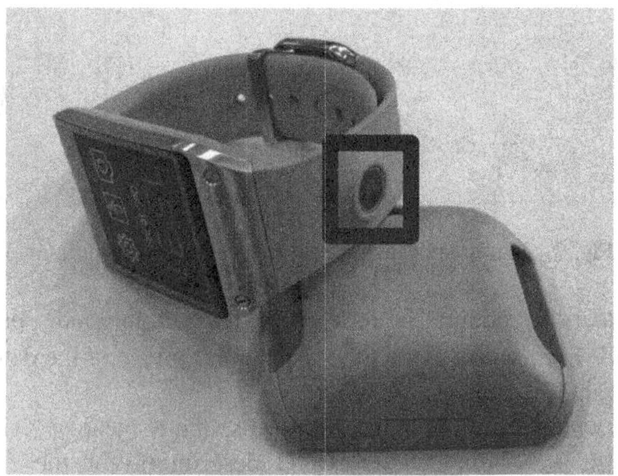

Fig. 1. The smartwatch used in our case study and its camera on the wristband (featured).

4 System Overview

The face recognition system we developed was named Gear Face Recognition (GFR), and it is aimed at helping visually impaired users recognizing people in their vicinity. The interaction flow with the application is the following: First, the user must open the app. There are two ways of doing this: through the S Voice application, or by setting a shortcut to open the application. In the first case, it is necessary to run S Voice by pressing the smartwatch's physical power/home button twice, and then giving the voice command associated to the app. In the second case, the user simply touches the top of the watch's display and slides it down. When the GFR opens, an audio feedback indicates that the app is running.

Then, the system uses the camera of the GEAR to perceive the user's surroundings. As soon as a face is detected, an audio feedback is given, indicating that a person's face is being framed by the camera. In this moment, the user and the camera have to stand still for a few seconds, to finish the framing. Next, the system performs the face recognition and provides an audio feedback that characterizes the identified person, such as a ringtone, a sound, or a personalized voice recording. Subjects must be previously registered in the system for the face recognition and a different audio can be associated to each person. Unknown subjects are mapped to a common audio feedback.

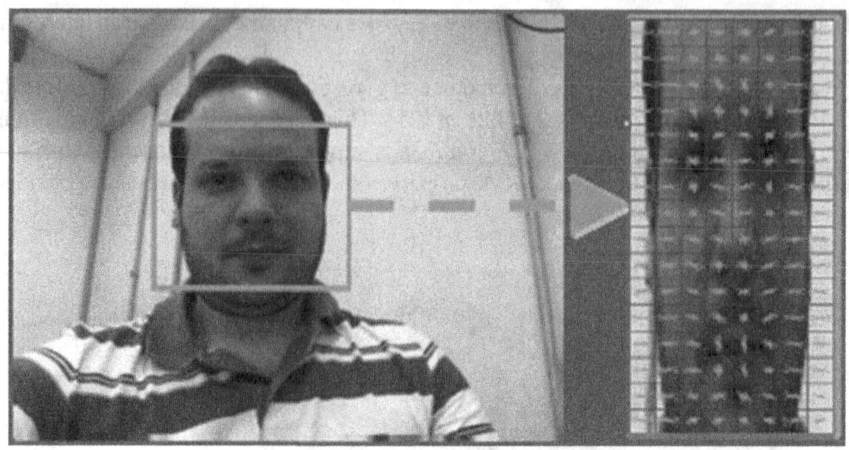

Fig. 2. Example of image conversion in HOG descriptor.

Our face detection module is based on the sample code provided by the OpenCV4Android[2] library. We extract the rectangular image of the detected face (face image) in video frames.

To run on the watch's limited hardware, we use the K-Nearest Neighbors (K-NN) algorithm [6] with 3,780-dimensional HOG descriptors for the face recognition approach. Figure 2 illustrates this conversion. The value of hyperparameter K can be set according to the amount of registered samples per person. Initially, as a default value we use $K = 1$, as we have only few samples per person.

HOG descriptors have shown good results to represent features set for face identification [23]. Moreover, HOG has a controllable degree of invariance to local geometric transformations, providing invariance to translations and rotations smaller than the local spatial or orientation bin size [7].

To improve the accuracy of the K-NN, we used temporal coherence over the video's sequential frames (sliding window) – we classify each frame within the temporal sliding window, and the most voted person is the final classification. Figure 3 summarizes the system architecture pipeline.

When the unknown person class wins the voting, the person being recognized may be classified as "unknown". A vote is computed for the unknown class when the distance from the sample to all the nearest neighbors is greater than a threshold distance. The threshold was set empirically based on observations of the distance values. The rationale behind this decision is that distances between samples from the same person tend to be smaller than the distances between samples from different people. The value for the threshold distance may vary depending on the camera resolution. The higher the quality and resolution of images captured by the camera, the smaller the threshold distance value. A more formal analysis shows that this hypothesis assumes that the classes are separable by a plane in the HOG high-dimensional space.

[2] http://opencv.org/platforms/android.html.

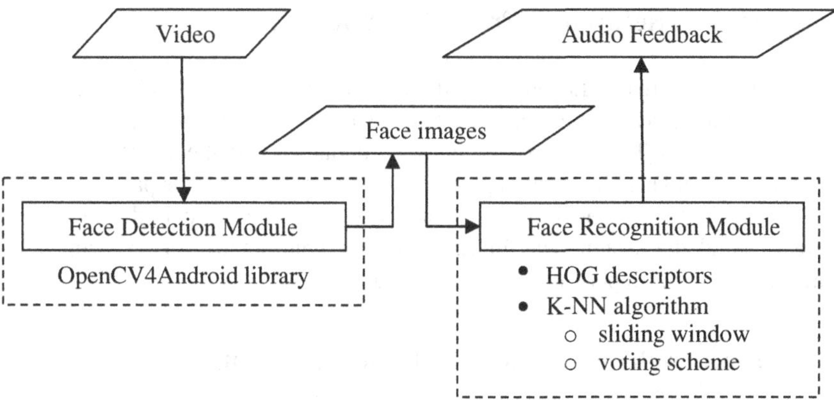

Fig. 3. System architecture pipeline of our approach.

We created a prototype with a simple interface for user interaction (Fig. 4). When the system detects an unknown face (unknown sample), we can add this sample to a new person or to an already registered person, simply by touching the smartwatch's display to capture the face being framed. If a new person is being registered, then the system asks to record an audio to associate with that person. To do so, we simply touch the display to start recording and then touch it again to finish.

If an already registered person is not recognized by the system, there is the possibility of adding new samples to that person's database. This serves to increase the robustness of the face recognition performed by the K-NN by adding new samples of the same person to the dataset, increasing the variability of the data for the same person. From the description, it is possible to note that the registration interface is not yet ready for visually impaired users. However, studies are being conducted to change that.

Fig. 4. Gear Face Recognition: an unknown person (left), adding a sample (center) and a recognized person (right).

5 Experiment Setup and Preliminary Results

Two experiments were conducted: 1) a pilot experiment with blindfolded users, representing people who have recently acquired the visual impairment, and 2) an experiment with low vision users. The pilot experiment was conducted with the intent of finding out critical technical and user interaction problems, and of adjusting some parameters of the same experiment before performing it with the real visually impaired. For this, and keeping in mind the system was in early development stages, the experiment was conducted with subjects performing the required actions.

5.1 Experiment with Blindfolded Users (Pilot Experiment)

The step-by-step of the experiment was the following:

1. A total of 15 subjects participated, 13 were registered in the database, leaving two to act as unknown;
2. For each registered user, five pictures were taken: one from a very short distance and four from the threshold distance. Of these four, two were sideways (one for each side) and two were frontal (one with a normal expression and one with a smile);
3. A participant was chosen to act as a blind user: first, the participants were taught how to open the GFR application, then they were blindfolded and, finally, they received a cane and instructions on what to do next;
4. In silence, four random participants were chosen to be placed in front of the blindfolded person, side-by-side and with their backs to a white wall (the same place where the samples were taken). At least one of these four people was not registered in the database, to act as unknown.;
5. Once the blindfolded subject was asked to start, the timer was set off and s/he had to enter the GFR application and recognize each one of the four people in front of them, by their name or as unknown. To facilitate, the blindfolded user started facing the four people to be recognized and was positioned in the threshold distance from them;
6. For each person the blindfolded user recognized, s/he had to say aloud who s/he understood that person was. This was necessary so that the accuracy rate could be calculated, especially in cases where framing issues caused problems, such as giving different feedbacks about the same person. Once all four people were recognized, the blindfolded user indicated s/he was done, and the timer was stopped;
7. The participant was kept blindfolded and taken back to the starting position. Steps 4 to 6 were repeated twice, with other two different groups of four people;
8. Steps 3 to 7 were repeated with a different blindfolded subject.

The previously described procedure was followed with 5 blindfolded participants, with the exception of the last participant, for whom the smartwatch's battery ran out before a third round could be executed. Additionally, another participant gave up before recognizing all four people, since s/he was not able to find one of them. Taking these two cases into account, in the end the experiment amounted to a total of 55 predictions, of which 46 were correct, giving an accuracy rate of 83.64 %.

Therefore, in terms of algorithms, the GFR system presented a high accuracy rate and a satisfactory performance.

Regarding the user interaction, several problems were raised during the recognition stages, especially considering the context of accessibility. The main complaints revolved around the audio feedback, as it presented only two types of feedback: one to indicate the application was framing a person's face and another to provide the result of the recognition (either a voice recording with the person's name or "unknown"). The "framing" feedback is a clue that the user needs to keep the wristwatch still, so that the system can analyze the captured face and, a few seconds later, provide the result of the recognition. However, the "framing" feedback was sometimes a false clue, either because the camera was not capturing a face or because the face being captured could not be analyzed. This caused frustration, as the blindfolded participant had to keep the arm elevated and bent at the elbow, to point the wristwatch's camera forward. This caused fatigue to be another issue reported by all users that were blindfolded, since after each round it became more and more tiresome to keep the arm elevated.

Despite these problems, a positive aspect of the user interaction was found by analyzing the times the blindfolded users took in each round of recognizing a group of four people. As it is possible to see in Table 1, every participant had their worst performance in their first round, when they were still learning to use the GFR application. Then, most of them have their best performance on the second round and an average one on the last round. "Blindfolded 3" was an exception because the application crashed on his last round, costing him some time. However, it is interesting to note that the average time for Round 2 was very close to the time of the expert (researcher that was already well-familiarized with the system and performed one round within the shown time). Additionally, the average for the first round is the highest and the average for the last round is the intermediate. Therefore, the decrease of average times from Round 1 to Round 2 indicates that the later interactions were easier, suggesting the system is easy to learn how to use. The increase in average times from Round 2 to Round 3 suggests the already mentioned fatigue issue.

Table 1. Time taken for each round of people recognition in the pilot experiment.

	TIME (MM:SS)		
	Round 1	Round 2	Round 3
Blindfolded 1	03:45	01:54	02:00
Blindfolded 2	02:36	02:00	01:30
Blindfolded 3	02:02	01:23	03:16
Blindfolded 4	04:26	01:17	01:24
Blindfolded 5	02:05	01:20	
Average	03:17	01:35	02:02

*Expert's Time = 01:29

Finally, the matter of the battery running out should be addressed. The experiment lasted about 2 h, including the time taken to register the 13 users in the database. Considering that the GFR system is intended to serve as an assistive technology for the visually impaired, battery life is a critical issue. However, we highlight the fact that the smartwatch's screen was turned on the entire time, to allow the researchers to analyze the application's behavior. In real contexts of use the screen would most likely be used very sparingly, increasing the battery life time.

5.2 Experiment with Low Vision Users

This experiment was conducted by following the same steps described for the pilot experiment, except that:

- A total of eleven people participated; nine were registered in the database and two were left to act as unknown;
- Two subjects with different high degrees of visual impairment (low vision) were the users of the GFR system. They wore their glasses during the experiment, which had different degrees for each eye. The first user's glasses have 12 degrees in the left eye and 23 degrees in the right eye, while the second user's have 15 degrees in the left eye and 16 degrees in the right eye;
- Due to time limitations, each user performed only one round of experiment.

In the end, the experiment amounted to a total of eight predictions. Five of these were correct, giving an accuracy rate of 62.50 %. The small amount of predictions made in this experiment (8) does not allow comparison to the pilot experiment.

On the positive side, low vision users reported that the system is easy to use and that it really helped them to recognize people. Although they use glasses (during the experiment and on a day-to-day basis), they reported having a hard time recognizing people and often mistaking people around them for others, suggesting the system is indeed useful to them, and not just to blind users. They also indicated that for people recognition they would prefer to use the watch instead of other devices. Additionally, both participants showed more interest and ability to use the shortcut to open the application. Sometimes they did not point the camera correctly at a person and one of them did not wait for the "framing" feedback before changing the position to recognize another person. The fatigue issue was also reported by one of them.

During the experiment, some difficulties were observed. Although the execution time of the low vision users was greater than the blindfolded users, as shown in Table 2, the visually impairment subjects experience other difficulties inherent of their condition. Both are teenagers and had difficulty pronouncing the voice command to open the GFR system, because of their shyness. Moreover, the environment was noisy. These two factors caused an increase in the time taken to complete a round of people recognition.

Regarding both experiments, the use of fewer samples in the training dataset is a well known problem as the *One Sample Problem* [24] or, more specifically, the *Single-Sample Face Recognition Problem* (SSFR) [33]. A sufficiently large training dataset is necessary for a robust face recognition. "For example [19], for a 100 × 100 face image being vectorized into a 10,000 dimensions, theoretically the number of training images

Table 2. Time taken by the low vision users for a round of people recognition.

	TIME (MM:SS)
	Round 1
Low Vision 1	04:29
Low Vision 2	03:07
Average	03:48

for each person should be at least ten times that of the dimensionality [12], that is, 100,000 images in total per person" [24]. This means that for the 3,780-dimensional HOG descriptors used in our approach, it would need at least 37,800 face images varying some attributes, such as angles, distance, lighting and facial expressions, which is impractical for the type of proposed system.

6 Conclusions and Future Work

In this paper we presented a wearable assistive real-time face recognition system to aid the blind and low vision people. Our prototype was built into a smartwatch with low processing hardware, featuring a 1.9 megapixel camera on its watchband. The developed system consists of two distinct modules: the face detection and the face recognition. The first one detects a face in the video captured by the camera and then sends the extracted face images to the second module. The face recognition module performs the face recognition and emits an audio feedback that either identifies a recognized person or indicates that s/he is unknown. In the face recognition approach, we used a variation of the K-NN algorithm to run on the watch's limited hardware. Finally, a case study was conducted to provide a preliminary evaluation of the GFR application in terms of system performance and user interaction. The case study consisted of two experiments, one (pilot) with blindfolded users and another with users with an actual visual impairment – low vision.

In the pilot experiment, the system showed a satisfactory performance, with a high accuracy rate of 83.64 %. The experiment with low vision users showed that the system is in fact meaningful to users with this disability, as it eases the difficulties they have with people recognition in their daily routine. Additionally, in terms of user interaction, both experiments were important to show usability and ergonomic issues that need to be addressed. The feedback that indicates a face is being framed needs more work so that it becomes a more precise clue as to where the user needs to point the smartwatch's camera. This is important not only to allow the system to be used as an assistive technology, but also to alleviate the fatigue issue reported by the participants. Other potential place for future enhancement concerns the interface to get data from people's faces, which still needs to be made accessible for blind and low vision users.

There is a lot of room to improve the actual accuracy of the system. To address this, we could use more sophisticated face detection algorithms or classifiers, and even use techniques of hallucinating exemplars from the existing data. Such techniques will reduce the SSFR problem and make the system more robust to noise and illumination conditions. In terms of the face recognition approach, we used the K-NN recognition directly over the HOG descriptors, which are on a high-dimensional space. This is quite unusual compared to what literature describes, as the K-NN (or any other classifier) is usually applied after a dimensionality reduction step, such as a PCA. The dimensionality reduction makes the system more robust, since, in a high-dimensional space, everything is far from everything. We avoided the PCA at this point because a PCA learns the subspace of interest from the training set. We are currently studying alternatives for a vanilla PCA, such as a self-updating PCA. This would use new exemplars, registered as the system performs, to estimate a more realistic subspace of operation. This will allow the system to start with a preregistered dataset, and improve its performance as it is used. Nevertheless, we can strongly declare that our objective in this paper was reached — it is technically possible to make a real-time robust face recognition system running exclusively on the low-performance hardware of the smartwatch.

Finally, we propose challenges for future work, including wearable systems for objects recognition, textual information recognition (e.g. signs, symbols) and a gesture recognition like [21], but processed within the smartwatch itself. Furthermore, we will conduct experiments to better analyze the system's energy consumption. Also, other experiments with visually impaired users will be conducted to further evaluate and improve the system as an assistive device.

Acknowledgements. The authors wish to express their gratitude to all the volunteers who participated in the experiments in this study, and also for Samsung Research that loaned the hardware equipment. Laurindo de Sousa Britto Neto receives a Ph.D. fellowship from CNPq (grant #141254/2014-9). Vanessa Regina Margareth Lima Maike receives a Ph.D. fellowship from CAPES (grant #01-P-04554/2013). Maria Cecília Calani Baranauskas, Anderson de Rezende Rocha and Siome Klein Goldenstein receive a Productivity Research Fellowship from CNPq (grants #308618/2014-9, #304352/2012-8 and #308882/2013-0, respectively). This work is part of a project that was approved by Unicamp Institutional Review Board CAAE 31818014. 0.0000.5404. This paper is an extended version of work published in [3].

References

1. Ahonen, T., Hadid, A., Pietikainen, M.: Face description with local binary patterns: application to face recognition. IEEE Trans. Pattern Anal. Mach. Intell. **28**(12), 2037–2041 (2006)
2. Astler, D., Chau, H., Hsu, K., Hua, A., Kannan, A., Lei, L., Nathanson, M., Paryavi, E., Rosen, M., Unno, H., Wang, C., Zaidi, K., Zhang, X., Tang, C.: Increased accessibility to nonverbal communication through facial and expression recognition technologies for blind/visually impaired subjects. In: 13th International ACM SIGACCESS Conference on Computers and Accessibility, pp. 259–260 (2011)
3. Britto Neto, L.S., Maike, V.R.M.L., Koch, F.L., Baranauskas, M.C.C., Rocha, A.R., Goldenstein, S.K.: A wearable face recognition system built into smartwatch and the visually impaired user. In: 17th International Conference on Enterprise Information Systems, vol. 3, pp. 5–12. Scitepress (2015)

4. Belhumeur, P., Hespanha, J., Kriegman, D.: Eigenfaces vs. fisherfaces: recognition using class specific linear projection. IEEE Trans. Pattern Anal. Mach. Intell. **19**(7), 711–720 (1997)
5. Chen, X., Flynn, P., Bowyer, K.: PCA-based face recognition in infrared imagery: baseline and comparative studies. In: IEEE International Workshop on Analysis and Modeling of Faces and Gestures, pp. 127–134 (2003)
6. Cover, T., Hart, P.: Nearest neighbor pattern classification. IEEE Trans. Inf. Theory **13**(1), 21–27 (1967)
7. Dalal, N., Triggs, B.: Histograms of oriented gradients for human detection. In: IEEE Computer Society Conference on Computer Vision and Pattern Recognition, pp. 886–893 (2005)
8. Freevoxtouch. the only smart watch in the world for the visually impaired. http://myfreevox.com/en/
9. Fusco, G., Noceti, N., Odone, F.: Combining retrieval and classification for real-time face recognition. In: 10th IEEE International Conference on Advanced Video and Signal Based Surveillance, pp. 276–281 (2012)
10. Gordon, G.: Face recognition based on depth maps and surface curvature. In: SPIE1570, Geometric methods in Computer Vision, pp. 234–247 (1991)
11. Hadid, A., Li, S.Z., Pietikäinen, M.: Learning Personal Specific Facial Dynamics for Face Recognition from Videos. In: Zhou, S., Zhao, W., Tang, X., Gong, S. (eds.) AMFG 2007. LNCS, vol. 4778, pp. 1–15. Springer, Heidelberg (2007)
12. Jain, A. K., Chandrasekaran, B.: Dimensionality and sample size considerations in pattern recognition practice. In Handbook of Statistics, pp. 835–855 (1982)
13. Kistler, D., Wightman, F.: A model of head-related transfer functions based on principal components analysis and minimum-phase reconstruction. J. Acoust. Soc. Am. **91**(3), 1637–1647 (1992)
14. Kramer, K., Hedin, D., Rolkosky, D.: Smartphone based face recognition tool for the blind. In: 32nd Annual International Conference of the IEEE Engineering in Medicine and Biology Society, pp. 4538–4541 (2010)
15. Krishna, S., Little, G., Black, J., Panchanathan, S.: A Wearable face recognition system for individuals with visual impairments. In: 7th International ACM SIGACCESS Conference on Computers and Accessibility, pp. 106–113 (2005)
16. Li, B., Mian, A., L., W., and Krishna, A.: Using kinect for face recognition under varying poses, expressions, illumination and disguise. In: IEEE Workshop on Applications of Computer Vision, pp. 186–192 (2013)
17. Luxand, Inc.: Detect and Recognize Faces with Luxand FaceSDK. https://www.luxand.com/facesdk/. Accessed 27 August 2013
18. Manduchi, R., Coughlan, J.: Computer vision without sight. Commun. ACM **55**(1), 96–104 (2012)
19. Martínez, A.M.: Recognizing imprecisely localized, partially occluded, and expression variant faces from a single sample per class. IEEE Trans. Pattern Anal. Mach. Intell. **24**(6), 748–762 (2002)
20. NEUROtechnology.: VeriLook SDK: Face Identification for Stand-Alone or Web Applications. http://www.neurotechnology.com/verilook.html. Accessed on 15 April 2014
21. Porzi, L., Messelodi, S., Modena, C. M., Ricci, E.: A smart watch-based gesture recognition system for assisting people with visual impairments. In: 3rd ACM International Workshop on Interactive Multimedia on Mobile, pp. 19–24 (2013)
22. Pun, T., Roth, P., Bologna, G., Moustakas, K., Tzovaras, D.: Image and video processing for visually handicapped people. EURASIP J. Image Video Process. **025214**(5), 4:1–4:12 (2007)

23. Schwartz, W., Guo, H., Choi, J., Davis, L.: Face Identification Using Large Feature Sets. IEEE Trans. Image Process. **21**(4), 2245–2255 (2012)
24. Tan, X., Chen, S., Zhou, Z., Zhang, F.: Face recognition from a single image per person: a survey. J. Pattern Recogn. **39**(9), 1725–1745 (2006). Elsevier, New York
25. Tanveer, M., Anam, A., Rahman, A., Ghosh, S., Yeasin, M.: FEPS: A sensory substitution system for the blind to perceive facial expressions. In: 14th International ACM SIGACCESS Conference on Computers and Accessibility, pp. 207–208 (2012)
26. Tistarelli, M., Grosso, E.: Human face analysis: from identity to emotion and intention recognition. In: Kumar, A., Zhang, D. (eds.) ICEB 2010. LNCS, vol. 6005, pp. 76–88. Springer, Heidelberg (2010)
27. Turk, M., Pentland, A.: Eigenfaces for recognition. J. Cogn. Neurosci. **3**(1), 71–86 (1991)
28. Viola, P., Jones, M.: Robust real-time face detection. Int. J. Comput. Vision **57**(2), 137–154 (2004)
29. Watanabe, H., Terada, T., Tsukamoto, M.: A sound-based lifelog system using ultrasound. In: 5th Augmented Human International Conference, pp. 59:1–59:2 (2014)
30. Wilder, J., Phillips, P.J., Jiang, C., Wiener, S.: Comparison of visible and infra-red imagery for face recognition. In: 2nd International Conference on Automatic Face and Gesture Recognition, pp. 182–187 (1996)
31. Wiscott, L., Fellous, J., Malsburg, C.: Face recognition by elastic bunch graph matching. IEEE Trans. Pattern Anal. Mach. Intell. **19**(1), 775–779 (1997)
32. World Health Organization: Visual impairment and blindness: Fact sheet N. 282 (2013). http://www.who.int/mediacentre/factsheets/fs282/en/
33. Yan, H., Lu, J., Zhou, X., Shang, Y.: Multi-feature multi-manifold learning for single-sample face recognition. NeuroComputing **143**, 134–143 (2014). Elsevier
34. Zhao, G., Pietikainen, M.: Dynamic texture recognition using local binary patterns with an application to facial expressions. IEEE Trans. Pattern Anal. Mach. Intell. **29**(6), 915–928 (2007)
35. Zhao, W., Chellappa, R., Phillips, P.J., Rosenfeld, A.: Face recognition: a literature survey. ACM Comput. Surv. **35**(4), 399–458 (2003)

Guidelines for Evaluating Mobile Applications: A Semiotic-Informed Approach

Flavio Nicastro[1(✉)], Roberto Pereira[1], Bruna Alberton[2], Leonor Patrícia C. Morellato[2], Cecilia Baranauskas[1], and Ricardo da S. Torres[1]

[1] Institute of Computing, University of Campinas (UNICAMP), Campinas, SP, Brazil
flavio.nicastro@attatecnologia.com.br
[2] Phenology Lab, Department of Botany, São Paulo State University UNESP, Rio Claro, SP, Brazil

Abstract. Portable devices have been experimented for data acquisition in different domains, e.g., logistics and census data acquisition. Nevertheless, their large-scale adoption depends on the development of effective applications with a careful interaction design. In this work, we revisit existing strategies for mobile application design and evaluation and use the Semiotic Ladder from Organizational Semiotics as an artifact to organize a set of guidelines. We propose a set of semiotic-informed guidelines with questions for evaluation of mobile application interfaces. We also propose a methodology for the evaluation of mobile application interfaces based on the proposed guidelines set. We demonstrate the use of the proposed methodology in the evaluation of four mobile application interfaces designed for phenological data acquisition in the field.

Keywords: Human computer interaction · Organizational Semiotics · Mobile application interface guidelines · Phenology

1 Introduction

Portable devices have been adopted in different domains to support data acquisition [1–3]. Key motivations for their use rely on the associated low costs, recent improvements in the hardware robustness, the incorporation of different sensors (e.g., for location, audio, image, and video acquisition) that provide useful contextual information for different purposes, and the availability of easy-to-use frameworks for developing applications.

However, the effective adoption of portable devices depends on the use of applications with careful interface design. An appropriate design should be associated with reduced mental and physical stress, reduced learning curve, and improved device operability [4]. The design and implementation of such interfaces deal with many constraints: small-size screens, data entry models, connectivity issues, and limited resources. Moreover, there are other factors underlying the user-system interaction that should also be considered, such as the social

S. Hammoudi et al. (Eds.): ICEIS 2015, LNBIP 241, pp. 529–554, 2015.
DOI: 10.1007/978-3-319-29133-8_26

implications of changing work practices. In this sense, the definition and use of appropriate interface design guidelines may help application developers to address part of these challenges.

Information and Communication Technology has evolved rapidly, shaping our relationships in the world (e.g., economic, social, laboral, interpersonal, and ethical). The relationship between people and information is changing at the same pace, mediated by that technology. Within this scenario, and as part of it, designing or evaluating an application demands a systemic view on the prospective product of that technology. For this systemic view on the design of computer-based applications, Organizational Semiotics (OS) [5] has been a fundamental theoretical frame of reference for our work.

By making use of several design cues, indicators, and signs, Semiotics, the doctrine of signs, enables us to search for a more accurate understanding of information as properties of signs. Anything that stands for something or is used to mean something to someone is an example of a sign: words, sentences, traffic lights, diagrams, a wave, a facial expression. Adopting Baranauskas' perspective to design [6,7], we take Semiotics beyond the study of how we use signs to communicate, to include shared knowledge and mutual commitment that establishes communication in the design process. In this sense, information, understood as signs, could be operated in distinct levels, meaning different operations a person can do upon the sign. These levels are represented as steps of a Semiotic Ladder (SL), or views of a semiotic framework [8].

In this work, we revisit existing mobile application design and evaluation strategies, and use the Semiotic Ladder from OS as an artifact to organize guidelines to support the design and the evaluation of mobile application interfaces. To the best of our knowledge, this is the first attempt to categorize existing guidelines according to the SL. The final guidelines set proposed, composed of 27 guidelines, is expected to support mobile interface designers, developers and evaluators in their daily tasks. We also propose a method for mobile application interface evaluation based on the defined set of guidelines. Another contribution of this work is that the proposed method can be conducted with the most interested parties: people from the application domain, not necessarily with knowledge on semiotics or in interface evaluations.

We demonstrate the use of the proposed methodology in the evaluation of four mobile application interfaces recently proposed in the e-Science domain. In these applications, we are interested in supporting data acquisition upon plant phenology in the field. Plant phenology concerns the study of recurrent life cycle events and its relationship to climate [9]. This discipline has been recognized as a strategic approach to climate change research [9]. Plant phenology studies are based on a well-defined methodology that has as main objective the identification and understanding of temporal changes in reproductive or vegetative events [10]. Plant phenology studies depends, therefore, on the continuous acquisition and analysis of data over time. Usually, plants are observed directly in the field, and the phenophases defined by the investigators (e.g., flower, fruiting, leaf flush) are visually identified and registered on paper sheets on the field. This task is time consuming and error prone. These issues have motivated the investigation upon the use of portable devices to support the phenological data acquisition process.

The remaining of this text is organized as follows. Section 2 provides the background on related topics. Section 3 introduces the proposed semiotic-informed guidelines set for support the evaluation of mobile application interfaces, while Sect. 4 describes a case study concerning the use of the proposed set of guidelines in the evaluation of application interfaces proposed for phenological data acquisition. Finally, Sect. 5 presents our conclusions and directions for future work.

2 Background and Literature Review

2.1 Phenology

Several research initiatives have recognized the importance of studying environmental changes. This is for example the main objective of Phenology, which investigates natural recurring phenomena and its relation to climate [9]. Phenology studies are dedicated to the observation of living beings and their relationship with meteorological data [11]. In the context of plant phenology, the budding of the leaves and the senescence are examples of important stages in the cycles of plants that usually are monitored in phenology studies dedicated to understanding several ecosystem processes such as growth, water status, gas exchange, and nutrient cycling [12,13]. In another scenario, plant phenology is important to the estimation of carbon balance and land productivity [14–16].

One important research venue in the Phenology is concerned with the specification and implementation of novel technologies for phenological observation [17–22]. This is, for example, the main objective of the e-phenology project,[1] which is a pioneer project in Brazil dedicated to performing phenology studies by considering information obtained from vegetation images. It is a multidisciplinary project that combines research in Computer Science and Phenology. The project is developed in the context of a collaboration involving the Laboratory of Phenology, Institute of Biosciences (IB), São Paulo State University "Júlio de Mesquita Filho" (UNESP) and the Recod Laboratory (Reasoning for Complex Data), in the Institute of Computing, University of Campinas (Unicamp). The main objectives are: (1) the use of the new technologies of environmental monitoring, (2) the creation of a protocol to a program of long-term phenological monitoring in Brazil, and (3) the proposal of models, methods, and algorithms to support the management, integration, and analyses of phenological data.

The current studies of the e-phenology project are based on a Cerrado area, located in the region of Itirapina, São Paulo, Brazil. The phenological data in this area have been obtained by biologists from Phenology Laboratory of UNESP since September 2004, and are related to the observations of the occurrence of biological phenomena in the life cycle of plants, called phenophases. The observed phenological phases are: flowering, fruiting, budding, and leaf fall.

[1] http://www.recod.ic.unicamp.br/ephenology/ (As of March 2015).

The production of flowers is divided into buttons and flowering itself, or anthesis (flower opening); the production of fruit is divided into development of fruits and unripe fruit, and the fruitification into period of ripe fruit and "ready to spread."

Every month researchers perform the field observation of several individuals. Each observer takes a clipboard with printed sheets. On these sheets, they register information of different individuals such as their identification number, family, type, and location. It also contains fields for the annotation of the intensity of the observed pehnophases of each individual, represented by the letters: Bot – Button, Ante – anthesis, FV – green fruit, FM – ripe fruit, Brot – budding and Qued – leaf fall. The stages are quantified according to three intensity classes: 0 – indicates that the phenology is not present; 1 – indicates presence of phenology at a lower intensity; 2 – indicates the presence of phenology at a higher intensity. After the researchers complete the observations of all individuals, they register observed data into digital spreadsheets. Later these worksheets are analyzed in order to detect inconsistencies in the data collected. For example, it is not correct the identification of flower without having registered the phenophase button in a previous observation. If an inconsistency is detected, it is considered that there is a problem of observation and based on the current observation, the value of the previous observation is modified. This process of collection began in 2004 and today, phenology studies have been performed by analyzing about a million records related to more than 2000 plant individuals.

2.2 Mobile Interfaces

New technologies provide power to people who are able to handle them properly. A technology becomes widely accepted and effectively used when well designed, and this means meeting the needs and capabilities of a target group. A key factor for the success of a particular technology relies on its interface with potential users. In this particular matter, one important concern consists in defining appropriate mechanisms to improve the way how people can use technology to think and communicate, observe and decide, calculate and simulate, and discuss and design. The Human-Computer Interaction (HCI) area addresses these issues by proposing appropriate approaches for the design of interface that may help people so that they can perform their activities with productivity, safety, and satisfaction [23].

With the exponential use of mobile devices, HCI researchers have dedicated to understanding and developing standards that improve the usability and the quality of interaction between human and portable devices. In particular, in this work, we aim to define an appropriate set of guidelines for mobile application interface design and evaluation based on the identification of existing research in the area. Table 1 summarizes some relevant work in the literature, without exhausting the subject. The literature studies point to different aspects that are relevant in evaluating mobile application user interfaces. In this work, we select and refine guidelines and questions proposed in those studies, classifying them according to the different semiotic layers.

Table 1. Literature overview on mobile interface design.

References	Overview
Nayeb et al., 2012 [24]	- this work analyses the state-of-the-art concerning the evaluation of the usability of mobile applications;
	- presents a methodology for usability evaluation;
	- suggests that there is little scientific research in this area.
Radia et al., 2012 [25]	- presents guidelines based on the latest research in industry and academia;
	- search design and development of successful mobile applications that can utilize the capabilities of next generation cellular network;
	- presents a model for developing client-server applications based on 4G technologies.
Zamzami and Mahmud, 2012 [26]	- states that there is little research focused on assessing the information quality on smartphone interfaces;
	- examines three main areas: mobile interface design, information quality, and user satisfaction.
Rauch, 2011 [27]	- discusses differences in usability research focused on desktops compared with what has been done for mobile devices;
	- summarizes emerging trends in usability studies for mobile devices;
	- suggests best practices for converting documentation to Kindle-compatible .MOBI format.
Ayob et al., 2009 [28]	- proposes a three-layer design model for mobile applications based on four existing guidelines.
Hussain and Kutar, 2009 [29]	- presents a usability metric framework for mobile phone applications;
	- proposes 6 guidelines with 21 questions and 30 metrics for usability evaluation;
	- include quality characteristics from ISO 9241-11.
Ryu, 2005 [30]	- presents usability questionnaires for electronic mobile products and decision making methods;
	- proposes an evaluation questionnaire containing 72 items.
Gong and Tarasewich, 2004 [31]	- presents guidelines for handheld mobile device interface design;
	- is based on golden rules of interface design.
	- one of the first attempt to organize a set of guidelines for the design of mobile devices interfaces.

In the following, these works are briefly outlined. In the paper of Nayeb et al. [24], the authors present the state of the art concerning the evaluation of the usability of mobile applications. They point out that is always important to consider three aspects of usability for all types of software: (a) More efficient to use: take less time to complete a particular task; (b) Easier to learn: operations can be learned observing the object, and (c) More user satisfaction: meets user expectations. Also, they attest that referring to evaluation methodology, three types are currently used in studies of mobile usability: (1) Laboratory experiments; (2) Field studies, and (3) Hands-on measurements. They state that there is little scientific research in this area and an evaluation methodology is presented to fill this gap.

In the paper of Radia et al. [25], the authors present some guidelines based on recent research from academia and industry, seeking the design and development of mobile applications that can use the capabilities of next generation of mobile network. They present a model for application development using a 4G-based client-server. Referring to the guidelines, the most important contribution from this paper to our work, the authors show that the extensive research has categorized the guidelines into three broad classes. The first class, "General UI Guidelines for Mobile Applications," is concerned with user interfaces. Some guidelines proposed in this class include: (1) provide shortcuts for experienced users and wizard for new users; (2) allow to maintain control by having the ability to control the application (or abort it) at any point; (3) create good dialogues by creating predictable and intuitive sequences of interaction with the application; (4) minimize dependence on user's memory through grouping information in "chunks" at a time, limiting the need for scrolling; among others. The second class, "Mobility Guidelines," is responsible for specific guidelines when dealing with mobility. Some examples: (1) allowing for multimodal interactions with the device; (2) allowing for convenient use with the ability to handle multiple and frequent interruptions with limited attention from the user; (3) providing an ability to synchronize the application with desktop and cloud data stores; (4) allowing privacy for single or multiple users; among others. And the third class, "Organizational Guidelines," is concerned with enterprise-specific and corporation guidelines. Some examples in this class are: (1) consistency with the organization's standards and systems; (2) support for business models; among others. The guidelines presented in the first and the second classes were very important on the set of guidelines proposed in this work.

A quite similar view by Nayeb et al. [24] is presented by Zamzami and Mahmud [26]. In their work, the authors state that there is little research to evaluate the quality of information in smartphone interfaces. They perform their analysis considering three key areas: design mobile interfaces, information quality, and user satisfaction. Regarding to mobile user interface design, they attest that there are three principals that need to be followed in designing user interface: (1) let the users be in control of the interface; (2) reduce user's memory load; and (3) make the user interface consistent. Also, they discuss some concepts concerning user satisfaction.

Also showing that much has to be researched and developed in the HCI area for mobile devices, Marta Rauch [27] addresses the distance of desktops in usability research when compared to what has been done for mobile devices. She summarizes the emerging trends in usability for mobile devices and suggests "best practices" for converting documentation to Kindle-compatible *.MOBI* format. She also presents a study based on the development of documentation on Kindle, Tablets, and Smartphones. Regarding to the guidelines, she brings the emerging usability guidelines for applications on these type of devices. Some usability guidelines pointed out include: (1) Consider the unique issues of mobile usability; (2) Analyze mobile user tasks; (3) Determine the target mobile device; (4) Help users avoid inadvertent actions; among others. She also discusses key requirements for professional communicators remember the guidelines. Example: for guideline 1: "When creating user assistance for mobile devices, ensure that the design is conducive to mobile use;" for guideline 2: "Determine whether a majority of your target audience will use your applications and documentation on mobile devices."

In Ayob et al. [28], the authors, in turn, propose a design model of three layers for mobile applications based on four existing guidelines. First, they raise the main issue of designing mobile application: "how to display all the information and elements in the small screen of mobile device?". The authors also present a discussion and a comparison about guidelines, which in turn are based on four existing set of guidelines named as: (1) Shneiderman's Golden Rules of Interface Design; (2) Seven Usability Guidelines for Mobile Device; (3) Human-Centered Design (ISO Standard 13407), and (4) Mobile Web Best Practices 1.0 (W3C). Some examples of guidelines from these four groups are: From group 1: (1) Enable frequent users to use shortcuts; (2) Reduce short-term memory load; (3) Design for small devices; among others. From group 2: (1) Meet user's need quickly; (2) Make user input as simple as possible; (3) Only show essential information; among others. From group 3: (1) Understand and specify the context of use; (2) Produce design and prototypes; among others. And for group 4: (1) User input; (2) Page layout and content; among others. Based on these comparisons, they propose a new guideline set divided into three layers called: (1) Analysis; (2) Designs, and (3) Testing. Some examples of the guidelines proposed: From layer *Analysis*: (1) Identify and document user's task; (2) Define the use of the system; among others. From layer *Design*: (1) Enabled frequent users to use shortcuts; (2) Design for multiple and dynamic contexts; among others. And from the third layer, *Testing*: (1) Usability testing; (2) Field studies; among others.

Another important work that addresses usability for mobile application is the one from Hussain and Kutar [29]. In their work, they present a usability metric framework for mobile phone application. This framework is composed of three main measures: effectiveness, efficiency, and satisfaction. Each measure has two guidelines. For example, for *Efficiency*, the guidelines Time Taken and Features are defined. In total, they proposed six guidelines, based on which 21 questions are defined. From these questions, 23 metrics for usability evaluation are developed. An example of this relation between measures, guideline, question, and metric considers the following structure: Measure: Effectiveness; Guideline: Simplicity; Questions: Is it simple to key-in the data? Does the application provide virtual keypad? Is the output easy to use? How easy is it to install the application? Is the application easy to learn?; Metrics: Time taken to key-in the data; Provide/not provide virtual keypad for touch screen device; Provide/not provide help when necessary; Optimized/not optimized the screen size; - Rating scale for satisfaction on output; Time taken to install; The number of interaction occurred while installing the application; Successful/unsuccessful installation; Time taken to learn each task; Number of mistake while learning. Also, the authors present a table with the most popular guidelines obtained from literature. Some of these guidelines are: (1) Completeness: the extent or completeness of user's solutions to tasks; (2) Less or no error: errors made by the user during the process of completing the task; (3) Simple: the application should be straightforward; (4) Ease to learn: the user interface must be designed for user to learn easily; among others.

In another similar study, Ryu [30] presents usability questionnaires for electronic mobile products and decision making methods. He also proposes an evaluation questionnaire containing 72 items for usability evaluation of mobile products. This questionnaire was divided into six groups: (1) Ease of Learning and Use; (2) Helpfulness and Problem Solving Capabilities; (3) Affective Aspect and Multimedia Properties; (4) Commands and Minimal Memory Load; (5) Control and Efficiency, and (6) Typical Task for Mobile Phone. One example of each group: (1) Is it easy to learn to operate this product? (2) Are the messages aimed at prevent you from make mistakes adequate? (3) Is this product attractive and pleasing? (4) Do the commands have distinctive meanings? (5) Is the data display sufficiently consistent? and for group (6) Is it sufficiently easy to operate keys with one hand? Some of these questions were used to compose our questionnaire for assessing the set of guidelines proposed in this work.

Finally, Gong and Tarasewich [31] published in 2004 one of the first attempt at a set of guidelines for the design of mobile device interfaces. They presented a guideline set for handheld mobile device interface design based on traditional guidelines for desktop user interfaces, the golden rules of interface design, and research with mobile device and applications. Some of the guidelines proposed in this study are: (1) Offer Informative Feedback; (2) Support Internal Locus of Control; (3) Design for multiple and dynamic contexts; (4) Design for limited and split attention; among others.

2.3 Semiotic Ladder

The Semiotic Ladder (SL) (illustrated in Fig. 1) consists of six steps representing views on signs from the perspective of the physical world, empirics, syntactics, semantics, pragmatics, and the social world. The physical, empirics, and the social world are Stamper's [8] contribution upon the traditional semiotic approach. Stamper introduced it in his work, as a way of looking at meaning, communication, and information from a semiotic perspective [32].

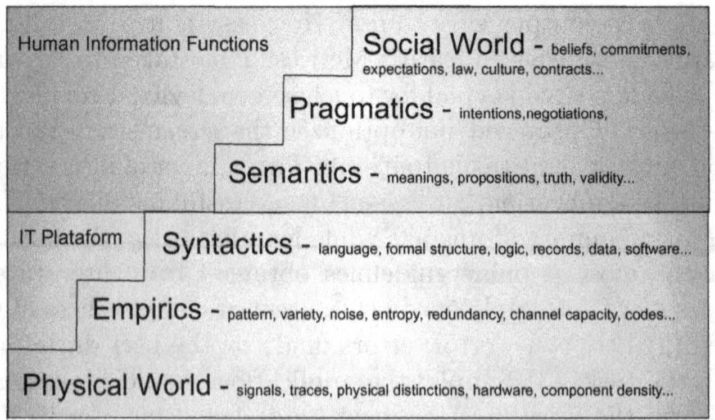

Fig. 1. Semiotic ladder steps. Figure adapted from Stamper [32].

The *Social World* is the layer in which we analyse the consequences of the use of signs in human activities. It deals, for example, with beliefs, expectations, commitments, law, and culture. *Pragmatics* is the layer studying the intentional use of signs and behavior of agents. Issues related to the intention and negotiation are objects of the pragmatic. *Semantics* deals with the relationship between a sign and what it refers to (its meaning); signs in all modes of signification. *Syntactics* deals with the combination of signs without considering their specific meaning. *Empirics* deals with the static properties of signs, when media and different physical devices are used. Finally, *Physical World* works with the physical aspects of signs and their marks (e.g., infrastructure issues).

In summary, the top three steps of the SL are related to the use of signs, how they work in communicating meanings and intentions, and the social consequences of their use. The three lower steps, in turn, answer questions related to how signs are structured and used, how they are organized and conveyed, and what physical properties they have, among others.

In the context of our study, the SL is an artifact that has been used for organizing the guidelines for system evaluation, covering aspects from its technological infrastructure (physical world, empirics, syntactic layer) to the system of human information (semantic layer, pragmatics, and social world). Therefore, this artifact supports both a wide and deep view of the different aspects that may be considered when evaluating interfaces for mobile devices. Other uses of the SL in different domains can be found in the literature, such as [33].

3 Mobile Application Interface Evaluation

In this work, we propose a set of guidelines for support the evaluation of mobile application interfaces. We discuss the process used for defining this guidelines set in Sect. 3.1. Another contribution of this work refers to the proposal of an evaluation methodology that takes advantage of the proposed guidelines set. This methodology is described in Sect. 3.2.

3.1 Proposed Guideline Set

From the analysis of literature concerning the mobile application design and evaluation strategies based on publications associated with ACM and IEEE conferences and journals (see Table 1), we classified existing guidelines and questions according to the Semiotic Ladder.

This step generated a total of 147 guidelines, distributed as follows: 15 into Physical World; 10 into Empirics; 58 into Syntactics; 26 into Semantics; 20 into Pragmatics, and 18 into Social World.

A novel set of guidelines was defined by merging similar ones and by discarding those considered non-pertinent to the application domain (13 in total). Examples of removed guidelines include questions such as:

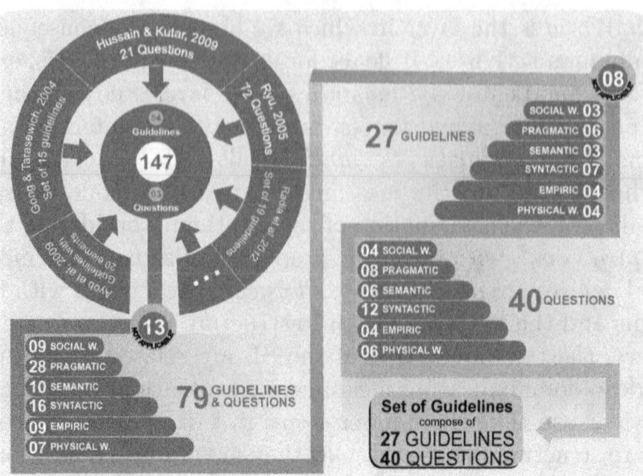

Fig. 2. The guidelines refinement process. The resulting set, composed of 27 guidelines, is presented in Table 2, while the 40 questions proposed to evaluate mobile interfaces according to the defined guidelines are presented in Tables 3–8.

- "Is it easy to change the ringer signal?",
- "Is it easy to check missed calls?",
- "Is it easy to check the last call?",
- "Is it easy to send and receive short messages using this product?",
- "Is it easy to use the phone book feature of this product?",
- "Can you personalize ringer signals with this product?".

Although those are general questions important to evaluate interaction and communication with the mobile device, they are not relevant for a mobile application interface evaluation in the domain considered. The resulting set included 7 guidelines into the Physical World, 9 into Empirics; 16 into Syntactics, 10 into Semantics, 28 into Pragmatics, and 9 into the Social World, totalizing 79 guidelines and questions.

Finally, these guidelines and their classification were re-evaluated and refined by 10 experts in the fields of OS and HCI, to eliminate redundancies and to come with more appropriate descriptions and a more cohesive set, resulting in a set of 27 guidelines distributed as follows: 4 into the Physical World, 4 into Empirics, 7 into Syntactics, 3 into Semantics, 6 in Pragmatics, and 3 into the Social World. Figure 2 illustrates the whole process for refining and organizing the guidelines. The final proposed guidelines set is presented in Table 2. Finally, a questionnaire was proposed to support the evaluation of mobile applications according to each defined guideline. The proposed questionnaire is presented in Tables 3, 4, 5, 6, 7, and 8. Each table refers to a different SL step. Note also that, more than one question can be used for a particular guideline in some cases. For example, for the fourth guideline related to the Physical World (*"Create design suitable for small devices with touch screen"*) – see Table 2, two questions are defined for the

Table 2. Proposed guidelines set composed of 27 guidelines.

Step on the semiotic ladder	Guideline description
Physical World	1 - Provide adequate contrast
	2 - Provide methods for easy and functional data entry
	3 - Create design suitable for small devices with touch screen
	4 - Easy operation with one hand
Empiric	5 - Implement planning on speedup
	6 - Keep recent data for reuse
	7 - Facilitate data exchange with other applications
	8 - Provide automatic application update
Syntactic	9 - Adequately provide information on system resources
	10 - Give control to the user of the application
	11 - Maintain consistency in the standards used both in data presentation as in how to perform each task
	12 - Facilitate the navigation between screens and information
	13 - Keep the user informed of what is happening through constant feedbacks
	14 - Provide shortcuts and wizards
	15 - Reduce mental efforts and memory requirements
Semantic	16 - Provide output of data easy to use
	17 - Provide appropriate documentation by means of manuals and helps
	18 - Design clear and understandable interfaces
Pragmatic	19 - Facilitate the discovery of new functionality
	20 - Design the application thinking about simplicity
	21 - Develop the application thinking in multiple contexts
	22 - Provide feedback to aid the prevention of errors and troubleshooting as well as provide means for reversing actions
	23 - Allow customization of the application by users
	24 - Facilitate application learning
Social World	25 - Implement security and privacy controls
	26 - Know your target audience in order to raise the application requirements, needs and "intrinsic" desires
	27 - Implement controls to avoid risks while using the application in motion (driving, walking, etc.)

Table 3. Questionnarie proposed - Physical World

Guideline	Question
1	1-Is the backlighting feature for the keyboard and screen appropriate in all contexts?
2	2-Does the application provide a virtual keypad?
	3-Does the application provide voice assistance?
3	4-Are pictures on the screen of satisfactory quality and size?
	5-Does the application provide appropriate menu button for touch screen?
4	6-Is it sufficiently easy to operate keys with one hand?

evaluation process: *"Are pictures on the screen of satisfactory quality and size?"*; *"Does the application provide appropriate menu button for touch screen?"*. For each question, the evaluator should indicate, in a Likert scale (from 1 to 5), whether the application is attending to the guidelines recommendations. In the scale: 1 means that the evaluator strongly disagrees; 2, disagrees; 3, neither agrees nor disagrees; 4, agrees; 5, strongly agrees.

Table 4. Questionnarie proposed - Empiric

Guideline	Question
5	7-Are the response time and information display fast enough?
6	8-Are data items kept short?
7	9-Are exchange and transmission of data between this product and other products (e.g., computer, PDA, and other mobile products) easy?
8	10-Does the application provide automatic update?

Table 5. Questionnarie proposed - Syntactic

Guideline	Question
9	11-How much information about system resources was displayed?
10	12-Are the HOME and MENU buttons sufficiently easy to locate for all operations?
	13-Are the letter codes for the menu selection designed carefully?
11	14-Are the color coding and data display compatible with familiar conventions?
	15-Can all operations be carried out in a systematically similar way?
12	16-Is the organization of information on the application screen clear?
	17-Is it easy to navigate between hierarchical menus, pages, and screen?
13	18-Does application provide feedback (haptic, audio, visual, etc.) constantly in order to keep the user engaged and attentive?
14	19-Does application provide shortcuts for experienced users and wizards for new users?
15	20-Does this application enable the quick, effective, and economical performance of tasks?
	21-Does interacting with this application require a lot of mental effort?
	22-Is it easy for you to remember how to perform tasks with this application?

Table 6. Questionnarie proposed - Semantic

Guideline	Question
16	23-Is the output data easy to use?
17	24-Are the documentation and manual for this application sufficiently informative?
	25-Does the application provide appropriate help?
18	26-Is feedback on the completion of tasks clear?
	27-Is the interface with this application clear and understandable?
	28-Is the design of the graphic symbols, icons and labels on the icons sufficiently relevant?

3.2 Evaluation Methodology

This section presents the proposed methodology for the evaluation of mobile application interfaces. The methodology is divided into four steps: definition of groups of evaluators; definition of application interfaces to be evaluated; evaluation of application interfaces; and performance of statistical tests.

Figure 3 presents the workflow of the proposed evaluation methodology. The first step (module labeled as A in the figure) is concerned with the definition of the application interfaces that will be evaluated. In our particular

Table 7. Questionnarie proposed - Pragmatic

Guideline	Question
19	29-Is discovering new features sufficiently easy?
20	30-Is it easy to access the information that you need from the application?
21	31-Does application allow convenient use with the ability to handle multiple and frequent interruptions with limited attention from the user?
	32-Does design of application is suitable for multiple contexts (home, business, travel, etc.) including support for runtime adaptation?
22	33-Are the error messages effective in assisting you to fix problems?
	34-Are the messages aimed at prevent you from making mistakes adequate?
23	35-Does application provide the ability to personalize the application to suit the user?
24	36-Is it easy to learn to operate this application?

Table 8. Questionnarie proposed - Social World

Guideline	Question
25	37-Does application allow privacy and security control for single or multiple users?
26	38-Does application have all the functions and capabilities you expect it to have?
	39-Is this application attractive and pleasing?
27	40-Is the application secure to use while driving or walking?

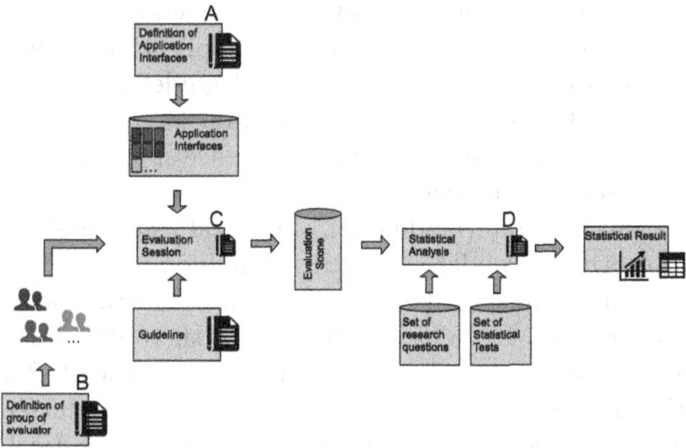

Fig. 3. Workflow of the proposed methodology.

methodology, we consider the possibility of evaluating both running and *mockup* interface designs. The second step (module B) refers to the definition of groups of evaluators. In our methodology, we consider that evaluators with different background and expertise can be invited to take part in the evaluation process. For example, experts from a target domain (e.g., Phenologists) and experts of HCI could be invited to evaluate mobile application interfaces (e.g., two prototypes named 1 and 2) to be used for data acquisition in the field. In this scenario, two groups of evaluators are considered.

The third step (module C) is concerned with the actual evaluation. In this step, the evaluators use the defined application (result of step A) according

Table 9. Summary of statistical tests. Adapted from Lazar et al. [34].

Experiment design	Independent variables (IV)	Conditions for each IV	Types of test
Between group	1	2	Independent samples t test
	1	3 or more	One-way ANOVA
	2 or more	2 or more	Factorial ANOVA
Within group	1	2	Paired-samples t test
	1	3 or more	Repeated measures ANOVA
	2 or more	2 or more	Repeated measures ANOVA
Between- and within-group	2 or more	2 or more	Split-plot ANOVA

Table 10. Examples of statistical tests for different types of questions.

Question	Type of test
Are there differences among the groups of evaluators	*t* test
Are there differences among the prototypes	Repeated measures ANOVA

to a pre-defined task. For example, evaluators use the application to register data collected regarding the intensity of specific phenophases of plants. After the evaluator performs the task in one or more application or prototypes, s/he fills out a questionnaire, based on the proposed guideline (see Sect. 3.1). The provided answers will be used to assess how certain interface is adherent to the items in the proposed guideline and how the interface supports the requirements of each step of the semiotic ladder.

In the fourth and last step (module D), statistical tests are performed. These tests have the objective of validating raised research questions. The first issue in this case refers to the definition of the research questions that will be addressed in the evaluation process. Examples include: "are there differences in answers among the group of evaluators?" (i.e., "is the evaluation of Prototype 1 by the group of HCI experts different from the evaluation conducted by Phenology experts?"). For answering these questions, a set of statistical tests has to be conducted based on the characteristics of the questions. Table 9 shows some commonly used significance tests for comparing means and their application context. In Table 10 we can see some possible questions with which each statistical test is used. For example, to answer the question "are there differences among the groups of evaluators?" a *t* test is the best choice.

The research questions considered in our methodology can be grouped into two categories: evaluator-centered and prototype-centered. The evaluator-centered questions aim to verify if there are differences among the groups of evaluators considering: (1) their general evaluation of the prototypes; (2) their evaluation of a particular prototype; (3) their evaluation of prototypes using a particular semiotic ladder step; and (4) their evaluation of a particular prototype according to a specific semiotic ladder step. The prototype-centered questions, in turn, aim to verify if there are differences among the prototypes considering:

(1) the complete set of guideline questions, i.e., all semiotic ladder steps altogether; and (2) a particular semiotic ladder step.

4 Case Study

This section presents the conducted case study that aims to demonstrate the use of the proposed evaluation methodology and guidelines. This case study concerns the evaluation of the interfaces of four prototypes designed to support the phenological data acquisition process in the field. We first describe the data acquisition process scenario in Sect. 4.1. Next, we describe the evaluated prototypes in Sect. 4.2. Finally, in Sect. 4.3, we present and discuss the results obtained from the evaluation using the proposed methodology.

4.1 Phenology Data Acquisition in the Field

Recently, phenology has been recognized as an important discipline for understanding the impact of climate change on living beings [35]. Phenology studies depend on the analysis of long-term temporal data. The common approach is the direct observation of plant individuals in the field at regular intervals (e.g., monthly or weekly) and the identification of phenophases (e.g., leafing, budding, flowering, and ripening) [10]. One widely adopted approach for data acquisition relies on using a qualitative method to assess the presence or absence of phenophase or using a quantitative method that assigns a different number (usually 0, 1, or 2) for a phenophase, depending on its intensity [36]. Usually, phenophase intensities are registered on paper sheets (in the field) and later inserted into digital spreadsheets (in the laboratory). This acquisition procedure can lead to errors and discrepancies in the collected data, which can delay data processing and analysis, as well as knowledge discovery.

Figure 4 presents the typical phenological data acquisition workflow. First, on-the-ground observations are planned. Multiple phenology experts may be involved in this process. Next, the in-the-field observations are performed by assigning intensity scores to plant phenophases. These scores are then registered in paper worksheets. In the lab, these data are stored in digital spreadsheets. At this moment, inserted data are checked with the objective of determining any inconsistency with previous annotations. If any inconsistency is identified, spreadsheets need to be updated accordingly. In this context, we have been specifying and developing new applications to support data acquisition in the field, based on the ongoing phenological observations carried out by the group from Phenology Lab at UNESP.[2] The objective is to design and implement applications for portable devices that may support phenology experts in the field by: (i) providing location-aware information regarding plant individuals; (ii) monitoring the evolution of the data acquisition process on real time; and (iii) implementing user friendly and loss-free mechanisms for data insertion and validation. The main challenges faced here

[2] Details from field site and sample methods can be found elsewhere [37,38].

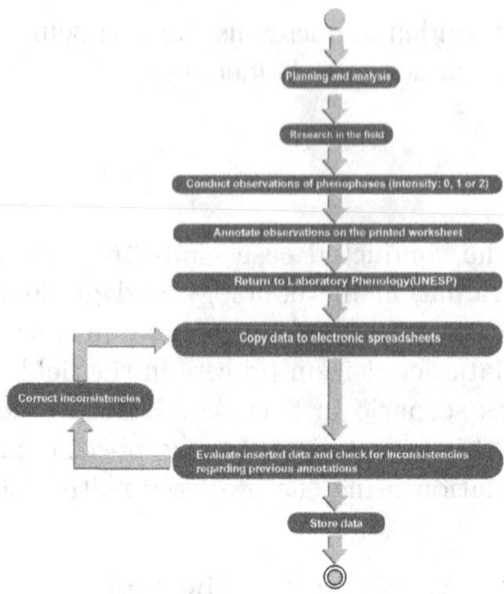

Fig. 4. Typical data acquisition workflow.

rely on both the design and the in-the-field validation of appropriate interfaces for data insertion using portable devices, as well as the implementation of protocols to guarantee that no data are lost in the whole data acquisition process. This section addresses the interface design evaluation of developed prototypes using the proposed set of guidelines.

4.2 Evaluated Prototypes

The prototypes of phenological data acquisition applications considered in this study were object of design within the scope of a graduate course in HCI (second semester of 2012) at the Institute of Computing, University of Campinas, Brazil. The methodology used in the design process was proposed based on recent studies of usability and inspired by Participatory Design practices and the Organizational Semiotics theory [7].

The design problem proposed to the students involved support to activities the biologists develop both in the lab (Planning and Analysis) and in the field (Field Work). The Planning and Analysis are activities in the lab to prepare the field work (pre-field), monitoring its execution, and analysing data after field work (post-field). Thus, the designing problem involved (a) the design of a (web) application to support the planning of field work, and receiving and analyzing the data collected, and (b) the design of an application to support biologists in the field work. Both applications should communicate. The object of discussion in this work is the mobile application to support the biologist field work.

A set of 25 students, organized in 7 groups, worked in the role of designers to conceive and develop the interface of the application. Four groups designed mobile interfaces and 3 groups designed web applications for supporting the process management. All the groups conducted the following activities: (i) problem

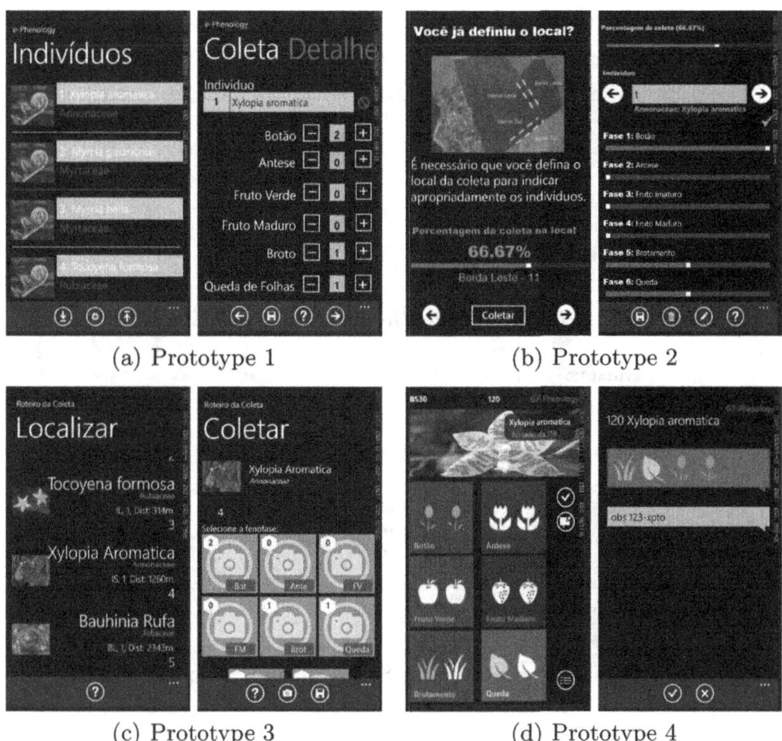

(a) Prototype 1

(b) Prototype 2

(c) Prototype 3

(d) Prototype 4

Fig. 5. Screen shots of prototypes.

clarification through participatory practices (e.g., Group Elicitation Method) and context analysis through Organizational Semiotics' artifacts (e.g., Stakeholder Identification Diagram, Evaluation Framework); (ii) organization of a first set of requirements, prototyping (low and high fidelity) and evaluation in an iterative cycle.

During the process, the participants communicated with the partner biologists both on-line and in face-to-face meetings: from the very start when the problem was being clarified to the validation of requirements and the evaluation of different proposals. At the end of the term, the groups presented their prototypes to two biologists from the Phenology Laboratory and two Computer Scientist from the Institute of Computing, University of Campinas. They were very excited with the great possibilities of the prospective applications to facilitate and add to their work in data acquisition in the field. Our challenge was then to evaluate these prototypes with a sound set of guidelines in order to discover which one (or what aspects of them) would best fit to the needs of experts within this domain (ePhenology Project).

In Fig. 5(a) to (d), we can see the screen shots of the prototypes considered in this evaluation. These screen shots refer to the main data acquisition process

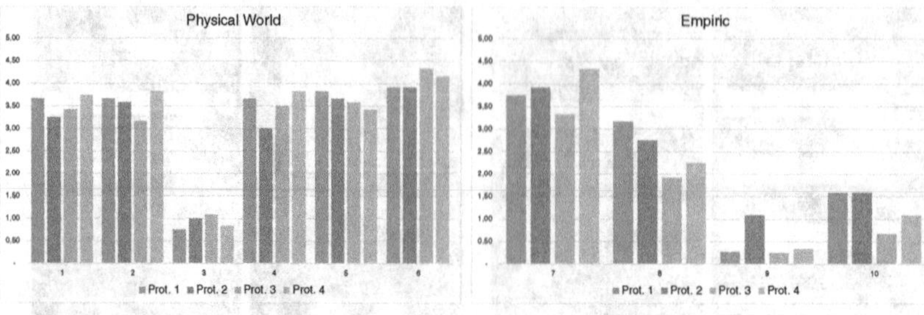

Fig. 6. Average results for the Physical World and Empiric step

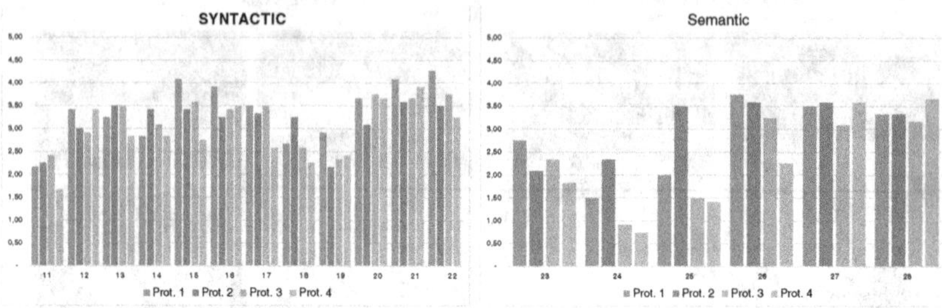

Fig. 7. Average results for the Syntactic and Semantic step

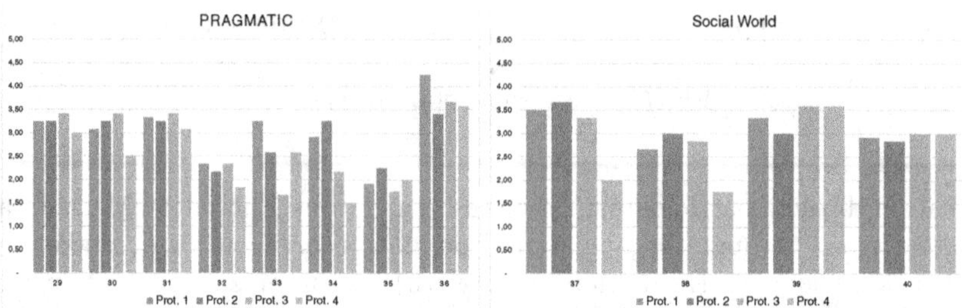

Fig. 8. Average results for the pragmatic and social world step

and some extra features implemented in each prototype. In the first prototype, Fig. 5(a), phenophase scores are defined using the "minus" (–) and the "plus" (+) buttons. In the second prototype, Fig. 5(b), the scores are defined using a sliding bar for each phenophase. In the third prototype, Fig. 5(c), the scores are defined by clicking in the icon for each phenophase. Finally, in the fourth prototype, Fig. 5(d), a quite different design is adopted, where phenophase scores are represented by painted icons: When only one icon is filled (see for example the leaf fall phenophase – *Queda* in Portuguese), then the intensity assigned to this phenophase is 1. When two icons are filled (see for example the flower bud phenophase – *Botão* in Portuguese), the intensity assigned is 2.

4.3 Results and Analysis

To evaluate the prototypes with the proposed guideline set, we invited a group of six specialists in HCI from the Institute of Computing, University of Campinas and six specialists in Phenology from São Paulo State University – UNESP. For this evaluation, the proposed questionnaire was constructed from the guideline sentences and answered in a Likert scale (1–5). Based on the specialists' responses, we computed the average scores for each question. Figures 6, 7 and 8 present these scores. Based on the evaluations, we highlight some important points:

- Regarding the Physical World step (see Fig. 6), we can notice the high performance of all prototypes regarding Q6 ("Is it sufficiently easy to operate keys with one hand?"). We can also observe low average scores of all evaluated prototypes regarding Q3 ("Does the application provide voice assistance?"). Furthermore, it is worth mentioning the low performance of Prototype 2, with regard to Q4 ("The pictures on the screen are satisfactory quality and size") and the slight superior performance of Prototype 1 regarding Q5 ("Does the application provide appropriate menu button for touch screen?").
- Regarding the Empiric step (Fig. 6), we can notice that all prototypes achieved relatively high average scores for Q7 ("Are the response time and information display fast enough?") and low average scores for Q9 ("Are exchange and transmission of data between this product and other products (e.g., computer, PDA, and other mobile products) easy?"). The results for Q7 are due to the fact that we are working with prototypes. In this case, the response is very fast because there exist little hardware processing. For Q9, the low scores are due to the fact that this specific features was not implemented in the prototypes. Also, it is worth mentioning the low scores for Q10 ("Does the application provide automatic update?") observed for all prototypes, specially for Prototype 3.
- Regarding the Syntactic step (Fig. 7), we can observe that Prototype 1 has the highest scores in 7 out of 12 questions. Another fact it is worth mentioning is that Prototype 4 has the lowest scores in 7 out of 12 questions. Also, we can notice that in questions Q11 ("How much information about system resources was displayed?") and Q19 ("Does application provide shortcuts for experienced users and wizards for new users?") all prototypes had scores below the media ("3.0 - Neither agree nor disagree") showing that this guideline was neglected by all of them.
- Regarding the Semantic step (Fig. 7), we can observe that Prototype 2 is much better than the other ones for question Q25 ("Does the application provide appropriate help?"). It is also worth mentioning the low scores observed for Q23 ("Is the output data easy to use?") and for Q24 ("Are the documentation and manual for this application sufficiently informative?") for all prototypes. In Q26 ("Is feedback on the completion of tasks clear?"), Q27 ("Is the interface with this application clear and underatandable?") and Q28 ("Is the design of the graphic symbols, icons and labels on the icons sufficiently relevant?") all prototypes had scores above media except for Prototype 4 in question Q26.
- Regarding the Pragmatic step (Fig. 8), there is no clear winner, except for Prototype 1 in Q33 ("Are the error messages effective in assisting you to fix prob-

lems?") and in Q36 ("Is it easy to learn to operate this application?"). It is worth mentioning the low scores observed for Q32 ("Does design of application is suitable for multiple contexts (home, business, travel, etc.) including support for runtime adaptation?") and Q35 ("Does application provide the ability to personalize the application to suit the user?") for all prototypes.

- Regarding the Social World step (Fig. 8), all prototypes need to be improved. We can observe, however, that Prototype 4 has the worst score for Q37 ("Does application allow privacy and security control for single or multiple users?") and Q38 ("Does application have all the functions and capabilities you expect it to have?"), in which it had scores below average.

Figures 9 and 10 show the average scores for each group of specialist and for each Semiotic ladder step, considering its questions. As it can be observed, there is no clear winner prototype regarding all criteria. That is true by taking into account the evaluation of HCI experts and all evaluators altogether. For Phenology experts, we can observe that Prototype 1 has the highest scores.

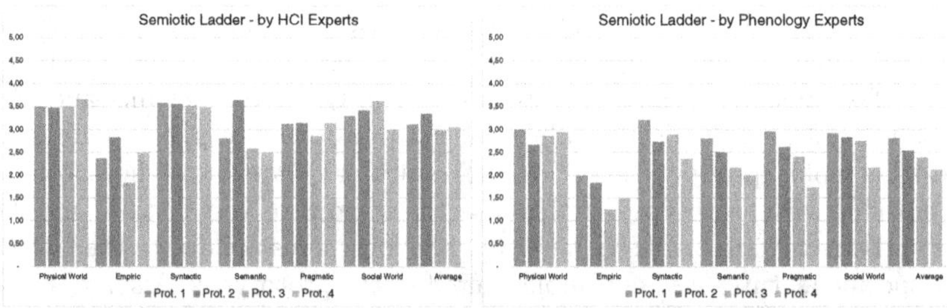

Fig. 9. Average results for each Semiotic ladder step according to the evaluation of experts

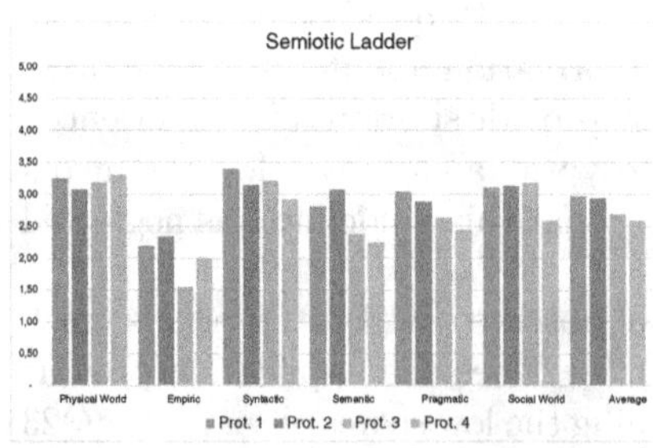

Fig. 10. Average results for each Semiotic ladder step considering both groups of evaluators (HCI and Phenology experts).

Observing the results for HCI specialists, we can point out that Prototype 1 is the best one in terms of the Syntactic step, while Prototype 2 is the best one in terms of the Empiric and Semantic steps. For the Physical World step, Prototype 4 is the best and for the Social World step, Prototype 3 has the highest average scores. For the Pragmatic step, we can notice that Prototypes 1, 2, and 4 have almost the same average scores. Observing the results for Phenology specialists, we can point out that Prototype 1 is the best one for all steps. Prototype 2 is the second choice, having the highest scores (disregarding Prototype 1) for all steps except for the Syntactic step, on which Prototype 3 has a better score (disregarding Prototype 1). When we analyze the global result (Fig. 10), i.e., considering both groups of evaluators altogether, we can observe that Prototype 1 is the best one in terms of the Syntactic and Pragmatic steps, while Prototype 2 is the best one in terms of the Empiric and Semantic steps. For the Physical World step, Prototype 4 is the best, while for the Social World step, Prototype 3 has the highest score. If we consider that the minimum acceptable score should be 4 ("Agree") and that none of them reached this score, we conclude that all prototype must be improved to meet the standards of evaluators. Figure 11 shows the evaluation scores of each prototype for each evaluator. Evaluators from 1 to 6 are HCI experts. We can observe that Evaluator 3 (an HCI specialist) gave the best scores for all prototypes (except for Prototype 3, but it was almost the highest). We can also observe lowest average scores given by Evaluator 11 (a Phenology specialist). Another fact worth mentioning is that scores provided by HCI specialists are better than those given by Phenology specialists. This is probably because usually the HCI specialist is looking for a non-functional prototype of an prospective application and, on the other hand, the Phenology specialist is looking at a product that s/he wishes to use.

The results of the evaluation through the proposed guidelines show that all the prototypes have interesting design decisions to be considered in the design of a final product. These results are even more important because they came from different design proposals that were created based on an informed and well-defined design process conducted by prospective designers in a participatory style.

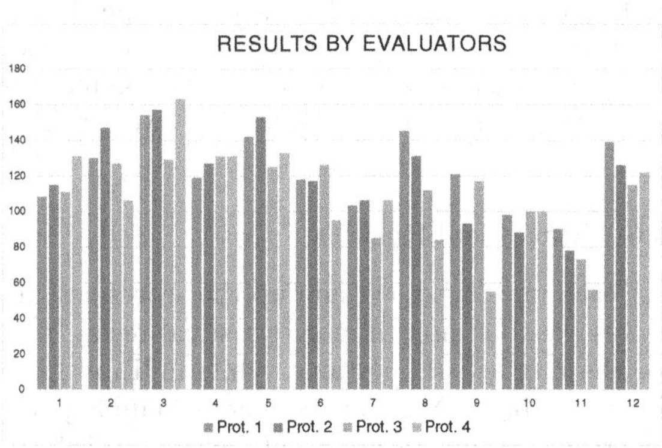

Fig. 11. Total points obtained by each prototype for each evaluator.

4.4 Statistical Analysis

Based on the results of the conducted evaluation, statistical analyses were performed in order to establish if there are differences among the evaluations of the different prototypes and also if there are differences between the two groups of evaluators (specialists in HCI and specialists in Phenology). These analyses were done using the evaluation methodology proposed in Sect. 3.2. Following this methodology, we characterize the performed statistical tests.

4.5 Overview

1. Definition of groups of evaluators.
   - Group 1: Six HCI experts from the Institute of Computing, University of Campinas;

  - Group 2: Six Phenology Experts from the São Paulo State University – UNESP.
2. Definition of application interfaces.
  - Four prototypes developed for in-the-field phenological data acquisition (for more details, see Sect. 4.2).
3. Definition of key research questions. The performed analysis addresses two research venues:
  (a) Are there differences between the groups of evaluators considering
    - their general evaluation of the prototypes?
    - their evaluation of a particular prototype?
    - their evaluation of prototypes using a particular semiotic ladder step?
    - their evaluation of a particular prototype according to a specific semiotic ladder step?
  (b) Are there differences among the prototypes considering
    - the complete set of guideline questions, i.e., all semiotic ladder steps altogether?
    - a particular semiotic ladder step?
4. Definition of statistical tests. - Based on characteristics of these questions, the statistical tests was selected according Table 9
  - For the first set of questions, we conduct t tests;
  - For the second set of questions, we use ANOVA Repeated Measures.

4.6 Statistical Results

For each prototype, we sum up the scores assigned by each evaluator. The final scores are then used in our statistical tests. In Table 11, we present the results for the first set of questions, while in Table 12 for the second set of questions. In these tables, "Yes" means that the null hypothesis was rejected, i.e., there are differences among the groups of evaluators (Table 11), or among the evaluated prototypes (Table 12). In all tests, we consider 95 % confidence.

We can observe that both groups of evaluators have different views regarding all prototypes (first column in Table 11). Furthermore, they also have different opinions regarding all prototypes (except for Prototype 1), when all steps are

Table 11. Result of t tests – Are there differences among the groups of evaluators?

	All prototypes	Prototype 1	Prototype 2	Prototype 3	Prototype 4
All steps	Yes	No	Yes	Yes	Yes
Physical World	Yes	No	No	No	No
Empiric	Yes	No	No	No	Yes
Syntactic	Yes	No	No	Yes	Yes
Semantic	Yes	No	Yes	No	No
Pragmatic	Yes	No	No	Yes	Yes
Social World	Yes	No	No	No	No

Table 12. Results of ANOVA tests – Are there differences among the prototypes?

	In general	HCI experts	Phenology experts
All steps	Yes	No	Yes
Physical World	Yes	No	No
Empiric	Yes	No	No
Syntactic	Yes	No	No
Semantic	Yes	No	Yes
Pragmatic	Yes	No	No
Social World	Yes	No	No

Table 13. Which one is the best Prototype?

	In general	HCI experts	Phenology experts
All steps	1	*	1
Physical World	4	*	*
Empiric	2	*	*
Syntactic	1	*	*
Semantic	2	*	1
Pragmatic	1	*	*
Social World	3	*	*

considered (first line). In fact, both groups of evaluators have the same opinion for all steps, regarding Prototype 1. For Prototype 2, there is statistical difference only for the Semantic step and when considering all steps. For Prototypes 3 and 4, sometimes they agree (for example, for the evaluation of the Physical World and Semantic steps), while for other steps they disagree (Syntactic and Pragmatic Step). In relation to the Empiric step, they have the same opinion with regard to Prototype 3, but, for Prototype 4 they have different points of view. Regarding the prototypes, there are statistical differences when the scores provided of HCI and Phenology experts are considered altogether (first column in Table 12). However, when only the opinion of HCI experts are considered, no differences are identified, regardless the Semiotic Ladder step (second column). For Phenology experts, the prototypes are different when all steps are considered altogether, or when only the Semantic step is taken into account. Finally, in Table 13, we present the statistical results concerning the identification of the best prototypes, considering the opinion of different groups of experts and different Semiotic Ladder steps. We can observe that when all steps are considered as well as the evaluation of all evaluators, Prototype 1 is the best one. For HCI experts, there is not a clear winner regardless the Semiotic Ladder step (cells marked with "*"). For Phenology experts, Prototype 1 is the best one when all steps are considered altogether, or when only the Semantic step is taken into account.

5 Conclusion

The large-scale adoption of portable device applications depends on the use of careful interface design. In this work, we analyzed strategies, guidelines and questions in literature on mobile application design and evaluation and proposed a novel set of guidelines composed of 27 semiotic-informed guidelines for supporting the evaluation of mobile application interfaces. This guidelines set served also as the basis for the proposal of a method for evaluating mobile application interfaces. Another contribution of this work refers to the fact that the proposed method can be applied to people working in the application domain, without specialized knowledge on semiotics or on methods for interface evaluation.

We demonstrate the use of the proposed method and guidelines in the context of the evaluation of four prototypes recently proposed for phenological data acquisition. The analysis of results from evaluations indicates that the proposed guidelines set is well suited for the evaluation of mobile application interface as it helps to identify positive and negative aspects of proposed designs, according to well-defined semiotic concepts of different information layers. A limitation of this study is the fact of having conducted the experiments with a not totally functional application. In this case, some questions are not applicable or not completely applicable, and this fact could have affected the results of our study. As future work, we intend to develop novel interface designs based on the findings related to the advantages and drawbacks identified in the evaluated prototypes, and to conduct experiments in which phenology experts will be able to evaluate the developed prototypes using the proposed guidelines. We also intend to evaluate whether the guidelines set proposed in this work are also useful for supporting the design of mobile application interfaces. We do believe that the set of guidelines is generic enough to be used for different application domains.

Acknowledgments. This research was supported by the FAPESP – Microsoft Research Virtual Institute (grants #2010/52113-5 and #2013/50155-0). LPCM, CB, and RST receive a Productivity Research Fellowship from CNPq (grants #306243/2010-5, #308618/2014-9 and #306587/2009-2). BA receives a PhD fellowship from FAPESP (grant #2014/00215-0). Also, we also thank CNPq, CAPES, and FAPESP (grants #2007/52015-0, #2007/59779-6, #2009/18438-7, and #2010/51307-0). We would like also to thank the HCI and Phenology experts for their help and participation in the evaluation process.

References

1. Abdallah, M.: Home healthcare devices: towards a scalable, portable, accurate, and affordable data acquisition instrument. In: 38th Annual Northeast Bioengineering Conference (NEBEC), pp. 9–10, March 2012
2. Hao, J., Kim, S.H., Ay, S.A., Zimmermann, R.: Energy-efficient mobile video management using smartphones. In: Proceedings of the Second Annual ACM Conference on Multimedia Systems, pp. 11–22 (2011)

3. Zarko, I.P., Antonic, A., Pripužic, K.: Publish/subscribe middleware for energy-efficient mobile crowdsensing. In: Conference on Pervasive and Ubiquitous Computing Adjunct Publication, UbiComp 2013 Adjunct, pp. 1099–1110 (2013)
4. Duh, H.B.L., Tan, G.C.B., hua Chen, V.H.: Usability evaluation for mobile device: a comparison of laboratory and field tests. In: Proceedings of the 8th Conference on Human-Computer Interaction with Mobile Devices and Services, MobileHCI 2006, pp. 181–186 (2006)
5. Liu, K.: Semiotics in Information Systems Engineering. Cambridge University Press, New York (2000)
6. Baranauskas, M.C.C.: O modelo semioparticipativo de design. In: Codesign de Redes Digitais - Tecnologia e Educação a Serviço da Inclusão Social. Penso Editora Ltda, pp. 38–66 (2013)
7. Baranauskas, M.C.C.: Social awareness in HCI. Interactions **21**(4), 66–69 (2014)
8. Stamper, R.: Information in Business and Administrative Systems. Wiley, New York (1973)
9. Schwartz, M.D.: Phenology: An Integrative Environmental Science. Springer Netherlands, Dordrecht (2013)
10. Morellato, L.P.C., Camargo, M.G.G., Neves, F.F.D., Luize, B.G., Mantovani, A., Hudson, I.L.: The influence of sampling method, sample size, and frequency of observations on plant phenological patterns and interpretation in tropical forest trees. In: Hudson, I.L., Keatley, M.R. (eds.) Phenological Research, pp. 99–121. Springer, Dordrecht (2010)
11. Rathcke, B., Lacey, E.P.: Phenological patterns of terrestrial plants. Ann. Rev. Syst. **6**, 179–214 (1985)
12. Negi, G.: Leaf and bud demography and shoot growth in evergreen and deciduous trees of central himalaya, india. Trees **20**(4), 416–429 (2006)
13. Reich, P.B.: Phenology of tropical forests: patterns, causes, and consequences. Can. J. Bot. **73**(2), 164–174 (1995)
14. Keeling, C.D., Whorf, T.: Increased activity of northern vegetation inferred from atmospheric CO2 measurements. Nature **382**(6587), 146–149 (1996)
15. Morellato, L.P.C., Alberton, B., Alvarado, S.T., Borges, B.D., Buisson, E., Camargo, M.G.G., Cancian, L.F., Carstensen, D.W., Escobar, D.F.E., Leite, P.T.P., Mendoza, I., Rocha, N.M.W.B., Silva, T.S.F., Soares, N.C., Staggemeier, V.G., Streher, A.S., Vargas, B.C., Peres, C.A.: Linking plant phenology to conservation biology. Biological Conservation (2015). doi:10.1016/j.biocon.2015.12.033
16. Rötzer, T., Grote, R., Pretzsch, H.: The timing of bud burst and its effect on tree growth. Int. J. Biometeorol. **48**(3), 109–118 (2004)
17. Almeida, J., Dos Santos, J.A., Alberton, B., Torres, R.d.S., Morellato, L.P.C.: Remote phenology: applying machine learning to detect phenological patterns in a cerrado savanna. In: 8th International Conference on E-Science, pp. 1–8, October 2012
18. Parmesan, C., Yohe, G.: A globally coherent fingerprint of climate change impacts across natural systems. Nature **421**(6918), 37–42 (2003)
19. Richardson, A.D., Braswell, B.H., Hollinger, D.Y., Jenkins, J.P., Ollinger, S.V.: Near-surface remote sensing of spatial and temporal variation in canopy phenology. Ecol. Appl. **19**(6), 1417–1428 (2009)
20. Rosenzweig, C., Karoly, D., Vicarelli, M., Neofotis, P., Wu, Q., Casassa, G., Menzel, A., Root, T.L., Estrella, N., Seguin, B., et al.: Attributing physical and biological impacts to anthropogenic climate change. Nature **453**(7193), 353–357 (2008)
21. Walther, G.R.: Plants in a warmer world. Perspect. Plant Ecol. Evol. Syst. **6**(3), 169–185 (2003)

22. Walther, G.R., Post, E., Convey, P., Menzel, A., Parmesan, C., Beebee, T.J., Fromentin, J.M., Hoegh-Guldberg, O., Bairlein, F.: Ecological responses to recent climate change. Nature **416**(6879), 389–395 (2002)
23. Baranauskas, M.C.C., da Rocha, H.V.: Design e Avaliação de Interfaces Humano-Computador. Nied/Unicamp, Campinas-Sp (2003)
24. Nayebi, F., Desharnais, J.M., Abran, A.: The state of the art of mobile application usability evaluation. In: 25th Canadian Conference on Electrical Computer Engineering (CCECE), pp. 1–4, April 2012
25. Radia, N., Zhang, Y., Tatipamula, M., Madisetti, V.K.: Next-generation applications on cellular networks: trends, challenges, and solutions. Proc. IEEE **100**(4), 841–854 (2012)
26. Zamzami, I., Mahmud, M.: User satisfaction on smart phone interface design, information quality evaluation. In: International Conference on Advanced Computer Science Applications and Technologies (ACSAT), pp. 78–82, November 2012
27. Rauch, M.: Mobile documentation: usability guidelines, and considerations for providing documentation on kindle, tablets, and smartphones. In: Professional Communication Conference (IPCC), pp. 1–13, October 2011
28. binti Ayob, N.Z., Hussin, A.R.C., Dahlan, H.M.: Three layers design guideline for mobile application. In: International Conference on Information Management and Engineering (ICIME), pp. 427–431, April 2009
29. Hussain, A., Kutar, M.: Usability metric framework for mobile phone application. In: 10th Annual Conference on the Convergence of Telecommunications, Networking & Broadcasting, PostGraduate Network Symposium (PGNet) (2009). http://www.cms.livjm.ac.uk/pgnet2009/Proceedings/Papers/2009013.pdf
30. Ryu, Y.S.: Development of usability questionnaires for electronic mobile products and decision making methods. Ph.D. thesis, Virginia Polytechnic Institute and State University (2005)
31. Gong, J., Tarasewich, P.: Guidelines for handheld mobile device interface design. In: Proceedings of DSI 2004 Annual Meeting, pp. 3751–3756 (2004)
32. Cordeiro, J., Filipe, J.: The semiotic pentagram framework-a perspective on the use of semiotics within organisational semiotics. In: Proceedings of the 7th International Workshop on Organisational Semiotics, pp. 249–265 (2004)
33. Piccolo, L.S.G., Baranauskas, M.C.C.: Climbing the ladder with energy: informing the design of eco-feedback technology with a social approach. In: The Fourteenth International Conference on Informatics and Semiotics in Organisations, pp. 187–194 (2013)
34. Lazar, J., Feng, J.H., Hochheiser, H.: Research Methods in Human-Computer Interaction. Wiley, New York (2010)
35. Menzel, A., Sparks, T.H., Estrella, N., Koch, E., Aasa, A., Ahas, R., Alm-kübler, K., Bissolli, P., Braslavská, O., Briede, A., et al.: European phenological response to climate change matches the warming pattern. Glob. Change Biol. **12**(10), 1969–1976 (2006)
36. Neves, F.F.D., Morellato, L.P.C.: Métodos de amostragem e avaliação utilizados em estudos fenológicos de florestas tropicais. Acta Bot. Bras. **18**(1), 99–108 (2004)
37. Alberton, B., Almeida, J., Helm, R., Torres, R.D.S., Menzel, A., Morellato, L.P.C.: Using phenological cameras to track the green up in a cerrado savanna and its on-the-ground validation. Ecol. Inform. **19**, 62–70 (2014)
38. Camargo, M.G.G., Souza, R.M.S., Reys, P., Morellato, L.P.C.: Effects of environmental conditions associated to the cardinal orientation on the reproductive phenology of the cerrado savanna tree xylopia aromatica (annonaceae). Biotropica **83**(3), 1007–1019 (2011)

Personalization of Privacy in Mobile Social Networks

Tiago Antonio Rosa(✉) and Sergio Donizetti Zorzo

Computer Science Department, Federal University of São Carlos, São Carlos, SP, Brazil
tiagorosapc@gmail.com, zorzo@dc.ufscar.br

Abstract. Mobile social networks are characterized by the sharing of user context information, such as the location of one's mobile device. The location information on a social network enables its operator to offer resources for socialization, such as suggestions of new friends, products, and services, in relation to the user's geographical area. While some users view such suggestions as a personal gain, others view them as an invasion of privacy. Since this location information is shared by the users on social networks, it can be accessed by the users' friends and service providers, but also by malicious users. Unauthorized access can pose several risks regarding privacy and security. On the other hand, sharing a user's location with a particular friend or group of friends while concealing this information from the service provider would guarantee the security and privacy of the user's information. This paper presents a mobile social networking model with privacy guarantees concerning the sharing of its members' locations. The model allows users to personalize their privacy by setting rules that determine to whom, when, and where their location information can be made available. The model provides three levels of privacy, personalized by the user, using techniques of anonymity and dissemination or setting the location to ensure the concealment of information before it is made available on the social network. A proof of concept for the proposed model, called RSMPrivacy, was developed for the Android platform. The performance tests showed that the delays generated by the use of RSMPrivacy were proportional to, and justifiable for, the privacy levels desired and chosen by the users. RSMPrivacy was evaluated by 50 users on the aspects of usability and evidence of the efficiency of the techniques in the proposed model.

Keywords: Privacy · Mobile social network · Privacy rules · Location-Sharing · Personalized privacy

1 Introduction

Social networks are immensely popular social media platforms. Conceptually, a social network is a framework of entities that are connected with each other through one or more specific types of interdependence, such as friendship, kinship, common interests, financial exchanges, empathy, or relationships grounded in shared beliefs, knowledge, or prestige [1]. Individuals, organizations, and groups are examples of such entities. The interactions between these entities are enabled via existing technologies and media, such as the Internet.

S. Hammoudi et al. (Eds.): ICEIS 2015, LNBIP 241, pp. 555–573, 2015.
DOI: 10.1007/978-3-319-29133-8_27

Mobile social networks (MSNs) are a subclass of social networks that users access using wireless communication via their mobile devices in order to interact with each other. MSNs arose as a result of the popularity of both social networks and mobile devices, and as the latter became increasingly affordable, this allowed for accessing, processing, and sharing information anytime, anywhere, thus providing ubiquitous access. In addition, the current mobile devices have high processing power, multiple network interfaces, a global positioning system (GPS), and various sensors, such as an accelerometer and magnetometer. Thus, these mobile devices allow for the execution of increasingly sophisticated applications and the ability to identify some aspects of users' contexts or even their current activity.

Using MSNs on their mobile devices, users can access (read), publish (write or insert), and share (transmit or disclose) contents created or obtained through the sensors on the device. Facebook[1] is an example of an MSN that had more than 680 million mobile users in 2014 [16]. Other popular MSNs are Twitter[2], Instagram[3], Foursquare[4], and WhatsApp[5].

An MSN is characterized by the addition of context information to the social network due to the ability of the mobile environment to obtain physical data via these sensors; thus, applications can combine context data and infer the state of the user. This makes it possible to improve the relationships between users or create new from common interests, such as sports played, frequented places, musical tastes, and posted messages, among others. Among such context information is the user's location.

The location sharing in an MSN enables the social network to offer recommendations—representing a personal gain for many users, but raising privacy concerns for others. Tosh et al. [2] and Benisch et al. [3] expressed concern about the release of location information in social networking applications affecting the willingness of users to adopt these applications. The provider of the social network uses this shared location information to offer socialization features, such as recommendations for new friends, places, products, etc. However, this provider can use this information inappropriately, therefore creating a risk to user privacy. Additionally, malicious users belonging to the social network have access to the locations shared by other users, and they, too, pose a threat to user privacy. On the other hand, sharing the location of a user with a particular friend or group of friends, while shielding this information from the social network provider and malicious users, could safeguard the information and ensure the user's privacy.

Some MSNs, like Facebook, already allow users to personalize their privacy settings when they use the application. This customization is performed through the established privacy policies that determine which users of the social network can view someone else's location and in which locations, dates, and times this information can be made available. Such policies established by the social networks, where they exist, are implemented with constraints in supply aspects or not the actual location of the user and the

---

[1] https://www.facebook.com/.
[2] https://twitter.com/.
[3] https://instagram.com/.
[4] https://foursquare.com/.
[5] https://www.whatsapp.com.

group of users that apply. In general, the policies are limited in the control of information collection, access to users' personal data, the security of the data transmitted, and the responsibility of the users.

This paper presents a location-sharing model for MSNs with privacy guarantees.

The model provides mechanisms aimed at ensuring the privacy of the individual user's location and the location of user groups formed within a social network. In the model, privacy is personalized by the user and can be configured using levels and rules. The model contains levels defining the accuracy of the location that will be shared and rules enabling users to define with whom, where, and when to share their location. All privacy mechanisms within the model run on the user's device. Thus, the model does not allow the real user's location to be obtained with high accuracy by either the provider of the social networking site or by malicious users. In addition, the socialization features offered by the social network can be altered depending on how the user customizes his or her privacy.

A proof of concept for the proposed model, called RSMPrivacy, was developed for the Android platform. RSMPrivacy allows the user to share his or her location with members of his or her social network or groups that are created by the user or are created in an automated way taking into account a certain context, such as the degree of kinship or geographical position. The performance tests showed that the delays generated by the use of RSMPrivacy were proportional and justifiable customizations performed by the user through the levels and privacy rules. Furthermore, RSMPrivacy was evaluated by a group of 50 users on the aspects of the usability and efficiency of the techniques present in the proposed model.

This paper is organized as follows: Sect. 2 presents the contextualization of privacy in the location sharing on MSNs; Sect. 3 presents the proposed model, its architecture, and its characteristics; Sect. 4 presents the implemented MSN prototype of the model, RSMPrivacy; Sect. 5 discusses the related work; Sect. 6 presents the results obtained from the performance testing and usability testing; Sect. 7 provides the conclusions regarding the work; and Sect. 8 proposes future work.

2 Privacy in Mobile Social Networks

In an MSN, the protection of information relating to a user's location is especially important due to the large number of applications that exploit this information to provide resources relative to the location of the user's mobile device. Indeed, these applications can misuse the information they acquire. Location privacy can be defined as the user's right to decide how, when, with whom, and for what purpose his or her location information may be disclosed to others [4]. Anthony et al. [5] identified the following location privacy categories:

- Identity Privacy: the goal is to protect the user ID associated or inferred from the location information; the location information may be provided to any entity, but the user's identity must be preserved
- Position Privacy: the goal is to hide the exact location of the user in order to protect his or her actual location

- Path Privacy: the goal is not to reveal the user's previous locations (i.e., the path traversed by the user).

All content posted, especially the location where it was posted, can be accessed or shared with other entities, representing possible sources of privacy attacks. Gao et al. [6] considered the following origins as security loopholes that can be classified in terms of access: (i) other users of the social network, (ii) third-party applications, and (iii) the actual service provider.

Other users of the social network pose a threat due to the ease with which attackers can join the social network, create an account with the service provider, and become real users. These malicious users can also produce false context information for the MSN that can be exploited by other malicious users to gain access to resources, adopt a temporary identity, and integrate into user groups created automatically by the MSN. When a user shares his or her location with a group created automatically by the MSN, these malicious users also have access to this information. They, in turn, can misuse the user's location and thus compromise user privacy. The misuse of information is characterized by monitoring the user's travel without his or her consent or knowledge, his or her current position, the places that he or she has attended, his or her routine as inferred from the location history, among others. This information may not only violate user privacy but potentially harm the users of the MSN.

Third-party applications are developed using the application programming interface (API) provided by the MSN. This API enables the creation of new resources for the MSN. Since these applications are developed by third parties, they are not always reliable. Some examples of third-party applications include games, music applications, photos and videos, and even the applications of advertising agencies conducting campaigns to promote products and services. These applications require the user to grant free access to his or her personal information, such as shared location and movement history.

The social network service provider is responsible for providing the necessary resources to the MSN users. The provider has access to all the personal information that the users have inserted or published. Moreover, the provider is responsible for managing and delivering the user's shared location with his or her friends or the groups to which he or she belongs. Thus, the provider also has access to the user's shared location. For this reason, social network users have been left to rely on the service provider without really knowing who is manipulating their shared locations.

The model proposed in this paper deals with the threats described above and allows users to customize their privacy settings by creating privacy rules. Furthermore, the model provides levels that deal with anonymous location accuracy and what is to be shared. Combining preferences and privacy levels allows users to minimize the risks associated with disclosing their location.

3 Model

Figure 1 illustrates the mobile social network model proposed in this work which provides a privacy guarantee. It is composed of a client application working in mobile devices, a social network server (SNS), a reliable proxy, and users.

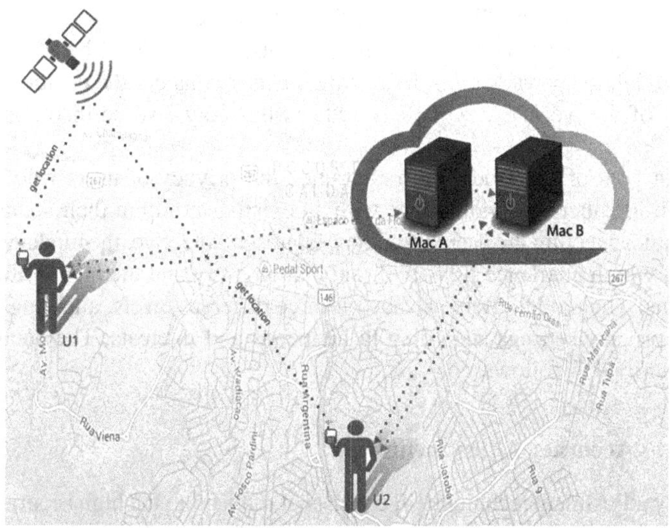

Fig. 1. Model architecture.

The application working in mobile devices must be able to connect to the internet through Wi-Fi networks or a data plan from operators, connect to servers, and determine its location through GPS, triangulation, and a Wi-Fi signal. Moreover, the devices must be able to receive location requirements and process rules and techniques which guarantee users' privacy.

The social network server, illustrated in Fig. 1 by Mac B, meets user requests.

The main goal of the server is to allow users to find the current IP address of social network members whenever they require send a request of location. For that, the server stores a list of its users, their contact lists, and the updated IP addresses of each user. Moreover, the server stores the current status of users. Users interact with the server when registering (only once), during the login phase (every time a user connects or disconnects), when downloading a list of contacts, when periodically informing the updated IP address and its status, and when sending location requirements to a member of their net.

In the model, users can be classified in two different ways: a requester, when sending a request to another user, or a target, when receiving a location-sharing request.

To increase communication safety, all requests made between users and the social network servers are encrypted with a public key certificate obtained from a reliable Certification Authority (CA).

To protect users' location privacy in relation to the server, none of the privacy techniques are applied by the server, but instead by the application in the users' devices. The information is sent to the server only after necessary alterations; this way, the server cannot know the real user location. This is a crucial aspect of the model, as it does not permit the server, which can be outsourced, to have any information relating to a user's location. However, the server knows their IP address and can, therefore, accurately infer their location (based on the IP-geolocalization). To solve this problem, users can hide their IP address using a reliable proxy which is illustrated in Fig. 1 by Mac A.

In this model, the privacy rules defined by the user consider the position, period (in hours), days of the week and whitelists. Other rules may also be incorporated in the model.

The main goal of the model is to guarantee the privacy of users who share their location with members individually or with an existing group in their social network. For that, besides meeting the users' preferences presented above, the model implements mechanisms which guarantee privacy through anonymity and the hiding of high accuracy positions. The model offers privacy on three different levels, allowing the user to personalize privacy settings according to his needs and interests. The details of each level are described as follows.

3.1 Level 1– Accuracy Adjustment

The accuracy adjustment technique [9] consists of modifying the high accuracy location so that this information about position represents different points inside a certain area. This adjustment is calculated based on the original location's random displacement for any direction inside a given radius, as shown in Fig. 2.

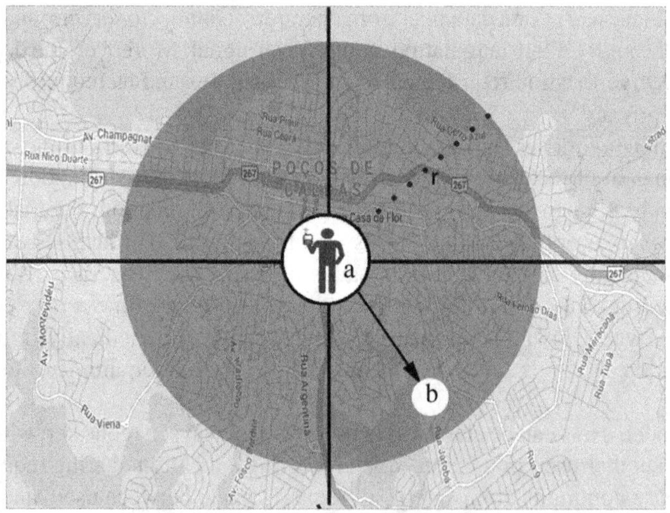

Fig. 2. Accuracy adjustment.

In Fig. 2, the real user location is illustrated by the center circle "a"; the displacement radius is illustrated by the letter 'r'. When the accuracy is adjusted, the user's location is randomly displaced for any direction inside the area illustrated by the smaller circle "b". The displacement radius or accuracy adjustment coefficient is defined by the user according to his preference.

To perform the accuracy adjustment, the formula below was used. It is based on the spherical triangle formed by the initial point, the final point, and the north pole [7].

Two sides of this triangle are already known: the side between the initial point and the north pole and the side referring to the displacement distance. In addition, the angle formed by these two sides is also known, and it is characterized by the displacement direction.

$$
\begin{aligned}
at2 &= \arcsin(\sin(lat) * \cos\left(\frac{d}{R}\right) + \cos(lat1) * \sin\left(\frac{d}{R}\right) * \cos(\theta)) \\
dlon &= arctan2(\sin(\theta) * \sin\left(\frac{d}{R}\right) * \cos(lat1), \cos\left(\frac{d}{R}\right) - \sin(lat1) * \sin(lat2)) \\
lon2 &= mod\,(lon1 - dlon + pi, 2 * pi) - pi
\end{aligned} \tag{1}
$$

In the formula above, the **θ** element represents the displacement direction where lat1 and lon1 are the coordinates of the initial point, and the angular distance is illustrated by d/R, where d is the adjustment distance set by the user and R is the Earth's radius. The goal of the module applied in the end of the formula is to accommodate cases in which the points are in opposite meridians. The resulting coordinates are illustrated by lat2 and lon2. This formula is valid only for cases in which the calculated distance is less than a quarter of the Earth's circumference.

After performing the accuracy adjustment in the user location information, the application sends the resulting coordinate to the SRS.

This technique guarantees that user location information shared with friends or a group of users inside a social network will not be a high accuracy location, and in this way, level 1 guarantees a certain amount of privacy to users.

Users can still match the accuracy adjustment in level 1 with the privacy preferences presented in Session 2 specifically to place, day of the week, and break time.

3.2 Level 2 – Anonymity

The model in level 2 guarantees user anonymity through a location information hiding technique. To hide information, information about the location of online users who are geographically near is used. In the case of a group defined inside a social network, the coordinates of the users in the group are used. To obtain the necessary locations so the anonymity technique can be applied, the application requests the locations of other users.

The hiding location is calculated by selecting one of the online groups' locations. This selection is made by calculating the fair point, a location which reduces the distance of any user related to all others. For calculating the fair point, the k-center problem was used. In the k-center problem, the goal is to find the k site among all locations shared so that the maximum distance of any user in relation to the others is reduced. Figure 3 illustrates an example of a scenario modeled with the k-center problem, where the fair point is calculated with four users.

In Fig. 3, the traced lines represent the maximum distances, while the full line represents the minimum distance among all the maximum distances. Therefore, in this scenario, the fair point is User U2.

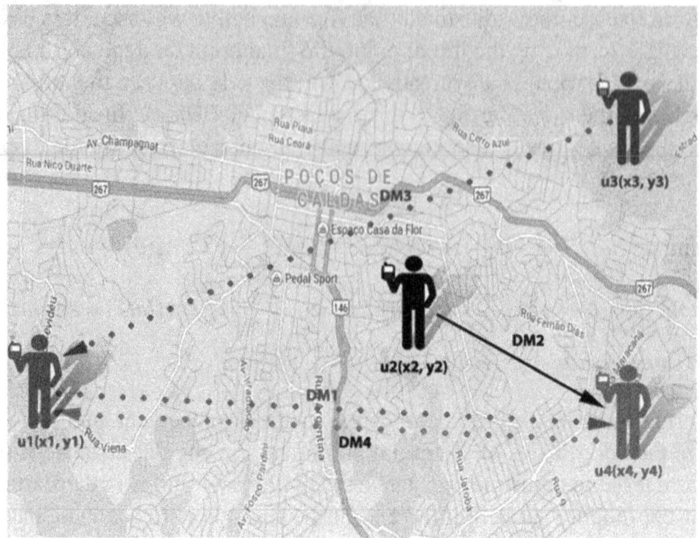

Fig. 3. Scenario modeled with the k-center problem.

After selecting the location which will hide the user's real position, the accuracy adjustment technique in level 1 is applied in the selected location and shared after being changed. The accuracy adjustment is necessary because the location which will be shared is a high accuracy location and is a valid location of a social network user.

The anonymity technique of this level cannot always be applied because it depends on the locations of other users within the group. If these locations are not obtained within 5 s, the application fine-tunes the current position of the user and conceals the actual location of the user.

3.3 Level 3 – Anonymity Guaranteed

In level 3, the model guarantees the existence of the anonymity group through the false location technique [9], as illustrated in Fig. 4.

The client application gets the current position of the user, shown in Fig. 4, at circle "a" using the device's GPS. From this information, the application generates four other false locations, shown in Fig. 4 by dark circles, using the characteristics of the level of precision adjustment technique 1. After this process, the application has five locations (four false and the current user). Then, the same technique is applied to compute the level 2. Anonymity is also applied at this level. The resulting location of anonymity, represented by circle "b" in Fig. 4, is fine-tuned and then shared in the social network. The model guarantees the user's privacy because the shared location will not be his real coordinate.

All techniques applied are performed on the user's device itself to guarantee the server cannot obtain the user's real location; the shared location is not real. Users can even combine privacy levels with their sharing preferences.

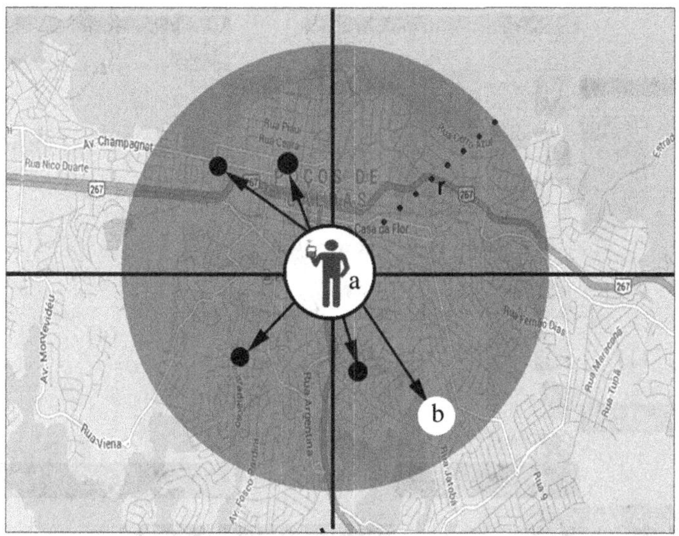

Fig. 4. Generation of false locations.

The proposed model was validated by the implementation of a prototype for a mobile social network called MSNPrivacy (Mobile Social Network with Privacy). MSNPrivacy allows the user to share his location with individual members of his social network or with groups created by him or automatically, taking into account a given context, for example, the relationship or geographic position. Details about MSNPrivacy's operation will be discussed in the next session.

4 MSNPrivacy

MSNPrivacy (Mobile Social Network with Privacy) is a mobile social network application prototype implemented in Android [10] which was developed with the aim of validating the proposed model. In the prototype implementation, the simple and intuitive natures of social networks were considered as far as usability. To compose the user's mobile social network, the prototype uses Facebook's friends lists. Figure 5 shows the main application interfaces where users can login and register, see the list of contacts and the status, require the location and see the feedback, and set their preferences and privacy levels.

In Fig. 5, the login (1) interface allows the user to register at first access or to login in at other accesses. The interface of the list of friends (2) allows the user to see all friends in his social network and their current status and to require their location and access the preferences setting interface along with privacy levels (4). When the user requires the location of a friend in his list, the feedback can be seen on a map (3).

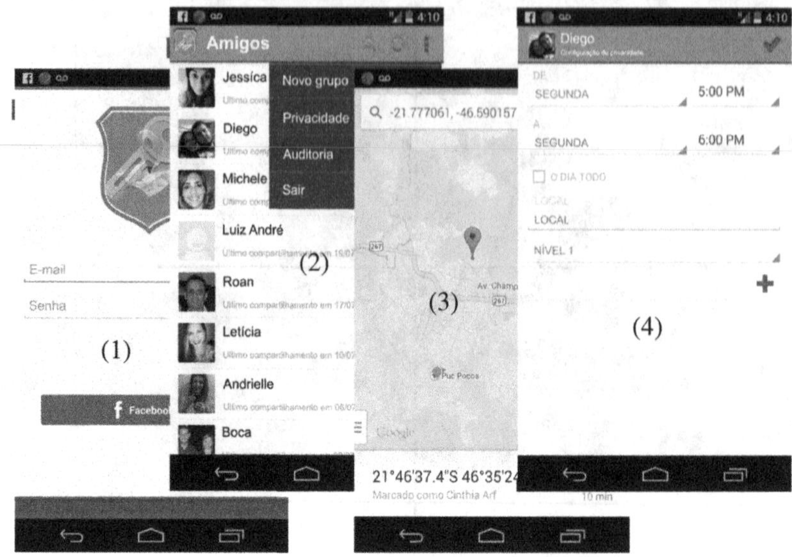

Fig. 5. Main MSNPrivacy application interfaces.

4.1 Operation Principle

MSNPrivacy works as follows: First, the user logs in or registers on the server, providing the access login and password. The application also provides the option to register directly through Facebook as shown in Fig. 5(1). If the user is connected to Facebook, the application directly captures the login information with no need for it to be typed by the user. At this point, in addition to sending the data to the server, the application starts a service which periodically updates the current IP address and also starts another service which monitors the reception of location requests from other users of the social network. After obtaining the user login data, the application sends it to the server. The server receives the data and, if the user is not registered, the server promotes integration with Facebook, looking for the user's list of contacts. After obtaining the contacts, the server stores them and sends them to the user's device which locally stores the contact list and presents it to the user. The process referring to the user's first access is presented in the sequence diagram in Fig. 6.

The user can set his preferences and privacy levels for each contact of his list and for the groups he is in (Fig. 5(4)). If this setting is not performed, the application uses level 1 as the pattern for all contacts and groups.

In a typical scenario, the User requests one of his online contacts' location by selecting him from his list. Next, the application prepares the request and sends it to the server. The server looks for the requested user's current IP, connects to the device, and sends the request. After receiving the request, the application verifies the privacy preferences set for the requested user, applies the privacy techniques on the obtained location, encapsulates the data, and sends it back to the server. The server directs the result to the Uses and shows the location on a map after receiving the information. If the

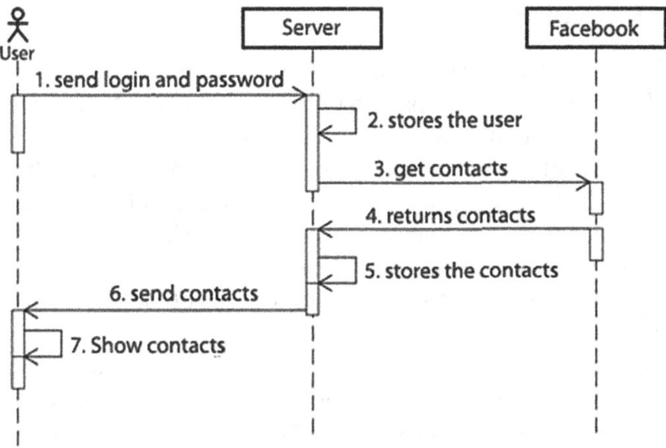

Fig. 6. First access sequence diagram.

requested user is not online at that moment, the requested user's application comes back to the main interface, and when the server receives the requested user's data, it sends it to the User's device. As soon as the application receives the feedback, it notifies the User. The requirement information received or sent is stored either in the server or in the user's device. This way, users can audit in the application or on the web. The process related to the location requirement is presented in the sequence diagram in Fig. 7.

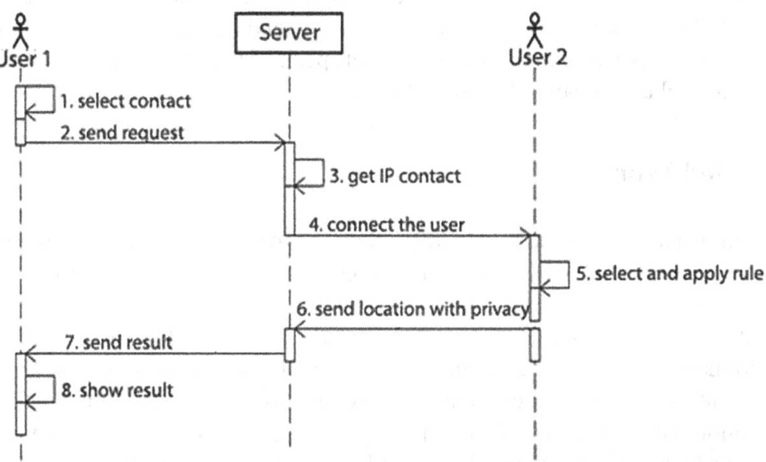

Fig. 7. Location request of a contact.

All privacy techniques presented in each level are processed in the user's device. This ensures the server does not have access to high-accuracy location information which is shared on the social net. However, the server still has the user's IP address which makes it is possible to infer his location. This issue can be easily solved using a reliable proxy as long as one is available.

4.2 Privacy Preferences Setting

The application allows the user to set his privacy preferences with each member of his social network and within the groups he has joined (Fig. 5(4)). Moreover, the user can match his preferences with the privacy levels offered.

The proposed model allows define rules to manage the privacy user. In MSNPrivacy some rules such as "Who", which allows the user to indicate which member of its mobile social network feels the urge to share his position, "Time", which allows to determine the period of schedule was implemented, "Where", which to determine the location and "days" which enables want to determine the day or days of the week that your location will be disclosed.

To better illustrate the privacy setting, a hypothetical user called "Alice" will be considered. Alice wants to share her location with friends in her social network when she is at home and on the weekends from 9:00 a.m. to 5:00 p.m. In this case, when creating a setting, Alice will have to indicate the location, the period of time, and the days of the week. Alice can even specify the privacy level. In case no level is specified, level 1 is automatically used. Alice will be able to create a rule for each member or group (individually) in her social network or set a rule for everybody.

The model deals with the conflict rules in two ways. In the first case, the model allows the user to only create rules that grant sharing your location and does not allow the creation of rules that deny sharing. For example, "Mary can see my location from 9 AM to 5 PM," but she is not allowed to specify, for example, that "my friends cannot see my location on the weekends." In the second case, the rule is checked before it is committed. This check is performed to prevent the rules from having conflicting parameters. For example, "Mary creates a rule that allows your friends to see your location on the weekend," so she failed to create a new rule that specifies that "your friends can see your location on weekends from 9 AM to 5 PM".

5 Related Works

A great effort has been made by several authors on the subject of information-sharing privacy in mobile social networks. Some of these works were imperative to developing the model proposed in this paper.

Smith et al. [11] carried out an initial investigation on technologies which allow people to share their location in mobile social networks. The result of this work was the development of a system called Reno. This system allows its users to manually share their location with other people and to pre-define locations or regions. Reno uses SMS to notify the location inside the social network, and the coordinates are obtained through the triangulation of cell phone towers. These technologies were used due to the high cost of the most modern devices with GPS. The privacy controls in the Reno system are performed only when the user decides to share his location. The proposed model in this paper, besides considering when the user wants to share his location, privacy levels are offered, with each having a defined characteristic to guarantee the high-accuracy location remains hidden.

Toch et al. [12] presented Locaccino, a location-sharing application for mobile social networks which allows the user to define rules to publish his location information. These rules are defined considering the person, the time, and if the user is willing to share his current position. However, the shared location is high-accuracy information. The proposed model, besides considering the aspects approached in the Locaccino application and also allowing for the definition of rules, applies algorithms which guarantee the current location's anonymity.

Bilogrevic et al. [13] investigated users' preferences in sharing their location in mobile social networks. The authors made use of users' behaviors when sharing their locations, and the result obtained was that users cannot specify correctly their location-sharing preferences. From that information came the creation of SPISM, a location-sharing system that (semi) automatically selects which rule must be applied when a user receives a request to share his information. Rule selection is made using machine learning algorithms. However, as with the other works, SPISM publishes high-accuracy location information. The proposed model does not use machine learning algorithms to select the best rule for the location-sharing requirement. Instead, it enables the user to manually set the rules to be applied with each user or one of his groups. Moreover, the model allows the user to match his sharing preferences with levels which apply algorithms to hide the high-accuracy location before it is shared.

Ribeiro and Zorzo [9] presented the LPBS (Location Privacy-based System), a system based on levels which guarantee users' location privacy in LBS. This system is divided into levels, with each level having distinct privacy characteristics that guarantee high-accuracy location anonymity. However, while the LPBS guarantees users' privacy in LBS, it is not applied in mobile social networks. The proposed model uses levels which guarantee a user's location anonymity and matches these levels with publishing preferences.

6 Results

Aiming to measure the model's performance, tests on the main options available in each level were carried out, such as the first access, where the integration with Facebook took place, location request, and the privacy techniques.

To perform these tests, the Android operational system emulator with IDE Eclipse and the ADT plugin were used to perform the application prototype. For the provider, a machine with a Windows 7 operational system (2 GHz CPU, 3 GB RAM) was used.

Figure 8 presents the model's performance when the user registers. The result indicates that running time increases in correspondence with the number of contacts the user has on Facebook. This happens because the moment the user registers, the application makes an authentication with the server. The server then promotes integration with Facebook with the goal of looking for and registering all the user's contacts that are popular in his mobile social network. Runtime time can also vary according to the internet connection used. As this action is carried out only when the user registers, it does not disturb the model's performance.

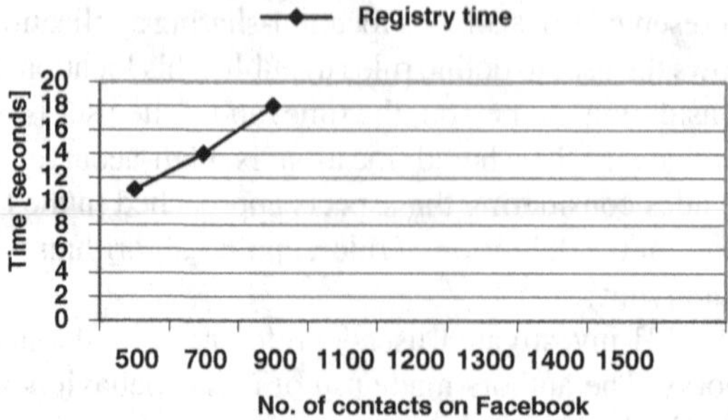

Fig. 8. Runtime time during user registration.

The following results show the model's performance for each privacy level.

Figure 9 presents the model's performance when applying the accuracy adjustment in level 1. As can be seen, the average runtime is constant, taking 0.3 s. This is because the accuracy adjustment calculation is always applied on the user's individual location and not in a group of users. Therefore, the number of users does not have an influence on the outcome. What can impact running time is communication with a GPS and the internet connection quality.

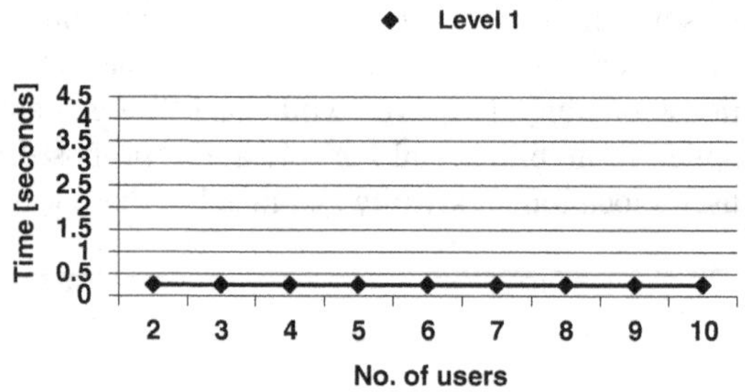

Fig. 9. Level 1 runtime.

Figure 10 shows the model's performance when applying privacy techniques in levels 2 and 3. As can be seen, as the number of users in a group increases, the runtime also increases. This happens because to have anonymity, the algorithm in these levels uses location information from all users in the group.

The difference in the runtime in level 3 occurs because, in this level, besides calculating the anonymity, the MSNPrivacy generates false locations using the accuracy adjustment and applies this same technique in the user's high-accuracy location.

As in the other results, the runtime in levels 2 and 3 can change depending on the internet connection quality or the GPS sign quality. Moreover, depending on the privacy rule set by the user, the running time can increase. However, this time does not put the model performance at risk.

Figure 11 illustrates the runtime results of the tests with rules. Tests to measure the performance of the model were realized based on the number and type of rule. These tests considered the worst-case scenario: one rule configured with all of the possible

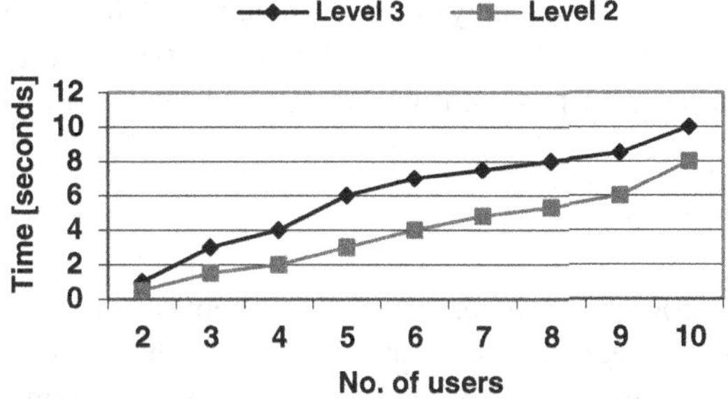

Fig. 10. Runtime in levels 2 and 3.

parameters and all of the rules with all of the possible parameters. In this test, we took three measurements based on the number of rules (10, 100, and 1,000 rules) configured with all of the possible parameters. The average time spent with 10 rules was 14 s; with 100 rules, the average time was 25 s; with 1,000 rules, the average time spent was 60 s. These results were plotted on a graph in Fig. 11. In this figure, we draw the trend line to get the behavior of the system performance based on the number of the rules.

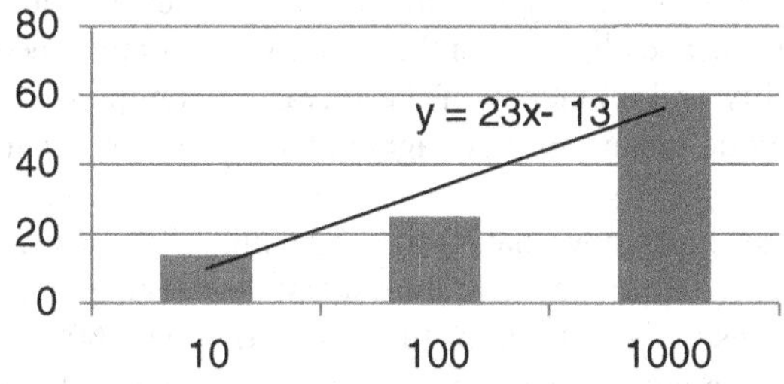

Fig. 11. Runtime time × number of rules.

Analyzing these results, we conclude that for a set of rules (n) to infinity, time behavior tends to increase linearly (i.e., the model runtime with no set rules is O (n)).

Based on the results obtained from the tests carried out in the privacy levels and testing with the rules, the average delay added by the implemented prototype was 35 s. This delay time is proportional to the implementation of level 2 and 3, with 10 users per group. The inserted delay can vary according to the number of users in a group. In a group with more than 100 users, the implementation of level 2 can become unwieldy. The solution to this problem is to adjust the amount of locations used in the calculation of anonymity. Level 3 is not compromised in this case because the locations used are generated by the application; the initial number of points generated is four.

Although a delay is inserted in the model performance, it is safe to say this delay does not damage the usability of the mobile social network, since the delay will only happen when the user receives a request for publishing his location. With the other functionalities, there will be no delays in performance. Furthermore, test results show that the delays generated by the privacy techniques offered are at proportional and justifiable levels; further, the privacy rules are desirable and chosen by users.

7 User Study

Usability study was conducted to get the users' perceptions of and measure the effectiveness of the privacy mechanisms the model offered. The study was conducted with 50 participants, aged 19 to 30 in the exact sciences, health, and humanities. A previous study found that many of the problems that are likely to occur in a given population were only identified by five participants [14]. We asked the participants to answer questionnaires. The issues addressed in the questionnaires were designed to measure user satisfaction related to privacy and usability.

The study consisted of two phases. In the first phase, participants answered an initial questionnaire composed of nine questions. The objective of the first questionnaire was to measure the level of participants' understanding of privacy in mobile social networking. In addition, the responses from this survey will be compared with the responses to the second questionnaire. In the second phase, participants used the main features of the prototype to create rules and privacy levels, location, and to request access to audit. Then, we asked participants to answer the second questionnaire, which contained 21 questions. The objective of this phase was to obtain feedback from participants on the usability and efficiency of the privacy techniques offered. A five-point Likert scale (where one means strongly agree and five means strongly disagree) was used.

The results of the study show that, at the beginning of the tests, 77 % of users had mistaken understanding of privacy in mobile social networking or did not worry about privacy issues. The results at the end of the tests show that 100 % of the participants believed that privacy safeguards were important and influenced location-sharing decisions in mobile social networking. Regarding the privacy techniques the model offered, 87 % of participants approved of its efficiency, while the rest of the participants (13 %) did not approve or were indifferent. On the usability of the prototype, 76 % found it difficult to configure privacy rules and levels the way the prototype offered. Overall, 80 % of participants would use the mobile social network prototype in their day-to-day lives.

8 Conclusion

Mobile devices now represent a simple way to quickly share information with others, including one's location. The use of MSNs is a form of location sharing. When a user shares his or her location with friends and family on a social network, this enables the information to be recorded by the social network, and the social network, in turn, uses this information to offer products and services according to the user's location. Many users view such offers as a personal gain, but others have concerns about their safety and privacy. Such concerns may decrease the motivation to use MSNs.

Section 2 discussed the privacy offered by the model presented in this paper by defining the rules and levels to prevent attacks. As the shared location information is hidden through these levels, malicious users cannot accurately detect the real position of the user. This also makes it difficult to infer the user's identity from his or her location. In addition, the social network provider does not store the history of shared locations and thus cannot be the way moths performed by users. The other members of the social network store all locations shared by their friends, but it is very difficult to obtain the user's path if policies and levels regarding sharing information are in place.

A relevant aspect to note is that the model does not fully committed services and recommendations offered by the social network, for users allow their location to be shared according to the rules. The location modified by the levels still belongs to the geographical area where the user is located. Thus, product and service recommendations based on geographic location can still be made. However, personalization is the user's responsibility; since the application allows the user's position to be shared, the services and recommendations made by the social network will not be compromised.

The results of the study showed that the model performed well, although there were delays. Analyzing the worst case, the model runtime to process an incoming request was, on average, 28 s. Nevertheless, this delay is acceptable if we compare the average time spent by the GPS to obtain the first location—that is, 30 s. The test results also showed that the delays generated by the use of privacy techniques were proportional to the levels of privacy desired by the user.

Besides the efficiency of the prototype, the results of the usability study conducted with 50 participants showed that the MSN users had mistaken or naïve views about privacy. They tend to share their location and other context information without worrying about security. Another important point regards the misunderstanding of the purposes of the permissions requested by the device operating system. Most participants believed that the applications were manipulating the data and resources of the device safely. The results obtained in the evaluation of users show three important points: First point is that users believe that, for the use of mobile social networks, supply and privacy safeguards is essential. The second point is that most users approved the efficiency of privacy techniques offered by the model. However, despite the privacy of efficiency is approved, the prototype needs improvements over its usability.

9 Future Work

The model ensures the privacy of its users' location information in an MSN through techniques that hide their real positions. This hiding, in most cases, is carried out through the actual shift in position to any point within an area. However, the model does not guarantee that the newly set position is valid; for example, it does not ensure that the new location is not in the sea. Validating the new generated position will be necessary to perform a mashup with some application maps, such as Google Maps [15].

Another important aspect of the model is offering privacy in the path taken by the user. This path is obtained through the history of shared locations. All levels within the model ensure the privacy of the user's movements. However, a study is required to analyze whether the path obtained through the history of hidden locations would enable someone to reach the end user. That is, if a mashup of shared points is done, can another malicious user get to the end point where the user is, even if the actual path is hidden? Such a study would indicate whether it is necessary to perform an optimization of the location obfuscation algorithms.

The rules in the proposed model allow users to set parameters that provide privacy with regard to location sharing in certain situations. This allows the users to continue to enjoy the socialization resources. However, the greater the number of rules defined by the user, the worse the application will perform. This problem must be solved in the future. One possible solution would be to create a more efficient rules engine analysis. An alternative implementation of this mechanism is to use a tree data structure.

In addition, an MSN with functionality and options similar to a social network like Facebook should be developed. Subsequently, tests can be conducted to analyze the impact of privacy, develop algorithms that ensure anonymity in order to optimize the runtime, detect users' conflicts and difficulties to define privacy policies, research and develop privacy techniques for other types of context information shared in RSM, and implement new techniques that guarantee user privacy in sharing location information.

References

1. Wasserman, S., Faust, K.: Structural Analysis in the Social Sciences. Cambridge University Press, Cambridge (1994)
2. Toch, E., et al.: Empirical models of privacy in location sharing. In: 12th ACM International Conference on Ubiquitous Computing, pp. 129–138 (2010)
3. Benisch, M., et al.: Capturing location-privacy preferences: quantifying accuracy and user-burden tradeoffs. In: Personal and Ubiquitous Computing, pp. 679–94 (2011)
4. Ardagna, C.A., et al.: Privacy-enhanced location services information. In: Digital Privacy: Theory, Technologies and Practices, pp. 307–326. Auerbach Publications (Taylor and Francis Group) (2007)
5. Anthony, D., Henderson, T., Kotz, D.: Privacy in location aware computing environments. IEEE Pervasive Comput. **6**(4), 64–72 (2007)
6. Gao, H. et al.: Security issues in online social networks. In: IEEE Internet Computing, pp. 56–63 (2011)
7. Smart, S.W.: TextBook on Spherical Astronomy, 6th edn., 415, p. Cambridge University Press, England (1977)
8. Williams, Ed.: Aviation Formulary 1.44. http://williams.best.vwh.net/avform.htm#LL. Accessed November 2013
9. Ribeiro, F.N., Zorzo, S.D.: LPBS – location privacy based system. In: IEEE Symposium on Computers and Communications, pp. 374–379 (2009)
10. Android. http://www.android.com. Accessed November 2013
11. Smith, I., Consolvo, S., LaMarca, A., Hightower, J., Scott, J., Sohn, T., Hughes, J., Iachello, G., Abowd, G.D.: Social disclosure of place: from location technology to communication practices. In: Gellersen, H.-W., Want, R., Schmidt, A. (eds.) PERVASIVE 2005. LNCS, vol. 3468, pp. 134–151. Springer, Heidelberg (2005)
12. Toch, E., Cranshaw, J., Hankes-Drielsma, P., Springfield, J., Gage, P., Cranor, L., Hong, J., Sadeh, N.: Locaccino: a privacy-centric location sharing application. In: 12th ACM International Conference Adjunct Papers on Ubiquitous Computing, pp. 381–382 (2010)

13. Bilogrevic, I., Huguenin, K., Agir, B., Jadliwala, M., Hubaux, J.P.: Adaptive information-sharing for privacy-aware mobile social networks. In: 2013 ACM International Joint Conference on Pervasive and Ubiquitous Computing, pp. 657–666 (2013)
14. Leon, P., et al.: Why Johnny can't opt out: a usability evaluation of tools to limit online behavioral advertising. In: SIGCHI Conference on Human Factors in Computing Systems, New York, NY, USA, pp. 589–598 (2012)
15. Google Maps. https://www.google.com.br/maps. Accessed March 2015
16. Facebook. https://www.facebook.com. Accessed March 2014

Enterprise Architecture

Modeling the Dynamics of Enterprise Architecture Adoption Process

Nestori Syynimaa[1,2,3,4](✉)

[1] Informatics Research Centre, Henley Business School, University of Reading, Reading, UK
[2] School of Information Sciences, University of Tampere, Tampere, Finland
[3] Enterprise Architect, CSC - IT Center for Science, Espoo, Finland
[4] Founder and Principal Consultant, Gerenios Ltd, Tampere, Finland
nestori.syynimaa@gmail.com

Abstract. During the last few years Enterprise Architecture (EA) has received increasing attention among industry and academia. EA can be defined as a formal description of the current and future state(s) of the organisation, and as a managed changes between these states. By adopting EA, organisations may gain a number of benefits such as better decision making, increased revenues and cost reduction, and alignment of business and IT. Despite of the benefits, EA is not widely adopted in organisations. One of the reasons for this is that the adoption has been found to be difficult. In this paper a model to explain the complex dynamics of EA adoption is introduced. The model of the Resistance during the EA adoption Process (REAP) is based on selected EA literature and on general organisational change and change resistance literature. The model introduces novel relationships between strategic level of EA, resulting organisational changes, and the sources of resistance during the planning and execution phases of the adoption. REAP is validated empirically using data collected from an EA-pilot conducted among 11 Finnish higher education institutions. Validation revealed that most of the resistance faced during the adoption was caused by the lack of EA knowledge. By utilising REAP model, organisations may anticipate and prepare for the organisational change resistance during EA adoption.

Keywords: Enterprise Architecture · Adoption · Change resistance · Strategic level · Organisational change

1 Introduction

During the last few years Enterprise Architecture (EA) has received increasing attention among industry and academia. In the modern information society an effective EA is critical to business survival and success [1]. It has been argued that in 21st century EA will be determining factor that separates the successful from the failures, the survivors from the others [2]. Adopting EA has some important strategic outcomes for organisations, such as better operational excellence and strategic agility [3]. Despite the benefits to be gained, EA is not widely adopted in organisations [4–6]. This is likely caused by the fact that EA has been found to be difficult to adopt.

S. Hammoudi et al. (Eds.): ICEIS 2015, LNBIP 241, pp. 577–594, 2015.
DOI: 10.1007/978-3-319-29133-8_28

From theoretical point of view EA adoption is an instance of organisational change aiming for realisation of the aforementioned EA benefits. However, about 70 per cent of organisational change initiatives fail [7–9]. Unfortunately, EA adoption is not an exception.

This study aims for increasing our understanding of the dynamics of EA adoption from organisational change perspective. To be more specific, we are seeking an answer to the question: *Why is Enterprise Architecture difficult to adopt?*

1.1 Definition of Enterprise Architecture

Enterprise Architecture (EA) has multiple definitions in the current literature. Due to these various, even ambiguous, definitions, EA is commonly misunderstood [10]. Therefore it is crucial that we first define the concepts used in this paper. The concept of *Enterprise Architecture* consists of two distinct terms, *enterprise* and *architecture*.

Definition of *enterprise* seems to be quite constant in the EA literature. Enterprise can be anything from a local team to a multi-level organisation of a global corporation [1, 11–13]. As such, it can be seen as a social system with an assumed purpose [12, 14] having a common set of goals [1]. As the term *enterprise* is usually used as a synonym of a business or company, later in this paper we will use the term *organisation* instead of it. *Organisation* covers both businesses and public sector and thus suits better to be used in this paper.

Similarly, definitions of *architecture* and *architecture description* are more or less constant. Architecture is a structure of the enterprise and an architecture description its representation [11]. To be more specific, architecture is seen as a *formal description* of an *enterprise* at a certain time [1, 2, 11], either from the current state or from one or more future states [15, 16].

Definitions of *Enterprise Architecture* are more diverse, but they also have some similarities. What is shared among the most of the definitions is the concept of *managed change* of the *enterprise* between the current and future states for a purpose [15–18]. According to EA specialists, this purpose is *to meet goals* of stakeholders and *to create value* to the organisation [19, 20].

Aforementioned definitions can be summarised to the following definition used in this paper. Enterprise Architecture is; (i) a formal description of the current and future state(s) of an organisation, and (ii) a managed change between these states to meet organisation's stakeholders' goals and to create value to the organisation.

1.2 Enterprise Architecture Adoption

The word *adoption* can be defined as "the action or fact of adopting or being adopted" where adopt refers to "choose to take up or follow (an idea, method, or course of action)" [21]. Similar concepts are *implementation*, "the process of putting a decision or plan into effect; execution" [21] and *institutionalisation*, which is to "establish (something, typically a practice or activity) as a convention or norm in an organization or culture" [21]. Following these definitions, in the EA context, adoption can be defined as the process where organisation starts using EA methods and tools for the very first time.

As a consequence, EA adoption is causing changes to the organisation. The organisation is adopting a new way to communicate (to describe) its current and future states, as well as a new managed way to develop the organisation to achieve its stakeholders' goals. Thus, we will adopt *organisational change* as the underpinning theory to explain the dynamics of EA adoption.

As noted earlier, organisations can be categorised as systems. Lee [22] states that systems may evolve from one state to another deliberately by design, or in a natural uninformed way (the default). Van de Ven and Poole [23] have recognised four ideal-types organisational development theories to explain organisational change processes (Fig. 1). These are *Life Cycle, Evolution, Dialectic,* and *Teleology*. *Life Cycle* theory sees change being imminent; organisation is moving from a start-up towards its termination through certain phases. Each of these phases is necessary, so the change is following always the same steps. Environment may influence this change, but it is not the driving force. *Teleological* theory sees that the change takes place because the organisation is trying to achieve a certain goal or purpose. Although this theory is also cyclical, fundamental difference is that there is no certain sequence of events to be followed. Moreover, the organisations do not "terminate", but are changing indefinitely. *Dialectical* theory assumes that organisation exist in the world of continuous conflicts. The change takes place when two or more opposing forces gain power enough to confront the status quo. *Evolutionary* theory sees change as a method to

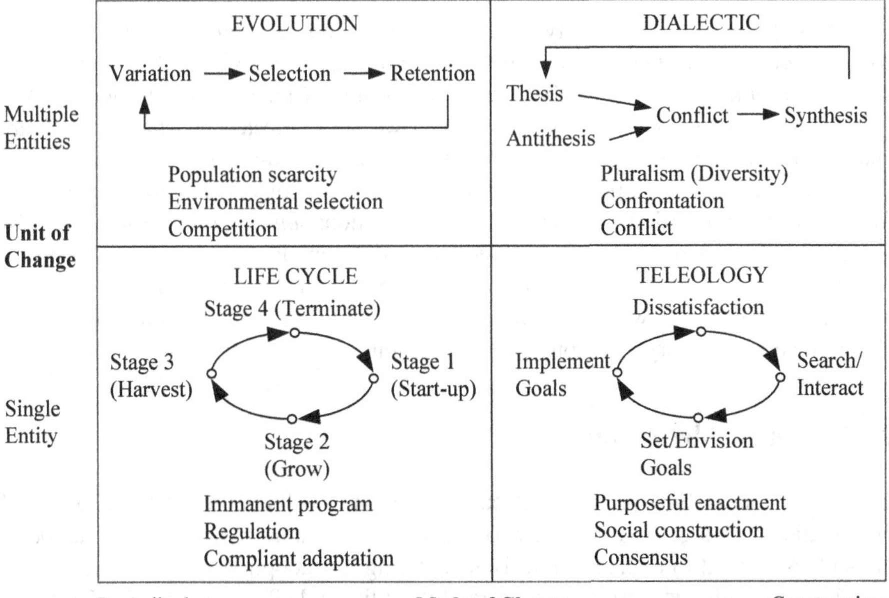

Fig. 1. Process theories of organisational development and change [23].

survive; competing from the same resources causes elimination of some of the organisations.

The most used theories in the current change management literature are life cycle and teleological theory [23, 24]. It can be argued that the latter one, teleological theory, explains the best EA adoption. First of all, EA is adopted in a single entity: an organisation. Secondly, EA adoption is constructive, as it is aiming to a specific goal e.g. the realisation of EA benefits.

According to Csribra and Gergely [25] there are two ways to predict future events in teleological change via goal attribution. These are an *action-to-goal* and *goal-to-action.* The former can be interpreted as a question: *What is the function of EA adoption?* In the same way the latter can be interpreted as a question: *What action should be taken to achieve EA being adopted?* A summary of differences of these two interpretation action can be seen in Table 1.

Table 1. The functions of teleological interpretation of actions [25].

Primary function	Type of inference	
	'Action-to-Goal'	'Goal-to-Action'
On-line prediction	Goal prediction: Predicting the likely effect of an on-going action	Action anticipation: Predictive tracking of dynamic actions in real time
Social learning	Discovering novel goals and artefact functions	Acquiring novel means actions by evaluating their causal efficacy in bringing about the goal

EA adoption can be of both types. If the organisation has a problem it tries to solve with EA adoption, it would be action-to-goal type; e.g. function of EA adoption is to solve the problem. If, on the other hand, organisation's main goal is to adopt EA it would be goal-to-action type. In this research we are interested in which actions are taken while adopting EA so the type of inference is goal-to-action.

Another dimension of predicting future events in teleological change is the primary function of the prediction [25]. There are two functions, *on-line prediction* and *social learning.* The former is aiming for prediction of either the goal or action based on ongoing actions. The latter aims to learning and finding of novel goals or means actions. In this paper, we are interested in increasing the understanding of the EA adoption so the primary function is social learning.

2 Research Methodology

In order to model Enterprise Architecture adoption, the literature related to EA and organisational change was reviewed. Based on the literature review, an EA adoption model was formed to explain the resistance during EA adoption.

Model's validity is a primary measure of its utility and effectiveness [26]. Therefore its validity needs to be tested using an appropriate validation method. Our model contains merely causal relationships and can therefore be validated using structure verification tests [27]. One of these tests is the *major behaviour patterns* -test where the model's accuracy to reproduce real-life behaviour is tested [27].

Our model is validated against empirical data gathered from a real-life EA-pilot. The validation is performed by analysing the empirical data using a *directed content analysis* approach. This approach is similar to the Grounded Theory approach by Strauss and Corbin [28]. The major difference is that the codes and keywords are derived from theory or from relevant research findings instead of data [29]. We are assessing the validity of the model by analysing the data by using the concepts of the model as codes and categories used during the coding. This way we are able to confirm the existence of the elements of the model in the data.

3 Enterprise Architecture Adoption Model

In this section we will describe the formulation of our conceptual model of EA adoption. First the three individual components of the model are introduced. The first component, *the strategic level of Enterprise Architecture*, is based on a selected Enterprise Architecture literature. Second and third components, *organisational change* and *change resistance*, respectively, are adopted from general organisational change literature. After introduction of the individual components, the conceptual model of EA adoption is presented.

3.1 Strategic Level of Enterprise Architecture

Enterprise Architecture is a relatively new phenomenon, having a multiple schools of thought. Lapalme [30, 31] has recognised three ideal schools from the current EA literature; *Enterprise IT Architecting, Enterprise Integrating,* and *Enterprise Ecological Adaption.*

Enterprise IT Architecting school is aiming to alignment of organisation's IT assets and business activities. This school often describes EA as "the glue between business and IT" [31, p. 38]. From a strategic point of view, EA is merely a tool to fulfil business objectives without questioning them in any way.

The goal of *Enterprise Integrating* school is to execute organisation's strategy by maximising organisation's coherency. Thus this school sees EA as "the link between strategy and execution" [31, p. 40].

For the *Enterprise Ecological Adaptation* school EA means designing all organisational facets, including bidirectional relationship to its environment. This school is interested also in what is happening outside of organisation's borders and is actively trying to change also the surrounding environment. Thus EA is described to be "the means for organisational innovation and sustainability" [31, p. 41].

Each of the three EA schools of thought can be seen being on a different strategic level. At the lowest level, EA is used merely as the glue between business and IT. On higher levels, EA is seen more as a means to executing organisation's strategy, but also as way to systemically change the environment of the organisation.

Strategic level decisions and choices are affecting the whole organisation. Organisations may take different tactical stance to achieve their goals and implementing their strategy [32]. This means that strategic decisions likely causes more changes than the tactical ones. As such, it can be argued that the higher the strategic level of EA, the more changes the organisation will face during the EA adoption.

3.2 Organisational Changes

Oreg *et al.* [33] have formed a model of change recipient actions (Fig. 2) based on a literature review of 79 quantitative organisational change studies conducted between 1948 and 2007. Their model suggests that the change and pre-change antecedents are linked to individual's explicit reactions and to change consequences. Also the explicit reactions are linked to change consequences. This model gives us a good starting point for our conceptual model of EA adoption. As noted earlier, EA adoption is an instance of teleological organisational change. Therefore it can be assumed that pre-change and change antecedents will result in organisational and personal consequences, either directly or indirectly by explicit reactions, also during EA adoption.

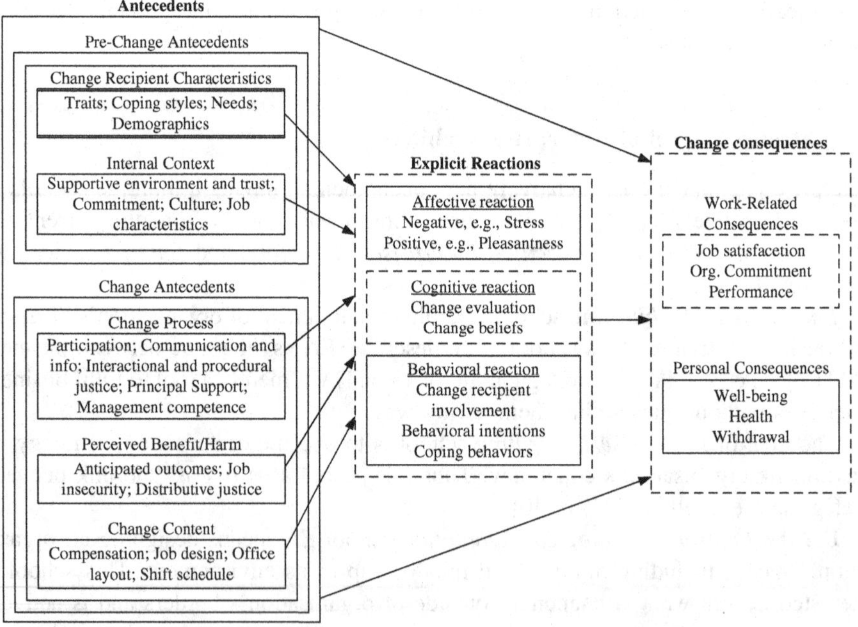

Fig. 2. Antecedents, explicit reactions, and change consequences of organisational change [33].

Organisational change can be categorised to four types [34, 35] according to what is the target of the change. These types of organisational change are; (i) *changes in processes*, (ii) *changes in functions* (structural change), (iii) *changes in power within the organisation* (political change), and (iv) *changes in values* (cultural change). This categorisation gives us a tool for classifying anticipated consequences and results caused by EA adoption.

It should be noted that the higher level change will likely result also to lower level changes. This means that changing the culture of the organisation also changes the power relations, structure, and processes.

3.3 Change Resistance

Every change, no matter how big or small, will face resistance. However, it has been found that the higher the impact of the change the higher is the resistance [36]. Change resistance can be defined as "any phenomenon that hinders the process at its beginning or its development, aiming to keep the current situation" [37, p. 152]. Following this definition, resistance during EA adoption refers to any phenomenon hindering the adoption. Resistance can be intentional or unintentional, can be recognised by target, or can be recognised by observer [38]. Another concept closely related to resistance is inertia, which can be defined as "a tendency to do nothing or to remain unchanged" [21]. In other words, for some reason, organisation resists changing the *status quo* of the organisation. One example of inertia is a *structural inertia*, which "refers to a correspondence between the behavioural capabilities of a class of organizations and their environments" [39, p. 151]. In the other words, the organisation has high structural inertia when the speed of reorganisation is lower than the speed of environmental conditions change. In our EA adoption model, conceptually we do not make difference between change resistance and inertia.

Pardo del Val and Martinez Fuentes [37] have recognised two types of resistance related to organisational change; *inertia during the planning stage*, and *inertia in the execution stage*. Reasons behind the former type of inertia are (R1.1) distorted perception, interpretation barriers and vague strategic priorities, (R1.2) low motivation, and (R1.3) lack of creative response. Reasons behind the latter type of inertia are (R2.1) political and cultural deadlocks, and (R2.2) other reasons. In the context of EA adoption, resistance can occur during the planning stage of the adoption and during its execution. Complete list of sources of resistance are listed in Table 2. Resistance in the planning and execution stages are referred as R1 and R2, respectively.

3.4 EA Adoption Model

The emerging conceptual model of Resistance in EA adoption Process (REAP) is illustrated in Fig. 3. The model is based on the EA and organisational change literature introduced in the previous sub-section.

Logical reasoning of the model is as follows. Enterprise Architecture can be used on different strategic levels [31]. The selected strategic level sets boundaries to EA adoption, e.g. what kind of objectives are set for the adoption and thus what kind of organisational changes may result [35]. In other words, the strategic level of EA influences the objectives of the adoption. These objectives (change antecedents) are

Table 2. Sources of change resistance [37].

#	Resistance
R1.1	Distorted perception, interpretation barriers and vague strategic priorities
R1.1.1	Myopia
	Myopia, or inability of the company to look into the future with clarity
R1.1.2	Denial
	Denial or refusal to accept any information that is not expected or desired
R1.1.3	Perpetuation of ideas
	Tendency to go on with the present thoughts although the situation has changed
R1.1.4	Implicit assumptions
	Assumptions, which are not discussed due to its implicit character and therefore distort reality
R1.1.5	Communication barriers
	Communication barriers, that lead to information distortion or misinterpretations
R1.1.6	Organisational silence
	Organisational silence, which limits the information flow with individuals who do not express their thoughts, meaning that decisions are made without all the necessary information
R1.2	Low motivation
R1.2.1	Direct costs of change
R1.2.2	Cannibalisation costs
	Change that brings success to a product but at the same time brings losses to others, so it requires some sort of sacrifice
R1.2.3	Cross subsidy comforts
	Need for a change is compensated through the high rents obtained without change with another different fact, so that there is no real motivation for change
R1.2.4	Past failures
	Past failures, which leave a pessimistic image for future changes
R1.2.5	Different interests among employees and management
	Different interests among employees and management, or lack of motivation of employees who value change results less than managers value them
R1.3	Lack of creative response
R1.3.1	Fast and complex environmental changes
	Fast and complex environmental changes, which do not allow a proper situation analysis
R1.3.2	Resignation
	Reactive mind-set, resignation, or tendency to believe that obstacles are inevitable
R1.3.3	Inadequate strategic vision
	Inadequate strategic vision or lack of clear commitment of top management to changes
R2.1	Political and cultural deadlocks
R2.1.1	Implementation climate and relation between change values and organisational values
	Implementation climate and relation between change values and organisational values, considering that a strong implementation climate when the values' relation is negative will result in resistance and opposition to change

(*Continued*)

Table 2. (*Continued*)

#	Resistance
R2.1.2	Departmental politics
	Departmental politics or resistance from those departments that will suffer with the change implementation
R2.1.3	Incommensurable beliefs
	Incommensurable beliefs, or strong and definitive disagreement among groups about the nature of the problem and its consequent alternative solutions
R2.1.4	Deep rooted values
	Deep rooted values and emotional loyalty
R2.1.5	Forgetfulness of the social dimension of changes
R2.2	Other sources
R2.2.1	Leadership inaction
	Leadership inaction, sometimes because leaders are afraid of uncertainty, sometimes for fear of changing the *status quo*
R2.2.2	Embedded routines
R2.2.3	Collective action problems
	Collective action problems, specially dealing with the difficulty to decide who is going to move first or how to deal with free-riders
R2.2.4	Capabilities gap
	Lack of the necessary capabilities to implement change
R2.2.5	Cynicism

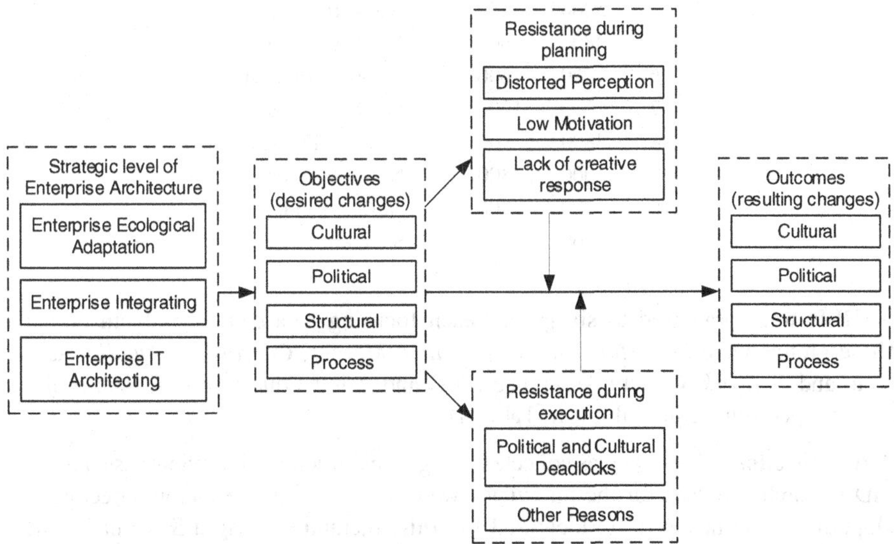

Fig. 3. Conceptual model of resistance in EA adoption process (REAP).

influencing the resulting changes directly and indirectly via explicit reactions of people [33]. During the planning and execution phases of the adoption, the change resistance (reactions of people) may distort adoption and thus influences the outcomes of the adoption [37].

3.5 Validation

Enterprise Architecture Pilot. In this sub-section our model is validated using empirical data collected from a real-life EA pilot (see [40]). The EA pilot was conducted in 2010 among 12 Finnish Higher Education Institutions (HEIs), which of two merged in the beginning of the pilot. During the pilot, EA was adopted by participating HEIs.

Demographic data collected from the public websites of the participating institutions can be seen in Table 3. Pilot participants represented 29 % of Finnish HEIs. Nine of the participating institutions were Universities of Applied Sciences (formerly known as Polytechnics) and two Universities.

Table 3. Pilot institutions.

HEI	Students	Employees	Location
1	8100	800	Southern Finland
2	2000	200	Northern Finland
3	2900	300	Northern Finland
4	5200	400	Southern Finland
5	4800	600	Northern Finland
6	7500	600	Southern Finland
7	16000	1200	Southern Finland
8	4800	400	Western Finland
9	3000	300	Northern Finland
10	15900	2900	Northern Finland
11	10000	800	Southern Finland

HEIs were organised to six groups each focusing to a certain problem domain. These groups were *Education*, *Adult Education*, *Merger*, *Consortium*, *Quality Assurance*, and *Network*. Quality Assurance (QA) and Adult Education (AE) sub-projects were merged during the pilot (see Table 4).

Data Collection. The data was collected using semi-structured interviews as a part of a PhD research. Themes for the interviews were derived from the factors affecting EA adoption. These factors were identified from the literature during a Systematic Literature Review conducted following the instructions by Kitchenham [41]. The review included 35 studies on EA adoption (see [42]). Identified factors were categorised under three categories; *Organisational* factors, such as organisational capabilities, *EA*

Table 4. Pilot groups.

Group	Institution(s)
Network	1, 4, 6
Education	7
Consortium	3, 5, 9
Merger	11 (12)
QA & AE	2, 8, 10

related factors, such as EA specific skills, and *environmental* (contextual) factors, such as possible external pressure. Following instructions by Kvale [43], questions listed in Table 5 were formed for interviews.

Table 5. Interview questions.

Think about some major change(s) your organisation have faced during the past few years. Describe such a change and how it was conducted. Which challenges, if any, the change faced
Describe the process how new information systems are defined, acquired or implemented, and introduced in your organisation
Describe how new development initiatives are introduced in your organisation. Who or which party is driving such initiatives? How important this is for the success of the initiative?
Describe on what basis are development initiatives given resources in your organisation
Describe how EA is organised in your organisation
Describe how communication is organised in your organisation. How about between external stakeholders?
About EA pilot, explain what are your or your organisation's expectations for the pilot. How are they related to your organisation's strategy?
Which kind of expectations from other stakeholders have you faced/know?
Explain how EA pilot or similar initiatives are related to the government level programs. How are such programs coordinated? What are the power relationships in such coordination?
Tell me about EA pilot, explain how was the used framework selected? Does the framework require any modification to suit your purposes? Explain. On which kind of principles is the EA pilot based on? Explain in your own words EA and related terms
Explain your and your organisation's EA experience. Has there been any training during the pilot? Which parts of EA, if any, you think your organisation has most challenges? Have you used contracted specialists/consultants during the pilot?

Interviews were performed between June and October 2010 by phone and were recorded to be transcribed later. Total number of 21 individuals were interviewed from three different roles; CIOs ($n = 9$), rectors and principals ($n = 8$), and Quality Assurance staff ($n = 4$).

Data Coding. Coding was performed using NVivo software package; Version 9.2.81.0 (64-bit). Transcriptions of the interviews were automatically organised as *nodes* using NVivo's *Auto code* feature so that each question formed a node. Each of these nodes contained all answers for the particular question from all interviews. The actual coding of each node followed the same process. Each answer were coded by searching for occurrences of the codes listed in Table 6. First each answer was analysed from the strategic level of EA point-of-view, next from changes point-of-view, and finally from the resistance point-of-view.

Table 6. Categories used in analysis.

Main category and source	#	Sub categories
Strategic level of EA [31]	S1	Enterprise Ecological Adaptation
	S2	Enterprise Integrating
	S3	Enterprise IT Architecting
Objectives [35]	C1	Cultural
	C2	Political
	C3	Structural
	C4	Processes
Resistance during planning [37]	R1.1	Distorted perception, Interpretation barriers, and Vague strategic priorities
	R1.2	Low motivation
	R1.3	Lack of creative response
Resistance during execution [37]	R2.1	Political and cultural deadlocks
	R2.2	Other reasons

4 Results

Illustrated summary of analysis on the group level can be seen in Fig. 4, where the analysis of each group (see Table 4) are combined to a single diagram. Boxes on the left represents strategic levels of EA, boxes in the middle the types of organisational change, and boxes on the right categories of sources of resistance. The legend for used abbreviations can be seen in Table 6.

Black and white circles represents findings from the analysis of the questions related to the *goals and objectives of the EA pilot.* A white circle indicates that the particular concept is found from the data. Solid black dot indicates that it is found from the data and *linked* to another finding. For instance in the Network group it can be seen that there is evidence in the data suggesting that the level of EA is seen as *Enterprise Integrating*. However, the same *respondent* has not mentioned any particular change, so there is nothing it could be linked to. It can also be noted that there is a link between *Enterprise IT Architecting* and *Process* change. In this case, the respondent has expressed both the strategic level of EA, and the actual change to be achieved. In some cases, such as in the Network group, there is also a link between the change and a source of resistance, supported by the data. Black and white squares represents findings from the analysis of the questions related to *past changes and challenges*, and diamonds to *possible sources of resistance* interpreted from answers.

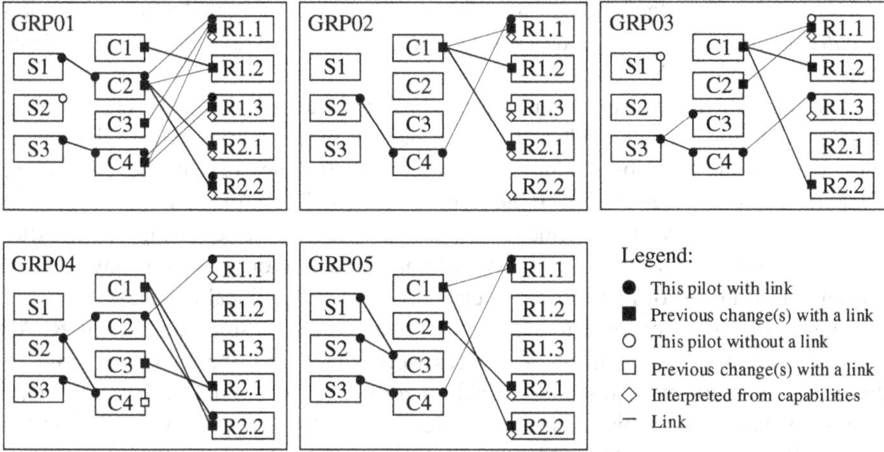

Fig. 4. Group level analysis.

Resistance during planning
Distorted Perception
Communication barriers
Perpetuation of ideas
Low Motivation
Different interests among employees and management
Lack of creative response
Inadequate strategic vision
Fast and complex environmental change

Strategic level of Enterprise Architecture
Enterprise Ecological Adaptation
Enterprise Integrating
Enterprise IT Architecting

Objectives (desired changes)
Cultural
Political
Structural
Process

Outcomes (resulting changes)
Cultural
Political
Structural
Process

Resistance during execution
Political and Cultural Deadlocks
Implementation climate and relation between change values and organisational values
Departmental politics
Forgetfulness of the social dimension of changes
Other
Capabilities gap
Cynicism

Logically deduced influence
Empirically validated influence

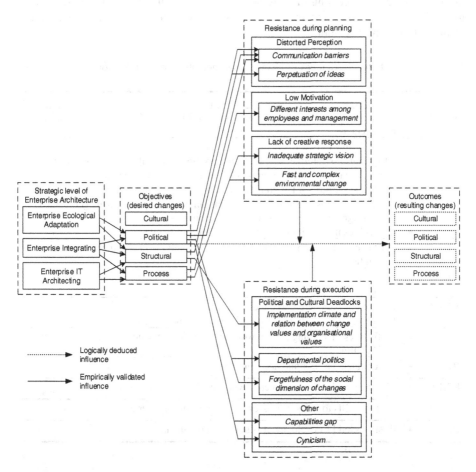

Fig. 5. Results of data analysis.

The summary of the findings are illustrated in Fig. 5. Dotted arrows indicates *logically deduced influence*, as described in the REAP. Solid arrows, in turn, indicate *empirically validated influence*.

Next we will briefly explain and discuss results in textual form. As suggested by REAP model, all strategic levels of EA were present in the data. However, there were no evidence of the adoption aiming for cultural changes in any organisation. Therefore *Cultural* change was removed from the results. One possible explanation for this is that as EA is used for the very first time, it is “safer” to focus on easier changes first. After all, as it can be seen in Fig. 4, previous cultural changes in organisations have caused resistance in four out of five resistance categories, as has political changes.

Sources of resistance were found in all five categories, as suggested by the REAP model. However, only 10 out of 24 sources were found from the data (see Table 7). This leaves 14 sources of resistance which were not faced during the EA pilot. One possible explanation for this is that such sources of resistance might not be faced in the Finnish HE sector at all. More likely explanation is that those sources of resistance were not met in this particular pilot but would likely be faced in other settings. For instance during the executing of cultural changes, political and cultural deadlocks are most likely faced. As noted earlier, there were no cultural changes executed nor planned during the EA-pilot.

Table 7. Sources of change resistance observed in EA pilot.

#	Description
R1.1.3	• Possibilities and limitations of modern IT/IM is not understood by the staff and management
R1.1.5	• Limited view to EA; EA understood as an equal to its outputs • HEI’s staff not familiar with EA concepts prevents “selling“ it to the business • Communication challenges caused by the management structure • Goals and purpose of EA adoption was not clearly communicated to stakeholders • Assigning the responsibility of EA communication to project manager instead of top-management does not guarantee communication • Difficulties in explaining IT and its possibilities to laymen
R1.2.5	• Staff and middle management doesn’t understand the importance of process descriptions
R1.3.1	• Due to fast environmental changes, change is performed without time for proper planning
R1.3.3	• EA used or seen barely as a tool • EA adoption is purely operative without relation to strategy
R2.1.1	• Difficulties in learning how to work with new organisation structure caused by staff’s attitude
R2.1.2	• Decentralised power and decision model
R2.1.5	• Moving people around is seen as very sensitive internal matter
R2.2.4	• Lack of skills to unify processes for instance during merging
R2.2.5	• Business led IT development is not seen convincing

An interesting detail is that the process changes caused resistance only during the planning, not during the execution. The HEI sector in Finland has faced a number of changes during the past decade. For instance, all HEIs have a Quality Assurance (QA) system in place which audited regularly by the government agency [44]. Therefore, execution of process changes may be so integral part of HEIs' operations that the resistance is not faced.

The REAP model is a qualitative model, e.g. it captures the resistance emerging from the data, but does not judge any source of resistance being more important than other. However, it can be noted that most of the resistance faced during the planning phase of the EA-pilot were related to understanding of EA concepts (R1.1.*). Other studies have also noticed the lack of EA knowledge in the Finnish public sector. For instance Lemmetti and Pekkola [10] argues that current definitions of EA are inconsistent and thus confusing both researchers and practitioners. This is also supported by Hiekkanen *et al.* [45]; EA is underutilised due to lack of understanding it properly. In general, poor communication have been found to be one of the factors contributing to EA adoption failures [46]. Moreover, perceived value of EA is directly influenced by how EA is understood in the organisation [47].

5 Conclusions

In this paper we have studied the complex dynamics of Enterprise Architecture (EA) adoption. A teleological organisational change was selected as an underpinning theoretical view to EA adoption. As a result, a model to explain the EA adoption was formed. The model of Resistance during EA adoption Process (REAP) is based on the selected EA literature, and to general organisational change and change resistance theories. Our model revealed previously unexplored relationships between the strategic level of EA and the objectives of the EA adoption. Also the relationships between these objectives and various sources of organisational resistance were identified.

The model was validated by analysing empirical data from a real-life EA-pilot. The analysis clearly indicates that the REAP model can be used to categorise the elements of EA adoption process. Thus it can be argued that the model is valid in this context, e.g. it predicted the real life behaviour found from the EA-pilot. However, as stated by Barlas and Carpenter [48], a valid model can be assumed to be one of the many possible ways to describe a real world.

5.1 Implications

The findings of the have implications to both science and practice. For science, REAP model provides a model to explain the dynamics of the EA adoption process from the change resistance point of view. In the paper, we have demonstrated that the resistance depends on the changes the EA adoption is causing, which, in turn, depends on the strategic level of EA. These relationships have not been previously explored. As such, the model is a novel contribution to the organisational science.

For the practice, the REAP model can be utilised as a tool to predict the possible sources of resistance. When the relationships between the strategic level of EA, resulting changes, and sources of resistance are known, one can prepare for and minimise the resistance during the adoption. For instance, the results of the analysis of the empirical data revealed sources of resistance which are likely to be faced during EA adoption in the Finnish higher education sector.

5.2 Limitations and Future Work

The empirical data used to validate the model was gathered from an EA pilot conducted among 11 Finnish Higher Education Institutions. Qualitative data is always contextually-bound, which limits the generalisability of the findings. However, similar challenges have been found also from other settings [49–51]. This supports our findings. REAP is based on general non-HEI-specific literature, and therefore is likely explaining the resistance during EA adoption also in a wider context. Therefore we are encouraging researchers and practitioners to apply and test the REAP model in other settings to increase its validity and generalisability. Especially interesting would be to study EA adoption in HEI sectors of other countries.

Author acknowledges that the REAP model is only one possible way to explain and describe the EA adoption. In other words, REAP is not necessarily comprehensive, i.e. there may be sources of resistance that are not captured by the model. Therefore we are encouraging researchers also to improve the model to cover other possible aspects hindering the adoption.

Analysing the empirical data with the REAP model revealed that most of the planning phase resistance was caused by the lack of EA knowledge. Thus one direction for the future research could be finding ways to overcome this type of resistance. See [42] for an example of the solution developed to minimise resistance identified by utilising the REAP model.

References

1. TOGAF: TOGAF Version 9. Van Haren Publishing (2009)
2. Zachman, J.A.: Enterprise architecture: The issue of the century. Database Program. Des. **10**, 44–53 (1997)
3. Ross, J.W., Weill, P., Robertson, D.C.: Enterprise Architecture as Strategy: Creating a Foundation for Business Execution. Harvard Business School Press, Boston (2006)
4. Schekkerman, J.: Trends in Enterprise Architecture 2005: How Are Organizations Progressing?. Institute for Enterprise Architecture Developments, Amersfoort (2005)
5. Scott Ambler. http://www.ambysoft.com/surveys/stateOfITUnion201001.html
6. Computer Economics. http://www.computereconomics.com/article.cfm?id=1947
7. Hammer, M., Champy, J.: Reengineering the Corporation: a Manifesto for Business Revolution. Nicholas Brearly, London (1993)
8. Beer, M., Nohria, N.: Cracking the code of change. Harvard Bus. Rev. **78**, 133–141 (2000)
9. Kotter, J.P.: A Sense of Urgency. Harvard Business Press, Boston (2008)

10. Lemmetti, J., Pekkola, S.: Understanding enterprise architecture: perceptions by the finnish public sector. In: Scholl, H.J., Janssen, M., Wimmer, M.A., Moe, C.E., Flak, L.S. (eds.) EGOV 2012. LNCS, vol. 7443, pp. 162–173. Springer, Heidelberg (2012)
11. ISO/IEC/IEEE: Systems and software engineering – Architecture description. ISO/IEC/IEEE 42010:2011(E) (Revision of ISO/IEC 42010:2007 and IEEE Std 1471-2000), pp. 1–46 (2011)
12. Dietz, J.L.G., Hoogervorst, J.A.P., Albani, A., Aveiro, D., Babkin, E., Barjis, J., Caetano, A., Huysmans, P., Iijima, J., van Kervel, S.J.H., Mulder, H., Op 't Land, M., Proper, H.A., Sanz, J., Terlouw, L., Tribolet, J., Verelst, J., Winter, R.: The discipline of enterprise engineering. Int. J. Organ. Des. Eng. **3**, 86–114 (2013)
13. Pragmatic EA Ltd. http://www.pragmaticef.com/frameworks.htm
14. Proper, H.A.: Enterprise architecture: informed steering of enterprises in motion. In: Hammoudi, S., Cordeiro, J., Maciaszek, L.A., Filipe, J. (eds.) ICEIS 2013. LNBIP, vol. 190, pp. 16–34. Springer, Heidelberg (2014)
15. CIO Council: A Practical Guide to Federal Enterprise Architecture. http://www.cio.gov/documents/bpeaguide.pdf (2001)
16. http://www.gartner.com/it-glossary/enterprise-architecture-ea/
17. GERAM: GERAM: Generalised Enterprise Reference Architecture and Methodology. Version 1.6.3. IFIP-IFAC Task Force on Architectures for Enterprise Integration. IFIP-IFAC Task Force (1999)
18. Pulkkinen, M.: Enterprise Architecture as a Collaboration Tool, p. 134. University of Jyväskylä, Jyväskylä (2008)
19. Syynimaa, N.: Taxonomy of purpose of enterprise architecture. In: 12th International Conference on Informatics and Semiotics in Organisations, ICISO 2010, Reading (2010)
20. Pragmatic EA Ltd. http://www.pragmaticea.com/docs/160-char-challenge-analysis.pdf
21. Oxford University Press. http://oxforddictionaries.com/
22. Lee, A.S.: Retrospect and prospect: information systems research in the last and next 25 years. J. Inf. Technol. **25**, 336–348 (2010)
23. Van de Ven, A.H., Poole, M.S.: Explaining development and change in organizations. Acad. Manage. Rev. **20**, 510–540 (1995)
24. Kezar, A.: Understanding and facilitating organizational change in the 21st century. ASHE-ERIC Higher Education Report. Wiley (2001)
25. Csibra, G., Gergely, G.: 'Obsessed with goals': functions and mechanisms of teleological interpretation of actions in humans. Acta Psychol. **124**, 60–78 (2007)
26. Groesser, S.N., Schwaninger, M.: Contributions to model validation: hierarchy, process, and cessation. Syst. Dyn. Rev. **28**, 157–181 (2012)
27. Barlas, Y.: Formal aspects of model validity and validation in system dynamics. Syst. Dyn. Rev. **12**, 183–210 (1996)
28. Strauss, A., Corbin, J.: Basics of Qualitative Research: Techniques and Procedures for Developing Grounded Theory. Sage Publications, Newbury Park (1990)
29. Hsieh, H.-F., Shannon, S.E.: Three approaches to qualitative content analysis. Qual. Health Res. **15**, 1277–1288 (2005)
30. Lapalme, J.: 3 schools of enterprise architecture. IT Prof. **PP**, 1 (2011)
31. Lapalme, J.: Three schools of thought on enterprise architecture. IT Prof. **14**, 37–43 (2012)
32. Casadesus-Masanell, R., Ricart, J.E.: From strategy to business models and onto tactics. Long Range Plan. **43**, 195–215 (2010)
33. Oreg, S., Vakola, M., Armenakis, A.: Change recipients' reactions to organizational change: a 60-year review of quantitative studies. J. Appl. Behav. Sci. **47**, 461–524 (2011)
34. Cao, G., Clarke, S., Lehaney, B.: A systemic view of organisational change and TQM. The TQM Mag. **12**, 186–193 (2000)

35. Cao, G., Clarke, S., Lehaney, B.: Diversity management in organizational change: towards a systemic framework. Syst. Res. Behav. Sci. **20**, 231–242 (2003)
36. Bovey, W.H., Hede, A.: Resistance to organizational change: the role of cognitive and affective processes. Leadersh. Organ. Dev. J. **22**, 372–382 (2001)
37. Pardo del Val, M., Martinez Fuentes, C.: Resistance to change: a literature review and empirical study. Manage. Decis. **41**, 148–155 (2003)
38. Hollander, J.A., Einwohner, R.L.: Conceptualizing resistance. Sociol. Forum **19**, 533–554 (2004)
39. Hannan, M.T., Freeman, J.: Structural inertia and organizational change. Am. Sociol. Rev. **49**, 149–164 (1984)
40. http://raketti.csc.fi/kokoa/pilotti
41. Kitchenham, B.: Guidelines for performing Systematic Literature Reviews in Software Engineering. Keele University, Keele (2007)
42. Syynimaa, N.: Enterprise architecture adoption method for higher education institutions, p. 262. Gerenios Ltd, Tampere, Finland (2015)
43. Kvale, S.: Interviews: an introduction to qualitative research interviewing. Sage Publications Inc, Thousand Oaks (1996)
44. The Finnish Education Evaluation Centre, FINEEC. http://karvi.fi/en/
45. Hiekkanen, K., Korhonen, J.J., Collin, J., Patricio, E., Helenius, M., Mykkanen, J.: Architects' perceptions on EA use – an empirical study. In: 2013 IEEE 15th Conference on Business Informatics (CBI), pp. 292–297 (2013)
46. Mezzanotte, D.M., Dehlinger, J., Chakraborty, S.: On applying the theory of structuration in enterprise architecture design. In: 2010 IEEE/ACIS 9th International Conference on Computer and Information Science (ICIS), pp. 859–863 (2010)
47. Nassiff, E.: Understanding the Value of Enterprise Architecture for Organizations: A Grounded Theory Approach, p. 135. Nova Southeastern University, Ann Arbor (2012)
48. Barlas, Y., Carpenter, S.: Philosophical roots of model validation: two paradigms. Syst. Dyn. Rev. **6**, 148–166 (1990)
49. Kaisler, H., Armour, F., Valivullah, M.: Enterprise architecting: critical problems. In: HICSS-38, Proceedings of the 38th Annual Hawaii International Conference on System Sciences (2005)
50. Pehkonen, J.: Early Phase Challenges and Solutions in Enterprise Architecture of Public Sector, p. 107. Tampere University of Technology, Tampere (2013)
51. Seppänen, V.: From Problems to Critical Success Factors of Enterprise Architecture Adoption. University of Jyväskylä, Jyväskylä (2014)

A Model-Based Approach for Retrospective Analysis of Enterprise Architecture Metrics

Manoj Bhat[(✉)], Thomas Reschenhofer, and Florian Matthes

Technische Universität München, Boltzmannstr. 3, 85748 Garching, Germany
manoj.mahabaleshwar@tum.de, {reschenh,matthes}@in.tum.de

Abstract. The Enterprise Architecture (EA) provides a holistic view of an enterprise and seeks to align the business and IT. As the change in the business goals and strategies of an enterprise is inevitable, managing the evolution of the EA is a key challenge for modern enterprises. Furthermore, the EA metrics are instrumental in quantitatively measuring the progress of an enterprise towards its goals. The retrospective analysis of the EA metrics empower practitioners to take informed decisions while planning and selecting efficient alternatives to achieve the envisioned goal. The tool support for the EA metric analysis is still in its infancy. In this paper, we propose a model-based approach to capture the temporal aspects of the EA metrics and extend a model-based expression language to compute the EA metrics at any point of time in the past. This allows the visualization of the evolution of the EA metrics and as a consequence the evolution of the EA.

Keywords: Enterprise architecture management · Metrics · Domain specific language

1 Introduction

Enterprises continuously change, improve, and evolve to respond to demands of their highly dynamic and competitive business and IT environment [1]. The enterprise architecture (EA) is an essential mechanism to capture requirements of their environment and it is widely accepted as a mechanism to achieve business and IT alignment [2, 3]. ISO Standard 42010 defines EA as the "*fundamental organization of a system [enterprise] embodied in its components, their relationships to each other, and to the environment, and the principles guiding its design and evolution*" [4]. Typically, an EA as an artifact documents the (a) current state of the EA model, (b) target state as an envisioned long-term perspective, and (c) intermediate planned states to achieve the target state [5]. By defining several planned alternate states with respect to an envisioned target state, decision makers can define efficient alternatives for the desired change and use an EA metric model to justify their decisions. The EA metrics which are part of an EA model enable the measurement of the EA management (EAM) endeavor and support the quantitative-based management of the EA targeting the predefined EAM goal achievement [6].

Managing the transformation of an enterprise from its current state to an envisioned target state via planned states is a non-trivial task [7]. A key aspect in analyzing the managed evolution of an EA is the understanding of the evolution of its EA metrics

S. Hammoudi et al. (Eds.): ICEIS 2015, LNBIP 241, pp. 595–611, 2015.
DOI: 10.1007/978-3-319-29133-8_29

which indicates the progress of an enterprise towards its target state. By considering EA metrics' evolution in a collaborative environment, decision makers can collectively reconfigure the planned states and select the appropriate alternative. Therefore, in this paper we focus on the temporal aspects of the EA metric model for analyzing the evolution of metrics and as a consequence the evolution of the EA.

In the domain of Software Engineering, the term *metric* is defined as a "*quantitative scale and method which can be used to determine the value a feature takes for a specific software product*" [8]. However, in the context of an EA, a clear definition of the EA metric does not exist. In general, EA metrics aid in planning and controlling the structural and behavioral aspects of an EA. The EA metrics corresponding to the structural aspects include quality and acceptance-oriented metrics such as the project's quality plan availability [9]. The EA metrics encompass Key Performance Indicators (KPIs) which correspond to the behavioral aspects of an EA (e.g. Application Criticality Rating). In this paper, the term metric refers to the EA metric that captures both the structural and behavioral aspects.

Even though metrics have been extensively used in Enterprise Performance Management systems for business intelligence, there exists a perception of the lack of metrics in EAM [6, 10]. This perception is changing as more and more efforts are being invested to formulate metrics and to map them with EAM goals [11]. The survey conducted by Hauder et al. [11], shows that the current EAM systems (85 % of the surveyed tool vendors) support the definition, calculation, and visualization of EA metrics and 23 % of the surveyed systems allow the customization of metrics with a domain specific language (DSL).

Although the current EAM tools support the definition of metrics through DSLs, these DSLs however do not have the flexibility to compute the metric at a point of time in the past. Furthermore, majority of the existing EA tools maintain version repositories of EA models as a sequence of architectural snapshots [7]. The issues with snapshot based versioning as indicated by Robbes and Lanza [12] are as follows:

- The data stored in versioning systems is not complete enough to perform quality retrospective analysis.
- A common approach is to download several versions from a repository and to process them all at once, which indicates that incremental processing is limited, and computations are long and resource-intensive.
- Changes between successive versions of the models and their instances are stored on explicit requests, which are not very frequent at enterprise level (quarterly, yearly, or only when significant changes are made to them). Thus, changes in the business objects which affect business decisions could be lost during subsequent versioning of the EA model.

Therefore, a means to index appropriate business artifacts for quick access becomes vital in understanding the continuous evolution of an enterprise over a given period of time. The contribution of this paper is twofold: first we conceptualize the temporal aspects of metrics in an EA model. We then extend an existing DSL [13] to facilitate the computation of metrics at any given time in the past by using the information model's history. In consequence, this allows the visualization of EA metrics' evolution for instance, on a time series graph.

Organizationally, Sect. 2 reviews the related work. Section 3 presents our approach to model the temporal aspects in an EA model. Section 4 presents a DSL to query the historized data and Sect. 5 presents the evaluation of our approach. In Sect. 6, we conclude with a short summary.

2 Related Work

Pourshahid et al. extend the Goal-oriented Requirement Language (GRL) with the *KPI* concept to measure business processes against business goals [14]. The meta-type KPI is modeled with attributes including *target value*, *threshold value*, and *worst value*. The concepts in the GRL model such as *goals*, *tasks*, and *actors* are associated with the KPI to provide the organizational context.

Popova and Sharpanskykh propose a meta-model to capture the goal structure, KPI structure and relations between them [15]. The meta-model captures the KPI as a concept with attributes including *name*, *definition*, *type*, *timeframe*, *scale*, and *threshold*. The attribute *type* captures the unit (continuous or discreet) used to measure the KPI. The attribute *timeframe* indicates the duration during which the KPI is defined and the attribute *scale* indicates the unit of measurement. The KPI *score* is acceptable if it above a minimum cutoff value. Further, the attribute *source* captures the internal or external source used to extract the KPI.

Strecker et al. present a method (MetricM) along with a DSL named MetricML [16]. The MetricM is integrated with the Multi-Perspective Enterprise Modeling method to enrich the description of the KPI with relevant enterprise context. The concept *indicator* in the MetricML meta-model refines the definition of the KPI as captured by Pourshahid et al. and Popova and Sharpanskykh.

To ensure consistency in defining, documenting, and retrieving KPIs, Matthes et al. introduced a uniform KPI description template to capture the *general structural elements* and *organization-specific structural elements* of a KPI [17]. The general structural elements and organization-specific structural elements of a KPI are listed in Tables 1 and 2 respectively. Furthermore, based on this template, an EAM KPI Catalog consisting of 52 literature-based and practice-proven KPIs was developed [9]. This catalog also lists EAM goals and maps them to KPIs. The "Application Continuity Plan Availability" KPI and its associated attributes are shown in Fig. 1.

Table 1. General structural elements of a KPI.

Property	Description
Title	A unique name of the KPI
Description	Detailed description of the KPI and its purpose
Goals	Each KPI is related to at least one of the EAM goals
Calculation	Textual description of how the KPI has to be calculated based on a certain information model
Source	Source of the KPI (literature or practice)
Layers	A KPI can be assigned to one or more EA layers

Table 2. Organization-specific structural elements.

Property	Description
Measurement frequency	The time interval between two measurement points
Interpretation	Description of how the calculated value should be interpreted (good, acceptable, or bad)
KPI consumer	The person who is interested in the value of the KPI
KPI owner	The person responsible for the KPI
Target value	The KPI values to be achieved while targeting the target value
Planned values	A KPI can be assigned to one or more EA layers
Tolerance values	The allowed deviations from planned and target values
Escalation rule	Steps to be taken when the target EAM goal is not achieved

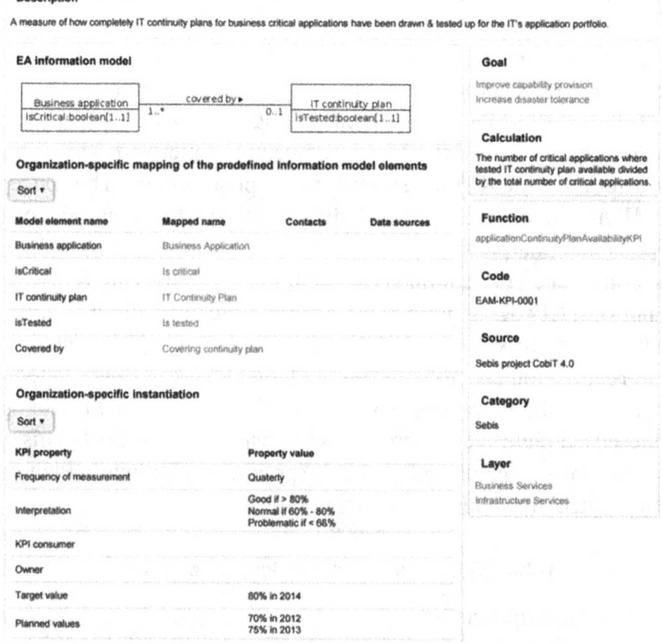

Fig. 1. An exemplary KPI instance from the KPI catalog.

There also exists a large body of knowledge on DSLs for ensuring non-functional requirements (e.g. safety-critical concerns and quality assurance) of information systems through appropriate metrics. For instance, in [18] authors propose a language for calculating metrics that determine the internal complexity, size, and quality of the domain models. Similarly in [19], a DSL for analyzing the source code of software systems is presented. In the context of an EA, Iacob and Jonkers [20] propose an approach based on the ArchiMate modeling language to quantitatively measure the performance of the EA models. Similarly, Johnson et al. [21] extend the influence diagram notation [22] to support the quantitative analysis of the EA model properties including information security, performance, availability, and interoperability.

Monahov et al. [13] propose a DSL named Model-based Expression Language (MxL) to formally define KPIs in the catalog [9] and to allow their automated calculation and evaluation. Figure 2, shows the implementation of the "Application Continuity Plan Availability" KPI using MxL. Furthermore, as shown in the lower part of Fig. 2, the KPI definition includes references to the information model. Any change in the information model results in the automatic redefinition of the corresponding methods. In other words, if the business type "Business Application" used in the above KPI definition is renamed to "Application", then the KPI definition is updated accordingly. The execution of this MxL expression results in the computation of the corresponding KPI. However, as discussed in [13], the current version of MxL is not able to access the information model's history to compute the KPI at a point of time in the past.

Custom MxL Function STATIC::applicationContinuityPlanAvailabilityKPI

Name	applicationContinuityPlanAvailabilityKPI
Description	A measure of how completely IT continuity plans for business critical applications have been drawn & tested up for the IT's application portfolio
Parameters	
Return Type	Number

Method Stub

```
/* Determine all critical applications */
let criticalApplications =
    find('Business Application').where('Is critical') in

/* Calculate proportion of covered critical applications */
criticalApplications.ratio('Covering continuity plan' <> null)
```

Outgoing MxL References

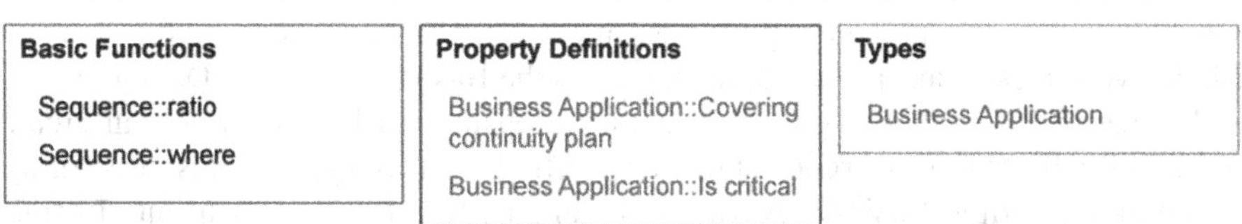

Basic Functions
Sequence::ratio
Sequence::where
Property Definitions
Business Application::Covering continuity plan
Business Application::Is critical
Types
Business Application

Fig. 2. The implementation of the EAM KPI shown in Fig. 1 using MxL. (cf. [13]).

Even though the aforementioned meta-models capture EA metrics and its properties, they do not consider the concept of time with respect to these metrics. Considering the temporal aspects in the meta-model is necessary for analyzing the evolution of metrics. Furthermore, it enables the extension of the existing DSLs to query the information model with respect to time and hence allows the calculation of metrics at any point of time in the past.

3 Capturing an EA Model's Evolution

A wide variety of EAM tools provide the capability to model an EA and to analyze the data in a collaborative environment [3]. However, to address the challenges including the rigid information structures and mismatch between unstructured information sources in an EA, a model-based hybrid wiki approach [23] was designed and an EAM tool Tricia[1] was developed. We extend Trica in our approach for the following reasons:

1. Tricia follows a model-driven approach to system implementation and has a flexible meta-model [24].
2. Tricia's MxL provides the capability to define and compute metrics.
3. Tricia's user-related services including access control, versioning, and schema evolution allows controlled access to the information model's history and enables the computation of EA metrics at any point of time in the past.
4. Tricia's extensive enterprise-level collaborative environment supports iterative development and management of quantitative models.

First, we will extend the EA metric meta-model with the temporal aspects. This is followed by a discussion on the extended version of the MxL that computes metrics at any point of time in the past by accessing the information model's history.

Figure 3, provides an excerpt of the EA metric meta-model with the focus on the metric and its temporal aspects. A description of the Tricia meta-model is discussed in [24]. In the following sub-sections, we will discuss the concepts relevant in our context and illustrate how these concepts enable to capture the evolution of metrics.

Business Type, Business Attribute Definition, Business Entity, and Business Attribute. The Business Type and Business Attribute Definition allow the definition of the information model's schema irrespective of the application domain. The Business Type is used to instantiate a domain specific concept and the Business Attribute Definition captures the properties of the concept. A user can create the domain specific information model at runtime by instantiating the Business Type and Business Attribute Definition. For instance, in the context of the EAM, the concepts such as the *business capability* and *application* are captured as Business Types (instances) and the relationship between these concepts are defined through the Business Attribute Definition.

Furthermore, as shown in Fig. 3, a *user* (constrained by the *Role*) can create multiple Business Entities representing a specific Business Type. A Business Entity can contain multiple Business Attributes belonging to a Business Attribute Definition. In other words, Business Entity and Business Attribute allow users to create instances of domain-specific concepts that were captured as Business Types and Business Attribute Definition. Therefore, these concepts in the meta-model allow users to create the domain-specific information model and its schema at runtime.

---

[1] http://infoAsset.de.

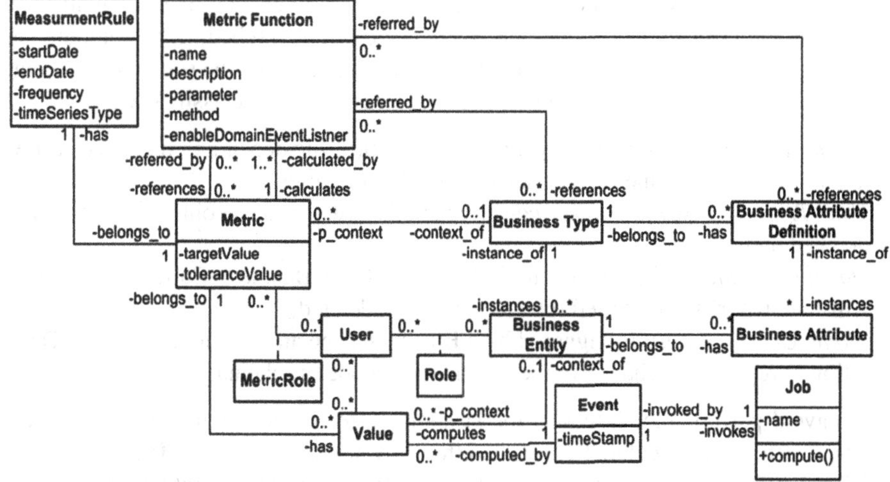

Fig. 3. Meta-model capturing temporal aspects of EA metrics.

Metric, Metric Function, Measurement Rule (MR) and Metric's Value. The concept Metric comprises of the general structural elements and organization specific structural elements as discussed in the previous section (not shown in Fig. 3). The temporal aspects of metrics are captured by its corresponding MR. The *frequency* information captured in the MR is used to trigger temporal *events* to recalculate metrics and the *timeSeriesType* information is used to visualize the evolution of metrics. The concept MR captures the following attributes:

- *startDate*: determines when to start monitoring a metric. The default value is the time when the metric was first defined.
- *endDate*: determines when to stop monitoring a metric.
- *frequency*: the interval between two measurement points; enumeration of values such as daily, monthly, and quarterly.
- timeSeriesType: enumeration of values such as continuous, discrete, linear, step-wise [25] for interpolation.

Furthermore, as shown in Fig. 3, a Metric is calculated by a *Metric Function* which refers to multiple Business Types, Business Attribute Definitions, and other metrics for its calculation. The attributes of the Metric Function are as follows:

- *name*: name of the Metric Function.
- *description*: description of the Metric Function.
- *method*: implementation script in a DSL.
- *enableDomainEventListner*: if the value is true, the Metric Function listens to domain events. When a business entity triggers a domain event to compute a metric, the Metric Function is executed and the new metric value is persisted.

Events. We explicitly model events in the meta-model to enable the recalculation of metrics. On occurrence of an event, a new job is created by a scheduler to compute the corresponding metric. For better readability, dependencies from the source of an event to a specialized event are not shown in Fig. 3. These events are classified as:

- *Temporal Event:* Is triggered by the Measurement Rule depending on the measurement frequency of a metric, i.e. daily, monthly or quarterly.
- *User Triggered Event:* A user can trigger this event at any point to accesses the updated metric value.
- *Domain Event:* A domain event is triggered by a Business Entity or Business Attribute when it is modified (created, updated, deleted).
- *Model Change Event:* Is triggered by a Business Type and Business Attribute Definition to represent a change in the information model's schema.

To avoid performance issues in the system due to frequent generation of domain events, a metric is recalculated only when the corresponding Business Type's attribute *canGenerateDomainEvent* and the Metric function's attribute *enableDomainEventListner* are set to true. In other words, domain events are propagated through the system and metrics are recalculated only when their corresponding flags are enabled. For instance, let us consider the scenario shown in Fig. 4. The metric "IT continuity plan for business applications (ITC)" depends on the ContinuityPlan and BusinessApplication Business Types whereas the metric "IT continuity plan for business applications supporting critical processes (ITCP)" depends on the CriticalProcess Business Type and the value of the ITC metric. As both enableDomainEventListner and canGenerateDomainEvent flags corresponding to the ITC metric and its corresponding Business Types are set to true any change in instances of these Business Types results in the recalculation and persistence of the ITC metric. On the contrary, changes in instances of CriticalProcess or values of the ITC metric does not result in the recalculation of the ITCP metric as the corresponding enableDomainEventListner flag is set to false.

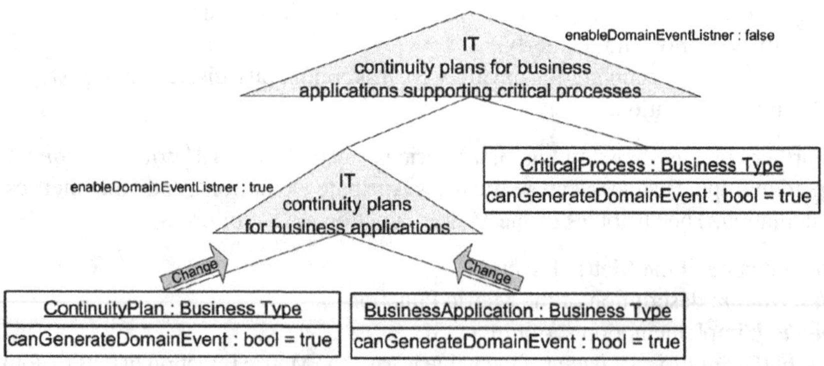

Fig. 4. Domain events.

Role of the User. Tricia provides access control and content authoring mechanisms to manage user permissions on the information model. The users or the group of users can read, write, or administrate content in the system. Similarly, user permissions and roles can be set on metrics defined in the system (through the *MetricRole* concept shown in Fig. 3). The metric consumers have read access, while the metric owners are responsible for defining metrics and have both the read and write access.

Capturing the aforementioned concepts in the model allows persisting metrics as its corresponding business entities evolve and as a consequence allows the visualization of the metrics' evolution (Fig. 11).

4 A DSL for Accessing an EA Model's History

By modeling the temporal aspects of metrics, we can query the value of metrics in the past and can visualize their evolution. However, if the temporal aspects of metrics are not yet modeled, their values in the past cannot be determined. In such scenarios, the information model's history needs to be accessed to compute the past metric values. Tricia manages versions of its entities and provides functionalities to compare versions and to restore previous versions of entities. As shown in Fig. 5, versions are managed in change-sets which not only capture the value of the entity before its change, but also its type, type of change (new, edit, delete), and modification date.

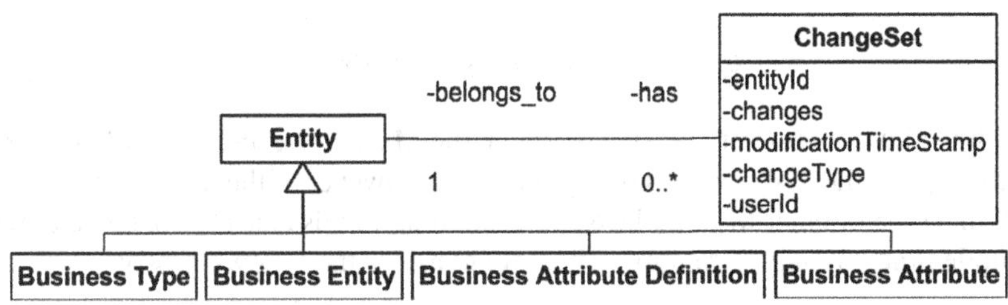

Fig. 5. Versions of entities.

An EAM tool that manages the information model's history and a DSL that can access the information model can facilitate evaluating a metric at any point of time in the past. As Tricia meets the above requirements, we extended the capabilities of the MxL to compute metrics at any point of time in the past. Furthermore, the MxL is independent of Tricia and can be integrated within other EAM tools. The MxL is specific to the EAM domain and is inspired by the Object Constraint Language (OCL) and Microsoft's Language Integrated Query (LINQ) leading to properties such as functional programming, object orientation, and sequence-orientation. A detailed description of the available data types, language constructs, and operations in the MxL with examples is documented in [13].

We extend the grammar of MxL by introducing a new literal "@" that retrieves the state of the object at a given time. That is, the MxL expression "Expression @ time" is not evaluated on the current state of the information model but on the information model's history and the state of entities at a given time.

The abstract syntax tree (AST) generated by the MxL parser containing the "@" literal sets the AtExpression as a node in the AST with one MxL expression as the left operator and the otherMxL expression representing date as the right operator. This is illustrated in Fig. 6 with a very simple example. The AST is passed to the MxL type checker to validate the static semantics of the language, which generates a Typed Expression Tree (TET) to be executed by the MxL execution engine. If the MxL expression refers to Business Types and Business Attribute Definitions, the MxL type checker ensures their existence in the information model's schema and retrieves them before generating the TET. Please refer [26] for a detailed description on the MXL type checker and the type system of the MxL.

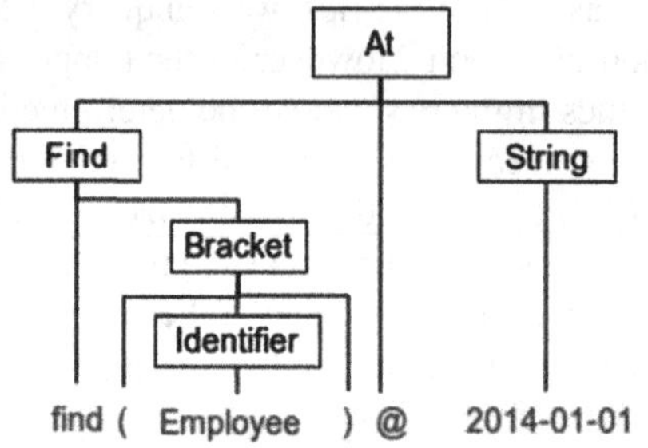

Fig. 6. The AST containing the At Expression.

With the introduction of the AtExpression, the MxL type checker now has to determine the type of the MxL Objects on a given date. However, if the date itself is an MxL Object, the type of other MxL Objects corresponding to this date cannot be determined at compile time but only at runtime. Thus, we consider the following two:

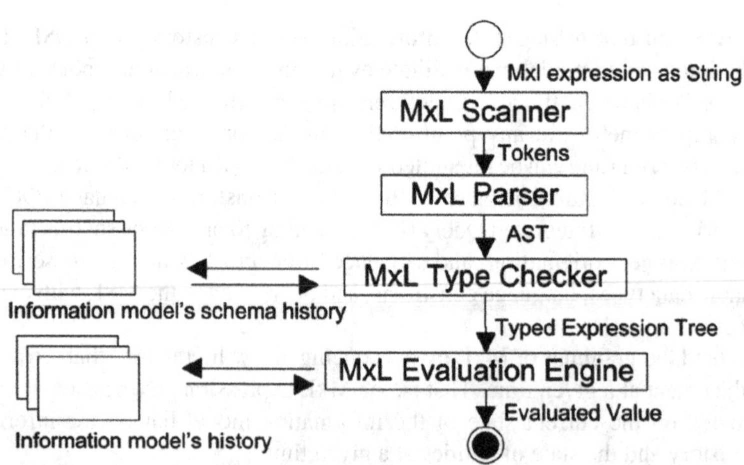

Fig. 7. Evaluating MxL expression with date as string.

Date at Compile Time: If the date is expressed as a string, the type checker ensures that the date is in a fixed format and determines the date at the compile time. As indicated in Fig. 7, the type checker queries the schema history and checks the type of the objects corresponding to this date.

Considering Date at Runtime: As shown in Fig. 8, if the date is an MxL Object, the type checker checks the type of all MxL Objects with respect to the current state of the information model's schema. At runtime, first the date is evaluated and then types of all other MxL objects are retrieved from the schema history and the expression is evaluated for this date.

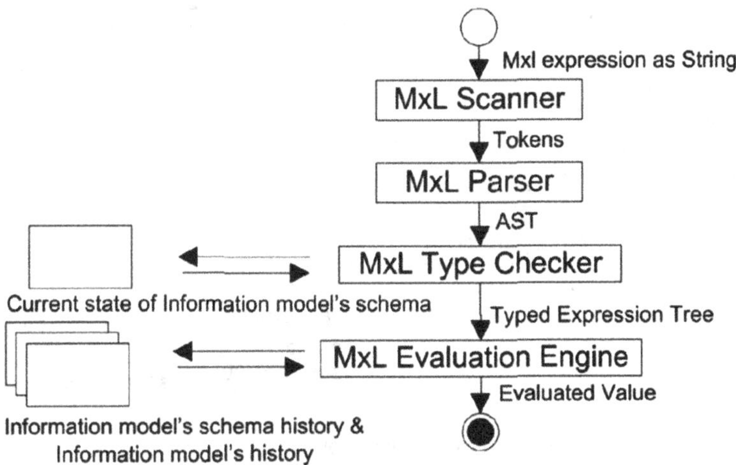

Fig. 8. Evaluating MxL expression with date as MxlObject/parameter.

Since Tricia maintains the change-sets of both the information model and its schema, it is possible to evaluate the expression irrespective of the change in either one of them. Let us consider an exemplary use-case to calculate a metric (*m* - "*find (Employee).where(salary>3000).count()*"). This metric computes the count of employees with the salary more than 3000. The MxL expressions corresponding to each metric *m*, *m1*, *m2*, *m3*, and *m4* are shown in Fig. 10. Furthermore, note that the value of the metric *m* changes as the business type *Employee* and its business attribute definitions *name* and *salary* evolve over time. As shown in Fig. 9, evaluating the MxL expression (1) corresponding to *m1* at the current point in time (Today), returns value: 3 which is based on the current state of system. However, executing the MxL expression (2) representing the metric *m2* at the current point in time returns value: 1, which is based on the state of the system at a point of time in the past i.e. pastDate1. Furthermore, Fig. 9 also shows that the schema itself is updated at some point after pastDate2 and executing the MxL expression corresponding to the metric *m3* with the date pastDate2, first checks for changes in the change-set representing schema change and returns the result corresponding to the schema at pastDate2. Also, the "@" literal can be followed by a sequence of dates, which returns a sequence of results corresponding to each date in the sequence as captured in metric *m4*.

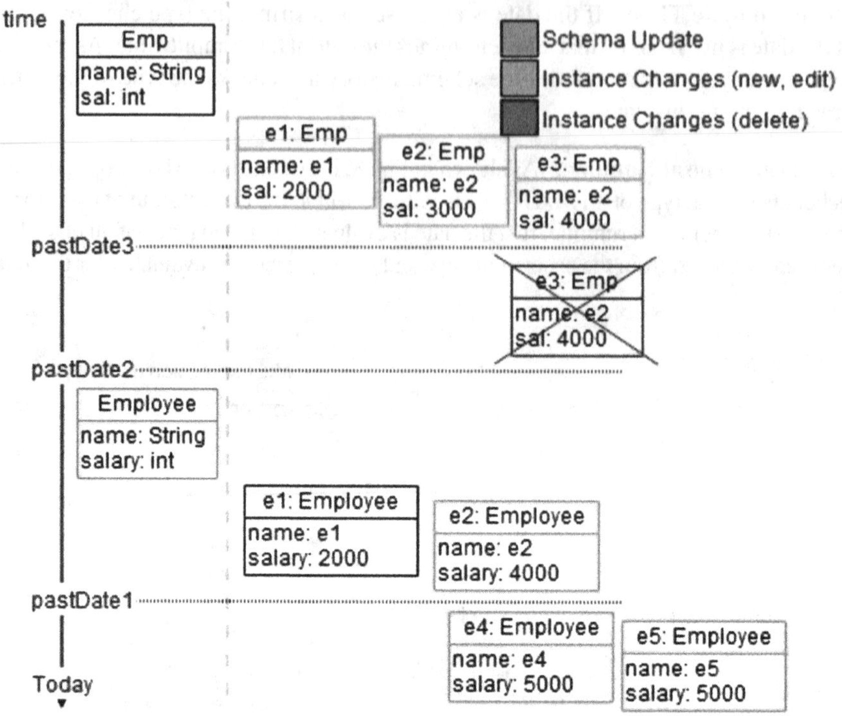

Fig. 9. Evolution of entities.

Furthermore, it should be noted that the definition of a specific metric itself adapts to changes in the schema. As briefly discussed in Sect. 2, the references in the MxL metric definition to its corresponding information model are maintained as first-class entities. Therefore the metric definition is updated when its corresponding information model evolves. For instance in the above example, the metric definition before pastDate2 is represented as *m` = find(Emp).where(sal>3000)*. At a point of time after pastDate2, the Business Type "Emp" is renamed to "Employee" and the attribute definition "sal" is changed to "salary". This results in the automatic redefinition of the metric *m`* to *m* ("*find (Employee).where(salary>3000).count()*".) Thus a user while defining the MxL expression with the "@" literal only has to consider the current state of the information model. Thus the metric *m3* which calculates the metric for the pastDate2 has references to "Employee" and not to "Emp" Business Type.

```
m1 = find(Employee).where(salary >3000).count()                 // 3
m2 = find(Employee).where(salary >3000).count() @pastDate1      // 1
m3 = find(Employee).where(salary >3000).count() @pastDate2      // 1
m4 = find(Employee).where(salary >3000).count() @
  [Today, pastDate1, pastDate2, pastDate3]                      // [3, 1, 1, 2]
```

Fig. 10. Exemplary MxL expressions.

5 Evaluation

5.1 Scenario 1: Visualization of the EA Metrics' Evolution

We conducted an analytical and observational evaluation [27] of the implementation of the MxL's At Expression. One of our industry partners in the financial sectors provided the historized data for the evaluation. Without losing generality, we imported the data with the timestamp of snapshots and updated the versions of artifacts to achieve a consistent view on the evolution of the information model. We then implemented metrics that are used to measure the complexity of the application landscapes (AL). These metrics (e.g., topology-based metrics and heterogeneity-focused metrics [28–30]), were identified by our research group in a related research activity. The metrics used to measure the complexity of the AL include the Number of Applications, Number of Information Flows, and Number of Applications per Customization Level (NACL) metrics. The customization level indicates the category of the business applications such as buy, make, and buy and customize. The historized data received from our industry partner was versioned quarterly from the first quarter of 2012 to the fourth quarter of 2013. Using the "@" operator to compute the Number of Applications in the past, the trend in the metric is visualized in the Tricia platform. Similarly, the Number of Information Flows metric is visualized on a time series graph and is used to analyze the complexity and connectedness of the AL. The complexity of the AL is directly proportional to the number of interfaces (information flows) in each application. The NACL metric determines the number of business applications in different customization levels. The trend in the NACL metric, as shown in Fig. 11, enables executives to compare and analyze where the company has been investing over the period of time.

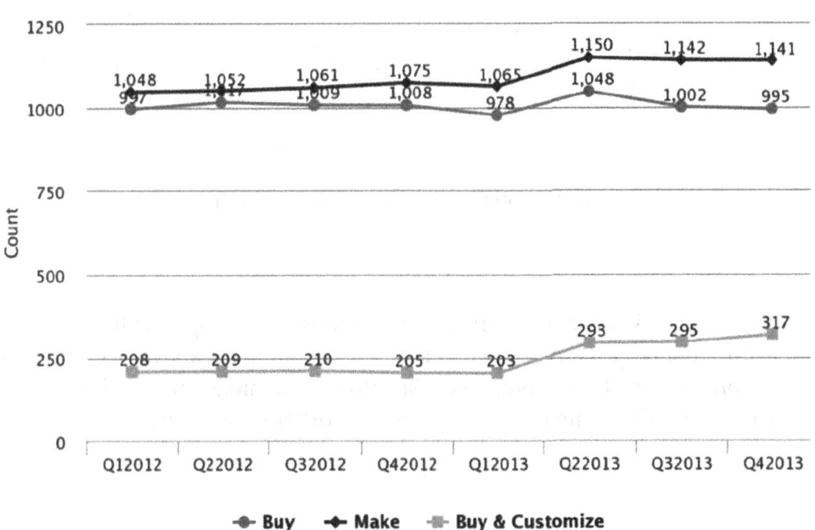

Fig. 11. Evolution of the NACL metric.

5.2 Scenario 2: Evolution of the Information Model

The business users are challenged with the need to support their decision on using a specific EAM tool. They achieve this by demonstrating the significant usage of the system across the enterprise. In our context, we use the Tricia platform to manage projects[2] of our industry partners and use the MxL to capture the evolution of the information model. Each project is managed in a separate workspace and the schema (i.e. Business Types and Business Attribute Definitions) is defined for the corresponding project. Figure 12, shows the evolution of the information model (i.e. Business Entities and Business Attributes) in one of the projects which has been maintained since January 1, 2013. This project has 14 Business Types and 375 Business Entities captured over time. The implemented MxL expression determines the count of Business Entities at a specific time by referring to the information model's history that has a total of 393,268 records. On executing and visualizing this MxL expression, it was interesting to note the drastic increase in the count of Business Entities in June 2013 (as depicted in Fig. 12). Upon investigation, it was concluded that these business entities were imported from an external data source and hence the history of their evolution is not available.

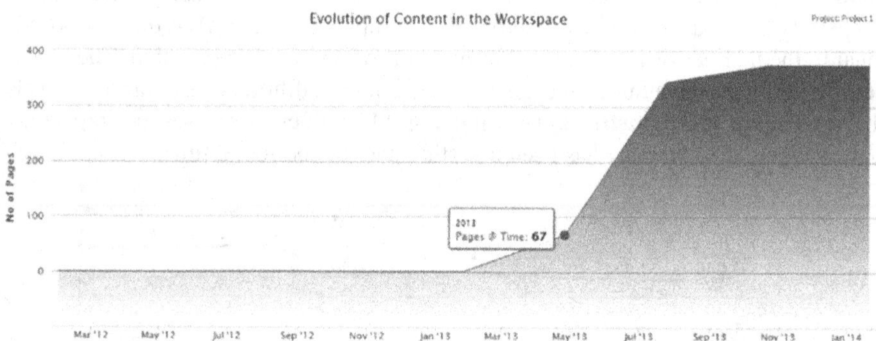

Fig. 12. Evolution of information model in Tricia.

Furthermore, our industry partners are also interested in comparing the evolution of content in different projects. As shown in Fig. 13, extending the above MxL expression allows the comparison of the evolution of the information model of two different workspaces. This allows capturing the activity trends in different workspaces.

[2] http://wwwmatthes.in.tum.de.

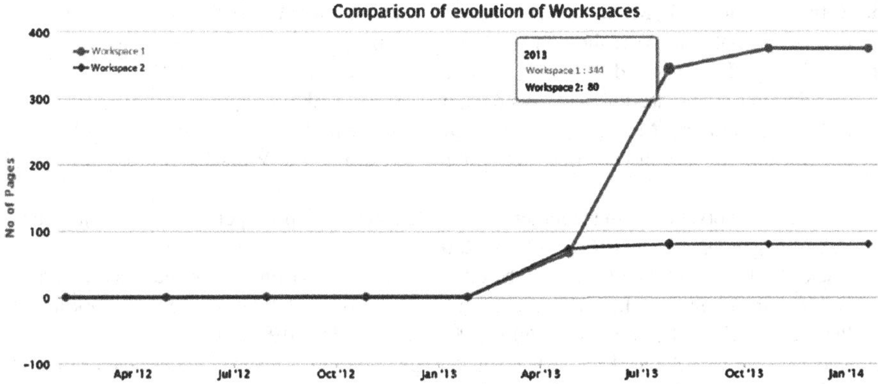

Fig. 13. Comparison of the evolution of the information model in Tricia's workspace.

6 Summary, Conclusions and Outlook

The business users heavily rely on the EA metrics to quantitatively measure the progress of an enterprise towards its goals, it is not only sufficient to define and capture the EA metrics in the EAM tools but there is also a need to perform retrospective analysis of these metrics to take informed decisions. In this paper, we have proposed a model-based approach to capture the temporal aspects of the EA metrics and extended a platform independent model-based expression language to compute the value of an EA metric at a point of time in the past. As discussed in Sect. 3, the proposed concepts in the meta-model support the re-calculation of the EA metrics on occurrence of specific events corresponding to the changes in the information as well as in its schema. Furthermore, through the extended model-based expression language named MxL, we can compute the past metric value based on the information model's history. This subsequently generates the time series model of the EA metrics, which will further enable us to predict the future values using evolutionary algorithms.

Even though we have evaluated the proposed approach using large datasets, we still need to study the usability and performance in a business environment to fully comply with the observational evaluation as defined in [27]. Furthermore, conducting interviews of enterprise architects in our partner organizations will provide necessary inputs to improve our system before testing it in their practical settings. We have proposed to further collaborate with our industry partners from the banking domain for evaluating our approach with their application landscape data.

References

1. Rouse, W.B.: A theory of enterprise transformation. In: Systems, Man and Cybernetics, vol. 1, pp. 966–972. IEEE (2005)
2. Matthes, F., Buckl, S., Leitel, J., Schweda, C.M.: Enterprise architecture management tool survey. Technical report, Technische Universität München, Germany (2008)

3. Roth, S., Hauder, M., Matthes, F.: Collaborative evolution of enterprise architecture models. In: 8th International Workshop on Models at Runtime (Models@ run. time) (2013)
4. IEEE 1471: Systems and software engineering - Recommended practice for architectural description of software-intensive systems, pp. 35–50. IEEE (2007)
5. Roth, S., Hauder, M., Farwick, M., Breu, R., Matthes, F.: Enterprise architecture documentation: current practices and future directions. In: Wirtschaftsinformatik, p. 58 (2013)
6. Bose, R.: Understanding management data systems for enterprise performance management. Ind. Manage. Data Syst. **106**(1), 43–59 (2006)
7. Buckl, S., Ernst, A., Matthes, F., Schweda, C.M.: Visual roadmaps for managed enterprise architecture evolution. In: Software Engineering, Artificial Intelligence, Networking and Parallel/Distributed Computing, SNPD 2009, pp. 352–357. IEEE (2009)
8. Radatz, J., Geraci, A., Katki, F.: IEEE standard glossary of software engineering terminology. IEEE Std. **610121990**(121990), 3 (1990)
9. Matthes, F., Monahov, I., Schneider, A., Schulz, C.: Eam KPI catalog v 1.0. Technical report, Technische Universität München, Germany (2012)
10. Kaisler, S.H., Armour, F., Valivullah, M.: Enterprise architecting: critical problems. In: 38th Annual Hawaii International Conference on System Sciences, HICSS 2005, pp. 224b–224b. IEEE (2005)
11. Hauder, M., Roth, S., Schulz, C., Matthes, F.: Current tool support for metrics in enterprise architecture management. In: DASMA Software Metrik Kongress (2013)
12. Robbes, R., Lanza, M.: A change-based approach to software evolution. Electron. Notes Theor. Comput. Sci. **166**, 93–109 (2007)
13. Monahov, I., Reschenhofer, T., Matthes, F.: Design and prototypical implementation of a language empowering business users to define key performance indicators for enterprise architecture management. In: EDOCW, 17th IEEE International, pp. 337–346. IEEE (2013)
14. Pourshahid, A., Amyot, D., Chen, P., Weiss, M., Forster, A.J.: Business process monitoring and alignment: an approach based on the user requirements notation and business intelligence tools. In: WER, pp. 80–91 (2007)
15. Popova, V., Sharpanskykh, A.: Modeling organizational performance indicators. Inf. Syst. **35**(4), 505–527 (2010)
16. Strecker, S., Frank, U., Heise, D., Kattenstroth, H.: Metricm: a modeling method in support of the reflective design and use of performance measurement systems. Inf. Syst. e-Business Manage. **10**, 241–276 (2012)
17. Schulz, C., Monahov, I., Matthes, F., Schneider, A.W.: Towards a unified and configurable structure for EA management KPIs. In: Aier, S., Ekstedt, M., Matthes, F., Proper, E., Sanz, J.L. (eds.) PRET 2012 and TEAR 2012. LNBIP, vol. 131, pp. 284–299. Springer, Heidelberg (2012)
18. Monperrus, M., Jézéquel, J.M., Champeau, J., Hoeltzener, B.: Measuring models. In: Model-Driven Software Development: Integrating Quality Assurance. IDEA Group (2008)
19. Klint, P., van der Storm, T., Vinju, J.: Rascal: a domain specific language for source code analysis and manipulation. In: 9th IEEE International Working Conference on Source Code Analysis and Manipulation, SCAM 2009, pp. 168–177 (2009)
20. Iacob, M.-E., Jonkers, H.: Quantitative analysis of enterprise architectures. In: Konstantas, D., Bourrières, J.-P., Léonard, M., Boudjlida, N. (eds.) Interoperability of Enterprise Software and Applications, pp. 239–252. Springer, Heidelberg (2006)
21. Johnson, P., Lagerström, R., Närman, P., Simonsson, M.: Enterprise architecture analysis with extended influence diagrams. Inf. Syst. Front. **9**(2–3), 163–180 (2007)
22. Expert, H.: Hugin API reference manual, version 6.4 (2005)

23. Matthes, F., Neubert, C.: Wiki4eam: using hybrid wikis for enterprise architecture management. In: Proceedings of the 7th International Symposium on Wikis and Open Collaboration, pp. 226–226. ACM (2011)
24. Büchner, T., Neubert, C., Matthes, F.: Data model driven implementation of web cooperation systems with Tricia. In: Dearle, A., Zicari, R.V. (eds.) ICOODB 2010. LNCS, vol. 6348, pp. 70–84. Springer, Heidelberg (2010)
25. Segev, A., Shoshani, A.: Logical modeling of temporal data. In: ACM Sigmod Record, vol. 16, pp. 454–466. ACM (1987)
26. Reschenhofer, T., Monahov, I., Matthes, F.: Type-safety in EA model analysis. In: EDOCW, IEEE 18th International, pp. 87–94 (2014)
27. von Alan, R.H., March, S.T., Park, J., Ram, S.: Design science in information systems research. MIS Q. **28**(1), 75–105 (2004)
28. Lagerstrom, R., Baldwin, C., MacCormack, A., Aier, S.: Visualizing and measuring enterprise application architecture: an exploratory telecom case. In: 47th Hawaii International Conference on System Sciences (HICSS), pp. 3847–3856. IEEE (2014)
29. Schuetz, A., Widjaja, T., Kaiser, J.: Complexity in enterprise architectures conceptualiza-tion and introduction of a measure from a system theoretic perspective. In: ECIS 2013 Proceedings, pp. 1–12 (2013)
30. Schneider, A.W., Reschenhofer, T., Schütz, A., Matthes, F.: Empirical results for application landscape complexity. Technical report, Darmstadt Technical University, Department of Business Administration, Economics and Law, Institute for Business Studies (BWL) (2015)

VASCO: Variability Specification in Business Process Models

Raoul Taffo Tiam[1,2(✉)], Abdelhak-Djamel Seriai[1], and Raphael Michel[2]

[1] LIRMM, University of Montpellier/CNRS, 161 rue Ada, 34090 Montpellier, France
{raoul.taffotiam,seriai}@lirmm.fr

[2] ACELYS, Business Plaza bat 3 - 159 rue de Thor, 34000 Montpellier, France
{raoul.taffo.tiam,raphael.michel}@acelys.fr

Abstract. Due to environmental factors influencing their business, information technology plays now a key role in competitiveness of enterprises. Software editors concerned by developing enterprise information systems are irreversibly affected with industrialization of reuse, in order to produce faster, better and cheaper. Software product line approach offers techniques to increase and automate reuse, by explicitly specifying and managing the common and variable features. Business processes constitute a key lever to accelerate strategic alignment and urbanization of enterprise information systems. Thus, variability should be expressed in business process models, with the aim of helping enterprises to overcome environmental fluctuations and editors to industrialize their production. Several models have been proposed to represent variable business processes, but they are far from being directly usable (operational) for production into software factories. We present these shortcomings herein and propose solutions to overcome them. The result is VASCO approach, an operational model of variable business process.

Keywords: Business process · Variability · Reuse · Software product line · Operationalization · Standardization · Completeness · Expressiveness · Separation of concerns · Feasibility · Industrialization

1 Introduction

Software Reuse is a way to increase productivity and enhance quality in software industries, especially when it is systematized. Two axes should be considered in order to improve software reusability, development for reuse and by reuse. Development for reuse relates to identification, specification and storage of reusable knowledge units in a "knowledge base". While development through reuse refers to search and selection of reusable knowledge units, their modification to fit new situations and their integration into new project. Several approaches have been proposed and help to achieve the goal of development for reuse: Software Libraries, Component-Based, Aspect-Oriented, Service-Oriented, Model-Driven, Software Product Line (SPL), Design Patterns, etc. While only SPL approach contributes to development by reuse in assisting and automating selection, configuration, and derivation of new products.

S. Hammoudi et al. (Eds.): ICEIS 2015, LNBIP 241, pp. 612–632, 2015.
DOI: 10.1007/978-3-319-29133-8_30

"*Software Product Line engineering is a way to engineer a portfolio of related products in an efficient manner, taking full advantage of the products' similarities while respecting and managing their differences*" [1]. SPL principle is to analyze common (similar) and variable (different) points between related products and represent them into a feature model. The originality of this approach is that it systematizes reuse, proactive reuse, through two complementary development processes: domain and application engineering. Firstly, domain engineering models reusable platform from which various products will be built by explicitly specifying both the common and optional features, complete with variable points. It can then produce artefacts (*assets*) for all these features. Secondly, application engineering allows to derive (configure) a desired product by selecting the appropriate features from the proposed platform. Both processes have the same development activities than conventional processes, such as specification, analysis, design, implementation or testing. Thus, artefacts may be, analysis or design models, design patterns, software architecture, source code, test plans, testing units, documentation, etc.

According to this approach, models of variable business process are among the artefacts produced during the analysis phase. A variable business process is the representation of common and specific elements of several variants for the same business process. Those different variants, or this variability, appear because of fluctuations around the business environment such as economy, society, technology, legislation or environment. It is therefore important for enterprises to withstand these changes in order to remain competitive, so they need to adapt their business processes without changing them completely. This is made possible through variable business process. So, it is necessary to express and manage variability to ensure better coverage of the target market. A business process linked to an enterprise information system or to a specific application, is a set of more or less related activities that collectively realize a business goal while defining the roles and relationships of each resource. The business process models capture that coordination of activities. They thus serve as relay between the requirements specification and software used to meet these requirements.

"*Significant research efforts have been made throughout the last decade, leading to an abundant production of variable business process models*" [2]. Despite this fertility, modelling variability in business processes remains a major challenge. Indeed, for such models to be really used in an industrial context, some criteria are essential. For example these models should not be owners but rather standardized, to enable integration with artefacts produced at other development stages. They must deal with variability in its entirety i.e. taking into account all types of variability, and propose solutions readily practicable. Unfortunately, many of these expected criteria, see Sect. 2, are not considered or completed in variable business process models proposed in the literature to make them operational [2–4]. Our work aims to bear most of these barriers by subscribing to the following goal: making an operational model of variable business process, i.e. truly usable in a software factories.

This paper is organized as follows: Sect. 2 outlines properties for an operational model of variable business process, Sect. 3 analyses previous related work, Sect. 4 details our proposal and Sect. 5 concludes the paper.

2 Criteria for an Operational Model of Variable Business Process

The goal here is to characterize a solution that takes into account essential and unavoidable properties to the operationalization of variable business process models. In this paper, we mainly consider the following properties: standardization, completeness, expressiveness, separation of concerns (requirements and business processes), and feasibility (validation and tools).

2.1 Standardization

Aim of standardization is to comply a product with a given standard or reference. Such an effort provides many benefits which rank commonality in terms and interpretation across people (uniformity) or tools (interoperability), scalability, adaptability, rising of technological feasibility and other profits of good practices. In a software factory, this criterion is essential as it brings together several activities and very often separate processes or existing tools. Therefore, the flow of information between the individual tools and its integrity from one tool to another usually follows the evolution of the tool, it is then performed improperly or not at all. Due to the lack of adequate equipped supports and integrated processes (lack of standardization), the same work is done repeatedly, with a lack of coherence and synchronization, as well as duplication.

About the variability we are seeing the emergence of a standard, CVL – Common Variability Language [5], proposed for its specification, both centred at the user level and realization of product. It is therefore recommended, even required, to refer to this standard too for specification of variability in business process models.

2.2 Completeness

Aim of completeness is to specify solutions for all aspects of an issue. It brings up lot of gains like fullness, fidelity and accuracy. In our software factory, completeness concerns the possibility to specify the variability in all components of the business process in which it may appear. The standard ISO ENV 40003 [6] defines four views to model enterprise business processes: functional, informational, organizational and resources. Thus, a business process is specified by its activities, events that trigger them, flows that interconnect them, actors involved, business objects that are used or produced and control nodes that coordinate the exchange of information. We must be able to explain the variability that can occur on any one of these components.

Partial specification of variability in business process models is an obstacle to operationalization because unconsidered components are ignored or at best, inappropriately treated.

2.3 Expressiveness

Aim of expressiveness is to provide native richness of a given language. The conferred benefits are for example clarity, legibility, understandability, and translatability. In our purpose, expressiveness in variability specification is ability to express naturally all types of variability that could appear in business process models. To offer a wide range of natively concepts not only contributes to the richness of a solution, but also to its simplicity. This criterion is especially important in an industrial context, where models are usually very complex and voluminous.

The general techniques for realization of variability are processed in [7], and categorized for business processes in [8]. We consider that the variability can minimally be expressed by the following forms:

- *basic:* adding/removing/replacing element, reorganization, typing, setting;
- *composite:* generalization/specialization, expansion/extension point, composition/ decomposition, generation, pattern design;
- or *conjunctural:* conditional, temporal.

To make operational models of variable business process, we are therefore concerned by the ability to express all these forms of variability.

2.4 Separation of Concerns: Requirements and Business Processes

Separation of concerns addresses the ability to separate components into elementary functions, so they are considered or performed separately. This criterion is even more important in industrial world as it increases the simplicity and reusability of designed artefacts, reduces errors and promotes teamwork. Variability discriminates the features of a product in four categories [9]:

- *mandatory*;
- *optional*;
- *variant*;
- and *external*.

Considering this decomposition, we evaluate existing solutions in terms of their compliance with these categorizations. Thus, for a solution to meet this criterion of separation of concerns, it is necessary that the considered elements are not only internal but also external to business processes.

2.5 Feasibility: Experimentation and Tools

Aim of feasibility is to ensure that a given solution is truly applicable in software factory. This last criterion is important for operationalization of variable business process models, and also validation, adoption or diffusion of an approach in industry. This is why we consider two aspects of feasibility, experimentation and tools. Experimentation concerns the implementation of a proposal on a real industrial case, with a preference when the concerned domain is validated by experts or issued from an authoritative repository. We are secondly interested by existence and availability of tools based on the approach.

3 Previous Work

Several research studies have focused on variability specification within business processes for nearly a decade. We selected five of the most representative and relevant approaches:

- C-EPCs (Configurable Event-driven Process Chains) proposed by Rosemann and van der Aalst [10], then enriched with the language C-iEPCs (C *integrated* EPCs) [11, 12];
- PESOA (Process family Engineering in Service Oriented Applications) or VRPM (Variant-Rich Process Models) [8, 13];
- BPFM (Business-Process Family Model) [14, 15];
- PROVOP (PROcess Variants by OPtions) [16, 17];
- Ayora et al. works [3, 18].

We analyse the match between models offered by these approaches and operationalization key criteria.

3.1 Standardization

C-EPCs approach uses its own C-iEPCs language for modelling variable business processes, making it an *ad-hoc* and proprietary solution which entails standardization.

This criterion is considered in PESOA and BPFM approaches which offer possibilities to use standards like BPMN or UML AD by proposing independent solutions of the business process modelling language. Therefore, they do not use the standard for variability specification, but languages inspired by FODA [19] also called «*FODA-like*» languages.

The PROVOP approach defines a set of structured blocks among others to represent the base model, its options and configuration context. It is an *ad-hoc* and owner language, thereby giving unstandardized properties.

Ayora et al. propose a solution independent of the business process modelling language and push this effort to standardize the variability specification language. However to specify variability, they use two formalisms: CVL standard and a *FODA-like* language. This clearly indicates a lack of uniformity in their variable business processes models, and a lack of standardization as well.

3.2 Completeness

With contributions of La Rosa and al., the C-EPCs approach allows to specify variability in roles (organizational resources) and manipulated objects. So, this approach is able to specify variability in every business process component, it is completeness.

PESOA approach does not allow to specify variability in control nodes (gateways), nor in the organizational resources (actors and roles).

BPFM approach can only specify variability in variable flow and activities of the business process, so it does not consider all business process components where variability can appear.

In PROVOP approach, it is only possible to specify the variability points at input or output of control nodes. Therefore, variability specification in organizational resources and objects is only partially treated as they are modelled as activities attributes.

Ayora et al. take this criterion into account from the beginning and manage all component parts of business processes, allowing them to validate completeness in variability specification.

3.3 Expressiveness

In C-EPCs it is possible to specify a variable model composed by union of all variants, which ignores for example information on reference model or default variants. This approach uses few basic mechanisms of realization of variability but not composite nor conjunctural technics.

PESOA models a reference business process in which it is possible to specify common, optional, variable, and default elements, as well as variability points. They use basic and composite mechanisms for realization of variability but not conjunctural ones.

BPFM is an approach that perceives the basic variability realization technics, but we deplore absence of several composite and conjunctural mechanisms.

The PROVOP approach offers basic mechanisms of variability realization but suffers from shortcomings regarding composite and conjunctural ones.

Ayora et al. works are expressive enough but that expressiveness failed for example to indicate variability on different abstraction levels such as with encapsulation (not achieving all composite variability mechanisms).

3.4 Separation of Concerns: Requirements and Business Processes

On this property we note that apart from the C-EPCs approach, there is no solution in related works that satisfies this separation of concerns between features of requirements and variable business processes. Indeed, in existing models of variable business processes the features considered are mainly internal to business process like uncorrelated to other artefacts produced by related activities of software factory as requirements specification or design. In the best case of C-EPCs approach those features are considered but buried within variable business process models.

3.5 Feasibility: Experimentation and Tools

C-EPCs approach satisfies both aspects of feasibility since it has been validated on a real case from film industry and is implemented by *Synergia* tool.

The PESOA approach for its part has been applied to an industrial hotel reservation case but is only partially implemented by an Eclipse plugin.

Meanwhile BPFM approach is not validated on an industrial case yet and its implementation via an Eclipse plugin is partial.

The PROVOP approach is partially implemented by *ARIS* tool and has two applications cases in automotive and health domains. However, the areas of these industrial cases were not validated by domain experts or issued from an authoritative repository.

Finally Ayora et al. works are applied to a business process of admission in university, so it is not an industrial case, and its implementation via the *MOSKitt* tool is not available yet.

3.6 Synthesis

We examine state of the art solutions in terms of key criteria for operationalization of variable business process models. This assessment is summarized in Table 1 below, where scores are assigned based on the level of satisfaction of the above criteria.

Table 1. Evaluation of existing approaches.

Criteria	C-EPCs	PESOA	BPFM	PROVOP	Ayora et al.
Standardization	0	0	0	0	½
Completeness	1	0	0	½	1
Expressiveness	½	½	½	½	½
Separation of concerns	½	0	0	0	0
Feasibility	1	½	0	½	0

1 ≡ satisfied criterion; ½ ≡ partly satisfied criterion; 0 ≡ unsatisfied criterion.

We note that no approach satisfies all the required criteria for an operational model of variable business process, in fact they all have at least one unsatisfied property. Thus, the specification of variability in business process models addresses an issue where the challenge remains topical.

4 Proposition

The following section detail our approach as well as our contributions to an operational model of variable business process.

4.1 Case Study

To ease understanding of our proposition, we introduce the case study, an industrial project of software product line in service center management. In Information Technology (IT) systems, a service center management tool is an interface between an IT service supplier, and the service customer which aims at processing requests for services through a centralized portal. The customer contracts a service catalog, allowing him to choose his service and to know his type parameters upstream for the control (expenses, unit of work, statistics…), rather than ordering services independently of each other. This tool allows service provider to standardize a framework for better management of service requests, capitalize on the provided services, receive feedback and thus improve both service delivery and profitability. ITIL repository defines twenty-two business processes for management and optimization of IT service centers. These business processes involve either services production, governance or management of their life cycles, and they harbor variability.

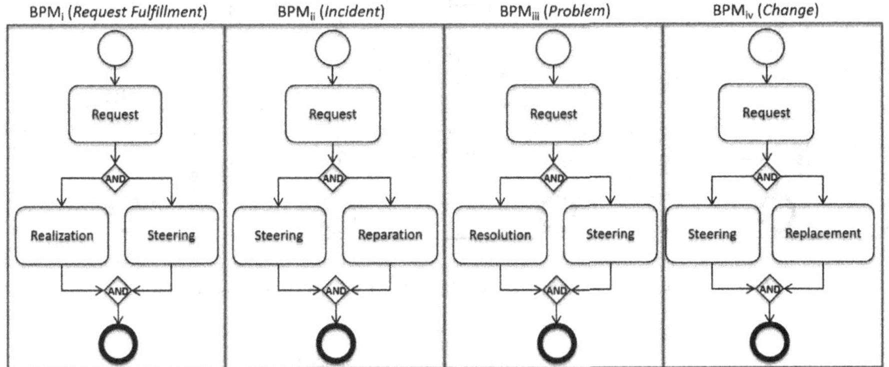

Fig. 1. Set of related business process models.

Figure 1 shows a set of models of business processes in service center. The first, *Request Fulfillment*, may occur for example in the case of a request for software installation (LaTeX). The second, *Incident*, is raise for example in case of a printer dysfunction. The third, *Problem*, occur for example in case of a blue screen problem. And the fourth, *Change*, may occur if there is nothing more to do with faulty screen. Those are "related" business processes because they all start with a *Request* activity carried out by the customer, follow up with the provider's synchronized activities: *Production* of service and a transversal *Steering*. When it is a *Request Fulfillment*, the *Production* consists in a service *Realization*; if it is an *Incident*, it would rather be a *Reparation*; *Resolution* when it is a *Problem*; and *Replacement* to a request for *Change*. All those options of *Production* activity are variability manifestations (see Fig. 2). Our approach should allow to express and specify this variability in a "variable" business process model. In addition, the model must take required criteria for operationalization into account.

4.2 Approach Overview

VASCO stands for Variability specificAtion in buSiness proCess mOdels, and the general idea of our approach is depicted in Fig. 3. Information systems produced by software editors allow enterprises to deploy, manage and optimize their business.

Because of fluctuations or changes in their business environments, these enterprises must adapt quickly to remain competitive, then they drift variants of their business processes. Software editors in charge of development must also take account of these business process variants in order to reduce costs and production time while increasing quality, through the reuse of common components.

Our approach, VASCO, then specifies the variability within business processes, so that the resulting models are used directly within a software factory. This is made

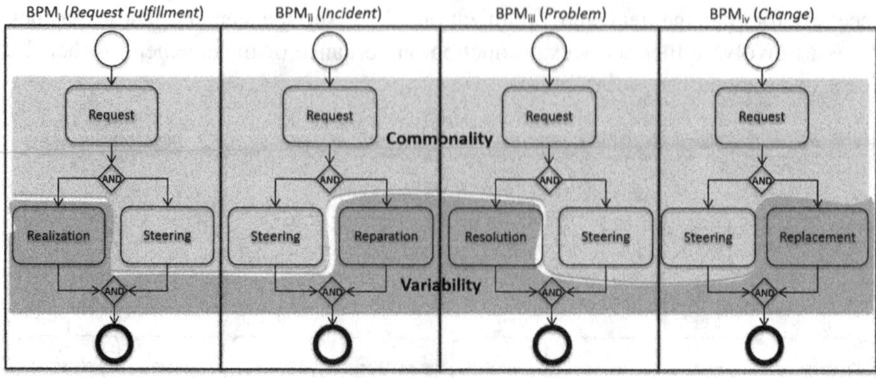

Fig. 2. Variability identification in related business process models.

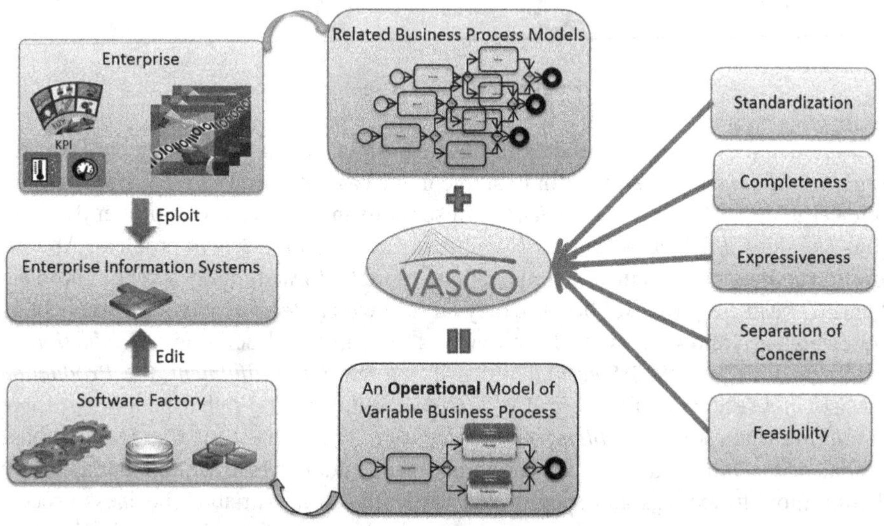

Fig. 3. Overview of the VASCO approach.

possible through the integration of key criteria for operationalization, namely standardization, completeness, expressiveness, separation of concerns and feasibility.

4.3 Standardization

To specify and represent variability in business process models, we implement the CVL standard for specification of variability. CVL is a generic and independent specification to model the variability in models throughout any DSL[1] defined based on the MOF – Meta Object Facility [20]. It is representative of ongoing efforts involving both the academic community and industry stakeholders to promote the standardization of

[1] Domain Specific Language.

variability modelling technology. This specification includes a CVL meta-model, semantics and concrete syntax for expressing variability. CVL consists of three models:

- *base model* – a model described in UML [21], BPMN [22] or any other DSL;
- *variability model* – a model describing the variability that exists within the *base model*;
- *resolution model* – the model that describes how to resolve the variability and create a new model in the base DSL.

The principle of using these models is as follows: a *base model* may have more *variability models* and each *variability model* can have multiple *resolution models*. With *variability model* and *resolution model* properly defined, the user can run a generic CVL model-to-model transformation to generate new resolved models that conform to the *base model*. To represent *mandatory* or *optional* features, with links *requires*, *excludes*, *xor*, *or*… and the cardinality at user-centered level, concepts such as *type*, *composite variability*, *constraint* or *iterator* are offered. While in product realization, concepts such as *placement/replacement fragment*, *fragment substitution*, *value substitution* or *reference substitution* are proposed to make the transformation of a variable model in a resolved one.

Our standardization effort in the variability specification in variable business process models consists in projection and adaptation of this CVL standard to business processes. Thus, we propose three independent models to specify common, optional and variable features: a *BaseModel* from which it is possible to build one (or more) *VariationModel*, which themselves can entail one (or more) *ResolutionModel*.

Our basic model – *BaseModel* – represents the common characteristics in business process "families".

The variability model – *VariationModel* – describes the variability in the *BaseModel*, in other words the variable characteristics. It indicates that variability using *placement fragments*.

The resolution model – *ResolutionModel* – describes how to resolve the variability and create a new model in the base DSL. It defines with *replacement fragments*, alternatives or options to resolve the variability indicated by *placement fragments*.

Those three models are represented in a synthetic model, a "*variable model*" of business process, which has both the common features of *BaseModel*, optional features of *ResolutionModel* and variable features of *VariationModel*. It is described in a DIML[2], which we define based on MOF. This business process modelling language inspired by UML AD and BPMN regardless of their fields, is proposed to bring together the respective communities of IT and business stakeholders.

To specify variability of our previous case study example of business process *Service Request*, we design its reference or variable business process model, including features from our three different models, see Fig. 4.

Request and *Steering* activities are common features as described before and *Production* is variable. Others activities *Replacement*, *Realization*, *Resolution* and *Reparation* are options (variants) to replace the variable activity.

[2] Domain Independent Modeling Language.

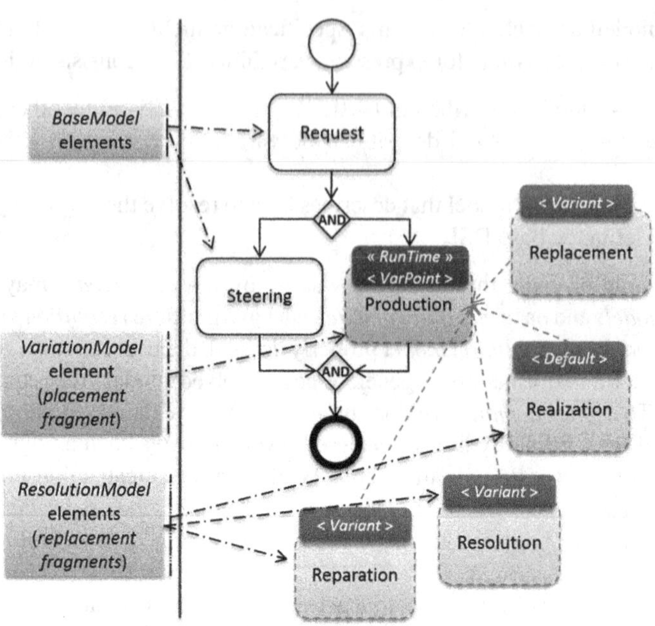

Fig. 4. *Variable model* of sample business processes.

We use these concepts uniformly for variability specification in all business process components.

4.4 Completeness

As mentioned, variability may appear in all components of business process, in activities, events, flow controls or gateways of the same business process as well as in manipulated objects and solicited actors. We propose to use our standardized models consistently across all these components.

Examples of Figs. 5 and 6 derived from our case study illustrate the variability that may appear respectively in roles (actors) for the same *Service Fulfillment* business process, or in objects (business entities) for *Service Fulfillment* and *Incident* business processes. This variability must be specified and represented in the objects and roles, by the same manner as in the variable activity of business process illustrated previously.

As regards the variability in objects and roles, we obtain the following variable model, see Fig. 7. Variable features are specified with *placement fragment* of *VariationModel* and optional features with *replacement fragments* of *ResolutionModel*.

4.5 Expressiveness

Variability is not expressed in the *BaseModel* which specifies common features, but rather on variable and optional features, so respectively through *VariationModel* and *ResolutionModel*.

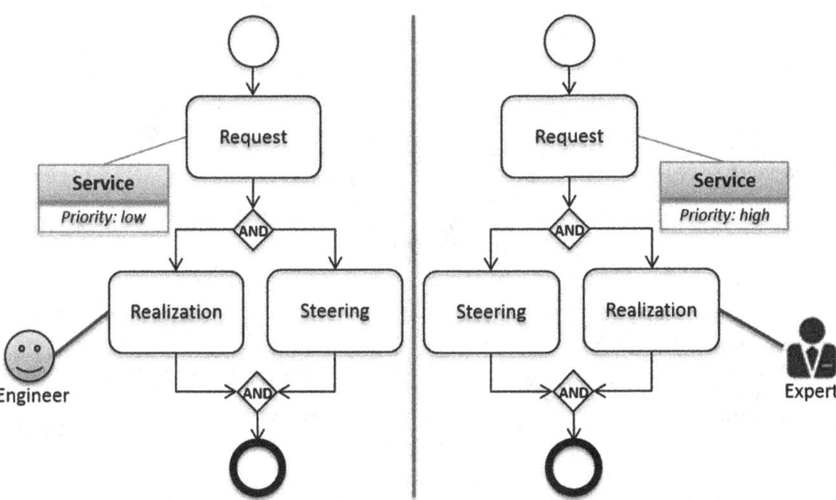

Fig. 5. Variability appears in roles.

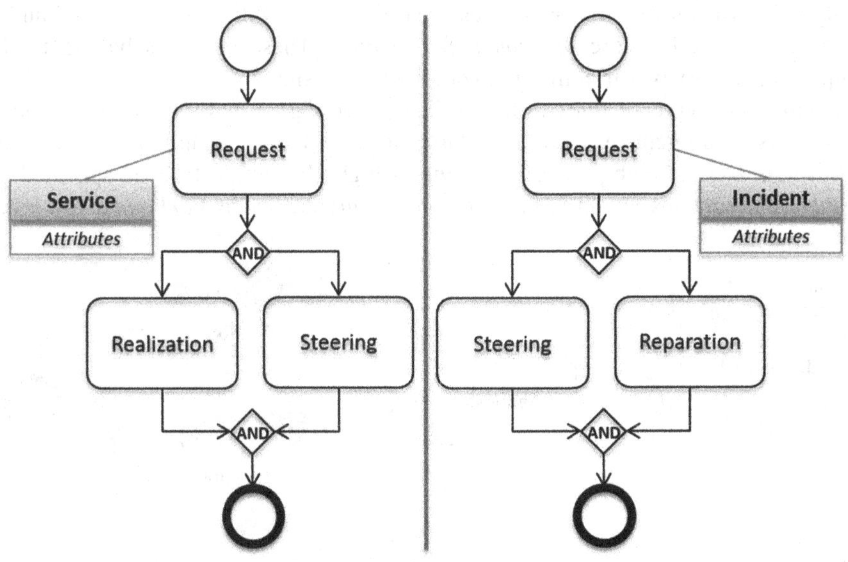

Fig. 6. Variability appears in objects.

Expressiveness in ***VariationModel*****.** To express variability in our *VariationModel*, several mechanisms proposed by CVL are implemented, such as *placement fragments* that correspond to the basic category (add/delete/replace feature).

However, there are different abstraction levels in business processes, corresponding for example to encapsulation of business sub-processes. We introduce two new concepts that specialize the concept of *placement fragment*, *Variable* and *VarPoint*, to manage variability specification on different abstraction levels. Thus, the

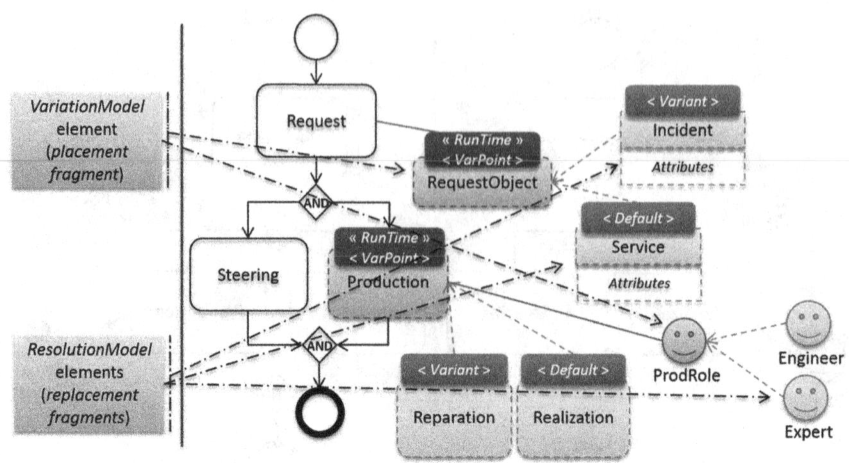

Fig. 7. *Variable model* with expression of variability in objects and roles.

Variable concept indicates variability at a high level, while *VarPoint* specifies variability at a lowest level. A *Variable* feature denotes variability at a high level and is composed of one or more *placement fragment*(s). These concepts belong to the composite category of variability realization mechanisms.

Examples of our case study in figures below, see Figs. 8 and 9, reflects variability that appears on different abstraction level in business process. Variability which appears on business activity (sub-process) *Steering* at high abstraction level is specified by *Variable*, and contains a variable task (activity) *Crop* specified by *VarPoint* at low level.

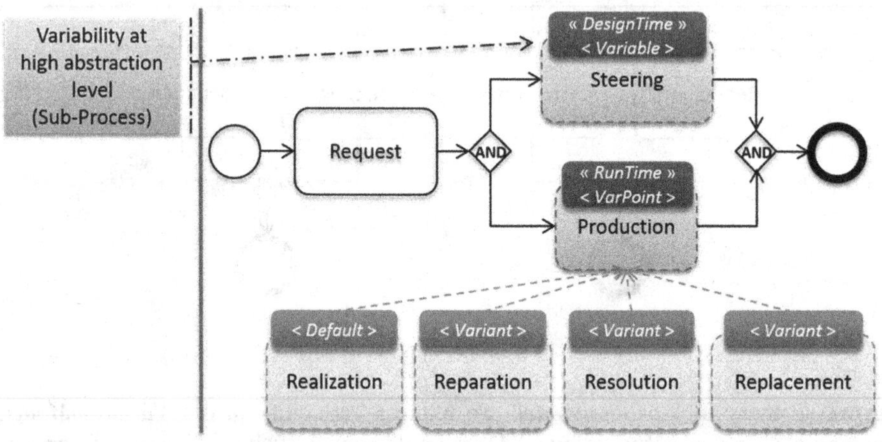

Fig. 8. *Variable* feature.

Environmental factors that characterize the variability in specified points are reified in item(s) which belong to *VariationModel* too, representing the context of variation – *VariationContext*. It is formulated by expressions – *ContextExpression*, which are

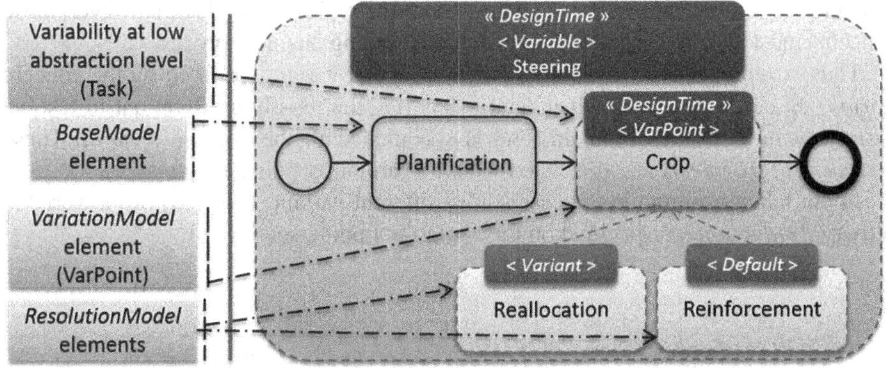

Fig. 9. *VarPoint* feature.

variables of considered domain. This is a conjunctural mechanism of variability specification, and conditional category more specifically.

For example in our case study, the availability of services should be taken into account as shown here in Fig. 10, specifying that an *Escalation* way in steering is required in case of power failure.

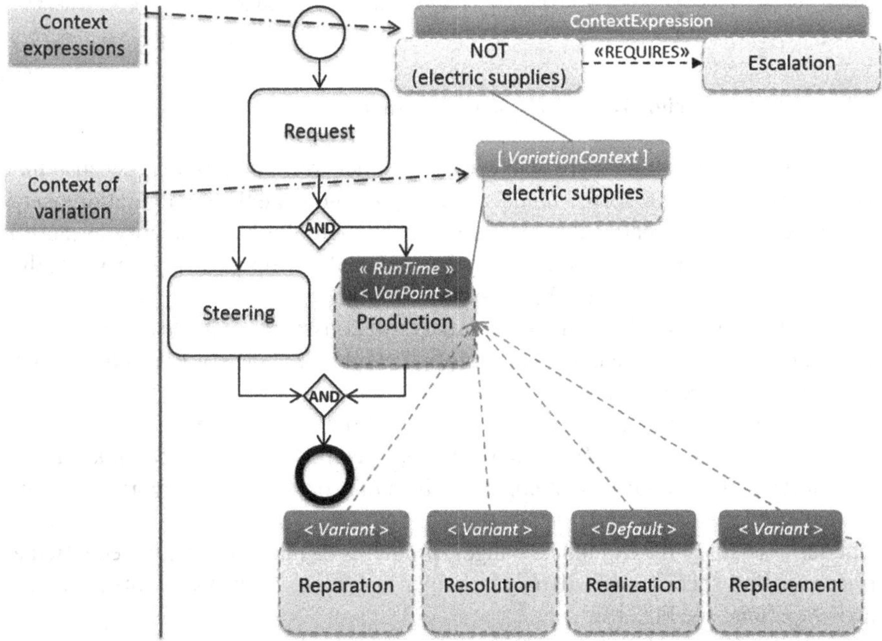

Fig. 10. Specification of variation context in our business process *variable model.*

Expressiveness in ***ResolutionModel*****.** Several variability realization mechanisms are also implemented in our *ResolutionModel*, like *replacement fragments* which correspond to the basic mechanisms of adding/removing/replacing artefact. However, these concepts must also be specialized to match the varying business processes.

Thus, a *replacement fragment* is either a normal variant specified by the concept *Variant*. In certain case default variant exists (i.e. the mostly used variant to resolve variability in a business domain) and is specified with the concept *Default*. These *replacement fragments* are associated with the variability points they resolve.

In our taken example in the case study, different variants (options) of the variable activity *Production* are specified on this variability point, see Fig. 11.

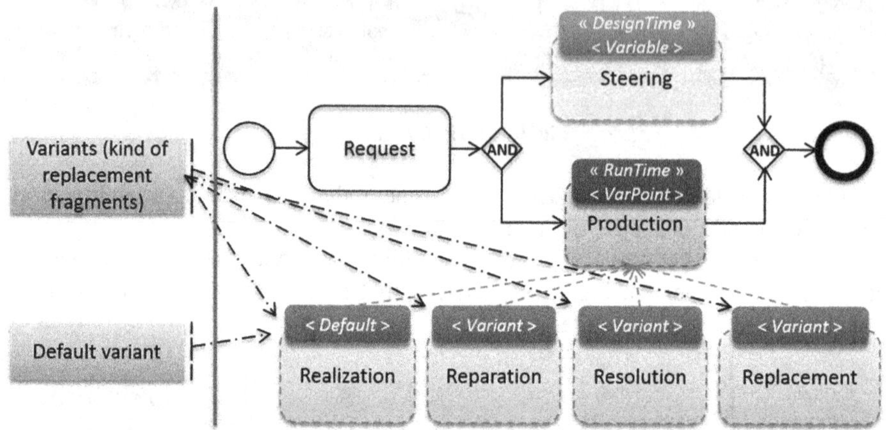

Fig. 11. *Variant* and *Default* variant specification.

Configuration constraints are also specified in our *ResolutionModel*, because they allow the validation of resolved models and help to automate the configuration operations. This variability realization mechanism belongs to the base category because it refers to reorganization. Constraints may be specified indiscriminately on variability points corresponding to variable business process components.

Figure 12 is an example from our case study, the constraints indicate that *Resolution* variants and *Realization* are in mutual exclusion, while the choice of *Resolution* variant requires the one of *Reparation*.

To manage the variability throughout the lifecycle of business process, the variability resolution time – *ResolutionTime*, must also be specified in *ResolutionModel*. It is a temporal form of variability, so it corresponds to the conjunctural category. That time is at analysis/design – *DesignTime*, or at execution – *RunTime*.

In our case study for example, changes, problems or incidents can be requested as services and thus specificities will only be known at runtime, so the variability resolution time is *RunTime*, see Fig. 13.

4.6 Separation of Concerns: Requirements and Business Processes

Elements considered so far to express and represent the variability within business process models are internal. We must then identify and treat separately the external

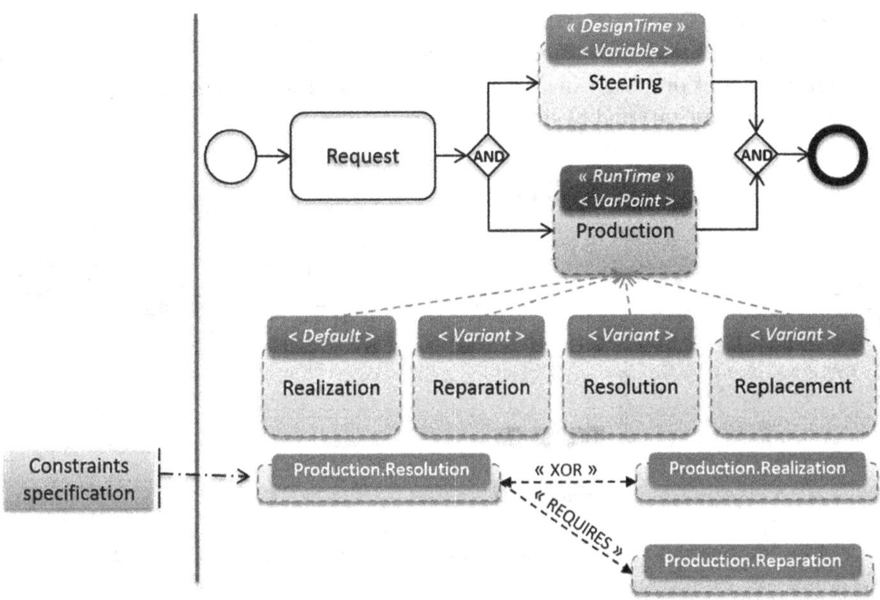

Fig. 12. *Constraint* specification in *variable model.*

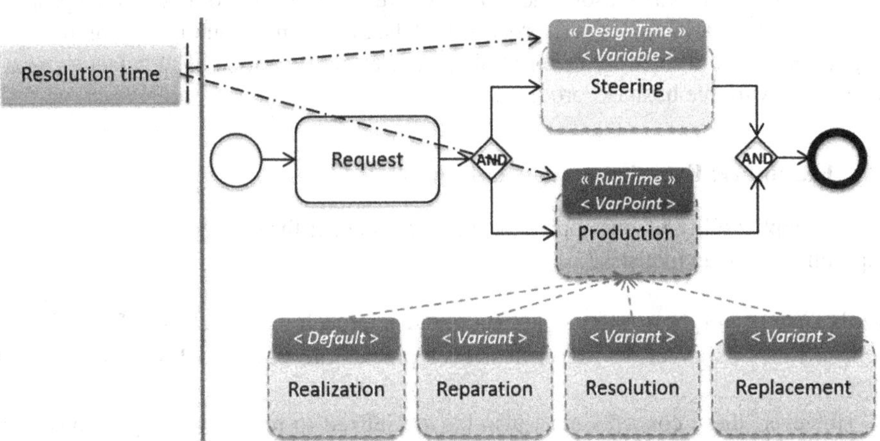

Fig. 13. Resolution time specification in *variable model.*

factors related to variability specification in business process models. In our concern, these external factors are requirements. Indeed in software factory activities, requirements specification precedes the modelling of variable business processes. Thus, during the product development, requirements specification according to customer particular needs influences the variability resolution in models of variable business processes.

This approach fits external features proposed in [8], with the particularity that information discriminated as external features in variable business process models is requirements. Therefore, when those features (requirements) are taken into account, separate model, cf. Fig. 14. In fact, this solution is structured through a traceability model proposed in our work, especially for the link between variable models of requirements and business processes.

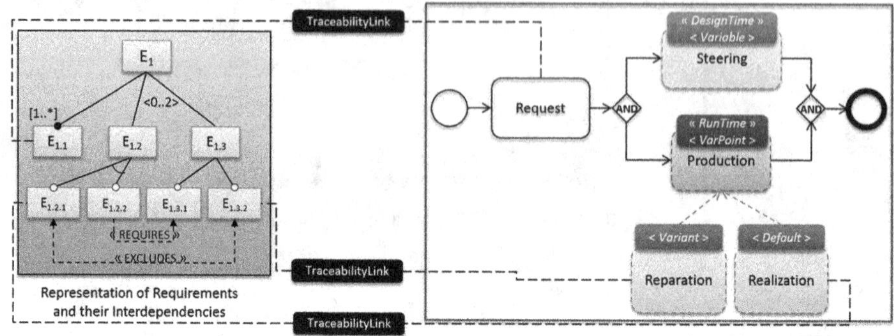

Fig. 14. Separation of concerns: requirements separate from business processes.

Now, choices of upstream requirements allow obtaining new constraints to consider for variability resolution of downstream variable business processes. This separation effort is essential for the reasons mentioned above in description of operational properties expected in variable business process models. Furthermore, automation of the variability resolution in software factories also requires consideration of such factors separately from variable business process models.

4.7 Feasibility: Experimentation and Tools

To rate applicability of our approach, we implement it through a prototype and also experiment it on an industrial case.

Tools. We prototype a tool to implement our approach using Eclipse PDE[3] with an Eclipse RCP[4] as target environment. Developments are based on EMF[5], GMF[6] and OCL[7].

However, these concepts must also be specialized to match the varying business processes.

EMF is used to define the abstract syntax, GMF the concrete syntax and OCL specifies static semantics, see Fig. 15. Component 1 defines vocabulary (concepts) and semantics of our modelling language (DIML) of variable business processes.

---

[3] Plugin Development Environment.
[4] Rich Client Platform.
[5] Eclipse Modeling Framework.
[6] Graphical Modeling Framework.
[7] Object Constraint Language.

Its development is based on the EMF framework. The sub-component 1 translates in OCL the rules and constraints to resolve variability. Component 2 defines the notation corresponding to previously proposed vocabulary. It is developed using the GMF framework. Component 3 designs the target platform for using previous components and model variable business processes. It creates four different views (perspectives) and toolboxes for designing these models. Its development is based on Eclipse RCP technology. Designed variable business process models are persisted in files conforming to standard XMI[8].

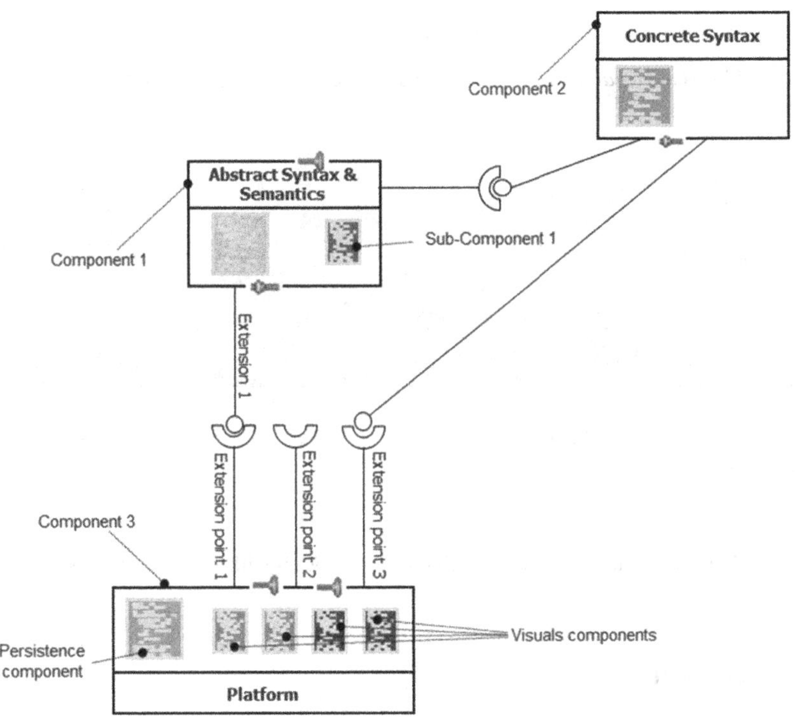

Fig. 15. Architecture of our tool.

Experimentation. The complete approach we propose has been implemented to specify the variability of business processes in an industrial case study described above. We illustrate some of the most representative results obtained with the prototype, see Figs. 16 and 17.

[8] XML Metadata Interchange.

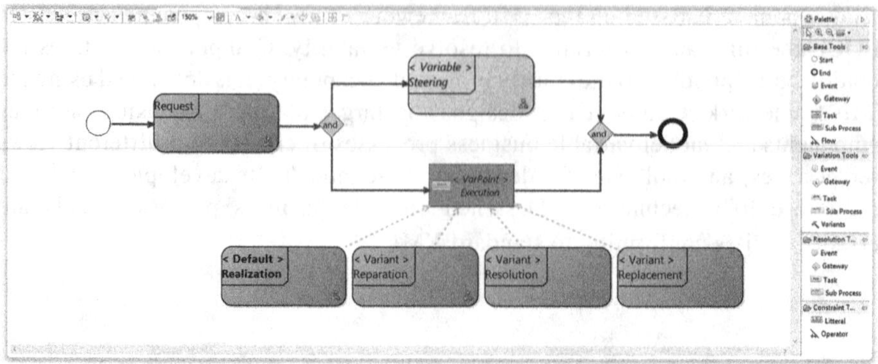

Fig. 16. *Variable model* of previous business processes in service center.

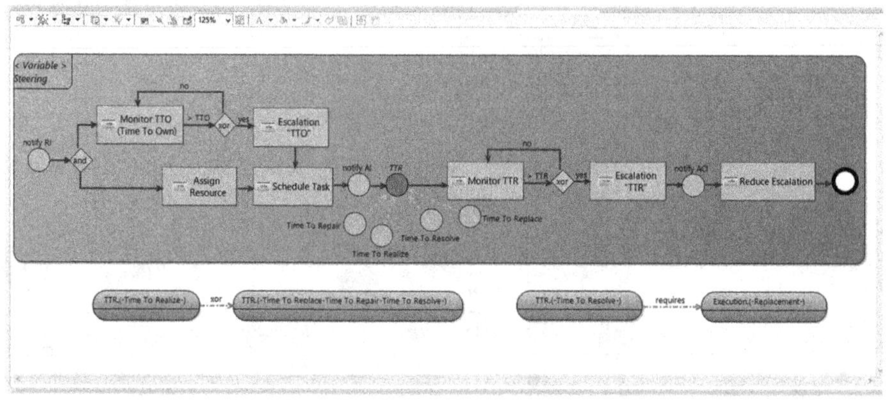

Fig. 17. Details of Steering sub business process with some constraints.

5 Conclusion

We highlight importance and urgency to propose an operational model of variable business process and respond to this need. By doing so, we show how critical is standardization in software factory due to uniformity or interoperability purposes, and perform an independent solution for variability specification compatible with BPMN or UML. Indeed, we project the emerging CVL standard for variability specification and adapt it to business processes. We expose pitfalls it may have by not treating variability on all components of business processes, because they help meet to key questions about business aspects. We then apply our proposition uniformly on all components of business processes where variability may appear. We explain why and how to take into account all types of variability that can occur in business processes. Our proposition offers then a native and natural way to specify different types of variability throughout all business process lifecycle. We analyze that requirements are often buried within variable business process models and establish a separation of concerns between these features, which contribute to modularity. For further feasibility validation of our approach, we prototype a tool that supports our proposition and we experiment our proposals to a case study corresponding to a real industrial project. Our approach, VASCO, satisfies thereby the key criteria required for operationalization of designed models of variable business processes.

In conjunction with this work, we address the problem of traceability between requirements and development models, particularly variable business process models. As requirements specification is treat separately from design and implementation activities in the development process, this separation affects negatively the time to market, product quality and customer satisfaction. So we operationalize the activity of requirements specification and propose a traceability model to link requirements and business processes. This effort allow us to take requirements into account as external features for variability resolution in variable business processes.

In further work, we will plan on variability specification in software architecture. Indeed to develop enterprise information systems, requirements specification allow answering to *why* questions, business process modeling answer to *what*, and software architecture designing answer to *how*. So after dealing with requirements specification and business process modeling, it will be timely to treat variability specification in software architecture.

Acknowledgments. We would like to thank the National Association of Research and Technology (ANRT in French) for its contribution to this research.

References

1. Krueger, C., Clements, P.: Systems and software product line engineering. In: Encyclopedia of Software Engineering, Chap. 112, pp. 1–14. Taylor and Francis (2013)
2. La Rosa, M., van der Aalst, W.M.P., Dumas, M., Milani, F.P.: Business process variability modeling: a survey. Technical report, ACM Computing Surveys (2013)
3. Ayora Esteras, C.: Modeling and managing variability in business process models. Ph.D. thesis at Polytechnic University of Valencia, Valencia (2011)
4. Reinhartz-Berger, I., Mechrez, I.: Modeling design-time variability in business processes: existing support and deficiencies. In: Bider, I., Gaaloul, K., Krogstie, J., Nurcan, S., Proper, H.A., Schmidt, R., Soffer, P. (eds.) BPMDS 2014 and EMMSAD 2014. LNBIP, vol. 175, pp. 378–392. Springer, Heidelberg (2014)
5. Haugen, O., Wasowski, A., Czarnecki, K.: CVL: common variability language. In: Tutorial, p. 277. ACM, New York (2013)
6. ISO: Enterprise Integration: Framework for Enterprise Modeling. Standard (2002)
7. Svahnberg, M., van Gurp, J., Bosch, J.: A taxonomy of variability realization techniques: research articles. J. Softw. Pract. Exper. **35**(8), 705–754 (2005)
8. Schnieders, A., Puhlmann, F.: Variability mechanisms in E-business process families. In: 9th International Conference on Business Information Systems, pp. 583–601 (2006)
9. van Gurp, J., Bosch, J., Svahnberg, M.: On the notion of variability in software product lines. In: Working IEEE/IFIP Conference on Software Architecture, pp. 45–54. IEEE Computer Society, Washington (2001)

10. Rosemann, M., van der Aalst, W.M.P.: A configurable reference modelling language. J. Inf. Syst. **32**(1), 1–23 (2007)
11. Mendling, J., Gottschalk, F., ter Hofstede, A.H., La Rosa, M., Dumas, M.: Beyond control-flow: extending business process configuration to roles and objects. In: Li, Q., Spaccapietra, S., Yu, E., Olivé, A. (eds.) ER 2008. LNCS, vol. 5231, pp. 199–215. Springer, Heidelberg (2008)
12. La Rosa, M., Dumas, M., ter Hofstede, A.H.M., Mendling, J.: Configurable multi-perspective business process models. J. Inf. Syst. **36**(2), 313–340 (2008)
13. Puhlmann, F., Schnieders, A., Weiland, J., Weske, M.: Variability mechanisms for process models. Technical report, BMBF-Project (2005)
14. Park, J., Moon, M., Yun, S., Yeom, K.: An approach to enhancing reusabilities in service development. In: 2009 International Conference on Hybrid Information Technology, pp. 143–150. ACM, New York (2009)
15. Park, J., Kim, J., Yun, S., Moon, M., Yeom, K.: An approach to developing reusable domain services for service oriented applications. In: 2010 ACM Symposium on Applied Computing, pp. 2252–2256. ACM, New York (2010)
16. Bauer, T., Hallerbach, A., Reichert, M.: Issues in modeling process variants with provop. In: Ardagna, D., Mecella, M., Yang, J. (eds.) Business Process Management Workshops. LNBIP, vol. 17, pp. 56–67. Springer, Heidelberg (2009)
17. Hallerbach, A., Bauer, T., Reichert, M.: Capturing variability in business process models: the provop approach. J. Softw. Maint. Evol. **22**, 519–546 (2010)
18. Ayora, C., Torres, V., Pelechano, V., Alférez, G.H.: Applying CVL to business process variability management. In: VARiability for You Workshop: Variability Modeling Made Useful for Everyone, pp. 26–31. ACM, New York (2012)
19. Kang, K.C., Cohen, S.G., Heiss, J.A., Novak, W.E., Spencer Peterson, A.: Feature-oriented domain analysis (FODA): feasibility study. Technical report, Software Engineering Institute (1990)
20. ISO/IEC: Meta Object Facility (MOF) Core 2.4.2. Information Technology – Object Management Group (2014)
21. ISO/IEC: Unified Modeling Language (UML) 2.4.1. Information Technology – Object Management Group (2012)
22. ISO/IEC: Business Process Model and Notation (BPMN) 2.0.1. Information Technology – Object Management Group (2013)

Time-Driven Activity Based Costing as a Service

André Machado[1(✉)], Carlos Mendes[1], Miguel Mira da Silva[1], and João Almeida[2]

[1] INOV, Lisbon, Portugal
{andre.machado,carlos.mendes,mms}@tecnico.ulisboa.pt
[2] Card4B, Systems S.A., Lisbon, Portugal
joao.almeida@card4b.pt

Abstract. Due to the global economic and financial crisis the application of cost saving techniques now receives even more attention than before. Organizations are searching for new ways of cutting costs, specially Small and Medium Enterprises (SMEs) that due to their small size and market exposure need cost awareness and efficiency more than ever. However, efficient and accurate costing methodologies are out of reach for most SMEs, since these methodologies usually involve hiring expensive consulting firms. In this research we propose that costing should be offered as a service to reduce the cost of cost analysis. Our research proposal is a cloud-based costing system that offers costing as a service using Time-Driven Activity Based Costing (TDABC) methodology and the concept of Business Process Costing Templates that together reduce the cost of cost analysis, especially for SMEs. This proposal was demonstrated in three Portuguese organizations from different industries. The evaluation based on experts and practitioners' feedback showed that the proposal has potential to contribute to the research problem.

Keywords: Costing · TDABC · Cost templates · Cloud computing · Cloud services · SaaS

1 Introduction

Enterprises are becoming increasingly complex and managing that complexity is a growing challenge. Competition is fierce among these entities that always tried to differentiate between themselves through a variety of factors, one of which is efficiency. Cost efficiency has always been a major concern to organizations but in the last few years its importance grew due to global economic and financial crisis. Due to their small size and market exposure, Small and Medium Enterprises (SMEs) need cost efficiency more than ever [1].

However, as organizational complexity grows, so does the complexity of cost analysis [2]. Information about how and where the money was spent is a concern of organizations across all industries. Knowledge about costs distribution and true understanding of overhead costs allocation is essential for an enterprise to focus on the most profitable products and services [3].

S. Hammoudi et al. (Eds.): ICEIS 2015, LNBIP 241, pp. 633–653, 2015.
DOI: 10.1007/978-3-319-29133-8_31

In order to obtain detailed information about costs and overheads distribution several cost methodologies were developed. These methodologies evolved and differentiated themselves from traditional cost accounting systems to better distribute overhead costs that have been rising inside organizations in recent years [4]. The increasing importance of overhead costs comes from the fact that the industry has evolved from manufacturing to services [5]. This development implied a substantial growth of overhead costs [4,5].

Organizations using these accurate costing methodologies know exactly where resources are being spent and what is the profitability of their products or services. However, the adoption of these costing methodologies is far behind of what would be expected. The lack of adoption is explained by the high costs of these methodologies for SMEs since they require time, expertise and expensive and complex software solutions that are out of reach for the most of these organizations [6].

2 Problem

Costing has been a major concern to all organizations since their genesis. As a competitive advantage, cost efficiency has been something that all organizations tried to achieve in order to increase their profit margins or reduce the price of their products or services. Cost efficiency is recognized as one of the most important aspects in respect to the competitive advantages of an organization.

Normally, organizations resort to cost accounting in order to analyse costs and achieve the desired cost reductions. This approach has a major issue: traditional cost accounting systems give low detailed information and lack the needed granularity to properly do cost analysis and, therefore, cost reduction. Not least, most accounting systems are focused on mandatory state-demanded reports [7] showing only large blocks of information totally misaligned with the organization's business processes. Therefore, when it comes to calculate the cost of a product or service, traditional methodologies give inaccurate values, mostly because they lack the needed granularity and differentiation of information [8]. Often, such information is inaccurate because of wrong distribution of overhead costs. Correct distribution of overhead costs is truly essential since they have grown from being a minor share of the total costs to the major one [5].

Presently, there are several costing methodologies to address the abovementioned problem. These methodologies resort to the activities that occur inside the organization to design the flow of costs from the inputs (e.g. material) to the outputs of an organization (products or services). This cost awareness allows organizations to take measures to improve their efficiency.

The problem with these accurate costing methodologies is that they require a lot of expertise and are normally supported by very expensive and complex software solutions [6]. Whereas large organizations can support the costs associated with the required expertise and software solutions, SMEs cannot [6]. It is crucial that SMEs have access to these accurate cost methodologies since they operate in a market that is more competitive [9] and they are more exposed to the effects of an economic crisis [1].

To solve this problem we propose that costing and cost analysis should be offered as a service instead of as an investment in a one-time project. This approach should enable organizations to access accurate costing methodologies because costs are diluted over time and the tools needed to perform this cost analysis are also offered as a service. Our proposal will also give organizations the ability to do on-demand cost analysis so that they can constantly evaluate the flow of costs as well as take measures to improve their cost efficiency.

3 Objectives

As we stated before in the problem section, the main issue with cost analysis is that it is too expensive for the majority of the organizations in both human and financial capital. However, we identified a clear need for cost analysis using accurate costing methodologies to help organizations stay aware of the flow of costs throughout the organization. This awareness would help the process of decision making since managers need correct and accurate information about costs and profitability so that they can decide which products or services should be improved or ceased, in order to maintain the sustainability of the organization.

We also identified another problem regarding cost analysis: it is often offered as a one-time big project instead of being offered as a service. Constant changes in business processes and in the markets where organizations operate urge the need of a costing service instead of a one-time analysis. Managers should be able to test new strategies as well as refine processes, activities and costs of resources, which also change frequently over time.

Therefore, the main objective of this proposal is to present a cost analysis service, targeted to SMEs, which solve the abovementioned problems. This service should be more affordable and easier to use than current solutions being also less dependent on external consultancy services. Our intent is that these characteristics will allow smaller organizations to conduct a bigger share of the cost analysis process.

Besides this main goal, we also want to achieve some other more specific objectives:

- The service should be easily available to organizations;
- The service should support any kind of organization or industry;
- The service should not require specialized expertise upon the moment of application on an organization;
- The service should be more affordable than traditional methods from the beginning of the cost analysis until its end, i.e., the moment when results are obtained.

4 Related Work

We will provide an overview of the tools and methods available that could contribute to solve the identified problem.

4.1 Cost Accounting

Cost Accounting (or costing) can be defined as the process of collecting, classifying, assigning and analysing the costs associated with the activity of an organization [10].

According to Vanderbeck [11], Cost Accounting provides the detailed cost information that management needs to control current operations and plan for the future. The goal of cost accounting is to gather all possible information so that it can be structured and used by management to take decisions and measure the organization's performance [12].

Information Systems built to support Cost Accounting are called Cost Accounting Information Systems. Main goals of these systems include recording transaction data and calculating the cost of the outputs of an organization [11].

4.2 Costing Methodologies

Activity Based Costing. ABC methodology defines an activity as an action executed inside an organization (e.g. packaging) that has a particular cost rate based on the cost of the resources allocated to that activity. Allocation of resources to activities and then to products or services is done based on interviews to those involved in the activities as well as in some estimates provided by the management team. This process results on splitting the costs related to the resources used by the activities using variables like percentage or headcount. Output costs are calculated adding the costs of all the activities that were needed to create the final product or service [10].

Traditional costing methodologies assign overhead costs by volume, that is, overhead costs are distributed by products using some variable (or driver) that reflects capacity usage (e.g. number of hours) regardless of the specificities of the product. On the other hand, ABC uses activities which mean that different products may use a set of different activities and therefore a set of different cost rates to calculate the final cost of a product or service.

Although ABC has some advantages over traditional costing systems it also has some pitfalls. First, costs are calculated using individual and subjective estimates. The accuracy of these estimates may be questionable since, in most cases, there is no evidence of correctness. Wrong estimates may distort measurements [13]. Second, ABC requires not only the creation of an activity for every task performed inside the organization but also its cost specification. Thus, the complexity of the model grows with the number of activities. Finally, since it is common to have activities with variable costs (e.g. special packing vs standard packing) and ABC defines activities as single tasks with fixed cost rates, models tend to have many similar activities just to simulate variable costs.

Time-Driven Activity Based Costing. Time-Driven Activity Based Costing (TDABC) [13,14] is an alternative costing methodology to ABC developed to calculate the profitability of products and services focusing on assigning overhead costs to these cost outputs. This methodology was created to address the ABC pitfalls described earlier.

The TDABC model simulates the actual processes used to perform work throughout an enterprise, therefore capturing far more variation and complexity than a conventional ABC model. Such variation and complexity is captured without significant demand for data estimates, storage, or processing capabilities. This model aims simplicity and flexibility while focusing on assigning overhead costs [13,14].

Targeting simplicity, TDABC assigns resource costs directly to the cost objects requiring only two sets of estimates, neither of which difficult to obtain: the cost of supplying resource capacity for the department and the capacity usage by each transaction processed in the department [13].

The cost of supplying resource capacity (or capacity cost rate) is the total expenses related to a particular resource (e.g. IT Department) divided by its capacity (normally expressed in time). Total expenses of a department may include costs such as personnel, supervision, occupancy, equipment and technology. On the other hand, capacity is the time available from the employees to actually perform the tasks. Capacity used by each transaction is the estimated consumption of capacity (typically unit times) needed to execute a particular activity. After estimating these two values it is possible to calculate the cost of an activity simply by multiplying the estimated consumption by the unit cost of a resource.

Regarding flexibility and concerning the limitations of ABC of each activity reflecting only one factor/condition [15], TDABC introduces the concept of time-equations. As we described earlier, ABC required the creation of a new independent activity for each small variation needed to drive the cost. However, in TDABC, linear equations are used to model the different resources consumed by an activity. An activity may have different consumption of resources (such as time) depending on the conditions that occurred in a particular instance of that activity. If we take as an example the packaging of an order that takes longer when gift wrapping is requested, in ABC there would be two activities: one for standard packaging and another for gift wrapping. However, in TDABC it is possible to express this variation with the following equation:

$$\begin{aligned} \text{Packaging} &= (3 + 5 * \varphi) * \text{Logistics Dtp. CCR} \\ \varphi = 1 \text{ if gift wrapping} &\vee \varphi = 0 \text{ otherwise} \end{aligned} \tag{1}$$

Finally, TDABC provides mechanisms to gather information about its own accuracy and to identify possible wastes or inefficiencies [13]. Given the capacity of a resource and the actual capacity used within a time period it is possible to calculate waste or inefficiency. If the sum of times used by a particular resource in the activities is below its total capacity it usually indicates that there is some sort of waste or inefficiency. On the other hand, if it is above, it normally indicates overuse. Indeed, discrepancies between capacity and its usage may also indicate errors in the model construction.

4.3 Business Process Cost Templates

Business Process Cost Templates is a method to reduce the costs of adopting efficient costing methodologies, such as TDABC, through re-utilization and standardization of business processes for organizations inside the same field or industry. The main goal of these templates is to dilute the costs associated with the analysis required to implement a costing methodology, in particular TDABC, making the adoption of such methodologies more affordable [16].

The method that creates a template for a particular field is composed of two distinct phases: a **Modelling Phase** and an **Application Phase**. The first is done only once and is where the field or industry is analysed and a generic cost model is developed. The second results of the application of the template produced. The template is instantiated and the specificities of the organization are set. These specificities may include addition or removal of activities, changing the coefficients in time-equations, or adding some unrepresented condition. This adjustment is crucial since not all organizations are identical, even though they belong to the same industry or field [16].

5 Proposal

We briefly describe our proposal **as a cloud-based costing service that uses TDABC and the concept of Business Process Cost Templates to reduce the costs associated with cost analysis.**

5.1 Costing Service Objectives

We highlight from our cloud-based costing service the following features: Time-Driven Activity Based Costing methodology, Business Process Costing Templates, Creation/Edition of Business Processes and Time-Equations, What-if Analysis, Data Integration, Data Visualization and Automatic Pre-configuration.

Offering a costing service in a cloud environment helped us achieve the needed technological cost reduction. Current solutions require local software installations that raise the costs of the service because, in addition to compelling the purchase of the technological equipment needed, it also implies operational costs. Those tools are also very complex and require expertise whenever modifications to the model are needed. These issues prevented managers from performing cost analysis as an ongoing process.

As for the costing methodology, we adopted TDABC for the reasons stated in the Related Work (4). TDABC is an accurate costing methodology that solves the problems identified in previous methodologies and that is simple to understand and implement, providing quick benefits for those who adopt it [17]. TDABC also has clear connections with BPM that helped us connect it with Business Process Costing Templates.

Regarding Business Process Costing Templates, we chose to use them within our service because they provide a way of creating cost templates to a given industry and distribute them for all the organizations that operate within that industry. These templates can be created and modified by an organization or by a cost analysis expert and included within our tool. Providing cost templates to more than one company leads to cost reduction, since the cost of creating a template can be distributed by multiple organizations. These templates can be later improved or adapted to the reality of the organization deploying the template. Even though the organization may incur in a cost by doing this, it will be a lower cost when compared to the cost of a complete analysis.

Finally, What-if Analysis, Data Integration and Data Visualization, are meant to provide means of assessing the organization's performance. Although these features are not directly related to the cost reduction of the cost analysis they are required to comply with the guidelines proposed by TDABC.

5.2 Costing Service - Analysis Process

Figure 1 shows the process of performing a cost analysis using the costing service. Users should start by configuring resources and resource pools and importing transactions. If the costing service is being used by more than one user, each one may be accountable for one of the activities. In the case of the resources, users should define, for every resource belonging to the organization, the name of the resource, its monthly capacity and the cost of providing such capacity. On the other hand, regarding resource pools, users should define the name of the resource pool and its classification, whether it is a support resource pool or a functional resource pool. Afterwards, users should configure the resource pool structure, that is, which support resource pools belong to which functional resource pools.

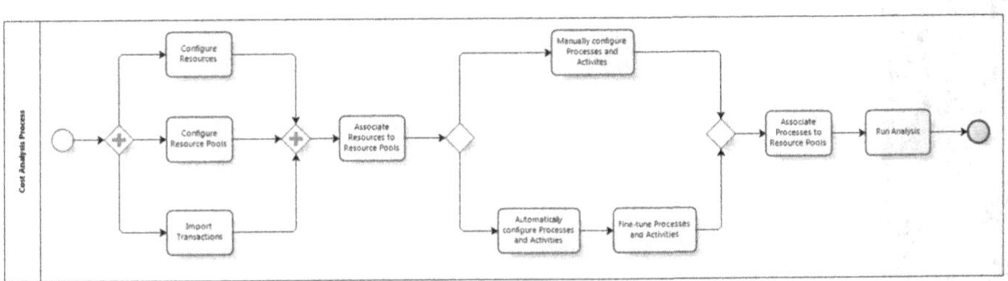

Fig. 1. Costing service - analysis process.

Users must also associate resources to resource pools. Resources can either be associated to support or functional resource pools. After completing these associations, resource pools will have their cost calculated so that users can know the costs of their resource structure before completing the analysis.

Afterwards, users should decide if they want to automatically configure business processes and activities or if they want to manually specify them. The main difference is closely related to the quality of the data available. If users know that their data matches the processes of the organization, they can let the tool automatically configure them. On the other hand, if users already have some sort of "optimized" business process template, they should manually configure the tool. Users may also let the costing tool infer business processes and then fine-tune them. We encourage users to perform an automatic configuration since this simplifies the process of analysis even further.

Finally, users should associate the functional resource pools to the business processes that those functional resource pools are accountable for and then compute the analysis. Running the analysis finishes the process of cost analysis. However, users may change resource cost values, fine-tune activities and business processes or change associations and then recompute analysis.

5.3 Costing Service Tool

We developed our costing tool according to the guidelines defined by both TDABC and Business Process Costing Templates meaning that they represented our requirements document.

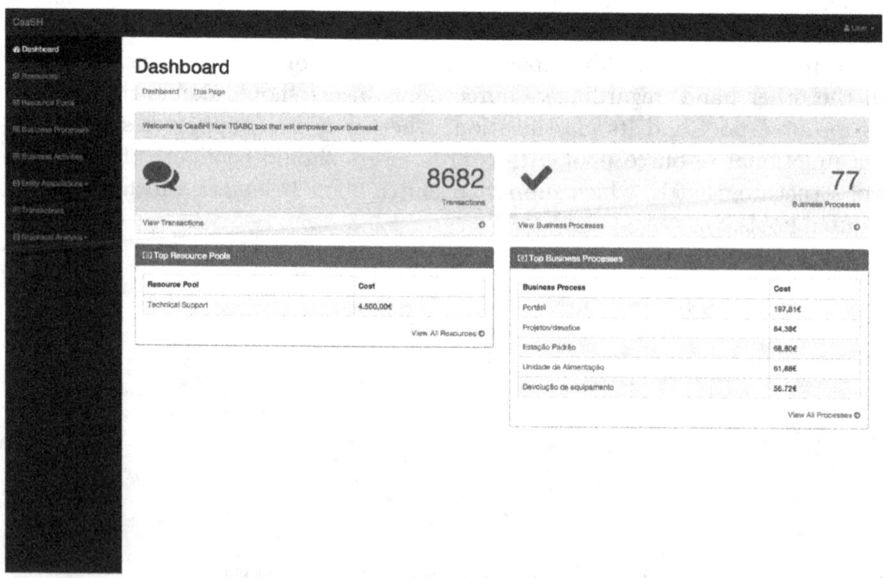

Fig. 2. CaaSH - Dashboard - costing tool.

Figure 2 shows the Dashboard of our tool. We provide information regarding the number of Transactions (8682) used to make the analysis, the number of Business Processes (77) identified and the list of the top five most costly Resource Pools and Business Processes.

6 Demonstration

We demonstrated our proposal by instantiating our artefact (the costing service) in three real world Portuguese organizations, namely "Social Security IT Institute", "Defence Data Center" and "Card4B".

The demonstrations consisted in instantiating the costing service, i.e., creating the cost template, within the costing tool, to the organization being tested. This includes the definition of resources, resource pools, business activities, business processes and the relationships between these entities to the particular environment of the organization being tested.

6.1 Social Security IT Institute

The Social Security IT Institute is a public institute, integrated in the indirect state administration, with administrative and financial autonomy. It is an organization with nationwide intervention. Although several state competences have been assigned to the Institute, we focused our demonstration in the service desk competences.

Following the process described in Sect. 5.2, we started by gathering relevant data to feed the transactional data needed to perform the analysis. We asked the Institute to provide us with a CSV file containing the data to be imported as transactions. We had access to 8682 **real transactions** to perform the analysis.

Regarding the resources, there are several resources involved in all the business processes and departments inside the organization. These resources are diversified and include technical and management staff, electricity, rents, material and equipments. Although all these resources and resource pools (such as the Technical Support department) are properly identified, the organization opted to avoid gathering the unit costs of each resource and their contribution to the resource pools. This decision was justified since the organization had been previously involved in a cost analysis project. From the results of this former project, the Institute knew the daily cost of the technical support staff. However, they were unable to link it to the execution of the business processes, which is the main objective of our demonstration.

Based on these limitations, we defined a resource and a resource pool that matched the daily value supplied. We knew that the monthly time capacity of this resource was 8 h/day and 22 days/month, which was converted in minutes with a 10 % waste on working hours, giving the final monthly time capacity of 9504 min for each technical support worker. If we assume (since we cannot disclose the real value) the cost of providing such capacity as 200€/day, the cost of providing 9504 min of technical support labour would cost 4400€. Since there is no other support resources or resource pools, this means that the capacity cost rate (CCR) of this resource is 0,46€.

From the 8682 transactions supplied, the automatic configuration of the costing tool was able to detect 77 business processes with 791 unique business processes instances. This means that the analysis was performed using data from 791 complete executions of a business process (from the 77 identified).

Figure 3 shows a sample of the results obtained from the analysis. The sample shows, for each business process identified, the average time and cost of execution as well as the number of instances that were identified for that business process. The red and green rectangles also show another interesting result from the cost analysis. The red rectangle shows a group of three business processes that were identified by the costing tool and that correspond to the same business process, as we were able to verify with the Social Security IT Institute management. This results from the wrong definition of workflows inside the IT Service Management software (EasyVista) which leads to wrong categorization of incidents/service requests in the service desk. The green rectangle shows the same problem described earlier but this time with an even minor difference (name pluralization).

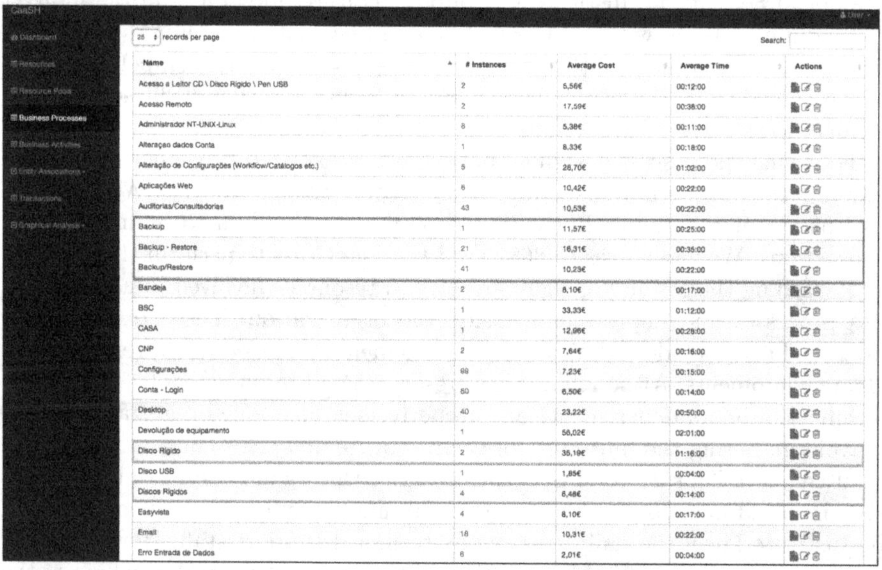

Name	# Instances	Average Cost	Average Time	Actions
Acesso a Leitor CD \ Disco Rigido \ Pen USB	2	5,56€	00:12:00	
Acesso Remoto	2	17,59€	00:38:00	
Administrador NT-UNIX-Linux	8	5,38€	00:11:00	
Alteraçao dados Conta	1	8,33€	00:18:00	
Alteração de Configurações (Workflow/Catálogos etc.)	5	28,70€	01:02:00	
Aplicações Web	6	10,42€	00:22:00	
Auditorias/Consultadorias	43	10,53€	00:22:00	
Backup	1	11,57€	00:25:00	
Backup - Restore	21	16,31€	00:35:00	
Backup/Restore	41	10,23€	00:22:00	
Bandeja	2	8,10€	00:17:00	
BSC	1	33,33€	01:12:00	
CASA	1	12,96€	00:28:00	
CNP	2	7,64€	00:16:00	
Configurações	99	7,23€	00:15:00	
Conta - Login	50	6,50€	00:14:00	
Desktop	40	23,22€	00:50:00	
Devolução de equipamento	1	56,02€	02:01:00	
Disco Rigido	2	35,19€	01:16:00	
Disco USB	1	1,85€	00:04:00	
Discos Rigidos	4	6,48€	00:14:00	
Easyvista	4	8,10€	00:17:00	
Email	18	10,31€	00:22:00	
Erro Entrada de Dados	6	2,01€	00:04:00	

Fig. 3. CaaSH - SS IT institute - business processes sample.

Not only the costing tool delivered what was expected, i.e., the cost of executing the business process that accomplishes the resolution of a service request or incident, but it also provided valuable insights to the organization regarding the workflows definition in the IT Service Management software. The organization can easily know the average time and cost of executing a business process. Moreover, the institute can further analyse the data and find **the cost for every execution of every business process**. The Social Security IT Institute management members considered these results very useful since they can now further analyse the different costs that the same business process generates. For instance, a desktop related incident has an average cost of 23,22€ but the minimum cost and the maximum cost of such incident was, respectively,

2,31€ and 70,83€. Having this information, the management may now try to understand what motivated such difference and take measures to mitigate the cause.

6.2 Defence Data Center

The Defence Data Center belongs to the General Secretariat of the Ministry of National Defence (Portugal) and among its several competences they are also responsible for service desk activities.

The Defence Data Center service desk uses EasyVista software for IT Service Management, i.e., the same software used by the Social Security IT Institute. It is also configured according to the best practices defined internally (ITIL). This means that the demonstration was almost identical to the previous case. Again, we followed the costing service process of analysis (Sect. 5.2), starting with the integration of the transactional data. This data was integrated through a CSV file exported from EasyVista, the IT Service Management software.

We had access to 34917 **real transactions** to perform the analysis. This represented over four times the number of real transactions available in the Social Security IT Institute. Still, the costing tool was prepared to handle high volumes of transactional data, so the performance of the solution was not affected and all the features remained functional.

From the 34917 transactions supplied, the automatic configuration of the costing tool was able to detect 453 business processes with 5340 unique business processes instances. This means that the calculations were performed using data from 5340 complete executions of a business process (from the 453 identified).

Figure 4 shows a sample of the results obtained from the analysis. The sample shows, for each business process identified, the average time and cost of execution as well as the number of instances that were identified for that business process. Again, the red rectangle shows a group of three business processes that were identified by the costing tool and that correspond to the same business process. As we stated in the previous demonstration, this results from the wrong definition of workflows inside the IT Service Management software (EasyVista) which leads to wrong categorization of incidents/service requests in the service desk. Once more, we assumed resource and indirect costs that **do not** match the real values provided by the Defence Data Center.

The costing tool delivered what was expected, i.e., the cost of executing the business process that accomplishes the resolution of an incident or service request. It also provided valuable insights to the organization regarding the workflows definition in the IT Service Management software.

6.3 Card4B

Card4B develops and operates integrated mobility solutions through interoperable contactless ticketing, passenger information, embedded systems and smartphones, systems integration and business intelligence. Presently, Card4B is

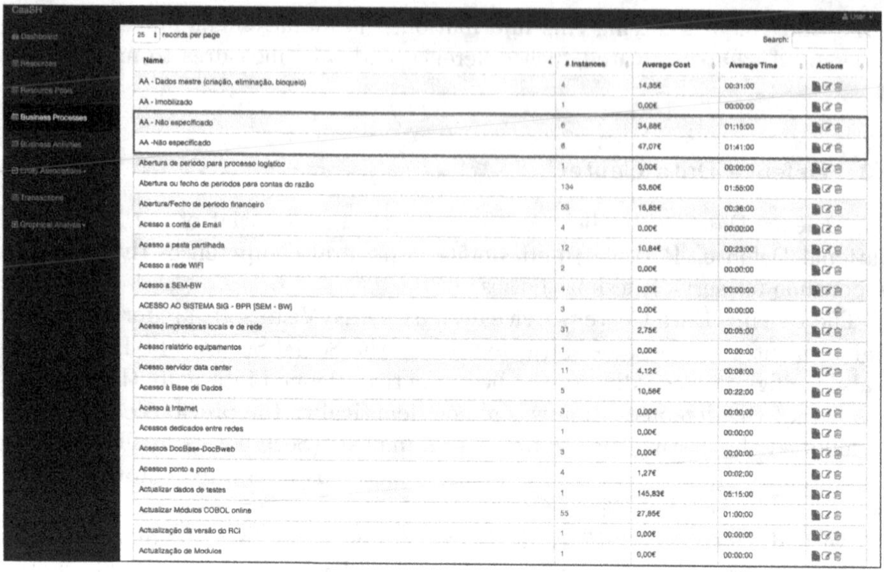

Name	# Instances	Average Cost	Average Time	Actions
AA - Dados mestre (criação, eliminação, bloqueio)	4	14,35€	00:31:00	
AA - Imobilizado	1	0,00€	00:00:00	
AA - Não especificado	6	34,88€	01:15:00	
AA -Não especificado	6	47,07€	01:41:00	
Abertura de periodo para processo logístico	1	0,00€	00:00:00	
Abertura ou fecho de periodos para contas do razão	134	53,60€	01:55:00	
Abertura/Fecho de periodo financeiro	53	16,85€	00:36:00	
Acesso a conta de Email	4	0,00€	00:00:00	
Acesso a pasta partilhada	12	10,84€	00:23:00	
Acesso a rede WIFI	2	0,00€	00:00:00	
Acesso a SEM-BW	4	0,00€	00:00:00	
ACESSO AO SISTEMA SIG - BPR [SEM - BW]	3	0,00€	00:00:00	
Acesso impressoras locais e de rede	31	2,75€	00:05:00	
Acesso relatório equipamentos	1	0,00€	00:00:00	
Acesso servidor data center	11	4,12€	00:08:00	
Acesso à Base de Dados	5	10,56€	00:22:00	
Acesso à Internet	3	0,00€	00:00:00	
Acessos dedicados entre redes	1	0,00€	00:00:00	
Acessos DocBase-DocBweb	3	0,00€	00:00:00	
Acessos ponto a ponto	4	1,27€	00:02:00	
Actualizar dados de testes	1	145,83€	05:15:00	
Actualizar Módulos COBOL online	55	27,85€	01:00:00	
Actualização da versão do RCI	1	0,00€	00:00:00	
Actualização de Modulos	1	0,00€	00:00:00	

Fig. 4. CaaSH - Defence Data Center - business processes sample.

developing a project, designated ecoDrive - Intelligent Eco Driving and Fleet Management, which is a multidisciplinary project, targeting the public transportation network, in which INOV is responsible for the identification of business processes (BPMN) and the cost analysis of those business processes using a TDABC approach.

The costing service described in the proposal (Sect. 5) was adopted as a solution for the ecoDrive project since it delivered all the needed features to accomplish the objectives defined. However, this project required that the identification of business processes and activities was done prior to the system deployment, meaning that we would only have access to real transactional data after the system enters in production, since there is no digital data from the past.

Starting with the business processes, we were able to identify 10 different business processes, each one with its distinct set of activities. For example, we identified a business process "Occurrences" that is related to the different events that may cause changes to the operational service of a bus. The activity list of this business process includes "Change Driver" and "Change Vehicle". Another example was the business process "Corrective Maintenance" that features activities such as "Repair of damage" and "Damage Report". These 10 business processes and respective activities are the ones that will constitute the foundation for the transactional data to be exported from the software being developed by Card4B for the public transportation industry.

As we stated before, we didn't have access to real transactional data since the system is not in production yet. In this particular case, our tool will import transactional data from JSON web services rather than from a CSV file, enabling the costing tool to get data in real time. As a result, after configured, the costing tool can pull data, in a given time interval, so that it can produce updated metrics without user intervention.

7 Evaluation

The goal of this evaluation is to determine if the solution proposed in the Proposal (Sect. 5) solves the problem stated in the Problem (Sect. 2).

The evaluation method will consist in the following steps:

1. **Interviews and Questionnaires:** Gather feedback from the proposal through the demonstration and identify improvements;
2. **Pries-Heje et al. Framework and Österle et al. Principles:** To formally evaluate the research;
3. **Demonstration's Critical Review:** To critically evaluate the research, objectives fulfillment and the demonstrations conducted;

7.1 Interviews and Questionnaires

After demonstrating our costing service, we conducted a small questionnaire to those involved so that we could obtain a more structured feedback. The questionnaire was made to five interviewees with the following business roles: Planning, Quality and Audit Manager, Budget Manager, Planning and Control Manager, Accountant for Client Support and an IT Director.

We carried out four questions to these professionals that helped us assess the artefact utility and the fulfillment of the objectives defined earlier. These questions were also defined having in mind the needed information to formally evaluate the research.

Figure 5 shows the questionnaire results which averaged 7,85 out of 10. We also gathered feedback from the interviews that provided us insights in different topics needed to evaluate this research as we will further detail in this section.

7.2 Pries-Heje et al. Framework

Alongside with Design Science Research guidelines and to better evaluate research artefacts, Hevner et al. proposed five different types of evaluation methods: Observational, Analytical, Experimental, Testing and Descriptive. Even though the authors provided these evaluation paths, not much more guidance was given on how to accomplish them [18].

Considering prior research done in the area of DSR evaluation, Pries-Heje et al. developed a framework to fill in this gap that could help researchers use and rigorously evaluate Design Science Research and its artefacts. This framework consists on distinguishing evaluation in two separated dimensions: one related to the form of the evaluation, the other concerns the moment of the evaluation [19].

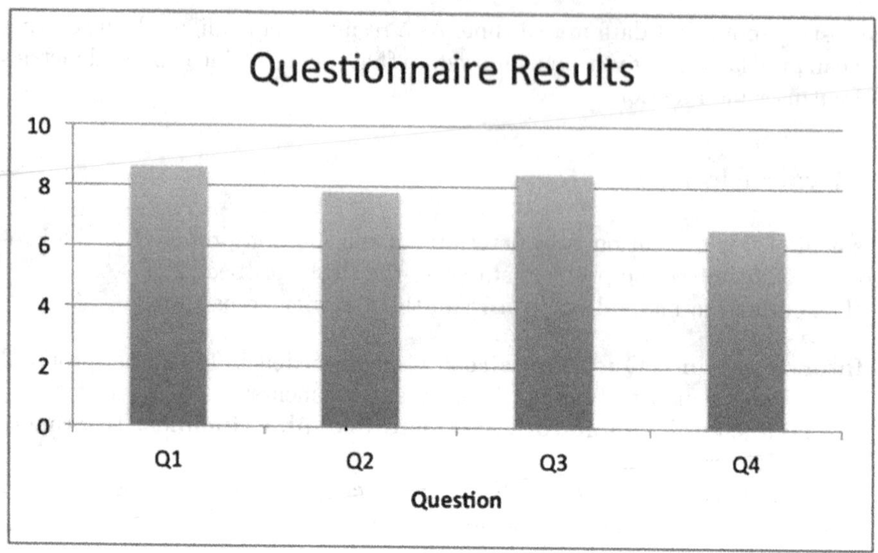

Fig. 5. Questionnaire results.

Regarding the form of the evaluation, it can either be artificial or naturalistic. In an artificial evaluation, the solution is evaluated in a contrived and non-realistic way (using for example simulations, laboratory experiments and mathematical proofs). In a naturalistic evaluation, a solution's performance is tested in real environments using real users, real systems and to solve real problems.

Concerning the moment of the evaluation, can be ex-ante or ex-post. *Ex-ante* means that the evaluation takes place before the artefact is developed, meaning that it is not absolutely necessary to construct an artefact to evaluate a theory. *Ex-post* means that when the evaluation is conducted the artefact is already developed. To further clarify, the artefact can be a design product or a design process.

In summary, there are three different aspects of a Design Science Research Evaluation [19]. In the case of our research, our evaluations have always addressed the three questions (What, How and When) the same way.

1. **What is Actually Evaluated?** The artefact evaluated is the costing service (a design product) proposed in (Sect. 5). We evaluated the results achieved by creating the costing tool that instantiates the costing service, the feedback collected among academics and practitioners and the results of applying this system in practice, i.e., the three demonstrations performed;
2. **How is it Evaluated?** The feedback gathered from experts and practitioners proved valuable to evaluate our proposal. We also implemented our proposal in three Portuguese organizations that represented a naturalistic evaluation since it was conducted using a real artefact, the costing tool.

3. **When was it Evaluated?** In the case of our research the evaluation was made *ex-post*, i.e., after the development of the design product. We first developed the costing service tool and only afterwards proceed to obtain feedback from experts and practitioners.

7.3 Österle et al. Principles

Österle et al. proposes an evaluation method based within four principles [20]. Our research met the four principles of Österle. This evaluation is based on the feedback received from practitioners, which were described in the previous sections.

1. **Abstraction:** The artefact we propose can be applied to the majority of the service-oriented or process-based organizations;
2. **Originality:** None of the interviewees had knowledge of any research or product similar to the proposed artefact. Similar research was not found regarding the costing service;
3. **Justification:** Our artefact is justified by the lack of a similar solution and from the positive feedback gathered during this research;
4. **Benefit:** According to the interviewees, at least in the industries consulted, there would be a valuable benefit, since it would provide an easier and more affordable way to perform a cost analysis.

7.4 Demonstration's Critical Review

We consider that our research was proper evaluated and tested with our demonstrations. We demonstrated our proposal in three Portuguese organizations, from two distinct industries, with the objective of providing those organizations with new ways to conduct simple and reliable cost analysis. The feedback gathered from the questionnaires and the formal evaluations from the previous sections validated the usefulness and the quality of the proposed costing service.

Our demonstrations targeted three organizations that are making clear efforts to consider business process costing a priority. Two of the three organizations (the service desks), already have their services oriented according to best practices such as ITIL and ISO 20000. That gave us an advantage regarding the costing service implementation. Although our service provides an easy way to start costing business processes and services, we do realize that the organizations deploying such service should have a considerable maturity in their architecture. Without such maturity the proposed service is much more difficult to deploy because the lack of transactional data. However, since many organizations are already service-oriented, our costing service is a solution that delivers clear benefits to those organizations, as emphasized by the demonstration.

We were able to deliver the average cost per business process and the real cost per business process instance. We consider the latter to be a benefit to service-oriented organizations since it enables organizations to comprehend the average cost of supplying a service or executing a business process but also the real cost for every business process instance executed. This helps organizations detect erroneous paths and singular problems that occurred at a given moment. With this knowledge organizations know their real business process costs and also know when and why some execution costed them more. Afterwards, organizations may try to investigate the real cause of the problem, knowing exactly which transaction and activity generated the issue. Therefore, our service can fulfill the objective of providing insights about the flow of costs and execution performance metrics.

Finally, every interviewee that saw the costing service configuration and use from the beginning of the process till it's end, considered the process of conducting a cost analysis using our tool very easy and understandable. This fact validated another objective aimed at providing a service that required low levels of expertise with both the service and costing methodology.

8 Conclusion

Over recent years, cost awareness and cost efficiency has been on the agenda of organizations from all industries around the world. Cost efficiency is now classified as a major concern of every department, process, product or service within an organization. It became crucial to assess and benchmark an organization's performance and to identify improvement opportunities across all sectors of the organization and over the cost stream. As we stated before, SMEs are particularly vulnerable due to their small size and market exposure. SMEs need cost efficiency more than ever [1].

However, traditional cost accounting systems fail to provide the needed data to perform such analysis because they are mainly focused on financial and tax accounting. New and innovative costing methodologies were developed to solve the problem but they are out of reach for the majority of the enterprises because they are too expensive to implement.

We followed the guidelines proposed by the Design Science Research Methodology to help us conduct this research. We started with the problem identification and motivation that led us to do research in costing, costing methodologies, costing templates and cloud services. From this analysis we made the choice of developing our artefact using concepts from accurate costing methodologies, cost templates and cloud services.

Our artefact is a cloud-based costing service meant to provide costing as a service. This means that our main objective was to develop a solution to reduce the costs associated with cost analysis so that SMEs can reach the accurate costing methodologies needed to assess an organization's cost efficiency and performance. We consider our solution is more affordable and less complex than those available in the market since we combine open source technologies, cloud services and costing templates. Respectively, this will lower licensing costs, implementation and deployment costs, and expertise or consulting services costs.

We validated our proposal in three Portuguese organizations belonging to two different industries: Services industry (two Service Desks) and the Public

Transportation industry. In all organizations we completed the demonstration by instantiating the proposed service using the developed costing tool. Following these demonstrations we formally evaluated the proposal using the Pries-Heje et al. Framework and the four principles proposed by Österle et al. We also conducted interviews with experts, practitioners and potential users. The feedback obtained was taken into account to improve the proposal and the implemented service.

In the next sections we will further detail our conclusions by presenting which were the lessons learned, the objectives we accomplished, the main contributions of this proposal, the limitations we identified and remained unsolved and future work that can be used to improve this research and that we believe would bring extra value to this proposal.

8.1 Lessons Learned

Our research raised several aspects worth mentioning. Some resulted from the Related Work and from the design phase of our research while others derive from the experience and feedback obtained during the demonstration and evaluation phases.

Regarding the lessons learned from the first stage of our work we observed that there is already a clear effort to model business process costs and cost structures to easily provide some methods of service chargeback and accurate cost allocation. We also noted that organizations are clearly trying to standardize their business processes according to widely accepted best practice frameworks such as ITIL/ISO 20000. This approach helped us note that inside the same industry some patterns emerge when such standardization is implemented.

However, aside from these praiseworthy efforts, we were still confronted with missing communication links inside an organization. We observed that management only wanted information that they could understand while others were only concerned with modelling and monitoring business process data. Almost completely unrelated with those described above, we have accountants calculating costs that are not related or explicitly linked to business processes. Finally, IT is supposed to just provide the needed data that feed the needs of those abovementioned.

Considering the demonstration step, the lessons learned were rather practical and closely related to the costing service implementation described earlier in the Proposal chapter. We observed that costing is a tough exercise. Since the accuracy given by the cost analysis is highly dependent on the quality of the data available, it is possible to model how each condition affects or influences the cost of a business process but it is only possible to evaluate them if they were somehow recorded. Data availability should be considered when cost modelling starts. We realized that cost analysis and modelling should be an incremental process since the analysis results encourage the organization to store and log more data so that the model and the analysis can be fine-tuned according to new expectations and questions.

Targeting these problems, ERP's, CRM's and Service Desk tools are used to store data needed to monitor and control business processes. However, we found cases where the information available was incorrectly introduced or missing. Still, first run results motivated the demonstration participants to store more accurate and broader data.

Finally, we also observed that organizations are not keen on providing data to the public domain, especially after the cost analysis is concluded. However, for research and development purposes the data was provided as needed.

8.2 Objectives Accomplishment

In the objectives section we described a set of objectives that should be accomplished in order to the costing service proposed successfully solve the identified problem. As a main objective, we defined that our proposal should present a costing service, targeted to SMEs, that should be more affordable and easier to use than current solutions. Regarding the main objective, we consider that it was fulfilled since our costing tool, that instances the costing service, is less demanding in terms of technology and expertise needed to run the costing service.

We also settled other more specific objectives that we shall now explain how and why they were accomplished. The following list describes the objectives defined earlier and the reasons why they were accomplished.

- **The Service should be easily Available to Organizations**
  - The costing service was created with the intent of being a cloud-based service. Organizations can get access to the costing tool, that instances the costing service, using a SaaS approach. Organizations may also deploy the service internally if they want to.
- **The Service should Support any Kind of Organization or Industry**
  - As we demonstrated, our proposal can be applied to different organizations and industries. Although we only tested three organizations from two different industries, we believe that our proposal can be applied to any kind of organization and industry since the models in which our costing service is based are generic and are not associated with any type of organization or activity.
- **The Service should Not Require Specialized Expertise Upon the Moment of Application on an Organization**
  - The costing service has a simple application process as described in Sect. 5.2. The costing service analysis process can be followed by any user without demanding significant or specialized expertise in costing. Moreover, the costing tool, which instances the costing service, was developed to be simple and easy to use. Both the proposal and the evaluation showed that the costing tool accomplishes the needed simplicity to be used by any organization or user.
- **The Service should be more Affordable than Traditional Methods from the beginning of the Cost Analysis until its end, i.e., the Moment when Results are obtained**

- Our costing service is less demanding regarding both human and capital costs. Demanding less specialized expertise upon the moment of application on an organization lowers both the human and the capital costs of the cost analysis. Furthermore, the costing service was created with the intent of being a cloud-based service which lowers the costs related to the technological aspects of the proposal. Since our costing service can instantiate existing costing templates for a given industry or organization, it will lower the particular or organization-specific costs of consultancy services needed to construct the cost model of analysis. Moreover, if the organization already has their business processes defined according to a best practice (such as ITIL), the costing tool can "infer" the business processes and activities, so that the cost analysis outputs match the business processes of the organization.

8.3 Main Contributions

We consider that our main contribution was delivering a costing tool capable of correctly and completely support TDABC and Business Process Costs Templates. This tool was more than just a simple prototype and it will be used as part of a bigger project regarding a management software solution for the public transportation network, which will be delivered by Card4B - Systems, S.A.

We believe that our proposal brings a valuable contribution in the context of costing and cost analysis. The resulting costing service allows organizations to conduct a bigger share of the cost analysis without demanding significant levels of expertise or capital.

The proposed costing service not only provided a solution to the problem of high costs of cost analysis but also delivered a costing tool capable of correctly and completely support TDABC and Business Process Costs Templates. These methods combined with the capabilities of our costing tool produced well-defined steps that act as a guideline for both analysts and managers looking for a cost analysis solution. The end result is a costing service capable of delivering the ability for an organization to do cost analysis with internal resources and expertise, without needing substantial investment.

8.4 Limitations

The limitations regarding our proposal can be divided into two groups, technical limitations and conceptual limitations.

Regarding the technical limitations, although we consider our costing tool to be more than just a prototype, we must state that it lacks some characteristics needed to be a full cloud-based costing service. The developed costing tool does not support integration and importing of tax and analytical accounting data. In order to avoid data input mistakes and to enable high volumes of data integration this would be mandatory. We also consider that the developed costing tool, although producing some useful metrics, lacks the ability to produce management reports.

As for the conceptual limitations, they are related to profitability, capital and investment characteristics that are needed to correctly reflect all the costs within the analysis. The research process and the interviews revealed that although costs and cost analysis are major concerns to organizations, they are strongly tied to capital costs, working capitals, return on investments and profitability. Although we excluded from the beginning of this research such concepts and metrics, we must acknowledge that the lack of such characteristics is a limitation that must be addressed in future research.

8.5 Future Work

In order to further validate the proposed costing service we consider that applying the service to more complex and different industries would be desirable. We achieved three full demonstrations but only in two distinct industries thereby restricting the validations done. However, our demonstrations were carried using a significant volume of transactional data which attested to the proper functioning of the applied algorithms.

Another interesting aspect would be to develop BPMN importing capabilities within our costing tool. Since some organizations already have their business processes modelled in BPMN it would simplify the process of cost analysis even further if they could import their models.

Finally, the costing tool should also be able to import business processes and activities specific drivers. This would enable the tool to produce different metrics other than just the cost of business processes and activities. Since our effort was to develop a service to reduce the cost of cost analysis, we opted to leave this feature as a future development because it would require transactional data to be much more specific than the datasets we had access to, conditioning the costing service validation and demonstration.

References

1. OCDE: the impact of the global crisis on SME and entrepreneurship financing and policy responses. Technical report (2009)
2. Wileman, A.: Driving Down Cost: How to Manage and Cut Costs-Intelligently. Nicholas Brealey Pub., Boston (2010)
3. Delloite: CIO survey report 2011 the Guerilla CIO: working smarter to add value. Technical report (2011)
4. Miller, J.G., Vollmann, T.E.: The hidden factory. Harvard Bus. Rev. **63**, 142–150 (1985)
5. Škoda, M.: The importance of ABC models in cost management. Ann. Univ. Petrosani Econ. **9**, 263–274 (2009)
6. Hall, O.P., McPeak, C., et al.: Are SMEs ready for ABC? J. Account. Finance **11**, 11–22 (2011)
7. Hicks, D.T., Costing, A.B.: Making It Work for Small and Mid-Sized Companies. Wiley, New York (2002)
8. Lambert III, S., Chen, K.H.: Overhead cost pools. Intern. Auditor **53**, 62 (1996)

9. Nandan, R.: Management accounting needs of SMEs and the role of professional accountants: a renewed research agenda. J. Appl. Manag. Acc. Res. **8**, 65–78 (2010)
10. Blocher, E.: Cost Management: A Strategic Emphasis. McGraw-Hill College, New York (2005)
11. Vanderbeck, E.J.: Principles of Cost Accounting. Cengage Learning, Boston (2012)
12. Cooper, R., Kaplan, R.S.: How cost accounting systematically distorts product costs. In: Accounting and Management: Field Study Perspectives, pp. 204–228 (1987)
13. Kaplan, R.S., Anderson, S.R.: Time-Driven Activity-Based Costing: A Simpler and More Powerful Path to Higher Profits. Harvard Business Press, Watertown (2007)
14. Kaplan, R.S., Anderson, S.R.: Time-driven activity-based costing. Harvard Bus. Rev. **82**, 131–138 (2004)
15. Dejnega, O.: Method: time driven activity based costing - literature review. J. Appl. Econ. Sci. **5**, 7–15 (2011)
16. Lourenço, A.G., Mira da Silva, M.: A cloud-based service for affordable cost analysis. In: 19th Americas Conference on Information Systems (2013)
17. Pernot, E., Roodhooft, F., Van den Abbeele, A.: Time-driven activity-based costing for inter-library services: a case study in a university. J. Acad. Librarianship **33**, 551–560 (2007)
18. Hevner, A.R., March, S.T., Park, J., Ram, S.: Design science in information systems research. MIS Q. **28**, 75–105 (2004)
19. Pries-Heje, J., Baskerville, R., Venable, J.R.: Strategies for design science research evaluation (2008)
20. Österle, H., Becker, J., Frank, U., Hess, T., Karagiannis, D., Krcmar, H., Loos, P., Mertens, P., Oberweis, A., Sinz, E.J.: Memorandum on design-oriented information systems research. Eur. J. Inf. Syst. **20**, 7–10 (2010)

Author Index

Printed in the United States
By Bookmasters